MW00674862

Mr. Cheap's
Atlanta

Mark Waldstein

Associate Editor
Erica Jorgensen

Assistant Editor
Tami Monahan

BOB ADAMS, INC.
Holbrook, Massachusetts

Published by Bob Adams, Inc.
260 Center Street, Holbrook, MA 02343

ISBN: 1-55850-292-0

Printed in the United States of America

A   B   C   D   E   F   G   H   I   J

Library of Congress Cataloging-in-Publication Data
Waldstein, Mark.
Mr. Cheap's Atlanta : bargains, factory outlets, off-price stores, deep discount stores, che
eats, cheap places to stay, and cheap fun things to do / Mark Waldstein.
    p.   cm.
Includes index.
ISBN: 1-55850-292-0 : $8.95
    1. Atlanta (Ga.)—Guidebooks. 2. Shopping—Georgia—Atlanta——Guidebooks.
3. Restaurants—Georgia—Atlanta—Guidebooks. 4. Bed and breakfast accommodations—
Georgia—Atlanta—Guidebooks. 5. Hotels—Georgia—Atlanta—Guidebooks. 6. Outlet
stores—Georgia—Atlanta—Guidebooks. I. Title. II. Title: Mister Cheap's Atlanta
    F249.A93W35   1994
    917.58'231—dc20   93-43270
                                                                      CIP

This publication is designed to provide accurate and authoritative information with regard to the subject matter covered. It is sold with the understanding that the publisher is not engaged in rendering
legal, accounting, or other professional advice. If legal advice or other expert assistance is required,
the services of a qualified professional person should be sought.
— From a *Declaration of Principles* jointly adopted by a Committee of the
American Bar Association and a Committee of Publishers and Associations.

This book is available at quantity discounts for bulk purchases.
For information, call 1-800-872-5627.

ACKNOWLEDGEMENTS

There is no way a project of this scale could be done alone! I would like to thank, first and foremost, my two hard-working assistants, Erica Jorgensen and Tami Monahan, who never complained in the face of many extra hours at deadline time. Thanks also to Laura Lieberman and Tracy White of the City of Atlanta's Arts Clearinghouse, making themselves and their vast information resources available to the Mr. Cheap team. To Doug Hamilton at Creative Loafing, for background material. And, a personal thank you to Gail Eaton, Jane Evans and Al Mazzocut, and Barbara Levitas.

From Erica, a big "Thanks, y'all!" to Jen Gardner and the whole Gardner clan, and to Kerrin McGillicuddy for her Southern hospitality. Also, thanks to Shannon McGlame, Bill Hopkins, Joe Veneracian, Deanne England, Rod Bain, Bill Carrier, Pam Lawrence and Rusty Johnson for their suggestions.

CONTENTS

A Few (Carefully Chosen) Words from Mr. Cheap

SHOPPING

A FEW (CAREFULLY CHOSEN) WORDS FROM MR. CHEAP

About this "cheap" business. I'll admit, there are more elegant ways to put the idea. Lots of folks want to save money, especially in these tough times. When it comes to low *prices*, few people know as many good places as I do. But, strictly speaking, that doesn't make these stores and restaurants "cheap." Nor does it make anyone who uses this book a "cheapskate." I think *thrifty* would be a better word. Or perhaps *frugal*.

After all, a cheap person, in my mind, is someone who has plenty of money to burn, and refuses to touch it; a thrifty person would probably spend the cash if he or she had it—expecially for something of good value. Most of us fall into the latter category, don't we?

Anyway, everyone loves a bargain, and it's my pleasure to pass these tips along. This whole idea grew out of my own personal experience, from years of living on the financial edge as a "starving artist." My background is in theater and writing; and, as most people know, actors don't make any money even with steady work. I learned to live "cheaply" out of necesssity, and developed my first book (*Mr. Cheap's Boston*) as a way to put this knowledge to good use, helping out folks in similar straits. That book wound up on the *Boston Globe* bestseller list; *Mr. Cheap's New York* soon followed. Suddenly, I discovered myself on a mission!

There is, by now, a research technique behind these books, but "cheaping" is hardly an exact science. Prices change all the time. Stores come and go. Restaurants change their menus. Sure, you won't find the exact same items on the shelves tomorrow that I found during my travels; but the descriptions in this book are sure to help you track down just about anything you may be looking for, at the lowest possible price.

A few words of caution. "You gets what you pays for." It's been said many times, and it's generally true. With new merchandise in particular, prices are always discounted for a reason. It may be that the item is simply a leftover from last year, yet still perfectly good; in other cases, if the price is low, the quality may not be far behind. I have tried to point out, wherever I could, items that are cheap because they are less well made, or because they are irregular or damaged. Even these "IR" goods may be useful to the reader who only needs them to last for a short time—students furnishing a dorm room, for example—or, to shoppers who happen to be handy with a hammer, or a needle and thread. Sometimes, the "truly cheap" is all you need.

I fully expect to hear from readers who insist I've left out their favorite diner, or some resale boutique they love. To these fellow bargain hunters, I say, Mr. C can't be *everywhere*; but I encourage you to please pass along the information, and I'll be happy to scout your suggestions out for our next edition. The address is:

Mr. Cheap
c/o Bob Adams, Inc.
260 Center St.
Holbrook, MA 02343

So, get ready to use the book—but be careful how you use the name! As you see, "cheap" can mean many things. And when you tell someone that you paid only $45 for your designer outfit, nobody will be laughing. They'll just want to know how you did it.

On to the goodies!

Mark Waldstein
a.k.a. Mr. Cheap

SHOPPING

The hundreds of stores in this section are all places which will save you money in some way. They actually cover a broad spectrum of discount shopping, from the latest designer clothing to thrift shops, new furniture and used, major brands and second-rate imitations. Mr. Cheap wants to cover it all, giving his readers as many options as possible for saving cash.

Whenever possible, Mr. C points out *why* an item is marked down—whether it's discontinued, second-quality (imperfect), or just plain cheap stuff. Thus informed, it is up to you to decide which stores and merchandise are for you.

The prices quoted, again, are based upon items Mr. C found at the time of his research. You shouldn't expect to find the same items, at the same prices, when you shop; these prices are just examples which are similar to what you may find. Even as prices go up overall, you should still find the book completely useful in comparing one place against another.

Many stores which sell several kinds of merchandise have been cross-referenced for you, appearing in each appropriate chapter; but remember to consult "Discount Department Stores" and "Flea Markets and Emporia" for many of the same items which have their own chapters. Similarly, the "General Markets" portion of the "Food Stores" chapter gives you more places to look for individual kinds of foods.

Okay, enough talking—*Go to it!*

APPLIANCES

AA Ideal Used Appliances
● 1665 Lavista Rd. N.E., Atlanta;
   634-2554

It sure is ideal, with savings from
40% to 60% off retail prices on used
appliances from Whirlpool, Hotpoint,
Kenmore, and other big brand names.
Selection is good in this 3,000-square
foot showroom, but Mr. C is told that
99% of the stock is late models, so be
careful before you buy.

Washers and dryers, priced at
$100 and up, are the most commonly
found units here. Carrier and Kenmore air conditioners start at about
$80, though most are in the $200
range; trash compactors, stoves, and
freezers are similarly priced, according to age and wear.

There's a 30-day guarantee on
parts and labor (fix-ups are done in
the store), and delivery is available
for a fee.

The store is closed Sundays.

Appliance and Furniture Exchange
● 1090 Howell Mill Rd. N.W.,
   Atlanta; 876-0017

The prices on new major appliances
and furniture in this store are decent,
if unspectacular; but, walk through to
the rear warehouse area, and you'll
find several neatly arranged rows of
used appliances at significant savings
indeed. Everything is clean, and in
working condition; nothing Mr. C
found seemed more than a couple of
years old.

He saw things like a Kenmore
washing machine for $99, a Hotpoint
dishwasher for $299—absolutely like
new—and a big Westinghouse side-
by-side refrigerator/freezer for the
same price. In general, refrigerators
and gas ranges start around $120,
electric ranges a bit higher (a Hotpoint for $169), and there is even a
selection of those little dorm-size
square refrigerators, all $49 each. Stu-

dents, take note!

Every one of these appliances has
a 90-day store warranty, in case there
are any problems their repair staff
has missed. Even after that period, if
anything goes wrong, the folks here
will only charge you for the replacement parts needed. Good deal. So is
an extra discount for paying by cash,
and free delivery within a 25-mile radius of the store. It's open from 9
a.m. to 6 p.m. daily, Mondays
through Saturdays.

Ashby Discount Sewing Machines
● 107 Broad St. S.W., Atlanta;
   688-7148

See listing under "Sewing and Fabrics."

Blalock Appliance Services
● 4960 Covington Hwy., Decatur;
   286-9451

Blalock is one of the Atlanta area's
main suppliers of appliances to land-
lords, selling "all makes and all models" of "reconditioned" used stoves,
refrigerators, and dishwashers to
some fifty different apartment complexes.

You can take advantage of these
same discounts, even if your rent
checks go out, rather than come in.
There are a few compromises,
though. Blalock doesn't do hook-ups
of gas appliances, so you'll have to
do that yourself—or find someone to
do it for you. You also have to pay
for delivery, or arrange it on your
own.

If you remain undaunted by these
points, you'll find some good deals
indeed. Nothing in the store is over
ten years old, and every item comes
with at least a 30-day or 60-day store
warranty. High sales volume, and in-
house repairs, allow Blalock to chop
prices on appliances from names like
G.E., Hotpoint, Kenmore, Amana,
American Chef, Whirlpool and West-

inghouse. Blalock's is willing to strike a deal, too—if you buy two or more appliances, for example, they'll discount the third, so be ready to haggle.

Open six days a week.

Bob Carroll's
- 2122 North Decatur Plaza, Decatur; 634-2411

Ovens are the big bargains at Bob's. An Amana "Radarange" microwave, priced at $199 ($50 off retail), and a Jenn-Air gas oven, listed at $169, selling here for $129, were just two of the recent deals here.

You'll also find good prices on dishwashers, like a Maytag unit selling for $429, a savings of $30 off the list price. Be sure to take a look at Carroll's closeouts and floor samples, too. Among these, Mr. C spotted an Amana refrigerator-freezer, with water and ice dispensers mounted in the doors, marked down by $200 at $1,299.

Cherian's
- Scott Village Shopping Center, 1707 Church St., Decatur; 299-0842

There are some surprising bargains to be found in this store. Catering to Decatur's Indian community, the store features an eclectic variety of imported items from overseas. So, along with bags of rice and tea and other grocery items, you'll find budget-friendly name brand electronics and small appliances.

Cherian's sells a mish-mash of small appliances, such as a Vidal Sassoon Mini Turbo Travel Dryer for $13.50, and a sharp-looking (no pun intended) Oskar food processor for $60. Both have been seen at higher prices in major department stores.

Be sure to carefully check the voltages on electronic items before you buy. Some are not compatible for use in this country. Because Cherian's is a direct importer, some products sold here are meant for customers who travel overseas, or those who send them back to family members in foreign countries.

Cherian's is open Tuesdays through Saturdays from 10:30 a.m. to 9 p.m., and Sundays from 1:30 p.m. to 9 p.m. It's closed on Mondays.

Circuit City
- 3400 Woodale Dr. N.E., Atlanta; 233-2060
- 1968 Greenbriar Pkwy. S.W., Atlanta; 349-5422
- 4512 Memorial Dr., Decatur; 299-2001
- 5495 Jimmy Carter Blvd., Norcross; 662-0557
- 1241 Morrow Industrial Blvd., Southlake; 968-1211

And other suburban locations

Sure you've heard and seen the ads (and you're probably plenty sick of them, too!), but Circuit City really does have a whopper of a low price guarantee. After purchasing an item, if you find the same product selling locally for a lower price, Circuit City will refund 110% of the difference.

One of the super bargains that Circuit City recently offered was a 13 cubic foot Kelvinator refrigerator/freezer for a mere $370.

The stores are open Monday through Saturday from 10 a.m. to 9 p.m., and Sunday noon to 6 p.m.

Roberds
- 4380 Memorial Dr., Decatur; 296-2040
- I-75 at South Loop 120, Marietta; 426-0868
- 6288 Dawson Blvd. N.W., Norcross; 449-4214
- 2000 Holcombwoods Pkwy., Roswell; 587-0703

And other suburban locations

Another biggie but goodie, Roberds promises to beat any competitor's price. Mr. C found bargains like a Whirlpool large-capacity dryer for $199, and a 4-cycle Whirlpool washer for $228. A self-cleaning electric range (again by Whirlpool), is $279, and a Kitchenaid built-in dishwasher with multi-level washing cycles, is $399.

Sewell Appliances
- 6125 Roswell Rd., Sandy Springs; 255-0640

Looking at the price tags at Sewell's may make you wonder if it's time to visit the eye doctor; but have no fear,

MR. CHEAP'S PICKS
Appliances

✔ **The Appliance and Furniture Exchange**—Keep your cash cool with a used refrigerator or other major appliance here, all guaranteed.

your vision is fine. So are these prices. Refrigerators and microwave ovens, along with harder-to-find appliances like trash compactors, are all well-stocked here.

Some of the bargains found by Mr. C's own eagle eyes included Amana heavy-duty washers; these were list-priced at $469, but selling here for just $399. Matching dryers, listed at $429, sell for $369.

You can cook up a storm with a floor-model KitchenAid "Selectra" self-cleaning oven, selling for $999 ($200 below retail), or an Amana smoothtop range, listed at $589, seen recently for $499. An Amana "Radarange" microwave oven, listing for $319, sells for $269; a GE "Dual Wave III" microwave, listing for $300, sells for $250.

To clean up your mess afterwards, how about a KitchenAid Superba dishwasher, $70 off retail at $659. You'll find similar savings on things like KitchenAid compactors and fancy Scotsman "Auto Ice" refrigerator-freezers. Save $90 on an Amana fridge; Sewell's even carries powerful Subzero refrigerator-freezers— one model, retailing for a whopping $4,128, was seen reduced to a cool $3,499.

Singer Sewing Products

- Lindbergh Plaza, Piedmont Rd., Atlanta; 261-4240
- 107 Broad St., S.W., Atlanta; 688-7148
- 5134 Old National Hwy., College Park; 766-0569
- 945 Windy Hill Rd., S.E., Smyrna; 432-5523

For used sewing machines, including built-in table models, by brands like Pfaff, Kenmore, and, of course, Singer, this is bound to be the source. The Lindbergh Plaza location is actually a factory outlet store, as well as a used machine shop, and definitely worth a trip if you're looking for to save some bucks on oh-sew-expensive sewing machines.

Repairs are done in the store, and their work is guaranteed. Meanwhile, this means that you can also find used vacuum cleaners here by Singer, Eureka and other brands. Mr. C saw a Kirby upright, several years old but still in great shape; selling for $400 when new, it was on sale for just $99. And a Singer 6.5-amp vacuum with headlight, originally selling for $139.95, was only $89.95. Always worth a look.

Troy-Bilt Official Factory Store

- 2744 Cobb Industrial Blvd., Smyrna; 433-2487

Almost all tillers, lawn mowers, chipper-vacs, chain saws, and leaf blowers are discounted at Troy-Bilt. The store is given a big break on volume, and, since there are no dealers to deal with, *you* get a further break on prices.

Just a couple of examples of the kind of savings found here: Top-of-the-line leaf blowers by Husquarna (you probably know these by the name "Husky") are priced at least 10% off retail, and chipper-vacs— with screen included—can help you turn wood into mulch at prices starting as low as $35.

BEDS AND MATTRESSES

Beds For Less
- 3853-B Peachtree Rd., N.E., Atlanta; 231-2188
- 5075 Austell Rd., S.W., Austell; 941-6030
- 4563 Memorial Dr., Decatur; 501-9274
- 220 North Cobb Pkwy. N.E., Marietta; 499-7060
- 6438 Dawson Blvd., Norcross; 242-0994
- 6474 Highway 85, Riverdale; 996-5132
- 1570 Holcomb Bridge Rd., Roswell; 641-1971
- 6319 Roswell Rd., Sandy Springs; 303-9546

And they *do* mean for less. This chain sells mostly Sealy, Serta, King Coil, and Spring Air mattresses and box frames. Because of the vast size of this chain, it can offer you not only great prices, but often free frames and delivery; they've even run newspaper ads with coupons worth up to $100 off mattress sets. Keep your eyes open for these ads, or call to see when the next sale starts.

Bear in mind that these perks often apply only to full, king and queen sets; but in these cases, bigger sizes may actually save you money compared to smaller sets at regulars store prices.

At the time of Mr. C's recent visit, Sealy and Serta firm mattresses were priced at $92 for a twin set, $172 for full, $199 for queen, and $249 for king size. Serta "Premium Super Plush" mattresses were on sale at half off retail: Just $199 per piece for a twin mattress or box spring, $239 for each full piece, $499 for the queen set, and $699 for the king pair.

Spring Air mattresses also sell for prices dramatically lower than retail. The "Fantasy" set was seen for $138 in twin, $199 full, $249 queen, and $349 for the king size set.

Most BFL branches are open from

10 a.m. until 9 p.m. weekdays, 10 a.m. til 6 p.m. on Saturdays and noon to 5 p.m. on Sundays.

The Great Futon Store
- 549 Amsterdam Ave. N.E., Atlanta; 872-2623

An unlikely addition to the Midtown Outlets is this small store selling beds and furniture. Opened in March of '93, it's already made quite a hit, with a limited selection of high quality merchandise at well below the prices at other specialty stores. A Mateo futon couch for instance, with a solid birch frame, was seen for $750 at the Home Store; here, the same item was recently selling for $539. And a handsome Charleston iron rail four-poster bed frame, listed at $599, was seen for just $259.

And what about the futons themselves? GF is the exclusive Atlanta distributor for Gold Bond futons, which start here at $99 in twin size. Full size is $125, queen $145, and king $199. That same price can get you a complete tri-fold frame and futon set, in full size; many of the wooden frames on display are made right here in the shop, while a variety of finished styles come from outside manufacturers. Futon covers are well priced too, such as $34.95 for a full size style—which you can get for half-price with the purchase of a futon.

There are some other home furnishings here too. Mr. C saw a butcher block kitchen table with a set of four chairs for $259; black metal bar stools, in an ultra-modern European design, for $39 each; and tower-style metal CD racks for the same price (reduced from $99). The idea is to carry just a few of the trendy items and styles that are currently found in the major stores, at better prices. They're shooting for a young-ish market here, the kind of folks who'll want to drive their purchases home in the car. Of course, if you'd prefer to have an item assembled and delivered, for a fee, that can also be arranged.

Also unusual is the fact that Great Futon is open seven days a week, one of the very few in this weekends-only enclave.

Haverty's Direct
- 5600 Buford Hwy., Doraville; 458-6700

See listing under "Furniture".

Kelly and Cohen Waterbeds Clearance Center
- 587 Cobb Pkwy., Marietta; 428-4334

Directly across the highway from their main showroom, Kelly and Cohen operate a smaller shop which includes their clearance outlet for floor samples, damaged items, and closeouts. It's all found at the rear of the store, with tags clearly denoting the original and sale prices. The amount of stock found here varies widely, since they can't really control the availability of these kinds of goods—or the chance of a sudden run on them by customers.

Still, the place is worth a look, along this suburban-sprawl shopping strip. Mr. C saw a discontinued twin size waterbed by Montrose, a four-poster with a pedestal base; it came complete with decking, heater, mattress, and liner for $299, reduced from its original $475. Some pieces are meant to be accessories to any bedding, like a solid cherry headboard with a built-in mirror, shelving, and cabinets, marked down from $899 to $480. And there are other kinds of pieces altogether, such as dressers, floor mirrors, and other bedroom furnishings.

Mattress King Discount Sleep Superstores
- 3651 Piedmont Rd. N.E., Atlanta; 233-4662
- 1715 Cobb Pkwy S.E., Marietta; 933-9226
- 6470 Dawson Blvd., Norcross; 416-8554
- 10997 Alpharetta Hwy., Roswell; 552-0231
- 2325 Highway 78, Snellville; 972-4476
- 6328 Memorial Dr., Stone Mountain; 879-1145
- 4773 Jonesboro Rd., Union City; 969-3001

You don't have to be royalty to afford regal bedding at Mattress King (also known in some locations as Mattress Giant). These stores specialize in selling Englander brand mattresses and box springs—but in a good selection of styles and firmness, at impressively low prices.

Buying direct from this manufacturer allows the stores to pass savings on to their customers. Mr. C spotted a queen size "Dreamer" bed and box spring set for just $349; to go with it, you may like a four-poster maple bed frame by Leggit and Plat for $399. Other selections at Mattress King include the Lady Englander "Anniversary" mattress set, priced at $339 queen, $490 king; both include a 15-year warranty.

Back on the subject of frames, a brass-plated bed frame was $339 in queen size and $499 in king, while a metal twin size frame for children, painted in either bright red or blue, was just $99. The "Sweetheart" twin frame, with its pretty scrolled metal headboard, was seen selling for $159. And an ornate oak-finish queen size Leggit and Plat wood bedframe is $439.

Mattress Warehouse Discount Sleep Stores
- 3761 Roswell Rd. N.E., Atlanta; 262-7923
- 2307 Browns Bridge Rd., Gainesville; 287-0353
- 7394 Tara Blvd., Jonesboro; 477-9661
- 976 Cobb Pkwy. S.E., Marietta; 424-4554
- 10800 Alpharetta Hwy., Roswell; 993-0117
- 4104 Lavista Rd., Tucker; 908-8002

Mattress Warehouse Discount Sleep Stores guarantee that their prices are the lowest available, and challenge you to find a better deal. The company offers hassle-free shopping, with features like same-day delivery and free layaway. There's no plush carpeting and soothing music in this true-to-its-name warehouse, but they make a point of keeping the stores well-stocked; if you want to buy a mattress and get it home in one day, there's usually no problem.

King Coils are in ready supply at the Warehouse, with even super firm styles available at good prices. The King Coil firm mattress starts at just $98 for a twin set, $150 for the full set, $189 for the queen set and $278 for the three-piece king size set with padded innerspring foundation.

The King Coil extra firms are $170 for the twin set, $258 full, $349 queen, and $449 for the king set; while the super firm style is $278 for the twin set, $348 full, $449 queen, and $549 for the three-piece king set. All of these come with a 15-year manufacturer's warranty.

Other brands, like Spring Air, are also sold here at comparable prices. All stores are open seven days a week.

Metropolitan Mattress

- 3690 Atlanta Hwy., Athens (Super Store); (706) 543-8001
- 3165 Peachtree Rd. N.E., Atlanta; 266-9131
- 1695 Church St., Decatur; 299-7186
- 1401 Johnson Ferry Rd., East Cobb; 971-9192
- 1690 S.E. Cobb Pkwy., Marietta; 850-8865
- 6520 Dawson Blvd., Norcross (Super Store); 416-1417
- 6746 Highway 85, Riverdale; 997-9401
- 11007 Alpharetta Hwy., Roswell (Super Store); 993-7410
- 6690 Roswell Rd., Sandy Springs; 250-1955
- 5370 Highway 78, Stone Mountain; 879-8082
- 4783 Jonesboro Rd., Union City; 306-1666

And other suburban locations

MR. CHEAP'S PICKS
Beds

✔ **Mattress Warehouse**—Rest assured that the deals found here are worth sleeping on.

✔ **Metropolitan Mattress**—A king-size set for under $200? Wow.

Metropolitan Mattress lays claim to the title of Atlanta's largest mattress chain; certainly, their high sales volume means savings for you. The fact that they manufacture their own mattress brand, Beautyedge, means even more good news for shoppers.

Beautyedge mattresses and box springs are sold individually, so you can buy only what you need. The firm style costs just $29 for each twin piece, $49 for each full piece, and $139 and $199 for the queen and king sets, respectively.

Simmons Beautyrest "Royalty," which received high marks recently in *Consumer Reports*, starts at $159 for each twin piece, $229 for each full, and $499 and $699 for the queen and king sets.

Other brands found here include Simmons, whose "Presidential" style is just $399 for a queen set or $549 in king; while the plush "Supreme" style is $599 for the queen set and $859 for king, with twin pieces $209 each and fulls just $259. Simmons adjustable beds are also stocked, with prices starting at $599.

Delivery is available seven days a week; if your purchase is in stock, same-day delivery is possible as well. Metropolitan Mattress also offers financing plans with no payments for six months, and layaways for up to a year. All stores are open seven days a week.

Rhodes Furniture

- 1680 Highway 138, Conyers; 922-9971
- 3655 Memorial Dr., Decatur; 289-2136
- 4363 Northeast Expwy. Access Rd., Doraville; 934-9350
- 5955 Stewart Pkwy., Douglasville; 489-5300
- 369 North Central Ave., Hapeville; 762-6181
- 119 North Cobb Pkwy., Marietta; 428-9401
- 633 Holcomb Bridge Rd., Roswell; 992-5143
- 2338 Highway 78, Snellville; 972-8289
- 6851 Shannon Pkwy., Union City; 964-7998

You don't need to be a Rhodes scholar to know that Rhodes is jam-packed with great values. From mattresses to dinette sets, you'll save plenty here. They've been in business for over a hundred years, so you *know* this is a store you can trust.

Queen-sized sleeper sofas are priced right, as low as $444 complete. Mr. C has seen similar quality ones for up to twice that price. Also for the bedroom, Rhodes was recently offering Simmons "Slumber Rest" queen mattress and boxspring sets for just $199, and the same model set in twin-size for just $99. And a Danish-style bedroom group, with dresser, mirror, chest, and head-board was almost $100 off retail at $577. Rhodes is also a great place for coffee tables, recliners, daybeds, hutches, and more.

One of the bonuses about shopping at Rhodes is that they offer a neat little satisfaction guarantee: If you're not happy with your purchase, return it within 30 days for a full refund or exchange, period. The stores are open from 10 a.m. to 9 p.m. Mondays through Saturdays, and from 1-6 p.m. Sundays.

Roberds

- 4380 Memorial Dr., Decatur; 296-2040
- 5300 Frontage Rd., Forest Park; 361-3288
- 550 Franklin Rd., Marietta; 426-0868
- 6288 Dawson Blvd., Norcross; 449-4214
- 2000 Holcombwoods Pkwy., Roswell; 587-0703

Sealy beds are (almost) a steal at Roberds. Whether you visit their vast home-base showroom in Norcross, or one of their chain store, you'll find the same competitive prices. Sealy "Satin Sleep" firm mattresses were recently selling for $58 per twin piece, and $98 per full piece, with the two-piece queen set just $248 and the three-piece king just $297. The "Satin Sleep Supreme" model goes for $194 for a twin set, $314 for a full, $397 for queen and $497 for the three-piece king set. "Satin Sleep Deluxe" mattresses and box springs by Sealy are $78 each piece in twin, $128 per piece in full, and $298 for the queen and $398 for the king sets.

The Norcross showroom also has a small clearance section at the back, where you may find some extra bargains on floor models from several of Roberds' departments—bedding, furniture and appliances. The selection, however, is not particularly large.

Roberds' Mattress Express service guarantees next-day delivery, and will also remove your old mattress. A unique feature offered by this company is its 30-day in-home trial: If you don't like your mattress and box spring after one month, you can return it without penalty.

All stores are open weekdays and Saturdays from 10 a.m. until 9 p.m., and Sundays from noon to 6 p.m. with deliveries made seven days a week.

BOOKS

You can save extra money on books by shopping for *used* editions. Atlanta is blessed with enough used book bookstores to give the hungriest bookworm indigestion; several are mixed into the listings below. Save even more by bringing in books that you no longer want. Most stores will give you a choice of cash or in-store credit; you'll usually get a higher figure by choosing the credit. It's a good, cheap way to check out new authors—and to keep your library lean.

A Cappella Books
- 1133 Euclid Ave. N.E., Atlanta; 681-5128

This Little Five Points mainstay sells new, used, out-of-print, and rare books; but it's the used books that are the real great buys. The store definitely sings to its own tune, including well-stocked sections of banned books, and gay and lesbian literature.

Classic works by Southern authors are also prominently featured, such as Flannery O'Connor and William Faulkner. O'Connor's *The Complete Stories*, listed at $8.95 for the paperback, was seen for just $4.50, in like-new condition. Tom Robbins' *Skinny Legs and All*, listed at $5.95 for the paperback, may be found for $3.

Among the other interesting finds: *Fiction of the Fifties*, with short works by Saul Bellow, James Baldwin, and others, in good shape for $4.95. *The Andy Warhol Diaries*, listed at $29.95 in hardcover, for $15. A fascinating biography on Jefferson Davis, by Clement Eaton, for $12.50 in hardcover. Taylor Branch's *America in the King Years, 1954-1963*, reduced to $12. Good selections on Civil War titles, too.

And, for the serious book collector, an eight-volume set of George Eliot's works is $100, while back issues of *The Paris Review* from the 1950s and 1960s go for $3.50 per copy.

Ageless Books
- 3369 Buford Hwy. N.E., Atlanta; 321-3369

Hidden like a bookmark among the storefronts of Northeast Plaza, Ageless Books is a quiet, cozy shop selling mostly used books. There's lots of fiction here, whether you're looking for big hardcovers by James Michener, Irving Wallace, Phillippa Carr, and James Clavell at less than half their original cover price; or paperback romance novels priced from 75 cents to $1.75. For that matter, there are also lots of used science fiction, horror, and mystery novels in paperback at the same low prices.

Other hardcover titles recently spotted here were John Fowles' *The French Lieutenant's Woman* for $1.95, and Sam Donaldson's witty memoir of his Reagan-dogging years, *Hold On, Mr. President*, reduced from $17.95 to $5.95. Open seven days a week, including evening hours.

Just a few doors down in this gigantic strip mall, **Frugal's Outlet** at 3363 Buford Highway (636-9085) is worth checking out for closeouts on new books in addition to their records and videos. Paperbacks, mostly pulp novels, start at 99 cents; hardcovers are mostly priced at $1.99 to $5.99. Almost all of these are brand new, but since they are publishers' overstocks, the selection is very limited. Both stores make good places to browse before or after seeing a $1.50 movie at the nearby Northeast Plaza 12.

Atlanta Book Exchange
- 1000 North Highland Ave. N.E., Atlanta; 872-2665

MR. CHEAP'S PICKS
Books

✔ **The Book Nook**—Lose yourself in these aisles of secondhand books, CDs, videos, and just about anything related.

✔ **The Book Warehouse**—Can't beat the bargains here. All remainders, all discounted dramatically, with all proceeds going to cancer research.

✔ **Chapter 11**—Even if you're filing, you can afford recently-remaindered bargain books here. Witty, knowledgeable staff.

✔ **Oxford Too**—Closeout book bargains, from art to world literature and everything in between.

One of a pair of related bookstores, Atlanta Book Exchange in Virginia-Highland specializes in new and used books of a fairly highbrow nature—literature, philosophy, American history, and the arts. Tall bookshelves and narrow aisles give it a crammed feeling, especially when cartons of newly arrived books are sitting in those same aisles.

The store has a particularly good selection of fine art books (the over-sized, color plate sort), such as one on Monet, reduced from an original $75 to a more reasonable $40. And H. W. Janson's *History of Art*, probably known to every art history college student, was recently spotted for just $29.95. Ah, if only you'd thought to look here before going to the campus bookstore!

Not everything at ABE strikes such a scholarly tone. Mr. C also found a copy of Lewis Grizzard's enjoyable *Elvis is Dead and I Don't*

Feel So Good Myself, in a used hardcover copy marked down from $11.95 to $5.95. And even a Frommer's guide to Washington, D.C.—the 1993 edition, seen during 1993—was found here, half it's cover price at $6.50. The store is open from 10 a.m. to 10 p.m. six days a week, plus Sundays from 1-6.

Barnes & Noble Booksellers
- The Peach, 2900 Peachtree St. N.E., Atlanta; 261-7747
- 7660 Northpoint Pkwy., Suite 200, Alpharetta; 993-8340
- 4776 Ashford-Dunwoody Rd., Dunwoody; 393-9277

This spiffy chain is related to B. Dalton and offers similar savings, but longer store hours in a more relaxed and refined setting.

Everything here, except for magazines and newspapers, sells for at least 10% below retail cover prices. Books on the *New York Times* bestseller list are sold at 30% off the cover price.

Special-ordering here is a breeze, and B&N's own publishing house offers classic hardcovers in easily-readable print at super savings. Their edition of Thoreau's *Walden*, for example, is only $4.98; same deal for titles like *Jane Eyre*, and many other great works of literature. And any art lover will appreciate B&N's *The History of Art*, an oversized, glossy edition bargain-priced at $24.98.

Overstocks are also super deals, and there's a wider selection here than in many of the other booksellers in town. A recently spotted example was the over-sized paperback *Bloom County 1986-1989* by Berkeley Breathed, selling for just $3.98.

The stores are open from 9 a.m. to 11 p.m., seven days a week.

B. Dalton Booksellers
- 24 Peachtree St. S.W., Atlanta; 659-1330
- Peachtree Center, 231 Peachtree Rd. N.E., Atlanta; 231-8516
- Underground Atlanta, 185 Lower Alabama St., Atlanta; 682-1797

- Lenox Square Shopping Center, 3393 Peachtree Rd. N.E., Atlanta; 231-1183
- 2968 North Druid Hills Rd. N.E., Atlanta; 634-4461
- 2100 Pleasant Hill Rd., Duluth; 476-8742
- Perimeter Mall, 4400 Ashford-Dunwoody Rd., Dunwoody; 394-4185
- 400 Ernest Barrett Pkwy., Kennesaw; 425-2817
- Greens Corner Shopping Center, 4975 Jimmy Carter Blvd, Norcross; 923-4484
- Northlake Mall, 4800 Briarcliff Rd., Northlake; 934-9292
- The Crossings at Roswell, 690 Holcomb Bridge Rd., Roswell; 998-7820
- Cumberland Mall, 1317 Cumberland Mall Rd., Smyrna; 435-3297

And other suburban locations
Sometimes, you just can't beat a national chain for great buys. B. Dalton is a sure-fire place to find reduced prices on *New York Times* bestsellers (hardcovers on the list are always are 30% off the list price). And, if you plunk down $10 to join their special "Book$avers Club," you'll get a further reduction of ten percent off every book, every day, even if it's *already* discounted. It may seem paradoxical to pay to save money, but if you're an avid reader, you'll more than make up for your investment.

Be sure to check out the bargain book table. Among the remainders and closeouts, Mr. C recently found *The Rodale Illustrated Encyclopedia of Herbs*—brought to you by the people who publish *Prevention*—reduced from a cover price of $24.95 to just $14.98. *The American Heritage Picture History of World War II* was seen for $19.99, Linda Ellerbee's *Move On—Adventures in the Real World* for $4.99 (list $21.95), and *Saint Maybe*, by the ever-prolific Anne Tyler, reduced from $21.95 to $5.99. For sci-fi fans, Douglas Adams' *The More Than Complete Hitchhiker's Guide to the Galaxy*, originally selling for a whopping

$51.80, is just $11.99—definitely a deal.

Also worth checking out is B. Dalton's in-house publication, "Discover Great New Writers," which profiles recently-published novels by impressive new talents.

Beaver's Book Sale
- 696-A Cleburne Terr. N.E., Atlanta; 876-1068

The flip side to Atlanta Book Exchange, Beaver's has a larger variety of more pop-oriented subjects. This shop gets lots of closeouts on recent fiction and non-fiction, plus used books, so that very little in the place goes much over $3-$5.

There's lots of stuff for various hobbies and activities, such as cooking and gardening. A range of Jane Fonda workout books, seemingly one for every aerobic fashion style, were all priced from $2 to $4 on a recent visit. Elsewhere on the testosterone scale, there is usually a good selection of Chilton's car repair guides—including books for older model years—all $3 each. Plus business, travel, computer guidebooks (*The 10 Minute Guide to Lotus 1-2-3* for $3), as well as lots of children's books.

In fiction, Mr. C found a new hardcover copy of John Updike's *Rabbit at Rest*, missing its paper dust cover, selling for just $2.95. There are special $1 sections with older major titles, plus shelves and shelves of used paperback mysteries and science fiction, selling for half the cover price. Even comic books, same deal!

Located on the tiny side street which runs between the Majestic Diner and the Plaza Shopping Center, this Beaver is busy from 10 a.m. to 10 p.m. six days a week, plus Sundays from 12 noon to 8 p.m.

The Book Nook
- 3342 Clairmont Rd. N.E., Atlanta; 633-1328

One moment inside the Book Nook was all it took before Mr. C was hooked. Cuteness aside, this is one of the most incredible stores any book or music lover could ever hope for. Located at the intersection of Clairmont and Buford Highway, these folks sell, buy, and trade books, magazines, comic books, books on tape, videos, records, tapes, and CDs. They've got so much of everything, they had to open a second store just to hold it all. Perhaps best of all, they're open until 10:30 p.m. every day of the week—presumably because it's so hard to stop browsing and leave.

The book section, about two-thirds of the store, is a homespun warren of shelves from floor to ceiling. Rolling stools, those little round ones you see in libraries, are used more as a place to perch and read than for actually climbing. Unlike libraries, or any other bookstore for that matter, books are strewn throughout the aisles like the leavings of some voracious bookworm. Interestingly, only one aisle is kept neat as a pin: Serial Romances. Here, new and used paperbacks are arranged in catalog order, by series—Harlequin, Bantam, Silhouette, and all the rest. Amazing.

Prices run generally as follows. Used paperbacks are sold at 40% off the cover price (30% off for science fiction), with a minimum of $1.80. Used hardcovers are marked on the inside, with even greater reductions. Hardcovers are in the minority here; most are recent and in very good condition. Magazines and new books are not discounted.

So, in paperback, you may find *The James Beard Cookbook*, with nary a stain on it, reduced from $12.95 to $7.75. Or Tom Clancy's massive *The Sum of All Fears* marked down from $6.99 to $4.20. *The 1993 Information Please Sports Almanac* was seen here recently, chopped from $9.95 to $6.00. And there are tons of computer guidebooks, like *Using Microsoft Word*, eight bucks off at $11.95.

In hardcover, John Jakes' *Heaven and Hell* was found as a new overstock, reduced from its original $19.95 to just $2.99. Same price for a like-new edition of Art Buchwald's hilarious *While Reagan Slept*. A used copy of Kitty Kelley's tell-all about

Frank Sinatra, *His Way*, was not $21.95, but $4.99. And *The Kodak Book of Practical 35mm Photography*, loaded with gorgeous color plates, could be snapped up for just $5.99. Lots of new and used children's books too, like *The Phantom Tollbooth* for $1.80. Talk about your Subtraction Stew.

Book Nook is also a haven for comic book fanatics, both for its selection of the latest releases—sorry, no discounts here—and for case upon case of older comics, all at half of the cover price, randomly mixed for maximum browsing potential. Speaking of bargain bins, don't forget the half-price book bins out front by the parking lot.

You can also sell your old books, comics, videos, and music, depending on condition and market demand; you'll be better off, though, if you choose what the store calls "universal credit"—good on anything in the store, new or used, except new magazines. Or, better still, consider swapping, which the store will do in almost any medium.

The store has been around for some twenty years; about two years ago, they opened up **The Bargain Trader**, at 4664 Lawrenceville Hwy. (Hwy. 29), Lilburn, telephone 564-9462; open seven days a week until 8 p.m. This store focuses primarily on the music side of things, with nearly 30,000 records, tapes, CDs, and videos.

Book Warehouse of Georgia

- 3097 Piedmont Rd. N.E., Atlanta; 237-1038
- 5370 Highway 78, Suite 515, Stone Mountain; 498-8077

Located not far from the Peachtree Road intersection, the Atlanta branch of this store is a bibliophile's paradise, with on average a quarter of a million books in stock at any given time. It's actually a converted car dealership, which should give you an idea just how huge the place really is. The warehouse atmosphere is at least softened somewhat by classical music wafting in the background.

Both stores offer so many fantastic book bargains that you can spend hours browsing—and buying—without blowing your budget. Shop in good conscience, too, since the Book Warehouse is a non-profit organization that sends all profits to the Holland M. Ware Cancer Research Laboratories at Emory University Hospital.

All books are unused, and most are in good shape; these are remainders and publishers' overstocks which have been rescued from certain death-by-shredding. The Warehouse buys in gigantic quantities (teachers and literary clubs, take note). Some of the hardcovers are a few years out of date, like Erica Jong's *Any Woman's Blues* ($5.99, listed at $18.95) and Stephen King's *The Dark Half* (marked down from $21.95 to $2.99); but these hardcovers can sometimes be cheaper than same titles in paperback.

The store has extensive shelves of children's books, as well as cooking, business, photography, literature, women's studies, health, biographies, and more. Some recent finds include Kitty Kelly's trashy *Nancy Reagan—The Unauthorized Biography*, reduced from a cover price of $24.95 to a super-cheap $1.99—how's that for trickle-down economics? For history buffs, Hedrick Smith's *The New Russians* was reduced from $24.95 to just $5.99. Armistead Maupin's *Sure of You* was marked down from $18.95 to $4.99.

The single-volume American Spectrum Encyclopedia was seen for $15.99, down from a whopping $85; and Exeter Books' weighty tome, *The History of Art*, was an amazing $19.99. It retails for over $60. If those are a bit too highbrow for you, perhaps you'd prefer Joan Collins' *Love & Desire & Hate*, just $2.99. And an unusual find here are Haynes automotive shop manuals, tucked in the back, selling for $12 per title.

Children's books include some of the most enduringly popular series, like the "Berenstain Bears" books (*The Messy Room, The Berenstain Bears Go to the Doctor*) at $2.99 per title; same price for Walt Disney's "Mickey Mouse" series, in hardcover. Alison Tharen's "Manners" books are also here, just $1.99 each. Robert Louis Stevenson's illustrated *A Child's Garden of Verses* was seen for $3.99. Imagine how cheaply that works out per poem!

The Book Warehouse stores are open from 9 a.m. until 9 p.m., Monday through Saturday; and from noon 'til 6 p.m. on Sunday.

Borders Bookstore
- Tuxedo Festival Shopping Center, Roswell Rd. N.E., Atlanta; 237-0707

Offering a 10% discount on almost every hardcover at all times, with a 30% slash off the prices of *New York Times* bestsellers, Borders is a mainstay in the Atlanta book market. It carries over 80,000 titles, with well-stocked sections from poetry to medieval history to "Esoteric Studies."

While you're almost always guaranteed good savings at Borders, the bargain books section is definitely a bonus. Mr. C saw a hardcover copy of the popular *Madonna Unauthorized* for $4.98, a quarter of its original price. *The Best American Short Stories of 1990*, listed at $20, was $4.98 (so what if the book is a couple of years old? You're getting masterpieces by Alice Munro and Madison Smartt Bell). At the other end of the intellectual spectrum, *With Love From Hell*—a postcard book by Matt Groening, creator of "The Simpsons"—was just $2.98. Same price for Sue Grafton's *"G" is for Gumshoe*, which listed originally for $16.95. And what would a book collection be without a bit of Mark Twain? Mr. Clemens's *Life on the Mississippi* was just $3.98.

Yet another perk offered by Borders is their book club registration program. Reading groups can save 25% on monthly bulk orders, when (and *only* when) the orders are placed in advance. Ask at the customer service area for more details—you could save your club big bucks.

Remember, too, to head for the Borders for author readings and book-signings. Children's book characters, like Madeline and Barney the Dinosaur, also make occasional appearances for book readings.

Borders Bookstore is open Monday through Saturday from 9 a.m. to 9 p.m., and Sunday from 11 a.m. until 6 p.m.

Chapter 11: The Discount Bookstore

- Ansley Mall, 1544 Piedmont Ave. N.E., Atlanta; 872-7986
- Briarcliff Village, 2100 Henderson Mill Rd N.E., Atlanta; 414-9288
- 2105 North Decatur Rd., Decatur; 325-1505
- Highland Plaza, 3605 Sandy Springs Rd. N.E., Marietta; 971-0744
- 6237 Roswell Rd. NE, Sandy Springs; 256-5518
- Snellville Plaza Shopping Center, 2274 Highway 78, Snellville; 736-0502

You certainly can't go broke shopping at Chapter 11 stores. All books here are sold at 11% off the cover price at all times; reductions are taken at the register. This reduction doesn't apply to their drastically reduced remainders, but these are so cheap (most hardcover novels are in the $5 range) that you'd hardly notice. *New York Times* bestsellers, like Jerry Seinfeld's *Seinlanguage*, are always slashed 30% off the list price.

Many of the books on the discount table are remainders and overstocks and may be a couple of years old, but they're also up to 75% off. Chapter 11 stacks and shelves even these closeout books neatly, keeping them in good shape. This is one bookstore that gets kudos from Mr. C for organization.

Among the goodies recently spotted here was *Jernigan*, the quirky fiction debut by *Newsweek* reporter David Gates, for just $4.99. John Updike's *Rabbit at Rest*, listed at $21.95, is just $6.99 here—a price that will let you rest easy, too.

Health books seen included Dr.

Miriam Stoppard's *Everywoman's Medical Handbook* at half-price, just $9.99. Elizabeth Kubler-Ross's *AIDS: The Ultimate Challenge*, considered one of the most important books on that topic, can be found here for $5.99, about two-thirds off the original cover price.

The section on parenting is especially well-stocked, with titles like Arlene Eisenberg's *What to Expect When You're Expecting* and Steve and Ruth Bennett's *365 Outdoor Activities You Can Do With Your Child*.

Keep on cooking with a copy of *Remarkable Feasts* by Leslie Forbes, a beautifully illustrated volume worth $30 but selling for just $15.99 at Chapter 11.

The staff at Chapter 11 tend to be voracious readers themselves, specializing in of out-of-the-mainstream books; be sure to check out their "Recommended Reading" displays to get ideas from their personal favorites. To give you an idea of just how much these folks enjoy reading, Mr. C would like to point out that there is even a "Recommended Book of the Day." Now, *that's* serious!

Children's Book and Gift Market

- 375 Pharr Rd. N.E., Atlanta; 365-0307

This Buckhead store primarily sells educational toys and books for children and young adults. Their selection of new books earned the store the honor of *Atlanta* magazine's "1993 Best Kids' Books" award, but the prices are certainly no bargain in Mr. C's book. Try the bargain section of Oxford Books right across the street instead; or, take the narrow staircase up to the second floor of the Gift Market for dramatically discounted books on slightly older paperbacks and hardcovers. Now, *here's* a story.

Up here, you'll find books for young and old alike. Libby Hathorn's *Thunderwith*, an acclaimed novel for young adults, was seen here reduced from $15.95 to just $2.95. A paperback copy of *In Country*, the novel-turned-movie by Bobbie Ann Mason, was cut from $5.95 to $3. And Kurt Vonnegut's *Slaughterhouse Five* was also half-price, at $3 for the paperback.

Books for tiny tots are also reduced by about half. For instance, books in the *My First Garden Tools* series by Joanne Barkan, regularly $4.95, sell for just $2 here. A book and tape set of that perennial procrastinator *Johnny Tomorrow*, goes for just $1, cut from its original list of $4.95.

The store recently expanded its hours. It's open from 9 a.m. to 6 p.m. on weekdays and Saturdays, and from 1 p.m. to 5 p.m. on Sundays.

Kendall's
* 2094 North Decatur Rd., Decatur; 633-6889

This jam-packed shop in the North Decatur Plaza is bursting with used copies of classics (many traded in by Emory students), romances, children's books, and much more.

Titles here tend to be priced according to demand; Alice Walker, Toni Morrison, and newer Stephen King books, for instance, are not reduced as much as works by other writers.

Most books go for about half of their original selling price. For young readers, a hardcover edition of *Little Men of the NFL* was seen for just $2. *Sweet Valley High* and *Sweet Dreams* romances for teens are $1.20 to $1.75 each, while *Silhouette* romances are $1.35 to $1.95 each. Mr. C loves how Kendall's organizes its romance books by number, so you won't have to search endlessly for a particular title.

Other great buys here may include Stephen King's *Misery*, the paperback version slashed (pun intended) from $4.50 to $3.50; and Alice Walker's *The Color Purple*, reduced from $5.95 to $4.20.

Classics like *Six Great Modern Plays* is just $4.95, while an out-of-print edition of James Joyce's *A Portrait of the Artist as a Young Man* is just $5.95, complete with introduction by Chester G. Anderson, an afterword, and extensive notes.

Self-help gurus will appreciate John Bradshaw's best-seller, *Coming Home*, cut from $12.50 to $8.75. Bill Cosby's *Fatherhood* is over half-off, reduced from $14.95 to $6.95. And psychology buffs will enjoy B.F. Skinner's *Walden Two*, in paperback for just $1.95. Many similar treasures await you here!

Oxford Books
* 360 Pharr Rd. N.E., Atlanta; 262-3333
* 2345 Peachtree Rd. N.E., Atlanta; 364-2700
* 1200 West Paces Ferry Rd. N.E., Atlanta; 364-2488

Book lovers, prepare to spend several hours at any of the Oxford Books locations. With mind-boggling selections from best-sellers to biography, aging, local authors, fine arts, sports, home and gardening, humor and children's books, the whole family is sure to find something to read here.

New York Times bestselling hardcovers and paperbacks are discounted by 30 percent, and they're sure to be always in stock here. And head to the discount tables for massive savings on everything from mysteries to children's picture books to coffee table books.

The *Where's Waldo* trilogy by Martin Handford is just $17.95; that will save you over $25, compared to buying the books separately. *Rolling Stone Magazine: The Uncensored Story* by Robert Draper is $4.98, down from $10.95. Mystery readers won't have to hunt for clues to savings here; not with the unabridged *Five Classic Murder Mysteries* by Agatha Christie for just $11.99, almost 80% off the combined list price of $49.75.

Another impressive collection spotted on the bargain book table was *The Globe Illustrated Shakespeare*. If you can carry this 2,300-page tome to the register, you'll pay only $29.98 for the Bard's collected dramas. That's less than a dollar a play!

The Pharr Road location is probably the most popular place in town to meet authors as they read and sign their latest releases; novelist Bobbie Ann Mason, poet James Dickie, and even former President Jimmy Carter have wowed the crowds at Oxford. The entertainment continues on Sundays at the Pharr store's Espresso Café, when local musicians play for free (see separate listings in the "Entertainment" section of this book, under "Readings and Literary Events" and "Music: Coffeehouses").

Be sure to pick up a copy of the store's own *Review*, a publication highlighting new releases from fiction to cookbooks, volumes on travel, spirituality, and psychology. And, for extra bargains on used books, check out **Oxford Too**, also in the Buckhead area (see listing below).

The staff at Oxford will happily search for out-of-print books for you, and special orders (even of foreign language magazines and newspapers) are not a problem. Rebinding services are also available, and gift wrapping is free.

As if all this isn't enough, the Oxford Bookstores are also an insomniac's paradise. The Pharr Road location is open until midnight on weekdays and Sundays, and until 1 a.m. (!!) Fridays and Saturdays. The other locations are open until 11 p.m. on weekdays and until midnight on Fridays and Saturdays. The Pharr Road store is also open an incredible 365 days a year.

Oxford Too
- 2395 Peachtree Rd. N.E., Atlanta; 262-3411

You don't need a degree from Oxford to figure out that this Buckhead store is probably *the* place in town for used books, whether you're looking for poetry, pop music or peace studies. Recent releases like Terry McMillan's paperback, *Waiting to Exhale*, or *Colony* by Anne Rivers Siddons, are priced at least 40% off their original list prices.

If you've shopped here before, you may have skipped over their $1 bargain book shelves due to their disheveled appearance. Take another look, says Mr. C. Tucked in here, you

may find a copy of Benazir Bhutto's autobiography, *Daughter of Destiny*, in paperback, or a hardcover edition of comic feminist Fay Weldon's *The Hearts and Lives of Men*.

Other used books may include *Princess Daisy* by Judith Krantz for just $3, *Plays* by W.H. Auden (just $17 for this rare copy), and, for sci-fi fans, Ursula K. LeGuin's *Sea Road*, which lists at $20, here just $6.98. Health-conscious Atlantans will like *Jane Brody's Nutrition Book*, and Robert E. Kowalski's *The Eight-Week Cholesterol Cure*, both around $4.

Mr. C also reminds you to not forget Oxford's remainders, especially in children's books and art. The Museum of Modern Art edition of *Seurat* listed for twice as much as its $37.98 price here; and the biography *Picasso: Creator and Destroyer* by Ariana Stassanopoulos Huffington is just $9.98, half off the $20 list price.

For the kids, a read-along book and cassette of *Mr. Tickle*, by Roger Hargreaves, is only $3.99, while Funk & Wagnall's *The World of Nature* is penny less than that. Lucy Maud Montgomery's 550-page collection, *Days of Dreams and Laughter*, is $10.

Cooks will like the *Duncan Hines Treasury of Baking*, priced at two-thirds off its $14.95 list price; and every parent can use a copy of the *Columbia University College of Physicians and Surgeons' Complete Guide to Early Childcare*, priced at half its $32.50 original price.

Starved for fiction? How about *Brightness Falls* by Jay McInerney (author of *Bright Lights, Big City*) for $3. And humor fans can chuckle over *The Best of Bombeck* for $9.98 (half-price) and Jay Leno's popular *Headlines*, same price, both in hardcover.

The store goes on and on. Old magazines offer a blast from the past for a paltry sum—back copies of *Life*, dating back to the 1960s, are priced at $2 to $4 each. Copies of *Rolling Stone* from the 1980s are $1.50, and late-eighties issues of *Esquire* and *Vanity Fair* go for $1 or $2.

This incredible store is open Sunday through Thursday from 9 a.m. to 10 p.m., and Friday and Saturday from 9 a.m. until midnight (!!).

Twisted Cover Book Shop
- 549-5 Amsterdam Ave. N.E., Atlanta

This may be one of the only book stores to turn up in Atlanta's many shopping outlet areas. Taking a cue from its neighbors, though, Twisted Cover takes a sort of outlet approach to books; everything in the store is priced at $1, $3, or $5, period. As appealing as the idea may be, unfortunately, the selection is very sparse. The stock is made up of an eclectic mishmash of overstocks, used college textbooks (evidently, the store's roots), and whatever else the buyers can get their hands on.

This leads to some unusual finds, like volumes of the *Congressional Record*, the *Supreme Court Reporter*, and other special-interest annuals. However, there are enough other (normal) subjects to make this store worth a look—including computers, travel, cookbooks, and history. There's a pretty good sports section, where Mr. C found a copy of Ted Williams' autobiography, *My Turn at Bat* for $3; some fiction, including novels by Ed McBain and Irving Wallace; and a good batch of books for children, from Dr. Seuss, Disney, and Sesame Street. Open Fridays through Sundays only.

CDs, RECORDS, TAPES, AND VIDEOS

You can save extra money on music by shopping for *used* items. Like used book shops, many of the stores below will allow you to trade in music you no longer want. Alas, they won't take just anything; used LPs, in particular, have become less marketable. Most stores will give you a choice of cash or in-store credit; you'll usually get a higher figure by choosing the credit. It's a good, cheap way to check out artists you might not take a chance on at full price.

Atlanta CD
- 2445 Cobb Pkwy., Marietta; 955-3177
- 4060 Peachtree Rd., Brookhaven; 239-0429
- 5495 Jimmy Carter Blvd., Norcross; 446-2339

Atlanta CD carries new and used discs in blues, jazz and rock. They do carry a few (*very* few) classical titles, but the store really caters to country fans (Conway Twitty's *Even Now* was seen for $4.97 used, while *Alabama's Greatest Hits* is $8.97) and alternative-rock lovers among the teen set.

The B-52's *Dance This Mess Around* is $9.97, while for $8.97 you may find such folk-rock titles as Suzanne Vega's *Days of Open Hand* or James Taylor's *Never Die Young*; R & B hits like Janet Jackson's *Rhythm Nation 1814* or Living Colour's *Time's Up*; and jazz picks like *Blue Interlude* with the Wynton Marsalis Septet or *The Last Set at Newport* by the Dave Brubeck Quartet. You won't be forgetting your budget if you buy Natalie Cole's *Unforgettable* CD for $10.97.

Oldies spotted by Mr. C include a new copy of Frank Sinatra's *Collectors Series* for $11.97, and, for the same price, *The Best of Rick Nelson*. You'll be able to afford to throw your own "Garden Party" with the money you've saved.

The clearance rack in the front of the store is also worth a peek. During Mr. C's visit, it featured *Jesus Jones Live* for $4.97, and *Rest of the Dream* by the Nitty Gritty Dirt Band for just $5.97.

27

MR. CHEAP'S PICKS
CDs, Records, and Tapes

✔ **Eat More Records**—One of the best local music selections around, at affordable prices.
✔ **CD Exchange**—From country to jazz to world beat, the CD Exchange has it, all with a quality guarantee.
✔ **Wuxtry Records**—For you LP collectors, this is a must-see. Great used alternative CD selection, too.

The stores are open from 10 a.m. to 9 p.m. Monday through Saturday and from noon to 6 p.m Sundays.

The Book Nook
• 3342 Clairmont Rd. N.E., Atlanta; 633-1328

One moment inside the Book Nook was all it took before Mr. C was hooked. Cuteness aside, this is one of the most incredible stores any book or music lover could ever hope for. Located at the intersection of Clairmont and Buford Highway, these folks sell, buy, and trade books, magazines, comic books, books on tape, videos, records, tapes, and CDs. They've got so much of everything, they had to open a second store just to hold it all. Perhaps best of all, they're open until 10:30 p.m. every day of the week—presumably because it's so hard to stop browsing and leave.

Like the books here, used music makes up the majority of the business. Used records and compact discs, in particular, offer almost as much selection as any full-price store; yet, most CDs are priced at $9, with bargain shelves of $2.99 discs. Cassettes are $3 used, with bargain bins of 99 cent tapes; used LPs are generally $2.50 to $4.50, depending

on their condition. New CDs tend to be $9.99, $11.99, and up. There is also a good selection of (new) books, magazines, and even sheet music covering everything from rock to Broadway.

There are plenty of used video movies, both on VHS tapes and the newer laser discs; you'll find top titles, like *E.T., Passage to India, Apocalypse Now, Star Trek: The Search for Spock*, and many others. VHS tapes are almost all priced at $9.50, while most laser discs are $16 each.

You can also sell your old books, comics, videos, and music, depending on condition and market demand; you'll be better off, though, if you choose what the store calls "universal credit"—good on anything in the store, new or used, except new magazines. Or, better still, consider swapping, which the store will do in almost any medium.

The store has been around for some twenty years; about two years ago, they opened up **The Bargain Trader**, at 4664 Lawrenceville Hwy. (Hwy. 29), Lilburn, telephone 564-9462; open seven days a week until 8 p.m. This store focuses primarily on the music side of things, with nearly 30,000 records, tapes, CDs, and videos.

CD Exchange
• 2280 Peachtree Rd., Atlanta; 351-7005
• 6690 Roswell Rd., Sandy Springs; 256-0057
• 4805 Briarcliff Rd., Northlake; 270-0057

After one visit, you may very well change your music store to the three-year-young CD Exchange. The chain offers Atlanta's largest selection of used CDs, and—get this—they even let you listen to your choices *before* you buy them, up to five CDs at a time. Every disc in the store, from Kiss to Kansas, is guaranteed, and each branch stocks over 6,000 titles.

Mr. C is told that about 60 percent of each store is devoted to rock 'n roll, with the rest of the selection split among jazz, blues, oldies and classical music. You'll find all your favorite rockers here: Eric Clapton, Rod Stewart, R.E.M., the Black Crowes, Lucinda Williams, Indigo Girls, and more. Jazz artists like Miles Davis and John Coltrane. All the big names in the classical world. You get the idea; it's a very complete inventory.

Titles are arranged in alphabetical order, so you won't go nuts looking for that one Travis Tritt disc which other used CD stores may tend to shelve haphazardly next to Kris Kross.

To further simplify your shopping here, all CDs are priced at $5.95 or $7.95 each, period. The higher-priced discs are in mint condition, and the lower-priced ones may have a few scuffs which merely affect their looks, not their sound.

Since all the inventory is computer-controlled, the sales help can tell you immediately, over the phone or in the store, whether the Exchange has any particular disc you nmay be looking for. And, if they don't have what you want, they'll take your name and call you as soon as a copy is traded in.

The CD Exchange will also pay you up to $5 each for your old CDs, depending on the condition and the number of identical titles they currently have in stock. Remember, you can extend their value by trading them for in-store credit. Gift certificates are also available.

CD Exchange stores are open from 10 a.m to 9 p.m., Monday through Saturday, and from noon to 6 p.m. Sunday.

Circuit City
* 4512 Memorial Dr., Decatur; 299-2001
* Town Center, 2801 George Busbee Pkwy., Kennesaw; 590-7444
* Southlake Mall, 1241 Morrow Industrial Blvd., Morrow; 968-1211
* 5495 Jimmy Carter Blvd., Norcross; 662-0557
* Cumberland Mall, 1968 Cobb Pkwy., Smyrna; 955-6866

You probably don't need Mr. C to tell you about megastores like this, but Circuit City can certainly save you some bucks on music, as much as the equipment to play it on.

The store's low price guarantee insures that if you buy something here, and then find the same product at a different store at lower price, Circuit City will refund you 110% of the difference. So, if you prefer not to take the "used" route to save money on CDs, cassettes, and videos, this is a good place to consider instead.

At the time of this writing, the store was selling every single-length CD for $12.95 or less—definitely a good start. U2's *Zooropa* was an unheard-of $9.99 ($7.45 for the cassette), as was *Janet* by Janet Jackson. That's almost as cheap as some stores charge for used CDs! Neil Young fans can find his *Unplugged* album for the same refreshingly low prices.

President Clinton could help the budget out by getting saxman Kenny G's *Breathless* CD for $9.99. UB40's *Promises and Lies* is just $10.45, and just $6.45 for cassette. Also for $9.99, you can get Luther Vandross's recent *Never Let Me Go*, or Toni Braxton's critically-acclaimed self-titled debut. Ziggy Marley and the Melody Makers' *Joy and Blues* is a bit more, at $10.45 for CD, while the *Sleepless in Seattle* soundtrack is just $11.95 for disc, and $7.45 for cassette.

The Circuit City stores in Lenox and Greenbriar Malls don't carry CDs, so if you're looking specifically for CD bargains, be sure to visit one of the five locations listed above.

Criminal Records
* 1101 Euclid Ave. N.E., Atlanta; 215-9511

It's a crime that other stores don't sell bargains as good as those Mr. C found at Criminal Records, a fantastic store smack dab in the middle of Little Five Points. This is the place for hard-to-find import CDs, arranged with impeccable organization.

Some of the steals Mr. C found here include a used CD copy of "The

Quintessence," featuring Quincy Jones and His Orchestra, for $7.99; and, for the same price, PM Dawn's *Of the Heart, Of the Soul and Of the Cross*, also on a used CD.

Other used discs include *The Rocky Horror Picture Show* soundtrack, seen for just $7.99, as was Bonnie Raitt's Grammy-winning *Nick of Time*. Peter Gabriel's *Greatest Hits* is a real deal—it crams 16 songs onto one CD for that same $7.99, used. *Hope Chest*, oldies and goodies from 10,000 Maniacs, is just $7.55.

Criminal Records gets another thumbs-up for its environmentally conscious recycling program. Keep your plastic bag when you shop here; bring it in the next time, and the store will give you 5% off your next cash purchase. Cool deal. The bags themselves are made from 100% recycled material, to boot. Mr. C thinks there ought to be a law that requires all stores to implement such programs.

Criminal's security system (kinda funny to say, isn't it?) is another way the store keeps prices low. Each CD jacket is displayed for customers to browse through, but the discs themselves are kept behind the counter, foiling would-be shoplifters—an expensive problem for many stores.

The store's hours are rather, um, casual. Mr. C. was informed that they open at "11-ish" in the morning, and close at "8-ish" in the evening, except on Sundays, when they close at "6-ish." Well, there ain't a law saying you have to have set hours, is there?

Eat More Records
- Sage Hill Shopping Center, 1799 Briarcliff Rd. N.E., Atlanta; 607-9122
- Carter Rockbridge Shopping Center, 1210 Rockbridge, Norcross; 717-8111

Perhaps they mean that you can show your good taste by shopping at Eat More Records, located near Emory University in Decatur. This is one of those little shops where the sales staff will talk about music with you for hours, suggest titles, inform you of upcoming concerts at Eddie's Attic

and other Atlanta venues, and generally gab.

The store's collection of used music leans toward folk, country, and rock; but there are quite respectable jazz and world beat sections as well.

Some of the recordings fall into the "oldies but goodies" category, like Fleetwood Mac's self-titled debut LP, selling for a mere $4 for a well-taken care of used copy. Same price for James Taylor's debut record, and Larry Gatlin's *Rain Rainbow* album (both used). Newer, less mainstream LPs like the soundtrack to the movie *Batman* are similarly priced.

Al Jarreau's *Soul Horizon* compact disc was seen recently for $6.99, *Hangin' Tough* by New Kids on the Block (remember them?) is just $5, while used CDs by Madonna, Michael Bolton, and Foreigner may go for as little as $3 apiece. Newer discs, like Reba McEntyre's *Sweet Sixteen*, Hank Williams, Jr.'s *Lone Wolf*, and *Siren* by Roxy Music are $7.99 each.

EMR also carries used cassettes. Check out the store's display of $1 cassettes, where Mr. C found a range of artists from Bon Jovi to Howard Jones.

You can shop more hours at Eat More Records, too, since they're open seven days a week; 11 a.m. to 7 p.m. Monday through Friday, 11 a.m. to 8 p.m. Saturday, and noon to 6 p.m. Sunday.

Frugal's Outlet
- 3363 Buford Hwy. N.E., Atlanta; 636-9085

Part of the Northeast Plaza shopping center, Frugal's—a name Mr. C just *has* to love—sells an interesting variety of new and used music and videos, as well as books. Interesting, because it's all such an odd mix of current titles, older closeouts, and leftovers that never sold in the first place. Perhaps, at 99 cents, some of these records will finally find a home, years after their release. There's a whole wall of them, mostly by totally unheard-of artists; though a

few by Chicago and the Oak Ridge
Boys stood out. Similarly, there are
cassettes from 99 cents to $3.99, and
CDs from $1.99 and up. There are
more current titles, priced about the
same as any mall store, with about
the same selection.

On the video side, there are more
useful bargains: Shelves and shelves
of "pre-viewed" movies, including titles like *Green Card, Housesitter, Pol-
tergeist,* and *Frankie and Johnny.*
Most of these are $10.99 each, about
half their original price or better.
You'll also find "classics," meaning
black and white films, for $3.99:
Comedies by Laurel & Hardy, and
Abbott & Costello were the best
deals seen in this section. These tapes
are closeouts again, not used. And
there are lots of new videos for kids,
like Peanuts, the Jetsons, and others,
selling for $5.99 each. Open seven
days a week.

Full Moon Records
• 1653A McLendon Ave. N.E.,
  Atlanta; 377-1919
Seemingly out of nowhere, in the
midst of this quiet neighborhood west
of Piedmont Park, you come upon a
block of artsy shops—like an enclave
that somehow hearkens back to the
sixties. Among these is Full Moon
Records, a secondhand shop which
manages to pack a lot into its tiny
storefront.

The pricing couldn't be easier: Unless marked otherwise, all LPs and
cassettes are $3 each (double-LP sets
are $5), and all compact discs are $7
each. Most of what you'll find here is
rock 'n roll, with some jazz and folk
mixed in. There are also several discount (!) bins, with albums for $1
and CDs for $3. Even in these,
among the many obscure titles, Mr. C
found a couple by well-known artists
like Simon and Garfunkel, Billy Joel,
Madonna, and others. Anyway,
they're just fun to browse through,
and the prices can't be beat. In fact,
the same can be said of the store in
general.

Rainy Day Records and Tapes
• 3005 North Druid Hills Rd., Toco
  Hills Promenade, Atlanta; 636-6166
Saving your pennies for a rainy day
to buy some great tunes? Here's the
place to spend them.

The store is worth a trip just to ad-
mire the vast collection of autographed photos, concert tickets, LPs,
and CDs amassed over the years by
the store's owner. From Webb Pierce
to Joan Jett to Peter Frampton, he has
enough memorabilia plastered along
the walls to open his own Hard Rock
Café.

There are some collector's items
worth hundreds, even thousands, of
dollars here at Rainy Day. A copy of
the Beatles' *Yesterday and Today,* recorded in mono (these are the very
original British releases), complete
with original cover, is priced at
$1000. Yikes! A rare copy of *Ella
and Louis* (Fitzgerald and Armstrong,
of course) is a bit easier to take at
$25. Mr. C is perfectly content, how-
ever, to check out all the $1 LPs, $3
double LP sets, and $2 CD singles
packed in to Rainy Day.

Everything, a 45rpm single by Atlanta's own Ellen James Society, was
seen for $2.95. LPs by bands like
Journey and Jackson Browne are just
$1, as is the *Flashback* soundtrack al-
bum. David Bowie's *ChangesBowie*
LP is $3. A copy of Joni Mitchell's
Wild Things are Free LP, in excellent
conditon, was spotted for $6, and *The
Beach Boys in Concert* LP for $7.

If you need to entertain the kiddies
when you're all cooped up inside on
a rainy day, stock up here on some
good children's records, such as Walt
Disney's *Happiest Songs,* for just $1.

Compact discs are in no short sup-
ply, with new and used editions
mixed together. *You Gotta Sin to Get
Saved,* the latest release by Maria
McKee, the former lead singer of
Lone Justice, is $8, while Randy
Travis' *Storms of Life* is just $4.
Other $8 discs seen here include Don
Henley's *The End of the Innocence,*
Steve Winwood's *Roll With It,* and
Jimmy Buffet's *A-1-A.* Same price
for CDs by local favorite Michelle

31

Malone, including *Drag the River* and *Relentless*. The store also carries lots of CD singles priced at $2 each, as well as plenty of used cassettes. Among these, you may find *The Swing* by Australia's INXS, priced at just $3, or Rickie Lee Jones' *The Magazine* for $4.

But wait—there's more! Every Saturday, the store holds a bargain-laden sidewalk sale, and at 3 p.m. that day there's usually a free in-store performance by local artists like Kodac Harrison and Shawn Mullins.

The store's hours are from 12-8 p.m., Sunday through Thursday; Fridays and Saturdays, they're open from 10 a.m. until 10 p.m.

Red Beans & Rice
- 2299 Peachtree Rd., Atlanta; 351-6163

You can savor the savings at Red Beans & Rice, the recently opened south Buckhead store specializing in blues, reggae and jazz music, along with soul imports and collectors' vintage jazz records.

Reduced-price used CDs have included Sting's *Ten Summoner's Tales* for $9.99, and an import of Sade's *Feel No Pain* for $13.99. *Diana Ross*, a 1970 LP which includes *There Ain't No Mountain High Enough*, was just $3.99. For the same price, you can find soul albums by the likes of Jermaine Jackson, Lionel Ritchie, and many others.

Collectors take note: the hard-to-find debut CD by (the man who used to be called, anyway) Prince was spotted here for just $12.99. It may be gone by now, but this gives you an idea of what goes on here. And check out RB & R's used LP section for super savings on rare jazz, like *The History of the Real Billie Holiday*, a two-record set seen here for $30.

Modern and service-oriented, Red Beans & Rice offers four headphone stations so that you can listen to the music before you buy. And free parking is available behind the store—a valuable commodity indeed for Buckhead. The store is open Monday through Thursday from 10 a.m. to 9

p.m., Friday and Saturday from 10 a.m to 10 p.m., and Sunday from noon to 6 p.m.

Sound Warehouse
- 5224 Memorial Drive (Memorial Bend Shopping Center), Stone Mountain; 294-9455
- 4101 Roswell Rd. (Providence Square Shopping Center), Marietta; 973-4725
- 5500 Jimmy Carter Blvd., Norcross; 449-4335
- 6320 Roswell Rd., Sandy Springs; 256-0344

Mr. C doesn't care for the trend toward music mega-stores; they have none of the quirky charms of individual shops. But Sound Warehouse—especially during a sale—is hard to beat for great buys. Rock is the language primarily spoken here, but you can also find a good selection of soundtracks, easy listening music, and jazz.

During sale promotions, new cassettes are often priced at $7.99 or so, and CDs are usually $11.99. You have to keep a sharp lookout, of course, for sales on a particular new release. Blind Melon's debut album, featuring the song *No Rain*, and Melissa Etheridge's *Yes I Am* both went on this kind of sale. So did titles like *Uptown MTV Unplugged*, Duran Duran's comeback release, *Duran Duran*, and Earth, Wind & Fire's *Millenium*. Radiohead's *Pablo Honey* CD premiered even lower, at just $10.99, and En Vogue's *Runaway Love* was priced at $9.99 as a new CD. *The Hits/The B-Sides*, the three-CD boxed set by the singer who used to call himself Prince, came out with a retail price of $50; it was seen here for $37.99.

So if you don't mind being bombarded by crowds (and being tempted by video rentals while you shop for CDs), give Sound Warehouse a look.

Target
- 2400 North Druid Hills Rd., Atlanta; 325-3211
- 3751 Floyd Rd., Austell; 436-3999
- 5025 Old National Hwy., College Park; 762-7711

- 1648 Highway 138, Conyers; 929-3300
- 4000 Covington Hwy., Decatur; 288-5000
- 5766 Buford Hwy., Doraville; 455-8900
- 2300 Pleasant Hill Rd., Duluth; 623-3519
- 6525 Tara Blvd., Jonesboro; 477-9690
- 805 Sandy Plains Rd., Marietta; 428-5100
- 610 Holcomb Bridge Rd., Roswell; 993-7500
- 235 Johnson Ferry Rd., Sandy Springs; 256-4600
- 2201 South Cobb Pkwy., Smyrna; 952-2241
- 2140 McGee Rd., Snellville; 979-4300
- 6425 Lawrenceville Hwy., Tucker; 934-9750

Here's another big, bland department store, but keep your eye on this Target for their CD sales. Discs normally priced at $13.99 and $14.99 are reduced to just $10.99 during sales on particular titles, which change weekly. These recently included Lenny Kravitz's *Are You Gonna Go My Way*, *Take A Look* by Natalie Cole, *It Won't Be the Last* by Billy Ray Cyrus, and *Human Wheels* by John Mellencamp.

Billy Joel's super-hot *River of Dreams*, which retails for $15.79, was cut to $11.99 soon after its release, as were new titles by Barbra Streisand and Tina Turner. So were such hits as *The Ballads of Madison County*, and Mariah Carey's *Music Box*.

Less current CDs, regularly priced at $11.99, sell here for $9.99. Among these titles, you may find James Taylor's *Greatest Hits*, *Elvis' Golden Records*, *Labour of Love* by UB40, and *Ten Strait Hits* by George Strait.

And don't miss (no pun intended) the section of budget CDs priced at $3.99 to $5.99 everyday—classics like Patsy Cline's *Walkin' After Midnight*, and *Reggae* by Bob Marley.

Tower Records

- Around Lenox Shopping Center, 3400 Wooddale Rd. N.E., Atlanta; 264-1217

Open until midnight every single day of the year, Tower is *the* place to run to if the baby won't stop crying and you think that playing a Frank Sinatra song just might do the trick, or if you're simply an insomniac yourself.

The nation's top-selling CDs and tapes are always discounted 30% off list price; newer releases, rising up the charts, also tend to be marked down—usually to about $10.99 for CDs, $7.99 for cassettes. And be sure to check the cut-out bins, where overstock music is always drastically reduced. You can usually find all varieties of music represented, from Patsy Cline to UB40, represented.

The store also stocks a bowling-alley-lane-long aisle of magazines, from *Sassy* to *Spin*. And, by the way, Tower opens at 9 a.m. for you early risers.

Turtles Music & Video Super Stores

- 3061 Buford Hwy. N.E., Atlanta; 633-2539
- 1605 North Buford Hwy. N.E., Atlanta; 932-0067
- 857 Oak St. S.W., Atlanta; 753-5655
- 29 Peachtree St. S.W., Atlanta; 524-6475
- 1536 Piedmont Ave. N.E., Atlanta; 607-1609
- 2625 Piedmont Rd. N.E., Atlanta; 231-4879
- 1039 Ponce de Leon Ave. N.E., Atlanta; 898-9441
- 1211 Powder Springs Rd. S.W., Atlanta; 514-3900
- 4429 Roswell Rd. N.E., Atlanta; 252-8541
- 7855 Roswell Rd., Sandy Springs; 698-2970
- 6235 Roswell Rd, Sandy Springs; 255-9406

And other suburban locations
Also:
- Turtle's Rhythm and Views, 2099 Peachtree Rd. N.E., Atlanta; 605-7131

Race over to Turtle's for great buys on new and collectors' series CDs and cassettes. On any given day, Turtle's will most likely have *some* kind of unique bargain. A recent month-long promotion offered sale prices on every title by a different artist each day. On Monday, every Eric Clapton disc was $1.96 off regular price; by Tuesday, every Beatles disc was discounted, and so forth.

Regular prices at Turtle's are okay, if not spectacular. Recent releases are often reduced, too. Bjork's debut was selling for $13.99 during Mr. C's visit, as was Sawyer Brown's *Outskirts of Town*, while *Rip Off the Knob* by The Bellamy Brothers was just $12.99 for CD and $7.99 for tape.

Turtle's often features good prices on "greatest hits" collections. *The Steve Miller Band Greatest Hits 1974-1978* was recently just $9.99 for CD. Same price for the *Collectors Series* of Ol' Blue Eyes, Frank Sinatra. Other easy listening classics, as well as classic rock from the 1960s and 1970s, are also discounted.

And don't be a slow poke if the store has one of their super tent sales. They're not always held at every location, but they're worth the trip if you have to make one. Compact discs normally priced from $9.99 to $16.99 will sell for $7 each, or two for $12; budget CDs regularly priced from $5.99 to $8.99 sell for an amazing $2.50, or five—count 'em, five—for $10. Cassettes that were in the $5.99 to $8.99 range suddenly sell for just a buck each or six for $5, and videos sell for $4 each or two for $6.

Wax 'n' Facts
- 432 Moreland Ave. N.E., Atlanta; 525-2275

Not for the claustrophobic, or the hearing aid crowd, Wax 'n' Facts is great place for used LPs, CDs, and cassettes in jazz, classic rock and soul music. Other areas, like folk, are less well-stocked. Meanwhile, this is one of the better places in town to try if you're looking to find releases by local bands.

If you can wend your way through the crowded aisles to the back corner of the store, you'll find new sampler and full-length CDs by local artists. Titles from Caroline Aiken, Cass Kennedy, Wendy Bucklew, Kristen Hall, and Michelle Malone are well-stocked and hover in the $11 price range.

W-n-F offers all kinds of R & B cassettes for your listening pleasure, most priced at $4, from Aretha Franklin to the Temptations. No wonder *Creative Loafing* voted this place the best shop in town for used cassettes. They have plenty of $4 LPs, too, from jazz greats like Chick Corea and Count Basie.

For just $3, you can take home *Michael Feinstein Sings Irving Berlin*, sweet tunes from the new darling of the Broadway and cabaret circuit. Mr. C also found an $8 CD by the Dirty Dozen Brass Band, and a slew of discs by jazz sax great David Sanborn priced from $7 to $9. Alternative music lovers will want to dig up *Fossils* by Dinosaur Jr., at just $7.50, or Nirvana's debut release, *Bleach*, a rare find and well-worth the $8 asking price.

For the thrill of discovery and some offbeat fun, rummage through the bins of no-one-wants-'em LPs. They're partially buried along the floor. *All I Need*, the LP by ex-General Hospital star Jack Wagner, is one of the oldies here, and all you need to take it home is $1. The boxes *do* contain plenty of clunkers, but Mr. C did find some easy-listening favorites (like the Beach Boys and the Carpenters) among these "Lost 45" titles.

Wuxtry Records
- 2096 North Decatur Rd., Decatur; 329-0020
- 197 E. Clayton St., Athens; (706) 369-9428
- 510 Baxter St., Athens; (706) 353-1894

Mr. C likes the bunches o'bargains to be had at North Decatur Plaza—Rainbow Foods, Chickibea's consignment clothing, Kendall's Books, and—not to be left out—Wuxtry Records. The shop is crammed full of used LPs and

CDs, and caters specifically to rock and alternative-music listeners.

Some of the big hits for tiny budgets include titles by Joe Jackson, Husker Du, and the soundtrack to *Wayne's World*, each priced at $3. New tapes by (Atlanta's own import!) Elton John start at just $6.99. And a used CD of the *Malcolm X* soundtrack was recently seen for $9.

Other deals found here included John McCutcheon's LP, *Mail Myself to You*, for $7.99, and Pete Seeger's *We Shall Overcome: The Live Carnegie Hall Concert* for $6. R & B fans can pick up a copy of Ashford & Simpson's *A Musical Affair* for a mere $3. Plus good prices on music by local artists.

Wuxtry's open from 11 a.m. to 7 p.m. Monday through Saturday and Sundays from noon until 5 p.m.

CAMERAS AND PHOTOGRAPHIC SUPPLIES

There are lots of places to save money on photography equipment in Atlanta. Some, unfortunately, are as far below repute as they are below retail. With merchandise that is imported from foreign countries, there is a greater possibility of shady deals, or inferior quality. Mr. C says this not out of any kind of prejudice, but because he wants you to be careful.

One of the best ways to protect yourself, if you have doubts as to *any* store's reliability, is to ask about their guarantee policy; make sure the item you want carries an American warranty. Since some stores deal directly with manufacturers in the Far East, their merchandise many carry a foreign warranty instead. Even for identical products, a foreign warranty can make repairs a hassle—unless you don't mind paying the postage to Japan! Remember, you are perfectly within your rights to inquire about this in the store.

Atlanta Camera Exchange
● 2682 Wiegelia Rd. N.E., Atlanta; 325-9367

If you're looking to save money on a camera, consider getting a used camera at the Atlanta Camera Exchange. Owner Bob Schadell is a former photojournalist who worked for such publications as *Sports Illustrated*, so you can be sure that he and his staff know their stuff. They've been at it for fifteen years. And, with anywhere from two to three hundred cameras in stock at any given time, you're bound to find something that's right for you and your budget.

Nikon, Olympus, Canon, and Minolta camera bodies and lenses are always available, in a wide selection of conditions, from good to excellent, and discounted accordingly. During Mr. C's visit, there were just four Leicas in stock; these are always in high demand. If you're seeking a particular camera and don't see one in the store, ask to be placed on a wait list and ACE will call you if one turns up.

One thing you *won't* find here, though, are cameras of the "point-and-shoot" variety—this is a store for "advanced amateurs to professionals." There are plenty of SLR cameras to choose from, and the store tries to carry only merchandise for which you can still find accessories. Buy one of their camera bodies or darkroom enlargers, and you can bet that there are still plenty of lenses and filters to go with them—many of which are probably available here at ACE.

Some of the other used equipment available here includes plenty of used Kodak slide projectors (along with empty carousels), projection screens, light stands, and tripods; also, 4 x 5 and 8 x 10 professional view cameras.

ACE also offers consultations to professional artists and amateur shutterbugs; feel free to make an appointment to discuss your photo-related questions. All equipment is warrantied for a minimum of 90 days after purchase, so you can buy these used items in good faith, and repairs are done on the premises. Such is the reputation of Atlanta Camera Exchange, in fact, that they actually receive mail order requests from as far away as California, especially for their hard-to-find panoramic cameras.

Buckhead Camera
- 3740 Roswell Rd. N.E., Atlanta; 266-1020

Mr. C didn't expect to make too many cheap discoveries in the Buckhead area, so this camera store came as a pleasant surprise. BC is staffed by knowledgeable, seasoned professionals who can answer any and all of your questions on equipment and developing. They also have plenty of new and used cameras and lenses to choose from, which do give you some money-saving options.

Cameras recently seen here ranged from a brand-new Canon EOS Rebel SII kit for $399.95 to a used Pentax MX 35mm camera for $159. There's an especially impressive selection of zoom lenses, like a new Fuji DL25 Plus for $59.95, a Pentax IQ Zoom 105R lens discounted from $319.95 to $297, or an Olympus Stylus zoom kit for $239. A used Olympus ST-20 flash unit would make a good addition for $49.

Some older camera bodies still in good shape are a Canon AE-1 body for $80 or a Ricoh XR6 body for $50. A used Pentax K-1000 body and lens could be snapped up for $249.95; or a Minolta XG-A camera with a 50mm, f1.7 lens for $105. Add a used Minolta 28mm, f2.8 lens to the kit for only $6. Another good item spotted was a used Olympus 50mm, f1.8 lens, looking absolutely like new, for $38.

Buckhead Camera is easy to find, located in Powers Ferry Square.

Camera Bug
- 1799 Briarcliff Rd. N.E., Atlanta; 873-4513

This store in the Sage Hill shopping center, just on the Atlanta/DeKalb border, is another good place to search for used cameras and lenses. Its proximity to Emory University is probably another reason why you'll find some bargains.

During a recent visit, Mr. C found a Pentax K1000 camera body, with a 50mm lens, in excellent shape; it was priced at $150. If you could find the same camera new, it would cost as much as $250. Meanwhile, the salesman was willing to haggle the price down a bit, to $125. Such a deal!

Another find was a Canon rangefinder camera body and lens—with flash—for $125. A Minolta Maxxum 50mm lens was spotted (actually, it was quite clean, ha ha) for a low price of $45. And a Gossen N100 hand-held light meter would complete the outfit for another $60.

You homemade movie aficionados should be sure to browse through the Camera Bug's movie and camcorder selection—Mr. C found a Canon Super-8 movie camera, part of a dying breed, for $75. They're open six days a week, closed on Sundays.

Camera Country USA
- 270 Hilderbrand Dr., Sandy Springs; 256-2595

Just off of Roswell Road, and just north of the Perimeter, Camera County USA offers solid values on a wide selection of new and used cameras and flashes. The store is not as huge as the name might suggest, but Mr. C found their stock of used cameras particularly impressive.

New equipment on the cheap includes a Star brand monopod for $15 (retail price $40), a Minolta "Weathermatic" waterproof camera for $219, a high-end Minolta 9XI 35mm camera for $799, a fully-automatic Olympus Stylus 35mm for $169, and a Ricoh Ultra-Dual automatic camera for $139.

Mr. C noted a used Gemini 80-100 zoom lens for $65, and a used Minolta MX-700 camera body for $250. Other bargains on previously-owned equipment included a Canon AE-1 Program camera, complete with 50mm lens, for $175; and a Canon FTb all-mechanical body and lens for $115.

A Vivitar XV-2, body only, was seen for $85; a Pentax KM camera with 50mm lens was just $115, while a Nikon AF with 35-105mm lens was $275. Camera Country even carries the occasional Leica. When Mr. C shopped there, a Leica R4 with 50mm lens and grip included, built in the mid-1980's, was $1,750; that may not exactly be your picture of cheap, but it's about $1,000 less than the new model nowadays.

Used flashes are in no short supply, either. A Pentax AF 160 flash was priced at a pittance ($25), while an Olympus Auto 310 flash was just $30, and a Sunpak 2000 DZ flash was just $35.

The store's open from 9:30 a.m. to 6:30 p.m. weekdays, 10 a.m. to 5 p.m. Saturday, and from noon to 5 p.m. Sunday.

Century Photographic Supply
- 8290 Roswell Rd., Sandy Springs; 992-9463

Moving further to the north, Mr. C discovered this tiny shop specializing in photographic development, especially black-and-white prints. They also happen to carry a limited but interesting selection of about fifty cameras, both new and used.

There are no used Leicas here, or much high-end merchandise, for that matter. The used cameras are primarily single-lens reflex models, with the new ones being mainly point-and-shoot. The average price for a used 35mm camera, including lens, is about $150. Used 35mm and zoom lenses, by brands like Nikon and Canon, start at around $50 each.

With its emphasis on photo development, CPS is also a good place to try for big savings on a used enlarger. The stock changes constantly,

MR. CHEAP'S PICKS
Cameras

✔ **Atlanta Camera Exchange**—A super-experienced staff will help you save big on used photographic equipment of all kinds.

though, so call ahead to check on their current selection.

CPS is open from 9:30 a.m. to 7 p.m. Mondays through Fridays, and from 9:30 a.m. to 5 p.m. Saturdays. The store is closed Sundays.

KEH Camera Brokers
- 188 14th St. N.W., Atlanta; 892-5522

This is America's largest *used* camera dealer, and while you can't walk into their Midtown location to shop, Mr. C thinks you should know about this underrated mail-order company. They sure do know their stuff, and they carry a truly amazing selection of merchandise, with brands from Bronica to Hasselblad to Mamiya and Pentax represented. Call KEH for their 60-page catalog.

All cameras and lenses sold by KEH are graded, by degree of wear. Codes range from "new" to "like new" all the way to "bargain" and even "ugly." Mr. C doesn't especially recommend the cameras categorized as "ugly", since these could be damaged enough to affect the quality of your photos; let's face it, there *is* such a thing as being *too* cheap.

Some of the better deals found in their latest catalog include a Bronica 250 f5.6 Zenzanon PG camera, in like-new condition, for $849. If it really were new, it would retail for $1,399. For less-serious picture-shooters, the basic Canon AE-1 models can run as low as $100 for one in good shape.

KEH offers a two-month warranty

on all its used equipment, and you may return your purchase within 14 days if there are any problems. The company also accepts trade-ins, which may be a further way to save yourself some money. Call KEH for more info.

Showcase, Incorporated

• 2323 Cheshire Bridge Rd. N.E., Atlanta; 325-7676

This recently-remodeled shop, near the Tara movie theater, is run by exceptionally knowledgeable salespeople who tailor advice to your abilities *and* your pocketbook. The store stocks both new and used cameras and lenses in everything from point-and-shoot to advanced SLR styles. They also have lots of camera bags, books, and accessories. The selection is so good, and the help so professional, that this store was chosen as the supplier to Clark Atlanta University photography classes.

New cameras and equipment are priced competitively, like the Canon EOS Rebel SLR with zoom lens for $399; a Nikon FM2 body for $525; or a Lowel total flood light for $143. Some of the used cameras available during Mr. C's visit included a Canon EOS 750 body for $250, an Olympus F280 with flash for $225, and a Canon AE-1 with a 50mm *and* 100-200mm zoom lens, plus a flash—a real bargain at $275.

For the truly serious photographer, a Nikon FE2 camera, complete with 50mm lens and motordrive advance, may go for as low as $425; a Rolleiflex SL 35mm camera with 50mm lens and 85mm portrait lens is $250, and a Leica R-4 with motor drive for a very reasonable $800. For those with simpler tastes, Showcase also has a Nikon F2 body only, (with no meter or lens), for $120. To organize it all, try the Tamrac Zoom System 4 deluxe case for $105, seen for over $40 more in other stores.

Film prices here rival those at many other discounters. Kodak Ektachrome Elite slide film sells for $6.22 for a 24 exposure roll; $8.65 for 36 exposures. Hard-to-find photo mailers in a variety of sizes are also for sale.

For do-it-yourself developers, a 16-ounce bottle of Kodak color developer starter is just $5.52, and 17 ounces of AGFA black-and-white film developer is $11.75, while gallon-capacity poly bottles for the darkroom are $3.50 apiece. Just about anything else you might need for the darkroom is available here.

Showcase is open from 9 a.m to 6 p.m. weekdays, and from 10 a.m. to 5 p.m. Saturdays. It's closed on Sundays.

Wolf Camera & Video

• 150 14th St. N.W., Atlanta; 892-1707
• 1579 Monroe Dr. N.E., Atlanta; 897-1111
• 117 Peachtree St. N.E., Atlanta; 525-1153
• Underground Atlanta, 168 Lower Alabama St., Atlanta; 524-1343
• 1197 Peachtree St. N.E., Atlanta; 898-8735
• Lenox Square Shopping Center, 3393 Peachtree Rd. N.E., Atlanta; 237-3388
• 2357 Peachtree Rd. N.E., Atlanta; 239-0303
• 1258 West Paces Ferry Rd. N.W., Atlanta; 233-3542
• 4441 Roswell Rd. N.E., Atlanta; 252-0893
• 231 Peachtree St. N.E., Atlanta; 614-1766
• 1450 Cumberland Mall, Smyrna; 434-5995
• Gwinnett Place Mall, Duluth; 476-0710
• 4400 Ashford-Dunwoody Rd., Chamblee; 394-2858

And other suburban locations
Bargain hunters: Don't be afraid of a big, bad chain like Wolf Camera. From serious high-end to everyday point-and-shoot cameras, to film, developing supplies, photo albums, and processing itself, you can huff and puff your way around town but will have a hard time finding better values than here.

Kodak film, for example, is nice and cheap; a three-pack of Kodak

Gold 24-exposure film sells for $13. Furthermore, when Mr. C was shopping, the store was offering a "buy three rolls, get one free" deal on 24-exposure rolls of Kodacolor ASA 200 film.

Professional-grade Leica cameras start at $300 (for the pocket-sized "Mini" automatic) to $2600 for an M6 edition 35mm camera with near-silent operation, complete with a three-year warranty.

Single-use cameras—you know, those disposable ones—are also inexpensive, like the Kodak "Funsaver 35" for just $6.74. Regular automatics are also smartly priced, like the Nikon "SmileTaker" auto-focus for $79.95, which includes a complete outfit of film, batteries, cleaning kit and case. The similar Fuji DL-7 outfit is just $29.95, with the case $10 extra, and the Minolta "Memory Maker," with red-eye reducing flash

and automatic date imprint, is $40. Accessories on the cheap include a Veblon four-section leg tripod for $39.99, and a Sunpak FK2 colored filter kit for $40.

The stores go on and on. Optical and video equipment are available here at competitive prices: Bushness 10 x 50 binoculars start at just $44.95, while 7 x 35 binocs start at only $29.95. A Panasonic PV-IQ203 camcorder costs $700, and Sony camcorder packages—complete with filters, three videotapes, a head cleaning tape and a Sunpak "Readylite 20" video light kit—start at $800.

Wolf Camera stores are open seven days a week. The main location in Midtown is open weekdays from 8:30 a.m. to 6:30 p.m., Saturday from 10 a.m. to 5 p.m., and Sundays from 12:30 p.m. to 5:30 p.m.

CARPETING AND RUGS

Everyone knows that Dalton, GA is the place to get real bargains on carpets. After all, if you want the best deals, you've gotta go to the source. But, if you're not able to make the trek up north, consider the following stores:

Carpet Mill Outlet
- Winn Dixie Shopping Plaza, 2076 Headland Dr., Atlanta; 763-0776
- 1169 Powder Springs Rd. S.W., Marietta; 590-9143

You don't necessarily have to go to Dalton to find a huge carpet showroom. Carpet Mill Outlet is the largest showroom in the perimeter area.

Because of low operating costs and giant-sized lot purchases, CMO can offer carpeting for as little as $3.99 per square yard. Broadlooms, many by name brand mills, sell here in hundreds of colors and dozens of styles.

If you have the chance to check in or call regularly, be on the lookout for periodic in-store specials. In one recent offer, complete installation of

carpet in three rooms (up to forty square yards) cost just $380.

Remnant choices can definitely save you up to hundreds of dollars, too; but be sure to check for boo-boos, stains, and uneven cuts before you buy. Next day installation is available, and Carpet Mill Outlet can offer instant credit to qualified customers.

Color Tile and Carpet
- 3141 Piedmont Rd. N.E., Atlanta; 237-2318
- 1475 Holcomb Bridge Rd., Roswell; 587-0321
- 4959 Memorial Dr., Stone Mountain; 294-1881

And other suburban locations

Color Tile is a national chain offering

good values on big name brand carpeting. Saxony carpets, treated with Anso Scotchgard, were seen here going for $28 per square yard; or, $40 a yard for their softest, most plush version. These prices include installation and padding. Sculpted-texture Saxony styles were $40 a yard, again with installation included.

DuPont Stainmaster Plus carpeting was $26 for textured finishes, and $37 a yard for MasterLife carpeting. Multi-colored wool berber rugs, completely installed with padding, are a well-priced at $26 a square yard. Big-loop berbers are $40 a yard, while patterned ones are $30 a yard.

Be sure to keep an eye out for Color Tile's once-a-year warehouse sale, when those berber rugs are slashed (well, not literally) to $10 a square yard, the plain Saxony to $12 a square yard, and carved Saxony to $25 a square yard.

Color Tile and Carpet's hours are 8 a.m. to 8 p.m. on weekdays, Saturdays from 8-6, and Sundays from 11 a.m. to 5 p.m.

1001 Rugs Persian & Oriental Rug Warehouse
- 4367 Roswell Rd. N.E., Atlanta; 256-1001

For a magical ride through the world of Middle Eastern and Oriental carpets, come here to 1001, located in the Roswell Wieuca Shopping Center. Don't be put off by the hoity-toity advertisements the shop places in *Atlanta* magazine. This is a true warehouse in size and price, but one with surprisingly unusual warehouse service.

If you don't know a Dhurry from a chainstitch, or a Chinese rug from a Pakistani rug, have no fear—the staff here will be more than happy to explain all of it to you. The selection in each type of rug, in sizes from runners to ballroom-size carpets, is nothing short of fantastic. And the direct-import prices won't leave you feeling trampled upon.

A diamond-pattern 6' x 9' chainstitch from Pakistan was seen for only $395, and worth about twice

that price elsewhere. A 6-foot round Dhurry rug, retail value $270, was selling for only $129, while the same type in a 5' x 9' size was priced at half off its $660 list price.

A 6' x 9' Persian pile rug (which Mr. C was told are among the finest carpets made), is $800—over half-off its retail value of $1,900. A Persian Bokhara rug, which retails for $2,160, is just $900. As a further cost-saver, you may want to consider an all-wool Romanian reproduction of a Persian carpet for $780.

1001 Rugs has plenty of exquisite Chinese needlepoint rugs. These babies take *years* to make. One 8' x 13' carpet of this kind, retailing for $11,000 (gulp!) was price-slashed to $5,000 here.

Want something a bit less daunting? A sculpted Chinese 2' x 4' throw carpet with a floral pattern, which would retail for a whopping $340, is only $90, while a fine 3' x 10' runner imported from India—perfect for a staircase—was $500, almost half off its $960 retail.

1001 Rugs also has a specially-lit display area, so the colors of the carpets aren't totally distorted by the fluorescents which light up most of the store. Nice touch. You can even take a rug home with you for a trial with no obligation, just to make sure that it really does match your furniture and wallpaper. Another plus is that delivery is free—why, it's almost like having your own personal genie.

The store is open from 10 a.m. to 6 p.m. Mondays through Saturdays, and is closed Sundays.

Oriental Rug Emporium
- 4475 Roswell Rd. N.E., Atlanta; 252-5694
- 2563 Washington Rd., Augusta; (706) 738-4166

The Emporium's direct importing brings dramatic savings right to you. Their prices may not be as super as at their neighbor, 1001 Carpets, located down the road, but it's still good stuff.

The owner preferred that Mr. C not list specific prices in this book, but let's just say that the Persian and

Chinese carpets range in size from 3'
x 5's to room-size, at up to hundreds
of dollars less than what some Buckhead boutique-style shops are trying
to charge. Chances are, if you're in
the market for these kinds of rugs,
you'll like what you see. The store is
open seven days a week.

Oriental Rug Factory Outlet (Oriental Weavers, USA, Inc.)
- 3293 Lower Dug Gap Rd., Dalton;
  (706) 277-9666 or 1-800-832-8020

This store will save you anywhere
from 30% to 90% off of manufacturer's suggested retail prices. Wool
and synthetic carpets come straight
from factories in Egypt to this outlet,
cutting out the middleman and saving
you big bucks. The limited store
hours also cut down on its overhead
costs.

These aren't likely to be the finest-
made Orientals you've ever seen in
your life (they're all machine made,
none of that super-expensive hand
knotted kind), but who'll really notice? With the money you save here,
you'll be able to afford a whole new
furniture set to put around them.

Carpets start at an unbelievable $5
(for little scatter rugs). Runners with
suggested list prices of $49-$199 sell
here for as low as $9-$49, and room-
size rugs with values of $100 to $700
and up sell for just $29 to $500!

The store is open weekdays only,
from 8 a.m. to 5 p.m., with occasional weekend special sales.

Park Avenue Rugs
- 3609 Roswell Rd. N.E., Atlanta;
  262-0544

Park Avenue imports so many Oriental rugs that they actually wholesale
them to other stores. You, meanwhile,
can shop here too, at the same wholesale prices. They carry a good variety
of sizes, from runners to 8' x 11'
room carpets, at far from Park Avenue (New York, that is) rates.

Many of these carpets come from
Belgium, like an 8' x 11' acrylic that
feels just like pure wool. Regularly
listed for $650, it was selling at Park
Avenue for $495. An American-made

MR. CHEAP'S PICKS
Carpeting and Rugs

✔ **1001 Carpets**—The savings at
this Persian rug warehouse are
simply magical.

version, with a similar pattern in the
same size, is just $145.

A more intricately-patterned carpet of pure wool, also 8' x 11', was
seen here for $1,250, a discount of
$400 below the retail price. The same
kind of rug in a 6' x 9' size is $780,
while a similar Chinese wool rug is
$650.

On the budget-priced end, a 4' x 6'
acrylic Crown carpet, also made in
America, was just $99, a savings of
$70 off its going retail price. A
tighter-weave polyester-acrylic Belgian rug is just as affordable at $117.
The same size Belgian in wool, retailing for $300, goes for $175; it's available with fringe or without, in a
variety of warm-colored patterns.
And if you need a throw rug, a 2' x 4'
American-made Oriental print is just
$30. (Mr. C always wonders: Do peo-
ple actually get these home and
throw them around the room? Ah, the
little mysteries of life...)

*A few more shops recommended by
Mr. C:*

Carpet Land Warehouse Stores
- 5376 New Peachtree Rd.,
  Chamblee; 457-7223

Carpet Liquidators
- 5105-C Peachtree Industrial Blvd.,
  Chamblee; 451-7513

Carpets of Georgia
- 1640 Powers Ferry Rd. S.E.,
  Marietta; 859-9238, or
  1-800-444-2259

CLOTHING—NEW

Know what you're buying! Clothes, like anything else, are sold at discount for many reasons. Let's quickly go over some basic terms.

With new merchandise, "First-quality" means perfect clothing—it has no flaws of any kind, as you would find in any full-price store. Such items may be reduced in price as a sales promotion, because they're left over from a past season, or because too many were made. Some stores are able to discount first-quality clothing simply through high-volume selling and good connections with wholesalers. "Discontinued" styles are self-explanatory; again, these are usually new and still perfectly good.

"Second-quality," sometimes called "irregulars," "seconds," or "IRs," are new clothes which have some slight mistakes in their manufacture, or which have been damaged in shipping. Often, these blemishes are hard to find. Still, a reputable store will call your attention to the spot, either with a sign near the items, or a piece of masking tape directly on the problem area.

If you're not sure whether you're looking at a first or a second, go ahead and ask!

MEN'S WEAR—GENERAL

Kuppenheimer's Men's Clothiers

- 3655 Roswell Rd. N.E., Suite 302, Atlanta; 231-3530
- 6525 Jimmy Carter Blvd., Norcross; 263-6146
- 688 Holcomb Bridge Rd., Roswell; 642-4122
- 2670 Cobb Pkwy., S.E., Smyrna; 952-1313

And other suburban locations
Make your friends think you shop at Phipps! This is one of those stores that eliminates the middleman to bring you big bargains in men's suits, and Mr. C does mean *big*.

Kuppenheimer's seems like any fancy men's careerwear shop, with its fawning sales help, and perks like in-house alterations. But, by making their own goods and selling them directly through their national chain of stores, they can save you hundreds of dollars on high-quality clothing.

These are classy suits in traditional American styles. Outfits that may retail for up to $450 in mall stores start here for just $200. Kuppenheimer's Sterling & Hunt line of wool blazers are $165, and S & H's cashmere-wool-polyester blend coats (you'll swear they feel like pure cashmere), are just $220.

All-wool slacks are $62.50 and up; cotton casual slacks are $32.50. Cotton-poly Oxford shirts are priced at just $25 to $28.50. Buy three, you'll get ten percent off the total. Kuppenheimer's own line of dress shirts, in cotton broadcloth, is priced from $19.95 to $29.95.

Men's Wearhouse

- 3255 Peachtree Rd. N.E., Atlanta; 264-0421
- 2131 Pleasant Hill Rd., N.W., Duluth; 623-6060
- 1425 Market Blvd., Roswell; 518-0253

- Sandy Springs Crossing, 6690 Roswell Rd., Sandy Springs; 252-8608

And other suburban locations

Buying in BIG lots for its 200 stores lets the Men's Wearhouse sell top names like Yves Saint Laurent, Ralph Lauren, Oscar de la Renta, and Givenchy at fractions of their retail list prices. The vast tie selection alone is worth a trip from just about anywhere.

These are first-quality, current fashions, at literally hundreds of dollars off retail. A Ralph Lauren "Polo" suit, listed at $750 (ouch!) would be a more comfortable $350 here. There's not a heck of a lot here for smaller sized or big and tall men; but if you're an average size, the stock is tremendous. The suits lean toward conservative, classic styles.

Mr. C found out that the lesser-known Vito Rufolo brand sold here is made by the same company as which manufactures Perry Ellis clothing. VR dress shirts, with retail list prices of $55, are just $35 here. The only difference that Mr. C could find between these shirts and Perry's is that the stripes on the Rufolo shirts weren't aligned as sharply on the collar, noticeable only at the very tips. But who's complaining if it saves you $50 or so?

Shirts from brands like Damon, Adolfo, John Clarendon, and Pattinni are also priced in the $20 to $30 range. Those ties, in 100% silk from Monterey County By the Sea, are $29; and slightly lesser quality Italian silk ties go for $22.99. Lizard-skin belts are $29, and Kenneth Cole socks are always $5 off retail.

Sounds good, right? It gets even better. Check out the Men's Wearhouse *Warehouse*, listed below!

The Men's Wearhouse Warehouse

- 1218-A Old Chattahoochee Ave. N.W., Atlanta; 351-1060

What a mouthful mouthful. Well, you'll get an eyeful when you walk into this store, newly relocated near the intersection of Chattahoochee and

---

MR. CHEAP'S PICKS
Clothing—New
General Wear

- ✔ **Gap Outlet Store**—It's casual, it's classic—and it's cheap!
- ✔ **K & G Liquidators**—Like a discount supermarket for men's suits.
- ✔ **Lana's Discount Designer Apparel**—Escada for the ladies and Armani for the men, all at drastically reduced designer-sample prices.
- ✔ **Muse's Outlet**—Save hundreds of dollars on some of the most expensive suits made.

Ellsworth. This national chain of 170 stores never runs clearance sales; instead, it sends all of its overstocks and closeouts to just three outlet stores, located in Dallas, Houston, and Atlanta. Lucky break, huh? You bet, because guys can choose from thousands of designer suits and other separates at big discounts.

So, a wool/silk blend suit by Bill Blass, which had retailed for $295, can be found here for just $120; an Austin Reed sportcoat, in a 100% wool tweed, may be marked down from $265 to $90. There is a wide selection of sizes and styles, including short and extra long sizes; simple alterations are available in-store. Complete the outfit with Adolfo dress shirts from $9.95, silk ties for the same price, and a pair of Pierre Cardin leather dress shoes, reduced from $125 to just $50.

Good savings too on outerwear, even in the fall; Mr. C saw a 100% camelhair topcoat by Chappell of Britain, marked down from $350 to $120. Do the math, folks—that's one-third of the original price. For sportier looks, you'll often find lots of leather coats, like a suede jacket by Collezione, marked down from $275 to $150. And a table of wool-blend cardigan sweaters was reduced twice, from $65 to $45 to a final price of just $10. There are also some racks of brightly colored sportshirts, jogging suits, and the like. Open seven days a week.

Wingate's Men's Suit Warehouse

● 1735 DeFoor Place N.W., Atlanta; 355-7733

Wingate's original location remains a great place for high-fashion suits at several budget levels; their shoe department recently departed for new, expanded quarters a block away (see listing under "Shoes and Sneakers"). Service, even in this warehouse environment, is attentive and friendly, without being high-pressured.

Wingate has long been known for fancy looks; most recently, they've found a couple of interesting new ways to save you tons o' cash on sharp European looks. At the high end, the store has begun to carry a select handful of brands which rival the very top-name designers like Armani and Versace; Wingate's names are not as famous, but they are made with the same standards and materials, saving hundreds of dollars over those fashion godfathers.

One smart-looking double-breasted suit, for instance, made of 100% wool with silk lining, would be comparable to a $500 suit in department stores; this version, by L. Pecci, sells for $198. A cashmere/wool blend blazer by Toscanini, seen elsewhere for $600, was half of that price at Wingate's. And a pair of triple-pleated, silk-lined woolen trousers by the same maker was seen here for less than half its retail value, just $80 (add a pair of eelskin suspenders, discounted from $80 to $39, and you really will be stepping out in style).

They take the same approach to other items. A traditional all-weather trenchcoat, by the same manufacturers which make London Fog, was recently seen here for $89. It's completely identical to the name brand; at $325, the name costs you a lot more than the coat.

For more budget-conscious men who still want European fashion, Wingate's also sells suits and blazers made by American factories with synthtetic fibers—but made in the same Italian styles. Many of these start at just $89 and $99 each, and may be just fine for guys who only wear such suits once in a while. Wingate's is open from 10 a.m. to 6 p.m. on Wednesdays and Thursdays, until 7:00 p.m. on Fridays and Saturdays, and from 12:30 to 6:00 p.m. on Sundays.

WOMEN'S WEAR—GENERAL

Ann's of Atlanta

● 4369 Roswell Rd. N.E., Atlanta; 843-8882

Ann's is a small, family-owned business that gets wholesale clothing samples and marks them up just a teensy bit; thus, you can buy high-quality women's clothing at 40% to 70% off retail. Plus-size clothing is a specialty here: Sizes range from 8W to 52W.

The merchandise is primarily casual sportswear, with some dresses and looks for the office, too. A spring-weight cotton sweatsuit by YS Sport was seen for $49; same price for soft ramie-cotton sweaters by Western

Connection. Extra-long T-shirts by Brazilia are among the store's biggest sellers, at $19 each, and Catalina sweaters are $26.

For career wear, Ann's was recently offering a rayon suit by Sharon Phillips that will keep you dressed for financial success at just $105. Or, a rayon-poly print dress by Chez California for $79, and a satin charmeuse top by Alyssa Carr for $25.

For special occasions, you may enjoy a sequin-trimmed dress by Anjali Jain is $149; and an all-sequin top by Kinei, with a retail price of $80, was seen here for just $39.

Ann's is open Monday through Saturday from 10 a.m. to 6 p.m.

Arthur's Ladies Sportswear

- 1710 DeFoor Place N.W., Atlanta; 355-2832

Big names and low prices made this a very busy place when Mr. C dropped in. Arthur's sells first-quality designer sportswear for women, fancy styles indeed, at anywhere from 40% to 60% off retail. Among the finds Mr. C spotted were a Harvé Benard blazer and long skirt, retail price $298, here $133; a gauzy "Black Tie" blouse by Oleg Cassini, embroidered with shiny black beads, not $188, but $79; and, for fall, a whole rack of *faux* fur coats (for the PC crowd) marked down from $290 each to just $160.

The store is open Wednesdays and Thursdays from noon to 5:30, Fridays from 10-6, and Saturdays from 10-5:30.

The Banker's Note

- Peachtree Center, 231 Peachtree St., Atlanta; 659-0336
- Lindbergh Plaza, 2581 Piedmont Rd., Atlanta; 233-5223
- 2100 Roswell Rd., N.E., Marietta; 565-9787
- 2965 Cobb Pkwy. S.E., Smyrna; 952-5600
- 3000 Old Alabama Rd., Alpharetta; 664-5544
- 2131 Pleasant Hill Rd., Duluth; 476-8934

And other suburban locations
Bargain hunters will want to take note of this shop for basic career fashions, from suits to blouses to accessories. The merchandise is of good quality for the price, with names like AK Collectibles and Nicola featured.

For suit prices that'll suit your budget just fine, how about a linen blend two-piece suit by Oleg Cassini for just $50, or a Liz Claiborne suit with contrast piping on the collar and pocket, for $100 (both prices are about half off retail). Suits by good brands like Kasper for ASL and Le Suit are similarly reduced.

Silky polyester print blouses, normally a good value at $34, were on

MR. CHEAP'S PICKS
Clothing—New
Women's Fashions

✔ **LoLo**—Bringing a New York style to Atlanta's designer outlet scene.

✔ **Natalie's Bridals**—Weddings don't *have* to break the bank—not when you make your arrangements here.

✔ **Yes Yes Yes**—For bargains on a select group of exclusive women's designers, you'd better believe it.

sale for just $26. Short-sleeve rayon shells, and tanks, available in over a dozen pastel and bright colors from A.K. Collectibles, sell here for $12.99. Poly-rayon skirts made by the store's own brand, in five seasonal colors, are $19.99. A dressy rayon print dress by Katie, listed at $90 retail, is only $73.

For more casual occasions, a black-and-white gingham checked rayon dress is $51 (25% off its $70 list price), and a funky-patterned rayon blouse by Krazy Kat is $25.95. And on those hot Georgia afternoons, relax in a Banker's Note linen blouse for $30, or a seersucker jacket by Casablanca for $19.99.

Most store locations are open weekdays from 10 a.m. to 9 p.m., Saturdays from 10-8, and Sundays from 1-6. That's better than most other banks.

Brody's

- 1735 DeFoor Place N.W., Atlanta; 350-0577

Among the Atlanta Outlet Park shops, this is one of the better-designed places to find better-designer women's clothing. They carry career and special occasion outfits that are not just current, but carefully chosen for up-to-the-minute styles. It's all first-quality, at discounts of 35% to 50% below retail. As owner Ron Yabroudy says, "We sell only what we think are fashions that are right for the time of year."

That may mean a snappy two-piece suit by Premiere, discounted from $150 to $69, or silk blouses by Cocoon—which look exactly like pin-striped men's dress shirts, until you get up close—reduced from $80 to just $29. For fall, perhaps a cashmere and wool blazer by Wheaton & Katz for $89, or a quilted silk jacket by Paolo Gucci for $49. Plus belts and scarves, and some jewelry to complete these outfits—again, not a vast amount to choose from, just the stuff that works with the clothing currently on the racks. Anything that would be superfluous has already been weeded out for you.

The store is open Wednesdays from 12 to 5:30 p.m., Thursdays 12-6, Fridays 10-6, Saturdays 10-5:30.

Cato
* Lindbergh Plaza, 2581 Piedmont Rd., Suite B-1300, Atlanta; 231-2056
* 7155 Highway 85, Riverdale; 996-4616

And other suburban locations
This is a good place for low-priced, good quality women's clothing in classic styles and the latest trendy looks. Regular, misses, and plus-sizes are both well-stocked.

Ramie-cotton cable knit sweaters by Carolina Colors, listed at $28 retail, and available in a slew of seasonal shades, are only $19.99. Cotton jeans by the same maker are just $29. A fancy pleated rayon dress by Applauzz, in a floral print, goes for $66. Similar dresses go for over $100 in the malls.

For misses sizes, Cato has a poly-cotton blend "grunge" vest by Bonkers for $17.99, and pretty poly-cotton lace-trimmed poet's blouses, listed at $25 retail, for just $17.99.

The Cato Plus section of the store features items like a drop waist, long-sleeved dress by Kathie Lee (y'know,

Gifford) for Plaza South Plus, for $75.

There is also a footwear section. Doc Marten-lookalike boots, made in the "Etc. by Cato" label, are just $19.99. Clogs by Gem Collection are $18, and fake leather flats designed by Studio C are just $9.99.

Dress Barn
* Loehmann's Executive Plaza, 2480 Briarcliff Rd., N.E., Atlanta; 329-0517
* Outlet Square Mall, 4166 Buford Hwy., N.E., Atlanta; 321-1837
* 6331 Roswell Rd., N.E., Sandy Springs; 303-9218

And other suburban locations
No, you won't look like a farm hand if you shop here; you'll just have more cash in hand, that's all. This national chain is a good place to stock up on basics like T-shirts and jeans.

The store's full of name brands, too, like Gloria Vanderbilt (her jeans are half off at $20). A double-breasted rayon plaid suit by Sasson was recently seen here, reduced from $175 to $125.

A cotton cable-knit sweater by Sweater Exchange was marked down from $38 to $30, and casual cotton pants by Westport Ltd. were selling for the same price—about one-third of their original retail value.

Stock up on basics here; cotton turtlenecks are two for $18, and crew socks are a bargain at $3 a pair.

Famous Garment Manufacturers
* 550-C Amsterdam Ave. N.E., Atlanta; 875-7053

How famous is Gilmor Trading? Well, they're working on it. This is the fourth outlet store for the Florida manufacturer of women's professional outfits. Their lines are already budget-oriented, but the prices and special sales at this Midtown Outlets store should make them plenty famous in no time.

Everything here is current, first-quality stock; from a basic heavy wool blazer in several earth-tone solids, twenty bucks off at $39, to a herringbone linen blazer reduced from $169 to $99. A cashmere-blend blazer and skirt outfit, in that smart, no-lapel Italian style, was recently seen for just $69, and a grey pinstripe blazer and trousers set was marked down from $139 to $79. Print blouses, in florals and abstracts, linens and rayons, start around $15; and there are lots of skirt and pants separates under $30.

There is so much of every style, in fact, that choral groups are among the frequent customers here—it's a good place to coordinate large groups of people in smart outfits on a budget. And each week brings special sales, when you may be able to get two $59 suits for $99, or blazers at two for the price of one. All sales are final, though there is a two-week exchange policy. The store is open from 10 a.m. to 7 p.m. on Friday and Saturday, and from 1-6 on Sunday.

Fashion Buys
- 1600 Ellsworth Industrial Blvd. N.W., Atlanta; 355-1487

The buys here are women's professional looks from a handful of top designers, plus many other brands that are just a notch or two below the big names. There are racks and racks of dresses, most priced between $60-$100; two-piece suits range from $100 to $225. Just about everything is first-quality and current season, except for the clearance racks at the rear of the store, where many items are sold at $39 or 50% off the tag price.

Of course, the prices in here are already up to 50% below retail, and sometimes more; on his visit, Mr. C found poly blouses by Adolfo, in shiny gold and silver, reduced from $60 to just $19.75. A petite-size dress by Leslie Fay was seen for $69.75 (there are, in fact, entire areas devoted to petite, missy, and large women's fashions, ranging from size 2 to size 24-plus). An embroidered red dress under the Kathie Lee Gifford label was selling recently for $79. Plus evening wear, along with the handbags and jewelry to complete any outfit. Open Thursdays from 10 a.m. to 5 p.m., Fridays and

Saturdays from 10-6, and Sundays from 1-5.

Loehmann's
- Loehmann's Executive Plaza, 2480 Briarcliff Rd. N.E., Atlanta; 633-4156
- 8610 Roswell Rd., Dunwoody; 998-2095
- 2460 Cobb Pkwy. S.E., Smyrna; 953-2225

Loehmann's means low prices on fancy women's clothing and shoes, plain and simple. These folks practically *invented* the designer closeout store years ago in New York; suave Manhattanites still schlep out to Brooklyn for their famous deals.

Mr. C found a rayon pantsuit by Karen Miller, which retails for $190, selling for just $90 here; and a Gillian wool coatdress, list price $270, here just $150. Two-ply cashmere sweaters are just $100, but get to the store early if these are advertised because they sell out *fast*.

Don't miss the better designer suits and evening wear in the now-famous Back Room. Here, a Bill Blass silk plaid dress with pleated skirt was slashed from an original $390 to an amazing $60, and a Bob Mackie silk blouse in women's sizes was just $80, less than half-price. Calvin Klein fashions can usually be found here too, like a pure cashmere sweater listed at $750 but reduced to $400.

At the time of Mr. C's visit, Loehmann's was running a special sale, offering a selection of suits at a ridiculously low *two* for $199. These were originally valued at $225 to $300 each, made by designers like Kasper for A.S.L. and Oleg Cassini.

It's definitely worth noting that petites can do very well for themselves here—with plenty of suits, dresses, and pants to choose from. A petite dress by Depeche was seen for almost $400 off the retail price at $299.

LoLo Ltd.
- 935-D Chattahoochee Ave. N.W., Atlanta; 352-9355

Raymond and Marlene Siegel had decided to move here from New York City. Both had impeccable credentials in the retail biz up there; Marlene, in fact, had managed the Burberry's shop near Fifth Avenue. In Atlanta, with all its off-price clothing shops, they noticed a distinct gap—no one, it seemed, was selling the kind of upscale, sophisticated women's clothing that is considered *de rigeur* in New York's trendy circles. Clothing that favors clean, tailored lines and the darker, simpler colors of the spectrum. Marlene calls it "understated."

And so, LoLo was born. As in low, low prices on better quality women's fashions. Ray and Marlene weren't about to commit overkill; you won't find thousand-dollar Armani suits here. They looked around, sized up the market, and created a small store in the Chattahoochee outlet district with a slightly more upscale look and feel than most bare-wall outlets. These walls are freshly painted in crisp white. The floor is carpeted. The friendly sales staff greets you and rushes to your side if you need anything, but doesn't put the pressure on.

The clothing, meanwhile, consists of first-quality, current season fashions that are truly elegant—and all sold at 50% to 60% below retail. A tailored pinstripe suit (by a designer whose name *everybody* knows), including a blazer with a matching skirt *and* trousers, was marked down from its retail price of $240 to $129. Brightly colored silk warmup suits were reduced from $110 to a svelte $49. And a blue blazer and skirt with beaded appliqué, by one of the big Italian designers, was not $600, but a more affordable $200.

There are plenty of inexpensive items, like cable knit sweaters with values of $40 and $50, selling for just $19; a black sequined vest, cut from $38 to $19; plus blouses and other accessories.

The idea behind LoLo must be a good one; the store was just a month old when Mr. C dropped in, and it was filled with customers singing its praises. Have a look for yourself, Thursdays through Saturdays from 10 a.m. to 6 p.m.

Midtown Designers' Warehouse
- 553-3 Amsterdam Ave. N.E., Atlanta; 873-2581

The specialty here is dressy, high-fashion women's clothing, including leather garments, at wholesale prices or nearly so. On the leather clothing in particular, this store can save you $200 or more over department or specialty store prices. Mr. C saw several different items of super-soft lambskin, in a variety of colors: Jackets with quilted sleeves and a suede body, reduced from a list price of $479 to just $249, and midi-length skirts, reduced from $239 to only $79.

The merchandise here is all first-quality, mostly past season closeouts. In other clothing, the looks are again dressy and high-toned; this is stuff for a big evening out. A bright red dress by Anne French, trimmed with gold applique, was reduced from $319 to $159. There were several different styles from this label, as well as Club France, and many others. And there are several clearance racks of clothes being sold on consignment from dealers in the Apparel Mart; not only are these exclusive deals direct from the makers, but they often sell here *below* wholesale prices. MDW also offers a quality selection of handmade costume jewelry to go with these fancy outfits, all selling at less than half of their original prices.

The store, in the Midtown Outlets area, is open Thursdays through Saturdays from 10 a.m. to 7 p.m., and Sundays from 1-6.

One Price Clothing
- 858 Oak St. S.W., Atlanta; 758-0590
- 3277 Buford Hwy. N.E., Atlanta; 633-7114
- 1289 Columbia Dr., Decatur; 288-5983
- 5762 Buford Hwy., Doraville; 455-4626
- 2066 Headland Dr., East Point; 209-1955

This is one store that stays true to its name. Budget-brand clothing for misses, juniors, and plus-sizes are all in good supply here, all at the same price of $7. Accessories are also included in the $7 one-price promise, though they're sold in multiples (two satin ponytail bows for $7, or three pairs of socks, for example). The quality of the clothing is not by any means superb, but it's good for everyday casual wear.

Some of the things $7 will get you here include all-cotton broomstick skirts; Justin Allen plaid cotton walk shorts; and silk tank tops and shorts by names like Manisha, Whistles, and Louise Paris.

All of the clothing here is first quality; there are never irregulars or seconds. One Price clothing stores are open weekdays and Saturdays from 10 a.m. to 8 p.m., and Sundays from 1 a.m. to 6 p.m.

S.E.C. Warehouse
• 1735 DeFoor Place N.W., Atlanta; 351-2509

S.E.C. imports many of its dressy fashions from India; sparkling sequined jackets and tops, which would retail elsewhere for up to $300, sell here for about $150. Leather jackets in various styles and lengths, with retail values from $250-$300 sell for $89 to $179. And there are plenty of American designers here too, including fancy dresses from Karen Miller, Tatiana, Affluence, and more, all at discount. These dresses, with retail prices up to $200, can be found here for $129 or thereabouts.

Some of the items here are past-season; a stylish spaghetti-strap dress by Weekend, with a black sequined blazer to match, was recently seen on the reduction rack—marked down from an original $180 to just $90. Open Wednesday and Thursday from 11 a.m. to 5 p.m., Friday and Saturday from 10-6.

Tamara's Ladies' Apparel
• 1735 DeFoor Place N.W., Atlanta; 355-0644

Walk in through Kids Wearhouse (see listing under "Children's Wear," below) and you'll find Tamara's, which is strictly for grownups. Women can find first-quality, current styles by top names at 30% to 75% below retail—

professional looks and snazzy evening wear. Some of these fashions could practically be called "artsy," decked as they are with flashy embroidery. The career wear, meanwhile, takes the high-end wool and linen route. Always worth a look. Open Tuesday 10 a.m. to 5 p.m., Wednesday through Saturday 10 a.m. to 6 p.m., and Sunday 12:30 p.m. to 5:30 p.m.

Wholesale Clubhouse
• The Balconies Shopping Center, 290 Hilderbrand Dr., Sandy Springs; 303-8244

You don't have to be a member of this "club" to save big on famous-name clothing you'll recognize in a second. But if you do buy a membership card (it costs $10 a year), you'll save about 20% more on the already-low prices in this tiny shop. Some of the clothes are past-season, but you'll still want to stock up on basics like solid-color sweaters, Express jeans, and more.

Mr. C saw a snazzy silk jogging suit by Robert Stock for $40, rayon skirts from India for $16, and a gangster pinstripe two-piece suit from Palmettos for $30. Palmettos jeans are just $17, and their yarn-dyed plaid cotton pants are $18. If you join the store's club, they'd only cost $12.

Knit pantsuits by Light House are $25, broomstick skirts are $15, and bodysuits by True Identity are $13 each. For $20, you can get a tricot knit sweater from Limited Express, or a cotton denim shirt from Essentials Sport.

Wholesale Warehouse
• 4300 Highway 20, Buford; 271-7883
• 5191 Old National Hwy., College Park; 766-9940
• 3517 Memorial Dr., Decatur; 286-4100
• 4746 Memorial Dr., Decatur; 292-8331
• 4735 Jonesboro Rd., Forest Park; 366-1364

This mall-based chain sells a colorful variety of inexpensive sportswear for women. You'll rarely find big name brands, but for everyday wear, there's a lot to see; some of these are irregulars. Among the deals recently found were blue jeans reduced from $48 to just $12.99; loose-fitting, baggy cotton sweaters for $9.99; leggings to go with them for $7.99; and knit pantsuits in bright colors decorated with faux gemstones and studs, just $14.99.

Yes Yes Yes
- 1190 Huff Rd. N.W., Atlanta; 355-4221

This outlet is a bit harder to find, being somewhat separated from its Chattahoochee neighbors. It's different in many other respects, as well. Owner Linda Weitzman is very particular about the designers she carries, bringing a very New York-ish sensibility to her store. In most cases, she is the sole distributor for such labels in the Southeast. For example, there is an entire room devoted to dressmaker Karen Alexander, whose in-demand fashions cater primarily to

taller women like herself. In here, you can find racks of $100-$300 dresses selling at half-price; such as a black crepe "Empire" style, with lace insets, reduced from $231 to $127.

Other names found here include knitwear by Joan Vass, like a purple turtleneck of cotton and cashmere, half-price at $75; Mosswear hand-painted silk dresses, marked down from $160 to $87 to just $43.50; and *noille* silk dresses by Eileen Fisher for $85. Her name was also one of many to show up on the past-season racks, where further reductions are taken. Linen blouses by Fisher were seen for just $20 each; some Karen Alexander dresses were going for $25 and $35.

YYY also has a nice collection of earrings, belts, colorful hosiery, and fun hats. If you want to see it all for yourself, plan carefully; the store is only open Fridays from 10 a.m. to 6 p.m., and Saturdays from 10-5.

MEN'S AND WOMEN'S WEAR—GENERAL

The Alley
- 1735 DeFoor Place N.W., Atlanta; 355-0205

Follow the signs for this one—it's at the lower end of the parking lot. Once inside, you'll find a vast assortment of trendy casual sportswear for men and women, all selling at discounts of 20% to 50% below retail. These are all current styles, first-quality only; and the store makes a point of carrying a deep selection of sizes on every item, including junior, missy, and plus sizes.

The fashions here can be as diverse as Jordache jeans, Lavon nylon jogging suits, cocktail dresses by Dave & Johnny, and other casual looks from Hang Ten, Gimme, and more. The emphasis is on cottons and washable fabrics; everything looks so comfortable, in fact, that you almost feel like diving into the tables these items are piled upon and rolling around for a while (now, now...). A few of those tables, by the way, are

$10 clearance tables—Mr. C found jeans, denim vests, sequined tops, etc.

There is a real warehouse look to the place, lined from floor to ceiling with racks; no-frills though it may be, there are fitting rooms among its few amenities. Credit cards are accepted, too. Hours are Wednesday and Thursday from 11 a.m. to 5 p.m., Friday from 10-6, and Saturday from 10-5.

Best Fashions
- Lindbergh Plaza, Suite B-800, 2581 Piedmont Rd. N.E., Atlanta; 261-2453

Best Fashions sells urban clothing and shoes for young men and women at discounted prices. These are the latest trendy looks, the kind of stuff you'll want for nightclubbing or the gym. A ladies' black tank dress, listing for $40 retail, sells for $25 here, and a cotton denim "car wash" dress, listed at $50, is $35. A rayon sheer sleeved blouse, with a retail value of

$45, is cut to $25, and an outfit with a fringed jacket with matching skirt, listed at $60 retail, is $50—and plastic earrings to go with it are just $1 a pair. Bicycle shorts, perfect for workouts, are $7.99; throw a cotton and satin warmup suit over them for $34, a savings of $16 off.

For the guys, Mr. C found an acrylic men's sweater by Salt Creek, listed at $40 retail, for $24.99; and a $30 polyester shirt by Diamond's for $20. Polyester slacks by Billion Bay, in hot looks for the dance floor, are reduced from $39.99 to $24.99; while casual, baggy colored jeans by Phenom, worth $40 retail, are $30. Men's huarache sandals listed at $29.99 sell here for just $19.99.

There's some children's clothing here, but not much; a little girl's rayon suit by Just Kids was seen here for $30, and a boy's dress shirt and tie by Wayne Scott was $19.99.

Best Fashions also offers in-house alterations.

Discount Depot

- 2775 Lakewood Ave. S.W., Atlanta; 559-8821
- 2508 North Decatur Rd., Decatur; 321-0119
- 5907 Stewart Pkwy., Douglasville; 489-8934

These plain-looking stores may not look too promising from the outside, but this book doesn't judge a store by its cover. Mr. C thinks the merchandise inside, especially their sportswear, will definitely surprise you; believe it or not, nothing is priced over $15.

Wilson tennis shorts, listed at $45, sell for an amazing $6. Wilson athletic shorts are reduced from $30 to $10, and Rossignol T-shirts are just $6. Ladies' cable-knit vests by Wimbledon, listed at $60 retail, are just $15, nylon Wilson tennis shorts worth $22 are just $10, and a Rossignol sweater priced at $30 is reduced to just $5 here.

A Lane Bryant cotton dress with coordinating belt, listed at $39, was seen recently for $10; a Spiegel shaker sweater, listed at $45 in their

catalog, was also just $10, and Levi's cotton twill skirts—retailing for $40—are just $14. For dressier occasions, cotton dress shirts by Aureus, worth $39, are an incredible $6, and men's silk ties imported from Italy, in paisleys and floral prints, range in price from $6 to $14.

These are closeouts and discontinued items, so the stock is ever-changing; at these prices, though, they will certainly not have reached the end of the line.

Gap Factory Outlet Store

- 3065 Headland Dr. S.W., Atlanta; 349-8600

This store sells irregular, discontinued, past-season, and store-damaged items, as well as some of the current Gap line.

If you're looking in the blooper sections, the staff will help you stay on the lookout for sun-faded spots, makeup, tiny holes, stains, pantlegs that are slightly different lengths, missing buttons, uneven stitching, broken zippers, and other boo-boos running from mild to very noticeable. Then, you can make an informed decision as to whether the price makes the blemish worth living with. Irregular or damaged items are automatically 20% to 40% off retail, and sometimes more.

Some of the clothes are so *slightly* damaged or defective that occasionally even the sales staff can't tell you what's wrong with it. Fortunately, almost everything is clearly labled with its problem. If there's no tape marking the imperfect spot on an irregular item, there may be a size irregularity; sometimes, only by trying it on will you know what the problem is.

Mr. C found a unisex denim jacket, marred only by a slightly frayed cuff that can be rolled up anyhow, for just $29.99 (that's reduced from $52). Irregular jeans (always try these on, for sure) sell for $9.99; they may have been as much as $44 at full price. The quintessential Gap t-shirt is available in half a dozen colors for just $7.99.

Men's green and white striped

swim trunks, selling for $24 in their prime season, were only $3.99. Seersucker shorts for men, $32 in the spring, can be found for $14.99 in the fall. You may also find leftovers for the youngsters, too, like girls' floral bathing suits for $3.99 (selling for $22 if first quality), and bright red sneakers for $9.99.

The store is open from 10 a.m. to 8 p.m., Monday through Saturday, and from noon to 6 p.m. on Sunday.

K & G Liquidation Center

- 1777 Ellsworth Industrial Blvd. N.W., Atlanta; 352-3471
- 3750 Venture Dr. N.W., Duluth; 623-9895

If you don't mind shopping for fancy suits in a supermarket setting, then you certainly won't mind K & G. These stores deal in what the clothing business calls "salvage;" don't worry, it looks much better than it sounds. These are clothes which manufacturers have to get rid of simply because they made too many, or because department stores ordered more than they could sell, or because they are "past season" (*you* may like to buy spring clothing in the spring, but major stores are already buying for the summer).

In any event, stores like K & G snap up these clothing deals—for men and women—and sell them off at great savings from their big, warehouse-type stores. It's all first-quality merchandise; "The only thing that's irregular here is us," said one of the store's quirkier clerks. Hey, a little personality goes a long way in a crowded, bustling place like this.

Men's suits make up the majority of the stock, from lots of big-name designers (the store prefers not to have these mentioned in print, to maintain good relationships with their sources), in sizes from 36 short to 50 extra long. Hand-tailored all-wool suits with retail prices of $350 sell here for $120, about as expensive as they get; wool blend suits, by lesser-known makers, start as low as $90. And there are walls covered with silk print ties to go with them,

most priced at just $7.90 each. Lots of the latest tuxedos, too, at around $100; alterations for all suits are available in the store.

K & G has other looks, including casual and sportswear, like cashmere sweaters reduced from $225 to $99, and full-length leather trenchcoats for half-price at $199. And there is a limited but good selection of shoes, dress and casual, at up to 40% off.

The selection for women is smaller, and available only at the Atlanta store; this department primarily offers professional outfits, like a classic European wool blazer in bright red (from a very well-known national specialty chain), marked down from $165 to a smarter $50. A rack of flowing rayon print skirts was reduced from $85 each to just $25, below wholesale cost. And there are sharp looks for going out, such as a 1960s-retro minidress in purple velvet ($45) or a black sequined vest ($39, down from $80).

There's a lot to see here, with new shipments arriving each week. The stores are open Fridays and Saturdays from 10 a.m. to 7 p.m., and Sundays from noon to six.

Lana's Discount Designer Apparel

- 3019 Peachtree Rd. N.E., Atlanta; 237-4225

Lana's is a well-hidden goldmine in Buckhead, chock-full of designer dresses, accessories, and even men's business clothing, most of it priced at about two-thirds off retail. The stock is made up of samples, used to show off new designs, but never previously used.

Mr. C found a wool jacket from Escada by Margaretha Ley, retailing for $1,500 (yikes!); it was selling here for $249. A DKNY jacket, with wool and leather trim, was reduced by $300 to a low $149.

Other deals spotted here recently included an August Silk dress, with a retail value around $300, selling for $129.99; a Liz Claiborne acetate dress with belt, seen for over $200 elsewhere, for $80; a simulated-silk acetate gown by Gillian, looking like something out of Liz Taylor's wardrobe, was also $80. A stunning beaded evening dress by Ellen Tracy was $280. For more casual occasions, a suede skirt by Sumiko is over half off at $60.

Men will also like Lana's for similarly incredible bargains, but they'll have to head for the nearly hidden back room. Here, ties by Hugo Boss and Giorgio Armani are $30 to $40 (over half off retail); and Girbaud jeans, available in many colors, are also below half price at $45.

Dress shirts with tab collars, by names like Club Room and Perry Ellis, are just $20; slacks by Austin Grey are $35, and suits by Perry Ellis Portfolio and Polo are just $200. Go.

Macy's Closeouts
• 3604 Memorial Dr., Decatur; 288-3882

Newly relocated from one end of the Avondale Mall to the other, MCO is the area's clearance center for men's, women's, and children's clothing. There is as much selection here as in many other full-price department stores; yet, prices on most of these tickets are marked down by as much as one-half. But there's more—because everything in the store is an automatic 40% off the lowest marked price (20% for shoes), and during special sales, some items may be 60% or even 75% off the lowest price. Whew! They're practically giving the stuff away...but then, that's the idea of a clearance center, right?

Women will find several designer names sprinkled among the many racks, like floral blazers and matching skirts from the Leslie Fay Sportswear collection. Originally $90 per piece, these have been reduced to $45—less another 40%, for a final price of just $27. A batch of Lizwear linen vests (Claiborne, that is), in powder blue with specks of pink, was once $66 each; here, they've come all the way down to $20. There is a full lingerie section, as well as several racks of splashy cocktail dresses.

For men, Mr. C discovered a real

buried treasure: A Polo sweater, in an exotic print on 100% wool, marked down from $335 to $167 to a final $100. There were a few sizes of loose-fitting black jeans by Willi-Wear, cut from $45 to $13, and lots of $40 Geoffrey Beene dress shirts for a snappy $11.25. There is a lot of stuff for kids, from basic infantwear at tiny prices, to boys' Perry Ellis "America" jeans for $9.60.

The shoe department favors the ladies; you can often find Bandolino, Sam & Libby, Naturalizer, Guess, and other more casual styles. A pair of white leather Ferragamo pumps was seen for $60, down from an original $175, and they looked just fine.

Macy's, as you may know, has been in bankruptcy protection for well over a year, so who knows what may become of this venerable retailer. Reports say that they've been effective in reducing their debts; that, coupled with this clean, new (and smaller) quarters in the rehabbed Avondale Mall may mean you'll be finding bargains here for a years to come.

Marshall's
• Buckhead Crossing, 2625 Piedmont Rd. N.E., Atlanta; 233-3848
• 3999 Austell Rd. S.W., Austell; 948-7276
• 2300 Miller Rd., Decatur; 987-1717
• 3675 Satellite Blvd., Duluth; 497-1052
• 425 Ernest Barrett Pkwy., Kennesaw; 424-2064
• 2211 Roswell Rd. N.E., Marietta; 971-2604
• 1096 Morrow Ind. Blvd., Morrow; 961-0612
• 6337 Roswell Rd. N.E., Sandy Springs; 252-9679
• 5370 Highway 78, Stone Mountain; 413-0945
• 6011 Memorial Dr., Stone Mountain; 469-4005

Well, you all know about Marshalls—Mr. C doubts that you need to "discover" this national chain by reading about it in these pages. Still, he could hardly write about discount clothing, shoes, and home furnishings without at least acknowledging the place, right? It is worth noting that, although Marshalls has been around for years, they have really worked hard recently to expand both the number of store locations, and the number of top-notch designer brands they carry there. Nowadays, finding names like Liz Claiborne, Calvin Klein, and Polo by Ralph Lauren, are quite standard; it's all become spiffier and better organized, too.

Muse's Outlet
- Buford Outlet Mall, 4166 Buford Hwy. N.E., Atlanta; 315-6221

You know Muse's. With three major stores in Atlanta, they've been selling fine—and expensive—clothing for over one hundred years. But it's only in the last year or so that they've opened up this clearance center in the Buford Outlet Mall. What began as a just-for-one-month experiment has become a thriving, permanent operation. Here, men and women can get some incredible deals on first-quality designer clothing that is past season. That is, as far as retailers are concerned. For us regular folks, these may still be quite current; and many of the men's suits are classics anyway, and they'll always look right.

So, after items have been on display in the regular branches, and perhaps on sale, anything left over comes here. Men may find a Harris Tweed sportcoat for $150, half its original retail price, or a Burberry all-wool suit, again half-price, at $290. Mr. C found a snazzy sportcoat by Hickey-Freeman, one of America's most highly regarded manufacturers. A blend of wool, silk, and cashmere, it was originally priced at $765; it had been on sale in town for half-price, $382.50—but here it was reduced by half again, to a final price of just $191.25. Whatta deal!

Other names found here include Aquascutum, Eagle, and more; and, worth noting for the big and tall set, men's suits range up to size 50. All the furnishings are here too: Shirts, ties, slacks, as well as casual tops and sweaters, most at half-price.

For women, there are similar bargains in professional outfits, though fewer of them. A petite-size black linen blazer by Pendleton was recently seen, reduced from $148 to $44; a Bentley Harris linen/cotton dress was marked down from $162 to $48; and there was an artists' palette of colors in 100% silk tops, originally $60, here $18 each.

All sales at the outlet are final, and credit cards are accepted. The store is closed Mondays and Tuesdays, with Wednesday-Saturday hours of 10 a.m. to 9 p.m. and Sunday hours from 12:30-5:30 p.m.

Tuesday Morning
- 3165 Peachtree Rd. N.E., Atlanta; 233-6526
- 3250 Satellite Blvd., Duluth; 476-0522
- 4502 Chamblee-Dunwoody Rd., Dunwoody; 457-3565
- 700 Sandy Plains Rd. N.E., Marietta; 428-1536
- 1115 Morrow Industrial Blvd., Morrow; 961-0707
- 1231 Alpharetta St., Roswell; 640-8146
- 2512 Spring Rd. S.E., Smyrna; 435-6678

And other suburban locations

We all know how much better Tuesday mornings are, compared to Mondays. TM's bargains will make you feel that much better any day, with discounts on everything from clothes to party supplies to toys to jewelry to luggage.

Mr. C found good deals on clothing basics, like Christian Dior socks for men, reduced from a retail price of $6.50 down to just $2.99; Givenchy six-packs of handkerchiefs, retail price $15, here $6; a three-pack of Eagle socks by Burlington for just $6; and Bill Blass pajamas, listed at $33, marked down to $16.

Men's dress shirts by John Henry are half price at $15, and a Christian Dior robe was seen for only $35 (still bearing its original $75 price tag). For ladies, an Eddie Bauer windbreaker, selling for $45 through their catalog, was going for only $19 at TM.

Save on generic and brand name accessories for all. An "America" by Perry Ellis handbag, in leather-look vinyl, was recently seen for half price at $15. Mr. C also spotted several Coach look-alike bags, in genuine leather, going for just $20. Get a Gallery One tote bag for $40, and a canvas bag by Capezio for just $12.99 (regularly $26). Open seven days a week.

BRIDAL AND FORMAL WEAR

Bridal and Formal Manufacturers Outlet

- 930-A Chattahoochee Ave. N.W., Atlanta; 355-0002
- 881 Jamerson Rd. N.E., Marietta; 516-0664
- 2348 Scenic Hwy., Snellville; 979-4888

This local company makes and sells its own lines of gowns for weddings, proms, and pageants, which are sold nationwide; here at their factory stores, you can buy the same dresses at discounts from 20% to 50% and sometimes more. Several other major bridal lines are also represented.

For current, reorderable dresses, the typical savings are in the 20%-30% range. The bigger savings come in dresses that are "off the rack"; that is, already made and in the store. If you find something in your size, you'll save 50%—such as an all-silk gown that was originally $1,350, selling here for $675. Many such dresses are as little as $275 or so. And in other kinds of women's formalwear, you may find an emerald green silk evening gown reduced from $688 to $379, or a black silk pantsuit, decorated by hand with shiny black beads, marked down from $750 to $395.

On all dresses sold here, full alterations are available in-house; catering, photography and floral services can also be arranged. The intown branch is open Tuesdays through Saturdays from 10 a.m. to 6 p.m., and Sundays from 1-6; the suburban stores are open Tuesdays through Saturdays from 10-8.

Natalie's Bridals

- 919 Chattahoochee Ave. N.W., Atlanta; 351-5285

There are two businesses under one roof here—at least. "Natalie's Bridals" offers over thirty designer labels in wedding gowns, with all of the current styles found in the latest bridal magazines, at discounts of 20% to 30% off retail. Over a thousand different dresses can be custom ordered, with all the service you'd expect at a full-price boutique; the place is ready for action, with fifteen fitting rooms and alterations available on the premises at reasonable rates. Every major bridesmaid's line is also here at 20% to 30% off.

On average, most bridal gowns sell here in the range of $500 to $800 each, though some can go as high as $5,000; but remember, that same high-priced gown would sell for as much as $8,000 at most other specialty stores.

The second business is called "Bridal Liquidators," which sounds like it should be the title of some movie in which Arnold Schwarzenegger goes around crashing weddings; not to worry, as this is hardly the case. If there's any truth in the joke, it's in the way prices are decimated and slashed on bridal gowns from these special racks. You never know what you may find in this section, but it has to be worth a look; some gowns start as low as $89—yes folks, that's not a typo. Most are priced under $400, and all are sold at 50% to 80% off their original prices. The catch? You won't find the latest up-to-the-minute styles, and if something you like isn't within one size above or below your own, it probably can't be fitted to you. And of course, none of these can be special-ordered—all of the actual dresses available at these prices are right there on the racks. Still, for many folks who can't afford a blowout wedding, these deals present lots of good options.

In addition, there is a comparable service in tuxedo rentals, again featuring the big designers like Pierre Cardin, Christian Dior, Raffinati, and others (since these are not being sold, Mr. C can tell you the names). Rent six or more tuxes, and the groom's rental is free. Then, there is a wedding invitation service, with designs from thirty major catalog books, all at a discount of 20% with the purchase of a dress. The idea is your basic "one-stop" bridal center. In all, this operation lays claim to being the largest bridal store in the south, drawing customers from five states; it certainly seemed very busy during Mr. C's visit, though Natalie just shook her head and called it a "quiet" day.

CHILDREN'S WEAR

Atlanta Kids Outlet Store
- 747 Miami Circle N.E., Atlanta; 233-1353
- 3455 Peachtree Industrial Blvd., Suite 210, Duluth; 813-8270
- 1401 Johnson Ferry Rd., Marietta; 565-6667
- 503 Crosstown Dr., Peachtree City; 631-8067
- 1425 Market Blvd., Roswell; 587-4170

These stores are all outlets for Frog Pond, a popular manufacturer of clothes for young boys and girls. Everything sold here is first-quality, current merchandise, at about 40% percent below national retail prices, and there is a good selection of basics and special-occasion outfits. The clothing here is appropriate for ages from three months to seven years (for boys) and to fourteen years (for girls).

A selection of appliquéd fall dresses for pre-teen girls, for instance, might retail for $70 in department stores, and sell for $42.50 here. And remember, what is "past season" for the big stores is current for us regular folks—in other words, you'll find spring dresses here in the spring, when you want them.

Other clothing recently seen here for girls included gold lamé pants for $23, Christmas and Easter outfits, and swimsuits. There is a similar, if more limited, selection for boys. The store also carries extra-large sizes on many items. Also of importance: The store does not take credit cards.

"Baby World" at Burlington Coat Factory
- 4166 Buford Hwy. N.E., Atlanta; 634-5566
- 3750 Venture Dr., Duluth; 497-0033
- 1255 Roswell Rd. N.E., Marietta; 971-6540
- 5934 Roswell Rd., Sandy Springs; 303-0505

See listing under "Discount Department Stores."

Baby Superstore
- Baby Superstore Plaza, 8801 Roswell Rd., Sandy Springs; 640-6155
- 1455 Pleasant Hill Rd. N.W., Lawrenceville; 279-BABY (2229)
- 1427 Roswell Rd. N.E., Marietta; 565-BABY (2229)
- 700 Highway 138, Riverdale; 473-0888

(See also listings under "Furniture" and "Toys and Games")
Baby Superstores will help keep your wallet from shrinking as your kids keep growing. Brand-name clothing for newborns to toddlers is well-stocked at this giant superstore, so you'll be sure to find something good (and inexpensive!) here.

For babies, Mr. C found a three-pack of terry drool bibs by Spencer for just $1.97, and a three-pack of Gerber snapshirts for $6.47. Spencer crew-neck T-shirts are just $4 each, and sleepers by Carter's sell for $13 a set. High-quality Health-Tex and Osh Kosh "Baby B'Gosh" tees are $12, and Wee Walker shoes were seen for just $9.97. Oh, and if you *really* want to get the kids dressed up, Baby Dior sleepers are $18.

For toddlers, Mr. C found Bugle Boy pants for $17; same price for a girls' Osh Kosh denim jumper; and leather L.A. Gear sneakers to go with either outfit for $26. Stadium jackets by French Toast (seen for over $45 elsewhere) are just $30 at the superstore.

Baby Superstores are open from 9:30 a.m. to 9 p.m. Mondays through Saturdays, and Sundays from 12 noon to 6 p.m.

Buy Buy Baby
- 1670 Lower Roswell Rd. S.E., Marietta; 977-4641

See listing under "Clothing—Used: Consignment/Resale Stores."

Children's Discount
- 27 Peachtree St. S.W., Atlanta; 521-1780
- Buford Outlet Mall, 4166 Buford Hwy. N.E., Atlanta; 321-1836

And other suburban locations
These stores indeed discount first-quality clothing for boys and girls, from newborns to age fourteen. Some of this is brand name stuff, though much of it is generic. There are racks and racks of everything from basics to fancy dresses and suits. You may find girls' sweaters by Health-Tex, reduced from $12 to $5.99, or red "bow and bell" party dresses by Martha's Minatures for $30 and up. Boys' double-breasted two-piece suits sell for $10 and $20.

CD has a good sports team section; Mr. C found boys' lined Falcons jackets by Stadium Apparel, originally $50, here $38. Going to the other extreme, this is a good place to stock up on underwear, like boys' Kids Kolors briefs at three pair for $3.99. Open seven days a week.

Kids Wearhouse
- 1735 DeFoor Place N.W., Atlanta; 352-5348

In the Atlanta Outlet Park, this shop has a wide selection of designer clothing for the kiddies at anywhere from 30% to 75% below retail prices. In fact, the store calls itself a "wholesale warehouse boutique," to emphasize the well-known name brands

they carry—which they asked Mr. C not to print. Needless to say, you'll recognize them when you get to the store. All are first-quality, current season items, in sizes from 0-7 for boys and 0-14 for girls. In addition to infant clothing, there is also a selection of accessories, crib toys, blankets, and the like. The store is open from 10 a.m. to 6 p.m. on Wednesdays and Thursdays, to 6:30 on Fridays and Saturdays, and from 12:30 to 5:30 on Sundays.

Samples Unlimited, Inc.
- Roswell Wieuca Shopping Center, 4373 Roswell Rd., N.E., Atlanta; 255-6934

For a seemingly unlimited selection of brand-name clothing for babies, toddlers, and little kids from playwear to dress-up styles, all at greatly reduced prices, this is the place. Manager Julia Halperin told Mr. C that the prices here are just 20% above wholesale cost.

Boys' romping pants made by Quality Fun Clothes, made with reinforced knees, are just $11. A cotton denim shirt by French Toast is $13.50. For formal occasions, dress pants by Jack Tan are $18.25, a tweed jacket by Christian Dior Jeune Homme Sportif is $54, and a Members Only sportcoat is $37.

For little girls, a portrait dress by Sophie Bess is $31, and a taffeta dress with jacket, made by Hollywood Babe, goes for $16. A denim jacket with real fur trim and lining is $65, a reversible rain coat by Rain Wave is $11.75, prewashed jeans by Used are $28, and cotton socks by Two Feet Ahead cost $3.25 a pair.

For babies, get a Buster Brown creeper for $12.50; another one by Babyra is $11. Health-Tex T-shirts are $4.50 each, and a hooded bath towel by Rosebud is $4.75. A pair of little girls' leggings by Tulip are $10.25.

It goes on and on. The store is open Monday through Friday from 10 a.m. to 6 p.m., and on Saturday from 10-5.

ACCESSORIES

Hattitudes
- Underground Atlanta, 60 Old
  Alabama St., Atlanta; 681-0086

If you think that Underground Atlanta is little more than a tourist trap, Hattitudes may change your attitude.

While their end-of-season clearance sales are definitely not to be missed, this store's everyday prices can still beat the pants off those in Atlanta's hoity-toity department stores. Or rather, the hats. Mr. C was asked not to publish specific prices, so you'll just have to visit to check out the values for yourself.

The selection ranges from baseball caps in cotton canvas or leather (!), to leather pill boxes, funky hats trimmed with fake-jewels, Jordache baseball caps, wide-brimmed felt Fedoras for a snazzy urban look, and straw hats with either leather or printed fabric bands.

Hats for men, ladies, and children are all well-stocked, so the whole family will be able to find something they like here. For you dapper gents, the shop also sells all kinds of ties—bow, bolo, silk print—at good value prices.

Lingerie Warehouse
- 1708 DeFoor Place, N.W., Atlanta;
  352-8719

Tucked in with all the stores selling big-deal designer clothing in the Chattahoochee outlet area, is this more unusual discounter. Lingerie Warehouse specializes in the fancy little fashions women like to wear underneath the fancy big fashions. And, like its flashier neighbors, it sells designer brands at major discounts.

The folks here preferred not to, er, reveal specific prices, but you'll definitely like what you see. Hmm, it sure is tricky to write about this stuff! Anyway, such famous names as Hanes, Olga, Calvin Klein, Christian Dior, Lily of France, and many others are all carried here on a regular basis. It's actually quite a large store, with clothing that ranges from hosiery and bras to teddies, bodysuits,

and sleepwear—all at near-wholesale prices. In spite of the great prices on these items, though, would you like to know what the store's hottest seller is? Well, right next to the cash register is a basket offering "Edible Underwear." These are available for both men and women, and they truly are edible. The manager told Mr. C that she has to refill that basket every time she looks at it.

Lingerie Warehouse is open Tuesdays through Saturdays from 10 a.m. to 5:30 p.m. (Fridays until 6:00).

Stone Mountain Handbag Factory Store
- 963 Main St., Stone Mountain;
  498-1316

And other suburban locations
You've seen them in stores like Rich's and Neiman Marcus for a hundred dollars and up. Here, you can get the same first-quality handbags for 20% to 50% off the suggested retail prices. The accessories sold in this shop are factory overruns and closeouts; and, since the bags are manufactured right here, no shipping costs are worked into the price, either.

Stone Mountain's leather handbags are available in tan, navy, hunter green, and other colors and trims, all with the company's trademark zipper-closure and multi-compartment style. Other products, such as leather-bound organizers, belts, wallets and eyeglass cases are sold here, too, in styles for men and women.

The store is open Monday through Saturday from 10 a.m. to 6 p.m., and Sunday from 1 p.m. to 5 p.m.

Sunglass Hut International
- Underground Atlanta, 180 Lower
  Alabama St., Atlanta; 577-0040
- Lenox Square Shopping Center,
  3393 Peachtree Rd., Atlanta;
  237-0931
- Market Square Mall, 2050
  Lawrenceville Hwy., Decatur;
  248-9220

And other suburban locations
Head to this hut for reduced prices on designer label sunglasses for sports

and general wear. Lens repair kits, cleaners, and cases are also reasonably priced.

Ray Ban styles are priced from $30 and up. Oakley frogskin glasses are $35 and up; shades by DKNY start at $49, and even Bollé and Vuarnet high-fashion sunglasses are similarly reduced from retail. Gargoyle "Killer Loop" glasses are $70 in a non-metallic finish, and $90 with mirrored lenses. Way cool, dude.

Sweats For Less

- 500 Amsterdam Ave. N.E., Atlanta; 875-9914
- 5225 Buford Hwy. N.E., Doraville; 451-0976
- 8037 Tara Blvd., Jonesboro; 478-1196
- 425 Barrett Pkwy. N.W., Kennesaw; 425-4777
- 2416 Atlanta Rd., Smyrna; 4346-6711
- 5370 Highway 78 S.W., Stone Mountain; 879-8429

Having recently opened its sixth store, in the Midtown Outlets complex, this blossoming little business is certainly not sweating things out. People love to come here and stock up on basics for the whole family—tees, sweats, socks, and novelty clothing, all at discount. First- and second-quality stock are both sold here, with irregulars clearly marked as such. There are plenty of name brands among the racks, though the merchandise turns over rapidly, so these are always changing.

Basic T-shirts, in that familiar palette of bright solid colors, start as low as $3.99 and $4.99 apiece; sweat shirts and sweat pants begin at $4.99 and $5.99. Mr. C also saw a rack of zip-up hooded sweatshirts for $7.99. Colored socks for children are just 99 cents a pair, or grab a six-pack of men's white athletic tube socks for $5.99. All of these prices meet or beat those found at most department stores.

In more decorative fashions, you may see women's scallop-neck T-shirts, in bright prints, for $4.99; full-length nightshirts; and stirrup-foot sweatpants, closeouts from a very famous catalog, reduced from $50 to just $11.99. Plus all kinds of novelty print socks for adults and kids, especially around the various holidays.

Speaking of prints, there is always a good selection of clothing featuring famous cartoon characters, as well as the insignia of most area colleges. Until the Hard Rock Cafe opened up its Atlanta restaurant and shop, this was one place where you could find deals on Hard Rock T-shirts; lately, they've been selling Planet Hollywood instead. And there is a vast assortment of heat-transfer designs on the wall, which can be mounted on any shirt, for $2 or $3 less than at the mall stores which do this.

Store hours vary; the Midtown Outlets branch is only open Fridays through Sundays. Call for specific times.

CLOTHING—USED

Used clothing is another great way to save lots of money—and don't turn up your nose at the idea. Recycling doesn't just mean bottles and cans, y'know. In these recessionary times, people are taking this approach to nearly everything, and it makes a lot of sense. There is a wide range of options, from trashy stuff to designer labels. Again, a few terms:

"Consignment" and "resale" shops are all the rage these days. Most sell what they call "gently used" clothing—the original owner wore the article only a few times, then decided to resell it. Often, these are fancy outfits in which such people don't want to be seen in more than that. Fine! This is how you can get these high fashion clothes at super low prices. Since they still look new, your friends will never know the secret (unless, of course, you want to brag about your bargain-hunting prowess).

You can also sell things from your own closets at these shops, if they are recent and in good shape; the store owners will split the cash with you.

"Vintage" clothing is usually older and more worn-looking, often still around from other decades. Sometimes it can cost more than you'd expect for used clothing, depending on which "retro" period is back in style at the moment.

Finally, "thrift shops" sell used clothing that has *definitely* seen better days. These items have generally been donated to the stores, most of which are run by charity organizations; in such places, you can often find great bargains, and help out a worthy cause at the same time.

CONSIGNMENT/RESALE STORES

Backstreet Boutique
• 3655 Roswell Rd. N.E., Suite 206, Atlanta; 262-7783

With a store like this, you can look like a million bucks for somewhat less than that. Billed as "Buckhead's upscale rescale", Backstreet resells well-kept designer fashions and accessories from names like Chanel, Gucci, and Yves Saint Laurent.

During his recent visit, Mr. C found a Donna Karan deerskin jacket for $500 (probably $1,000 off its original price), as well as a wool Anne Klein coat selling for just $169. A two-piece knit suit in a cotton/linen blend by Adolfo was seen for $199, and a fox and mink coat by Ralph Ripley for $149.

Because this merchandise is of such high quality to begin with, some of these items are still priced in the hundreds of dollars; whatever you purchase, though, you *will* be saving half off or better compared to the original retail prices.

Some of the other deals included a tan Gucci handbag for $59, about $200 off retail; a pair of Bandolino patent leather pumps, scuff-free, for just $22; and a Chanel satin charmeuse blouse for $169.

Backstreet is open Tuesdays through Fridays from 11 a.m. to 6 p.m., and Saturdays from 10 a.m. to 5 p.m. It's located in the Tuxedo Festival Shopping Center.

Buy Buy Baby
• 1670 Lower Roswell Rd. S.E., Marietta; 977-4641

About one block below Roswell Road in East Cobb, on this residential street, is one house with a difference: It's been turned into a very successful store, selling secondhand clothing and accessories for children. Fran Lloyd has been presiding over this operation for about eleven years now, filling her store with what she refers to as "pre-loved" clothing. And she puts a lot of love in herself. Clearly enjoying the sight of a little girl popping out of a fitting room, enthralled with a "new" party dress, Fran was beaming as much as the girl's own mom.

Each tiny room of this ranch-style house is positively crammed with clothes; each room has a different focus, from infant clothing to boys to girls, ranging up to about size 10. She prices everything by starting at half of the retail value, and then adjusting that price up or down depending on the condition. So, a size 7 velvet and taffeta dress by Jessica McClintock, which might go for $100 in department stores, sells for

$50 here. Honestly, you'd never know it was used. Young girls would also love a pair of red leather ballet slippers by Sam and Libby, just $20; as well as fashions by Laura Ashley, Monday's Child, and others.

For boys, Mr. C found a Gap sweatshirt for $6.50, plus baseball jackets, jeans, shoes, and sneakers; and the newborns' room featured such respected names as Health-Tex and Carters. A little girl's jogging suit, just as cute as can be, was seen for $5.50. You can also find some furniture here, though it always goes fast; also strollers, carriages, car seats, and the like. A Kolcraft stroller was selling for $42.50, easily half its original price. Considering how durably made these are, and how briefly they may be needed, why *shouldn't* you buy a used one if you can?

You can buy and buy here from 10 a.m. to 5 p.m., Tuesdays through Fridays, and Saturdays from 10 a.m. until 3 p.m. "or whenever," admitted Fran.

Chickibea
- 2130 North Decatur Rd., Decatur; 634-6995

Since 1972, Chickibea has been a fixture in Atlanta's upscale resale consignment clothing trade. Owner Chicki Lipton will be more than happy to help you find whatever specific items you're looking for, among the career wear and evening clothes packed into her store in the North Decatur Plaza.

Mr. C saw great bargains like an Ann Taylor linen/rayon two-piece suit, selling for $99 (worth $300, easily), or a never-worn fuchsia silk Casual Corner blouse for just $32. A Liz Claiborne angora cardigan, worth $100, was only $40 here.

Denim lovers can take their pick from Calvin Klein jeans for $59 (these go for over $100 at Neiman Marcus), a Donna Karan New York jean skirt reduced to $49, or a pair of Marithé and Francois Girbaud jeans for just $39.

The shoes at Chickibea are, for the most part, in good shape. A pair of

---

MR. CHEAP'S PICKS
Clothing—Used

✔ **Backstreet Boutique**—You won't believe it until you see it. *The* place for gently worn Chanel and Anne Klein designs at miniscule prices.

✔ **The Clothing Warehouse**—Somewhat more-used vintage clothing. Great for cheap, broken-in leather jackets.

✔ **Sweet Repeats**—For the little ones, clothes from super names like Saks Fifth Avenue and Taffy's sell for a few bucks each at this Buckhead shop. Pharr out!

Naturalizer pumps, with real leather uppers, was selling for just $24, and a pair of "i.e." Nike Air cushioned suede flats was seen here—during their inaugural season on the market—almost half-price at $18.

The eveningwear section of the store featured a black lace gown by Scott McClintock for just $59, a shirred rayon dress from Saks Fifth Avenue for $100, and a velvet evening gown and cape by J. Reynolds Designs for $249. There are plenty of sequin-decorated dresses to choose from, too.

Accessories like a $39 Gucci bag (really!), a $62 crocodile bag by Saks, and $20 silk scarves should help to complete any of these outfits, without finishing off your budget. Chickibea is open weekdays from 10 a.m. to 5 p.m. (Thursdays until 6 p.m.), and Saturdays from 11 a.m. to 5 p.m. The store is closed Sundays.

Circles Unlimited
- 1720 DeFoor Place N.W., Atlanta; 352-8563

Along this tiny street lined with outlet stores, here's something unusual; Circles Unlimited is the only one on the block selling secondhand designer clothing and samples for women. This cozy little frame house-turned-store boasts an even greater variety—and better bargains—than its neighbors. Knowing the league she is playing in, owner Faye Rittelmeyer is every bit as discerning about what she will sell as any retailer.

Okay, so it's not current season stuff. Everything here is close to it, never more than a year or two old, and all in great condition. Relying on what people pull out of their closets, the store's merchandise is always changing, which is part of the fun; among the finds recently discovered here was a two-piece dress in pink satin, with a rhinestone bow, designed by Raul Blanco for Neiman Marcus. It was selling here for $65. A Nicole Miller dress was seen for $25, a black wool blazer by Anne Klein II for $60, and a Jones New York wool skirt in dark plaid for $28.

Samples, of course, have never been worn, and CU gets a good supply of these on a regular basis. Mr. C saw a rack of tartan plaid silk blouses by British Khaki for $50 each. There are also lots of secondhand shoes in good condition; bag a pair of brown suede Bandolino heels, almost like new, for $30. Plus accessories and jewelry, much of which are new. The store is open Wednesdays through Saturdays from 10 a.m. to 6 p.m.

The Consign$hop
• 2899-A North Druid Hills Rd., Atlanta; 633-6257

Prices at the Consign$hop are up to 75% off retail, for fashions that are as nearly current as used clothing can be. The stock on display is always geared to the season at hand; unlike some shops, you won't find a floor full of wool suits in the middle of August here. Everything is neatly organized by size, too, so you won't waste half the day rummaging.

For women, Mr. C saw a mohair/acrylic blend sweater by Express

for $28, a wool double-breasted blazer by J.H. Collectibles for $32, a beautiful velvet blazer by Rafaella for $49, and an Esprit overcoat for $30. A wool-rayon blend bouclé jacket from Ann Taylor was $45. In addition to these big names, solid brands like J.G. Hook and Norton McNaughton pop up frequently in the racks, keeping the quality consistent.

More deals for gals: A black merino wool and cashmere dress by Vanessa Van Cleeb for $42, a sleeveless wool pinstripe suit by Larry Levine for $36, and a leather bomber by Express for $99.

Some of this merchandise has never been worn—Lee jeans with the tags still on are just $12, while brand-new looking wool pants by Benetton were recently on sale for $22.

Men, too, can look dapper for just dimes—thanks to such items as a Woolrich fleece jacket for $29, or dress shirts by Christian Dior Monsieur for $14, and Van Heusen for $10.

Got a special occasion coming up? The Consign$hop sells black tuxedo jackets for $65, wool jackets by Polo University Club for $49, a plaid suit by Hart Schaffner & Marx for $48, and dozens of $6 ties, made by the likes of Geoffrey Beene and such.

For more casual wear, Mr. C did find a never-worn Izod Lacoste windbreaker for $18, Duck Head pants for $12, Gap jeans for the same price, and cotton chinos for $14.

The store offers plenty of consigned shoes, nearly all of which are in very good condition. Anne Klein slippers are $15, Unisa silk flats are $16, and Joan & David pumps are $22. For men, Bass Weejun penny loafers are $16 and Reebok pump sneakers are $39.

The store openly accepts consignments on a 50/50 split, but only takes items that are in excellent condition. It's located in the Toco Hills Shopping Center, and is open weekdays and Saturdays from 10 a.m. to 6 p.m., staying open until 8 p.m. on Thursday evenings.

Elegant Trash
- 3180 Roswell Rd. N.E., Atlanta; 233-3877

Here's yet another Buckhead consignment shop for those who wish to look like they spent $1,000 on an outfit, but can't afford to drop that kind of dough. If you were wondering what ever happened to Hodge Podge, by the way, wonder no more. Elegant Trash has replaced that shop, and now sells not only consignment clothing and furs, but unusual furniture and decorative items as well.

Many of the items seen here are slightly more worn than the stuff in other consignment shops around town; but if you hunt around, you'll find bargains like a Talbots wool bouclé suit in plaid for just $20, or a cotton sweater by Jones New York for only $14.

This store sells a good selection of consigned fur coats as well. These tend to be priced in the $500 range, while a pair of silver fox-lined gloves were seen for $125.

And, not to be left out in the cold themselves, men may find things like or a glen plaid wool suit by Polo University Club for just $85, or dress pants by Imperial for Haggar for just $16.

Mr. C thinks the prices for accessories and furnishings in the other part of the store are a bit on the pricey side, but he did spy a terrific Louis Vuitton garment bag for $250.

Play It Again
- 273 Buckhead Ave. N.E., Atlanta; 261-2135

You'll want to shop at this store again and again, with its super prices on better designer brand career and casual wear. But, you must remember this: Play It Again only deals in women's clothing. Sorry, Bogey.

Mr. C spotted incredible deals like a $32 rayon blend suit by Kasper, an Ann Taylor silk suit for $72, and jeans by Guess?/Georges Marciano for $18.

For special occasions, Play It Again had a taffeta and velvet evening gown by Opening Night! for $62, and an all-sequin Lord & Taylor jacket for $62. Accessorize these with $8 Monet *faux* pearl earrings and $32 high heels by Salvatore Ferragamo.

Don't miss the sale area in back, which has unbelievable specials like a $4 silk dress (no, that's *not* a typo), made by Richard Warren for Neiman Marcus; also, a cotton skirt by Esprit for just $2.

The store is open weekdays from 10 a.m. to 6 p.m. (Thursdays until 7 p.m.), and Saturdays from 10-5.

Sweet Repeats
- 321 Pharr Rd., N.E., Atlanta; 261-7519

Sweet savings on used, consigned maternity and children's clothing fill this Buckhead store. All the stuff here is in truly exceptional shape, and most of it looks as if it has never been worn at all.

For moms-to-be, a rayon dress by Mother's Work is just $32, a Saks Fifth Avenue velvet number with puff sleeves is $75, and a shaker sweater by Motherhood, which would easily cost $60 in the mall, is just $32.

For toddlers, Mr. C found a pullover by A Pea in the Pod for $6.50, and a striped rugby pullover by Chesterfield for just $9.50. A girls' knit jacket by Tiny Tots is just $10, while a white fake fur overcoat by Millicents of San Francisco was $18.50.

Moving up to slightly bigger kids, there was a pair of girls' overalls by Imp Originals for $8.50, a cotton dress from the Gap for $14, and a fleece pajama set by Kidding Around for $6. Young boys will enjoy things like Pony soccer cleats (a score for $9.50), Osh Kosh velcro-close sneakers ($6.50), and a flannel tweed suit by Michael James ($32).

Accessories like crib bumper pads for $15, or an Aprica stroller for $25, are also great values. The shop often gets fun stuff in too, like a tutu for $5 (or is that fivefive?), or a pair of Taffy's tap shoes for $8.50. With these, you won't mind so much when your budding ballerina quits after three classes.

Sweet Repeats is easy to find, located right across the street from Oxford Books at Pharr, and is open from

10 a.m. to 5 p.m., Monday through Saturday.

VINTAGE CLOTHING STORES

Aunt Teek's
• 1166 Euclid Ave. N.E., Atlanta; 525-0630

Aunt Teek's will keep you in cool vintage garb without making you look like you raided your Aunt Mildred's closet. Some of the clothes are on the kooky side—like a $45 leopard-print coat—but there are plenty of classically trendy vests and jeans here, too.

Mr. C saw a Scottish wool kilt, and a velour jacket, both of which could be considered unisex, both priced at $15. Lots of Levi's here, both ripped and unripped, in shorts and regular lengths; most were priced around $16 or so, depending on the condition (jeans must be one of the few items in which wear and tears can actually increase the price). Denim jackets, by Levi's, Lee and Wrangler, are $20 or so each, and casual, kinda worn-out overalls by Lee are just $12.

Aunt Teek's also sells nightclub wear like $10 bustiers (try these on for size, Madonna). The shoe selection is not outstanding, however, and some of the boots Mr. C saw did actually look like antiques in their own right. But again, for certain buyers, that's the idea.

The Clothing Warehouse
• Toco Hills Promenade, 2971 North Druid Hills Rd., Atlanta; 248-1224

For vintage looks from basic to funky, The Clothing Warehouse is jam-packed with bargains. Be sure to check out their denim and leather jacket sections, way down in the back of the store. Men and women will find equally huge selections of goodies here, and there are also some children's items, to boot.

Men can wade through tons and tons of ties, from far out extra-wide, extra-loud stripe styles, to sedate classic styles by Givenchy (just $3 each).

You can afford to really dress up with a pinstriped Brooks Brothers suit, in a pure wool, for just $36; a Jos. A. Bank dress shirt for $7.99, or a rayon Claiborne shirt for 99¢; or Perry Ellis linen slacks for $1.95. A men's long leather coat by McGregor, in pretty good shape (call it "broken in") was seen for a mere $34.95.

For more casual wear, flannel shirts by Levi's and Dickies are priced in the $4.95 range (and could cost up to $50 each if bought new at the malls). Go for the grunge look with gas-station workshirts for $6.95 each, vintage striped shorts for $2, and faded Levi's jeans for $9.95.

Ladies will like the $9.50 price tag on the cotton floral skirt by Lady Van Heusen, a $9.95 cotton drop-waist dress by Express, the $40 satin prom dress by Gunne Sax, and the 99¢ corduroy overalls by Alyssa. A cotton turtleneck by Cambridge Dry Goods, perfect under those overalls, was seen for just $8.99. Not to mention sweaters from brands like Forenza and Rafaella priced at two for $12, and a Gap sweatshirt spotted for $3.50. Great stuff.

Stefan's
• 1160 Euclid Ave. N.E., Atlanta; 688-4929

For dressy vintage clothing, especially for men, Stefan's is simply swell. None of these clothes are shabby looking; the store only accepts items which have been well taken care of.

Mr. C saw an all-cashmere coat by Kashmira for $145 (it would sell for at least $800 at Macy's or Rich's if new), and a wool plaid overcoat by Robert Hall for $85.

An all-silk sharkskin suit was recently available for $145, an all-wool dress jacket for $60, a paisley robe for $26, and a Hemingway-style straw fishing cap for is just $12. For special occasions, a tuxedo jacket from Rich's is $55, and a Manhattan brand ruffled shirt to go with it was $20.

Women's fashions are represented here, too; this is a great place to find a basic black evening dress. Why spend hundreds of dollars at Phipps or Lenox when you can get one here for $12? A sleeveless black crepe dress, just the sort of thing you'd see on Audrey Hepburn, was seen for only $55—and that was among the most expensive dresses in the house. An aqua-colored satin princess-seamed dress, with cap sleeves, was seen for only $20. A gorgeous satin and lace wedding gown that looked like it's never been worn was $95.

Accessories like $10 cat's eye sunglasses and a $20 wool felt hat by Wall Street also make great buys. The tie and suspender selection is stupendous, and at about $10 a pop, you can afford to stock up. And be sure to check out the cuff links, tie tacks, and, for ladies, the flashy-to-gaudy costume jewelry selections.

The store is open from 11 a.m. to 7 p.m., Mondays through Saturdays, and from noon to 6 p.m. Sundays.

The Junkman's Daughter
• 1130 Euclid Ave. N.E., Atlanta; 577-3188

The Junkman's Daughter is not, as you may have expected, full of trash. The looks here are definitely grunge-style, though, and the store's splatter-painted walls and super-loud sound system, along with its selection of vinyl clothing and nose rings, may scare off the faint of heart.

The clothing here tends toward retro nightclub styles. Used platform shoes are priced at $15 and up, silver heels are $7.50, while a satin baby doll dress was seen for $26. The store also has a lot of vintage lingerie, like 1940's-ish camisoles for $20; and sleeveless tees for $6.

For guys, gas pump attendant shirts are here for $15, and wild paisley button-down cotton shirts are $10. Levi's jeans, available in both men's and women's styles, are usually priced in the $16 range.

The jewelry selection is eclectic to say the least, with everything from mood rings for $6—the ultimate in retro— to hematite stone earrings for $14.

Junkman's Daughter is open weekdays and Saturdays from 11 a.m. to 7 p.m. or so, and Sundays from noon to 6 p.m.

The Thrift House of the Cathedral of St. Phillip
• 2581 Piedmont Rd. N.E., Atlanta; 233-8652

For true thrifty shoppers, this benefit shop for various local charities is a must-see. The small selection of used books and toys isn't that fantastic, but the bargain buys on donated clothing certainly are.

Mr. C saw a Champion sweatshirt for just $2, and Arrow dress shirts for men for $3. Levi jeans will cost you no more than $5.

For $2.50, you can take home a ladies' crocheted wool-angora cardigan, or, for $3.50, a nylon pullover windbreaker. A woman's twill skirt by Dockers is selling for only $3.

The store tends to get packed with bargain hunters, so you never know what kind of buys you'll find. Leather pocketbooks, Kenya bags, and costume jewelry are hot items that sell almost as fast as the staff can put them on the sales floor.

The store is open Monday through Saturday from 10 a.m. to 4:30 p.m. They'll gladly accept any clothing items (if in reasonably good condition). Any items which the store is unable to sell after a certain period of time are ultimately given away at the Union Mission.

THRIFT STORES

Amvets Thrift Store
• 3651 Memorial Dr., Decatur;
  286-1083

There is a surprising amount of clothing and housewares to be seen in this shopping center store, at some of the lowest thrift prices around. Mr. C found a three-quarter length rabbit-fur coat for just $50; a navy blue pin-stripe blazer by Pierre Cardin, wrinkled but quite restoreable, for $1.48 (that's not a typo—$1.48!); women's Pappagallo sandals for $1.98, and a whole section of dresses, all 99 cents each. Occasionally, Amvets gets a deal on some new clothes, like a rack of '93 Braves T-shirts, right after the season, marked down to $7.

This is also one of the better stores for small appliances, glassware, books, and television sets. Mondays, by the way, offer a 25% discount for senior citizens. The store is open seven days a week, including every night but Sunday until 9 p.m.

Goodwill Thrift Stores
• 2575 Bolton Rd. N.W., Atlanta;
  352-0119
• 888 Abernathy Blvd. S.W., Atlanta;
  755-9131
• 2201 Glenwood Ave. S.E., Atlanta;
  373-5815
• 3160 E. Main St., East Point;
  761-6459
• 854 Southway Dr., Jonesboro;
  478-4970
• 5396 Jonesboro Rd., Lake City;
  361-3844
• 508 Grayson Hwy., Lawrenceville;
  963-7793
• 5291 Highway 29, Lilburn;
  564-1751
• 6114 Gordon Rd. S.E., Mableton;
  941-3154
• 1365 Roswell Rd. N.E., Marietta;
  509-7395
• 752 Sandtown Rd. S.W., Marietta;
  428-6667

Goodwill is one of the country's foremost thrift stores, with a large selection of clothing in good condition and at very low prices. There is al-ways enough stock on the floor, it seems, to make sure that you never leave here empty-handed. Women's two-piece professional outfits start as low as $6.95 and up; men's suits from $9.95; lots and lots of blue jeans from $4.95, dress shirts from $2.95, outerwear from $9.95, and much more. Often, the stores get closeout deals on new clothing as well. And just about every day brings a different special: All dresses become half-price for the day, all items with green tags are reduced to $1, all shoes go for 25% off the tagged price, and so on—pick up a calendar at the front of the store, so you'll know in advance when to go and stock up.

Tuesdays are senior citizen days, when they get 25% off their total purchases. And at the Glenwood Avenue store only, there is a "flea market" held every Friday, Saturday, and Sunday, in which all items are 99 cents each. All stores, meanwhile, are open seven days a week. The funds raised through Goodwill stores help support this organization's programs which give job training to people with disabilities.

Last Chance Thrift Stores
• 4420 Jonesboro Rd., Forest Park;
  361-3740
• 4841 Highway 78, Lilburn;
  978-1905
• 6025 Gordon Rd., Mableton;
  944-0478
• 720 Sandtown Rd., Marietta;
  422-0142
• 201 Norcross-Tucker Rd.,
  Norcross; 662-5616

Yet another of Atlanta's many thrift store chains, Last Chance serves the Perimeter suburbs with clothing for men, women, and children. You can find lots of good deals on jeans and sweaters, jackets, dresses, suits, shoes, and more, all in "fair to mid-dling" condition. If you're looking to get a ton of stuff cheap, give this place a chance.

Nearly New Shop
- 2581 Piedmont Rd. N.E., Atlanta; 233-6639

True to its word, this thrift store—in the unusual location of a major shopping center—has lots of donated clothing that is in very good condition. The quality is somewhat better than that of your average thrift, including the comfortable shopping atmosphere. You'll find good names mixed in on the racks; Mr. C found a men's suit by Jos. A. Bank, a classic navy pinstripe, in good condition for just $35—and a Brooks Brothers dress shirt to go with it for another $5. Just about all shirts, for men and women, are priced at $5; like a rack of women's cotton turtlenecks in an artist's palette of colors.

Jeans, for men and women, range from $5-$10, as do women's skirts. Fancier outfits, like a shiny green dress from Maggy Boutique—pleated below the waist and on the sleeves—may go for only $10-$20. And shoes to complete the look, with names like Evan-Picone and Saks Fifth Avenue, still have some life in them at $3-$5 a pair.

There are lots of $1 clearance sale racks, as well as some children's clothing and toys, though not as much as thrift stores usually have. This, of course, may vary from week to week. Nearly New also has extra special sales at certain dates through the year, like a winter coat sale each November; pick up a flyer in the store for more details.

In spite of the Piedmont address, you'll actually find the store off of Sidney Marcus Boulevard, next to a K-Mart. It's run by the Junior League of Atlanta; proceeds from the shop benefit its many programs in the areas of child welfare, the homeless, environmental concerns, education, and more.

Value Village
- 1899 Stewart Ave. S.W., Atlanta
- 1320 Moreland Ave. S.E., Atlanta
- 2555 Bolton Rd. N.W., Atlanta
- 1599 Memorial Dr. S.E., Atlanta
- 3503 Memorial Dr., Decatur
- 4298 Old Jonesboro Rd., Forest Park

Telephone for all stores: 416-1110
Perhaps the biggest and best among Atlanta's thrift shops, Value Village approaches the selection and scope of a full-price department store. Mr. C found lots of good clothing for women, men, and children; suits for $10-$20, dresses for $5-$10, and shoes for $3-$5—even a few pairs of western boots for $3!

The store Mr. C visited had a whole wall of color televisions, most of which were up and running, priced at $80 and $90. These are in such good condition that, unlike most thrifts, they sit behind a protective barrier—but if you're interested in one, you can ask to see it up close. V.V. also has an especially good stock of toys and games for kids. Picture a game of "Pictionary" for $1. All branches of the store are open seven days a week, including weeknights until 9:00.

COSMETICS AND PERFUMES

The $1 $uper $tore
- Cub Foods Shopping Center, 2179 Lawrenceville Hwy., Decatur; 315-9350

Right at the intersection of Lawrenceville and North Druid Hills Road, this store is chock-full of cheap stuff you can definitely use. Cosmetics are in good supply here, including such items as Ethnique Monaco nail polish and lipstick, Candler hair mousse, baby shampoo, conditioner, and body lotion.

The store is open Monday through Saturday from 9 a.m. all the way to 9 p.m., and on Sundays from 11 a.m. to 6 p.m.

Perfumania
- Northpoint Circle Mall, Alpharetta; 410-9766
- Gwinnett Place Mall, 2100 Pleasant Hill Rd., Duluth; 813-0335
- Cobb Town Center, 400 Ernest Barrett Pkwy., Kennesaw; 590-9799
- Northlake Mall, 4800 Briarcliff Rd., Northlake; 723-1404

Perfumania is a national chain of 150 stores (and growing); their vast buying power enables them to sell top-name designer perfumes at cut-rate prices. You can save as much as 60% off retail on names like Elizabeth Taylor's "Passion" and Cher's "Uninhibited," as well as colognes by Alfred Sung, Paco Rabanne, Ralph Lauren, Paloma Picasso, Halston, and many others. Price tags are color-coded to show you which bottles are selling at 20%, 40%, and 60% off.

You can sample as many of these as you like; the staff is extremely knowledgeable and relaxed. The scents are sprayed onto special papers, which are then labeled for you with the respective brand; this way, you don't walk out of the store wearing ten contrasting fragrances.

The store also specializes in boxed gift sets, again, at up to half off or more. In many cases, you can get a cologne set, with matching lotion, shower gel (or whatever), for the same price as the perfume alone. There are some cosmetic gift sets as well, such as eye shadow color kits. And you can always find a good selection of gifts here for under $10. Open seven days a week.

The Perfume Outlet
- 132 Mitchell St. S.W., Atlanta; 653-1013
- 7471 Highway 85, Riverdale; 997-3505

This is a retail perfume outlet, not a warehouse, so all the perfumes sold here are in their regular packages, and ready for gift-giving. Some men's colognes and aftershaves are sold here, but the store mainly caters to women.

Dozens of designer fragrances are sold here, including Red, Giorgio Beverly Hills, Elizabeth Taylor's "Passion," Bijan, Chloé, Liz Claiborne and more. You probably won't find the very latest creations, but plenty of recognizable and classic brand names are kept in stock. Men's aftershaves like Ralph Lauren's "Polo" and Calvin Klein's "Obsession" can be found here.

The Perfume Outlet requested that Mr. C not put the actual prices in writing, in order to protect their relationships with the manufacturers. But they did say that their perfumes are generally marked 10% to 15% (and sometimes more) below department stores like Macy's and Rich's.

The store also sells hair care products from Paul Mitchell, Redken, and Nexxus; but, alas, these are sold at regular retail prices.

Here's an extra bargain-hunting tip: Bring your own empty bottles into the shop, and you'll save even more. A half-ounce of perfume which may sell for $10 in bulk would be reduced to $8 if they can put it into your own container. Considering the fact that their prices are already lower than other perfumeries, these savings can really add up!

Sally Beauty Supply
- 3728 Roswell Rd. N.E., Atlanta; 233-9438
- 2973 Headland Dr. S.W., Atlanta; 346-1226
- 2954 Canton Rd., Marietta; 427-9012
- 10705 Alpharetta Hwy., Roswell; 992-7714

And other suburban locations
A more accurate name for this chain might be "Sally's Hair and Nail Care Supply," but no matter, for on these particular products there are bargains galore. From shampoos to fake nail sets to perming equipment, you'll find it here. And because this is a large national chain with big buying power, their prices are among the best around.

At the time of this writing, a twelve-pack of Styling-Ese straight perm rods was selling for just 79¢, and Jheri Rhedding's "One for All" acid perm kit for $3.99. All Set hair spray in the twenty-ounce can cost $1.29, and a pint of Queen Helene Strawberry Shampoo was $2.19. And you can get a whole quart of Tresemmé European Remoisturizing Conditioner for just $2.44.

There is a full selection of quality products geared toward African-American customers here too. These include such hair care items as Dark & Lovely's Cholesterol Conditioning Treatment for $1.99, and the same brand's No Lye Relaxer System for $4.69.

Sally's own brand, Beauty Secrets, will save you even more money. Cotton balls, for example, are just $1.39 for 100 triple-size balls; that's about 75¢ off what you can expect to pay for the same product in a grocery store or regular drug store. Beauty Secrets Nail Glue is just $2.99.

In addition to treatment supplies, Sally also sells pro-grade equipment at salon industry prices. A Conair "Grand Champion" professional styling dryer is $34.99; Helen of Troy's hot curling iron with brush is $8.99; and you can even get a Curlmaster Curling Iron for an incredible $2.99.

Sandy's Hair Care Co.
• 2625 Piedmont Rd. N.E., #53, Atlanta; 239-9387

For salon-quality hair care products, from shampoo and conditioners to mousses and more, Sandy's has it all, and at dandy prices, to boot. Even some harder-to-find brands are stocked here at the same discounted rates.

Mr. C found oodles of bargains here, like Focus 21 Sea Plasma Conditioner; it was priced at $5.59 for the eight-ounce bottle. KMS Gelato hair gel was $3.77 for four ounces, and Redken Climatress deep conditioner in the 8.5 ounce tube was seen for $11.99.

Back Alive Curl Revitalizer is a good deal at $5.99 for the sixteen-ounce bottle; so is a thirteen-ounce can of Sebastian Shaper Hair Spray at $8.95, and a big twenty-ounce bot-

---

MR. CHEAP'S PICKS
Cosmetics and Perfumes

✔ **Perfumania**—In the suburbs, this national chain reigns supreme with a vast selection for women and men.

✔ **Perfume Outlet**—Simply sweet deals on your favorite fragrances.

---

tle of Infusium 23 Hair Treatment is $6.88—which is about half of the retail price.

Soft Sheen Super Optimum Relaxer Care System is reduced from $9.98 to just $7, and Joico Ice Gel is $6.65 for an 8.8-ounce tube. Have a look for yourself!

Scentsations
• 1777 Ellsworth Industrial Blvd. N.W., Atlanta; 355-2584

This "shop" is actually little more than a counter inside of the women's department at K & G Liquidators (see separate listing under "New Clothing: Men's and Women's General Wear"). Scentsations carries a selection of designer colognes for men and women at discounts of about 10% to 40% off retail prices. Most items will save you in the range of $5-$10 a bottle; but a 3-oz. spray bottle of Oscar de la Renta perfume, which lists for $52, costs only $36.95 here. Other women's fragrances include a 2.5-oz. spray of Perry Ellis eau de toilette, reduced from $37.50 to $29.95; a 1.7-oz. Romeo Gigli perfume reduced from $50 to $34.95; and the same size eau de toilette by Paloma Picasso, $7 off at $41.95.

Men can save $5 on longtime favorite Z-14 by Halston, $19.95 for a 1.9-oz spray bottle; four ounces of Guess for Men cologne are marked down from $40 to $31.95; and Paco Rabanne saves you about $6 on the

1.7-oz spray bottle.

Scentsations also carries lotions, powders, and other skin care products; they can design custom gift baskets, and ship anywhere in the country. Open Fridays and Saturdays from 10 a.m. to 7 p.m., Sundays from 12-6 p.m.

Tuesday Morning
- 3165 Peachtree Rd. N.E., Atlanta; 233-6526
- 3250 Satellite Blvd., Duluth; 476-0522
- 4502 Chamblee-Dunwoody Rd., Dunwoody; 457-3565
- 700 Sandy Plains Rd. N.E., Marietta; 428-1536
- 1115 Morrow Industrial Blvd., Morrow; 961-0707
- 1231 Alpharetta St., Roswell; 640-8146
- 2512 Spring Rd. S.E., Smyrna; 435-6678

And other suburban locations
We all know how much better Tuesday mornings are, compared to Mondays. TM's bargains will make you feel that much better any day, with discounts on everything from clothes to party supplies to toys to jewelry to luggage. They also tend to have similar deals on cosmetics and perfumes, though the selection varies, depending on what closeouts they can snap up. Whatever you do find, it'll probably be as much as 50% off the retail price.

By the way, if you're worried that these liquid liquidation bargains may be a bit old, Mr. C has heard from experts in the business that perfume doesn't begin to lose its potency until *after* it has been opened. As long as it's sealed, it's fresh. Tuesday Morning stores are open seven days a week.

DISCOUNT DEPARTMENT STORES

Big Lots
- 3291 Buford Hwy. N.E., Atlanta; 320-7299
- 5437 Riverdale Rd., College Park; 991-0419
- 4181 Snapfinger Woods Dr., Decatur; 288-6226
- 4851 Jonesboro Rd., Forest Park; 361-6467
- 1720 Roberts Rd. N.W., Kennesaw; 499-2466
- 2745 Sandy Plains Rd. N.E., Marietta; 973-8947
- 1863 Roswell Rd. N.E., Marietta; 977-4256
- 3791 South Cobb Dr. S.E., Smyrna; 438-8321

And other suburban locations
Go ahead—call this place cheap. They love it. They have *fun* with it, in signs all over the store that say "We must be crazy..." and so forth. Over forty aisles are packed with closeouts, salvage from other stores, discontinued items, knock-off brands, and every other way they can think

of to be cheap. They have a huge selection, as much as any department store, as much as the major liquidation places Mr. C has seen in New York and other cities.

You never know what they may have here. As with any store specializing in closeouts, you can't *expect* them to have exactly the item or brand you want. But you'll probably find something comparable. Or, as many folks do, you can go in just to see what's there—no doubt, a few things you can really use, at rock-bottom prices.

You want toys? They got toys, like a "Slap II" electronic basketball game, originally $125, now just $50; or Mattel "Plush Pets" reduced from $20 to $7.99. Need some sneakers? Maybe you'll find Adidas running shoes for $15.99. What about hair care? You can get those generic copies of salon brands like Paul Mitchell and Nexus for $1.49 a bottle, or go for the real thing with Jhirmack and

Revlon for a buck each.

Not to mention domestics and other home furnishings, hardware and tools, sports equipment, household products, a 15-pound sack of kitty litter for $1.99, greeting cards at 40% off the printed price, and several aisles of reduced-price grocery items. BL is also a good place to check out for seasonal items, like Halloween costumes and Christmas decorations—discounted before the holidays, not after. All stores are open seven days a week.

Burlington Coat Factory

- 4166 Buford Hwy. N.E., Atlanta; 634-5566
- 3750 Venture Dr., Duluth; 497-0033
- 1255 Roswell Rd. N.E., Marietta; 971-6540
- 5934 Roswell Rd., Sandy Springs; 303-0505

Not content with being a popular clothing discounter for the entire family, Burlington Coat Factory stores have expanded from within to become something almost like actual department stores. They are quite large, and in each one, you'll not only find discounted clothing for the whole family, but also shoes, jewelry, linens, and infant furnishings.

Most folks know of Burlington for its clothing. They carry big names at good prices; some are very good bargains indeed. You can outfit yourself from top to toe here, inside and out, in conservative or stylish looks. True to its name, you can find all kinds of coats here—like a Pierre Cardin lambskin bomber jacket, list priced at $300, for just $180, or racks of simulated fur coats for women. How about a *faux* fox, reduced from $200 to $120?

But there's more here than meets the elements. Underneath those coats, guys could be wearing a Harvé Benard double-breasted suit of 100% wool, discounted from $400 to $180. Or creations by Ralph Lauren, Perry Ellis, Nino Cerruti, and Christian Dior at similar savings. For the gals, perhaps a nifty black two-piece Oleg Cassini set, not $270, but $150. A

Jones New York turtleneck sweater, reduced from $140 to $90. Or 100% silk blouses for $12.95. Size selection is good here, from petite to plus sizes for women, as well as big and tall sizes for men.

Then, there are all the fashions for children, from tots to teens. Boys' Jordache ski jackets were recently seen reduced from $70 to $40; girls will look smart in a dressy red coat by London Fog, marked down from $110 to $80. Both can save ten bucks or so off Levi's jeans, Guess denim fashions, and others.

You can also stock up on basics and accessories here, like ties, hats, and underwear (particularly Burlington hosiery, at $1-$2 off all styles). There is also a small but serviceable jewelry counter, selling gold chains, bracelets, watches, and the like at permanent discounts of 40%-50% off retail prices. And don't forget to look for the clearance racks in every clothing department!

Now, let's move on to the specialty stores-within-the-store. **The Capezio Footwear Outlet** extends these savings to all kinds of basic and classy shoes for men, women, and kids; it's not just for dancing anymore. Current styles in dressy shoes and boots are mostly sold at $10-$20 off list prices; for deeper discounts, though, look over on the long self-service racks, arranged by size. These are mainly closeouts and overstocks, all perfectly good. You may find a pair of red leather pumps by Bandolino, reduced from $72 to $39; men's dress loafers by Johnston and Murphy, marked down from $165 to $98; or Wrangler cowboy boots for $70 (not leather, obviously, but good looking). There is a more limited selection of sneakers, like ankle-high tennis shoes by Reebok for $49; plus kids shoes by Sesame Street, Fisher Price, and Hush Puppies.

Baby World sells discounted clothing, furniture, and accessories for newborns and small children. Along with good prices on infant and maternity wear, you can find things like a white crib set, complete with a

Simmons mattress and colorful print sheets, reduced from $350 to $205. Not to mention plenty of soft and cuddly toys to fill those cribs. Also, such diverse items as a Little Tykes plastic table and chairs, for toddler tea parties; Graco strollers, like the "Elite" model, discounted from $140 to $99; a Snugli car seat, reduced from $62 to $36; and clothing not only for newborns, but also for maternity moms.

Luxury Linens does the same deal for home furnishings, many by designers and name brands, at 20% to 50% below retail. Mr. C found things like Ardsley goose down comforters, in full or queen size, reduced from $140 to $90; Laura Ashley flat sheets, discounted from $32 to $12, along with names like Utica, Martex, and Bill Blass; towels by Dundee; plus bed pillows (including orthopedic styles), throw pillows, shower curtains, decorative baskets, and more—stacked from floor to ceiling.

50 Off Stores
- 803 Ralph D. Abernathy Blvd. S.W., Atlanta; 753-4878
- 2841 Greenbriar Pkwy. S.W., Atlanta; 349-7148
- 3850 Jonesboro Rd. S.E., Atlanta; 363-2799
- 3445 Memorial Dr., Decatur; 284-4565
- 1365 Roswell Rd. N.E., Marietta; 565-9797
- 2532 Atlanta Rd. S.E., Smyrna; 435-9079

The name says it all here. 50 Off sells closeouts on all kinds of clothing and home furnishings at big discounts. How much? Guess! The stock is always different, depending on whatever deals are out there on the liquidation circuit. You may see, as Mr. C did on his visit, Jordache sweaters for women, just $15; men's dress shirts by Botany 500 for $10; plus lots of midgrade brands of clothing and shoes for men, women, and children.

In housewares, there are often such deals as a Corning "Visions" six-piece cookware set for $23, full-sized Cannon sheets sets for $14 and comforters for $20, brass-finish coat trees

for $12.50, as well as toys, decorative items, bathroom accessories, and the like.

Whatever you're looking at, remember—take 50% off the tagged price (in the above descriptions, Mr. C has already done the math for you). Senior citizens get an additional 10% discount off their total purchases on the first Friday of each month. Open seven days.

MacFrugal Stores
- 2581 Piedmont Rd. N.E., Atlanta; 237-1919
- 2685 Stewart Ave. S.W., Atlanta; 762-5449
- 2975 Headland Dr. S.W., Atlanta; 349-1616
- 2738 Candler Rd., Decatur; 241-34866
- 1375 Roswell Rd. N.E., Marietta; 565-6208

Not to be confused with the car rental people, MacFrugal is another chain store offering big reductions on closeout items found in many area shopping plazas. They tend to have less clothing, and more hard goods, than the 50 Off stores; MacF is more like a "real" department store, and the discounts here run anywhere from 40% to 70% off retail prices.

The clothes they do carry are usually irregulars, and rarely name brands; thus, you may see women's jeans for $7.99, children's print T-shirts for $2-$3, etc. You're better off in housewares, where Mr. C was impressed with a 25-piece "Freeze, Heat, Serve" cookware set by Anchor Hocking for just $9.99. Along with lots of kitchen gadgets, MacFrugal's also stocks closeouts on packaged foods which are at or near expiration, but probably still quite edible.

The store is particularly good for toys, like Cabbage Patch Kids for $14.99, as well as lots of cars, sports games, and model kits. For bigger kids—and you know who you are—there is a well-stocked hardware and tools aisle. Check MacF's out for cosmetics and hair care products, too. They've got a little bit of everything. Open seven days.

ELECTRONICS

AUDIO/VIDEO EQUIPMENT

There are lots of places to save money on appliances and electronics in Atlanta. Some, unfortunately, are as far below repute as they are below retail. With merchandise that is imported from foreign countries, there is a greater possibility of shady deals, or inferior quality. Mr. C says this not out of any kind of prejudice, but becasue he wants you to be careful.

One of the best ways to protect yourself, if you have doubts as to *any* store's reliability, is to ask about their guarantee policy; make sure the item you want carries an American warranty. Since some stores deal directly with manufacturers in the Far East, their merchandise many carry a foreign warranty instead. Even for identical products, a foreign warranty can make repairs a hassle—unless you don't mind paying the postage to Japan! Remember, you are perfectly within your rights to inquire about this in the store.

Capitol TV
• Sandy Springs Shopping Center,
  6125 Roswell Rd., Sandy Springs;
  256-9081

You know you can trust a place like this—they've been around since 1965. Must be doing something right. By selling just one thing and lots of them, they can bring you great deals; in this age of "superstores" selling three models of every electronic item under the sun, it's nice to find these smaller, older shops—where selection is still a virtue.

Some televisions here are year-old closeouts; but, in most cases, you can hardly tell the difference between them and their newer versions. Mr. C found a 19" Sony color TV for $295, complete with stereo sound. The cable-ready version's just $40 more. A similar RCA model, again with a 19" screen, was seen for $329; or $399 for the 25" size. Be sure to check out their floor samples, too, for even better bargains.

Capitol can also finance your purchase of large-screen TVs, like the RCA Home Theatre ($595), or a Sony projection TV with Surround Sound (a floor sample was on sale for $650). And, for families who always fight over what to watch, there's a dual screen Sony with wireless infrared earphones (!) for $995. Who says TV doesn't bring families together anymore?

Cherian's
• Scott Village Shopping Center,
  1707 Church St., Decatur;
  299-0842

There are some surprising bargains to be found in this store. Catering to Decatur's Indian community, the store features an eclectic variety of imported items from overseas. So, along with bags of rice and tea and other grocery items, you'll find budget-friendly name brand electronics and small appliances.

A Casio single CD player, seen for $200 elsewhere, may sell for only $169 at Cherian's. A Nintendo control deck with joysticks was also seen here under $170. Mr. C also spotted a ten pack of TDK 90-minute audio cassettes, which would sell for over $20 in music stores, going for $9.50 here.

Be sure to carefully check the voltages on electronic items before you buy. Some are not compatible for use in this country. Because Cherian's is a direct importer, some products sold here are meant for customers who travel overseas, or those who send them back to family members in foreign countries.

Cherian's is open Tuesdays through Saturdays from 10:30 a.m. to 9 p.m., and Sundays from 1:30 p.m. to 9 p.m. It's closed on Mondays.

Electronics Liquidators

- 1750 Howell Mill Rd. N.W., Atlanta; 351-1414

Just off of I-75, and around the corner from the clothing outlets of the Chattahoochee area, this small shop is filled with truly wonderful bargains on all kinds of electronics for the home or office. Open only since June 1993, the store snaps up equipment that is being cleared out from department stores. These are items which may have been returned for some reason, and repaired; but laws prohibit them from being sold as new, so the stores and manufacturers are eager to get rid of them through resellers like this. So, just about everything in this store is new, and is sold at 50% to 60% below retail. Many are even sold below wholesale cost.

Most of what you see here are brand-name items; many others are "private labels," made by the same manufacturers, but sold under a department store name like Sears or J.C. Penney. Electronics Liquidators sells these with a six-month warranty on parts and labor; they do their own repair work. Major brand items still carry the original factory warranties. In other words, even though some of these are returns, there is no more risk involved here than anywhere else.

Okay, so what've they got? Well, it's always different, of course, but Mr. C found a Sony CD player, with remote control, which originally sold

for $199, selling here for $109. Same price for a portable walkman-style CD player by Panasonic. A Sharp 20-inch color TV reduced from $389 to a sharper $239. And a video camcorder, made for J.C. Penney, selling for just $359. Plus car stereo units, like a removable CD player/radio marked down from $299 to $159.

For the home or office, there was a Sony cordless phone for $79, an AT&T answering machine reduced from $149 to $89, and a Toshiba notebook computer, with a built-in fax/modem unit, less than half its retail price at just $700. Also pagers, word processors, and even some home appliances, such as microwave ovens and vacuum cleaners.

Whew! There's a lot to see. In fact, by the time you read this, Mike and Igor—the guys who started the place—plan to have expanded into a warehouse space behind the store. They also offer an inexpensive repair service for anything you may bring in. Speaking of which, you can even trade electronics in for credit toward a purchase. That creates the potential for working some incredible deals.

HiFi Buys Outlet Store

- Buford Outlet Mall, 4166 Buford Hwy. N.E., Atlanta; 633-8557

This is the clearance center for the well-known chain, with over a dozen stores in the Atlanta area. From this location in the Buford Outlet Mall, they sell off demo models, samples, and returned/refurbished units, all at well below their original prices. Many of these still carry the full manufacturers' warranties, which may last from one year to five years (on some speakers). Refurbished items, repaired in the store, have a 90-day warranty—about as good as you can get on these. There is also a fourteen-day exchange policy, so you can't really get stuck with a lemon.

The store has a wide selection of just about everything sold from their retail stores: VCRs, TVs with screens of up to 35 inches diagonally, home and car stereos, you name it. Among the things Mr. C found were a Sony

Trinitron color TV, with a ten-inch
screen, for $199; a Sharp six-head
"Artificial Intelligence" VCR for
$239; a pair of Kenwood three-way
speakers, four feet tall, for $140; a
five-disk CD changer, also by Ken-
wood, for $169; and a Panasonic
compact stereo system—with a dual
cassette deck, tuner, graphic equal-
izer and built-in speakers—reduced
from $400 to $199. Even a Sony
Watchman personal TV, originally
$400, was found here for $250.

Some pieces are on sale here because they are missing their remote
control units; these are marked "as
is," but the repair department can
often find you a suitable replacement.
The folks here are really friendly,
happy to demystify the latest techno-
logical advances if you wish. It's nice
to find such low prices *and* such
good service together under the same
roof. Open seven days.

Recycle Electronics
• 6624 Dawson Blvd., Norcross;
  449-1872

Part of the Georgia Antique Center
and Market, with a separate entrance
from the west side parking lot, Recy-
cle buys and sells used stereo and TV
equipment. They also do their own repair, and even accept trade-ins toward a purchase. Thus, they have an
ever-changing selection of recent and
not-so-recent (but certainly not antique) models of every kind. You may
see a brand-new, 26-inch RCA Color-

COMPUTERS

CompUSA Computer Superstore
• Around Lenox Shopping Center,
  3400 Wooddale Dr. N.E., Atlanta;
  814-0880
• 3825 Venture Dr., Duluth; 813-8565
• 2201 Cobb Pkwy., Marietta;
  952-1042

Mr. C isn't in the habit of discussing
superstores, since you probably know
about them already. But, with its high-
volume sales, CompUSA is hard to
beat on new computers and accessories including software packages,

MR. CHEAP'S PICKS
Electronics

✔ **Electronics Liquidators**—Two
guys snapping up closeout
bargains directly from
manufacturers and department
stores, and selling them
incredibly cheap.

✔ **HiFi Buys Outlet Store**—The
clearance center for the big
local chain is filled with factory
refurbished stereo and video
components, all warrantied.

trak 2000 wood-console TV for
$497; or a used Zenith 19-inch color
TV for $175. Or a used Zenith VCR
for just $139. Mr. C also found an
Emerson compact stereo system, with
a tuner, dual cassette deck, and speakers, for a mere $88; perfect for a col-
lege dorm, perhaps. And there was a
large selection of car stereo speakers,
all new and in their original packages.

Everything sold here comes with a
30-day in-store warranty, during
which these folks will make any necessary repairs for free. They're open
seven days a week.

printers, and more.

That is, if you can find the store.
The Buckhead location, at any rate, is
practically hidden in a tiny shopping
center near the Swissotel next to
Lenox Square Mall. Once you find it,
though, you 'll find goodies like an
Apple Mcintosh IIvx computer with
CD-ROM, listed at $1,600, but seen
here for $1,199 (monitor and key-
board sold separately). A Compudyne
IBM-compatible 486 system, with
Windows and MS-DOS software installed, was recently selling for just

$849 (without monitor). Business leasing is available on these items, as well as laptops, at rates as low as $40 a month.

Other necessities at good prices include things like fax/modems, trackballs, cables, software, books, and more. A MicroSpeed "MicroTRAC" ball for laptops was seen for $64 (but up to $80 elsewhere), while 3 1/2 " double-sided high-density diskettes—already formatted—sell for 69 cents apiece when you buy 25 or more at a time. You can also save big on paper and printers (a Hewlett Packard LaserJet model was recently on sale for $349, down from $600).

A friend of Mr. C's, who is a high-tech expert, loves CompUSA because the store puts all of its hardware out on display. Everything's up and running, from desktops to laptops to fax machines, so you can compare models and play with them to your heart's content.

The stores are open weekdays and Saturdays from 9 a.m. to 9 p.m., and Sundays 11 a.m. to 6 p.m.

The Consumer Expo
- 740 Holcomb Bridge Rd., Roswell; 643-9750.

Talk about a success story. Trac Distributors, an electronics wholesaler, began a business experiment last fall, selling a small portion of its merchandise to the public at factory-direct prices. Beginning in a warehouse space at the rear of their Northeast Expressway offices, Trac quickly realized they had a potential goldmine. And so, in early '94, they switched to a new name, a new location, and more room—a former car dealership in Roswell, with 26,000 square feet ready to be filled with some of the best deals on computers and office equipment in the entire Atlanta area.

Here are just a few of the incredible finds seen on an early visit: A Compaq 386SX desktop computer, with monitor, for $699; it included DOS 5.0, Windows 3.1, and a one-year warranty. (You could also purchase that software set for $49.) Dell 14-inch computer monitors, non-inter-

laced, fully warrantied, for $229. A Digital "PostScript" laser printer, capable of running out four pages per minute, for $699; in stores, it sells for as much as $900.

Of course, by the time you go, there may be very few of these particular items left. The stock is always going to be changing. Many items are current models; The Consumer Expo holds back a small portion to be sold at this outlet. Others are overstocks and closeouts. Open Thursday and Friday from 11 a.m. to 7 p.m., Saturday from 9 a.m. to 6 p.m., and Sunday from 12-6.

Delta Electronics
- 5147 Buford Hwy., Doraville; 458-4690

Put some changes into your computer system by shopping at Delta. The company's been around for eighteen years, and has more recently gotten into the computer biz by purchasing IBM compatibles in volume, and then reselling them at big discounts. You can also save by mixing and matching components; the staff will help you put together just the system you need.

Mr. C was told that a 386 unit, with a single floppy disk drive and keyboard, can be had for as little as just $299; while a Samsung color monitor could be added for only $255. Mouses and laptops are also budget-priced. A 486 computer system, with IBM motherboard, and keyboard, color monitor, and three-button mouse, plus DOS 6.0 and Windows 3.1 installed, was selling for $1,439. Of course, prices on 486 computers are falling rapidly now; call or stop in to find out the current prices, which have probably improved already. Delta's a favorite of both small and large businesses, since all hardware products are sold with a 30-day money-back store guarantee as well as a one-year manufacturer's warranty.

MicroSeconds
- 6125 Roswell Rd., Sandy Springs; 252-7221

With the booming growth of the computer business, a new kind of store has evolved: The secondhand computer reseller. Because the manufacturers are bringing out newer, fancier models almost every day, you can save lots of money on these big-ticket purchases by going with used equipment. After all, a model that's only a year old may be *passe* to some hackers, but it's still got a lot of life in it.

MicroSeconds is one of the best examples of this kind of store Mr. C has found in the Atlanta area. It's a consignment store, with a young, friendly, and knowledgeable staff that really helps its customers get exactly what they need. Whether you're buying new or used, you can put together your own IBM-compatible or Mac system, paying only for what you need. All of the used equipment has been beautifully well-kept, and the in-house repair crew has cleaned and checked every unit, erasing the memory and testing for viruses.

IBM-clone 286-based systems are priced from just $300 complete; and 386-based systems from $550. That's right—for as little as $300, you can get an entire system, with disk drive, keyboard, and monitor, everything you need to go home and start computing. No, it's not as powerful as the latest generation; but for many folks—grad students writing a thesis, say, or parents who want to get their kids started—this may be all you'll need.

Some pieces are a few years older yet, but still perfectly useful; IBM-type "XT" systems, five years old and more, sell for $150. You can get an IBM Personal System 2 monochrome monitor for only $30. Back to the present, Mr. C found a WYSE 386 system with 2 MB of RAM, an 80 megabyte dual drive, and a 14" VGA color screen for $600. A Zenith 386 Notebook with 62 megabyte hard drive and trackball was seen for $1,100, while a Macintosh Plus "UltraDrive 20" with keyboard was $550.

Now, MicroSeconds does also sell new IBM-clone systems, too; at the time of Mr. C's visit, their basic pack-

MR. CHEAP'S PICKS
Computers

✔ **The Consumer Expo**—An importer which sells to department stores has decided to sell to the public as well. Super bargains on computers, printers, and some office machines.

✔ **MicroSeconds**—As in *secondhand*, a great way to save hundreds of dollars on this expensive equipment. They do their own repairs, and guarantee them.

age for a new 386 system was priced at $790 complete. From there you can mix or match, substituting higher- or lower-grade components. Want to make it a 486? That's an extra $120. Would you like it with more memory? Upgrade it from 40 MB to 170 MB for another $85. A sharper monitor? Add $40. Meanwhile, *any* complete 486 system for under $1,000 is currently a good deal indeed.

The store usually has a good selection of new and used peripherals to choose from, like a Toshiba "3-in-1" dot matrix printer for $120; or, you can go high-tech with an Apple Imagewriter II laser printer for $1,000. Used software is also for sale here, such as Apple's "Style Writer" for $225, "MacDraw" ($25), and "Lotus 1-2-3 for DOS" ($230).

New computers carry a one-year warranty; used items are guaranteed for thirty days, during which they'll patch up any problems they may have missed. MicroSeconds is located just half a mile north of the Roswell/Perimeter intersection.

PC Warehouse

- Peachtree & Piedmont Crossing Shopping Center, 3330 Piedmont Rd. N.E., Atlanta; 240-0004
- Peachtree Corner Shopping Ctr., 7050 Jimmy Carter Blvd., Norcross; 448-6633

It's not your typical mile-high-ceiling "warehouse," but there's still plenty of selection, plus a super-knowledgeable staff, at this national chain.

Brand names can be found throughout the store, like a Toshiba "Satellite" notebook (seen recently for $1,599), or an IBM "ThinkPad" 486 notebook with 4 MB of RAM, a 125 MB high-density drive, and a TrackPoint II trackball, plus DOS and Prodigy installed—all for $1,999.

Printers and other peripherals are well-stocked here and quite affordable, like a Panasonic KX-P1150 dot matrix printer recently on sale for $139; an Epson "Stylus 800" InkJet for $269; and even laser printers. The Sharp JX9400 Laser Printer, capable of six pages a minute, was recently seen here selling for $499.

FLEA MARKETS AND EMPORIA

A Flea An' Tique

- 1853 Cheshire Bridge Rd. N.E., Atlanta; 872-4342
- 222 S. Main St., Alpharetta; 442-8991

Yes, this store is a bit of both. Over fifteen different vendors have banded together to create this wonderfully eclectic shop, filled with furniture, vintage clothing, collectibles, and of course, bric-a-brac. Would you believe a like-new solid oak dining table, with a removable center leaf and six chairs, plus a matching china cabinet, all for $975? Sure, but wait—that cabinet just isn't complete without the $12.50 cow-shaped teapot. Or, perhaps a set of eight glass tumblers from the 1950s, embossed with what must have been a fashionable design of the times, complete with metal caddy for $15.

For fashions that never go out of date, check out the vintage dresses—like a full-length black crepe gown for $45. Grab a shiny gold beaded handbag to complete the outfit for $24. You'll probably even find a selection of feather boas.

The Alpharetta store has even more to browse through—having just recently doubled its space to a total of 7,000 square feet. Both emporia are open seven days a week.

A-Ta-Z Salvage

- 240 East Trinity Place, Decatur; 377-9576

No, that's not a misspelling! The name of this store should give you some indication of its merchandise. Whether the stuff is really worth salvaging is up to *you* to decide.

This garage-like shop is right near the entrance to Agnes Scott College, just south of the center of Decatur; you should have no trouble finding it. However, you *will* have trouble making your way around the store. It's soooo cluttered with toys, furniture, and miscellaneous doo-dads that there's barely enough room to walk.

If you're just (just *just*) starting out on your own, and need a super-cheap sofa, desk, or other furniture, this can be a great place to look. You may find a (kinda dusty, but okay) three-piece wicker bedroom set, including dresser, night table, and mirror, all for $259. A three-piece wrought iron patio furniture set was seen for just $139. The store accepts cash only for special deals like these; but then, think of how much cash you'll save in credit card fees and bank charges!

Other furniture Mr. C saw included a curio cabinet for $32.50 (slightly scratched, and not solid wood, as you'd expect with a price like that); and an oak-finish bedroom set with nightstand, bedframe, chest and double dresser for $139.95. A dinette table with six leather-covered chairs (yep, real leather this time) is just $160.

Moving on: There are plenty of kitchen and household items, like a Hamilton Beach blender for $17.95, a Proctor-Silex steam iron for $7.95, and a Hoover toaster for $6.95. Didn't know that Hoover makes toasters? Neither did Mr. C. Guess you could call this place educational, too. Anyway, if the thing toasts, then what the heck?

For the kiddies, A-Ta-Z has games like an "Aim & Shoot" basketball set (y'know, the kind you hook over the back of a door) for just $2.95, a used Playskool xylophone and drum set for $3.99, and a crazy mish-mash of dolls, Frisbees, and Tinker Toy-type items. There was even a slightly rusty tricycle for $15.

What else? How about some LP records, like Waylon Jennings for $2.49 and the Judds for $1.95. Considering the rough condition of the covers, though, you may be wise to leave these alone.

A-Ta-Z offers a thirty-day layaway plan on its furniture, an extra convenience not often found at this kind of establishment. It's open Monday through Thursday from 11 a.m. to 6 p.m., and on Friday and Saturday from 12 noon to 6 p.m.

Atlanta Swap Meet Flea Market
• Storey North 85 Twin Drive-In, 3265 Northeast Expwy. Access Rd., Chamblee; 233-3889

Every Saturday and Sunday, the parking lots of this drive-in movie theater become one of the biggest flea markets in the area. From racks, tables, the back of their trucks, and sometimes just blankets spread on the pavement, vendors sell new and old clothing, jewelry, toys, home furnishings, electronics, the ever-present bric-a-brac, and even fresh produce. Just a few of the items Mr. C scoped out on his visit: A pair of used jeans

MR. CHEAP'S PICKS
Flea Markets and Emporia

✔ **A Flea An' Tique**—Lots of good bric-a-brac, from clothing and furniture to records and magazines, representing over fifteen dealers under one roof.
✔ **Bargainata**—Only held twice a year, but bargain fans count the days.
✔ **Everything's a Dollar**—And they ain't lying. One of the best of the city's many "dollar" stores, carrying name brand necessities and goodies.

for $6, an old Zenith color TV console for $65, a brand-new full size sheet set for $15, with new goose feather pillows at $15 a pair, and an 8mm camcorder, also new, for $499.

Plus crew socks in bulk quantities, antique jewelry, Spanish music cassettes and CDs, printed T-shirts for $5, and lots (*lots*) of junk. If flea markets are your thing, you've gotta see this one. There's also a playground area for kids, and the movie theater's snack bar is open. Free parking is available, though it gets jammed up early; better to park along the highway access road and walk in. You'll find the market between the Shallowford Road and Chamblee/Tucker exits, heading north on I-85. Open every Saturday and Sunday from 8 a.m. to 5 p.m.

Bargainata
• 791 Miami Circle N.E., Atlanta; 262-7199

This is not a store, but a twice-a-year bargain fest, organized by the Atlanta division of the League of Jewish Women. If you're reading this book, you probably know about it already; Bargainata has taken on hallowed significance over its twenty-year history.

Every March and November, there is an almost Pavlovian response to the approach of this sale—you can see shopping fans almost drooling with anticipation.

When opening day arrives at last, folks don't just line up at the door waiting for the 11:00 a.m. start; they bring lawn chairs and camp out from the early morning hours, hoping to be among the first people to gain entry. Getting tickets to a Grateful Dead concert is easier than this. Anyway, once the doors open, the warehouse and adjoining tent become so crowded that security personnel actually have to hold people back at the door, letting more shoppers in a few at a time as other satisfied customers finally make their way out.

Can you believe it? You'd better! The reason for all the fuss is that some pretty fancy closets get emptied for donations to this event. One of the organizers told Mr. C that, for their upcoming sale, a foreign diplomat based at an Atlanta consulate had donated 45 suits. Men's and women's designer clothing and shoes are indeed the main attraction at Bargainata, though you can also find linens, luggage, jewelry, toys, and housewares. And, while almost all of these are used items, they are classy, in "gently-worn" condition, and priced *very* cheaply. Lots of articles are under $10. And, on the last day, anything that hasn't sold yet goes for half-price.

The funds raised by these sales help the League's various educational programs, many of which are geared toward helping newly-arrived American citizens settle into their new homes. In fact, all clothing left over from each Bargainata is given directly to these immigrants.

To find out when the next sale is scheduled, or for information on making your own tax-deductible donations to the event, call the phone number listed above.

Best Flea Market
- 2707 East College Ave., Decatur; 377-0133

Mr. C isn't exactly sure that this is *the* best flea market he's ever seen, but it certainly is a fun place to rummage through.

From a $5 Samsonite suitcase to a $15 Zebco fishing rod and reel to a $25 Spalding golf set (complete with nine clubs and carrier), you never know what you'll find here. The merchandise is actually geared mostly towards guys; but, with a bit of children's clothing, plus toys and gadgets, you can find something for everyone in the whole family here, without blowing the budget.

Some of the fun items Mr. C found here include Nintendo game cartridges for just $8 each, a little girl's "Barbie Bike" for $15, and a baby carrier-rocker by Century for only $12. For the home, candle holders made from real copper are just $5, while a 13-inch RCA color television set was recently available for only $80. Ladies will like the 75¢ sunglasses and the $10 Gucci leather loafers. Plus packs of last season's baseball cards, used compact discs by the likes of Kenny G. and Hammer, and lots more.

Best Flea Market is closed on Mondays; store hours are Tuesdays through Thursdays from 10 a.m. to 7 p.m., Fridays and Saturdays from 10-8, and Sundays from 11-5.

Buford Highway Flea Market
- 5000 Buford Hwy., Chamblee; 493-7348

This is probably not what you think of when you hear the term "flea market." It's more like a Middle Eastern bazaar, with individual vendors set up in booth after booth, mostly selling new merchandise cheap. The booths—over 300 of them—are neatly arranged into grids, with the aisles humorously named after the area's major thoroughfares—Lenox Road, Cheshire Bridge Road, and so on. All of this, meanwhile, is completely indoors, in a building which clearly began life as a supermarket. This also means plenty of free parking in its huge front lot.

Inside, you may find tremendous

bargains or tremendous junk—it's your call. Maybe you'll snap up a leather jacket for $75, or four silk ties for $20. Perhaps a Seiko or Bulova watch at 20% to 30% below retail. One gentleman repairs and sells used stereo equipment, complete with a 30-day warranty; Mr. C found good deals on quality components like a Yamaha CD player for $99, as well as Bose speakers and JVC cassette decks.

What else? Tons of clothing buys, from brightly colored jeans to African dashikis and kufi hats. Low priced reproductions of designer colognes and handbags. Furniture that looks as cheap as it costs, but sometimes, what the heck. Children's bikes and tricycles. Comforters and linens. Shoes and boots. Even a tattoo parlor (at a discount? Mr. C did not inquire). Not to mention cheap food, i.e. hot dogs and such, when you need to take a breather from it all. The market is only open on weekends: Fridays and Saturdays from 11:00 a.m. to 9:30 p.m., and Sundays from noon to 7:00 p.m.

Everything 99 Cents
- 2575 North Decatur Rd., Decatur; 371-0444
- 7981 Tara Blvd., Jonesboro; 471-3663
- 91 Highway 138, West Stockbridge; 474-4901

A pretty good version of the marketing concept that's sweeping the nation. Here, you can find overstock, closeouts and leftovers in everything from costume jewelry and hair decorations to packaged foods, household cleaning products, coffee mugs, toys, and lots more. You never quite know what they'll have, but you *always* know how much it'll cost!

Everything's A Dollar
- Underground Atlanta, 96 Lower Alabama St. S.W., Atlanta; 681-1416
- Buford Outlet Mall, 4166 Buford Hwy. N.E., Atlanta; 315-1079
- 3700 Southside Industrial Pkwy. S.E., Atlanta; 361-0529

- 1355 East-West Connector S.W., Austell; 819-8995
- 2050 Lawrenceville Hwy., Decatur; 636-2581
- 400 Ernest Barrett Pkwy. NW, Kennesaw; 421-1932
- 337 Shannon South Pk., Union City; 969-0790

And other suburban locations
This is one of the best "dollar" stores, a good place to stock up on simple necessities like shampoo, snacks, and kitchen utensils, as well as seasonal items like wrapping paper and holiday decorations. This chain carries many name brands you may actually recognize, as opposed to the oddball "copy-cat" labels most dollar stores tend to carry. Everything really is priced at a buck here, too, except smaller items which are sold in multiples for $1.

Mr. C found plenty of cosmetics here, like Bonne Bell blusher, Clean & Clear hair gel, and Almay eye shadow. Novelty hair items, like bows and ponytail holders, are always stocked in mega-quantities. Nylons in many different shades, and athletic socks for men and women, are also carried.

And don't forget Fido! You can find products like Wagtime Dog Treats, as well as Alpo dog food and cat food.

If you're going to buy people food here, do be careful. If it's August and you're looking at green and red foil-wrapped chocolates, you can bet that these have been hanging around some warehouse since last Christmas. You'd probably be better off going to the grocery store for less ancient stuff. Some of the food Mr. C saw actually had price labels on them from department stores like Target; while these give you an immediate idea of the savings, be sure to check for an expiration date. Of course, with all the preservatives used in most foods nowadays, you probably can't go too far wrong. Some of the safer-looking items Mr. C saw were fruit sours, hard candies, potato chips, breath mints, mint chocolates, and even Slim Fast Cheese Curls.

Miscellaneous other items in store include fake flowers, woven baskets, beach balls, frying pans (that's right, for $1), Christmas tinsel (in September!), and four-pack Panasonic "C" batteries. How much? You know.

Gwinett Flea Market

- 5675 Jimmy Carter Blvd., Norcross; 449-8189

Right at the intersection of this popular shopping thoroughfare and I-85, the Gwinnett looms large both literally and figuratively. This vast two-story building is filled with dozens of small, individually owned store-booths selling clothes, shoes, jewelry, toys, Oriental rugs, antiques, electronics, and gifts.

The stores may come and go over time, but here are just a few of the goodies Mr. C noticed at different shops: A comforter with matching curtains for $65. A six-foot halogen torch lamp for $25. Cheap telephones for $12.99 each. Silver and turquoise earring studs for $5. Oriental porcelain vases for $10 each. And there's even a designer clothing reseller, who had things like an Oleg Cassini dress for $12—in great shape.

Because everyone picks up a share of the overall operating costs, it's less expensive to run a business here than in a private store; consequently, they can often charge lower prices than competitors. Still, don't assume that everything in here is automatically a bargain; shop just as carefully as you would in regular stores. A lot of the stuff in here can be as cheaply made as it is cheaply priced. Look for recognizeable brand names, and do a bit of price comparison if you have time.

The market is open Wednesdays, Thursdays and Sundays from 12 noon until 7 p.m.; Fridays and Saturdays from 11-8. There's tons of free parking, too.

The $1 $uper $tore

- Cub Foods Shopping Center, 2179 Lawrenceville Hwy., Decatur; 315-9350

Right at the intersection of Lawrenceville and North Druid Hills Road, this store is chock-full of cheap stuff you can definitely use.

Cosmetics are in good supply here, including such items as Ethnique Monaco nail polish and lipstick, Candler hair mousse, baby shampoo, conditioner, and body lotion.

Running low on bingo markers? Thought so. Pick up a pair for a dollar. Also, rolls of masking tape, telephone extension cords, work gloves, pencil-type tire pressure gauges, and longnose pliers. And you can spruce up the house with bud vases, glass votive candle holders (two for $1) and a three-piece pastel plastic bathroom set, complete with cup, toothbrush holder, and soap dish.

Household products found here tend to be generic knock-offs of better name brands. Instead of Windex, try Touch of Glass cleaner in the 33-ounce size; McAuley's Carpet & Room deodorizer, in a big 20-ounce box, will save you money over Lysol and such.

Novelty school sets, with ruler, pencil, eraser, and pouch might just get the kiddies interested in their homework. There are also plenty of toys to keep the young'uns entertained, like a Multicopter wind-up flying action toy, Teenage Mutant Ninja Turtles playing cards, troll dolls, plastic boomerang, magnifying glasses, flash card sets, and cardboard Simpsons stand-ups. Little Golden Books of *Beauty and the Beast* and *The Little Mermaid* were also well-stocked on a recent visit.

Some of the kitchen gadgets you'll find here are spices, pizza pans, cookie sheets, and plastic containers by Storekeepers. If you're planning a barbecue, you'll want to pick up a few citronella patio candles, too.

The store is open Monday through Saturday from 9 a.m. all the way to 9 p.m., and on Sundays from 11 a.m. to 6 p.m.

Onion Dome Imports

- Shops of Buckhead, 2221 Peachtree St. N.E., Atlanta; 352-3881

This interesting emporium offers plenty of exotic—and not overly expensive—doo-dads for your home. That in itself is a rare find for *this* neighborhood.

Mr. C warns you, though, that should you start a conversation with owner Edna Hughes, you may well be talking for hours. She's a real character, who's been in business since 1962; and she's accumulated stories galore from her world travels.

Onion Dome is mostly taken up with little, relatively inexpensive toys for children. Some are priced as low as ten cents each. This is a great place to check out for kooky stocking stuffers, and gifts for hard-to-please kids.

Among the goodies spotted here were a little piggie pencil sharpener for only $1, and toy binoculars for $1.50; plastic sharks are 50¢, while a plastic snake is a whopping $3. Straw placemats are $1, and ceramic bird whistles are 50¢. What else? Collapsible drinking cups for 25¢, leather hair clips for $2, fabric-covered elastic ponytail holders for $3, and decorative folding paper fans imported from Japan are $1.25.

This is the place to find those plastic recorders and flutes you probably tooted on as a kid yourself. They're still around, looking pretty much the same, for $2. Little tambourines go for $1.50.

Some of the more expensive—but high quality—items at Onion Dome include woven Mexican peasant shirts for just $10, straw safari hats for $3, and genuine sterling silver rings for $20. A strand of copper bells for your door is $6, while brightly colorful woven Guatemalan bed throws are $35.

The store is named after the onion-shaped domes of St. Basil's Cathedral in Moscow's Red Square, but the only obviously Russian items that Mr. C found at here are brightly-painted Matrioska dolls (you know, the ones with a doll inside a doll inside a doll...), priced at $30. It seems that Hong Kong is more responsible for many of the gifts found in here; but no matter, it's just plain fun.

Scavenger Hunt on Clairmont
• 3438 Clairmont Rd. N.E., Atlanta; 634-4948

This name fits perfectly. In true flea market style, twelve collectors have crammed every nook of this shop just off the Buford Highway with a treasure trove of antiques and collectibles. Bins and bins of old record albums (Barry Manilow, for some reason, seems to be at the front of each one), books, old magazines and license plates, mirrors, framed art, sets of china, brass objects, and all kinds of furniture...any of which can make for an offbeat gift idea. How about a special edition Coke bottle, commemorating the University of Georgia football team's undefeated 1980 season? The soda, now *really* classic Coke, still sits inside the never-opened bottle, which is imprinted with the score of each game—all for $3.50.

There are also lots of used televisions and radios, most of which are up and running; Mr. C noticed a new-looking black-and-white model selling for just $29.50. Others are scattered around the store, which is open from 10 a.m. to 6 p.m. every day of the week.

FLOWERS AND PLANTS

Many of the great deals you'll find on roses are only available for cash-and-carry purchases. If you want your flowers delivered, you'll probably wind up paying at least $10 more than the prices described below, plus an additional delivery charge. Also, be aware that while some florists advertise long-stem roses, they may not always be available in red; or if they are, they may sell out early in the day. Mr. C advises you to call ahead to find out for sure.

American Fare
• 1701 Mountain Industrial Blvd., Stone Mountain; 938-0151 (Floral department: 939-5043)

While you may hedge (ha ha) at buying your plants at a giant grocery store of sorts, your budget will fare well if you give American Fare a try.

Holly, juniper, and privot plants are just $2.29 each; a Japanese dwarf holly in a three-gallon pot goes for $10.97. Hardy mums are yours for $1.99, and three-gallon hibiscus plants for a very reasonable $11.

Japanese boxwood plants are also $11 in the three-gallon size pot. To keep your yard safe, American Fare also sells that ever-necessary Dexol Fire Ant Killer, $3 for a four-pound bag.

For the lawn, try Scotts Turf Builder fertilizer, enough to cover 6,000 square feet of grass, for just $8. Rebel II and Rebel Supreme grass seed is just $5.97 for a five-pound bag, while Lime-Rite pelletized lime is $1.99 for a big forty-pounder.

Other equipment for the yard is also sold here at great prices. K-Gro bamboo rakes are only $5.88 each, while their smaller garden rakes and hoes $2.97 each.

Art Moods
• 1058 Mistletoe Rd., Decatur; 325-2334

Art Moods gets its name from the fact that it's also a custom picture-framing shop. You may have driven by this place a hundred times on your way to the Market Square Mall in North DeKalb, without ever noticing it. The store is right off North Druid Hills Road, down a hill and around a corner from the drive into the mall parking lot.

It's worth the little hunt, though, if you're looking for fresh, long-stem roses at a nice price. A dozen red long-stem roses cost only $16.95, while medium stems in a variety of colors are priced at $10.95 per dozen. Spruce up any bouquet by adding baby's breath for just $1.50 extra.

This store is unusual, in that its long-stems tend to be available *only* in red; most other discount florists seem to overstock the pink, white or peach ones. These prices are cash-and-carry; delivery, within a five-mile range of the store, is $7 extra.

Atlanta State Farmer's Market
• 16 Forest Pkwy, Forest Park; 366-6910

This is the *professional* farmer's market. Your own supermarket or corner store probably gets its produce here. Mini-vans and eighteen-wheelers zip around the rows and rows of semi-enclosed stalls, delivering or filling up with fruits, vegetables, and more. So, can you pull up in your little ol' Hyundai and buy just a pound of tomatoes? Yes you can!

Located at exit 78 from Interstate 75, this massive, state-run complex divides neatly into two sides as soon as you drive in: To your left are the rows of stalls, where farmers stand waiting to sell their wares—while the warehouses to the right are for purchasing in wholesale quantities. Both sides offer the chance to get better deals than your local stores; naturally, the wholesale area has the absolute lowest prices, and if you (or your school, business, etc.) can shop in case quantities, you are most welcome.

Meanwhile, at the very end of the stalls side, closest to the highway, is the newer Garden Center. Down here, you can get great deals on everything from sod to straw, and a particularly fine selection of locally grown annuals and perennials. Choices (and prices) vary from season to season, but you may find things like flats of pansies at $8 for a tray of 48 plants.

Don't forget to check up and down the rows of farmers' stalls; there are some florists mixed in here, too. Some may offer a ten-inch potted ficus for $7.50, or a pot of chry-

santhemums for a mere $5.50. The
price for the mums would blossom to
more than twenty dollars in town.
Why so cheap here? No fancy pack-
aging (though some dealers will add
this for an extra few bucks) and no
deliveries. This keeps their costs, and
prices, low. To paraphrase Sgt. Joe
Friday: Just the flowers, ma'am.

You can cover a lot of ground—literally and figuratively—for little
cash by coming to this one place. The
Farmer's Market itself is open twenty-
four hours a day, though you're not
likely to find much action on the
farmers' and garden side after 9 or 10
p.m.; late nights are the truckers' do-
main. Weekdays, of course, are the
quietest and easiest times for regular
folks to shop here.

Atlanta Wildflowers
- 3872 Roswell Rd. N.E., Atlanta;
  814-0454 or 1-800-758-6102

They're just wild about floral arrangement at Atlanta Wildflowers. If you
haven't got a clue as to what kind of
bouquet you want, they'll be happy
to suggest lots of choices to fit any
budget. They also specialize in
flower arrangements for men here, in
minimalistic styles and earthy color
schemes, so if you want to surprise
the man in your life, give 'em a try.

The store is conveniently located
in the Buckhead Court shopping center. Cash-n-carry roses are just
$12.95 per dozen here, in selected
colors only. If you don't call early to
order your bunch, you may wind up
with pink or white, but at least the
price will keep your budget from going into the red.

Boxed roses are considerably
higher, though pretty good at $38 a
dozen, while a single rose arrangement with vase is $9.95; single roses
are $1.75 to $2 each, depending on
color. Single carnations are $1, and a
dozen plain carnations are $5.95,
while a dozen in arrangement with
baby's breath and ferns is $21. An-
other interesting option is a dozen
dried roses for $12. Ferns and baby's
breath can be added to any arrangement for an extra $2.95.

MR. CHEAP'S PICKS
Flowers and Plants

- ✔ **Artmoods**—In the mood to
  spend just $11 on a dozen
  roses? This is the place!
- ✔ **Flora Dora**—Incredibly
  lifelike silk flowers, wholesale
  to you.
- ✔ **Florida Tropicals and
  Roses**—Ficus trees, ferns, and
  other fun stuff at prices that
  will warm you right up.

The store also sells big helium bal-
loons in a variety of colors for $1.50
a pop (no pun intended). If you do
want to spring for delivery, there's a
$25 minimum order, not including
the additional delivery charge.

A Blooming Earth Florist and Greenhouse
- 2403 Lawrenceville Hwy.,
  Decatur; 321-4409

People drive miles out of their way to
get floral arrangements here, and for
good reason. The parking lot is often
full, and pulling back out onto
Lawrenceville Highway can be a
death-defying experience; but when
you can buy roses for $9.99 a dozen,
who cares?

Mr. C does want to point out that
these are medium-length stems, but,
if you think about it, you're going to
chop a foot off to get them into the
vase anyway. They're available at
this price in pink, yellow, and white
only; red roses are still a bargain at
$12.95 a dozen. So much so, in fact,
that these often sell out quickly each
day.

A Blooming Earth does get a limited stock of long-stems for just $25
a dozen. They don't offer delivery on
these, since they're often in short supply. Medium-stems arranged for delivery are $30, plus a low $4 delivery

fee. Makes sense to present them yourself, no?

Other flowers available here include carnations for just $1.25 each ($6.99 a dozen), and snapdragons for $2.50. The store is open from 8:30 a.m. to 6 p.m. weekdays, and from 8:30 a.m. 'til 4 Saturdays. They're closed Sundays.

Flora Dora

- 503 Amsterdam Ave. N.E., Atlanta; 873-6787

At the rear center of the Midtown Outlets, this large warehouse offers something unique in the world of flower shops, or for that matter, outlets in general. This company makes silk flowers and plants, so stunningly lifelike that you can't tell them from the real thing unless you stand right next to them. They create this faux flora for stores, business offices and buildings, movie companies, and other commercial clients; but you can shop here too, and get the same great direct-from-the-source prices.

Many of the "plants" sold here, in fact, are rentals which have been returned; these are sold off at cost, since they need to make room for new stock. The flowers themselves are made of fine Chinese silk, which are assembled here at the factory. Stalks of snapdragons are reduced, for instance, from an original $12 each to just $7.

These guys don't stop at flowers. They "make"over 70 different types of trees, attaching silk leaves to actual wood trunks and branches. This enhances the illusion, yet you never have to water anything! A seven-foot tall ficus tree will cost in the neighborhood of $59. You can even find copies of house plants, like Swedish ivy; formerly priced from $12-$14, they are marked down to $5-$8 each. Again, especially if they're up in a hanging planter, you'd scarcely know they were fake.

Speaking of planters, this store is a great source for all kinds of pots, baskets, and bowls of all sizes and shapes. You can even get things like solid-colored marbles, perfect for filling crystal bowls and glass jars. Plus lots of other glass giftware items, as well as Christmas ornaments and decorations (many of which depict African-American Santas, a rarity), all at great prices. And don't forget Christmas trees, far better than any artificial tree from a department store, starting around $39 for a four-foot tree.

Service is just as important to the folks at Flora Dora as their carefully crafted copies of Mother Nature. Owner Tony Pernice points out that, since the company's main activity is designing displays for corporate clients, good relations are crucial. "We built this place on service," he says proudly, and he means it. You can return any purchase for a full refund, or work with the staff to get exactly the right look for your home or office. And, unlike most of the stores in this outlet complex, Flora Dora is open seven days—weekdays from 9-5, Saturdays from 10-6, and Sundays from 1-6.

Floral Boutique Inc.

- 2179-K Lawrenceville Hwy., Decatur; 633-2381

This busy shop near the local Po Folks restaurant sells *arranged* roses for a reasonable $40 a dozen. The location may be a bit out of the way for you, but the price is definitely right if you want to give something fancier than plain, paper-wrapped roses. Floral Boutique is a particularly convenient shop if you need flowers for someone staying at the nearby DeKalb Medical Center or Decatur Hospital.

A super-low $4 delivery charge will get your flowers sent within a limited Northside/DeKalb area.

Florida Tropicals & Roses

- 2459 Piedmont Rd., Atlanta; 261-5231
- 4765 Memorial Dr., Decatur; 296-7673
- 5250 Buford Hwy., Doraville; 457-1392

And other suburban locations
Let us not forget how our neighbor state to the south got its name. These

shops are sure-fire spots for savings not only on floral arrangements, but on tropical house plants, too.

Pretty snapdragons cost $14 per dozen or $1.50 each, while handsome blue irises are $2 each or $14 a dozen. Lilies are $22 per dozen, or $2.50 each. And healthy-looking long-stem roses are just $12.95 a dozen. These flowers are priced on a cash-and-carry basis, though delivery is available at an extra charge of $8. With their city and suburban locations, there's bound to be one that delivers in your area.

Make your lady happy with a low-maintenance "Pink Lady Jane" plant (or *anthurium*, for you botany fans) priced at $16, or a big potted peace lily for $19. Of course, Florida Tropicals is also the place to go for ficus trees, with or without braided stems. A four-foot braided ficus costs $34.95, while an impressive six-footer is only $59.

The stores tend to be a bit crowded, and some plants can be hard to reach, but they're all carefully maintained.

Please note that checks are absolutely, positively, not accepted—this keeps prices low for you, since bounced checks and the ensuing bank charges are thus pruned from the stores' overhead costs.

Mr. C also wants to note that some Florida Tropicals stores do *not* carry roses—check the phone book for the Florida Tropicals *& Roses* stores if you're looking for a bouquet.

The Flower Shoppe
- 4980 Roswell Rd., Atlanta; 255-1001 or 1-800-241-0571

This store is kinda messy, and some plants are more on the frond side; but poke around, and you will find bargains sprouting up all over.

The store stocks more house plants than cut flowers, but the prices on all items are good to great. Cash-and-carry roses are just $12.95 for medium-to-long stems. Arranged roses are $45 a dozen on telephone orders, a bit pricey; but you can get a $5 discount if you come into the

store and pay at the time of your order. Not so bad. A dozen carnations, meanwhile, are a mere $5. Delivery for any floral arrangements is an additional $6.

Peace lilies (in small 4" pots) are just $3.49, while a Madagascar palm tree is $14.95 (and take it from Mr. C—it's almost impossible to kill one of these babies). Ficus plants (trees-to-be) are $10.95 each, with healthy, full-grown ficus trees quite reasonable at $24.95. Aboricolas—good for low-light areas—are just $9.95. To turn your apartment into a miniature rain forest, try a truly gigantic Majestic fern for $75.

The store is open from 9 a.m. to 6 p.m. on weekdays, and from 9 a.m. to 4 p.m. Saturdays.

Maud Baker Flower Shoppe
- 252 West Ponce de Leon Ave., Decatur; 373-5791 or 1-800-221-3674

Near West Ponce Place and a short walk from the Courthouse, Maud Baker sells roses and some hardy house plants at good prices. Boxed, long-stem roses are $45 a dozen arranged—which may sound like a lot, but it is cheaper than anyplace in the Peachtree Center or Buckhead areas. And since delivery within the Metro Atlanta area is only $5, this becomes a good deal when you want to send a bouquet somewhere downtown.

Some of the houseplants Mr. C saw include a $20 Christmas cactus, a huge chrysanthemum for $25, and a big peace lily for $20. All of these look radiantly healthy, so you probably don't need to be a green thumb to take care of them.

Maud Baker is open seven days a week—definitely a rarity for floral shops. The hours are 8 a.m. to 6 p.m. Monday through Friday, 10 a.m. to 4 p.m. Saturday, and 8 a.m. to 4 p.m. Sunday.

Pike Family Nurseries
- 3935 Buford Hwy. N.E., Atlanta; 633-6226
- 2431 Bolton Rd. N.W., Atlanta: 355-7292

- 4020 Roswell Rd. N.W., Atlanta; 843-9578
- 2426 Fairburn Rd. SW, Atlanta; 349-8900
- 1380 South Cobb Dr. S.E., Marietta; 428-4133
- 7865 Roswell Rd., Sandy Springs; 396-0921

And other suburban locations
Green thumbs know that Pike is a great place to stock up on all kinds of gardening supplies, perennials, and indoor plants. Wicker baskets for 10" plants are under $5, and potting soil costs as little as $1 for a twenty-pound bag. African violets are just $2 each, and tiny angel plants (in 3" pots) are only 97¢; while medium-sized house plants like philodendrons, arboricolas, ficus plants, and China dolls are just $7 (on sale, they can be under $4). Ficus trees, rubber plants, and schefflera are around $15 each, but go on sale for as low as $7. Boston ferns in hanging baskets are $6, while Swedish ivy plants are $4.

For the yard, try mums or azaleas (starting at just $1), or potted junipers for $1.75. Bulk tulip or daffodil bulbs are priced at $3 for ten.

Keep your lawn healthy with Sta-Green starter fertilizer, $9.97 per bag, and Atlanta Blend lawn seed is $35 for a 25-pound bag. Regular Kentucky fescue lawn seed by Pennington, though, is considerably cheaper at $13 for the same size bag.

Pike even offers a "horticultural consulting service," and will send a real live horticulturalist to your home to assess your gardening needs. They'll answer questions relating to your lawn, landscaping, or even insects and diseases affecting your plants. Call (404) 594-2813 to schedule an appointment. Doctors don't make house calls anymore, but these folks do.

The nurseries are open seven days a week. Hours are from 8 a.m. to 7 p.m. Mondays through Saturdays, and from 10 a.m. to 6 p.m. Sundays.

Shelton's Flowers and Gifts
- 1573 North Decatur Rd. N.E., Atlanta; 378-3900

A dozen plain roses cost just $15.95 at Shelton's, located across the street from Kroger in Emory Village. That price is for cash-and-carry; but delivery costs just $5 (!), so overall, you still get quite a good deal. It's very convenient for sending flowers to someone on the Emory or Agnes Scott campuses, or the nearby VA Hospital.

Furthermore, the shop is not too far from the Virginia-Highland area; if you're on your way to visit someone in ViHi or Morningside, you can stop in at Shelton's on the way and save some serious cash over the inflated prices of stores in those areas.

Mr. C does want to note that other flower arrangements are not priced as spectacularly low (for example, arranged roses are $49.95 a dozen with baby's breath, $42.95 without). But since you save so much on delivery, the store is sure worth a try for simple arrangements, plain roses, and carnations, and of course, those cash-and-carry bouquets.

FOOD STORES

Quoting prices on fresh foods, like meat and produce, is about as smart as quoting politicians on *their* promises. Neither seems to keep very long. The prices mentioned herein, like everything else in this book, are simply examples which should give you some idea of each store's general pricing.

However, it's important to note that the shops below were all visited at the same time year; because of this, you can certainly use these descriptions for comparison with each other.

Finally, remember that many of the foods listed under individual categories can also be found at stores in the "General Markets" section of this chapter.

BAKERIES

Arnold Bakery Outlet/Best Foods Bakery Outlets

- 1950 North Highway 85, Jonesboro; 460-5448
- Toys 'R Us Plaza, 501 Roberts Ct., Kennesaw; 424-4636
- Drug Emporium Plaza, 11060 Alpharetta Hwy., Roswell; 992-3393

Arnold and Thomas's baked products, plus cookies by President's Baking, are sold here at drastic price reductions. These are packages which have gone unsold in grocery stores, but which are still a few days shy of their expiration dates. Some of the jumbo-sized food service packs may be overwhelming for the average consumer, unless you're shopping for a large family; but your basic loaf of bread here is priced 50% to 75% lower than at the supermarkets.

Sovex cereals, spotted in health food stores for $3-$4, are just $1.79 to $2.50 at these outlets. Loaves of bread that would sell for $1.89 in regular stores are two or even three for $1.89, with occasional "buy two, get one free" specials on Arnold products. Thomas's English Muffins were recently selling at three packages for $1.49.

Don't let these low prices, or the approaching expiration, scare you away. Due to small (but effective) amounts of preservatives used these days, bread products actually have twice the shelf life retail stores give them. They only show up in stores like this, and several others described below, because the bakeries keep cranking out newer loaves—which have replaced those on the shelves.

Hard-to-find Southeastern Mills mixes are also discounted here (these are the folks that make that great

gravy for Cracker Barrel restaurants). Southeastern gravy mix, enough for five cups, is just 99¢. Cornbread and biscuit mixes are also super-cheap. Hours vary by store.

Atlanta Baking Company/Flowers Baking Company Thrift Stores

- 7420 Douglas Blvd., Douglasville; 949-4440
- 2879 East Point St., East Point; 766-1278
- 4764 Jonesboro Rd., Forest Park; 363-9062
- 605 Indian Trail-Lilburn Rd., Lilburn; 564-1361
- 2601 South Stone Mountain-Lithonia Rd., Lithonia; 482-8451
- 136 Powers Ferry Rd. S.E., Marietta; 973-5200
- 6866 Highway 85, Riverdale; 997-7066
- 4745 Hugh Howell Rd., Tucker; 938-1902

Another bakery outlet, this chain "clears out" Sunbeam and Roman Meal breads, as well as several other kinds of packaged foods, at less than half-price. Pick up three loaves of Sunbeam thin-sliced white bread for 99¢, or two packages of their bake and serve dinner rolls for a buck; "Nature's Own" whole wheat bread, which sells in supermarkets for $1.45 a loaf, can be found here for at two for $1.59. Same price for loaves by Roman Meal, in various flavors.

You may also find foods here such as Jubilee brand whole pecan pies for $2.69 each; or their apple danish, in a package of six, for $1.89. There are always lots of different snack cakes, packaged individually for sale at convenience store counters, selling here at four for a dollar; plus things like sugar-free candies and no-salt potato chips. Store hours vary.

Bernie the Baker

- Toco Hills Promenade, 3015 North Druid Hills Rd. N.E., Atlanta; 633-1986

No muppets here. That's *Bernie* the Baker, a name you won't soon forget if you head on over to Toco Hills to check this place out.

Even full-size cakes are affordable here. Poppy seed cakes sell for just $4.50, an overflowing apple pie is just $4.95, and big coffeecakes—in lemon, chocolate, and marble varieties—are just $5.50 for a generous-sized cake. Bernie even has Boston cream pies for an amazing $6.

If you don't feel like bringing home a whole pie or cake, many are available by the slice—more than at your typical bakery, that's for sure. Apple strudel slices ($1.25), apple crumb squares ($1), and cherry turnovers ($1 each), are super buys. Linzer tortes are just 70 cents each, and almond horseshoe cookies—a house specialty—are $1.50 each. Big slices of carrot cake are just $1.20, too.

And there's more here than meets the sweet tooth; Bernie's is a good place to look for bargains in day-old bread, which is just as good here as some bakeries make fresh. Day-old bagels and loaves of bread are available in "buy one, get one free" deals.

Bernie's is open from 7:30 a.m. to 6:30 p.m. Monday through Friday, and from 8 a.m. to 4 p.m. on Sunday. They're closed Saturdays.

Colonial Bakery Store

- 350 Moreland Ave. N.E., Atlanta; 521-2742
- 2572 Gresham Rd. S.E., Atlanta; 241-1566
- 3212 Glenwood Rd., Decatur; 284-7477
- 2821 South Cobb Dr. S.E., Smyrna; 432-0209

Continuing our tour of bakery factory outlets, Colonial sells its bread and pastries at incredible savings here. Get five "Big" loaves of their white sandwich bread for $1.69, or four "Giant" loaves for $2.59. Who can

use that much bread at once? Well, if you're not making lunches for a gaggle of growing teenagers, you can probably get comparable deals on just a loaf or two.

On the sweet side, Mr. C recently found things like a package of six cherry-filled sweet rolls selling for $1.09. You can also find almost a supermarket's worth of related products, from dinner rolls to bread crumbs, and from pretzels to candies. Hours vary by store.

Entenmann's Thrift Cake Bakery

- 1451 Scott Blvd., Decatur; 378-5546

Just a little bit down the road from the North Druid Hills Road intersection, you can save BIG on great desserts, breads, and other bakery items from this well-known brand.

This store actually marks items down twice. The first time, they're "redlined," meaning that the original supermarket price sticker is slashed with a red marker. These are the freshest items in the store, and are indistinguishable from brand-new. So strict are the labeling rules, Mr. C was told here, that supermarkets often take food off the shelves even when it's still perfectly fresh.

Some redlined items Mr. C saw include a six-pack of bagels for $1, and and a pound cake (which weighed twelve ounces, but let's not be picky) reduced from $2.49 to just $1.90. An apple strudel, selling for $2.79 if ultra-fresh, is cut to $2.15 here.

Then, there are the "blacklined" items, which are more than just a couple of days old (although Entenmann's doesn't sell anything past the expiration date). Blacklined breads will probably be okay for just a few days longer—or, they're perfect for making croutons, crumbs, and bread pudding. Blacklined items that Mr. C saw included English muffins (99¢ for a package of six), a Louisiana crunch cake for $2.60 (down from $3.39), loaves of Italian bread or dill rye bread for 79¢ each, and fruit cakes reduced from $6.99 to $5.50. A

14-ounce fudge brownie cake, originally selling for $3.19, is a sweet deal at just $2.

Check out the dollar rack, too, for coffee cakes, banana lemon crunch cakes, and Boboli bread shells (designed for making your own pizza). The store is open weekdays from 10 a.m. to 6 p.m., and Saturdays from 9 a.m. to 4:30 p.m.

Henri's Bakery
- First Union Plaza, 999 Peachtree St. N.E., Atlanta; 875-1922
- 61 Irby Ave. N.W., Atlanta; 237-0202
- 6289 Roswell Rd., Sandy Springs; 256-7934

Owner Henry Fisius hails from the French province of Alsace-Lorraine, so you know his croissants are to die for (and just 75¢ each); but it's his lemon squares ($1.50 each) that have garnered national press. They're almost 350 calories each—ouch!—but quite worth the dietary splurge.

Breakfast and lunch items are available, including the $2.49 breakfast plate: Two eggs with grits, plus sausage, ham, or bacon, and a biscuit or small croissant. For lunch, choose from several light entrees, like the "make your own" stuffed potato (for an equally light price, $1.85). But it's the bakery items that will really make you say, *"C'est magnifique!"* Loaves of sourdough rye or herb onion, or honey wheat breads are just 99 cents each. Six-grain loaves are $2.95. Lemon crunch cakes ($5.75) and cheese strudel ($3.65) are always big crowd pleasers.

No time to cook? No problem. Pick up a dozen of Henri's stupendous chocolate macaroons or chocolate chip cookies for $5.40, or some caramel brownies (55¢ each). Whole black forest cakes ($13.95), carrot cakes, Swiss mocha, or turtle cakes ($8.95 each) may not sound exactly cheap, but are great values.

For the calorie-conscious and those with food allergies, Henri's has a listing of recipe ingredients and nutritional information for many of the breads.

MR. CHEAP'S PICKS
Bakeries

✔ **Bernie the Baker**—In Toco Hills, surprisingly good prices on wonderful breads, cakes, and pastries.

✔ **Entenmann's Outlet**—Save money on yummy pastries that are a few days old, but far from stale. One of the area's many such outlets, including Arnold, Flowers, Colonial, and Pepperidge Farm.

✔ **Royal Bagel Shop**—As close as you're gonna get to New York style.

International Bakery
- 2165 Cheshire Bridge Rd. N.E., Atlanta; 636-7580

If you're looking for sweet treats cheap, this place will hit the spot. True to its name, the International Bakery whips up not only Greek pastries—the nationality of the man in charge—but also pastries from France, Germany, and other corners of the Western world.

Baklava dripping with honey is certainly the main specialty here, in several different varieties. The basic versions are priced at just 95 cents—for *two* pieces, and they are yummy. You, however, may prefer profiteroles; they're here too, topped with chocolate and just 50 cents apiece. Chocolate eclairs are 95 cents, with "mini" eclairs (perhaps meant for cheating on your diet?) just 45 cents. Or, you can get a good ol' apple turnover for 85 cents.

International also makes cakes to order, in large and small sizes, starting at $8.00. And they carry fresh and packaged food items, mainly Greek, like feta cheeses, orzo, creme caramel mixes, and extra virgin olive oil ($10.65 for a gallon can). Watch carefully for the bakery as you whizz by, tucked into one of the many little shopping centers along Cheshire Bridge Road.

Our Daily Bread and Cobbler Shop
- 879B Ralph D. Abernathy Blvd. S.W., Atlanta; 753-2777

This bright, cozy cafe in the West End is kind of a cross between a bakery and a luncheonette. Stop in for a quick muffin or a just-baked meat pie, or order up a full hot lunch and find a table by the big glass window. The food is wonderful, the service comes with a smile and it's all done fast and cheap.

And creatively. Among the unusual varieties of freshly baked loaves, all priced between $1.49 and $1.79, you'll find honey wheat bread, jalapeño bread (look out!), and cheddar cheese bread. Plus baguettes and many of the more standard flavors. Muffins, including poppyseed, raisin bran, and banana nut, come in two sizes. The larger size ($1.25 each) is so big, it's been dubbed the "Bruffin—our breakfast muffin that you can eat all day."

Meanwhile, there's something here for every kind of sweet tooth, from walnut-oatmeal-raisin cookies (50 cents each) to German chocolate cake ($1.55 a slice) to—of course—cobblers, cobblers, cobblers. Oh sure, they've got your basic apple, cherry, and so forth. But how about pear almond? Or plum custard, banana rum, or even mango? They're all about $1.50 per slice, and all yummy.

ODB opens up at 11:30 in the morning (presumably, they're baking like mad until then); they only serve until 5:00 in the afternoon. However, being near the West End MARTA station, they do sell food to take out until 7:30 on weeknights. Closed all day Sunday.

Palace Bakery
- Toco Hills Shopping Center, 2879 North Druid Hills Rd. N.E., Atlanta; 315-9017

Eat your cake and be able to afford another one, too. Breads, cookies,

and specialty pastries are cheap, but delicious, at this Palace.

Loaves of seven-grain bread cost just $1.89, while the very popular rye bread loaves are $1.69 apiece. Cream cheese brownies are among the cheapest around—just 75¢ each—while generous slices of apple strudel will only put you back $1.30. Raspberry jelly rolls sell for $2.59 each.

Lace cookies and rainbow torte cookies are both $6.19/lb., while the rugelach pastries, which attract shoppers from miles away, are $8.19/lb (and perfect if you're cooking dinner for someone you need to impress!) They come in cinnamon pecan, raspberry, and apricot chocolate flavors. Up to twenty pounds of this stuff can sell in an afternoon, so you may want to call ahead to see if it's still available before you hop in the car.

Pepperidge Farm Thrift Store
- Pharr Road Shopping Center, 318 Pharr Rd. N.E., Atlanta; 262-7580
- 5495 Chamblee-Dunwoody Rd., Dunwoody; 394-3400

Pepperidge Farm remembers when bread wasn't priced so ridiculously. The stuff here, like that of Entenmann's, is a little older than supermarket quality, but still fine. A one-pound loaf of Pepperidge Farm white bread is just 84¢, and fancy Milano and Lido cookies, once $2 for a half-pound package, are reduced to $1.50. Goldfish crackers (do you known anybody who doesn't like these?), are available in the giant 20-ounce carton, cut from their $4.19 original price to $3.14.

Other yummies are available, like a six-pack of puff pastry shells ($1.79), "Family Request" cookies ($1.85, originally $2.49), and poppyseed or onion rolls (a mere 94¢ a package). Twin French loaves, at just 89¢, are yet another of the incredible buys in this tiny (but stocked to the ceiling) shop.

The thrift store also offers "Frequent Shopper Bonus Cards" which you may have punched after every purchase, entitling you to "save up" for free bread, rolls, and even layer cakes. The store is open from 9:30 a.m. to 5:30 p.m., Mondays through Saturdays.

Royal Bagel Shop
- Ansley Mall, 1544 Piedmont Rd. N.E., Atlanta; 876-3512

Most folks consider these to be the best bagels in town. They line up on weekend mornings, newspapers in hand, hoping to get one of the plastic tables by the glass storefront (or, weather permitting, just outside) so they can nosh and watch the world go by. Many others prefer to bypass the scene and get a "Royal Dozen" to take home.

Whichever you choose, you can choose from a dozen or more flavors of bagel, from your basic poppy to garlic, herb, cinnamon-raisin, and "Great grain." These go for $5.40 a dozen; or get a bagel with cream cheese, freshly whipped up in the store (and kosher, by the way), for $1.25. Put some egg salad on it instead for $2.95; or lox, whitefish, and tuna spreads, even peanut butter. Whatever.

The bakery also has challah loaves for $1.99, sourdough loaves for $1.25, and all kinds of pastries, cakes, and pies at similarly reasonable prices. This is about as close to the New York experience as you're likely to get here, folks—even if you do have to go to a mall to find it.

CANDY AND NUTS

The Candy Barrel
- Underground Atlanta, 118 Lower Alabama St., Atlanta; 577-2905

You don't need barrels-ful of money to stock up on sweets at this shop. Sure, it's in Underground Atlanta, but their big-volume purchases mean good news for your wallet and your sweet tooth, too.

All the candy is attractively displayed in giant barrels, in penny candy shop-style (of course). It may be a good idea to leave the kiddies at home when you shop here, or they may drive you crazy picking stuff randomly out of all these barrels.

Well, nobody sells candy for a penny anymore, but Mr. C did find goodies like Mary Janes, coffee bonbons, Tootsie Rolls, Super Bubble bubble gum, and Jelly Bellys (in 24 flavors!), for $5.98 a pound. Bit-O-Honeys, fruit slices, caramels, salt water taffy (in 15 flavors), chocolate nonpareils, and lollipops are the same price. Low calorie and sugar-free candies (even in exotic flavors, like pina colada) are clearly marked, too. The store's open seven days a week.

The Candy Company
- 2550 Sandy Plains Rd., Marietta; 973-MINT (6468)

This ten-year old store is heaven on earth. It's a favorite of businesspeople who just don't know what to get the boss or a co-worker for a gift; CC's custom-designed gift baskets are a quick and delightful solution. Gourmet flavored popcorn and sugar-free candies are also available, for weight-conscious customers.

There are over 35 flavors of Jelly Belly jellybeans, including Mai Tai, cream soda, cantaloupe, and pink grapefruit. Chocolate can be molded by these folks, at your request, into a variety of shapes—golf clubs, pizza pies, or even your company logo. "Adult" designs are also available, for naughtier gag gifts.

Racy designs notwithstanding, the Candy Company also hosts children's birthday parties. Here, among other treats, the kiddies get to make and take home their own goodies. Call the store for reservations.

Everything Special Shoppe
- Southlake Mall, 1101 Morrow Rd., Morrow; 961-0750

Everything you could possibly need to make your own candies, cookies, and cakes is value-priced here. The store prefers to not have its prices listed in Mr. C's book, but let's just say they're spectacular.

Wilton brand cake pans, springform pans (for cheesecakes) and other baking gear are all well-stocked. And for cake decorating, there are icings galore, prompting many engaged couples to shop here and save a little dough for the honeymoon by making their own wedding cakes. They've even got the bride and groom cake toppers.

Chocolate molds, lollipop and hard candy flavoring syrups, and diabetic candies are also big sellers among the equipment and ingredients found at this delightful shop. It's open seven days a week.

Maggie Lyon Chocolatiers

• 6000 Peachtree Industrial Blvd., Norcross; 446-1299

This store, just outside of the perimeter, specializes in gourmet chocolates at great prices.

If their chocolate chips haven't sold out for the day by the time you get there, you can get a pound for just $1.75 (in white or milk chocolate). That's less than half what you'd pay for the same amount in the grocery store!

Truffles are $16 a pound, and are available in champagne, lemon, Grand Marnier, dark chocolate, lemon, and chocolate chip varieties. Heck, things like that are *never* going to be cheap, but comparatively speaking, these prices are quite reasonable. Other chocolate specialties, like fudge and caramels, are priced as low as $6 a pound.

Funky items, like chocolate-covered potato chips, are priced up to $15 a pound, which may sound like a lot; but again, for the amount of chips you get, it's a sweet deal. The store's open from 9 a.m. to 6 p.m. weekdays, and usually from 10 a.m. to 2 p.m. Saturdays (call ahead to check, since this changes occasionally).

Rainbow Natural Foods

• North Decatur Plaza, 2118 North Decatur Rd., Decatur; 636-5553

You never know what you'll find under this Rainbow, but you can bet it'll be a bargain. Carob candies, sugar-free candy bars, and fruit-sweetened treats line the aisles; and the nut

prices won't make you nutty, either. A pound of dry roasted peanuts is just $1.56 a pound here, and whole cashews, available roasted, salted, both, or plain, are a good deal at $3.42 a pound. Organic raisins (hey kids—a good source of fiber!) will fill you up for just $1.84 a pound. Maybe there really is a pot of gold at the end of the rainbow.

Russell Stover Candy Outlet

• 2941 Buford Hwy. N.E., Atlanta; 636-2468

You don't need Mr. C to tell you about Russell Stover Candies. They're probably one of the most popular gift boxes in the country. What you may not know, however, is that this particular store is the only one in the entire state where you can purchase "seconds" at big savings.

And just what makes a candy imperfect? Well, little problems like flawed shapes, or too much filling—oooh, what a shame! That's all it takes—the candy tastes perfectly good, but it cannot be sold at full price.

So, you can get a sweet deal, like three pounds of assorted seconds for a mere $2.97—easily half the retail price. They come in a plain box, but who cares about the box? There are lots of similar bargains on bulk chocolates of various kinds. You can also save on hard candies, like fruit sours and jelly beans, by the pound at 20% off regular prices. And there are usually some smaller items, like individually wrapped pecan rolls reduced from $1.10 to a mere 59 cents apiece.

Another item sold here is "intermediate" candy, which does mean regular assortments in the familiar boxes—candies that have gone just past their expiration date. Not enough to be life-threatening, don't worry. Gift assortments, like the milk chocolate or dark chocolate varieties, sell at just $3.68 for a one-pound box.

In case you were wondering, the store does sell fresh candy at regular prices along with the seconds.

The Southern Candy Company
• Underground Atlanta, 112 Lower Alabama St., Atlanta; 577-3697

You know you're in for a sweet surprise when you see the fifty-pound bags of sugar lined up in the window of this store. Bring the kids—you can watch these folks making pecan rolls and peanut brittle, and purchase classic chocolate concoctions and Georgian specialties. It's an especially good place to try if you're stuck looking for a gift idea—and this is the only candy store in Atlanta to ship worldwide, they say.

A one-pound box of Georgia pralines is $9.95, and pecan brittle is $5.25 a pound. Fudge comes in plain, vanilla, maple nut, amaretto, chocolate swirl, rocky road, and peanut butter varieties, in prices starting at $9 a pound.

Half-pound pecan log rolls are only $3.25 (small ones are just 99¢), and huge peanut butter cups are just $1.25 each. Take that, Reese's! And chewy caramel-packed turtles are just $9 a pound.

Stock up on salt water taffy at just 99 cents a pound, caramel apples ($2.25 each) and candy apples (just $1.25 each). Yum!

Gift baskets are a specialty here; if you're in a big hurry, you can even phone an order in and have it shipped. A pound and a half of assorted candy, arranged in a basket, starts at $15.

CHEESE AND DAIRY PRODUCTS

For cheese bargains, your best bets really are the giant places like Your DeKalb and Harry's Farmer's Markets (see below). However, Mr. C did find one other shop he wants you to know about:

Mathis Dairy
• 3181 Rainbow Dr., Decatur; 624-0600

How about it, folks, a dairy that still makes deliveries! Mathis products are so fresh that many restaurants brag about carrying their milk, chocolate milk, and yogurts. You can get the same great stuff for yourself, right here at the farm.

Homogenized milk is $2.99 a gallon, and $1.99 a half gallon. A half-gallon of their super orange juice is $2.43, and fresh whipping cream can be delivered right to your door, too ($4.25 a quart). Yogurt is just 80¢ a cup, and available in peach, mixed berry, plain, strawberry, strawberry/banana, and vanilla varieties.

A dozen Grade A large eggs costs just 99¢, and Mathis's super sour cream is just $1.39 a pint.

COFFEES AND TEAS

Barnie's Coffee and Tea Company
• Underground Atlanta, 50 Upper Alabama St., Atlanta; 577-1703
• Lenox Square Shopping Center, 3393 Peachtree Rd. N.E., Atlanta; 233-3556
• 4800 Briarcliff Rd. N.E., Atlanta; 939-9737
• Market Square at North DeKalb, 2050 Lawrenceville Hwy., Decatur; 633-6406

And other suburban locations

Not to be confused with Bernie the Baker, Barnie's is a gourmet coffee shop, granted, but without the gourmet price tags.

Hawaiian Kona coffee, often priced up to $30 a pound in other specialty shops, sells for just $15.99 a pound here. The store's "Special Blend" is $7.99 per pound, as is its Kenya AA blend. Espresso roasts start at a reasonable $6.99 a pound. Not the cheapest coffee you'll find anywhere, but this grind ain't bad for Underground Atlanta or Lenox Square.

Blue Ridge Coffee Company

- 145 South Columbia Dr., Decatur; 378-6961

This company supplies Rainbow Natural Foods with its incredible fresh coffees. If you order a minimum of five pounds of coffee (you can mix varieties), it can cost as little as $3.95 a pound for the house blend. And they'll even ship your order right to your doorstep.

Swiss water process decaffeinated coffee is just $5.45 per pound. Flavored roast coffees cost as little as $4.25 a pound; or, you can jazz up your java yourself by purchasing Blue Ridge's flavoring additives, just like the kind found nowadays in fancy coffee "bars." These come in vanilla, chocolate almond, and Irish creme flavors, among others.

Blue Ridge Coffees and products also make great gift ideas, since they can be shipped anywhere in the United States.

Coffee Plantation

- Fountain Oaks Shopping Center, 4920 Roswell Rd., Sandy Springs; 252-4686
- Toco Hills Shopping Center, 2205-F LaVista Rd., Atlanta; 636-1038 (or 1-800-252-8211 for mail orders)

Awarded *Creative Loafing*'s "Best of Atlanta" award for the best neighborhood coffee shop, Plantation Coffee will get you a pound to go without giving you (or your budget) the jitters.

The house blend is just $5.99 a pound, while Columbian Supremo goes for $6.99. The sweet Swiss Chocolate blend is $7.99, as is the Amaretto-flavored roast; getting more exotic, Jamaican Blue Mountain is $24.99 per pound.

Gourmet teas are also reasonably priced here, sold loose by the pound. "Imperial Gunpowder," a flavor similar to Lapsang Souchong, sells for $11.95 per pound; same price for Darjeeling from India. Assam and Yunnan black teas are good deals at just $7.25 a pound each; another good buy is the mild jasmine tea, at $8.95 per pound.

Globe Foods & Video

- North DeKalb Square, 2179 Lawrenceville Hwy., Decatur; 633-6540

The folks at Globe Foods & Video didn't want their prices listed in this book, but Mr. C assures you that the prices are great here. This section of Decatur is home to a number of Indian-run businesses, many of which are family-operated. That often means low overhead, and great prices for the customer.

Mr. C found goodies like a one pound can of Lipton's Finest Darjeeling tea, and the same size of Lipton Yellow Label (the regular brew). But hey, when in New Dehli...why not be more adventurous? Try some of the imported varieties such as Mamri, Nirau, and strong-scented Laxmi. They all come here straight from India. Some of these teas are much stronger than the typical teas found in American supermarkets; the folks at Globe will be happy to explain the differences for you.

Rainbow Natural Foods

- North Decatur Plaza, 2118 North Decatur Rd., Decatur; 636-5553

There are so many varieties of coffee under this Rainbow's roof that it could take you an hour to decide what to get. Kenya AA coffee sells for $6.89 a pound; Hawaiian Kona is a remarkable $8.77 a pound, and Mocha Java will get you jiving for low $5.87 a pound. Organically-grown Mexican coffee is a definite deal at $5.87 a pound as well.

Teas are also bargain priced—remember, this is one of Atlanta's favorite health food stores, and their high volume of sales means low prices for you. Celestial Seasonings teas, in 24-bag boxes, are often found in supermarkets for $2.30 and more; here, they're $1.90. Twinings teas, seen for $3.50 and up elsewhere, are just $2.82 for the 25-bag box. Who needs snooty, gourmet "boutiques", anyway?

GENERAL MARKETS AND PREPARED FOODS TO GO

Atlanta Municipal Market
- 209 Edgewood Ave. S.E., Atlanta; 659-1665

Here's the place to save on farm-fresh produce and meats when you're downtown, and can't get out to the farm. Since 1918, in what has been declared an historic building, this marketplace has existed in some form or another; in fact, it's currently being renovated so that, perhaps, the decor will look as fresh as the food.

Inside this cavernous structure are dozens of individual vendors, a curious mix of Americans, Asians, and Hispanics, each working in several languages. Some sell off of wooden tables, others from behind glass refrigeration counters. Around the perimeter, there are a few snack bars selling junk food; there's also a discount grocery store. Downstairs, a "Merchant's Mart" carries the same idea to housewares, furniture, and other home furnishings, sold in liquidation.

You can buy every part of the pig here, from tongue to tail, whether you want slab bacon by the pound, or a thirty-pound box of frozen baby back ribs for $45; whether you want it turned into chitlins or homemade sausage. Fly off with chicken wings at 99 cents a pound, or some chopped chicken liver. Several vendors sell great-looking greens, fruits and vegetables in season, Georgia peanuts and pecans, and even some homemade jams and preserves.

The Market is open Mondays through Thursdays from 8 a.m. to 5:45 p.m., Fridays and Saturdays until 6:45 p.m.; it's closed on Sundays.

Globe Foods & Video
- North DeKalb Square, 2179 Lawrenceville Hwy., Decatur; 633-6540

The folks at Globe Foods & Video didn't want their prices listed in this book, but Mr. C assures you that the prices are great here. This section of Decatur is home to a number of Indian-run businesses, many of which are family-operated. That often means low overhead, and great prices for the customer.

Along with great prices on coffees and teas (see listing above), you can save money buy purchasing bulk ingredients like cloves, cumin seeds, widely used in Indian and Thai dishes, or crushed Nirav chilis (try them on pizza).

Stock up on staples here, like a forty (!!) pound bag of Basmati rice. Soup makers will especially like the two pound bags of dried garbanzo beans (also called chick peas), or red kidney beans. Whole yellow peas and black-eyed peas, perfect for soul food side dishes, are also super-cheap when bought in bulk.

Harry's Farmers Market
- 1180 Upper Hembree Rd., Alpharetta; 664-6300
- 2025 Satellite Point St. N.W. Duluth; 416-6900
- 70 Powers Ferry Rd. N.E., Marietta; 578-4400

Wow. Look out, America, here comes the next generation of supermarket. Decatur has "Your DeKalb," and a wonderful place it is (see listing below); but Harry's, which is something of a spinoff, blows the roof off of just about any supermarket you've ever seen. Or, to paraphrase Pogo: We have seen the future of this business, and it is gorgeous—and in many areas, it is even cheap!

You see, besides making a quantum leap in quantity purchasing, which keeps prices low, Harry's is a gleaming, glistening, brightly lit, white-walled palace. It's a massive place, selling not only the freshest-looking produce you've ever seen, but everything else you'd find at any other supermarket—again, beautifully presented, quality stuff, often at warehouse prices. Plus hot foods, liquors, glassware, cut flowers, plants, firewood...it's the "superstore" approach to supermarkets.

Of course, it's futile to print exact prices on foods like these, which fluctuate all the time. Suffice it to say, you can do very well here if you spend carefully—and especally if you, like Harry, can purchase in bulk. In the coffee bean section, Mr. C did find a three-pound bag of in-store ground Columbian roast for $7.99, as well as two or three gourmet flavors at weekly special prices of $2.99 and $3.99 a pound. He also noted heads of iceberg lettuce being sold in pairs, for the price most other stores charge for one. You get the idea. It's quantity *and* quality.

Even the layout of this store is revolutionary. Instead of the usual grid of aisles, there is one, winding path which takes you through the entire place, like a giant game board. In fact, that's exactly what the printed map, handed out to you upon entering, looks like. As one of Mr. C's friends pointed out, this is all very shrewd on Harry's part—it's hard to just run in for one item and head for the register. Suddenly, you're saying, "Hey, we *do* need some Belgian endive at home—and just look at the price!" Well, maybe.

Even more cunning is the placement of the bakery/hot coffee/juice bar as the first station you come to on the long and winding road. There didn't seem to be one kid in the whole place who wasn't nibbling something sweet. For that matter, there are little stands in many sections where friendly folks have bites of food for you to sample. This store is such a production, that official tours for foreign businessmen are frequently seen winding along with the shoppers. Can it be long before Harry's produce is sprouting up all over Atlanta? Stay tuned.

Harry's In A Hurry
- 1875 Peachtree St., N.E., Atlanta; 352-7800

More than a yuppie grocery store, Harry's In A Hurry is the answer to all your eating-on-the-run dilemmas. Meals are prepared using fresh ingredients from Harry's Farmers Market, and packaged—much of it in microwaveable form—for those of you

who just don't have the time to cook.

Did you ever think you could have a sushi dinner for $3.29? Pasta dishes like spaghetti and meatballs or macaroni and cheese start at $3 each. Roast turkey and vegetarian lasagna dinners all go for under $5. Goat cheese pesto pizzas are $4.99, too.

"Briefcase" lunches, like the 28-ounce fruit plate ($3.99) or brie cheese and fruit ($4.49) are good buys. If you're shopping for basics such as bread, fruit and vegetables: A loaf of focaccia bread costs just $1.39, and seedless grapes are pre-washed and ready to go for $1.59 a pound. Two pounds of organic carrots sell for just $1.29.

Having a party, but no time to cook? Wow your guests with a two-pound marble cheesecake (for $9.99), or a custard pie (for only $6.99). Dark chocolate and banana creme pies are under $8, too.

Oh, and to really win points, you can even pick up a dozen roses on your way out, for just $8.99. Beat that, A & P!

International Farmer's Market
- 5193 Peachtree Industrial Blvd., Chamblee; 455-1777

This is the farmer's market for the northeast crowd. In a no-frills warehouse setting, there is a huge selection not only of fresh produce, but of everything else you'd find at any supermarket—much of it at terrific prices. Weekly sale items are even better bargains. During Mr. C's visit, these included New York strip steaks at $3.99 a pound (normally $5.69), imported sharp cheddar cheese reduced from $3.99 a pound to $1.99, and whole watermelons at 23 cents a pound. Many of the aisles have central tables laden with more unadvertised deals.

But the IFM goes beyond these foods to sell liquor, flowers, live seafood, freshly baked breads, and more. There is a hot coffee/pastry counter toward the rear (small cappuccino, just 75 cents!). Speaking of coffee, this is a good place to buy gourmet beans, with many varieties priced at a low $3-$5 per pound. Also, in the meat and produce departments, you may inquire about wholesale price deals if you're purchasing in large quantities.

The market is open seven days a week, from mid-morning into the early evening; it's a popular stop on Sundays after church, when families stream in to stock up for the week.

Market Grocery
Atlanta State Farmer's Market
- 16 Forest Pkwy., Forest Park; 366-6910

Hidden inside the Atlanta State Farmer's Market (see listing under "Produce" below), which is completely open to the public, is the real hidden treasure of the whole place: The **Market Grocery**. It's a true warehouse for supermarkets, but you can shop here too. In this cavernous space, there are package deals on just about every kind of grocery item, making this a particularly great place to shop for large families. There are all kinds of sodas and juices; get a case of Coke—24 twelve-ounce cans—for just $5.99, or a quarter apiece. Mr. C noticed a case of Van Camp's pork and beans, again 24 cans, for $9.90. In the meat and dairy section, you may find slab bacon at $1.19 per pound—or just 79 cents a pound if you can buy a thirty-pound case (maybe you've got a big freezer, or a company cookout coming up). Extra-lean ground chuck may sell as low as $1.59 a pound, and locally grown baby lima beans—in frozen, five-pound bags—as low as $5.

Plus bulk household supplies, such as laundry detergent and toilet paper; pet foods, like a 25-pound bag of Purina Dog Chow for $9.90; even a case of Quaker State motor oil, twelve quarts for $15.40. Many items are packaged for resale, like a box of 36 two-ounce packs of Famous Amos cookies for ten bucks, or six-pack "bricks" of Tylenol or Band-Aids.

The whole marketplace runs twenty-four hours a day, but the grocery is open from 8 a.m. to 5 p.m.

MR. CHEAP'S PICKS
General Markets

- ✔ **Harry's Farmer's Market**—Taking the "superstore" approach to supermarkets: Dazzling selection and surroundings.
- ✔ **Market Grocery at Atlanta State Farmer's Market**—Buy where the grocery stores buy, and at their prices.
- ✔ **Your DeKalb Farmer's Market**—A legend in Decatur, this world-beat supermarket has warehouse prices in an appropriate setting.

daily. Weekdays, of course, are the quietest, easiest times to shop here. After you've driven into the main Farmer's Market entrance, take the first right; go all the way down this central drive to building "K", and turn right again for the southern end of the building.

Preferred To-Go
- 2221 Peachtree Rd. N.E., Atlanta; 352-8099

If you've got no time to eat, but don't want to eat just junk, make a quick trip to this Buckhead "emporium." All sorts of prepared salads are sold by the pound here, from hummus ($6.50/lb) to spinach fettucine ($6.95/lb) to couscous ($5.95/lb). The black-eyed pea salad is a popular one, selling for $6.25 a pound.

Hot and cold entrees change daily, featuring elaborate (but not elaborately priced) dishes like stuffed chicken Florentine ($5.95), chicken-Boursin sandwiches ($4.95), and grilled eggplant ($4.95). Stacked-high sandwiches like turkey or ham sell for under $4. And if you've got room for dessert, Mr. C suggests the truffle mousse pat, selling for $5.25 a pound (a typical-sized serving will cost you about $2).

The store is open from 10 a.m. to 8 p.m. on weekdays, and from 10 a.m. to 5 p.m. on Saturdays. They're closed for Jewish holidays.

Your DeKalb Farmer's Market

- 3000 East Ponce de Leon Ave., Decatur; 377-6400

Get ready to be overwhelmed—by great values, that is. Your DeKalb Farmer's Market is as big as two (yup—two!) football fields, filled with terrific values along every yard.

The deli will delight you, with especially good deals on seafood. Jumbo shrimp was recently seen for a tiny $7.99 per pound, whitefish for $2.99, and steamed crab for is an incredible dollar a pound. Even delicacies like frog legs are here (these jump off the counter at $7.99 per pound). The dairy department is equally impressive, with treats like German brie for $6.39 a pound, along with more basic staples. All cheeses that are over two weeks old are automatically marked down an additional 20% off their already-low prices. All cheeses can be sliced, cut, or shredded to order, too.

And what could be better to put some of that cheese on, than the Market's pasta—like their soft, fresh spinach linguini ($1.15 a pound), wheat noodles ($1.30), and ready-to-cook lasagna (just $1.15 a pound).

The produce selection is simply astounding, with selections flown in from all over the world. From broccoli to bok choy, apples to endive, everything is farm-priced. You can even buy in bulk quantities; a 25 pound bag of carrots is yours for just $6! Of course, most customers who don't own rabbits, a restaurant, or both, prefer the five-pound bag, at around $1.39.

The Market's bakery is simply out of this world, too, with four big peanut butter muffins for just $1, or a three-pack of whole wheat (!?) croissants for 75 cents. Save more with day-old breads, like an organic-grain French loaf just 65 cents. For just a nickel more, you can buy a pound of fresh bread crumbs, too. A six pack of bagels, available in six varieties, are just $1.19. DeKalb, truly a store for the recession-strapped, health-conscious '90s, also lists out the ingredients on most bakery items.

If you're going to have fresh bread, you need some wine to go with it. The Market's extensive (and Mr. C means it when he says *extensive*) wine and beer selections include Newcastle Brown Ale in the big 18.6-ounce bottle for just $2.09, and China Five Star beer for $7 a six-pack. Champagnes, too—Freixenet's Cordon Negro, which goes for up to $10 in some liquor stores, is $6.79 here. Wines from as far away as Greece, Lebanon, Spain, Portugal, Argentina, and Chile are here for the choosing. Some of the recently spotted special deals included $8.99 bottles of Raymond Napa Valley chardonnay and cabernet sauvignon (seen elsewhere for $14), $5.29 bottles of Caliterra cabernet sauvignon from Chile, and Weibel Black Muscat red dessert wine for $9.

And speaking of dessert, sweets are also sweetly priced, with Danish butter cookies for $2.19 a pound, Lindt caramel just $1.29 for the 4-ounce package, roasted in-shell peanuts selling for $1.39 a pound, and chocolate-covered almonds for $4.79 a pound.

The market's open weekdays from 10 a.m. to 9 p.m. and weekends from 9 a.m. to 9 p.m. They also have a sit-down cafeteria for weary shoppers, or anyone who seeks out the truly international flavor of this unique kind of store (see "Market Cafe" listing under "Restaurants").

An extra note from Mr. C: Don't forget your local farmer's market when it comes to saving big bucks on fresh fruit, veggies, and even plants! Some locations are only open on a seasonal basis—call ahead to

SHOPPING   FOOD STORES

make sure they're open. Here are some good ones to check out, along
with their specialties:

Adams Farms
• 1486 Highway 54 West,
  Fayetteville; 461-9395
Vegetables.

Berry Patch Farms
• 786 Arnold Mill Rd., Woodstock;
  926-0561
Blueberries, pumpkins, Christmas
trees.

Ellis Brothers Pecans
• Route 3, Vienna; (912) 268-9041
Pecans, peaches, peanuts.

Flintwood Farms
• 516 McDonough Rd., Fayetteville;
  461-4643
Plants, cut flowers.

Gardner Farms
• U.S. 23/Georgia 42, Locust Grove;
  957-4912
Peaches, blueberries, blackberries.

Harp's Farm Market
• 1692 Highway 92 South,
  Fayetteville; 461-1821
Herbs, berries, peaches, pumpkins,
Christmas trees.

Pete's Little Idaho Tater Farm
• Route 2 (Hog Mountain Rd.),
  Auburn; 867-8096
Potatoes (what else?), beans, okra,
peppers.

Whimsy Haven Farm
• 552 Highway 279 (Old National
  Hwy.), Fairburn; 461-6742
Blackberries, vegetables, herbs, flowers.

Yule Forest Inc.
• 13 Reagan Rd., Stockbridge;
  957-3165
Berries, pumpkins, Christmas trees.

For a complete listing of the state's farmer's markets, call or write
the Georgia Farm Bureau Federation's Marketing Department, P.O. Box
7068, Macon, GA 31298; telephone (912) 474-8411 or 1-800-342-1192.

HEALTH FOODS AND VITAMINS

**Bill Stanton's Health Food
Market**
• Lindbergh Plaza, 2581 Piedmont
  Ave N.E., Atlanta; 814-9935
Health food stores often have surpris-
ingly good buys on staple items—
such as cooking and baking
ingredients—and Bill Stanton's
Health Food Market is no exception.

Mr. C found turbinado (un-
bleached) sugar for $1.29 a pound,
navy beans for $1.49 a pound, and
jumbo prunes on the cheap at $3.69
a pound. Poppy seeds, $1.59 for four
ounces, and sunflower seeds, $2.19 a
pound, are also good (and healthy)
buys.

Bulk spices are real bargains, like
poultry and seafood seasoning mixtures, going for $4.69 a package. Jas-
mine tea is only $2 for a four-ounce

package, while UniTea Herb's herbal
teas from Boulder, Colorado are $7
for each four-ounce bulk purchase.

You can even find health-conscious cosmetics here. Many high-
end organic products are reasonably
priced here, as compared to the
prices found in general grocery stores
and drug stores. Kiss My Face olive
and aloe moisturizer, for instance, is
$6.60 for a one-pint bottle, but it
could easily be more expensive elsewhere. The Market's open seven days
a week.

Nuts 'N Berries
• 4274 Peachtree Rd. N.E., Atlanta;
  237-6829
*(See also listing under "Restaurants:
Decatur and Northeast Atlanta.")*
Within walking distance of the Brookhaven MARTA, Nuts 'N Berries will

101

keep you from going crazy from other stores' ridiculously high prices on health food.

As you'd expect, they do sell nuts and dried fruits in bulk. Pumpkin seeds ($3.99/lb), soybeans (39¢/lb), shelled walnuts ($5.99/lb), and hazelnuts ($1.39) are cheaper here than any grocery store. Sliced almonds (who has time to slice almonds these days?) are just $5.39 a pound.

Save big on bulk black beans (say that ten times fast!), which sell for just 89¢ a pound. Freshly made peanut butter is just $1.79 a pound—cheaper than what you'd pay for that preservative-laden stuff in the supermarket!

Other unusual and well-priced items include Annie's Raspberry Vinaigrette salad dressing for $2.99 a bottle, Eddie's organic durum wheat spaghetti ($3.19/lb), and bulk Basmati rice ($1.65/lb). And, for you health nuts (no pun intended), a quart of Natural High brand aloe vera gel is $6.39.

You can forage in Nuts 'N Berries from 9:30 a.m. to 8:30 p.m. Mondays through Saturdays, and Sundays from 11 a.m. to 6 p.m.

Rainbow Natural Foods
• North Decatur Plaza, 2118 North Decatur Rd., Decatur; 636-5553
Organic and health food lovers take note—you never know what you'll find under this Rainbow, but you can bet that it's a bargain.

Mr. C found staples like whole spelt for 99¢ a pound, a box of New Morning Fruit-E-O's cereal for $2.99, and Mori Silken tofu for an incredible 90¢ a package (tofu's got to be the benchmark for any health food store, right?). Six big blueberry muffins from the Masada Bakery go for $3, while you can do some of your own tasty baking with Rainbow's turbinado sugar, selling for just $1.49 a pound.

Harvest all your fresh veggies at Rainbow, where organic lettuce was recently seen for just 79¢ a head. However, if you feel like going on a "junk" food binge, Garden of Eatin'

blue corn chips are a natural way to do it, just $2.15 a bag.

Cosmetics, like Beauty Without Cruelty Gentle Herbal Facewash, are also reasonably priced. The eight ounce bottle of this item sells for $5.98, several dollars cheaper than you'd pay in a specialty store.

Maybe there is gold at the end of the Rainbow, as the legend goes. You'll certainly have more change in your pocket after shopping here, at any rate!

Return to Eden
• Cheshire Square Shopping Center, 2335 Cheshire Bridge Rd. N.E., Atlanta; 320-EDEN (3336)
There's so much more than just apples in this Eden! It's hard to find organic and vegetarian foods much cheaper than this. Mr. C noted organic raisins for just $2.19 a pound, dried peaches for $3.49 a pound, Bartlett pears for 25¢ each, and garbanzo beans (chick peas) for a mere $1.79 per pound—why, these chick peas are just chicken feed compared to grocery store prices!

Nuts are also super-cheap, like whole cashews for $6.49 a pound, almonds for $4.89, Spanish peanuts for $1.99, sunflower seeds for $1.09, and mixed nuts for $5.99. Mammoth-sized California pistachios were seen for only $4.79 a pound, too.

Other good buys include Weetabix cereal for $3.39 a box; one liter of Edensoy Soy Drink for $1.69; and Lightlife tempeh for $1.49 a package.

Coffees by Cafe Tierra and Frontier Coffee sells for just $5.99 a pound in over 32 different blends, including Dutch Bavarian chocolate, decaf Mexican Azteca, French roast, and Irish cream. Teas from Traditional Medicinals sell are priced at $2.75 for the 16-bag box; and Great Eastern Sun's Organic Japanese Green Tea costs $3.79 for 25 bags (this brew helps prevent cancer, they say).

You can also find cruelty-free cosmetics on the cheap here, such as Nature's Gate toothpaste ($3.89 for a seven-ounce tube) and Beauty Without Cruelty's facial moisturizer, selling for $6.29 a pint.

Sevananda Community Owned Natural Foods Market

- 1111 Euclid Ave. N.E., Atlanta; 681-2831

As the name implies, Sevananda is actually a food co-op, which means you can save extra cash if you choose to join. Membership involves a $20 annual fee, which entitles you to 5% off everything in the store, not to mention a slew of other benefits. Co-ops are run by the members, so everyone here helps to choose which products will be carried. Prices are already reasonable; but, if you choose to work as few as three hours a week, you will get an extra 20% discount on store purchases.

Sevananda carries everything you'd find in a regular grocery store, and then some. You can find anything here from bread to shampoo to vegetarian dog food (just $1.49 a pound!). The produce section includes both strict and "transitional" organic fruits and vegetables. The "transitional" varieties are cheaper than true organic food, coming from farms that are slowly changing over to organic methods; this produce may still have some chemical residues.

Locally-grown organic muscadine grapes were recently seen here for $2.99 a pound, Rome apples in season for just 69¢ a pound, and organic carrots for $1.09 a pound. Other vegetarian staples on the cheap include Edensoy soy drink (1 liter for $1.59), and alfalfa sprouts at 59¢ for a four-ounce package.

Bulk spices are also a smart buy here, such as allspice for $7.19 a pound, or celery salt for $3.59 a pound (if these prices seem a bit high, don't forget that you're likely to need only a couple of ounces at a time).

There's a whole aisle of regular and herbal teas at reasonable prices, from Celestial Seasonings, Stash, Twinings, and more. Plus plenty of homeopathic health products and cosmetics. Nature's Gate keratin shampoo, in the big 18-ounce bottle, is only $3.79.

Sevananda is open Mondays through Saturdays from 10 a.m. to 9 p.m., and Sundays from noon to 9 p.m. There's plenty of free parking out back, so you don't have to worry about searching for a spot in ever-crowded Little Five Points.

MEAT AND FISH

For butcher bargains, your best bets really are the giant places like Your DeKalb and Harry's Farmer's Markets (see above). However, Mr. C did find one other shop he wants you to know about:

Harold's Butcher Shop

- 322 Pharr Rd. N.E., Atlanta; 262-1730

This Buckhead butcher knows his stuff, and has attracted a loyal following of local customers who want the best for less. From steaks to seafood, Harold's is a good place to know. Everything in here is super-fresh, and cut the way you want it.

In addition to good values on sirloin steak, rump roast, and the like, Harold's also sells fresh seafood—like whole rainbow trout (recently seen for $3.49 a pound!), silk snapper, yellowfin tuna, jumbo shrimp, and little neck clams (35¢ each). Oysters go for as little as $3.99 a dozen.

The store is open Monday through Friday from 10:30 am. to 6:30 p.m., and Saturday from 10 a.m. to 6 p.m. It's closed on Sundays.

PRODUCE

Atlanta State Farmer's Market
- 16 Forest Pkwy., Forest Park; 366-6910

This is the *professional* farmers' market. Your own supermarket or corner store probably gets its produce here. Mini-vans and eighteen-wheelers zip around the rows and rows of semi-enclosed stalls, delivering or filling up with fruits, vegetables, and more. So, can you pull up in your little ol' Hyundai and buy just a pound of tomatoes? Yes you can!

Located at exit 78 from Interstate 75, this massive, state-run complex divides neatly into two sides as soon as you drive in: To your left are the rows of stalls, where farmers stand waiting to sell their wares—while the warehouses to the right are for purchasing in wholesale quantities. Both sides offer the chance to get better deals than your local stores; naturally, the wholesale area has the absolute lowest prices, and if you (or your school, business, etc.) can shop in

case quantities, you are most welcome.

On the stalls side of the road, you can stroll up and down to find the best deals on locally grown produce in season, though everyone is pretty competitive with each other. Prices fluctuate through the year, but perhaps you'll find a bushel of ten big, red apples for $3.50, or a bunch of bananas for $1.25. And of course, pecans by the truckload, at $1.50 a pound—in five-pound bags, or the economical fifty-pounder. Many of these small businesses also sell homemade specialty items, such as honey, pickled onion relishes, or even hickory-smoked hams. All the way to the side, at the highway end of the market, is a new garden section, for things like sod and flowering plants.

The whole place is open twenty-four hours a day, though you're not likely to find much action on the farmers' side after 9 or 10 p.m.; weekdays, of course, are the quietest, easiest times to shop here.

FURNITURE

This chapter combines stores selling new and used furniture, for the home as well as the office. Many of your favorite retailers operate clearance centers, where you can find leftovers and slightly-damaged models at drastic savings—if you're patient.

A caveat to the cash-conscious: Be very careful when you're shopping for any leather products. The quality of leather used in making sofas can vary widely, and this can determine how durable your sofa will be in the long run. If you see lots of very obvious flaws in the grain of the leather, think twice before buying.

NEW FURNITURE

Baby Superstore
- Baby Superstore Plaza, 8801 Roswell Rd., Sandy Springs; 640-6155
- 1455 Pleasant Hill Rd. N.W. Lawrenceville; 279-BABY (2229)
- 1427 Roswell Rd. N.E., Marietta; 565-BABY (2229)
- 700 Highway 138, Riverdale; 473-0888

(See also listings under "New Clothing" and "Toys and Games")
High-quality, name-brand cribs, cra-

dles, rockers, and more are for sale at significant discounts in this incredible store. Mr. C found an Okla-Homer Smith cradle in cherry and oak, listed at $170, selling here for just $129; and an Ascot Rose cradle, complete with quilt, bumper, and sheets, is a great value at $60. A solid wood Brooks rocking chair was seen for $160 (down from $200). Cosco high chairs with foot stools are just $19.97, while larger high chairs by Graco are $35.

Bassett brand shelving units, perfect for the kiddies' toys, are $190 (and made from solid wood). An oak-finish changing table was recently seen for just $104, a maple high chair by Simmons for $220, and a baby-sized pine chest, also by Bassett, for under $200. Training beds are also well-stocked, like the metal-finish "My Little Bed", by Fisher-Price, which sells for just $39.97.

Bernhardt Home Furnishings
• 1919 Piedmont Rd. N.E., Atlanta; 897-1919

Wow. Every so often, Mr. Cheap comes across a store which, on first glance, just *cannot* possibly belong in his books. Bernhardt is a manufacturer of very high quality furniture, which is sold in this very high quality setting. But don't be put off by the "power" appeal of this place; the sales staff is very friendly and down-to-earth, while the prices on everything you see are 30% to 50% off retail.

How can such a gorgeous shop be a discounter? Well, it's almost, but not quite, a factory outlet. Bernhardt does not own the store itself; co-owner Joe Tufano created the place just over a year ago, with the intention of carrying this line exclusively. Devoting the whole store to one vendor means that the profits come from volume sales, not the markups on individual pieces. Hence, automatic markdowns of 40% off the suggested retail prices seen for the same items at finer department stores.

Okay, end of Econ 101. So, what've they got? Simply every kind of look for the bedroom, dining room, and living room—18th century, country and lodge, Oriental, European, and the contemporary fashion which Joe calls "Neo-Classical." He also calls it his biggest selling style overall—blending graceful, traditional features into a modern look that is bright, spare, and definitely elegant. And while it's not cheap—a dining table and six chair set lists for $6,000—you *can* get it here at 40% off, or closer to $3,500. Is this a bargain? You bet it is.

Not everything is at this high end of the price scale, though nothing here is "cheap" in any sense of the word. Another dining set, in oak, was reduced from $1,377 to a very reasonable $825. A six-piece sectional sofa with reclining end units, in genuine white leather, retails for $9,029; it sells here for $5,418, while a similar set in a linen finish was also seen for $3,089.

Walk around, through room after completely furnished room, and you'll find mahogany tables, hutches, leather couches ("There is no vinyl in this store...") sleigh beds, day beds, four-posters, and more. Handsome wall units whose doors slide away to reveal computer furniture and entertainment centers. Plus all the lamps, rugs, and side tables you'll need to finish off your own rooms.

Many of these items—lamps, mattresses, rugs, etc.—are not made by Bernhardt; but they are still good deals, all selling at 30% below retail. Joe also sells Bernhardt closeout items at 50% off. A traditional recliner of the softest leather you've ever touched, was recently reduced from $2,625 to $1,179—simply because the burgundy color was discontinued.

On the regular merchandise (the upholstered items, that is) you also have a choice of over 1,200 different fabrics, all of which are on display. There is even a computer, linked directly to the warehouse, which will tell you exactly how long any custom-ordered item will take to be delivered. There is a charge for delivery, but what service! They do all the necessary assembly at the factory, wrap everything carefully in cloth, put it exactly where you want it in the room, and then do a kind of unveiling—followed by a last-minute polishing job. Customer satisfaction is a big emphasis at Bernhardt, not often true of a discount store.

See for yourself, Mondays through Saturdays from 10 a.m. to 6 p.m., and Sundays from 1-5.

Brownlee's Furniture

- 309 Maltbie St., Lawrenceville; 963-6435

You wouldn't think that a huge, two-acre showroom would be hard to find, but it is. Once you get there, though, you'll be glad you stayed with the hunt. There are over 1,000 sofas and loveseats in stock at this mammoth place; more than 150 bedroom and dining room sets, too.

The remote, low-overhead location—and lack of amenities, like carpeting and air conditioning—allow Brownlee's to sell their merchandise at slightly-above wholesale prices. Names like Lane, Stearns & Foster, Hooker, Bassett, Broyhill, Craftmaster, and Fairfield are all here, all at great discounts. There is a charge for delivery (they are out in the boonies, after all); but, after you save hundreds of dollars on the furniture itself, you'll still come out way ahead on the deal.

Brownlee's Furniture is open weekdays from 10 a.m. to 9 p.m., Saturdays from 10-6, and Sundays from 1-6.

Casual Style Furniture

- 1028 Alpharetta Hwy., Roswell; 642-6911

This is a boutique-y looking specialty shop which specializes in outdoor furniture. It may look un-Mr. Cheapish, but with a small overhead, its good prices have made it a well-reputed area favorite.

The showroom is actually split between a barn built in 1840, and a house built in 1912, lending it a unique character even before you look at the furniture. Casual Style preferred to not have any of its prices published in print, but take it from Mr. C—these are bargains. Wrought-iron barstools, coffee tables, end tables, lamps, and patio sets, plus indoor wicker furniture, are all reasonably priced, with featured brands like Woodard, Meadowcraft, Winston, Lloyd/Flanders All-Weather Wicker, and Cumberland Crown. Floor samples are special bargains, if you're lucky enough to find some when you visit; keep an eye out for their twice-a-year special sales, too.

Aluminum pool-area chairs and accessories are stocked here, as well. They also carry those ubiquitous plastic stackable chairs and other cheapo furniture, too, at prices that are even better than Pace's and such.

The store is located about a mile south of Holcomb Bridge Road, and is open Mondays through Saturdays from 10 a.m. to 6 p.m. (closed Wednesdays, though) and from 1-6 p.m. Sundays.

Designer Fabrics, Inc.

- 741 Miami Circle N.E., Atlanta; 233-1725

In the spring of '93, this 26-year-old wholesale business opened its doors to the public, selling closeouts in designer fabrics at 60% to 80% off retail. Now, you can buy material for your home projects, or select patterns to be used on furniture made by this company—getting you brand-new upholstered furniture at near-wholesale prices.

The owner's brother runs a factory in High Point, which makes high-quality chairs, sofas, and loveseats. You can choose from hundreds of fabrics here in the store, and have these custom-built to order. The average price for woven fabrics is around $14.95 to $19.95 a yard, with prints averaging a few dollars less. In the end, you can save lots of money by coming here—where interior decorators and designers get their materials.

The store is open from 9:30 a.m. to 6 p.m. weekdays; Saturdays from 10-5; closed Sundays.

Furniture Mart

- 6624 Northeast Expressway
  Access Rd., Norcross; 449-0307

Part of the gigantic, sprawling Georgia Antique Center, this store sells a large quantity of dining room, living room, and bedroom furniture, often at good prices. They carry a mix of name brands (Singer, Bassett, Ashley) and lesser-known makers; and of new, current lines mixed with some floor models and closeouts. Not everything here is likely to be a super bargain, but Mr. C did find a good deal on a Victorian living room set by Kimball—a large sofa, two side chairs, two end tables, and a marble-top cocktail table for $2,499. These were all in a high-backed, gracefully curved design, with floral print and wood trim along the top. In a similar vein, the store had a batch of Queen Anne-style living room chairs made by Classic Originals in North Carolina (where all the good stuff comes from). They were closeouts, upholstered in a variety of solid colors, reduced from a list price of $649 to just $219 each. Certainly worth a look.

Gateway Furniture

- 6624 Northeast Expressway
  Access Rd., Norcross; 441-1739

Another store found in the Georgia Antique Center, Gateway manufactures its own line of solid oak furniture in old-fashioned styles. These are not meant to fool you into believing that they're antiques or anything; but, if you like period dining tables, rolltop desks, and such, you'll enjoy looking at all the choices in their showroom. And you can save money, because you're buying at "direct from the factory" prices.

Among the pieces Mr. C saw on his visit were an oak rocker, high-backed with arms, selling for $169; a 42-inch round drop-leaf kitchen table for $259; a 44" x 24" secretary's writing desk for $395; and swivel-seat bar stools for $95 each. Plus china cabinets, hutches, benches, coat trees, planters, and many other kinds of items. Many of these have handles, knobs, and other details in solid brass.

MR. CHEAP'S PICKS
Furniture

✔ **Bernhardt Home Furniture**—Save big on fancy furniture by getting it direct from this prestigious maker.

✔ **Carriage House**—Terrific buys on used furniture, and orphaned new pieces from big-name manufacturers.

✔ **Naked Furniture**—Hold on to your hats, folks when you check out these values!

✔ **Treasures for Your Home**—You'll treasure the value-priced name brand furniture here, from bedroom sets to sofas.

The packed showroom, which is accessible from inside the market or from the parking lot, actually spills over into several smaller rooms as well, giving you plenty to look at. And if you don't see exactly what you want, ask—chances are, they can custom-build it at well below other furniture store prices. Open Thursdays through Mondays only, from noon until early evening.

Haverty's Direct

- 5600 Buford Hwy., Doraville;
  458-6700

Go directly to the source for super deals on sofas and more at this incredible clearance center.

A Simmons sectional sofa, with reclining end units and a queen-sized sleeper, was seen recently for just $700 (down from its original $1,000 retail price). La-Z-Boy recliners start at $130, and a black iron canopy bed frame was seen for $200.

You can find Thomasville furniture at half-price or better here; Mr. C saw a loveseat, originally selling for

$1,600, marked at just $750 (!!), while a cherry-finish dining room set with four chairs was $397. And you can certainly sleep easy with Sealy Posturepedic and Serta Perfect Sleeper king-size mattress and box spring sets, worth up to $1,300 retail, selling for as little as $300.

The store's open Monday through Saturday from 10 a.m. to 9 p.m., and Sunday from 12 noon to 6 p.m.

La-Z-Boy Furniture Galleries
- 6478 Dawson Blvd., Norcross; 242-7313
- 2359 Windy Hill Rd. S.E., Marietta; 988-0690
- 1335 North Highway 85, Fayetteville; 461-3457
- 11060 Alpharetta Hwy., Roswell; 594-9914
- 3685 Atlanta Hwy., Athens; (404) 659-5172

La-Z-Boy recliners, during special sales, are priced as low as two for $499 at these factory-direct show-rooms. Swivel rockers can be found at $399 a pair; and their "Classic Series" chairs, with styles like Chippendale and Queen Anne, go for $599 a pair. Presumably, you can also talk to the folks here about buying individual chairs at comparable prices.

Sofas are also value-priced, starting at $499, with reclining sofas from $599, and La-Z-Boy leather sofas from $1,499. The stores are open Mondays through Saturdays from 10 a.m. to 8 p.m., and Sundays from 1-6.

Leather Sofa Factory
- 4600 North Buford Hwy., Norcross; 447-9779
- 911 Cobb Pkwy. North, Marietta; 427-9118
- 2970 State Rd. 138W, Riverdale/Fayetteville; 997-3433

This store is so confident that they have the lowest prices around, that they'll give you your sofa *free* if you find it priced higher anywhere else. By specializing in selling one product only, they keep their costs low and pass the savings along to you.

Some of the colors veer a bit toward the wild side—jade, red, and yellow, for instance—but with over five hundred colors in stock, you're bound to find something to fit into almost any decor. While their everyday prices are impressive enough, recent special offerings at LSF included an all-leather three-piece sectional selling for just $1,499 (seen elsewhere for up to $5,000), and an all-leather sofa and loveseat pair, selling for up to $3,500 in other stores, going for $1,300. Sleeper sofas are priced as low as $600.

Financing is available, with no payments required for 90 days. The stores are open weekdays from 10 a.m. to 8 p.m., Saturdays from 10-7, and Sundays from 12-6.

Major Furniture
- 1158 Euclid Ave. N.E., Atlanta; 524-1931
- 488 Flat Shoals Ave. S.E., Atlanta; 522-2093

Get ready for some major savings at this store, which has been helping budget-conscious shoppers since 1968. It's the place of choice for young folks just starting out, perhaps looking for their first dining room table or bedroom set.

A wrought-iron patio chair set sells here for $120, leather chairs for only $100, and a gorgeous pine wardrobe for a very reasonable $250. A big dresser was recently seen for only $55—at that price, you'll still be able to afford some clothing to put inside it!

Mr. C also found a five-piece dinette table and chairs for $175, a glass-topped coffeetable for the same price, and a funky black-and-white print chaise lounge for $200. A corner hutch will unclutter your dining room for $350.

Overhead is low, which keeps their costs (and therefore, prices) down. What this really means is no air conditioning; but for all the money you'll be saving, you won't even care. A lot of the sale-priced items on display here are samples or special purchases, so if you see something you really like, grab it!

Major Furniture is open from 10 a.m. to 6 p.m., Monday through Saturday; and from 1 p.m. to 6 p.m. on Sunday.

Naked Furniture

- 6438 Dawson Blvd., Norcross; 417-1233
- 11060 Alpharetta Hwy., Roswell; 594-9686

The prices at Naked Furniture will make you (almost) jump out of your clothes with glee. Naked Furniture is a true bargain spot, selling high-quality—but affordably priced—wooden tables, chairs, and bookcases, along with other handy handcrafts like compact disc holders, magazine racks, and wine racks. Most are made of solid pine, with some other woods mixed in. Why "naked," and why the savings? Because this is unfinished furniture. Take it home, throw on a coat of stain or lacquer, and you've got a handsome, natural wood bargain.

Some furniture is ever-so-slightly chipped in spots, but nothing too major. Other items were marred by being constructed of heartwood, which means lots of knots; you decide whether these features are charming or flawing. Knots may also make furniture (especially beds and bookcases) weaker, depending on where they appear, so be careful. Heartwood is also less likely to absorb a finishing stain evenly.

Otherwise, everything in this store will save you lots o' cash. Prices listed are for the items in their unfinished states only; you can choose to keep the furniture plain, have the store finish it for you, or finish it yourself with their all-you-need kits—suitable for creative types and novices alike. In addition to classic finishes, the store offers novelty patterns, like sponge painting and faux-marble finishes. In fact, if you bring in a photo or sample of a particular look you want, the store can duplicate it for you.

Mr. C saw a very practical bookcase/desk combination selling for $270 ($370 if the store finishes it for you). Elsewhere around this huge showroom, there was a ten-compart-

ment entertainment center selling for $380; a queen-size, mission-style bedframe for $400; and a walnut dining table set with six chairs for $1,300 complete. There are lots of sofas and upholstered pieces, too, like a sleep sofa with a funky southwestern print fabric for $689.

Floor samples make for even better bargains. Case in point: A large, maple-finished armoire with two glass doors was spotted here recently for $800. Another sample seen was a blue and white-striped queen sleeper sofa, for only $400. That's easily less than half of what you'd spend for a plain couch at many stores.

Other advantages here include free parking, as well as layaway and financing plans. Naked Furniture is open weekdays and Saturdays from 10 a.m. to 6 p.m. (Mondays and Thursdays 'til 8), and Sundays from 1-6.

Rhodes Furniture

- 1680 Highway 138, Conyers; 922-9971
- 3655 Memorial Dr., Decatur; 289-2136
- 4363 Northeast Expwy. Access Rd., Doraville; 934-9350
- 5955 Stewart Pkwy., Douglasville; 489-5300
- 369 North Central Ave., Hapeville; 762-6181
- 6851 Shannon Pkwy., Union City; 964-7998
- 2338 Highway 78, Snellville; 972-8289
- 633 Holcomb Bridge Rd., Roswell; 992-5143
- 119 North Cobb Pkwy., Marietta; 428-9401

You don't need to be a Rhodes scholar to know that Rhodes is jam-packed with great values. From mattresses to dinette sets, you'll save plenty here. They've been in business for over a hundred years, so they must be doing something right.

Queen-sized sleeper sofas are priced right, as low as $444 complete. Mr. C has seen similar quality ones for up to twice that price. A dinette set with a solid wood-top table and four fan-back chairs was seen for just $488, while a glass-top dinette with upholstered chairs was just $149. Rhodes is also a great place for coffee tables, recliners, daybeds, hutches, and more.

One of the bonuses about shopping at Rhodes is that they offer a neat little satisfaction guarantee: If you're not happy with your purchase, return it within 30 days for a full refund or exchange, period. The stores are open from 10 a.m. to 9 p.m. Mondays through Saturdays, and from 1-6 p.m. Sundays.

Rich's Furniture Clearance Center
- Cobb Center, 2144 South Cobb Dr., Smyrna; 392-4601

Formerly found at Rich's Stone Mountain branch, this clearance center sells closeouts, samples, and floor models from its many stores around the Atlanta area. Major brands of indoor and outdoor furniture, as well as bedding, some Oriental rugs, and a few televisions, are sold here at reductions of 30% to 50% off original retail. To keep things moving, an additional 20% is knocked off the price every 45 days, until the item sells.

Some of these pieces are slightly damaged, and are sold "as is"; but, if you're not too fussy, you can find incredible deals like a rattan sofa marked down from $629 to $278, a country-style white pine dresser reduced from $830 to $470, and even a burled walnut "sleigh bed" frame, once a whopping $5,400, here just $1,730. There are even leather sofas and loveseats, tables, patio furniture, and some accent pieces.

Mattresses are sold in sets only, and are rated in overall firmness and quality as "good, better and best." In full size, these range from $149 for a good set, to $299 for better, and $379 for best. Delivery on any item is available for a fee; the store will not hold an item for you, or offer layaway plans. You'll find the clearance center up on the second floor.

Southern Home Furnishings
- 2409 Piedmont Rd. N.E., Atlanta; 237-2585
- 4747 Memorial Dr., Decatur; 292-8558

Southern Home Furnishings sells first-quality furniture at Yankee-cheap prices. It's a no-nonsense, sky-high ceilinged warehouse store, with barely enough room to squeeze through the rows and rows of sofas—also well worth checking out if you need a love seat, coffee table, or bed frame. The intown location is directly across the street from the Lindbergh MARTA station.

Mr. C found a white damask sofa, listed at $795 retail, selling here for $525. A very pretty floral print sleeper sofa, also $795 retail, was an incredible $495. A good (though not stupendous) quality leather sofa, with a suggested retail of nearly $1,000, was reduced to just $598.

A grey art deco chair was half off (at $129), and a black console for a full-size bed is just $159 (and listed at $275). One of the best deals in the store was the rice-carved four-poster bed frame, listed at $1,350 retail, but priced here at just $895.

Other unique items that Mr. C liked included a black lacquer-finish coffee table, normally reduced from $525 to $329, and placed on sale for just $289; and a three-foot-tall Bassett mirror, with a scroll work pine frame, reduced from $239 to $149. Nice stuff.

Storehouse Clearance Centers
- 3106 Early St. N.W. Atlanta; 233-4111
- 6368 Dawson Blvd., Norcross; 446-2646

You probably know Storehouse, the regional chain of contemporary furniture stores based in Atlanta. You may *not* know about their two clearance centers, where you can save money on floor samples, overstocks, and other leftovers for every room.

The stock always varies, but you can find a pretty good selection of one-of-a-kind pieces. On his visit to the Norcross branch, Mr. C liked a handsome oak rocking chair selling for $179, a savings of $50 off its regular price. A comfortable looking Chesterfield sofa, upholstered in tan-colored linen, was reduced from $1,099 to $899. And a seven-drawer pine dresser was $150 off at $449.

There was a wide selection of butcher block table tops in a variety of sizes and shapes; presumably, the people here can find you the bases to match. And there were plenty of Windsor-style chairs, in maple with a white lacquer and natural finish, to go along with them too—or, they make excellent side chairs on their own.

Mr. C found a cedar hope chest (with a couple of teeny chips), regularly $429, selling for $299. A wardrobe once selling for $600 was half off, while a Lane cherrywood Shaker table with a retail value of $2,600 was reduced to just $1,899. For just $70 you may take home an oak teak bookcase. Artsy scrolled table lamps, originally selling for $89 in their first season, were also seen for $70. For the kids, how about a solid ash or maple bunk bed ($147), an oak table ($119), or a set of Lane nightstands, (cut from $719 to just 499).

It's a bit of mix-and-match here, and when there's a lot of stuff, everything is crammed in rather tightly; some of these items are slightly damaged. But, if you're willing to poke around, you may come up with a good bargain. Open seven days a week, including weeknights until 9:00 p.m.

Treasures for Your Home
• Suburban Plaza, 2597 North
  Decatur Rd., Decatur; 373-0777
If you can't find a bargain here, Mr. C has to doubt whether you can find one anywhere. This two-level shop is literally jam-packed with dinettes, sofas, tables, bedroom sets, and accessories, many of them from fine brand-name makers, and all at discounted prices. The sales volume is high, the overhead is low (it's just one big warehouse-style room, but without too much of that warehouse

feel), and many items are special purchases. All of these factors help you save money.

A Hooker mahogany chest, listed at $423, was seen here for just $264. A framed watercolor by Frederick Carl Frieseke, with a retail value of $263, was $175, while a Tempo ceramic lamp, listed at $120, was reduced to $75. In the showroom downstairs, Mr. C found a plant stand by Lane, originally $300, reduced to just $160 (this was a special closeout). A Berkshire daybed frame, meant to sell for over $300, was an unbelievable $80, and a mahogany-finish Fairfield chair was cut by $150 down to $267.

Sofas will save you big bucks, like a Clayton Marcus model (reduced by half to $700), and a Broyhill club chair (cut from $437 to $273), or the Delft love seat (originally $813, reduced to $513). Even a Taylorsville sofa, valued at $1,313, was reduced by over a third—to $814.

Delivery is free to a large area, but Treasures for Your Home cannot accept layaways. The store is open Monday, Thursday, and Friday from 9:30 a.m. to 9 p.m.; Tuesday, Wednesday, and Saturday from 9:30 to 6 p.m.; and Sunday from 12:30 p.m. to 5 p.m.

Windsor Furniture Liquidators
• 764 Miami Circle N.E., Atlanta;
  814-0770
All the way at the end of this street lined with furniture wholesalers and a few other assorted discounters, Windsor has three huge rooms filled with furniture closeouts and floor samples. Mixed in with budget brands, you may find pieces by such manufacturers as Virginia House, Henredon, Lane, and Regency, often at wholesale prices.

The styles seen here range from traditional American to contemporary European, as well as Oriental looks. A large dining table, for instance, a formal Italian style in green marble, was seen here selling for $658—an incredible price anywhere. Originally, it was priced at $1,400. In the bedroom area, a full-size solid cherry bed frame and headboard were seen for $399. A plush easy chair, which doubles as a recliner and rocker, was selling for $289.

Many items are sold in groupings, like a contemporary linen print sofa, loveseat, and chair for $899. During Mr. C's visit, there was a "weekly special" set in solid oak: A dining table with six chairs, and a matching china cabinet/buffet sideboard, reduced from $1,395 to $950 for the entire set. Conversely, you can also find individual pieces here to add to whatever you've got at home; there is an entire room filled with chairs of every size, shape and purpose; they're stacked on the floor and hanging from the ceiling.

Not everything you'll see here is of the highest quality. Many of the couches have foam-filled cushions; some of the wooden furniture is of the pressed-wood-and-veneer sort, which looks great but may not hold up under heavy use. Still, these may be fine for shoppers on a tight budget, or perhaps for that rarely-slept-in guest room. And there's so much to see here that the place is definitely worth a look. Hours are from 10 a.m. to 6 p.m. Monday through Saturday and noon to 5 p.m. on Sunday.

USED FURNITURE

Carriage House Consignment Gallery
• Town & Country Shopping Center, 1305 Roswell Rd. N.E., Marietta; 973-7100

A funny thing happened on the way to running an antiques shop. See, a couple of years ago, a friend asked owner David Herckis if he would sell off a piece of used furniture (non-antique) in the store. Not only did it sell quickly, making a bit of cash for both Herckis and his friend, but this led to a complete change of focus for the store. Now, David and his wife,

World of Wood
• 5645 Jimmy Carter Blvd., Norcross; 368-0000

From their new location next to the Gwinnett Flea Market, this store discounts "better quality" furniture by 30% to 70% off retail. These are not necessarily name brands, but they are good stuff, made from solid wood. Mr. C liked a cherry wood four-poster bed frame, reduced from $599 to $360; other matching pieces were available, if you care to add a mirror or a dresser. Another good deal seen recently was a kitchen table and four chairs, made from solid ash in a natural finish; the table was also topped with white ceramic tiles, and the set was marked down from its retail price of $559 to just $319.

WOW also sells a big selection of unfinished pine furniture, which is a good way to save money on well-constructed chairs, dressers, bookshelves, and more. Get them at these low prices; stain or lacquer them yourself; they'll look great and hold up for years. Thus, you can get a double dresser, not for $339, but for $195; or an antique-style rocking chair for only $87. Open Mondays through Saturdays from 10-6, and Sundays from 1-5. Be careful driving into their parking lot, by the way; it's right at the intersection of Jimmy Carter Boulevard and the I-85 off-ramp. Any closer, and it would be *in* the intersection.

Elaine, run a business that has grown into a huge, rambling shop jam-packed with used furniture and decorative items, some still in great condition, selling for a fraction of their original values.

A regular classified advertisement in local papers keeps a steady flow of goods coming into the store as fast as pieces move out. You may find an Ethan Allen sofa, originally $1,000, selling for $499. A country-style "refractory" solid oak library table by Century, once $3,000, now $799. And Mr. C absolutely loved a handsome secretary's desk by Drexel, with a leather top and a built-in clock—which could easily have been $5,000 new—selling for $1,499. Yes, it's got a few scratches, but it's still a high-quality, unique piece with a lot of character. Room after room is filled with easy chairs, bedroom and dining room sets, wicker parlor chairs, lamps, framed paintings, and more—in styles from old-fashioned to contemporary.

But there's more to the story. Some of the major furniture manufacturers, for which the South is so well known, heard about the place. They asked if Herckis would be interested in selling off some of *their* unwanted merchandise, too—perfectly good pieces that were shipped to department stores with the wrong color finish, or returned for some similar reason. It would be easier and cheaper, rather than shipping them back to tne factory, to just have Carriage House sell these and split the cash. And so, you will also find some incredible bargains on gorgeous, brand-new furniture by some of the biggest makers in the country. Mr. C was asked not to print specific names and prices, to protect these relationships; but he saw some real knockout deals that can save you hundreds of dollars.

All items are sold "as is," and sales are final. The store is open seven days a week; they're so busy, in fact, that they may open a second store in the Atlanta area, perhaps by the time you read this. Carriage House will also evaluate any item you'd like to sell on consignment, and pick it up at no charge.

OFFICE FURNITURE

Academy Desk Company
• 342 Peachtree St. N.E., Atlanta; 524-5414

Just a few blocks from the heart of downtown, Academy sells a mix of new and used furniture and other accessories for the office. Most of the items are in good to fine condition,

DHS Sell-Out Center
◆ 1374 Moreland Ave. S.E., Atlanta; 622-1800

In the Moreland Center shopping plaza, this vast store buys up furniture and furnishings from hotels when they renovate their rooms. Then, they turn around and "sell out" the stock at incredibly low prices. Sure, these items have seen better days; some pieces are in good condition, some are not. But if you doubt there's a market for this stuff, guess again. The place gets a steady stream of shoppers. And, twice a year, when DHS holds its half-price sale on everything in the store, it becomes a mob scene.

So, think about your average hotel or motel room. Whatever you'd find there will be on sale here: Bedding, tables, chairs, lamps, the pictures on the walls, the carpeting under your feet. And it's all super-cheap. Get a king-size Sealy mattress and boxspring for $95 *per set.* Plush side chairs in every color and shape imaginable (so it seems) from $20 and up. Circular glass tables with lamps built into the center for $25. Framed prints from $15. A huge piece of rolled-up carpeting for $45. You get the idea.

Occasionally, DHS also gets deals on new items too; on Mr. C's visit, there was a special on mahogany (veneer) nightstands, with drawers, for $39 each. These were still in their original boxes, and there were tons of 'em. Plus lots of other unusual items, including a bit of a sideline business in vintage clothing and collectibles. It's a fascinating place, run by friendly folks. Check them out; they're open seven days a week.

with only a few scratches here and there—like on an otherwise handsome credenza of solid cherry wood with brass trim, seen here recently for $595. A perfect-looking gooseneck side chair would look perfect next to it; upholstered in maroon leather, it was seen for $450, or $200 off its list price.

There are usually plenty of the popular ergonomic chairs, many of which are new; basic steno models (no pun intended) start around $140, while a fancier model with side arms and gas lift was reduced from $350 to $240. And a Cole two-drawer lateral file cabinet, which listed originally for $450, was marked down to $289. Plus all kinds of chalkboards, both traditional and the new, magic-marker variety; schedule boards; computer furniture, and other office accessories. It's friendly and casual in here, and even at these prices, prompt delivery is promised.

Alpha Business Interiors
● 2133 Mountain Industrial Blvd., Stone Mountain; 934-2229

This four-year-old warehouse store is small business heaven. They sell new and used famous-brand office furniture, from desks to electric filing systems, at fractions of their original prices. The high sales volume allows them to keep selling this stuff amazingly cheap.

Alpha's prices on new furniture are good, but the real story here is its deals on used items. Some of the highest quality brands are found here; desks and chairs by Steelcase and Herman Miller sell here for just 10 or 25 cents on the dollar. A five-year old Steelcase file cabinet, for example, which sold for $1,000 when it was new, may go for just $250 here. And if you know office furniture, you know these babies last forever—five years is a drop in the bucket! Bookshelves, data racks, free-standing cubicle panels, and work stations also sell here at true bargain prices.

The store's open six days a week, from 10 a.m. to 7 p.m.; they do close up at 5 p.m. on Wednesdays, though.

Artlite Office Furniture Outlet Center
● 1860 Cheshire Bridge Rd. N.E., Atlanta; 872-6279

In its main stores, Artlite sells not only the humblest paper supply, but also major office furniture as well. In this newly-opened clearance center,

you can find extra bargains in floor samples, closeouts, and discontinued models. Some have a few scratches, but there is a goodly amount of pieces to look at in this small but packed store.

Mr. C found a slightly scuffed executive's desk, in a good-quality walnut laminate veneer, reduced from $550 to $279. A brand-new oak veneer computer desk and hutch unit, of the assemble-it-yourself variety, was seen for $285. A solid mahogany credenza, meanwhile, was also spotted by your intrepid bargain hunter for $875, from an original price of $1,635.

New ergonomic stenographers' chairs start at $79, while older styles can go as low as $35. A high-backed side chair in white leather upholstery was reduced from $685 to a mere $325. There were even some architectural flat files, marked down from $550 to $285. Guess you never know what'll be available here, but it seems there's always a good basic selection. Open daily from 8:30 a.m. to 4:30 p.m., Saturdays from 10-3, and closed Sundays.

Business Furniture Liquidators
● 890 Chattahoochee Ave. N.W. Atlanta; 355-9493

This gigantic store is divided into two sections. The front room displays new and practically-new office furniture of very high quality, at discount. Here, you may find such items as a Hooker credenza in rich walnut, with brass trim, selling at $500 off its retail price, or $999; handsome Paoli side chairs, in cherry wood with teal upholstery, reduced from $540 to $280; or a mahogany executive's desk, with just a nick or two, marked down from an original $1,240 to $795.

Walk through to the much larger back warehouse area, and it's as though you've entered another world. In a storeroom as big as the proverbial football field, older furniture is stacked as far and as high as the eye can see. Much of it is still in good, useable condition, even if it wouldn't win any beauty contests. Many other pieces have undoubtedly seen their last coffee break. Still, for starting up an office on a dime—attention, budding entrepreneurs—this place is bound to have whatever you need. How much do these items cost? Who knows. Nothing is marked. Presumably, this gives you an opportunity to sharpen your negotiating skills. Generally, chairs start around $25 and up; file cabinets start at $60 or thereabouts; and so on. In any event, you'll have a good time just poking around back there. Open every day but Sunday.

Ivan Allen Company
- 1503 Northside Dr. N.W., Atlanta; 352-2422

From this rather quiet West Side location, Ivan Allen Company sells a good selection of used office furniture, as well as new items that have been slightly damaged in shipping. The new items are in fine condition indeed, especially the wide variety of contemporary desk chairs—many of which are still wrapped in plastic. There are often enough of each kind to be arranged in rows of identical seats, good for anyone looking to furnish an office uniformly on a budget. Ergonomic steno chairs by Steelcase, for example, were recently seen for $175 each, nearly half of their retail price. And a Global high-backed "Obus Forme" chair, in mint condition, was reduced from $1,030 to $579.

There are complete areas of this loading dock warehouse sectioned off for similar deals on desks, tables, bookshelves, and file cabinets. A large shipment of Hon two-drawer "AccuGlide" vertical files, still in their cartons, was marked down from $275 to $130 each.

The desks, from exec to secretary, and various-sized tables, tend to fall into the "used" category; some have very noticeable scratches and chipped corners. But, when you can get a cherry wood credenza—originally valued at $1,750—for just $329, it's hard to complain. Other

---

MR. CHEAP'S PICKS
Office Furniture

✔ **Alpha Business Interiors**—New and used bargains; the used items in particular, are astoundingly cheap. Great for startup companies.

✔ **Recycled Office Interiors**—The furniture and surroundings are so nicely kept, you'll think you're in a "new" store.

---

desks start as low as $30 and up. Many of these could easily be refinished, looking like new and still costing far less than they might have. Service is very friendly and helpful; the store is open weekdays from 8:30 to 5:30.

Recycled Office Interiors
- 1800-B Northeast Expressway Access Rd. N.E., Atlanta; 634-4500

This is easily the fanciest used furniture store you'll ever see. Very shrewdly, they have designed the place with carpeting, muted flourescent lights, and cloth cubicle partitions—in other words, like an office. So, instead of taking the warehouse/back of a truck approach, ROI lets you see its furniture as it will probably look wherever you're going to use it. Smart, huh?

The merchandise itself falls into three basic categories: New pieces, samples, and floor models from the parent retail store, Office Expo, sold at 50% below list price; refinished pieces, made to look like new again, at 60% to 70% off; and used pieces in fair to good condition at even further discount. All of these are contemporary in style, and there is a large stock to choose from.

Among the new items, Mr. C was shown a Haworth mahogany execu-

tive's desk with a 36" x 72" top, originally retailing for $2,500, on sale for
$1,245. If that's still too pricy for
you, many other (used) desks start
from as little as $100. If you wish,
you can have these refurbished by the
ROI staff, in a variety of finishes, for
a total cost that will still be well below original retail. Not only that, but
the company guarantees its materials
and workmanship for one year.

There are always dozens of chairs
to see, from older vinyl steno chairs
for $35 to the latest ergonomic, cloth-
covered fashions. "Task" chairs by
Workspace, originally retailing for
$325, sell here for $160 each. Some
have been reupholstered, and look absolutely like new, yet are still about
half-price. Mr. C also saw rows of
four-drawer vertical file cabinets
priced at $80 each; these were used,
and looked it, but included such rock-
solid name brands as Hon and Cole
Steel. You may also find conference
and breakroom tables, with chairs to
match; computer tables and typing tables; even drafting tables, like a big
37" x 54" model for $400. These
folks can even make formica table
tops for you, which can be laid across
a pair of two-drawer file cabs, for a
look that is truly functional and truly
cheap.

Open weekdays from 8-5.

Wholesale Office Furniture
- 645 11th St. N.W., Atlanta;
  873-5491

Here's an out-of-the-way place selling a good selection of used office
furniture, as well as new furniture
from major catalogues, all at reduced
prices. "We don't sell junk that eventually falls apart," says owner Laura
Kamenitsa. Indeed, the warehouse offered lots of good deals, on a variety
of ergonomic steno chairs from $30
and up; desks from $25 (for the ba-
sic, black metal sort) and up; and
used executive desks, like a three-
piece desk, credenza and bookcase
set for $1,100, several hundred dol-
lars below its original value. From little accessories, like letter trays and
waste baskets, to big workstations,
like a Herman Miller setup for two
people (originally $6,000, here
$2,300), there's a lot to see.

WOF also carries brand-new lines
from over 250 national manufacturers, from budget to high-end brands.
You can get discounts on desks by
Jasper, chairs by Hickory, and White-
hall upholstered side chairs; plus
products from Sam Moore, Hooker,
Lane, Highpoint, and many others.
Open weekdays from 9-5, and Saturdays from 10-3.

HOME FURNISHINGS

DECORATIVE ITEMS, KITCHENWARE, LIGHTING, LINENS, PAINT, WALLPAPER

Americolor Paint Depot
- 2862 East Ponce de Leon Ave.,
  Decatur; 373-7284

The Depot is one of those tucked
away no-frills places. You could miss
it altogether, with its small, unpaved
drive and tiny sales floor; the savings, though, are enormous. The store
sells its own brand of paint, available
in several finishes, at wholesale
prices.

Latex "one-coat" scrubbable wall
paint is just $7.99 a gallon for white
and in-stock colors, reduced to $7.49
if you buy five gallons or more. Light
tints are $8.99 a gallon; again, save
an extra fifty cents each on five gallons or more.

Latex semi-gloss enamel is $9.99 a gallon for white and stock colors, $10.99 a gallon for light tints, $12.49 for dark tints, and $12.99 for accent tints for trim. Alkyd semi-gloss enamel for woodwork, cabinets, and furniture starts at $12.99 a gallon, going up to $15.99 for accent colors.

The Paint Depot also sells Polyurethane varnish for $13.99 a gallon (available in satin or glossy finish), porch and deck enamel for $12.99 in stock colors, and semi-transparent wood stain for just $11.99 a gallon. Exterior acrylic paints start at just $9.99 for flat paints, $10.99 for gloss finishes, and $14.99 for oil-based one coat house paints.

All the supplies and tools you'd need to make use of these paints are well-stocked, too. The store is open from 8 a.m. to 5 p.m., Mondays through Fridays only.

Beverly Bremer Silver Shop
• 3164 Peachtree Rd. N.E., Atlanta; 261-4009

Bremer's wins a silver medal for savings of up to 75% off regular retail prices on fine sterling silverware and silver accessories. (Should be a gold medal, but then the joke wouldn't work...)

Most of their silver has been obtained from years of shopping at estate sales, and even more items have been traded in, giving the shop an inventory of one thousand flatware patterns. Unlike some other silver shops in town, not everything here is antique or near-antique age. As a result, many sets of flatware and other items are surprisingly low-priced.

Tea services, jewelry, trays, candlesticks, cigarette cases, picture frames, wine coolers, and punch bowls are regularly in stock. Have a look for yourself! The shop is open Monday through Saturday, from 10 a.m. to 5 p.m.

The Container Store
• 3255 Peachtree Rd. N.E., Atlanta; 261-4776

Hallelujah! A store for both the organizationally-impaired *and* the budget-impaired, with items for

home and office. Many of these would also make great gift ideas, by the way...

Clean out your closet, throw away those dreadful ties Aunt Henrietta gave you, and put all the good ones onto a super-duper tie rack by Xtendables, priced at $14.99. All kinds of clothes hangers and garment bags, too; and a canvas L.L. Bean lookalike tote bag is a bargain at just $9.99.

For the kitchen, how about a big acrylic recipe box for $12.99, or clamp-top mason jars for $6. And how have you managed all these years without an ostrich feather duster for $9, a 28-spool thread holder for $6, and a $2.50 magnetic box for straight pins?

For work, pick up a sturdy metal two-drawer file cabinet for $79, a 14-ounce flat-bottomed "commuter" coffee mug for $10.99, one of those big write-on-wipe-off marker boards for $10, or a $2.99 plastic drawer organizer for those pesky piles of paper clips.

Furniture for home and office is bargain-priced to help you get your act together. Big plastic modular stacking shelves are $20 each, a metal bookcase by Adeptus is $90, and a nine-shelf tower for books is $60. Vinyl-covered trunks, perfect for kids heading to college, are $60, a 44-disc CD rack is $15, and a solid oak audiotape rack is just $12.

Plus basics like wrapping paper and cardboard shipping boxes ($3.49 for a huge 18" x 18" x 28" size), too. Now that you've gotten your life so organized, you can pack up all the junk and ship it off to Kalamazoo.

Decorative Arts Wholesale
• 764 Miami Circle N.E., Atlanta; 231-4332

Way up at the end of the Miami furniture run, this new shop is a great discovery for anyone whose taste runs to the Oriental. Massive quantities of decorative items are stocked on shelves, and many are simply spread out on the floor, in fresh-off-the-boat style; and all of it sells for less than half of the retail price. Of course, with this type of merchandise, you don't have many opportunities to see if *anybody* sells it at retail prices, but this is good-quality stuff.

There are tons of enameled porcelain vases, for instance, in several color schemes. Mr. C saw several in the traditional blue and white design, list priced at $97, but selling for $39; the former price would probably be way too much, but the actual price is probably just fine. Table lamps with similar porcelain bases are almost all $79, reduced from $199; get some tall porcelain candlesticks to match at $9.50 apiece.

They also have a treasure trove of chests, large and small; beautiful black wooden lacquered chests, about a foot square, with decorative paintings inlaid on their lids, are marked down from $470 to $188; smaller versions in cherry wood, suitable for holding jewelry, range from about $35 to $60. And if a seven-foot black lacquer folding screen is just what your living room cries out for, there are lots of designs to choose from here—both modern and traditional. Even at the half-off price of $1,000, though, these are not exactly what you'd call cheap.

Georgia Lighting Clearance Center
- 1510 Ellsworth Industrial Dr. N.W., Atlanta; 875-7637
- 735 Highway 138, Riverdale; 994-0138
- 1207 Alpharetta St., Roswell; 552-5438

No doubt you've heard of Georgia Lighting. But, you may not be aware of these clearance outlets, where they sell factory closeouts, special purchases, and discontinued items that have been taken off the floors of their regular retail showrooms. These sell at reductions of 10% to 70% below retail prices. The Atlanta store has that genuine warehouse ambiance—it's like an airplane hangar, inexplicably strung with gorgeous lights.

Most of GL's lines are traditional in style, though there are some contemporary models here and there. Flush-mount lanterns in polished brass, for your front door, start as low as $19.95; a five-lamp brass chandelier was seen recently for $59.95. Plus ceiling fan/lights from $39.95, table lamps, floor lamps, strip lights for bathroom mirrors, and lots of bulbs, globes, and shades to go with them.

The clearance centers also get deals on other home furnishings, like framed paintings and mirrors, as well as some accent furniture pieces like plant stands, end tables, and coat trees. The knowledgeable staff is ready to answer all your questions, technical and esthetic; amazingly, they seem to know every single item in this vast store by name and number. The intown store is open Mondays through Saturdays from 10 a.m. to 4 p.m.; the suburban stores are open seven days a week. Stock tends to vary from one store to another, so if you don't see quite what you're looking for, ask them to call around.

Lechter's Homestores
- Market Square at DeKalb, Lawrenceville Hwy., Decatur; 325-0358
- Phipps Plaza, 3500 Peachtree Rd., Atlanta; 261-4244

And other suburban locations
Lechter's is a national leader in discount home necessities, from picture frames to kitchen utensils and small appliances to laundry bags and drawer organizers. They really seem to have a little bit of everything.

A Rubbermaid basting brush is just $1.99, while a shower caddy by the same brand is $8. A wooden spice rack is only $7.99 (add your own spices), and an Ecko sifter, retailing for $4.99 and up elsewhere, is just $3.49 here.

You'll be cooking up a storm with Pyrex cookware, like a pint-sized measuring cup or a nine-inch pie plate, each priced at $1.99. To go with all of these, of course, you'll need a real chef's hat by Chef's Club, selling for just $6.99.

Get yourself organized with a

handy three-tier plastic storage cart by Sterilite for only $9.99. Decorative hanging baskets are $3.99 each, and 5" x 7" wooden picture frames are priced at two for $10.

For further bargains, Lechter's also has clearance outlet centers in Commerce and Calhoun.

Linen Loft

- Akers Mill Square, 2971 Cobb Pkwy., Atlanta; 952-6929
- Gwinnett Place Mall, 2100 Pleasant Hill Rd., Duluth; 476-7770
- Lilburn Market Place, 4805 Lawrenceville Hwy., Lilburn; 279-9302
- Toco Hills Center, 2915 North Druid Hills Rd. at Lavista; 633-9354
- Roswell Mkt. Place, 10800 Alpharetta Hwy. at Mansell Rd., Roswell; 587-0915

And other suburban locations

Prices at the Linen Loft will surely be uplifting to your spirits. Sheets and comforters by designers like Bill Blass (his individual twin sheets cost $8.49, for instance) and Laura Ashley ($11.04 a twin sheet) are priced well below retail. Dan River sheets are priced at $6.79 each and up. Of course, you'll find complete package sets, at great savings as well.

Comforters sell for a comforting $70-$150 off their retail prices. Recently, Mr. C noted a super offer on down comforters—a special group was selling for just $70 each, in any size from twin right up to king. Pillows, towels, and window treatments are similarly discounted.

This is a particularly good place to check out, by the way, when you're looking to furnish the kids' rooms. Linen Loft offers lots of brightly colored novelty prints that may actually make the little ones *want* to go to bed.

Most locations are open from 10 a.m. to 9 p.m., Monday through Saturday, and on Sundays from noon to 6 p.m.

Linen Supermarket

- 2325 Cheshire Bridge Rd. N.E., Atlanta; 636-9157

MR. CHEAP'S PICKS
Home Furnishings

✔ **Americolor Paint Depot**—Great discounts on—what else?—paints.

✔ **The Container Store**—Everything you need to help store all the stuff you've bought with this book!

✔ **Georgia Lighting Clearance Center**—Fantastic closeout deals on all kinds of indoor and outdoor lighting.

✔ **Tuesday Morning**—Closeout bargains on cookware, linens, and doodads.

Just opened in the fall of '93, this is the first store in Georgia for this successful Texas and Florida chain, selling all kinds of domestics and hard goods for the home. Though it's as fully stocked as any department store, you'll save as much as 70% on sheets, comforters, and towels by such makers as Cannon, Martex, Dan River, and more. Some items are seconds and closeouts. A recent special featured reversible comforters by Cannon and J.P. Stevens, with retail prices of up to $60 in full/queen size, selling for just $24.99; Stevens' bath towels were going for a clean $1.99 each. Stack these on a white wicker two-tier rack, just $9.99.

For the living room and dining room, synthetic Oriental rugs were seen at just $49.95, and designer linen tablecloths were marked down from $19.99 to $7.99. And, not to leave the kitchen out, there is a wide assortment of deals such as 20-piece dinnerware sets reduced from $60 list to $19.99, glassware and flatware sets at less than half-price, and a set of three different no-stick frying pans for $8.88. This is also a great place for gift ideas. And, unlike the outlets, this is a regular retail store, open seven days a week.

Linens and Wares
- 2480 Briarcliff Rd. N.E., Bldg. 11, Atlanta; 634-9360

At this store in Loehmann's Executive Plaza, you'll find accessories for bedroom, bathroom, and more. Brand name items from the likes of Utica, Rubbermaid, and Martex are all discounted here.

Utica and Springmaid sheet sets and comforters are priced at 20% below retail. Brightly printed comforters from Colours by Alexander Julian, listed at $100, thereby sell for $80. And the king-size Dan River "Bed in a Bag" set, retailing for $175, was reduced to $119.

Other goodies in store include Borman lamps, reduced from $25 to $19, Battenburg lace tablecloths by Handmaid Lace for $13, and Martex bath towels for only $8. Mr. C also found a snazzy Bill Blass shower curtain, listed at $45, for just $34, and other unusual designs, like one featuring a map of the world, for $20.

Plenty of items for the kitchen, too; Rubbermaid Servin' Savers bottles, with list prices of $3.50, are just $2.99, and T-Fal non-stick frying pans listed at $30 sell for just $22.

The store is open Mondays through Fridays from 10 a.m. to 8 p.m., Saturdays 10 a.m. to 6 p.m., and Sundays noon to 5 p.m.

"Luxury Linens" at Burlington Coat Factory
- 4166 Buford Hwy. N.E., Atlanta; 634-5566
- 3750 Venture Dr., Duluth; 497-0033
- 1255 Roswell Rd. N.E., Marietta; 971-6540
- 5934 Roswell Rd., Sandy Springs; 303-0505

See listing under "Discount Department Stores."

Plej's Textile Mill Outlet
- 1737-20 Ellsworth Industrial Dr. N.W., Atlanta; 355-4893

In a humble, true-outlet style, Plej's ("pronounced 'Pledge's'," the sign says) sells a bit of everything for outfitting your home. First-quality, ir-

regulars, and closeouts are mixed together, as are name brands with unknowns. Mr. C did notice Dan River among the table of fitted bed sheets, selling at $9.99 in king-size, half its retail price. Martex thermal cotton blankets were marked down from $30 to $12.99. And a full-size comforter by Rosecliff was reduced from a list price of $130 to just $79.99.

For the living room, how about a country-style woven accent rug by C.S. Brooks, of synthetic fibers, marked down from $45 to $29.99—or vinyl mini-blinds from just $8.88. In the bathroom, you can get nonbrand bath towels for as little as $2.99 each, or an Elizabeth Gray double swag linen shower curtain, with a floral design, reduced from $55 to $30.

The store is open Thursdays from 12-5, Fridays and Saturdays from 10-6, and Sundays from 12-6.

Southern Textile Outlet
- 900-B Huff Rd. N.W., Atlanta; 355-1172
- 500 Amsterdam Ave. N.E., Atlanta; 872-3584

With one location in the Chattahoochee outlet area and another in the Midtown outlets, you could say this company has got the bedspread market covered. They get their down comforters from the same mills which supply stores like Bloomingdales—but at far more comforting prices. These come in your choice of four grades, depending on how much down you need, and the type of stitching. The basic twin-size model is just $59.99, ranging up to $89.99 in king-size—very good prices indeed. The top-of-the-line prices range from $149.99 twin to $219.99 king. Good deals on down pillows, too.

STO will also custom-make comforters and duvet covers, using any fabric you bring them; prices are typically less than half of what such a service might cost at a specialty store. They also make bed skirts, shams, and decorative pillows. It's no wonder that decorators shop here for their clients.

There is a limited selection of linens, such as cotton sheet sets by Utica, at prices that are often better than Macy's or Rich's, even during sales. You can find the popular Battenburg lace styles here, in shower curtains (from $29.99) and bedding; as well as bath towels by Martex and others. There are some seconds mixed in (and marked as such) with the linens only; otherwise, everything here is first-quality. The Huff Road store is open daily from 10 a.m. to 5 p.m., except Sunday; the Midtown Outlets branch opens Friday and Saturday from 10-7, and Sunday from 1-6.

Tuesday Morning

- 3165 Peachtree Rd. N.E., Atlanta; 233-6526
- 3250 Satellite Blvd., Duluth; 476-0522
- 4502 Chamblee-Dunwoody Rd., Dunwoody; 457-3565
- 700 Sandy Plains Rd. N.E., Marietta; 428-1536
- 1115 Morrow Industrial Blvd., Morrow; 961-0707
- 1231 Alpharetta St., Roswell; 640-8146
- 2512 Spring Rd. S.E., Smyrna; 435-6678

And other suburban locations
We all know how much better Tuesday mornings are, compared to Mondays. TM's bargains will make you feel that much better any day, with discounts on everything from clothes to party supplies to toys to jewelry to luggage.

For the home, you may find a queen-sized quilted comforter by Impressions, reduced from $200 to $90; and an Eileen West king-size sheet set, marked down from $165 to $60. Low-priced doo-dads for around the house include a Chantal omelette pan, half-price at $30; and a Vigaro teapot, listed at $35, and selling for $15. Porcelain by Rosenthal of Germany is just $9 per dinner plate (down from $21), and only $30 for a server (regularly $88). Linen damask tablecloths are half-price at $30, and four cloth placemats are just $13 (about half their going retail price).

You can also go the disposable route, with a package of 42 plastic utensils or a dozen 12-ounce tumblers, each priced at $1.99.

Occasionally, Tuesday Morning gets special deals on larger items for the home, like a recent special on Weider home workout gyms, which were priced at just $49. These can sell out quickly, though, sometimes within one day; so if you see or hear an advertisement for a great bargain like this at TM, you may want to head right on over. Open seven days a week.

Wallpaper Atlanta

- 3230-B Peachtree Rd. N.E., Atlanta; 266-0011
- 455 Grayson Hwy. S.W., Suite 116, Lawrenceville; 963-1467
- 4920 Roswell Rd. N.W., Suite 18, Dunwoody-Sandy Springs; 303-1205
- 2846 East Ponce de Leon Ave., Decatur; 377-9206

And other suburban locations
Wallpaper Atlanta? These guys probably could! Volume purchasing allows this chain to offer some great discounts on plain and fancy designs. Discontinued closeouts and overstock items make for even better bargains.

Warner paper, retailing for $21 per roll, sells for $10.99 a roll here, and a country-style floral pattern by Waverly is only $12.99 a roll—that's also half off the retail price. Fancy-looking marble prints by C & A are just $9.99 a roll, down from $20.99 retail.

Muted stripes and floral prints by Birge in an oversized 56-square foot roll are $9.99, down from their $16.99 list prices. Attractive prints by generic makers go for $8.99 a roll and less.

For wallcoverings special-ordered from the store's books, fabric wallpaper is reduced by 15% off retail; designer styles are 20% off retail, and all regular styles are 30% off retail list prices, every day.

Finish the room off with borders by York, for $7.99 a roll (listing at $15.99). Fabric-backed vinyl wallcoverings by Ashbury Place, just the thing for soggy bathrooms, are reduced from $17.99 a roll to just $8.99.

And don't forget to check the flower pots in the back of the store for those closeouts on regular-sized rolls and borders, starting at just $1 a roll and up.

Wallpaper Plus!

• 5000 Roswell Rd. N.E., Atlanta; 252-1329

This shop's run by an interior designer who knows his stuff. And he knows how to price it well enough to rival any of the city's mega-chain wallpaper stores.

Designer wallpaper orders from the store's books are always discounted. Patterns by Stroheim & Roman, and Schumacher, are 30% off list price; Waverly is 35% off. Any special order from other sources will automatically be slashed 35% off retail.

Pre-packaged wallpaper and border paper is priced low everyday, too. A double roll pack of a Waverly floral print may go for just $11.99 (that's down from $25.99 retail), and 56 square feet of Linden St. Gallery wallpaper is priced $10 off retail, at $18.99.

Bright striped paper by Village is also $10 off, selling for $11 per roll; a willow print by Eisenhart, $25.99 elsewhere, is $10 for two rolls, and water-resistant prints by Rosedale Waldex, normally selling for $15.99 or more, are just $4.99 a pack. The popular Waverly American Classics line, regularly selling at a hefty $23.99 for a double roll, is just $11 here. Add five yards rolls of border prints for $9.99 each.

Wallpaper Plus! also pledges to match any advertised prices listed by mail-order companies, too.

Not satisfied yet? Then you may also want to check out:

The Hill Street Warehouse Sample Store

• 2050 Hills Ave. N.W., Atlanta; 352-5001

Myron Dwoskin's Outlet Store

• 3535 Memorial Dr., Decatur; 288-4914

Outrageous Bargains

• 1397 Roswell Rd. N.E., Marietta; 578-6944

JEWELRY AND CRAFTS

Shop for gold and gems very carefully! Diamonds vary greatly in quality, especially clarity and color; there is a very intricate set of official ratings, far more detailed than the "A, B, and C" grades some stores use. Be sure to have the jeweler explain any diamond's rating to you before you decide to buy. There are similar ratings for other gemstones, too.

AJS Shoe Warehouse

• 1788 Ellsworth Industrial Blvd. N.W., Atlanta; 355-1760

In addition to great values on imported shoes for women (see listing under "Shoes and Sneakers"), AJS sells a distinctive collection of accessories, such as leather bags and hand-

made jewelry.

The jewelry, in particular, is gorgeous—and a far cry from the usual "accessories" found in other shoe stores. Their buyer is an artist, someone who once lived among native American Indians, and whose taste in sterling silver handcrafted earrings, necklaces, bracelets, and rings makes this small part of the store worth the trip by itself. There are lots of items, many set with semi-precious stones, and plenty to see in the $10-$20 range and up. The prices stay reasonable, again, because the high volume of sales means very little markup is needed.

The store is only open Fridays from 10 a.m. to 6 p.m. and Saturdays from 10 a.m. to 5 p.m. sharp.

Asia Jewelers
- 1707 Church St., Decatur; 294-1646

Located in the Scott Village shopping center, Asia Jewelry deals primarily in gold jewelry for women—mostly necklaces, with some earrings and bracelets. Oriental motifs, naturally, are seen in many of these pieces; there are also some very basic styles. Mr. C was told that all jewelry in the store is made from 22-karat gold, which they can certify for you.

Some of the bargains Mr. C found were a ladies' gold rope chain necklace for an amazing $35, and medium-sized gold hoop earrings for $50. A heavy gold necklace, ornately trimmed with pieces of coral, is only $30. Among the few items for men was a thick chevron-patterned bracelet for $60.

Direct importing is one key to the store's great prices; also, it's not located in a fancy stretch of town, which helps keep overhead costs down. The store is located a short distance from the Marketsquare at North DeKalb, near the intersections of Scott Boulevard and Church Street.

Buckhead Jewelry
- 935-B Chattahoochee Ave. N.W., Atlanta; 352-9001

In spite of the name, this store is not in Buckhead, but rather the Atlanta Outlet distict. It's an interesting shop. Here, you can find 14-karat and 18-karat gold, platinum, watches, and even diamond jewelry at about 50% to 70% below retail values.

Now, these can be very tricky items when it comes to such price comparisons, but hear Mr. C out.

MR. CHEAP'S PICKS
Jewelry

✔ **Coyote Trading Company**— You'll howl with delight at the buys on turquoise and silver jewelry at this new L5P store.

✔ **Solomon Brothers**—Direct importers and cutters of diamonds can save you big bucks in Buckhead.

Jack, the owner, is a goldsmith by trade; he makes his own designs, right in the shop, which of course keeps the overhead costs low. And he's a real master of the art, as one look at his creations will tell you. His particular expertise is in gold rings—wide bands with ornate designs and inlays, for men or women. Have something in mind? He'll design it for you. Seen something you like in a magazine or catalog? Bring it in to him—and in a week's time, Jack will produce a replica that is nearly indistinguishable from the picture, with the same materials (even diamonds, thanks to a family contact in the New York gem trade)—for hundreds of dollars less than it might have cost. He showed Mr. C one such ring, an intricate pattern set with tiny diamonds, first in a pricy catalog—where it was listed for $3,125. Then he brought out his version, which might just as well have been the real McCoy; his price was $750.

The store also sells basic gold chains and silver rings, from $15 up into the thousands; plus bracelets, necklaces, and earrings; and Pulsar watches at discount. And they offer expert repairs, often while you wait. Open Thursday through Saturday from 10 a.m. to 6 p.m.

Coyote Trading Company
- 439 Seminole Ave. N.E., Atlanta; A new addition to the Little Five

Points scene, this Native American art shop near the Point is chock-full of beautiful yet relatively inexpensive jewelry. Most pieces are made with sterling silver and turquoise, and some of them are fashioned into intricate beaded patterns.

Mr. C saw liquid sterling silver earrings for $12, and a $9 pair of earrings made from beads and cut porcupine quills. Triangular-shaped turquoise earrings on hanging sterling posts are $15. One of the more interesting items in the shop is a Navajo ghost bead necklace, which is traditionally used to keep away bad spirits. At just $5, it will certainly keep the creditors away from your door.

Coyote also sells belt buckles, bolo ties, bracelets, and rings, most of which are quite moderately priced.

Cumberland Diamond Exchange

- Cumberland Crossing Shopping Center, 2772 Hargrove Rd., Smyrna; 434-GEMS (4367)

The Cumberland Diamond Exchange has been busily importing diamonds for over twelve years. Thus, the store can offer low prices for two reasons: No middlemen and volume purchasing.

Tennis bracelets start at $399 for a one-carat total weight bracelet, up to $1,599 for a four-carat total weight style. Diamond earrings start as low as $119 for $\frac{1}{5}$-carat stones, $179 for $\frac{1}{3}$-carat stones, and $799 for 1-carat diamonds. And engagement rings start at a modest $199 for a $\frac{1}{4}$-carat style, $249 for a $\frac{1}{3}$-carat, $349 for a $\frac{1}{2}$-carat, and $599 for a $\frac{3}{4}$-carat stone.

Even more dramatic savings can be found on their rings of one carat or more. A 1$\frac{1}{4}$-carat ring is $1,299; a 1$\frac{1}{2}$-carat is $1,899; a two-carat is $2,299, and a hefty three-carat ring is $2,999. Heavy as those prices sound, they could well be much higher at . many other stores.

CDE offers delayed payments and 90-day financing. The store is open Mondays, Wednesdays and Fridays from 10 a.m. to 6 p.m., Tuesdays and Thursdays from 10 a.m. to 8 p.m., and Saturdays from 10 a.m. to 5 p.m.

It's About Time

- 225 Peachtree St. N.E., Atlanta; 523-2501
- 3373 Peachtree Rd. N.E., Atlanta; 233-0357

And other suburban locations

It's about time that someone started selling watches at half-decent prices, and doggone it, this store did it. Pulsar and Seiko are the major brands stocked here. You'll also find stylish clocks for the home and office, as well as accessories like Colibri cigarette lighters.

A Rolex-style watch made by Timex is just $45, and a Rolex-style Seiko is $185. A man's Pulsar, with 18-karat gold overlay, is $92; and a ladies' Lasalle, listed at $325, sells for just $162.50 (both come with three-year warranties). IAT also carries novelty watches, like ones with the logo from Super Bowl XXVIII (the one Atlanta just hosted).

Mr. C, always on the go himself, liked a travel clock by Casio. It gives you the hour for any time zone in the world, all for a mere $26.95. Seiko and Citizen travel alarms are priced in the $40 range.

A giant (four foot tall) wall clock by Howard Miller is $280, but most normal-sized kitchen and living room clocks are in the $40 area. Yes, if you've got the time, this store has, er...got the time.

Sam Fowler Jewelers

- Sandy Springs Shopping Center, 6125 Roswell Rd., Sandy Springs; 255-2480

Just north of the perimeter, this store has been selling diamonds and watches to people from all over the Atlanta metropolitan area since 1955. All the merchandise is new, but it varies widely in quality.

Mr. C saw plenty of unusual bargains here, like cameo brooches and coral pins in the $75 price range. A beautiful cultured pearl bracelet was seen for $99, and an opal and gold ring for $95. A gold tennis bracelet, set with diamonds, was reasonably priced at $485, while sterling silver lockets were just $29.

In men's jewelry, Mr. C saw a 14-karat gold ID bracelet for $300, a chunky gold nugget bracelet for $225, and a leather-banded Speidel watch for $149.

Sam Fowler's also offers well-priced watch and jewelry repairing services, as well as engraving.

Friedman's Jewelers
- Market Square at North DeKalb, 2050 Lawrenceville Hwy. Decatur; 248-0324

Not to be confused with the equally bargain-laden Friedman's Shoe stores (see listing under "Shoes and Sneakers"), Friedman's Jewelers is equally focused on value and exceptional customer service.

Most of the gold jewelry in the store is of 10 or 14 karat quality. A ruby ring, set in 14 karat gold, was seen for $119 (it's retail value was estimated at $149), and an 18" flat chain of 14-karat gold was $224, valued at $320. A braided rope chain of 14-karat gold is $595 (list price, $850). And gold-plated hoop earrings are priced as low as $10.

Bulova watches and diamond tennis bracelets and other jewelry are available at similar discounts. Mr. C saw a 1-carat total weight double rope tennis bracelet for $799 (retail $999), and a similar 2-carat bracelet worth $1,750 reduced to only $975.

A half-carat total weight triple-row ladies wedding band, intended for a 30-year anniversary, was recently selling for $100 of the retail price, at just $399. A marquis-cut $1/4$-carat solitaire ring is only $299 (about $75 off retail).

Gold and Diamond Gallery
- Market Square at North DeKalb, 2050 Lawrenceville Hwy., Decatur; 636-5690

Elsewhere in the Market Square, this family-owned shop has been around for almost 25 years. The Gold and Diamond Gallery can offer you great prices on more than just the baubles in its name. And, if a particular item is just a bit over your budget, you may find these folks willing to make a deal with you.

The savings here are the result of direct importing, cutting out middle-man markups. Thus, a truly gigantic diamond ring, with a total weight of five carats—which would retail for $9,650—costs $3,299 here. Similar savings can be found on a three-carat ring, which retails for over $5,000, but sells for a lighter $2,000. Don't worry if these prices are stil out of your range; a $1/2$-carat diamond ring is just $199, while Ruby rings start at $39, emeralds at $69, and amethysts at $99.

Looking for something more unusual? Show your Braves spirit with a tomahawk charm for $49, in 14-karat gold; or a pair of 10-karat tomahawk earrings for $24. You can also find a pair of emerald-and-gold earrings for just $79, or classic cameo pins for $119.

Items for guys: Gold tie tacks, priced from $30 and up. Onyx and gold rings from $99 and up, and and a hefty Claddagh ring in 14-karat gold for $229.

Midtown Designers' Warehouse
- 553-3 Amsterdam Ave. N.E., Atlanta; 873-2581

The specialty here is dressy, high-fashion women's clothing, including leather garments, at wholesale prices or nearly so. On the leather clothing in particular, this store can save you $200 or more over department or specialty store prices.

In addition, MDW offers a quality selection of handmade costume jewelry to go with these fancy outfits, all selling at less than half of their original prices. Mr. C was shown a three-piece, gold-plated necklace and earring set—solidly made, not the flimsy junk often sold as an afterthought with clothing—selling for $23, down from its retail price of $60. Some of the jewelry is made with semi-precious stones, such as a handsome necklace of green malachite chips. Long enough to be worn at full or doubled-over length, it was reduced from $40 to $12.99.

The store, in the Midtown Outlets area, is open Thursdays through Saturdays from 10 a.m. to 7 p.m., and Sundays from 1-6.

Oglewanagi Gallery

- 842-B North Highland Ave. N.E., Atlanta; 872-4213

More than just a lovely jewelry and gift shop, this address is home to the American Indian Center, a resource center for Native Americans to gather for educational and creative purposes. In the gallery itself, you can find beautiful jewelry in sterling silver and turquoise, made by members of tribes like the Navajo, Comanche, and others. Some of these items are expensive, and no doubt worth it, given the incredible skill and handcraft that go into making them. Still, you may also want to stop in to check out their cases of rings and earrings which start as low as $5-$8 and up; also, wonderfully creative crafts and ceramic pottery in an inexpensive to moderate price range.

Pavé Villa Unreal Jewelry

- Underground Atlanta, 50 Upper Alabama St. S.W., Atlanta; 577-2117

Yes, believe it or not folks, Mr. C has found you a bargain in Underground Atlanta! The low prices at Pavé Villa are for real; the "gems" in its jewelry are not, but only you need to know the truth.

Most of the jewelry is made with Austrian crystal. But until you get extremely close up, it's sure hard to tell this stuff from actual rose quartz, emeralds, sapphires, amethysts, and even diamonds. The gold isn't solid, either (it's overlay), so you can buy jewelry that looks like it costs hundreds or thousands of dollars—for prices that hover in the $50 range.

For example, a *faux* ruby and diamond bracelet was seen here for just $28. If you bought the real thing at Maier and Berkeley, it would cost at least $1,000. Yet, this doesn't look like cheap costume jewelry.

A pair of 18-karat gold overlay earrings with fake diamonds and sapphires go for $76. A fake rose quartz

necklace is $42, a "pearl" and "diamond" stickpin is $29, and the same "jewels" were seen mounted in a brooch/scarf clip for $40.

Get the idea? Other bargains include a *faux* pearl and onyx bracelet with Austrian crystals for $28, and an heirloom-type drop-emerald portrait necklace for $66. Of course, when you wear one of these fancy fakes out on the town, the trick will be to keep from telling your friends how much it really cost you!

Puttin' on the Glitz

- Peachtree Center, 231-233 Peachtree St., Suite B-33, Atlanta; 525-0624

Here's another store for cheap costume jewelry that doesn't *look* cheap. Styles range from *faux* pearls—good enough to wear with any business outfit—to wild, oversized plastic baubles, like red plastic earrings for just $5.99. Lots of the jewelry is made by the store, and sold under its own label.

Mr. C found cloisonné earrings in the $10 range, an $18 copper-tone bracelet, and faux pearl necklaces for only $4.99 and up. An imitation Monet gold-plated set, with bracelet, necklace, and earrings, goes for $15.95.

"Enhancers" are another interesting idea to consider. These are pieces set with fake rubies, emeralds, etc., surrounded with diamond-like crystals. They can be attached to a plain chain or pearl necklace, flashing it up considerably for only $16.

Solomon Brothers Manufacturers

- Tower Place Buckhead, 3340 Peachtree Rd. NE, Suite 1700 (17th floor), Atlanta; 266-0266

Solomon Brothers touts itself as offering Atlanta's largest selection of diamonds at the most affordable prices. They certainly have a lot to see; and since they are diamond cutters, Solomon lets you buy direct and save big.

Emerald cut diamond rings start around $899 for a half-carat stone. A 1½-carat emerald cut ring is $2,550. Princess-cut diamond rings (round-shaped) sell at $675 for a half-carat, while one-carats range from $2,000 to $3,400. Two-carats range in price from $6,000 to $9,000.

There are lots of tennis bracelets, in a variety of settings. A one-carat total weight bracelet is just $249, a three-carat total weight goes for $900, while a whopping ten-carat total weight bracelet is yours for a mere $6,000. But it *could* cost a lot more!

Pearls are also available here in 6mm to 8mm sizes, almost half off their suggested retail prices.

Parking is free. The store is open Mondays through Thursdays from 10 a.m. to 6 p.m., and Fridays and Saturdays from 10 a.m. to 5 p.m.

Tuesday Morning
- 6325 Spalding Dr., Norcross; 447-8872
- 1231 Alpharetta St., Roswell; 993-6176
- 1901 Montreal Rd., Tucker; 934-1616

We all know how much better Tuesday mornings are, compared to Mondays. TM's bargains will make you feel that much better any day, with discounts on everything from clothes to party supplies to toys to jewelry to luggage. At these three particular branches only, TM has its "Fine Jewelry Centers," where you can save hundreds of dollars on first-quality closeouts from designers and well-known brands.

A recent sale, for example, offered stylishly sculpted rings in 10K gold, set with pearls or semi-precious stones. The retail values of these rings ranged from about $200 to $500, but here they were all selling for prices under $100.

Another style, the narrow "stack" ring, meant to be worn in groups, was on sale for $29.99 each. There were several versions to choose from, decorated with rows of tiny emeralds, sapphires, garnets, amethyst, and more; they had originally retailed for as much as $89 each.

Of course, Tuesday Morning sells closeouts on discontinued styles, the

selection can be limited. Not all sizes may be available in all designs. Should you decide to gamble on something here as a gift, and it does not fit, TM does have a thirty-day return policy; just remember to keep your receipt!

All stores are open seven days a week.

Walter R. Thomas Wholesale Jewelers
- Toco Hills Shopping Center, 2891 North Druid Hills Rd., Atlanta; 634-3197

Walter Thomas is another direct importer, bringing in much of its jewelry from Antwerp. Eliminating the middleman allows them to offer you super buys on diamonds and other precious stones.

A tennis bracelet, decorated with two-carats' worth of diamonds, sells for $1,300. A 14-karat gold ring with sapphire, carrying a retail price of $600, costs $300 here, and a seven-carat emerald studded with over four carats' worth of diamonds is $5,600—about half its retail price tag of $10,500. And a large opal, set in 14-karat gold with two diamond baguettes, is $210, but worth $900.

Loose diamonds are also dramatically reduced, like a .60-carat brilliant round stone, internally flawless for $5,300 (again, half of retail value). A 1.01-carat SI2 round-cut diamond, with color rated between I and J, is $3,799 (retailing for $4,500). A diamond valued at $21,300 (it's a big 1.11 carats, rated E VVS2) is reduced to $10,650 here. As you can see, Thomas can offer you near-wholesale prices in many instances. Layaway and financing are also available.

Worth the Weight
- 231 Peachtree St. N.E., Atlanta; 681-4653

This tiny counter-top shop in the Peachtree Center Mall is worth a trip downtown for bargains on 14-karat gold rope chain necklaces, bracelets, and the like.

There are a variety of thicknesses and cuts available: Diamond cuts from smooth to brilliant, braided ropes, and more. Prices start at $11.95 per gram, depending on thickness. A man's thick rope-style gold necklace, weighing about 21 grams, costs $249 here. A comparable-length necklace would cost over $500 in

fancy department stores.

Sterling silver chains start at $9.95 a gram, although there's not as large a variety of cuts as compared to the gold chains. Other goodies seen here include gold nugget rings, with a retail value of $40, selling for $19.95.

LIQUOR AND BEVERAGES

All-American Package Store
- 15-A Moreland Ave. S.E., Atlanta; 688-9223
- 1238-A Pryor Rd. S.W., Atlanta; 627-6752
- 4465-A Roswell Rd., Atlanta; 255-6826
- 1220-A Clairmont Rd., Decatur; 633-5250
- 4467-A Glenwood Rd., Decatur; 284-5111

High prices for liquor? Why, that would be positively un-American!

This chain gives you many ways to save. They offer a five percent discount on half-cases of wine, and ten percent reductions when you buy a whole case. You can find French merlot wines for $5.99 a bottle, and Robert Mondavi Sauvignon Blanc 1991 California wine is $8.99 for 1.5 liters. A large bottle of Moet & Chandon champagne is $26.99. And good ol' Sutter Home chardonnay or cabernet is $9.99 for a big 1.5 liter size.

Liquor bargains may include Taylor Golden sherry for $4.99 a bottle, Dekuyper amaretto at $9.89 for a 750ml bottle, Peachtree schnapps by the same maker for $8.99 a bottle, and Bacardi Light rum at $11.99 for a 750ml bottle. Again, hard liquor in quantities of three or more may entitle you to a further price break—just ask the sales staff.

Mr. C spotted many good deals on beer, like a 12-pack of Rolling Rock for $7.99, a suitcase of Bud Light for $13.99, and a six-pack of Miller Genuine Draft bottles for $4.59. The

specials are ever-changing, but you're always sure to find something good on sale.

Cheers Beer & Wine
- Loehmann's Executive Plaza, 2490 Briarcliff Rd. N.E., Atlanta; 321-7777

Cheers is sure to cheer you up with its great prices. The selection isn't as extensive as some of the other liquor stores Mr. C visited, but the values found here are sure worth a special trip.

A big 1.75 liter bottle of Smirnoff vodka is $17.99, while you can go wild with a liter of Wild Turkey Bourbon at $19.99. (Don't overdo it, now.)

1991 vintages of Sutter Home red wine were recently seen for just $4.99 a bottle, while a bottle of Ernest & Julio Gallo Gewurtzraminer (bless you!) white wine was $3.99.

Beer is similarly discounted—a 12-pack of Moosehead Special is $7.99, and a 12-pack of Fosters Lager is $8.99. Speaking of Cheers, these are prices even ol' Normie could love.

Bulk discounts are also available, but the store does not provide delivery.

Green's Package Stores
- 739 Ponce de Leon Ave. N.E., Atlanta; 872-1109
- 2612 Buford Hwy. N.E., Atlanta; 321-6232

An undisputed leader in liquor sales, Green's can save you lots of green on all kinds of beverages. They must be doing something right, since they seem to be permanently packed; on a recent weeknight, people were pulling up to the Ponce store in every-thing from BMWs to bicycles. Inside, the store was bustling with shoppers snapping up bargains like twelve-can cases of Heineken beer for $9.99, and six-packs of Grolsch for $4.79; 750ml bottles of Cuervo tequila for $12.29, and the same size bottles of Jagermeister for $15.99; and more.

Green's has a large wine section as well, with quite a variety of well-known names and their own "discov-eries." You can pick up a newsletter, "Green's Grapevine," devoted to their latest acquisitions. Money-sav-ers recently included lesser-known domestics from Washington State, like Hedges 1991 Cabernet Merlot for $7.99 a bottle, and Trentadue non-vintage red table wine from Sonoma County, California, for $5.99. Of course, you can also find bargain brands, such as Beringer white zinfan-del, $4.49 for a 750ml bottle.

Inquire in the store about their ex-tra discounts on beer and wine by the case.

Habersham Winery
- Underground Atlanta, 122 Lower Alabama St., Atlanta; 533-WINE (9463)
- Roswell Mill, 85 Mill St., Building A, Roswell; 641-0160

Habersham specializes in wines pro-duced at its own vineyards in nearby Baldwin, Georgia. At their two stores, you can save money by buy-ing direct from the company; so you can afford these wines (many with special labeling for gift-giving pur-poses) more easily.

Cherokee rose, for example, sells at $7.99 for a 750ml bottle. Purchase it by the case, and the price goes down to $6.99. Granny's Sweet Red Grape Wine is also $7.99 a bottle, and also available with the case dis-count. And a 1990 Georgia chardon-nay is $12.99 a bottle, while a chablis is $7.99.

You can visit Habersham's Vine-yards in Baldwin, too, and see the whole operation. This tiny village is located about twenty miles north of Commerce, where you'll probably

---

MR. CHEAP'S PICKS
Liquor

✔ **Green's Package Stores**—The place is always packed. Must be some good prices here.

✔ **Tower Beer & Wine**—Great wine and beer values, especially if you're purchasing in quantity.

---

want to stop for more bargain hunt-ing! Give Habersham a call for more info, at (706) 778-9463.

Harry's Farmers Market
- 1180 Upper Hembree Rd., Alpharetta; 664-6300
- 2025 Satellite Point St. N.W., Duluth; 416-6900
- 70 Powers Ferry Rd. N.E., Marietta; 578-4400

See listing under "Food Stores: Gen-eral Markets."

Jax Beer & Wine
- 5901 Roswell Rd. N.E., Sandy Springs; 252-1443

Here are the facts, Jax: This store will certainly surprise you with its ex-cellent wine selection, and its liquor and beer prices are also hard to beat. The store is easily accessible from I-285.

Among the scores of different wines here, recent deals included Corvo red wine from Sicily, regularly $9.99, selling for $6.99, and Valdivi-eso cabernet sauvignon from Chile, same deal. Firestone chardonnay (no, it doesn't taste like a tire!) was re-duced from $12.99 to $9.99. Cabernet sauvignons by Clos du Bois or the Australian Black Opal brand were $7.99 each.

Carlo Rossi California Burgundy is only $9.48 for the jumbo four-liter bottle. And for real bargain prices, consider wines from less likely parts of the world. Avia chardonnay, imported from Slovenia, is only $2.99 a bottle.

Sake lovers will adore the $6.99 price tag on Gekkeikan; and you'll be toasting up a storm when you bring home Bollinger Special Cuvee Brut champagne (just $25.99), or Korbel Brut for $9.69.

Buying hard liquor here won't be hard on your budget, either. Grand Marnier is $28.99 for a 750ml bottle, Cointreau is $27.99, and Emmets Irish Cream Liqueur is $9.99 for that same size. Absolutely, you can pick up a bottle of Absolut vodka for $23.98 in the big 1.75 liter bottle. And, if you're having a big bash, don't forget Jose Cuervo margarita mix, only $3.99.

Jax has a mind-boggling beer selection, from six-packs of Bud Lite for $4.49 to a six-pack of Natural Light in bottles for $2.89. Lowenbrau is $7.69 for a twelve-pack. Other good prices were found on brands like Telluride beer from Colorado, Lone Star from Texas and many others.

Peachtree Road Liquor Store
* 1895 Peachtree Rd. (at Collier Road), Atlanta; 355-4990

This South Buckhead package store, located near Harry's In A Hurry, offers a wide selection of wine and liquor at good value prices.

For example, a three-liter jug of Gallo Chablis Blanc wine, was recently seen for just $7.99. Sutter Home white zinfandel from 1992 was selling for $4.59 a bottle. And a 1991 bottle of Robert Mondavi sauvignon blanc was $4.99 a bottle.

Seagram's wine coolers in several flavors are just $3.99 for a 4-pack. On a more celebratory note, a 750ml bottle of Korbel Brut Champagne was a decent $9.99.

Mr. C also found plenty of other liquor on the cheap, like a liter of Bombay Dry Sapphire gin for $19.99; Jack Daniel's in the 375ml size for $7.69; and the same size of Cuervo tequila for $7.49.

Beer bargains included a twelve-pack of Molson Golden or Molson

Light for $7.99, and a twelve-pack suitcase of Rolling Rock in bottles for $7.69.

Toco Hills Giant Package Store
* 2941-A North Druid Hills Rd. N.E., Atlanta; 320-1903

Giant store, giant savings, what more could you ask for? Head for the hills—Toco Hills, that is—for super buys on beer, wine, and liquor. The beer selection from around the world is impressive, and volume discounts are available—just ask.

Mr. C saw a six-pack of Newcastle Brown Ale in bottles for just $6.99, George Killian's Red for just $4.69 a six-pack, and a 34 ounce "minikeg" of Kronenbourg for just $2.99. Steinlager from New Zealand is only $2.49 for 25 ounces—talk about having a g'day, mate!

For wine drinkers, Beringer white zinfandel is $6.99 a bottle, and a 1991 Pouilly-Fuisse white burgundy (is that possible?) is just $9.99. Geikkeikan sake from Japan is $7.99 for a 750ml bottle.

Good heavens! Heaven Hill Kentucky bourbon is $8.49 for a liter, Crown Royal Canadian Whiskey is $21 for a 750ml bottle, and Southern Comfort is $10.29 for the same size. Liqueurs like Bailey's Irish Cream and Kahlua are reasonably priced, too.

For the big party, basics like Daily's Margarita mix ($5.49), and two-liter bottles of Canada Dry Ginger Ale ($1.29 each) will also save you big bucks.

Tower Beer & Wine Stores
* 223 Moreland Ave. S.E., Atlanta; 688-2774
* 2161 Piedmont Rd. N.E., Atlanta; 881-0902
* 3196 Bankhead Highway, N.W., Atlanta; 799-8685
* 5877 Buford Hwy., Doraville; 458-3272

You won't find any towering prices here, that's for sure. These stores sell a stupendous variety of wines, from California to France, Germany and Australia, along with an incredible selection of beers and hard liquors—all at warehouse prices, but without the warehouse feel.

In addition to its regular prices, Tower has a quantity discount policy on wines. All bottles with a price ending in "9" ($7.99, $4.99, etc.) are an extra five percent off if you buy six bottles, and ten percent off if you buy twelve or more bottles. That means you can do very well on Riunite Blush Bianco, priced at $4.79 for 750ml; a bottle of Black Silk from Australia for $6.99; or a bottle of Veuve du Vernay Blanc de Blancs French sparkling wine, just $5.49. The four-liter jug of Carlo Rossi California Chablis is $9.98 and not subject to this volume-purchasing offer, but is a bargain enough in itself.

Beer drinkers will be impressed with the $7.49 price on a twelve-pack suitcase of Bud Lite or Bud Dry in bottles, or the $14.29 price tag on a case of Bud cans. Even fancier specialty brands are reasonably priced, like Sam Adams Double Bock at $6.29 for a six-pack.

For mixed drinks, how about a 375ml bottle of Galliano for $14.69, or 750ml of Chambord for $19.99? A one-liter bottle of Appleton Jamaican rum is just $13.99, so hey mon, why not stock up on some for your next party. Other deals Mr. C saw include a 1.75 liter bottle of Finlandia vodka for $17.97, and the same size bottle of Jack Daniel's for $24.95. Along with Green's Liquors, Tower came out on top in a recent Creative Loafing readers poll. Drop in yourself, and you'll see why.

Your DeKalb Farmer's Market

- 3000 Ponce de Leon Ave., Decatur; 377-6400

See listing under "Food Stores: General Markets."

LUGGAGE

Bentley's Luggage & Gifts

- Phipps Plaza, 3500 Peachtree Rd. N.E., Suite E-28, Atlanta; 841-6247
- Market Square at DeKalb, 2050 Lawrenceville Hwy., Decatur; 633-9323
- Gwinnett Place Mall, Duluth; 497-8447
- Town Center at Cobb, Kennesaw; 422-9406
- Shannon Mall, Union City; 969-0970

You sure don't have to drive a Bentley to afford luggage here. Yes, the store is in Phipps Plaza, but it really does offer good discounts on fine brands like French, Tumi, Boyt, and Delsey.

A bit of an old-fashioned emporium, Bentley's is definitely male-oriented, and geared toward the corporate customer. A man's leather briefcase with combination lock, made by Mark Phillip, was recently seen discounted from $200 to $159. Mr. C also saw an Eiffel Travelpro rollaboard suitcase reduced from $200 to $149, and an Atlas double combination attaché case for $200 off, at $650.

There are some items for the ladies, such as a more feminine-styled briefcase with three big inner compartments and a top zipper. List priced at $225, it sells here for $140. You'll also find luggage suitable for the whole family here, like a Hartmann leather-trim suitcase marked down from $350 to $210, and a Hartmann garment bag, selling for $198 (retail price, $330).

As these places tend to do, Bentley's also stocks fine-maker pens by Parker, Cross, and the like; as well as other travel necessities like pill cases and shaving kits, all at competitive prices.

Leather & Luggage Depot

- 1151 Chattahoochee Ave. N.W., Atlanta; 351-7410

This one-year-old shop is filled with

MR. CHEAP'S PICKS
Luggage

✔ **Bentley's Luggage &
Gifts**—Even the Buckhead
branch of this local chain offers
special bargains on travel bags
and briefcases.

---

a wide variety of inexpensive luggage. The store does not carry big-
name brands, but rather focuses on
budget brands which are good values,
if not likely to become heirlooms.
Hey, you gotta have a niche, y'know?

What they do have, they sell at
about half the retail prices—the same
prices, in fact, as you'd get at the Apparel Mart, if you could shop in that
wholesale-only center. You can get an
entire five-piece ensemble of suitcases, overnighter and garment bag
for as little as $65. Most sets, though,
are in the $100 to $185 range, and
are made of more durable materials.
Speaking of which, have you seen
those brightly colored, hard-plastic
suitcases by Echolac? They're here,
ergonomically designed to roll easily
even through Hartsfield, and reduced
from a list price of $180 to just $99.
Get 'em in eye-catching blue, yellow,
and red.

Mr. C did find one well-known
name here, John Weitz. His "Pea-
cock" garment bag was on sale from
$160 down to $60. You'll find some
knapsacks here too, including a Mal-
lard leather backpack for $12.90. And
L&L has a good selection of leather
and synthetic briefcases. These range
in price from $60 to $300, with most
under $100.

The other part of the store's name
refers to its limited, but funky, collec-

tion of leather clothing for men and
women—from belts to jackets and
pants. Open Fridays and Saturdays
from 10 a.m. to 6 p.m., and Sundays
from 12-5.

Tuesday Morning
- 3165 Peachtree Rd. N.E., Atlanta;
  233-6526
- 3250 Satellite Blvd., Duluth;
  476-0522
- 4502 Chamblee-Dunwoody Rd.,
  Dunwoody; 457-3565
- 700 Sandy Plains Rd. N.E.,
  Marietta; 428-1536
- 1115 Morrow Industrial Blvd.,
  Morrow; 961-0707
- 1231 Alpharetta St., Roswell;
  640-8146
- 2512 Spring Rd. S.E., Smyrna;
  435-6678

And other suburban locations

We all know how much better Tuesday mornings are, compared to Mondays. TM's bargains will make you
feel that much better any day, with
discounts on everything from clothes
to party supplies to toys to jewelry to
luggage.

Among the well-priced travel gear
Mr. C found on a recent visit, there
were Samsonite duffel bags—available in an assortment of neutral colors—reduced from $90 to $40. A
Samsonite soft-sider suitcase was reduced from $220 to $80, while a
smaller, wheeled suitcase was
marked down from $150 to $70.

Leisure Luggage brand carry-on
tote bags, listed at $90 retail, were
just $30 here; and a Pierre Cardin
carry bag sells for $90—half its origi-
nal retail price. Garment bags are
also well-stocked, with brands like
Ascot and Samsonite, starting as low
as $40. All sell for at least half of
their retail prices.

If it's Tuesday, this must be Belgium. If it's Tuesday Morning, this
must be the way to travel there. All
stores are open seven days a week.

MUSICAL INSTRUMENTS

Here's another category in which you can save money by "going used"—though many instruments actually increase in value as they age. Often, a top-quality used instrument which can repaired is a better investment than a cheaper, newer version. It will sound better and last longer.

Baldwin Factory Showrooms
- Gwinnett Place, 2100 Pleasant Hill Rd., Duluth; 476-7481
- Family Music Center, 1825 Cobb Pkwy. S.E., Marietta; 952-7982

Got a grand notion to get yourself a fancy piano? Baldwin grand pianos, one of the biggest names in the business, are priced under $8,000 at these direct-to-you factory stores. May not exactly sound cheap, but you can save some money here. The store is open from 10:00 a.m. to 10:00 p.m. on weekdays and Saturdays, and from 1:00 p.m. to 5:30 p.m. Sundays.

Cooper Music Superstore
- 1610 N.E. Expressway Access Road N.E., Atlanta; 329-1663

This is *the* place for pianos, and it's hard to miss—just look for the huge store with the big piano sticking up into the air. Some of their Steinways are of vintage or heirloom quality (yep—way out of Mr. C's budget); but new and restored pianos, from brands like Kawai, Mason & Hamlin, Weber, Kohler & Campbell, Kimball, and Knabe, plus Yamaha and Baldwin, are on sale at reductions that will be music to your ears. Area churches often come here to purchase budget-priced organs; the store sells everything from upright acoustic pianos to digital keyboards.

The company didn't want Mr. C listing prices in this book, but if you've got an instrument to trade in, or if you're looking to buy, you can call them for a price quote.

The store is open from Monday through Saturday from 10 a.m. to 5 p.m. (Mondays until 8 p.m.), and Sunday from 1-5.

Emile Baran Instruments, Inc.
- 117 Clairmont Ave., Decatur; 377-3419

This is where schoolchildren from over fifty school systems in the area buy and trade in their instruments. That means smaller sizes along with smaller prices. There are lots of half-size and three-quarter-size violins, with the appropriate bows; plus violas, basses, cellos, and lutes; and almost any other common instrument, too. As owner Emile Baran told Mr. C, they sell "Just about anything a high school band or orchestra uses". The stock goes on to include piccolos, flutes, French horns, tubas, clarinets, drums, and trombones, plus tuning instruments.

Parents shop here when they don't want to buy their growing children a brand-new instrument, only to need a new one the next season. Since about fifty percent of this store's business is done in the month of September, you'll probably find good specials during the off-months, when business is a bit slower.

Baran's sells about 750 string instruments a year. Suzuki violins are available in 1/10 to full size, Germans from 1/4 to full, and cellos from 1/4 and up.

Mr. Baran told Mr. C that a child's used German violin or viola would go for $475 or so, and a high-quality Gibson acoustic guitar is just $269. Instruments are obtained from all over the country, and vary in quality and price; but they must all match the company's standards before being taken in. You can also rent instruments here, or have them repaired. The store is staffed by former band

and orchestra directors who know their stuff and really care about the kids.

Emile Baran's is open from 9:30 a.m.to 5:30 p.m. weekdays, and from 10 a.m. to 5 p.m. Saturdays.

England Piano & Organ Warehouse Showrooms
- 359 Pike St., Gwinnett; 963-5159
- 1873 Cobb Pkwy., Marietta; 984-1124

This store is making noise (pun intended) in the Atlanta area for offering some of the lowest prices on pianos around, guaranteed in writing. New, used, and display models are all offered; Mr. C does stress that you carefully check out the floor display models for scratches and the like, though these don't always affect the sound of the instrument.

The Warehouse stocks Yamaha, Kimball, Kawai, Wurlitzer, Roland, Baldwin, and Young Chang pianos, organs, and digital pianos. Some recent sales included grand pianos priced under $5,000, digitals under $700, and console pianos under $2,300.

The store is open seven days a week: Monday through Saturday from 10 a.m. to 6 p.m., and Sunday from 1 p.m. to 6 p.m.

Famous Bargain Music
- The Balconies Shopping Center, 290 Hilderbrand Dr., Sandy Springs; 252-1427

This is where Dunwoody's own Black Crowes used to shop—before they got rich and famous, that is. New and used guitars and even banjos are stocked, along with used amplifiers and speakers. The professional staff gives honest information about what instruments and equipment would be best for you; parents of budding Jimi Hendrixes can feel welcome shopping here, even if they know little about these instruments themselves.

Bently GTR acoustic guitars, list priced at $175, sell for $139 here. The Ovation Judas guitar is $300; a Goya acoustic, listed at $200, was recently seen for just $100 (thanks to

an accidental double-order), and a Jackson Soloist six-string electric, listed at $500, was $399. A used Alvarez left the shop in the blink of an eye for $199, and two teens enjoyed trying out a used Peavy T-40 bass, priced right at $299.

A used Marshall Model 710 Series 9000 amp was selling for just $200, while a Crate GX-15 amp was a mere $100, complete with a five-year warranty (and a two-year warranty on the speakers). Mr. C also found a Peavy 20-watt "Audition Plus" amp, a with 12" speaker—perfect for newer players—selling for a decent $150.

Get a famous bargain for yourself, anytime from 10 a.m. to 7 p.m. on weekdays, and from 10-6 on Saturdays.

Galaxy Music Center
- 6167 Memorial Dr., Stone Mountain; 879-8381

Galaxy lays claim to being the largest used music equipment dealer in town, and Mr. C would be hard-pressed to debate the point. A large volume of sales activity enables this place to sell drum sets for as little as $99, and acoustic guitars from a mere $49. Now, *that's* cheap!

Galaxy also carries bargain-priced band instruments, like flutes and clarinets, and the occasional French horn; plus string instruments from violins to mandolins to banjos. In fact, they always have 700 to 800 guitars in stock *alone*. And, though they no longer give lessons, they do have a big selection of music books, too.

They really do seem to have everything under at least one sun here. As an employee told Mr. C, "We carry every imaginable instrument known to man." The store's open Mondays through Fridays from 10 a.m. to 7 p.m., and Saturdays 10 a.m. to 6 p.m.

Midtown Music
- 3326 North Druid Hills Rd., Decatur; 325-0515

Lots of local bands trust Midtown for their acoustic and electric guitar needs, as well as for amps. The occasional used drum set shows up from time to time, but guitars are the real name of the game here. There are about 100 new Alvarez electrics and 150 new acoustics in stock at any given time.

The store's low overhead helps keep prices low too (it's in a tiny house-like building along a residential stretch of North Druid Hills Road). The staff knows what's up, too. They can recommend just the right used Gibson, Martin, or Guild guitar for your needs. New Alvarez models, for the serious (and rich!) musician, are also available. Vintage guitars, like the $2,700 Fender Stratocaster from the 60s, can be found here too, but they ain't gonna be cheap.

Mr. C saw a Roland synthesizer for $375, a used Applause six-string guitar for just $195, and a used 50-watt Marshall amp for $475 (Mr. C was told that it would cost up to $800 if new). A crate amp, worth $500 brand new, was seen just $345 and in incredible shape.

A 1970s Rickenbacker bass was priced at $500 for you collectors, but bargain-hunters would be wiser to keep their eyes open for used Gibson and Martins, priced around $150. The turnover is high on these items, so frequent visits (or perhaps bribes to the staff!) are a good idea.

The occasional violin also appears here; there were four used ones in stock during Mr. C's visit, with prices from $100 and up for the German models.

Midtown is open Mondays through Saturdays, from 10 a.m. to 6 p.m.

The Music Trader
• 3964 Lawrenceville Hwy., Tucker; 934-7919

The Music Trader deals only in used instruments and equipment, from sound systems to keyboards, basses, electric, and acoustic guitars, and drum sets. The stock is ever-changing, and always worth a look.

The store is open from 10 a.m. to 6 p.m., Mondays through Saturdays.

MR. CHEAP'S PICKS
Musical Instruments

✔ **Emile Baran**—From big-band brass instruments to the house specialty—violins—you can save with previously-owned music makers here.

✔ **Rhythm City**—Good discounts on a wide range of guitars, keyboards, and the electronics to wail on them with.

Rhythm City
• 1485 Northeast Expressway Access Rd. N.E., Atlanta; 320-7253

This vast store just off I-85 almost seems to be too successful for its own good (we all know that can't happen). Even though Mr. C dropped in late in the afternoon on a weekday, the place was packed; shoppers were waiting for any of a dozen salesmen to become available; and the phone never stopped ringing. They do such a booming business here that the "phone" is in fact a switchboard, with a receptionist who answers each line, then pages the staff: "Guitars, line four, long distance..."

In other words, if it's this hard to shop here, it *must* be good. And it is. There are over 5,000 guitars in stock here, both new and used. Prices start as low as $150 for some of the used models; new axes are significantly discounted, too. Mr. C noted a Gibson electric with a list price of $1,000 selling here for $650, and a Fender "Jazz Bass" reduced from $1,099 to a groovy $675. New Washburn acoustics begin at $225. Among the various types of drum kits, there was a Pearl "Export Pro" set, selling for almost half-price at $695.

In a smaller side room, you can try out dozens of digital keyboard units, like a Roland JW50 (with a 16-track sequencer on board) marked down from a list price of $2,300 to just $1,595. Still a lot, yes, but better. Computers, for MIDI interfacing, are available here too. In another side room, much more private, RC shows off its collection of simulated electronic baby grand pianos. Did you know that Hyundai makes more than just cars? Mr. C heard one of their five-foot grand pianos, sounding for all the world like the real live thing. It was priced at $6,000, a savings of $3,000 off retail.

All the way to the back, there's yet another private room. This one's an *auditorium*, no less. Presumably, rock bands can test out entire packages of instruments, amps, and related concert gear in this "hall." Rhythm City really is a full service store.

They also sell monitors, amps,

mixers, four-track tape recorders, PA equipment, and—yes—karaoke machines (shudder). Needless to say, you can also get all the cases, strings, sticks, tapes, and other accessories you could possibly want. You can save money by purchasing some of these in quantity; a twelve-pack of drumsticks, for instance, was selling for $58; if you bought six pair individually, they would have cost $72.

About the only thing in short supply here are band instruments, although they make an effort with a few saxes, flutes and trumpets. But it really is more of a rock 'n roll store. And, busy as they are, the salespeople really are helpful—once you get one.

Rhythm City is open six days a week, into the early evening.

PARTY SUPPLIES

In addition to the stores listed below, don't forget to check out the liquidation stores listed in the "Department Stores" chapter: Big Lots, MacFrugal's, and the like, as well as just about any "dollar" store you come across.

Card & Party Super Store
- Loehmann's Plaza, 2480 Briarcliff Rd. at North Druid Hills Rd., Atlanta; 315-1940
- Mall Corners, 3616 Satellite Blvd., Duluth; 476-4450

For super savings on greeting cards, party decorations and plastic tableware, head to the Super Store. Birthday, seasonal, and general greeting cards are always sold at 50% off the marked price here—so now you have no excuse not to write!

The staff here knows their stuff. If you haven't the foggiest notion what you need for your bash, just ask. Mr. C found many bargains worth celebrating, like a giant plastic table cover for $1.99, huge latex balloons for 79¢ each, and lawn placards for $3 which announce your party to all who drive by.

Wrapping paper, in a zillion styles,

is as little as 33¢ a foot. A five-pack of personalized, rainbow-painted pencils costs $2.25, and those big paper honeycomb decorations, the kind that fold up flat, are $3.83. You can get a package of 250 three-ply cocktail napkins—perhaps all you'll ever need—in bright colors for $7.25; and 500 feet of crepe paper is $4.50. And, for a truly "out of this world" party, how about a glow-in-the-dark planet Earth for $6?

The Card & Party Super Store is open seven days a week.

In Any Event...
- Roswell-Wieuca Shopping Center, 4413 Roswell Road, N.E., Atlanta; 256-4033

This paper and party supply shop is tiny, compared to other stores Mr. C found, but it's jam-packed with bargains.

Contempo brand plastic plates, in bold colors and pastels, are $2.39 for a pack of ten. Plastic table covers go for $2.35 a pop, and big plastic salad servers are just 50¢ each. Sturdy ten-ounce tumblers by Beverage Ware are $1.89 each; a dozen plastic utensils by Oak Hill, available in bright colors, are $1.00; and fifty dinner napkins are $3.89.

A package of ten plates decorated with the University of Georgia Bulldog are $2.99. Plastic bowls are 30¢ each. To liven up the house, try 500 feet of crepe paper streamers, available in a wide assortment of colors, for $4.25.

In the gift wrapping section, a five foot roll of wrapping paper is $1.79, and 250 yards of colored ribbon are $3.75.

In Any Event... will keep you well supplied for any children's bash, with tons of cute party favors by Unique. Most sell under $2, like a four-pack of big chalk sticks, or a six-pack of plastic bracelets. Those noisemakers used New Year's Eve are 39¢ each, as are metal horns decorated with fun confetti patterns.

Don't miss the store's gag and joke section. Some of the tricks Mr. C found were SALT water taffy, with an emphasis on the salt, for $1.49; plus fake beer, sneezing powder, and trick candies that turn your mouth blue—all available for under two bucks.

Party City
- Sandy Springs Crossing Shopping Center, 6690 Roswell Rd., Sandy Springs; 303-8100
- Killian Hill Merchants Shopping Center, 4051 Highway 78, Gwinnett; 979-0700

Wherever your city may be, Party City is worth the trip when you're getting ready for a big bash. This metropolis-sized store is set up warehouse style, with floor-to-ceiling displays, but without the cold warehouse feel. And it's prices are amazing.

Be sure to pick up a shopping checklist when you first walk in—a

MR. CHEAP'S PICKS
Party Supplies

✔ **Party City**—If you can't find what you want in this metropolis-sized store, give up! Significant savings on all your celebratory supplies.

✔ **Card & Party Super Store**—You just can't beat their 50% everyday discount on greeting cards.

breakthrough idea. There are lists for wedding receptions and showers, children's birthday parties, retirement parties, and seasonal events; the lists are arranged by aisle, making shopping here a breeze.

Newlyweds can put more money toward their honeymoon by shopping here for wedding decorations and accessories. Champagne glasses, which can be engraved, are $3.99 and up. Wedding cake toppers start at $14.99, and a "Wedding Treasure Masters" set gives you glasses, a cake server and plate, garter belt, and guest book, all for $42.99.

Basic party supplies are incredibly well-stocked here. A box of a dozen thank-you notes is $1.99. A pack of eight shower invitations, listed at $2.95, sell for $1.50. A nine-foot "Happy Birthday" banner, covered with metallic glitter, is $4.99. You can get fancy napkins and a matching tablecloth at good prices, or save even more with the store's own brand, available in an impressive array of brights, darks, and pastel shades.

Need some gift wrap? A hundred square feet of wrapping paper by the Gift Wrap Company is $7.99. Taper candles are 69¢ each, and scented votive candles are 59¢ each. And, to make sure your party packs a punch, an eight-quart plastic punch bowl with server is just $5.99 at the City.

Bargains on kid stuff include a Big Bird-shaped cake pan for $9.77, two-foot balloons for $9.99, an eight-pack of party blowouts for $3.29 (list $3.85), and an eight-pack of "Party Loot" bags for $1.49. A tissue paper clown, to be used as a table center-piece, is $1.88. Napkins and paper plates come decorated with a variety of characters, like Thomas the Tank Engine, the Little Mermaid, Beauty and the Beast, Snow White, 101 Dalmatians, and Cinderella. Most are priced at $1.59 for a set of sixteen.

Super-embarrassing cardboard placards ("Look Who's Forty!" (Fifty!, Sixty!, etc.) are just 88¢, while a huge "Look Who's 30!" button is $2.97. And an "Over The Hill" talking doormat is $9.99. Better hope the guest of honor has a good sense of humor.

Party Station
- 5290 Roswell Rd., Sandy Springs; (404) 255-9477

Hop on board for savings at the Party Station! This store sells tons of decorations you can use to really set a theme for your party. There are more wedding supplies in stores like Party City, but try the Station for offbeat fun.

Some of the theme-oriented decorations here include Chinese lanterns for $5.99 each, plus hand-held Chinese folding fans for 69¢ each. Get a six-foot tall cardboard palm tree for $5, plastic leis for 25¢ each, with a realistic adult-sized raffia hula skirt for $7.99, and who needs an expensive trip to Hawaii? Piñatas, in parrot, donkey, and even cruise ship designs, start at $9.99.

To handle all the munchies, 50 forks by Gala are $3.99, plastic table covers in over a dozen bold shades are $3.19 each, and nine-ounce sturdy plastic cups by Gala are $2.49 for 20. Buying in volume will save you bundles here: fifty 12-ounce Gala cups are only $3.79, and 50 12-ounce bowls are $2.49.

Get a cardboard juke box for $2.99. Bandannas for playing "Pin the Tail on the Donkey" or those piñata games, are $1.49 each. A spray can of Party String is $2.99, and bags of multicolored glitter are $2.69 each. Gift-wrapping ribbon is $3.99 for a huge 550-yard roll, and 500 feet of C.A. Reed brand streamers are $3.99. For the joker in all of us, a rubber chicken is $7.99.

Party Warehouse
- 3330 Piedmont Rd. N.E., Atlanta; 231-4111

Yes, believe it or not, Mr. Cheap finds more savings in Buckhead.

This Warehouse isn't exactly done up in the kind of warehouse style that Mr. C usually sees (it's carpeted, for example), but it sure is packed to the ceiling with great, fun and unusual party supplies at unusual savings for this part of town.

Mr. C found reusable paper table-cloths, reinforced with plastic, in several pastel and bright shades for $2.79 each. Plastic dishes in a variety of shell shapes, perfect for chips and dips, are just 59¢ to 95¢ each, while a 20-pack of dinner napkins in dozens of colors are $2.49 each. And for dressing up the table, how about 12 gold foil doilies by Paper Art for $1.90, or two dozen plastic utensils for $2.29.

Crepe paper by C.A. Reed is just $3.45 for 500 feet; a big jar of glitter by Highlander is $8.50; and, for those Hawaiian-themed parties, a hula skirt is $4.98. There's also a super selection of piñatas, in seasonal and classical Mexican designs, starting at about $10. For wedding showers and receptions, paper wedding bells are just $1.99 each.

Wrap your gifts in glitzy sheets of metallic mylar paper, $1.75 each, or tissue paper for 15¢ a sheet. A handy ribbon curler for $1.25 will make your wrapping look truly professional.

This store wins big points for its great selection of party favors for the kiddies. Puffy stickers are just 10¢ each, a four-pack of crayons are 20¢ each, and little erasers, dice, plastic magnifying glasses, and those obnoxious little New Year's Eve party pop-pers are all 20¢ each or less.

The store is closed on Sundays.

Winn Dixie
Locations throughout Atlanta
Unless you already shop at one of the
South's biggest supermarket chains,
you may not be aware that Winn
Dixie sells greeting cards at 40% off
the printed price every day. The size
of the card aisle varies from one store
to another, but there's always at least
a decent selection of cards for all occasions—birthdays, holidays, thank
yous, etc.

The store actually carries only one

line, the Gibson brand; but they make
as much of a variety as any other
company, whether you want your
message to be silly, sentimental, or
just plain straight. There are also
cards with famous figures on the
front, from Mickey Mouse and the
Little Mermaid to characters from
television shows like "Designing
Women." Since Winn Dixies are everywhere, this is a great little tip to
store away for that time when you're
late for the party and need to grab a
card on the way.

PET SUPPLIES

These are some of the best places to buy pet foods and supplies
around the metro area. Mr. C also suggests that you check out some of
the "dollar" stores (see listings under "Discount Department Stores"),
since many of them sell reduced-price canned food, and sometimes even
leashes, collars, and doggie and kitty toys.

The Aviarium
- Market Square at North DeKalb,
  2050 Lawrenceville Hwy.,
  Decatur; 634-5930

The Aviarium, as its pedigreed name
hints at, specializes in birds and fish,
plus everything you'll need for their
care; though they do carry a variety
of products for other types of animals, too. It's located in the Marketsquare at North DeKalb.

Here, a chrome bird cage by Hoei,
with a retail price of $53.99, sells for
$42.99. A two pound bag of L/M saf-
flower seed for hookbill birds is
$2.39. Perfect-A-Scene, the plastic-
coated photography which presumably tricks pet fish into thinking that
they're back in the ocean, is $1 a
foot. Tetra-Min Flake Food costs
$2.99 for the 20-gram canister.

The Aviarium also carries some
dog and cat supplies, like 69¢ cans of
Iams cat food, four-pound bags of
Iams Dog Biscuits for $5.19, and six
pounds of Nutro Max Cat Lite cat for
$10.49. For gerbils, hamsters and

guinea pigs, a whopping three bush-
els of L/M Animal Farms brand red
cedar bedding is a cozy deal at
$10.99.

Cheshire Pet Supply
- 2855 North Druid Hills Rd. N.E.,
  Atlanta; 325-4945
- 501 Roberts Court, Kennesaw;
  499-0861
- Providence Square Shopping
  Center, 4101 Roswell Rd.,
  Marietta; 565-5779
- 6595A Roswell Rd., Sandy
  Springs; 256-9166
- 5236 Highway 78, Stone
  Mountain; 498-9760
- 1929 Mountain Industrial Blvd.,
  Tucker; 934-7632

You can't miss Cheshire Pet Supply—
look for the giant cat painted on the
building. CPS boasts that it has the
largest selection of discount pet supplies in the Southeast—and even the
ol' Cheshire Cat would find nothing
to smirk at about this.

You'll probably spot a Spot or two
while shopping here, since pets are al-

ways welcome with their owners (beware, those out there with allergies). Mr. C saw no less than three cats and a golden retriever while visiting the Toco Hills store. CPS doesn't actually sell any pets, except for tiny animals like gerbils and hamsters, though—they mostly deal in pet supplies.

Your own grinning tabby will love prowling around in a "Carpeted Cat Condo" by Doskocil, for just $19.90. Does this double as cheap housing? Add Doskocil's big self-feeder for $11. Speaking of which, Whiskas cat food in the 5.5-ounce can is 39¢, and Iams cat food is 72¢ each six-ounce can, or $17.20 for a case of 24 cans. And an 18-pound bag of Luv My Cat flushable cat litter is just $3.90.

You'll bark for joy when you see the bargains here on dog food. Hill's Science Diet for senior dogs is $6.85 for the five-pound bag, Kal-Kan Pedigree food is 75¢ a can, and 14-ounce cans of Cycle are 67¢ a can. Forty pounds of Purina Puppy Chow are just $20.55.

Canary seed may be for the birds, but these prices aren't—two pounds of Vita-Vittles Gold Canary bird food is $2.15, and five ounces of Sun Seed bird treat is $2.30. For your outdoor feathery visitors, wooden bird nests made by Hope Farms are $17 and up.

You can also find food for less-common pets here, like Kellogg's Bunny Brunch rabbit pellets, $2 for five pounds. Zoo Menu iguana food is $2.25 for six ounces. Kay-Tee guinea pig food is available in bulk for 30¢ a scoop, and FortiHamster food is 35¢ a scoop, while Cockatiel & Parrot mix is 48¢ a scoop. Plus tanks, hutches, pens, and domiciles for all these little creatures.

Cheshire Pet Supply delivers orders, Monday through Saturday only. The store is open daily except Sunday at 10 a.m., and is open until 7 p.m. Monday through Thursday, until 8 p.m. Friday, and until 6 p.m. Saturday. Sunday hours are from noon to 5:30 p.m.

Market Grocery at Atlanta State Farmer's Market
- 16 Forest Pkwy., Forest Park; 366-6910

See listing under "Food Stores: General Markets."

Pedigree's Pet Care
- 1365 Clairmont Rd., Decatur; 634-7020
- 2936 Canton Rd. N.E., Marietta; 426-7015

For great buys on food, general pet and grooming supplies, and especially doggie beds, take a trip to Pedigree. The Decatur store is right near Athens Pizza, not far from the Emory University campus.

Pedigree's is involved with the manufacturing of Canine Cushions, a brand of those cedar-filled beds for dogs. Direct-from-the-manufacturer selling lets the store charge ridiculously low prices, considering the quality of the beds. Prices, in sizes for poodles all the way up to Old English Sheepdogs, range from just $19 to $59. That's about half as much as you'd pay at other pet stores, or through some fancy mail order catalog.

Other bargains include discounts on Iams cat and dog food, as well as deals on necessities like Ponderosa pine shavings, just $2.19 for 100 cubic centimeters. Pedigree's has good prices on small pets themselves, like finches for $9.99, parakeets for $11.99, gerbils and hamsters for just $3.99 each, and black Tetra fish for just $1.59 each.

The Pet Set
- Loehmann's Executive Plaza, 2480 Briarcliff Rd. N.E., Atlanta; 633-8755

You thought Loehmann's was only for us? This store, close by in Loehmann's Plaza, is where wealthy Atlantans come for costumes to dress their dogs and cats for nights on the town—really. Mr. C isn't kidding, although he almost wishes he were.

However, Pet Set's prices for basics like cat litter and pet food aren't as outrageous as you might expect. A four-pound bag of Iams kitten food is

just $7.50. The store also offers regu-
lar patrons a discount program: When
you buy ten bags, you'll get one free.

Twelve pounds of Ever Clean cat
litter are just $9.99, and Science Diet
dog food in the "small bite" variety is
$20.92 for a twenty-pound bag. Since
this store is as much for the elite set
as the pet set, they offer a wealth of
grooming services as well; from
whirlpool baths to hot oil coat treatments to "complete makeovers."
Come to mama, Poopsie.

Petsmart

- 3803 Venture Dr., Duluth; 813-8400
- 860 Cobb Place Blvd., Kennesaw;
  424-5226
- 2150 Paxton Dr., Stone Mountain;
  985-0469
- 4023 Lavista Rd., Tucker;
  414-5126

You can really save big on pet food
at this big, bright "superstore" chain
in the suburbs. A gigantic forty-
pound bag of Purina Hi-Pro Dog
Food is $12.99 here, and Alpo Beef
Dinner is $11.97 for a fifty-pound
bag. Choo Hooves treats are 78¢
each, while Alpo, Cycle, Pedigree or
Grand Gourmet dog foods are all just
38¢ a can. Skippy premium dog food
was on a special sale recently, four
cans for $1.

Other bargains include Litterguard
cat litter at just 69¢ for a ten-pound
bag; a ten-gallon aquarium with hood
for $17.99; and Tetra Min fish food
flakes, $3.95 for the 1.85 ounce box.

Petsmart also offers free pet nail
trims every day, along with other
grooming services at reasonable
prices. All stores are open Mondays
through Saturdays from 9 a.m. to 9
p.m., and Sundays from 10 a.m. to 6
p.m.

Petstuff

- Parkaire Landing, 4880 Lower
  Roswell Rd., East Cobb/Marietta;
  509-7270
- Parkside Shopping Center, 5920
  Roswell Rd., Sandy Springs;
  256-4580
- Windy Hill Plaza, 2108 Cobb
  Pkwy. SE, Smyrna; 988-0811

MR. CHEAP'S PICKS
Pet Supplies

✔ **Cheshire Pet Supply**—You'll
be madly grinning, too, when
you see how much you can
save here.

✔ **Petsmart**—The superstore
approach to animals, their care,
and feeding.

- Stone Mountain Square, 5370
  Highway 78, Stone Mountain;
  469-4677

Petstuff is headquartered in Atlanta,
which helps guarantee that its prices
stay nice and low. So, whatever you
may pick up here for your dog, cat,
bird or fish, you can bet that it's a
good deal.

Rover can tuck into a 40-pound
bag of Hill's Science Diet food for
$18.39, four pounds of Milk Bones
for $3.78, and Cycle dog food in 13
ounce cans for 40¢ each. Eukanuba
Adult dog food is priced at $27 for a
40-pound bag, and a 25-pound bag of
Come 'N Get It food is just $7.89.
Accessories include medium-sized
Dogloo cedar beds for $22.99, and a
three-foot long dog carrying crate for
$100.

For felines, 9-Lives and Friskies
cat food is just 14¢ for a 5.5 ounce
can. Iams cat food is $17.45 for a 20-
pound bag, and Fresh Step cat litter
is $6.69 for a 21-pound bag.

And don't forget our feathered
friends. Nutrition Plus bird food for
cockatiels is $4.79, and $5.49 for par-
rots. You'll find "8 in 1" cuttlebones
for $1.49, and Booda Byrdy perches
at $3.99 for small birds and $6.99 for
large ones. Mixed seed bells are just
99¢, and an attractive cedar outdoor
bird feeder was seen for $11.99.

Petstuff also offers obedience training programs, and even a portrait stu-

dio! The stores are open weekdays from 9 a.m. to 9 p.m., Saturdays from 8 a.m. to 9 p.m., and Sundays from 10 a.m. to 6 p.m.

SEWING AND FABRICS

Ashby Discount Sewing Center
- 107 Broad St. S.W., Atlanta; 688-7148

This family-operated store has been at the same location for an amazing 53 years. Expect to find great bargains on used brands like White, Viking, Pfaff, Singer, and Baby Lock. All of the used models are obtained through trade-ins, which have been carefully checked out before being accepted.

According to the experts here, machines manufactured in Japan are better-made than those from Thailand, two of the main suppliers of equipment; Mr. C suggests that you keep this in mind when you shop, and if you're interested in a particular machine, don't be afraid to inquire.

Ashby keeps about 125 machines in stock at any given time, so you'll always have a good selection from which to choose—including regular pedal-controlled machines and even backstitch machines. Mr. C was asked not to list specific prices, since the stock is ever-changing; but he can tell you that used Singer sewing machines generally start as low as $99, depending on their quality and degree of wear and tear.

You can get good deals on new machines here as well; Ashby makes purchases in high volume, allowing them to offer discounts of up to 25% off suggested retail prices. Guess you could say that they've got bargains all sewn up.

Cloth World
- 1395 Roswell Rd., Marietta; 973-3220
- 10711 Alpharetta Hwy., Roswell; 992-7575
- 5861 Memorial Dr., Stone Mountain; 294-5224

And other suburban locations

Get into vogue at Cloth World (as in Vogue patterns, that is) as well as those by New Look, McCall's, Simplicity, and Butterick, which are always sold at 50% off retail here.

Other bargains may include *faux* suede material selling for just $4 a yard, while similar deals can be found on satin (as low as $2 a yard), Waverly drapery prints ($10 a yard), and calicos ($5 yard). Velour, great for making bathrobes, regularly sells for a low $4 per yard; but it's occasionally on special sale for as low as $1.75. Durable corduroy, in a rainbow of solid shades, sells for an affordable $4 a yard, too. And you'll like CW's low prices on notions like thread (five spools for just $1) and high-quality Fiskars scissors ($11 a pair—seen for up to $15 elsewhere).

The stores are open from 9 a.m. to 9 p.m., Monday through Friday, from 9 a.m. to 6 p.m. Saturday, and from noon to 5 p.m. Sunday.

Designer Fabrics, Inc.
- 741 Miami Circle N.E., Atlanta; 233-1725

In the spring of '93, this 26-year-old wholesale business opened its doors to the public, selling closeouts in designer fabrics at 60% to 80% off retail. Now, you can buy material for your home projects, or select patterns to be used on furniture made by this company—getting you brand-new upholstered furniture at near-wholesale prices.

The fabric area of the store has remnants that actually start as low as $1 a yard—and they're nice materials! Sizes vary, but many have at least a few yards. Other closeouts include designs which retailed for $20-$40, now selling for as low as $4 a yard, in a good variety of solids and prints, in natural and synthetic fibers.

Another room is filled with current styles, all competitively priced; designer patterns from Waverly, P. Kaufman, Royal Doulton and others start from $9.95.

The store is open from 9:30 a.m. to 6 p.m. weekdays; Saturdays from 10-5; closed Sundays.

Discount Fabric Center
- 3145 Piedmont Rd. N.E., Atlanta; 231-8685
- 1899 Stewart Ave., S.W., Atlanta; 758-6196
- 3451 Memorial Dr., Decatur; 289-8811

The name is no-nonsense, and so are the prices here at DFC. This store is one of those hard to find spots, around the corner and behind the Men's Wearhouse building. But, as Mr. C often says, poor locations mean low rent—and thus better prices for you. The material ranges from the roughest-looking (and feeling) upholstery to softer cotton-olefin blends and fine quality silks.

Drapery fabrics are $7.99 a yard. Rayon-cotton-poly blend sheer material, just right for curtains, is just $1 a yard. And you'll probably agree that the savings you'll get here are sheer joy.

Mr. C found several bolts of acetates, all selling for $5 a yard—many in holiday colors and plaid patterns. Per yard, satins are just $1.99, velour is only $3.99, lamé and other metallic fabrics are just $5.99, and silk dupioni is a bargain at $12.95. There are some brand name fabrics to be found—Mr. C saw one roll of wool knit material by J.G. Hook, for example.

In the remnant sale area, pieces of broadcloth—perfect for men's dress shirts—are just $1.66 a yard; muslin goes for $1.50 a yard, and upholstery remnants start at $2.99 a yard. And don't miss the quilted fabrics, priced at just $4.99 a yard.

The sewing essentials section makes the Center look like a dollar store—among the bargains are rolls of twine for $1, spools of thread at five for $1, three yards of lace trim

---

MR. CHEAP'S PICKS
Sewing and Fabrics

✔ **Designer Fabrics, Inc.**—On Miami Circle—material fabrics from a dollar a yard, and designer fabrics as low as $4 a yard.

✔ **Fabrics Direct**—Go directly to *this* source for an impressive selection of fabrics, from cotton calicos to upholstery material, and a talented staff to answer all your questions.

✔ **Lewis Textiles**—Like a factory outlet for better (and some designer) fabrics.

---

for $1, Simplicity cotton batting ($2 for a 206 cm x 204 cm package), cotton interfacing ($1 for four yards), and shoulder pads (two pairs for just $1). The store also holds a few surprises, like slightly irregular comforters, priced at $80 for a queen size and $34.95 for a full size. Open six days from 10 a.m. to 6 p.m., and Sundays from 1 p.m. to 6 p.m.

Fabrics Direct, The Decorative Fabrics Superstore
- 6690 Roswell Rd., Sandy Springs; 255-0255

Head straight for Fabrics Direct if you're looking for super savings on better and designer fabrics, from the lightest lace to the sturdiest burlap. The store specializes in drapery and upholstery textiles, although some of the satin-like fabrics and laces could be used for making clothing as well.

Cotton chintzes, with retail values of up to $12.95 a yard, are just $5.98 a yard here. Drapery fabrics in 100% cotton are $10.75 a yard, down from $21.95 retail, and rayon-polyester blend window treatments go for $10.95 a yard, again about half of the retail price.

Polyester lace is just $7.45 a yard (retail value $14.95), and cotton acetate moiré fabric, suitable for prom and bridesmaid's gowns, is available in a super selection of colors at just $5.95 a yard, down from $11.95.

Upholstery fabric is also incredibly reduced here. Poly olefin-cotton material is over $10 off suggested retail prices per yard, selling for just $11.95. A cotton-rayon blend of "Tivoli" oyster pattern material, perfect for children's furniture that will get loads of wear, is just $11.95 a yard, reduced from $23.95. And Mr. C found a heavy burlap-like upholstery fabric to be surprisingly soft to the touch; retailing for $31.95 a yard, this cotton-rayon blend is just $15.95 here.

Be sure to check out the back of the store for remnants. You never know what sorts of materials and looks can be found here, super-cheap.

The store sponsors occasional seminars on various sewing techniques, and will also complete projects for you, like window treatments and upholstering, for a charge. Delivery is also available. FD is open weekdays from 9:30 a.m. to 7:30 p.m., Saturdays from 9:30-6:00, and Sundays from 12:30-5:00.

Lewis Textile Company
- 912 Huff Rd. N.W., Atlanta; 351-4833

This place, in a real warehouse, is like a discount outlet for gorgeous fabrics. So much of what you see here is dazzling, like black and gold lace fabric selling for $9.98 per yard; or shiny solid color satins for $2.98 and $4.49 a yard. There are lots of eveningwear fabrics, made with sequins and beads, as well as basic wool suiting for $9.98. Bright rayon challis prints go for $5.98 a yard; and there are some designer names in here as well, like Ellen Tracy printed silks for $15 a yard and up.

There is a large and amazingly organized remnant area; the pieces are actually hung on suspended racks, like clothing. Among these, Mr. C

found more Ellen Tracy (these were wools), solid color moires for $3.98 a yard, and upholstery rems for $5.98. Most of these are very large pieces, giving you plenty of material to work with. The staff will cut anything to size for you. Open Mondays through Saturdays from 9-5 (Saturdays until 4).

Hancock Fabrics
- 2581 Piedmont Rd. N.E., Atlanta; 266-0517
- 5512 Peachtree Industrial Blvd., Chamblee; 451-4600
- Suburban Shopping Center, 2655 North Decatur Rd., Decatur; 378-8220
- Cedar Village Shopping Center, 5265 Jimmy Carter Blvd., Norcross; 449-1393
- Roswell Village Shopping Center, 619 Holcomb Bridge Rd., Roswell; 998-1432

And other suburban locations
Serious seamstresses seek Hancock for its guaranteed low prices on everything from gabardine to gingham prints to grosgrain ribbons. Everyday prices are just great; and if you buy a whole bolt, they go even lower.

Mr. C saw lovely calicos for just $3.47 a yard ($3.17 if you get the whole bolt). All-polyester gabardine fabric was just $2.67 a yard, and cotton broadcloth—for spiffy-looking dress shirts—was a mere $1.67 per yard. Fancy bouclé wools, perfect for ladies' suits, were value-priced at $16 yard (these have been seen elsewhere for over $30).

Other craft-making necessities, like felt ($3 per yard), as well as patterns by Vogue and Butterick (usually 20% off list) are priced to sell quickly. Even heavy-duty fabrics, like drapery remnants ($5 a yard) and upholstery remnants ($2 a yard) are available cheap.

The stores are open from 9:30 a.m. to 9 p.m. six days a week, and Sundays from 1 p.m. to 6 p.m.

Kala Niketan Fabrics
- 1707 Church St., Decatur; 296-1001

Traditional Indian fabrics are for sale

here in sari-sized swatches (these are usually six yards long). Most of the material is silk and silk chiffon, with some embroidered cottons, most in bright colors and patterns. While the material may be meant for making saris, it's also perfect for pillows and other smaller sewing projects.

Printed silk chiffon ranges from $25 to $35 for the six yards, depending on the design's degree of intricacy, and solids are just $18 for the same size. A sturdy silk organza in floral and traditional Indian prints is $25. Hand-embroidered cotton cloth averages out to just $5 a yard. If you're looking for something out of the ordinary, this may be the place.

Piece Goods Shop Fabric and Crafts

- 1580 Holcomb Bridge Rd., Roswell; 587-9203
- 5203 Memorial Drive, Stone Mountain; 879-8000
- 3804 Roswell Rd. N.E., Atlanta; 237-9129

And other suburban locations

Where else can you get wool gabardine for $5 a yard? The Piece Goods Shop is known for its incredible everyday prices, even though the quality may not always be comparable to some of the top-notch fabric stores in town.

Cotton calico prints sell for just $4 a yard, polyester jacquard prints (with both floral and animal designs available) for just $6 a yard, and solid or printed challis goes for $5 per yard. And you can fool your friends with suede-like polyester fabric for just $6 a yard. These stores are open daily from 9:30 a.m. to 9 p.m., and Sundays from 1 to 6 p.m.

Singer Sewing Products

- Lindbergh Plaza, 2581 Piedmont Rd. N.E., Atlanta; 261-4240
- 107 Broad St., S.W., Atlanta; 688-7148
- 5134 Old National Hwy., College Park; 766-0569
- 945 Windy Hill Rd., S.E., Smyrna; 432-5523

For used sewing machines, including built-in table models, by brands like Pfaff, Kenmore, and, of course, Singer, this is bound to be the source. The Lindbergh Plaza location is actually a factory outlet store, as well as a used machine shop, and definitely worth a trip if you're looking for to save some bucks on oh-sew-expensive sewing machines.

Among the deals seen on his visit, Mr. C found a used Kenmore machine, originally $299, selling for just $69 here. A used Universal machine is only $59.95. A Touch-Tronic 2010 Memory Machine with built-in table, originally $1,499.95 (that's right!) is reduced to $129.95 (that's right, too!).

All repairs are done in the store, and their work is guaranteed. These stores don't sell only used equipment, though. A new Singer Feather Weight Plus machine, retailing for $249.95, is discounted to $199.95. And a new Singer Magic Press presser, with a suggested price of $399.95, is only $269.

It should be pointed out that some of the used machines are really decades old, and some really look it, while others don't. The scratchiest ones, as well as the ones that could pass for antiques, are probably best avoided.

SHOES AND SNEAKERS

Abbadabba's

- 421-B Moreland Ave. N.E., Atlanta; 558-9577
- 322 East Paces Ferry Rd. N.E., Atlanta; 262-3356

The savings you'll find here might leave you at a loss for words—maybe that's how they named the place, after their delirious, happily babbling customers. Or, possibly, they just like the Flintstones.

Abbadabba's caters to the young, flavor-of-the-month crowd, offering decent prices on high-end casual shoes. Brands found here include Clarke's, Birkenstock, Rockport, and others. They also carry the trendy, industrial Doc Martens, as well as platform shoes, and wilder creations for nights out on the town. The store's high-volume purchasing translates into discounts passed on to you.

AJS Shoe Warehouse

• 1788 Ellsworth Industrial Blvd. N.W., Atlanta; 355-1760

Art Schneider wants no part of the outlet craze. "This is not an outlet," he says passionately, "it's a warehouse." And there is a difference. He and his wife Vicki, who run this booming business together, don't sit around waiting for overstocks to roll in; they shop in Europe, where the best shoes are made. And they can sell these at discounted prices because of the crowds which pack the store during the fifteen hours a week that it's open.

In fact, when the Schneiders began their store ten years ago, they *thought* they had picked the most tucked away, far-from-the-outlets location they could find. They just prefer not to be lumped in with that other kind of business. But, as fate would have it, the outlets found them anyway—creeping in and around the Chattahoochee/DeFoor/Ellsworth area until AJS was surrounded. Oh well.

Identity crisis aside, such developments (oops—no pun intended) seem to have only helped these folks out. People have come to know that this is one of *the* places in all Atlanta for women's shoe bargains. Yes, you'll find designer labels here, with names like Kenneth Cole, Joan & David, Calvin Klein, and many others; but Art is more proud of the fact that shoppers rely on him for quality, not name-dropping. Those factories he visits in Spain and Italy are often the same places which manufacture for the big designers. But, since Art gets

shoes directly from the makers, he can sidestep the whole label issue and sell the same desireable fashions for less.

Everything here is all current stuff, no irregulars, with no man-made materials. You've probably seen the newspaper ads; they never mention labels or prices. All Art has to say is "Two thousand new pairs this weekend," and folks come running. They know they can save 50% or more on "better quality" shoes; perhaps $200 off retail on a pair of leather boots; and similar savings on imported leather handbags, as well as handmade jewelry (see listing under "Jewelry and Crafts").

The overall look of AJS is further proof that you are not in an outlet. It *looks* like a real store—yes, a high-ceilinged, techno-industrial sort of place, but one with bright splashes of color and a comfortable feeling overall. By the time you read this, in fact, Art and Vicki will probably have expanded into the building across the street, where they plan not only to add more casual footwear, but perhaps even a cafe as well. Meanwhile, don't forget that the store is only open Fridays from 10 a.m. to 6 p.m. and Saturdays from 10 a.m. to 5 p.m. sharp.

Army Surplus Sales

• 342 Peachtree St. N.E., Atlanta; 521-2227

Alas, the phrase "army surplus" doesn't automatically mean the kind of bargain shop it once did. Still, there are some deals to be found in a traditional store like this one, especially in footwear. Whether you're the outdoor type, or perhaps looking to get into the "grunge" look with a pair of military boots, you'll be sure to find something here at a good discount.

Work boots in brown brushed leather, with rugged cut soles by Georgia Boot, sell here for $65 a pair. The same boots may go for as much as $115 to $140 in department stores. Shiny black patent leather uniform shoes, as much as $70 elsewhere, can

146

be found here for $49.99, along with a range of inexpensive alternatives to Doc Marten's and the like. Hiking boots by Timberland and Northlake, some in discontinued styles, add to the bargain options.

There is, of course, lots of clothing to be seen here too, but not much of it is cheap. Some searching may prove worthwhile; you will find good prices, for example, on pea coats, which are making their periodic return to high fashion. They start from just $95 here, from $75 in women's styles, and as low as $67 for children.

Bennie's Discount Shoes

- Lindbergh Plaza, 2581 Piedmont Rd. N.E., Atlanta; 262-1966
- Cumberland Square North, 2441 Cobb Parkway, Smyrna; 955-1972
- Brook Hollow Center, 5192 Brook Hollow Pkwy., Norcross; 447-1577

Attention gentlemen: Looking for fine imported dress shoes by brands like Cole-Haan and Bally of Switzerland, or casuals from Bass and Foot Joy? Search no further. Bennie's means bargains.

The store is bursting with great brand names, like Bostonian, Giorgio Brutini, Sebago, Sperry, Johnston & Murphy and New Balance. The big bonus here is that big sizes are always stocked; Mr. C saw a size 15C pair of Foot-Joy leather dress shoes with tassels, list priced at $190, but selling here for just $45.

Other styles seen recently included a $24.95 pair of Dockers lace-up casuals, a $45 pair of New Balance running shoes, and Brooks hi-tops for $35 (listed at $85). Sperry Classic Double Sole Topsiders were marked from $80 down to $50, while $39 was the price on a pair of deck shoes by Sebago.

More dress shoe deals: A pair of Giorgio Brutini tassels, listed at $75, for $60. Same price for lace-up "jazz shoes" by Florsheim. Wing-tips by Steeple Gate, listed at $120 retail, were reduced to $100. And Italian loafers by Bruno Magli, retailing for a *fortissimo* $205, were only $119.

Mr. C reminds you that the best

MR. CHEAP'S PICKS
Shoes and Sneakers

✔ **AJS Shoe Warehouse**—Unlike the outlets, these folks scour Europe for fantastic deals and quality.

✔ **Bennie's**—Men who don't shop here must not know that they're missing deals on names like Rockport, Sperry, and Giorgio Brutini. Hard-to-find sizes, too.

✔ **Friedman's**—Great buys on brands from 9 West to Chanel to Florsheim. Wide and large sizes are a specialty.

✔ **Shoemakers' Warehouse**—More designer bargains for men and women, in the Midtown Outlets.

finds in all shoe stores are often hidden in the back—Bennie's is no exception. Don't miss their bargain-laden table, piled high with deals like a $20 pair of Bally sneakers, and a $40 pair of Rockport walkers, (which were ever-so-slightly scuffed). Some of these shoes have obviously been worn once or twice, and returned; check them carefully for blemishes. You may well decide that a scratch here or there—which is gonna happen anyway, let's face it— is worth it at these prices.

The Lindbergh Plaza location is open Mondays through Saturdays from 8 a.m. to 6 p.m., while the Smyrna and Norcross stores open an hour later.

En Vogue Shoewarehouse

- 935-C Chattahoochee Ave. N.W., Atlanta; 352-4333

If En Vogue is somewhat less spectacular than many of its shoe outlet counterparts, it was no less busy during a Saturday afternoon visit. The store discounts shoes by lesser-known makers, targeting the true budget crowd; Mr. C was asked not to mention them by name, which is okay, since you might not have recognized them anyway. But what this means is that you can buy the latest American and European looks for far less than the big brands, even on sale.

A flashy pair of silver lamé sandals, for instance, decorated with fake colored stones, only retails for $32 to begin with; here, you can get them for $10. A silver-studded black boot shoe was reduced from $98 to $59, and a pair of flats in multicolored patches of suede was marked down from $56 to $35. Everything is clearly identified, with all the boxes stacked along the floor.

Famous Footwear
- 2152 Henderson Mill Rd. N.E., Atlanta; 908-2144
- 4166 Buford Hwy. N.E., Atlanta; 634-2257
- 4101 Roswell Rd., Marietta; 565-7429
- 425 Ernest Barrett Pkwy., Marietta; 423-2236
- 1425 Market Blvd., Roswell; 552-8548

And other suburban locations
Always selling shoes and sneakers at 10% to 50% off manufacturer's suggested retail prices, Famous Footwear can make you look like a celebrity for less. With the money you save, perhaps you can afford that chauffeur you've been meaning to hire....

All shoes are first-quality, with savings provided to customers by cost-cutting within the company on shipping, billing, and such. Recent bargains found at Famous Footwear include women's Esprit sandals for an unheard-of $5, L.A. Gear sneakers for $39 (listed at $46), Naturalizer high heels reduced from $57 to $32, and Mootsies Tootsies shoes for $10.

Doc Marten boots, listed at $120 a pair, were marked down to $100 here. Nike cross-trainers and Reebok high-tops for girls sell for about $10 off retail, and girls' Tretorn tennis

shoes scored an ace at twenty percent off retail, only $30.

Men can jog out of the store having saved big on Saucony Jazz running shoes, ten bucks off at $50, and Fila high-tops, regularly $85, selling for $75. Boys' Air Sonic basketball sneakers by Nike, with a suggested retail of $70, were only $60.

There's plenty of stuff for your famous child here, as well. Playskool sneakers for toddlers, for example, sell for $20, which is almost $10 off the list price.

Almost as impressive as the savings was the fact that the sales floor was extremely neat and organized—despite the massive sales event which happened to be taking place during Mr. C's visit.

Florsheim Factory Outlet Store
- 201 Peachtree St. N.E., Atlanta; 523-6221

A Florsheim retail store for decades, this location just became a clearance outlet for the famous manufacturer in April of 1993. Now, you can find incredible prices on the same great shoes for men and women, along with similar bargains on other brands. The deals are mixed around throughout two floors, combining first-quality closeouts with irregulars. Men can save as much as $20-$100 on a pair of shoes; women, anywhere from $10-$50, depending on the style.

Guys may find Florsheim's "Royal Imperial" dress shoes, a rock-solid black leather slip-on with tassels for a European look, reduced from $190 to just $99. Or, a pair of "Outdoorsman" hiking boots—Florsheim's answer to Timberland—at $20 off the original price. Other deals seen here were a pair of casual brown suede lace-ups by Oleg Cassini for $60, Rockport's "DresSports" shoes for $80, and even some athletic shoes, like Converse All-Stars, that classic canvas basketball look, for $29.

Women will find plenty to try on, too; Florsheim's basic patent pumps, in a palette of colors, reduced from $54 to $39; two-tone flats by Etienne Aigner, marked down from $67 to

$59; several designs from Nine West's "Spa Collection" at $10-$15 off; and their "9 & Co." boot shoes for $29.90.

Downstairs, the bargains get even better—the real clearance racks, with discounts of up to 70% off retail prices. Again, there is lots to see for men and women, as well as some kids' styles (little girls' dress shoes, $5). Many of these are lines from past seasons which have gone out of date. For the women in particular, there are some garish colors—were these *ever* in style? But there are classic looks mixed in as well, including such names as Nickels, Enna Jeticks, Madeline Stuart, and others. For men, there is the full range of Florsheim fashions, plus some other brands. All sales are final; though you may return shoes for an exchange.

The manager told Mr. C that he intends to restructure the somewhat scattered layout of the store, so that all the men's shoes will be on one floor, and women's on the other; this would make things a bit less confusing. It may already have happened by the time you read this. Whatever the arrangement, the bargains are terrific—and you don't have to trek out to the outlet malls to find them. The store is located right across from the Westin Hotel, and near several others, in downtown Atlanta.

Friedman's Shoes
- 209 Mitchell St. S.W. (men's only), Atlanta; 523-1134
- 223 Mitchell St. S.W. (women's only), Atlanta; 523-1134
- 4340 Roswell Rd. N.E. (mixed), Atlanta; 843-2414

Open since 1929, Friedman's claims the title of Atlanta's first discount shoe store. It's probably lasted that long because they still specialize in customer service, along with good prices; they'll even provide van service to those customers who don't drive.

High-quality designer and name brand shoes are stocked, some in only petite and small sizes, others only in average sizes. The inventory is ever-changing. If you see something you really like, grab it; who knows if it'll be there on your next trip?

Pairs of men's Rockport loafers, seen for $100 or so at Macy's, sell here for $85. Friedman's own label of wingtips and tassel shoes are $75 a pair, as are those by Steeple Gate. Zengara buckled dress shoes are $65, and Zodiac casuals are $70. Aztec huarches are only $25. Sebago saddle shoes are $80, and their Docksiders are $70; super-comfortable Boks loafers, made by Reebok, are $70 a pair. All of these are at least $10 off the suggested retail price.

Ladies will love Evan-Picone sequined sandals for $40, Unisa leather sandals for $25, and sling-back shoes by Shoe Strings for $15. Etienne Aigner sandals are $40, flats by Aerosole are $30, and crocodile-print pumps by Nicole are $40 a pair.

Further up the scale, Mr. C noted patent leather shoes by Paloma Picasso for $75, and suede pumps by Van Eli at $72. Anne Klein II leather heels were $65, over 50% below the retail price; and a pair of metallic high heels by Chanel was seen for $100, again more than half off retail—*ooh la la*!

Loehmann's
- Loehmann's Executive Plaza, 2480 Briarcliff Rd. N.E., Atlanta; 633-4156
- 8610 Roswell Rd., Dunwoody; 998-2095
- 2460 Cobb Pkwy. S.E., Smyrna; 953-2225

Loehmann's means low prices on fancy women's clothing and shoes, plain and simple. These folks practically *invented* the designer closeout store years ago in New York; suave Manhattanites still schlep out to Brooklyn for their famous deals.

Funky shoes, boots, and high heels are reduced, like DKNY platform heels (listed at $158, selling for $70), and ankle boots by Zodiac, (listed at $78, selling for $35). Calvin Klein pantyhose, listed at $8, are just $5 a pair. Other accessories include colognes and jewelry at up to 50% off!

Piedmont Shoes/Piedmont Shoe Outlet

- Lindbergh Plaza, 2581 Piedmont Rd. N.E., Atlanta; 233-5554

This store sells women's shoes only, with many made by better designers. Styles range from professional looks to walks on the wild side.

Woven-pattern leather flats by Bellini, made in Brazil, sell for $29.99, a substantial reduction from their original list price of $69. Flats by Cameo, with grosgrain bow trim, are only $9.99.

Genuine suede pumps by Jasmin, which retail for $36, are only $25 here, while high-quality kidskin pumps by Jazz are $29.99. Mr. C has seen these in department stores for upwards of $80.

More casual styles include suede and leather loafers by Lady Cameo, which are meant to sell for up to $42 but can be gotten here for just $24.99. Same price for lace-up casuals by Flirtations, listing at $40.

Piedmont focuses on the average size range for its stock; there isn't a huge selection of large and small sizes. If this store fits you, though, be sure to keep an eye open for their sidewalk sales, too.

Rack Room Shoes

- Market Square at North DeKalb Mall, 2050 Lawrenceville Hwy., Decatur; 315-0014

The whole family can find footwear at Rack Room Shoes. From tots to moms and pops, everyone will save big on popular lines of casual and dress shoes. Let's start small and work our way up:

Infants' Reebok shoes with retail prices of $24 sell here for $20, and little girls' patent leather "Mary Jane" shoes by Borelli Sport are $10 off, selling for $20. Little boys' velcro-close sneakers by Osh Kosh are $7 below retail at $30. Bigger boys' Asics gel running shoes are $57, over $10 off what you'd pay in a sporting goods shop or department store; similar savings can be found on girls'

Nike cross-trainer sneakers.

Men—you don't have to walk to Maine to save big on Rockport walking shoes. Styles retailing for $70 and more sell around $55 here. Dexter shoes are also reduced, to $57 for the normally $67 pair. And men's Reebok sneakers, retailing for $63, are $53 at the Rack Room.

For women, clogs by Unisa were seen for $40 ($7 off retail), and Candies sneakers are $15 ($9 off). Etienne Aigner heels are $58, down from $70, while black leather ankle boots by White Mountain are just $45—that's $11 off their regular price. Keds canvas sneaker/shoes, seen for $32 in department stores, are $22 here. Mootsies Tootsies suede flats are $5 off at $29. Shoes by Esprit and Mia are also featured.

S & H Shoes

- 1240 Old Chattahoochee Rd. N.W., Atlanta; 350-0861
- Loehmann's Plaza, 2840 Briarcliff Rd. N.E., Atlanta; 633-7774

It's moved around a bit over the last fifteen years, but S & H is one of Atlanta's very first shoe discounters. In fact, the business—with a handful of stores up and down the East Coast—began where *all* outlet shopping began: Reading, Pennsylvania. And the family that started S & H is still running the stores today.

The stores sell some eighty name brands of women's shoes, all at discounts of 20% to 70% off retail. You'll find the latest most comfortable casuals from Aerosole, like their "Weave It" suede flats, reduced from $42 to $30; and fancy dress pumps by Bandolino, marked down from $74 to $40. Big names like Stuart Weitzman can save you big bucks, such as a pair of his Victorian-style high-heeled ankle boots, in black suede, reduced from $178 to just $99. And perhaps one of the best deals seen recently was one of the cheapest—good ol' Keds basic white canvas sneakers for $15.

Other brands typically found here include Kenneth Cole, Anne Klein, Nickels, Rockport, Unisa, Life Stride

(for which S & H is the city's only
discounter), and more, in sizes from
5-12. There is also a decent selection
of handbags, and lots of cute, colorful hats in a variety of styles. And
some of you shoe addicts may want
to join the "Frequent Buyers Club":
After you buy any nine pairs of
shoes, you get the tenth pair free—
valued at the price of the *most* expensive of the other nine.

The new Chattahoochee location,
at the corner of Ellsworth, is open
Wednesdays through Saturdays from
10-6, and Sundays 12-5; the other location, at Loehmann's Plaza, is open
seven days a week.

Shoe Depot
• 1735 DeFoor Place N.W., Atlanta;
609-9903
Another part of the Chattahoochee
outlet trail, Shoe Depot offers fun,
casual women's shoes, in season, in
sizes from 6 1/2 to 12. They carry the
latest lines from brands like Via
Spiga, Paloma, Jazz, Nickels, and
more. Among the examples Mr. C
was shown were Kikit "boot shoes,"
retailing for $68, but selling here for
$39.90; "Rani" shoes by Nickels, list-
ing for $96, were here for $59.90;
and a pair of Seychelles boots were
hot sellers, reduced from $100 to just
$49. They also had Nike's latest in-
vention—shoes, called "i.e."—discounted from $35 to $29.90
immediately upon their introduction
to the market.

Shoe Depot also has a large "sale
wall" area, where shoes from the past
season sell for $19.90, $35.90, and
up; here too, were brands like Nickels and Via Spiga.

Open Thursdays through Saturdays from 10 a.m. to 6 p.m.; Sundays
from 1-5.

Shoemakers' Warehouse
• 500-A Amsterdam Ave. N.E.,
Atlanta; 881-9301
Part of the Midtown Outlets complex, Shoemakers' Warehouse is one
of the city's largest and best-laid-out
shoe discounters, with a big selection
of hot fashions for men and women.
Its owner is a former buyer for

Macy's and Rich's, giving her some
fantastic insider connections. The
stock, in boxes lined up along the
floor like low building-block walls, is
all first-quality; it divides into current
season styles from well-known manufacturers, and past-season leftovers
from the big designer labels. Sorry, Mr.
C can't say just who, but trust him—
just about all of the biggies are here.

Ironically, of course, the very latest looks—especially for women—
have been copied from the 1960s.
You'll find plenty to choose from,
like a pair of strap-back heels in
black suede, by a very famous designer, with those thick heels that
flare out just at the bottom. These
were marked down from a list price
of $195 to just $120. A pair of gold
lamé pumps by the same designer
was seen at half-price, $79.99. And
genuine leather western boots, in several colors, were reduced from $165
to $80.

There are lots of handbags, again
in leather by major designers; a huge
black saddlebag-style model was
seen reduced from $200 to $130,
while a silver-sequined clutch purse
was marked down from $42 to $30.
And you can save 20% across the
board on famous maker socks, tights,
and pantyhose.

Over on the guys' side, lots of Italian leather dress shoes were nearly
half of their retail prices, like one
pair reduced from $110 to $70. Mo-
torcycle-style leather boots kick-
started at $110, about $40 off; and
black patent leather shoes—you
know, that clunky British maker
adopted by the grunge crowd—sell
for about 20% below retail.

There are clearance racks in both
the men's and women's sections,
with everything cut down to $29.95;
as well as a special sizes area with
narrow and wide sizes. Every stack
of shoes is clearly identified with a
sign noting the maker, the list and
sale prices, and sizes available. For a
no-frills store, Shoemakers' Warehouse is about at civilized as bargain
hunting gets. Open Fridays and Saturdays from 10-7, and Sundays from 1-6.

SHOES AND SNEAKERSSHOES AND SNEAKERS   SHOPPING

The Sports Authority
- Akers Mill Square, 2963 Cobb Pkwy. N.W., Atlanta; 955-6662
- 3450 Steve Reynolds Blvd. N.W., Duluth; 418-9354
- 1360 Morrow Industrial Blvd., Jonesboro; 968-8787
- 850 Cobb Place Blvd. N.W., Kennesaw; 426-1444
- 3230 Northlake Pkwy., Northlake; 270-1644

See listing under "Sporting Goods."

The Sport Shoe
- 3732 Roswell Rd. N.E., Atlanta; 231-0430
- 4101 Roswell Rd. N.E., Marietta; 971-6958
- 10506 Alpharetta Hwy., Roswell; 642-8122
- 5370 Highway 78, Stone Mountain; 498-6085

And other suburban locations
You jock types have got to love the Sport Shoe. From tennis to soccer to running to basketball sneakers, there's savings galore for you here, as there have been for some twenty years.

Some of the deals Mr. C liked on his recent visit included Asahi canvas tennis sneakers, marked down from $35 to $20; same price for a pair of Rebook jogging shoes ($10 below list price), Brooks youth basketball sneakers for $17 (half off list), Converse hi-tops reduced from $45 to $20, and Mitre youth soccer shoes for $15, down from $25.

For the ladies, Etonic Clay Court tennis sneakers—with a retail price of $55—were seen for only $30 here. Classic leather oxfords by Keds were $10 off the $40 list price. And Nike's newly created line of casual sneaker/shoes, listed at $30, were $23.

Sport Shoe stores are open weekdays from 10 a.m. to 9 p.m., Saturdays from 9-7, and Sundays from 12-6. The Buckhead store, however, closes at 7 p.m. Monday through Saturday.

Wingate's Men's Shoe Warehouse
- 1218-B Old Chattahoochee Ave. N.W., Atlanta; 355-7745

Recently spun off from Wingate's Men's Suit Warehouse a block away (see listing under "New Clothing: Men's General Wear"), Wingate's is another shoe clearance center which has put some of the frills back into no-frills shopping. This spiffy new store (in spite of the address, you'll see it from "regular" Chattahoochee) is clean, bright, and staffed with sales clerks who offer full service. They really know their stock, as well as what's coming in, and can place custom orders for you, too.

Wingate buys directly from manufacturers, selling first-quality dress and casual shoes in season, mostly to the business and professional crowd. You'll find top brands like Johnston & Murphy, Florsheim, Nunn Bush, and many more. They always have a big selection of Italian leather dress shoes, priced at $60 and up; and Mr. C found a pair of Pierre Cardin "Espace" leather lace-ups, with a basket-weave look, discounted from $135 to $70. If you want to get really fancy, check out a shiny pair of Fratelli snakeskin shoes, reduced from $310—as frightening as any rattler—to a much calmer $160.

Speaking of exotic skins, you can save $100 on a pair of lizardskin cowboy boots by Dan Post—tops in the biz—at $250, in four different colors. Dingo soft leather boots were seen here too, mate—reduced from $110 to $80 a pair. And, if hiking boots are more your speed, try on a pair of Wolverines (by Hush Puppies), marked down from $78 to $60.

In casuals, you may find multicolored "sneaker/shoes" by Travel Fox, cut from $88 to $50; or Easy Spirit suede shoes—but they feel like sneakers!—half-price at $49. And there's a whole wall of socks, from Cardin silks to splashy, colorful styles, all discounted by as much as 50%. Unlike many of its Chattahoochee neighbors, Wingate's is open seven days a week; from 10 a.m. to 6:30 p.m. Mondays through Thursdays, to 7:00 on Fridays and Saturdays, and from noon to 6 p.m. on Sundays.

152

SPORTING GOODS

The Athletic Exchange
- 240 Cobb Pkwy. S.W., Marietta; 422-7457

This independent store buys, sells, and trades sporting goods of all kinds. Owners John Muldoon and Joe Greenfield take in new and used gear on consignment; their store is just packed with things for every team sport, as well as exercise machines, golf clubs, bicycles, skis, rollerblades, camping equipment, and more.

Mr. C found a Fitness Master ski/walker machine, originally $300, selling for $150, and exercise bikes from as low as $25, up to a LifeCycle electronic bike reduced from $2,200 to just $600. Real bicycles included a Raleigh women's ten-speed for $60. A pair of Rossignol "Excel" skis were seen for $75. Plus tennis and squash racquets, baseball bats for $8 and up, rollerblades for $25...you get the idea. You can get bigger savings, of course, by trading something in. Open seven days a week, including weeknights until 9:00.

Outback Outfitters & Bikes
- 1125 Euclid Ave. N.E., Atlanta; 688-4878

A self-proclaimed "outdoor adventure store," Outback sells a good selection of backpacking, biking, and camping gear at prices that are definitely down-to-earth.

Mr. C saw men's and women's Avocet Cross 40 all-terrain bicycle shoes, listing at $64.99, selling here for just $49.99; and novelty silkscreen shirts with humorous bicyclist scenarios, designed by Louis Garneau, for $15 each. Use these on a Cannondale M400 bike, priced $40 below its suggested retail price at $579, or a Bridgestone XO-3 mountain bike similarly discounted to $399.

Women's mountain boots by Nike were reduced to $40 (about $20 off the retail price), and a comfy zip-up sport top, in warm fleece, was reduced from $74 retail to just $49.

Be sure to check out their sale racks and discount tables, too. You'll generally find lots of athletic shorts and tops, made by Nike and other big brand names, for as little as $10 each. Shimano bicycle racing shoes, spotted on the discount table, were just $10 a pair.

Outback is open Mondays through Saturdays from 11 a.m. to 7 p.m. (Thursdays and Fridays until 8:00), and from 1 p.m. to 6 p.m. Sundays.

Play It Again Sports
- Chastain Square, 4279 Roswell Rd. N.E., Atlanta; 257-0229
- Merchants Exchange Shopping Center, 4400 Roswell Rd., Marietta; 565-5200
- 1825 Rockbridge Rd., Stone Mountain; 413-7333

And other suburban locations

From humble beginnings in Minneapolis, this has grown into a national chain of some 400 stores—all buying, selling and trading new and used sports equipment. The merchandise gets swapped around between stores, insuring a large, balanced selection in every store.

PIAS gets good deals on new items that have been discontinued (but hey, how much can a baseball glove change?). Among these, Mr. C saw an Alpine Tracker exercise machine, reduced from $160 retail to a *svelte* $99.95. A pair of Ultra Wheels in-line skates was $25 off at $150. And a Mizuno baseball mitt, worth over $100, was selling here for $59.

About 60% of the stock consists of used equipment. Seen recently were a boy's mountain bike for $69.95, a pair of K2 downhill skis for $89.95, billiard cues from $11.95, and a set of Tommy Armour .845s golf irons, valued at $1,000, selling

MR. CHEAP'S PICKS
Sporting Goods

✔ **Play It Again Sports**—New and used gear, all at incredible prices; save even more by trading your old stuff in.

✔ **The Sports Authority**—National mega-store prices on equipment, clothing, and team memorablia.

for $399. Plus hockey sticks, basketballs, baseball bats, footballs, shoulder pads for linebackers of all ages, tennis racquets, and lots more. Best of all, you can trade in your old stuff toward anything in the store—even new items.

Open seven days a week.

Pro Golf Discount
- 5810 Buford Hwy., Doraville; 455-8809
- 1671 Cobb Pkwy. S.W., Marietta; 955-9500
- 11230 Alpharetta Hwy., Roswell; 442-3033
- 4959 Memorial Dr., Stone Mountain; 294-0818

High-volume sales make for under-par prices on new golf equipment, from clubs to cleats. The sales staff, clearly duffers themselves, are ready to help you choose from the walls of club sets, which on Mr. C's visit included things like a set of eight Wilson 1200 midsize irons, list priced at $600, reduced to just $290. An Allied Classic 17-piece bag and club set was marked down on a special sale from $320 to $199. And, you can save even more with used clubs, like a set of three Spalding "Centurion"drivers for $60; or, perhaps something from the $5 club bin.

There are lots of sale-priced shoes; one example was a pair of Nike "Air Classics," retailing for $120, on sale

for $80. Plus similar discounts on balls and accessories, and clothing. There's even a demo area in the store, where you can try out your swing with that new Titleist you've been eyeing.

Soccer Alley
- 3265 Roswell Rd. N.E., Atlanta; 266-0762

The prices here on sportswear and shoes by big names like Umbro and Mitre should be right up your alley. The merchandise is primarily geared to sizes for children and young teens.

Bounding through these aisles, Mr. C saw shorts by Umbro, which sell for over $20 in department stores like Rich's, selling for just $16.99; reversible shorts by Lotto for $22.99; and T-shirts imprinted with "World Cup" designs, by Le Coq Sportif, for $16.99, about $5 off retail.

The soccer shoe collection is good, with Diadora turf shoes selling for $52.99. Indoor soccer shoes by Mitre are sold at 25% off suggested retail prices, with pairs recently seen for $35.99.

The Sports Authority
- Akers Mill Square, 2963 Cobb Pkwy. N.W., Atlanta; 955-6662
- 3450 Steve Reynolds Blvd. N.W., Duluth; 418-9354
- 1360 Morrow Industrial Blvd., Jonesboro; 968-8787
- 850 Cobb Place Blvd. N.W., Kennesaw; 426-1444
- 3230 Northlake Pkwy., Northlake; 270-1644

Now listen up, all you sports junkies! Sports Authority has rolled into town with several branches of its superstore chain in the last few years. Brand-name sports equipment and clothing from makers like Champion, Russell Athletic, BIKE and Weider are discounted here. The mere sight of this mega-market can bring a tear of joy to the eye of any sports fan.

Sports Authority sells a good selection (of brands, though not necessarily deep in every brand) of equipment, uniforms, shoes, and official team paraphernalia. Mr. C saw a Weider 16-in-1 lifting bench, with adjustable seat, lat pull, and butterfly extension, for a lean $80. A Tunturi electronic stair-stepper was selling for $150 (complete with a ten-year manufacturer's warranty), and Vitamaster's "AIRmaster" exercise bike was seen for under $100. Not to mention basketballs, footballs, hiking and fishing gear, bicycles, helmets, and more, at high-volume-discount prices.

Ladies' leotards by Marika sell for just $16; men's nylon running suits by Frank Shorter will help you slim down while leaving your wallet a little fatter, at just $30. Baseball caps feature several Braves designs, as well as those for every other major league team in baseball, football, basketball and hockey; these start at around $12, higher in all-wool. Shoes also offer many good buys here, like women's Avia cross-trainers selling as low as $25, and men's Reebok "Scrimmage" mid-height cross-trainers for $70 (they've been seen for up to $100 elsewhere).

The stores are open Mondays through Saturdays from 10 a.m. to 9 p.m., and Sundays from 11 a.m. to 6 p.m. (the Northlake location is open from noon to 5 p.m. on Sundays).

Sports Town
- Northeast Plaza, 3349 Buford Hwy. N.E., Atlanta; 634-9439
- Gwinnett Mall Prado, 2300 Pleasant Hill Rd., Gwinnett; 623-8703
- Cobb Crossing Center, 50 Powers Ferry Rd., Marietta; 971-0446
- Sandy Springs Promenade, 6690 Roswell Rd., Sandy Springs; 847-9727
- Hairston Memorial Crossings, 5855 Memorial Dr., Stone Mountain; 299-7530

This is one of the biggest discount chains around town for game equipment, workout gear, and clothing, with frequent sales you should keep an eye out for.

Women's Everlast T-shirts sell for as low as $15; men's fleece shorts by Soffe, great for the basketball court, are affordably priced at $13 each.

Sports Town is a good bet for general equipment too, like Wilson's "Pro 1000" basketball, just $20 (and recently on sale for $15). Want to put up a hoop in the driveway? Spalding's "Pro Flite" backboard with all-steel construction was seen here for just $99.

Tennis enthusiasts will love the Prince "Pro III" racquet with a prestrung aluminum frame for $45, along with other tennis, racquetball and squash gear; while in-line skaters will appreciate the low price on Rollerblade's "Bladerunner Pro 2000," just $80 (and seen for well over $100 in other shops).

The stores are open daily from 10 a.m. to 9 p.m. (Saturdays from 9-9), and Sundays from 12 noon to 6 p.m.

STATIONERY, OFFICE, AND ART SUPPLIES

Artlite Office Supply
- 1851 Piedmont Rd., N.E., Atlanta; 875-7271

For over thirty years, Artlite has been one of the city's great resources for large and small office supplies, fine-quality mechanical pens, and gifts. Even though it's an independent store, they do enough high-volume sales to offer good discounts. You'll save money here whether you're buying a single elegant Cross pen, or a whole batch of Bics.

Those classy pens are perhaps Artlite's prime calling card, with so many brands and models to choose from that they get their own room. Mont Blanc, Sheaffer, Waterman; ballpoints, fountain pens, mechanical pencils, in men's and women's styles; they're all here, at discount. A Parker "Sonnet" fountain pen, for instance, with an 18-karat gold tip, was recently seen for $89.50; it regularly sells for up to $125 elsewhere.

Cross pens start as low as $9.99 in chrome, but if you really want to improve your writing style, perhaps the quickest method would be to get yourself a 14-karat solid gold ballpoint. It retails for $500, but sells here for $369. The folks at Artlite can engrave these for gift-giving; they also offer personalized stationery.

Other essentials for the exec-on-the-go include Filofax organizers; the handsome leather "Winchester" model is discounted from $155 to $116.25. Lower-priced brands are here too—Rolodex makes a similar leather-bound version, seen here for $59. For that matter, Rolodex has its "Electronic 10K Personal Organizer," in which you type in data on a small keyboard. Slightly larger than a calculator, it's marked down from $40 to $31.50.

Meanwhile, Artlite has every kind of old-fashioned office need from paper clips to manila folders. Buying in quantity will keep the boss extra happy (especially if you're self-employed); get a dozen legal pads for $3.48, or a dozen PaperMate stick pens for 96 cents. "Post It" pads are as low as 33 cents for the 3" x 3" square size. And you can save about a dollar off the retail price on packages of smart-looking Southworth watermark writing paper.

Artlite is open Mondays through Fridays from 8:30 a.m. to 6:00 p.m., and Saturdays from 9:00 a.m. to 1:00 p.m. only. For office furniture bargains, visit their clearance center around the corner on Cheshire Bridge Road (see listing under "Furniture").

Binders Discount Art Center
- 2581 Piedmont Rd. N.E., Atlanta; 233-5423
- 206 Johnson Ferry Rd. N.W., Atlanta; 252-1203
- 2320 Pleasant Hill Rd. N.W., Duluth; 233-5423

Binders can definitely help keep your budget from falling apart. Good as their rates are, they offer to match any competitor's price; feel free to challenge them with advertisements

from other art stores. These guys also win points for their own sense of organization—there's plenty of room between aisles, and the merchandise is arranged meticulously, unlike some supply stores.

For the serious artist, a watercolor easel by Corona is $324, though it's listed at $405 retail. A Nielsen & Bainbridge ready frame, in the 18" x 24" size, with a suggested retail price of $34.25, is just $22.26. Forty-sheet packages of Strathmore colored art paper, listed at $6.25 retail, are $4.69. Plus faux marble contact paper, spray mount, and lots more at discount.

For your kids (or the kid in you), a 48-pack of Crayola crayons is $3.67. Rich Art Fresco powder tempera paints, a good non-toxic choice for childrens' art projects, is just $2.80 a pound (retailing for $4). Binders also sells its own brands, for additional savings on many items.

There are plenty of other creative ways to keep the kiddies busy, like jewelry-making kits, and an Origami paper-folding kit by Altoh; listing for $6, it sells for $4.50. A Walter Foster cartoon drawing kit, appropriate for older children, teens, and adults, is marked down from $12.95 to $9. And on those crazy rainy days, try Activa Scenic Sand, for making landscape-like designs in glass jars—it sells for $1.35 a bag, available in a dozen colors.

Pearl Artist and Craft Supply
- 3756 Roswell Rd. N.E., Atlanta; 233-9400

Pearl is one of the country's leading art supply houses—Mr. C thinks of it as an art supply department store. They seem to sell everything under the sun, all at discount; whether you want to decorate your office, a blank canvas, or a cake, you're sure to find whatever you need for the job.

"Art Markers," by Design, retail for $2.75 each but sell for $1.29 at Pearl. Fifty-sheet newsprint sketch pads by Morilla, in the 24" x 36" size, are $13.13, while sheets of marbelized paper, perfect for giftwrapping or construction, are $3.50 each.

The store has tons of ready-made white canvases: An 8' x 18' canvas by Dixie, listed at $240, sells here for $118. A sixty-piece Rembrandt soft pastel set was recently on sale for $70, half its retail price; you'll also find paints, brushes, airbrush kits, the works.

Finish off your masterpiece with a wooden picture frame with a beveled-edge mat, for $11.26. And to carry all your art around, you'll need a portfolio, like a cordura nylon model by Roz Art, selling here for $47. Pearl has briefcases, too.

Jazz up your walls with a decorative stencil kit for $11.67. A 16.9 ounce jar of Winsor & Newton acrylic paint to use with it is $12, reduced from $17.95. Sea sponges, about a dollar off at $2.42, are great to use instead of paintbrushes to give walls a textured look, without the expense of wallpaper.

Getting into crafts: Make a lamp into a piece of art with paintable lampshades by Design-A-Shade, for $6.12 each. A box of tiny beads by the Bead Shoppe, perfect for jewelry making and other projects, is $1.35. For you cake bakers, a spring form pan from Wilton, perfect for cheesecakes, is $8.70; and don't forget the above-mentioned cake decorating accessories.

Pearl also has an extensive collection of art guidebooks and manuals; the comprehensive *Artist's Handbook*, full of information about the latest techniques and technologies in the art world, sells here for $10 off its $30 cover price. And then there's furniture—easels, drafting boards, flat files, storage systems, and more. It's all contained in an attractive catalog; the store does an extensive (but not expensive) mail-order business here and around the world. Open seven days a week.

Suburban Picture Frames
- 2573 North Decatur Rd., Decatur; 373-3544

This frame shop is actually combined with both a gallery and a trophy company; sharing the space cuts down on

MR. CHEAP'S PICKS
Stationery, Art and Office Supplies

✔ **Pearl**—A true gem of a shop for all—and they mean *all*—your art needs.

overhead, which leads of course to lower prices for you.

Frames, from sedate to ornate, are well-stocked here. You can buy them ready-to-use, or unfinished; others are metal, or have metallic finishes.

A 14" x 18" gold-tone frame is just $28.50. Mr. C also saw an 8" x 10" plain wood frame for $10, and an intricately carved 5" x 7" one for $11.

Framing can be finished in the store or you can take it home to do it yourself and save even more cash. The store is open from 9:30 a.m. to 5:30 p.m. Mondays through Fridays.

Tuesday Morning
- 3165 Peachtree Rd. N.E., Atlanta; 233-6526
- 3250 Satellite Blvd., Duluth; 476-0522
- 4502 Chamblee-Dunwoody Rd., Dunwoody; 457-3565
- 700 Sandy Plains Rd. N.E., Marietta; 428-1536
- 1115 Morrow Industrial Blvd., Morrow; 961-0707
- 1231 Alpharetta St., Roswell; 640-8146
- 2512 Spring Rd. S.E., Smyrna; 435-6678

And other suburban locations
Don't forget that among the aisles and aisles of flashy closeout bargains for which Tuesday Morning is so popular, there are also great buys on plain and fancy office supplies. You can find incredible deals on fine-maker pens and pencils, fountain pens, and rollerball pens. They also have lots to see in quality stationery

sets; there's generally a good variety of colors and thicknesses. Packages of seasonal greeting cards are also priced right.

Cross writing instruments are usually about half price, while some Sheaffer sets were recently marked down from $35 to a mere $15. Both ladies' and men's styles, sold singly and in sets, tend to be well-stocked; but remember, when this store advertises a special in the paper, you can expect them to sell out fast.

TOYS AND GAMES

In addition to the stores listed below, don't forget to check out the liquidation stores listed in the "Department Stores" chapter: Big Lots, MacFrugal's, and the like.

Baby Superstore
- Baby Superstore Plaza, 8801 Roswell Rd., Sandy Springs; 640-6155
- 1455 Pleasant Hill Rd. N.W., Lawrenceville; 279-BABY (2229)
- 1427 Roswell Rd. N.E., Marietta; 565-BABY (2229)
- 700 Highway 138, Riverdale; 473-0888

(See also listings under "New Clothing" and "Furniture")
Baby Superstores will help keep your wallet from shrinking as your kids keep growing. Brand-name games and toys are stocked to the rafters in this giant superstore. You may just want to find a babysitter before shopping here; if you actually bring the kiddies, they may never let you leave!

Classic Raggedy Ann and Raggedy Andy dolls were recently selling for $8.97 here, while Sesame Street bean-bag "Bean Pals" were just $3.97, and My First Cabbage Patch dolls were priced at $14 a kid.

For slightly older children, how about the Baby Puffalumps doll ($13), or a High Back Toddler Swing ($22)? Colorforms (remember those?) Barbie Dress-Up sets are just $1.97 a pack, Playskool's Fire Chief sets sell for $22, and the Little Tykes "Easy Hit Baseball Set" will get your budding Braves started early for only $15.

Not everything here is just for fun—you can hear what your child's doing even if you're not in the same room with a Sound 'N Lights monitor system, selling here for only $40. The store has a similarly vast selection of clothing and furniture, too. Baby Superstores are open from 9:30 a.m. to 9 p.m. Mondays through Saturdays, and Sundays from 12 noon to 6 p.m.

Eddie's Trick Shop
- 3655 Roswell Rd. N.W., Atlanta; 264-0527

Boy, does Mr. C love a good joke shop. Not only will you get a hoot out of the stuff they sell here, but you'll be able to bring lots of it home without spending all your loot.

Eddie's sells oodles of gags, magic tricks, and costumes (it's a great place to check out as Halloween approaches). For the kid in all of us, Eddie's sells those gigantic sunglasses (Elton John, eat your heart out!) for only $2.50. And you don't need big bucks for fake buck teeth—plastic bunny teeth are just 49¢.

$2.95 gets you a can of Festival Serpentine Spray, a copy of Silly String. Hand someone an exploding pen, just $1.95. Whoopie cushions are only $1.29, just one of several, er, scatological gags.

Speaking of practical jokes, Eddie's has joker's candy for $1.95 (it will turn your mouth temporarily blue). They also have garlic chewing gum, or those packs that spring upon your victim's finger, for just 99¢ each; not to mention plastic cockroaches, fake spiders, and rubber mice. Eek!

Of course, Eddie's is ready to handle all your rubber chicken needs—perhaps the most expensive toy in the house at $7.95.

Eddie's Trick Shop is easy to find, located in the big Tuxedo Festival Shopping Center, next to Borders books.

Kiddie City
- 6285 Roswell Rd., Sandy Springs; 252-2904

Kiddie City (it's just fun to say out loud, isn't it?) is one of Atlanta's most complete toy stores, with a huge sales floor with everything from dolls, toys, and games to novelty clothing and tricycles. The selection is vast and the prices are very low, whether it's the latest rage (Barney) or a classic we grew up with (Radio Flyer). KC also specializes in Lionel train sets and accessories. Geared toward volume purchasing, they even offer a "Frequent Shopper's Club" which allows you to save up extra discounts.

Plush-A-Rama
- 7274 Roswell Rd., Sandy Springs; 512-0916

You know those crazy arcade games, in which you try to win a stuffed animal by picking it up with a crane-like contraption? Want to cheat 'em and just buy the animals instead?? This is the place to get them, at wholesale cost—a buck apiece—if you call ahead to place your order.

Plush-A-Rama normally sells only to carnivals and retail stores, but they told Mr. C that, as long as you give them enough time to bag your order in advance (at least a day or so), they'll have it ready for you to come in and pick up. It's a lot easier than trying to bag a tiger the other way, and you won't even have to get sick on cotton candy.

This is a great idea if you're throwing a birthday party and need prizes to give out, or perhaps for nursery schools and daycare centers.

MR. CHEAP'S PICKS
Toys and Games

✔ **Baby Superstore**—From Barbie dolls to Playskool sets to Tonka trucks, Baby Superstore has it, and has it discounted.

✔ **Toy Liquidators**—Solid bargains on lots of the big names for little people.

Toy Liquidators
- Buford Outlet Mall, 4166 Buford Hwy. N.E., Atlanta; 315-7657

Here's a toy store that parents will enjoy just as much as their kids. That's because toys by Fisher Price, Playskool, Disney, Nintendo, Child Guidance, Milton Bradley, Tonka, and many other popular brands are all discounted by up to 50% and sometimes more.

Remember Spirograph? Well, it's still around, only now it's "Mega Spirograph." Toy Liquidators has it at half-price, just $9.99. Other game deals include the ever-popular "Chutes and Ladders," "Parcheesi," and "Don't Break the Ice," each only $5.99.

There are lots of different Sesame Street toys, like a Kermit coin bank (certainly can't call it a "piggy bank," can we?) discounted from $10 to $6, and a 16-piece "Circus Set" reduced from $20 to $12.99. Not to mention a "Where's Waldo?" activity set, marked down from $12.99 to $4.99. And, for parents' peace of mind, a Disney nursery audio monitor system was also recently seen at half-price, just $20.

Then there are Barbie dolls, Ninendo game cartridges, Lincoln Logs, and Tonka trucks; also, some sporting goods, like Frisbees, Voit soccer balls, and Nash skateboards. Let's go, Mommy!

Tuesday Morning

- 3165 Peachtree Rd. N.E., Atlanta; 233-6526
- 3250 Satellite Blvd., Duluth; 476-0522
- 4502 Chamblee-Dunwoody Rd., Dunwoody; 457-3565
- 700 Sandy Plains Rd. N.E., Marietta; 428-1536
- 1115 Morrow Industrial Blvd., Morrow; 961-0707
- 1231 Alpharetta St., Roswell; 640-8146
- 2512 Spring Rd. S.E., Smyrna; 435-6678

And other suburban locations
We all know how much better Tuesday mornings are, compared to Mondays. TM's bargains will make you feel that much better any day, with discounts on everything from clothes to party supplies to toys to jewelry to luggage.

Tons of toys for girls and boys are bargain priced at TM, whether your child wants dolls or darts. A Kool Aid Kid doll is just $8, while a Barbie for Girls makeup set, which retails for $6.50, is just $3.25; and a Bath Bopper inflatable toy is just $3.

Simplicity doll quilt kits, meant to sell for up to $20, are only $8 here. Gund-like stuffed animals by the Manhattan Toy Company are less than half their retail price: A stuffed bear, listed at $60, sells here for $25. Teenage Mutant Ninja Turtle figures are priced in the $4 range, as are G.I. Joe Survival kits (which retail for $8).

You'll find sports games here, too. Electro-Darts, selling for up to $50 in fancy toy stores, were recently seen for only $25; and a Pro Sports Basketball set, originally $35, was only $15.

UNUSUAL GIFTS

This is Mr. C's "catch-all" chapter, in which he's put some of the stores which just don't fit anywhere else in the book. Many of the stores below are places to find truly nice gifts, while others fall more into the realm of the fun and decidedly offbeat.

Art By God

- Underground Atlanta, 50 Upper Alabama St. S.W., Atlanta; 577-7311

The name of this shop may be lofty, but its prices on semi-precious jewelry sure aren't. Art By God calls itself "a museum store of natural wonders"—it's full of fossils, relics, and collectible artifacts of all sorts. Mr. C should warn you, though, that not all of the items in the store are appropriate for little children. Some of the skulls here, from humans to hippos, may scare even the most Jurassic-crazed kiddies.

The jewelry prices aren't nearly as scary, though. Necklaces made from stranding together chips of semi-precious stones, like malachite and quartz, are just $6 each. Necklaces

with solid gemstones are just $4 more. A similar style made from dark, shiny hematite is $16, and others made from polished blue sodalite are $20.

Mr. C found plenty of other unique gifts, including real petrified dinosaur droppings (yep!), polished "worry stones" for a dollar, and chunks of fool's gold, petrified wood, and soapstone, all in priced around a couple of bucks each. Art By God is located in the upper exchange of the Underground, near the escalators. It's open from 10 a.m. to 9:30 p.m., Mondays through Saturdays, and from noon to 6 p.m. on Sundays.

Boomerang

- 1145 Euclid Ave. N.E., Atlanta; 577-8158

Once you visit Boomerang, you'll definitely want to return again and again (ha ha) to check out their eclectic collection of handmade jewelry and funky decorative items. This is the place to try if you've looked *everywhere* for a gift and just can't find something that Aunt Betsy would like.

Admittedly, the furniture also sold in the shop is not what you'd call cheap—uniquely hand-painted, hand-carved wooden dressers and tables, for example—but the artsy vases, frames and accessories are worth a trip.

Mr. C saw a good-sized wall mirror, trimmed with fancy stained glass, for just $12, and a hand-blown colored glass vase for $20. Multi-colored glass candlestick holders are $11, and dainty glass perfume bottles with swirled-glass stoppers are $15.

Cloisonné earrings shaped like cats are $14, while a painted oak double picture frame made to hold two 3" x 5" pictures, is only $12. Teach the kids geography by buying globe designs for just $3.50. And you would be crazy to pass up a real cuckoo clock for just $16, wouldn't you?

China Cabinet
- Northeast Plaza, 3363 Buford Hwy. N.E., Atlanta; 634-8091

For nearly twenty years, designer Judy Appel has been filling her Cabinet with the most beautiful objects she could find—and selling them at well below retail prices. Her business has grown and grown—this is her third, largest location. Judy won't say exactly how she does it, but she discounts only brand-new, top-quality accessories and decorative pieces for the home. In many instances, she is the sole Atlanta retailer for many of these items.

The selection is always changing. You may find a sterling silver hors d'oeuvre tray, selling for one-third off its retail price, at $40; a pair of hand-cut leaded crystal candlesticks, reduced from $75 to $46.50; or a mahogany box, suitable for holding decks of playing cards, for $12.99.

Crystal from Astral , Limoges, and

MR. CHEAP'S PICKS
Unusual Gifts

- ✔ **Art By God**—A saving grace among the tourist-trap stores of Underground Atlanta.
- ✔ **China Cabinet**—Unique and beautiful artsy items for the home, at reduced prices.
- ✔ **Now & Again Consignment Shop**—Little, artsy heirloom pieces—and you don't have to be rich to acquire them.
- ✔ **Studio 5**—Funky painted shirts, and pottery, and photographs, and jewelry, and...well, you get the idea—all in one L5P shop.

Spode, porcelain from Royal Worcester, silver from International, and many other top crafters are all represented here, in decorative items large and small. Vintage animal print portraits, in burled wood frames, were seen reduced from a retail value of $380 to $210; an ornately hand-tooled, wooden bird cage was marked down from $300 to $160. Or, you can find interesting cards and small gifts, like bags of potpourri (recently on sale, two for the price of one at $8.39).

China Cabinet also offers a full design service for your home; by appointment, you may consult with Judy and her staff, free of charge.

Coyote Trading Company
- 439 Seminole Ave. N.E., Atlanta; 221-1512

A new addition to the Little Five Points scene, this Native American art shop near the Point is chock-full of beautiful yet relatively inexpensive jewelry. Most pieces are made with sterling silver and turquoise, and some of them are fashioned into intricate beaded patterns.

Mr. C saw liquid sterling silver earrings for $12, and a $9 pair of earrings made from beads and cut porcupine quills. Triangular-shaped turquoise earrings on hanging sterling posts are $15. One of the more interesting items in the shop is a Navajo ghost bead necklace, which is traditionally used to keep away bad spirits. At just $5, it will certainly keep the creditors away from your door.

Coyote also sells belt buckles, bolo ties, bracelets, and rings, most of which are quite moderately priced.

Crystal Blue
- 1168 Euclid Ave. N.E., Atlanta; 522-4605

Mr. C sees savings in your future if you shop at Crystal Blue, yet another artsy store in Little Five Points. This shop caters to the new-age crowd, featuring crystal balls, incense, funky jewelry, and wind chimes aplenty.

A box full of colorful, tumbled stones is $2.50, while incense sticks available in dozens of scents are $1.75 for a pack of twenty. Honeycomb-patterned beeswax candles are $2.30 a pair, and talisman charm necklaces are $11.

Chunks of amethyst crystals are $3 each, while the always-fun glass prisms are only $5; make beautiful music with a medium-sized metal wind chime for $16. Bookends in rose quartz, fluorite, and malachite are among the more expensive items in the store, selling for $33.

Georgia Grande General Store
- Underground Atlanta, 50 Lower Pryor St. S.W., Atlanta; 577-3335

This shop appears to be a tourist-trap if ever there was one, but don't pass it up; it actually stocks some great gift items, especially if you're shopping for older relatives who remember the good ol' days.

Many nostalgic reproductions of classic household products are sold here, like bars of Octagon soap for $1.29, or cookie tins for $7 decorated with old-fashioned advertisements for Smith Bros. Cough Drops and Hershey's candy.

Don't miss the penny candy

counter (okay, it's actually $4.95 a pound, but you'll get a lot of jelly beans, red hots, Sugar Daddies and gummy bears for all those pennies). Traditional striped candy sticks, in flavors from orange and lime to peppermint, are also sold here for just 14¢ each. Freshly made pecan logs are $3.

Other goodies sold here are eight-ounce jars of peach jam for $3.99, and bottles of Mayhaw syrup, made from apple-flavored berries that grow right in southwestern Georgia. These are $5 each. Mr. C was told here that this stuff is just super on vanilla ice cream! Keeping with the Georgian theme, peach potpourri sells for $4.19 a bag.

The Georgia Grande General store is also a good place to try if you're hunting for old-fashioned wreaths and baskets, Christmas tree ornaments, and other household decorations around the holidays.

Identified Flying Objects
- 1164 Euclid Ave. N.E., Atlanta; 524-4628

Don't go throwing good money out the window when you're trying to find unique gifts! IFO in Little Five Points is a great place to try when you want something inexpensive for a hard-to-please kid or a space-case adult who's still young at heart.

IFO is, appropriately enough, run by a Grateful Dead-head, lending a laid-back, pressure-free atmosphere to the shop. Mr. C found lots of fun stuff, like those way cool glow-in-the-dark stars that stick to your ceiling. They're just $5 a package—a neat way to get your kids into astronomy! Miniature frisbees, perhaps the original IFO, are just $1 each; a real live boomerang is $11; and a juggling kit is just $5. You must be from Mars if you don't love these prices!

But wait, there's more. For just $5.20 you can bring home a miniature helicopter toy that really flies. Small delta kites, perfect for a breezy afternoon in Piedmont Park, are only $3. A huge kite is priced at $16, with medium and even bigger versions also available in a variety of colors and patterns.

Jamtego
- 426 Seminole Ave. N.E., Atlanta; 681-9418

Walking around in Jamtego is like a cheap, quick getaway to the islands. Caribbean creations range from jewelry to pottery to bags and decorative items, all reasonably priced. They're yours to be had, *if* you can find this closet-sized store, practically hidden by a Fellini's Pizza.

Bob Marley figures prominently here, as you might well imagine. Posters of the Rastaman are $7 each. Woven coasters in red, green and yellow straw, the colors of the Jamaican flag, are just $5 a set.

Off-beat earrings made from copper, beads, and shells are only $5 and up, while charm necklaces with little glass amulets are only $6 and up. Plus caps to keep away the Atlanta rain ($14), leather coin holders ($9), handmade purses ($10), and many more unusual items, mon.

Now & Again Consignment Shop
- Andrews Square, 56 East Andrews Dr. N.W., Atlanta; 262-1468

Since this is a consignment shop, you never know what you may find. It looks more like some kind of a museum; and, for the high-quality antiques and heirloom items you can find here, it's an incredible bargain.

Mr. C found a 3" by 3" pewter picture frame for a mere $12, and a miniature glass salt and pepper shaker set for $3.50. An Imari laquered hinged box, perfect for holding jewelry, was $22, and a silver plated hors d'oeuvres plate was an incredible $10. At the other end of the price scale a reproduction Louis XVI is about $2,500; whether or not this is a bargain is up to you. Just pretend you didn't see it, stick with the collectibles and knick-knacks, and you'll find plenty of memorable gifts.

The shop is open Mondays through Saturdays from 10 a.m. to 5 p.m.

Oglewanagi Gallery
- 842-B North Highland Ave. N.E., Atlanta; 872-4213

See listing under "Jewelry."

Onion Dome Imports
- Shops of Buckhead, 2221 Peachtree St. N.E., Atlanta; 352-3881

This interesting emporium offers plenty of exotic—and not overly expensive—doo-dads for your home. That in itself is a rare find for *this* neighborhood.

Mr. C warns you, though, that should you start a conversation with owner Edna Hughes, you may well be talking for hours. She's a real character, who's been in business since 1962; and she's accumulated stories galore from her world travels.

Onion Dome is mostly taken up with little, relatively inexpensive toys for children. Some are priced as low as ten cents each. This is a great place to check out for kooky stocking stuffers, and gifts for hard-to-please kids.

Among the goodies spotted here were a little piggie pencil sharpener for only $1, and toy binoculars for $1.50; plastic sharks are 50¢, while a plastic snake is a whopping $3. Straw placemats are $1, and ceramic bird whistles are 50¢. What else? Collapsible drinking cups for 25¢, leather hair clips for $2, fabric-covered elastic ponytail holders for $3, and decorative folding paper fans imported from Japan are $1.25.

This is the place to find those plastic recorders and flutes you probably tooted on as a kid yourself. They're still around, looking pretty much the same, for $2. Little tambourines go for $1.50.

Some of the more expensive—but high quality—items at Onion Dome include woven Mexican peasant shirts for just $10, straw safari hats for $3, and genuine sterling silver rings for $20. A strand of copper bells for your door is $6, while brightly colorful woven Guatemalan bed throws are $35.

The store is named after the onion-shaped domes of St. Basil's Cathedral in Moscow's Red Square, but the only obviously Russian items that Mr. C found at here are brightly-painted Matrioska dolls (you know, the ones with a doll inside a doll inside a doll...), priced at $30. It seems that Hong Kong is more responsible for many of the gifts found in here; but no matter, it's just plain fun.

Princess Pamela's Tchotchka Palace
- 1141 Euclid Ave. N.E., Atlanta; 222-9514

This store is definitely not for older folks—it's loud, campy, and more than a bit irreverent; but, to find gifts for surly, hard-to-shop-for teenagers, it's a pleasure palace.

Rock concert T-shirts featuring bands like 10,000 Maniacs and Depeche Mode are $10 to $15, depending on how long ago the tour actually took place. Used CDs and tapes are in good supply, like a cassette of the Rolling Stones' *Tatoo You* for $3.25, or *Strange Fire* by Indigo Girls for $6. Midnight Oil's disc, *Earth and Sun and Moon*, was seen recently for $7.95, and *Oranges & Lemons* by XTC was $8.50.

What else? There are fun cartoon "flip books" for $4, and Venus flytrap plants for $5. Big racks of celebrity postcards, from James Dean to Madonna, are fun to flip through, too. For those scientifically-inclined kids on your shopping list, you can get a "Build & Erupt Your Own Volcano" kit for just $12. Just remember to tell them to play outside.

Pop culture is the reigning force in this palace, so you can expect to find lots of paraphernalia from TV shows like Speed Racer, the Brady Bunch, the Simpsons, and whatever else happens to be the trend of the day. These images adorn shirts to clocks to stand-up placards, all at good, cheap prices.

Studio 5
- 1103 Euclid Ave. N.E., Atlanta; 524-5223

This tiny split-level art gallery and gift shop near the Variety Playhouse is chock-full of regional folk art, including pottery, paintings, photography, and clothing. It even sells works by Howard Finster, a clergyman known to folk art fans for his second gig creating album covers for the Talking Heads, among other projects.

A smallish Finster painting, which would fetch $400 or more in a trendy New York gallery, sells here for only $100. Limited edition black-and-white photographic prints are also selling for a fraction of what you'd expect to pay elsewhere.

For those of you not into art collecting (read: not-so-rich), how about a funky $15 silkscreened T-shirt, or a $12 coffee mug, signed by their artists? There are vases and plates galore, too, in earth tones or bold colors. Also plenty of hand-painted frames in the $10-$20 price range, and collapsible wooden baskets, too, by artists who have shown their goods at fairs like the Arts Festival of Atlanta and others.

Studio 5 has a counter filled with intricately designed earrings, some sterling silver, some made from glass or clay, and many priced under $10.

This store-gallery is open Mondays through Thursdays from 11 a.m. to 7 p.m.; Fridays and Saturdays from 11 a.m. until 8 or 9 p.m.; and on Sundays from noon to 6 p.m.

Urban Nirvana
- 15 Waddell St. N.E., Atlanta; 688-3329

Could any place be more appropriately named? Here, in the middle of a major city, you pass through an ordinary-looking gate—and suddenly, there are wind chimes jingling in the breeze, sheep and fowl poking about in a pen, and bright southwestern colors everywhere. Urban Nirvana is an art gallery, a ceramics shop, a garden, and sometimes even a coffeehouse.

What it really is, every bit of it, is the playground of artist Christine Sibley. Inside this old industrial building at the corner of Waddell, DeKalb, and nowhere, she has truly created an oasis. In a room off to one side as you enter, there is a sort of vault, whose shelves are crammed with Sibley's own creations: Rough-hewn ceramic pieces mainly intended for your own urban garden. There are distinctive planters and flowerpots of every size, priced from about $25 and up; lawn and garden decorations such as angels, cherubs, and rabbits, many of which are around $10; herb markers for $7; and plaques in the form of seashells, inscribed with words of inspiration or whimsy ("She gathers seashells by the seashore..."). Many of these show the influence of classical sculpture, with a bit of mysticism tossed in.

Everything is produced in mass quantity, which means that if you look around long enough, you're sure to find something in the size, shape, and color you prefer. It also means that you can even find "seconds," slightly defective or broken items at a discount. Yet, even with this mass-produced art, each piece is a signed Christine Sibley original.

Hours for Urban Nirvana are weekdays from 9 a.m. to 5 p.m., Saturdays from 10-5, and Sundays from 1-4 p.m.

OUT OF TOWN OUTLETS

Mr. Cheap has focused his book primarily on the metro Atlanta area, but he knows that there are many more bargains to be found in them thar' hills beyond the Perimeter. Too miserly to give up the space needed to describe them in detail, he nevertheless cannot leave this part of the book without at least mentioning a few more of the South's best outlet centers. In some cases, they offer deals on products or brand names that are not available at discount anywhere in town.

Boaz Factory Outlet Stores
• Boaz, Alabama; (205) 593-8154
Mr. C knows Bo—Boaz, Alabama, that is. This is one of the largest assemblages of manufacturer-to-you stores around, making it well worth the three-hour drive from Atlanta.

Some of the dozens of shops in the town include:
Clothing and Accessories
Liz Claiborne, Jones New York, Anne Klein, London Fog, Ralph Lauren/Polo, Bugle Boy, Geoffrey Beene, Eddie Bauer, Chaus, Fila, Boston Trader Kids, Carter's Children's Wear, Osh Kosh, Gold Toe Hosiery, Arrow Shirts, Van Heusen, Jerzees, Casual Male Big & Tall, Jockey, Capezio, Danskin, Polly Flinders, L'eggs/Hanes/Bali, Fruit of the Loom, Maidenform, Barbizon, Cape Isle Knitters.
Shoes
Evan-Picone, Johnston & Murphy, Etienne Aigner, Capezio, Hush Puppies, Bass, Naturalizer, Totes.

Jewelry
The Jewelry Outlet, Boaz Wholesale Jewelry.
Cosmetics
Prestige Fragrance, Perfumania.
Home Furnishings
Fieldcrest/Cannon, Global Rug Outlet, Corning/Revere, Oneida, Pfaltzgraff, Mikasa, Brass Factory.
Miscellaneous
Remington, Book Warehouse, American Tourister, Samsonite, Rocky Mountain Chocolate Factory, Toy Liquidators, Wilson Discount Fabrics, Wal-Mart, Black & Decker.

Most of the stores in the outlet area are open weekdays and Saturdays from 9 a.m. to 9 p.m., and Sundays from noon or 12:30 p.m. to 5:30 or 6 p.m.

For a brochure with a map and a complete listing of all the stores in the outlet area, call 1-800-727-6885.

Commerce, Tanger Factory Outlet Center
- Commerce, Georgia; (706) 335-6352

Located near exit 53 on Interstate 85, this factory outlet area attracts shoppers from all over Atlanta, South Carolina, and Tennessee. All stores here are owned and operated by the manufacturers, getting you the real thing at prices up to 70% off retail.

Stores here include:

Clothing and Accessories

Liz Claiborne, Van Heusen, Cape Isle Knitters, Adolfo II, Bugle Boy, Gitano, Multiples, Jerzees, Just Kids, Geoffrey Beene, Capezio, Generra Sportswear, London Fog, Harvé Benard, Barbizon, L'eggs/Hanes/Bali, Maidenform, The Wallet Works by Amity.

Shoes

Banister, Reebok, Bass, Capezio.

Home Furnishings

Farberware, Oneida, Welcome Home, Corning/Revere, Fieldcrest/Cannon, Famous Brands Housewares Outlet.

Miscellaneous

American Tourister, Toy Liquidators, The Paper Factory.

The outlet center will send you a map and listing of all the shops if you call the above number.

ENTERTAINMENT

Atlanta has so much to see and do, and it seems there is more coming along all the time. Lots of entertainment is inexpensive and often free. Movies, concerts, theater, museums, nightclubs . . . you name it, there's a way to experience it on the cheap. Nearly everything in this section of the book is free, or only a few bucks; in some cases, Mr. C has found activities that are a bit more expensive, but discounted from their full prices.

To find out the latest information about the shows particular groups and venues are offering these days, Mr. C suggests that you call the Atlanta Arts Hotline at 853-3ART. With a touch-tone phone, you can hear the current offerings from dance troupes, theater companies, art galleries, and much more. And here's why Mr. C really likes this service—it's FREE! Hey, there is no reason why a limited budget should keep anyone from enjoying the arts.

ARTS CENTERS

These centers are great places for a variety of fun and inexpensive activities—whether you're just viewing, or actually participating. Many of the programs and classes are designed for adults, children, or both.

Atlanta Arts Festival
- Piedmont Park, Atlanta; Information, 885-1125

This first listing is not an arts center, but an annual arts gathering which offers tons of fun for the whole family.

You'd never know that this forty-year old event got its start as a get-together of artists in a Buckhead backyard. It now attracts over 300 artisans from all over the country, and performers from as far away as Japan. In addition to the paintings, sculptures, jewelry, and decorative items for sale, there are also plenty of performing arts events for both adults and children. And, with free general admission (donations are gladly accepted; most people donate at least $1 for a commemorative pin), you just can't beat the price!

The Artists Market is like an outdoor museum, with booths displaying everything from inexpensive pen-and-ink drawings to paintings selling for thousands of dollars. Lots of crafts, too; you can buy directly from the artists, or feel free to just browse around and take it all in as a visual experience.

Performers at last year's festival featured the Theatrical Outfit's popular production of "Beowulf," a concert by the Sarah Skaggs Dance Company of New York, and a "poetry slam" by members of the Nuyorican Poets Cafe, also from the Big Apple. An exotic highlight of the week was the performance of Theater Katiaisha, a Tokyo-based experimental movement-theater company.

Restaurants all over the perimeter bring their specialties to the concession stands here, including plenty of ethnic foods from such eateries as Touch of India and El Toro.

The festival runs for a week in mid-September and is usually open from 11 a.m. to 9:30 p.m. daily. Free MARTA shuttle buses run frequently from the Arts Center station. Some children's craft activities require pre-registration (keep an eye on the newspapers for details), and a few of the more popular performance events charge a minimal admission fee ($5 at the most); some require advance ticket purchases.

Callanwolde Fine Arts Center
- 980 Briarcliff Rd. N.E., Atlanta; 872-5338

Callanwolde Fine Arts Center, a magnificent Tudor-style mansion, is home to a number of fun and inexpensive activities for young and old alike. Callanwolde offers classes in the performing arts, including theater, dance, and music; as well as in the visual and literary arts like painting, pottery, photography, and writing. The fee for most classes is a modest $10 per class, with the length of sessions varying from one week to eight weeks or more.

If you and your children are more interested in enjoying the other people's work, Callanwolde has something for you, too. Regular programs include poetry readings, held on the second Monday of each month at 8:15 p.m., and storytelling on the fourth Wednesday of each month at 7:30 p.m. Admission to these events is just $2 and $5, respectively. They also have regular theater performances and recitals, many featuring young students from the performing arts classes.

Callanwolde also has an art gallery, which is free and open to the public. Each year, the gallery presents eight solo exhibits by local artists. The gallery is open from 10 a.m. to 3 p.m., Mondays through Saturdays. For more information about any of Callanwolde's programs, or to get on their mailing list, call them at the number above.

Chastain Arts Center
• 135 West Wieuca Rd. N.W., Atlanta; 252-2927

The Gilbert House
• 2238 Perkerson Rd. S.W., Atlanta; 766-9049

Southeast Arts Center
• 215 Lakewood Way S.E., Atlanta; 658-6036

These three arts centers are all run by the City of Atlanta's Bureau of Cultural Affairs, offering classes in a variety of visual arts and crafts at very affordable prices. The Chastain Arts Center offers the largest variety of classes, some thirty in all; most run eight weeks, and the fees work out to less than $10 per class. Recent offerings included "Beginning Pottery" ($60 for eight weeks) and "Framemaking," ($76). Chastain also offers after school programs for kids, including workshops in areas like clay sculpting.

The Gilbert House and Southeast Arts Center each offer fewer classes than Chastain, but their programs can be even less expensive. The Gilbert House recently offered an eight week class in picture framing for just $30, and one in silkscreen printing for $40. They even offered a class, "Walking for Wellness," for free!

Southeast Arts Center has some of the cheapest classes of them all: A recent class in ceramics cost just $22 for eight weeks. That's $2.75 per class! They also offered an advanced photography class, at $30 for eight weeks.

Again, it is thanks to city/county funding that all three arts centers are able to keep their prices so low. Thank goodness someone still thinks of the arts as an essential, not a luxury. To get more information on these

MR. CHEAP'S PICKS
Arts Centers

✔ **Chastain Arts Center, The Gilbert House, and Southeast Arts Center**—Three city-run arts centers all offering the cheapest arts classes around.

programs, or to get on their mailing lists, call the respective numbers above.

Southeastern Center for the Arts
• 1935 Cliff Valley Way N.E., Atlanta; 633-1990

The Southeastern Center for the Arts teaches courses in photography, computer graphic design, and creative writing. While their classes are not necessarily cheap (though they are certainly reasonable), they do host a monthly lecture series on photography which is completely free and open to the public.

Speakers include SCA faculty members, as well as area photographers; the talks are usually held at the center from 7:30 to 9:00 on Friday evenings. There are occasional exceptions, as with the recent Thursday night lecture on collecting photography which was given by Jane Jackson at her gallery in Buckhead (described in the "Jackson Fine Art" listing in this book, under "Art Galleries"). Other recent lecture topics have included "Travel Photography" and "Holiday Picture-Taking Techniques." Call them for more info.

Spruill Center for the Arts
• 5339 Chamblee-Dunwoody Rd., Dunwoody; 394-3447

Here at the Spruill Center for the Arts you won't have to spend a lot of money to pick up a new hobby, or have fun learning to express yourself through various art forms. Spruill has classes in the performing, literary, and visual arts. Learn to build and play a dulcimer; learn how to use fabrics to redecorate your home. Take a class in swing dance, or directing for the stage.

Spruill has classes in painting, photography, landscape design, jewelry making, woodcarving, and much more. They even teach the practical side of the arts, like "Theater Techniques for Business People" or "How to Sell Your Art." Class fees vary, but most are about $10 per class with sessions of varying length. Some classes can be very expensive; they recently offered "Katazome and Tsutsugaki: The Art of Japanese Resist Dyeing" at a fee of $150 for five classes. But, with over a hundred courses to

choose from, you shouldn't have much trouble finding something both interesting and affordable.

The Spruill Center also has its own art gallery, mounting eight new exhibits every year. Some are geared for kids, like the recent "Trash to Treasure"; like the activities, though, Spruill caters to all ages. But wait, we're not through yet! You can also visit the recently opened **Spruill Center Gallery and Historic Home**, at 4681 Ashford-Dunwoody Road in Dunwoody. Exhibits at this gallery have included works in wood and fabric. The Spruill Historic Home also includes a gift shop and history room.

Call them to get more information on their programs or to be placed on their mailing list.

ART GALLERIES

Most city dwellers know that browsing through art galleries is one of the truly enlightening an (best of all) free cultural activities around. For no more than the price of an espresso at a nearby cafe—you have to do that, right?—you can while away a fine afternoon or early evening.

Some galleries may require you to buzz in, only for security purposes. Don't fear that you're being kept out because of an annual income below that of, say, Ross Perot; go on in! After all, the richer people are, the less they have to care about their appearances—for all the gallery owners know, someone in torn jeans could be an eccentric millionaire. Be sure to sneer at one or two paintings, as though you *could* buy one if you wanted to.

Buckhead, naturally, is the heart of Atlanta's high-priced fine art scene; but there are lots of other interesting galleries all over town. Some are tucked away in unlikely places. With the development of the "Arts Corridor" gathering steam in the Northwest part of Atlanta, more will certainly follow!

Ann Jacobs Gallery
• 3500 Peachtree Rd. N.E., Atlanta; 262-3399

Since 1968, the Ann Jacobs Gallery has been showing a variety of contemporary artwork, from paintings and sculptures to American folk art, including carvings and handmade

gifts. Most of the works they show are produced by southern artists and craft people. Their exhibits have included the work of William Houston, Sallie Marcucci, and Jim Jonson.

Located in Phipps Plaza, a popular shopping center in Buckhead—which is, of course, the popular place to browse through galleries in the city— Ann Jacobs is open seven days a week. Hours are Monday through Saturday from 10 a.m. to 9 p.m., and Sunday from noon to 6 p.m.

Art Forms
- 887 West Marietta St. N.W., Atlanta; 264-0246
- 22B East Andrews Dr. N.W., Atlanta; 264-0246

This pair of galleries, in the western and northern parts of town, focus on what can best be called "art furniture." In other words, look—but don't sit! Exhibits range from the semi-functional to the truly wild, blending elements of sculpture and craft, and using a variety of materials. The downtown branch, formerly located next to the Homage Coffeehouse on Trinity Avenue, has recently moved out to the new King Plow Arts Center just west of Midtown; the other branch is in Buckhead— naturally, *dahling*.

Artists' Atelier
- 857 Collier Rd. N.W., Atlanta; 355-6710

An art gallery at the shopping mall? Sure, why not! A few blocks in from Howell Mill Road, in a plaza called Howell Mill Village II, artists have taken over three of the storefronts and turned them into mini-studios and galleries. And it's all free and open to the public. Over forty artists, working in various media, rent space in this not-for-profit cooperative— which has grown from just one "store" back in 1985 (on Cheshire Bridge Road) to its present location and size. The French word "atelier" means workshop, as artist Joy Hartsfield, who runs the place, will tell you; it derives from the phrase "in process," which seems appropriate not only to these artworks, but to the very place itself.

As you wander around through this rambling maze of small studios and slightly larger gallery areas, you'll see the artists at work on watercolors, oil paintings, sculptures, textiles, crafts, and more—there's sure to be something different every time.

There is a small gift shop area, where you can buy jewelry and small crafts at direct-from-the-artists prices (of course, the same is true for the major artworks on the walls). There are also classes offered on a regular basis; several of the residents here teach at colleges in the area.

Meanwhile, as Mr. Cheap often says, it don't cost anything to come here and look. You can easily spend a delightful hour or two browsing through the studios and perhaps chatting with the artists. Or, call to get information on the next gallery exhibit opening, and rub elbows with Atlanta's art crowd. The Artists' Atelier is open weekdays from 10 a.m. to 5:30 p.m., and on Saturdays from 12-4; gallery openings are usually held on Sundays.

Atlanta International Museum of Art and Design
- 285 Peachtree Center Ave. N.E. (2nd Floor), Atlanta; 688-2467

Hidden inside the Marriott Marquis Hotel, up the escalators of Tower Two, is this elegant and serious gallery focusing on arts and crafts from around the world. It's stated desire is to promote better understanding among different peoples by displaying their art; only the steady stream of international tourists and conventioneers staying at this and other glitzy downtown hotels makes the location seem appropriate.

Among the recent exhibits filling the handful of small rooms at the A.I.M. have been displays of textiles and traditional folk costumes from Turkestan; the woven Japanese art called Tsuzure-Ori; a show simply entitled "Silver: New Forms and Expressions," and works from Guatemala, the Philippines, and the United States. The museum is open Tuesdays through Fridays from 11 a.m. to 5 p.m.; admission is by donation.

Atlanta Photography Gallery
- 75 Bennett St. N.W., Atlanta; 609-9484

Part of the TULA Art Centre (see listing below), this gallery is the public side of the Atlanta Photography Group, which works to bring photographers together to, um, develop their art. APG runs educational workshops, informal discussion groups, and even presents its members' portfolios to prospective buyers and exhibitors. At the gallery, you can see the work of its members, many of whom are winners of prizes and grants from around the country and around the world. It's open Wednesdays through Saturdays from 11 a.m. to 4 p.m.

Dorothy McRae Gallery
- 3193 Roswell Rd. N.W., Atlanta; 266-2363

The Dorothy McRae Gallery specializes in contemporary fine art. The emphasis is on sculpture with a figurative or narrative approach, as opposed to abstract works; the media used include clay, glass, wood, and metal. Artists such as Leonard Baskin, Verne Funk, and Sherry Sanabria have all been exhibited here.

The McRae Gallery spices up their offerings with occasional lectures by artists and museum curators, usually in conjunction with the opening of an exhibit. Regular hours are Mondays through Saturdays from 10 a.m. to 6 p.m.

Fay Gold Gallery
- 247 Buckhead Ave. N.E., Atlanta; 233-3843

Described by one of Mr. C's experts as "the blue-chip gallery in town," Fay Gold is indeed a place to see some of the finest quality exhibitions by contemporary and other 20th century artists, sculptors, and photographers. If you're looking to buy, it ain't gonna be cheap. If you're just plain looking, it won't cost you a cent. There are several rooms in this large gallery, offering two or three different exhibits on any given visit. When Mr. C dropped in, there were new paintings and drawings by Robert Jessup on view; also, portraits by Louise Dahl Wolfe, a photographer who worked in Hollywood during the golden age of movies, and snapped many celebrities in casual settings; and a room filled with a variety of Picasso prints. The gallery is open Mondays through Saturdays from 9:30 a.m. to 5:30 p.m. (they open at 10 a.m. on Saturdays).

Hammonds House
- 503 Peeples St. S.W., Atlanta; 752-8730

Nearly ten years ago, the late Dr. Otis Thrash Hammonds, a longtime Atlantan and collector of art, purchased a vacant house on a quiet street in the West End. Rundown and somewhat "Addams Family" in style, it was often referred to as "the ghost house." Hammonds set about restoring it to its former beauty, though alas, he did not live to enjoy it; and so, it was acquired by the Fulton County Arts Council and turned into a gallery specializing in the works of African-American and Haitian artists.

Today, Hammonds House is not only one of the city's leading galleries, but it sits in a part of town that is poised for an urban renaissance. The West End, always a proud and historic neighborhood, is fast becoming recognized as one of Atlanta's most interesting—with more homes being renovated in all their Queen Anne glory, new restaurants, and museums like Hammonds.

Inside, there are two floors of handsome rooms showing special exhibits and items from the permanent collection of some 250 works. The sun porch at the back features Haitian artists. And, do take a moment to examine the wonderful touches put into the restoration of the house itself—one of the oldest in the city—like the hand-tooled craftwork of the arches over the doors.

All this for a $1 donation as you enter. Also, the museum frequently hosts panel discussions with prominent artists and educators; these are free and open to the public. Hammonds House is open Tuesdays through Fridays from 10-6, Saturdays and Sundays from 1-5, and closed on Mondays.

High Museum Folk Art and Photography Galleries

- 30 Houston St. N.E., Atlanta; 577-6940

Located at the rear of the Georgia-Pacific building at 133 Peachtree Street, the High Museum of Art's downtown galleries have just been renovated and re-christened; they are now solely dedicated to folk art and photography. As always, they are free and open to everyone. It's all gorgeous—both the exhibits and the rooms themselves—two long, narrow levels, outfitted with the *de rigeur* track lighting and natural wood floors. The entire place is fully wheelchair-accessible, as you can move between the upper and lower levels by elevator or by long, gradually inclined ramps.

The inaugural exhibits featured 19th century American quilts, as well as an eclectic sampler tracing the history of photography, all culled from the High's permanent collections. The photos included works by Walker Evans and Cindy Sherman, along with early daguerreotypes and some fascinating views of Atlanta during the reconstruction. It's a comfortable, quiet oasis in the center of the bustling city. Gallery hours are Monday through Saturday from 10 a.m. to 5 p.m.

Tours are scheduled for 12:15 p.m. on the first and third Wednesdays of the month from October through April, and from May through September, the tour is given at the same time but only on the third Wednesday of the month. Reservations aren't necessary. Call ahead at least three weeks to arrange free guided tours at other times, though.

The Georgia-Pacific branch also runs the High Noon series of films lectures, and concerts on the second Tuesday of the month, also starting at 12:15 p.m. Their innovative program, *Art After Work*, is used for some exhibitions; call for details.

Illumina

- 1529-D Piedmont Ave. N.E., Atlanta; 233-3010

MR. CHEAP'S PICKS
Art Galleries

✔ **Artists' Atelier**—Art at the mall? Sure, and it's a fun way to relax between spending sprees.

✔ **The Mexican Consulate**—Another amazing gallery in an unexpected location.

✔ **Nexus Arts Center**—The unofficial leader of Atlanta's modern art scene.

✔ **Urban Nirvana**—You don't have to go very far to reach Nirvana—like stepping into another world.

At Illumina, you will see art that is meant to be worn. While the jewelry on display here may be no more affordable than the paintings for sale at other galleries, you can certainly enjoy the artistry of these one-of-a-kind handcrafted pieces. Most of the artwork here is done in silver and gold, and many pieces include colored gemstones. Works by local artists, including Victoria Greenhood, Laura Powers Hill, and cloisonné pieces by Ricky Frank, are often the focus; but international works, such as pieces by German goldsmiths, have also been shown here.

Illumina is located in the Clear Creek Center plaza, and is open seven days a week. Monday through Saturday hours are from 11 a.m. to 9 p.m., plus Sundays from noon to 5:30.

Jackson Fine Art

- 515 East Paces Ferry Rd. N.E., Atlanta; 233-3739

Jackson Fine Art is dedicated exclusively to the art of photography. They show some 19th century work, but of course, the camera was still in its infancy then; most of what's on view here is from the 20th century. You'll find works by emerging artists, mixed in with some of the great masters in this field, including Ansel Adams, Irving Penn, and Robert Doisneau. Jackson Fine Art, in Buckhead, is open Mondays through Fridays from 10 a.m. to 6 p.m., and Saturdays from 11 a.m. to 5 p.m.

King Plow Arts Center
- 887 West Marietta St. N.W., Atlanta; 449-6444

The brand-new King Plow Arts Center, part of the "art corridor" being developed in this industrial area just west of Midtown, is as beautiful as any former plow factory can be. Long, two-story brick warehouses—built at the turn of the century—have been handsomely converted into a complex inhabited by artists' studios, galleries, violin makers, and even a modeling agency (no, that's not why King Plow is listed here). You can wander around here, indoors and outside, enjoying the classy renovation; it's filled with neat little touches, like a tiny landscaped stream flowing along the narrow space between two buildings.

At the time of Mr. C's visit, workers were still busy getting the place up and running; there are already a couple of galleries to see, such as **Human Arts** in studio J-103 (telephone 724-9141), which was showing works by a number of women artists from the Southeast in its debut exhibit. Several other galleries are relocating to King Plow; and, perhaps by the time you read this, there will be an outdoor cafe where you can sip espresso and such. A theater is also in the works, the new home of the Actor's Express troupe, which is moving here from Little Five Points. Check this place out now, and keep your eye on it as it grows; within a couple of years, King Plow should be one of the premier arts centers in the city.

The Mexican Consulate
- 3220 Peachtree Rd. N.E., Atlanta; 264-1240

It isn't uncommon for consulates—in Atlanta and in other cities—to display art from their native countries. The Mexican Consulate in Buckhead is unique, though, in that they have a permanent art gallery space. What they put into that space is truly amazing. That you can see it all for free is even more so.

Here, you can learn about Mexican art and culture and have fun at the same time. In fact, a recent show examined the idea of fun; called "Mexican Toys," it included over 500 items from the collection of renowned storyteller Eduardo Robles Boza. The exhibit included dolls, animals, miniatures, and paper toys from many different regions of the country.

Not everything that is shown in this gallery comes from Mexico; some exhibits focus on related subjects, with works by artists from other nationalities. A recent exhibit, "Borders," featured the work of American artist David Zeiger. His photos detailed fences and border points between the United States and Mexico.

The Mexican Consulate is involved in other artistic and cultural events. Give them a call for more info, or stop in to visit. The exhibits change quarterly, so there's something to see every few months. One note: You will have to be buzzed in. Don't worry, it's just a security measure, standard at any such building.

Modern Primitive Gallery
- 1402-4 North Highland Ave. N.E., Atlanta; 892-0556

The Modern Primitive Gallery specializes in folk art, primitive art, and something they call "outsider" art. This can best be described as work by artists outside of the mainstream; most are self-taught, and use primitive materials, like mud or found objects. Often, these pieces are intended to be functional, as much as artistic.

Modern Primitive has shown work by a number of established artists, including Howard Finster, known in the avant-garde world for creating album covers for the rock group the Talking Heads. Other recent exhibits have included works by Jim Sudduth and R.A. Miller. Exhibits change

every month or so; there's often
something new to see.

Modern Primitive Gallery is open
Tuesdays through Thursdays from 12
noon to 9 p.m.; Fridays and Saturdays from 12 noon to 10 p.m.; and
Sundays from 1 p.m. to 9 p.m.

Nexus Contemporary Art Center

* 535 Means St. N.W., Atlanta;
  688-1970

Recently celebrating its 20th anniversary, Nexus began as a small but dedicated group of photography artists
who opened a small storefront gallery
in Virginia-Highland. Two decades
and two locations later, they have become one of Atlanta's leading forces
for cutting-edge art in all media. Not
only does their newer, larger home
present major exhibitions of photography, painting, and sculpture; but also
live music, performance art, video,
and all kinds of classes for adults and
kids. Next door, the Nexus Press pub-
lishes books of art, as well as books
about art.

The gallery itself, a former body
shop (the words "Truck Repair" can
still be seen over the door) has been
gloriously renovated with skylights,
glass brick windows, and interiors of
white walls and exposed brick. It's
large enough to display artworks created on a grand scale. Artists also
rent studio space in the adjacent
building; many of them open their
doors to visitors. A sign inside the gallery directs you to the particular studios which you can visit on any
given day.

When you stop in, you can check
the bulletin boards and pick up flyers
and newsletters about all the different
happenings at Nexus. They are many
and varied indeed, and always exciting.

Trinity Arts Group

* 315 East Paces Ferry Rd. N.E.,
  Atlanta; 237-0370

The directors of several downtown
galleries have banded together to
form this impressive new gallery in
Buckhead. Opened in the fall of '93,
Trinity Arts Group exists in a newly-
renovated, two-story building which

is simple and unassuming on the outside—the gray stucco exterior could
just as easily house a clothing store
or medical office—but inside, there
are several large, comfortable rooms
to wander through. The street level is
for major exhibitions, which can feature artists and sculptors from Atlanta
and around the world; upstairs, you
can explore selected items from the
permanent collection.

There's a little something for everyone here; the staff has chosen not
to focus exclusively on contemporary
art, but also to display masterworks
from previous centuries. So, you may
see creations by such current artists
as David Fraley and William Ludwig,
but there are also wonderful pieces
by Chagall, Dali, Renoir, and lesser-
known artists from the 17th century
onwards. The upstairs gallery is also
outfitted with couches and chairs for
a relaxed atmosphere. TAG is open
from 10 a.m. to 6 p.m. Tuesdays
through Saturdays, including Fridays
until 9 p.m.

TULA Art Centre

* 75 Bennett St. N.W., Atlanta;
  351-3551

This fascinating, hidden jewel is actually several art galleries and studios
under one roof. Located on a small
street (just barely a street) behind the
Mick's on Peachtree Road as you approach Buckhead, the TULA complex is a place where you can while
away an hour or two exploring the
very latest streams in the art world.
This makes a delightful alternative
to, say, the same couple of hours
shopping at the plaza next door along
Peachtree—and far less expensive.
Unless you buy one of the paintings,
of course.

Wander around through galleries
on two floors; the building, recently
renovated, is open at the center, with
a handsome atrium. It's an art lover's
heaven to look up from the lower
level and be completely surrounded
by galleries. There are several working studios here too; at any given
time, artists may be "home" with the
doors open, and you'll be welcome to

drop in to chat and see their works-in-progress.

Among the several established galleries here are the **New Visions Gallery** (609-7200), featuring works by local artists; **Liberal Arts** (605-0310), which focuses on architectural and design arts, including workshops for children and adults; **Galerie Timothy Tew** (352-0655), which shows recent works by national and international artists; **The Atlanta Photography Gallery** (described in a separate entry above); the **Kiang Gallery** (352-5477), specializing in works by Asian artists, such as its recent show of lithographs from Beijing; and **Lowe, The Gallery** (352-8114) which alerts you to its importance simply by moving "the" into the middle of its name.

Most of these galleries are open Tuesdays through Saturdays only; weekday hours tend to be 10-ish to 5-ish, while Saturdays begin around noon. Before you reach TULA, by the way, there is a nice cluster of antique shops, which can add to your outing; and, down at the very end of the street is one more gallery, the **Eve Mannes Gallery** at 116 Bennett Street (351-6651), which again features contemporary art and sculpture.

Urban Nirvana
* 15 Waddell St. N.E., Atlanta; 688-3329

Could any place be more appropriately named? Here, in the middle of a major city, you pass through an ordinary-looking gate—and suddenly, there are wind chimes jingling in the breeze, sheep and fowl poking about in a pen, and bright southwestern colors everywhere. Urban Nirvana is an art gallery, a ceramics shop, a garden, and sometimes even a coffeehouse.

What it really is, every bit of it, is the playground of artist Christine Sibley. Inside this old industrial building at the corner of Waddell, DeKalb, and nowhere, she has truly created an oasis. The gallery, all the way into the building, displays works which have a primarily Central American

folk art flair; paintings, crafts, sculptures, and mixed-media installations by many different artists. The room itself, lit by natural skylights, is painted in a blend of green, blue, and purple, with a large garden fountain splashing in the center. It is, in every sense of the word, a trip.

On frequent occasions, the gallery hosts evenings of music, poetry, and other performances, many of which are organized by Sylvia Cross, who until recently presented such events in her own establishment, the Atomic Cafe. When it closed, she transferred some of that scene to Sibley's place, and everyone involved seems to find it a perfect match. Call to find out about any upcoming events. Regular hours for Urban Nirvana are weekdays from 9 a.m. to 5 p.m., Saturdays from 10-5, and Sundays from 1-4 p.m.

Vespermann Glass and Craft Gallery
* 2140 Peachtree Rd., Atlanta; glass gallery: 350-9698, craft gallery: 350-9545

As you can see from the dual telephone numbers, Vespermann is really two separate galleries, each with its own particular bent. The craft gallery includes jewelry, textiles, paperweights, perfume vials, kaleidoscopes, and more, while the other side focuses on glass as an art form. Some of these pieces hail from artisans in California and Washington State—where the glass movement is said to have gotten its start—including works from the 1950s by Jon Littleton and Kate Vogel, two founders of this genre. The gallery has also shown work by international artists, including Italian glass by Lino Pagliapietra. They even have a section devoted to "corporate art," where you can see glass awards created for use by companies like Coca-Cola.

Vespermann Glass and Craft Gallery is open Monday through Saturday from 10 a.m. to 8 p.m.

CHILDREN'S ACTIVITIES

See also the "Museums" and "Outdoors" chapters for listings of other activities suitable for children and families.

ABRACADABRA! Children's Theatre

- 420 Courtland St. N.E., Atlanta; 897-1802

Every Saturday at 10:30 a.m., and again at 2 p.m., ABRACADABRA!— the children's theater side of the On-stage Atlanta troupe—presents plays for kids ages 3 and up. Admission, for any age, is just $6. ACT's repertoire includes classics like *Winnie the Pooh*, *Charlotte's Web*, *The Littlest Angel*, and *Aesop's Falables* (no, that's not a typo, it's a pun; the troupe mixes in a dash of wit, for the grownups). Each production runs four to seven weeks; give them a call to see what's coming up.

Atlanta-Fulton Public Library

- One Margaret Mitchell Square N.W., Atlanta; 730-1700
  And many other branches

With 33 branches, the Atlanta-Fulton Public Library has lots of activities for children to enjoy. Many branches host story hours, at regularly scheduled times each week. Some even have their own themes, such as "Animal Tales Story Time," held at the College Park branch. They also sponsor several craft programs, like "Color Me Crafts" at the Perry Homes branch and "Fabulous Fall Crafts" at the South Fulton branch.

The library is also a great place to see films for free. There are regular lineups of after-school films, back-to-school films, and special seasonal festivals. They also have the occasional film series for grown-ups, as well as series for senior citizens.

While this may not fall under the heading of "fun," another valuable program offered at the library is "Homework Help." Several branches, including the Cleveland Avenue

branch and the Techwood branch, actually have "homework assistants" available in the afternoons, ready to help in various subjects, free of charge.

Library hours and programs vary from branch to branch. Some programs require advance registration. To get more info and a calendar of upcoming events, call the central branch in Margaret Mitchell Square.

The Center for Puppetry Arts

- 1404 Spring St. N.W., Atlanta; 873-3391

There are two kinds of ways to entertain your kids here. The Museum at the Center for Puppetry Arts is home to over 200 puppets from around the world. Here, you'll see some of the most famous puppets of all time, from Punch and Judy to Jim Henson's Muppets. You'll also be introduced to less well-known examples, such as realistic African figures. The museum presents special exhibits, such as a recent one titled "Trick Marionettes." And don't miss "Puppetworks," the "please touch" exhibit that gives your kids (or you) the chance to be a puppeteer. Admission to the museum is just $3 for adults, $2 for children under 14, and senior citizens.

But then, what would a place like this be without actual puppet shows? The Center's performances use a wide variety of puppetry styles and some live actors to entertain, dazzle, and delight. Recent shows include crowd-pleasers *Aladdin* and *Alice in Wonderland*.

Performance tickets, not included with museum admission, are $4.50 for children aged two to fourteen, and $5.50 for adults. However, museum admission is free with perform-

MR. CHEAP'S PICKS
Children's Activities

✔ **Atlanta-Fulton Public Library**—With free activities that are both fun and educational, the library is a great place for kids and adults alike.

✔ **The Center for Puppetry Arts**—Fun museum exhibits and exciting performances, all rolled into one place.

---

ance admission on the same day. Shows are presented Monday through Saturday; the actual times vary, so check newspapers or give them a call.

Oh, and one more option: The CPA offers hands-on workshops for children, such as the always-popular "Create a Puppet Workshop." At the end of this class, kids ages four and up will have designed and made a puppet which they can take home. Workshops cost a mere $2 per person; they're held Monday through Friday at 10 a.m. and 12 p.m., and Saturdays at 11:30 a.m. and 1:30 p.m. Reservations are recommended. As with performances, free same-day admission to the museum is part of the workshop fee. It's a double bargain!

The Center for Puppetry Arts is open Monday through Saturday from 9 a.m. to 4 p.m. In addition to its box office number, it has a 24-hour information hotline at 874-0398.

The Children's Festival
• Woodruff Arts Center, 1280 Peachtree St. N.W., Atlanta; 892-3600

This one-day annual festival is filled with fun activities for kids, including art workshops, storytelling, puppet shows, music, and more. All events are free, though some performances

require that you pick up free tickets in advance.

The day's events emphasize things that children can make and do themselves, so your kids certainly shouldn't get bored. They'll learn to build puppets, create still-life drawings, paint wearable pins and big murals, and participate in theater games. Events take place all over the Woodruff Arts Center—including Symphony Hall, the Alliance Theatre, and the High Museum of Art. It's a great way to get your kids acquainted with these places at an early age. Call the number above to find out when the next festival is to be held.

Hobbit Hall
• 120 Bulloch Ave., Roswell; 587-0907

The newsletter from this children's bookstore announces that "Reading is a good Hobbit." And they've also figured out that it is a hobbit—er, *habit* that is best cultivated early. Every Wednesday at 10 a.m., they present a storytelling time for preschoolers.

For slightly older kids who are in school during the week, the store has programs on Saturdays at 10 a.m. These are mostly author readings and signings, and have included Douglas Wood, author of *Old Time*, and Ruth Tiller, author of *Cinnamon, Mint and Mothballs: A Visit to Grandmother's House*. Another frequent visitor is composer and musician Mark Eskola.

Hobbit Hall will also host birthday parties, and schools can bring in classes for story hours. Call them for more info.

The Kids Comedy Theatre
• The Balconies Shopping Center, 280 Hilderbrand Dr., Sandy Springs; 256-KIDS (5437)

Daytimes at the Punchline, a popular comedy club, the Kids Comedy Theatre offers fun for the younger set. Their shows pack in a whole lot of fun and laughs, and you won't have to spend a lot to join in the merriment! Tickets are only $4 for the kids and grown-up kids get in for half-price. Recent shows, all of which are performed by professional actors and comics, include *Androcles and the Lion, Snow White and The Seven Dwarves, The Elves and the Shoemaker,* and *The Boy Who Cried Wolf.*

But the fun doesn't end there. The place also shows cartoons, not to mention a "Funny Faces" video, which is taped as the audience enters, and then played back with hilarious results. All the while, kids can enjoy snacks served up by the actors themselves.

Showtimes are Mondays through Fridays, 10 a.m. and 12 noon; Saturdays at 10 a.m. and 12:30 p.m., and Sundays at 12:30 p.m. and 3 p.m. Group discounts are available, as well as special deals for teachers, and more.

Stage Door Players
* North DeKalb Cultural Center, 5339 Chamblee-Dunwoody Rd., Suite D, Dunwoody; 396-1726

Along with exciting musicals and dramas for grown-ups, the Stage Door Players also have a Children's Theatre program. Each show has a four to five week run and performances are on Saturday at 1 p.m. For just $6 each you and the little ones can enjoy shows like *The Just So Stories, Robin Hood,* and *The Red Rose.* These and others are sure to amuse small (and not-so-small) imaginations. Give them a call to find out the current schedule.

The Wren's Nest
* 1050 Ralph D. Abernathy Blvd. S.W., Atlanta; 753-8535

The Wren's Nest is the historic home of Joel Chandler Harris, author of *The Uncle Remus Tales.* This beautiful Victorian home has been lovingly restored to look exactly as it did in 1881. You can tour the house, complete with original Harris family furnishings, books, photographs, and memorabilia, for $4; $3.50 for seniors and teens, $2 for children. Visiting hours are Tuesdays through Saturdays from 10-4, and Sundays from 1-4.

And, every Saturday at 2:00 p.m., the folks at Wren's Nest present storytellers who bring Uncle Remus to life. The cost is an additional $1 per person. During the summer, storytelling is offered three times a day, five days per week. That's a lot of Br'er Rabbit!

In addition, there are a number of special events throughout the year, such as the Christmas celebration which is always held on the second Sunday of December. This event (which also commemorates Harris's birthday) includes storytelling, choir singing, and a chance to see the home all decked out in authentic Victorian Christmas style.

COLLEGE PERFORMING ARTS

The many college campuses of the Atlanta area offer a wealth of music, dance, theater, and films which don't require much personal wealth to attend (unlike the colleges themselves). Many events are free to students, of course (don't forget your ID!); but most are also open to the general public, also for free or a very small charge. If you want to put culture into your life on a regular basis, this is a great way to do it.

Agnes Scott College
* 141 East College Ave., Decatur; 371-6430

Agnes Scott College has a number of dance, theater, and music events going on each month, most of which are free or cost just a few dollars. Some of the events that have been offered for no charge include chamber music recitals, a concert by New Life Presbyterian Church Choir, and regular performances by the Agnes Scott

College Community Orchestra.

The school has quite a strong local reputation for the quality of its theater productions. Many of these events charge no more than a few dollars, like the Agnes Scott College Blackfriars' recent theatrical presentation of *The Princess Trilogy*, with tickets for just $2. Same price for concerts featuring the Agnes Scott College Studio Dance Theatre. And admission of just $1 was charged for productions in ASC's "WomanEyes" drama festival.

Guest performers usually bring higher ticket prices, though these are still quite reasonable. Tickets to hear the Chicago Brass Quintet were just $12 recently, as were tix to a performance by the troupe Dance Alloy. Tickets for Theatre Gael's *The Lady and the Poet*, were just $10. Call the number above for a schedule of upcoming events.

Clayton State College
• Spivey Hall, 5900 North Lee St., Morrow; 961-3683

Clayton State College's Spivey Hall (pronounced with a long *i*, as in *blimey*) is renowned for the wonderful acoustics of its auditorium, and the school's calendar is full of world-class musical events. Of course, such treats do not always come cheaply; some of their concerts are quite expensive. But there are plenty of opportunities to enjoy great music in a great hall and not spend a fortune.

First of all, full-time students, from any school, get half-price on all tickets at all times with ID. For the rest of you, Spivey presents many concerts at reasonable ticket prices. While it may cost you $25 a pop to see Robert Shaw conduct his chamber singers, you may instead choose to hear the Atlanta Singers, an *a cappella* choral group, for $10. Other recent concerts in this price range have included pianist Kenneth Thompson performing jazz, ragtime, and Latin American music; the Morehouse College Glee Club, the Gwinnett Festival Singers, and the Tara Choral Guild.

But wait, there's more! Spivey Hall is also the place to be for a num-ber of free concerts during the year. They offer a noon concert series, for instance, featuring students from Atlanta's Southern Crescent area schools. In addition, faculty and students from the CSC music department present recitals throughout the school year. These are always free and open to the public. To get more information about either the noon concert series or the music department concerts, call 961-3683.

Emory University
• 1380 South Oxford Rd. N.E., Atlanta; 727-6123

If you are interested in the performing arts—whether it be music, dance, or theater—look no further than Emory University. Their calendar is jam-packed with events in all areas of performance, and even includes some literary events, featuring both professional and student artists. From September through May there are at least one or two events per week, sometimes as many as ten, and several of these are free. But even ticketed events are quite reasonably priced. Here's a quick look at some of what Emory has to offer:

Music at Emory: Professional music concerts here have presented the Rustavi Choir, American Bach Soloists, the Boston Chamber Music Society, the Atlanta Winds, the Billy Taylor Trio, and many others. Tickets to these shows are never more than $15 and most are either $8 or $10. While Mr. C thinks these are great prices already, there are discounts to be had. The best deal is for students; with a valid ID from any institution, all concerts are just $4. Non-students, meanwhile, can save 20% on ticket purchases when they buy tickets to four shows or more per season. That's like getting subscription rates, without having to commit to a full subscription. It also means that you can make up your own "series" by choosing only the concerts which appeal to you. Mr. C highly approves of this opportunity!

Emory also presents a variety of free concerts every year. Recent performances seen for free include: The Chamber Orchestra of the San Pedro Theatre, organist Peter Planyevsky, the Atlanta Youth Wind Symphony, the Emory Wind Ensemble, the Atlanta-Emory Orchestra, and the Emory Early Music Consort. For more information on music programs, call the box office at 727-6187.

Theater at Emory: Theater Emory produces professional and student theater at Emory University. Tickets to these performances are very cheap; tickets were just $10.50 for the recent presentation of *Agamemnon and Electra*, directed by Tim Ocel, associate director of the Sacramento Theater Company. Tickets to other productions were just $8.50.

But if even these prices don't jibe with your budget, don't despair; there are plenty of opportunities to enjoy theater absolutely for free. Recent presentations that didn't require tickets included Aristophanes's *Lysistrata*, performed by the intern company of the Alliance Theatre; Henrik Ibsen's *Ghosts*, and workshop performances of new scripts in development. Some productions offer "pay-what-you-can" performances, as was the case with a Wednesday evening performance of *Agamemnon and Electra*. For more info about theater at Emory, call the box office at 727-6187.

Dance at Emory: While there are not as many dance offerings at Emory as theater, they are definitely worth checking out. The dance program generally offers about four concerts per year, including works with guest artists and choreographers; tickets are generally priced between $4.50 and $8.00. Call the department of dance at 727-2835 for more info.

Creative Writing at Emory: "The Reading Series of the Creative Writing Program" brings celebrated contemporary authors to the campus for readings, lectures, workshops, and colloquia. Writers who have taken part in this program include Kurt Vonnegut, Maxine Kumin, and Gloria Naylor. More recently, Emory has

---

MR. CHEAP'S PICKS
College Performing Arts

✔ **Clayton State College—** Spivey Hall has some of the best concert acoustics around, and CSC lets you enjoy them inexpensively.

✔ **Emory University—**With a calendar full of theater, dance, music, and literary readings, you can't get bored—or go broke—at Emory.

✔ **Kennesaw State College—** Another local college with plenty to see and do, KSC has lectures, music and theater events, dance concerts, and more.

---

presented poet Frank Bidart, playwright Arthur Kopit, and novelist and short story writer Randall Kenan. For more information on this series, call 727-4683.

Georgia State University
- University Plaza S.E., Atlanta; 651-2000

The school of music at Georgia State University offers dozens of concerts each semester, most free of charge. Recent free concerts have featured the Atlanta Symphony Brass Quintet, GSU Orchestra Festival, GSU Jazz Band, and the University Singers. A few concerts each semester do require tickets but they're usually no more than $12. In fact, tix to a concert by the Altanta Brassworks were just $8. Call 651-3676 for more information.

The GSU Players present three or four dramatic productions each year. Tickets are just $5 general admission, $3 for students, and free for GSU students. Recent performances have included Bertolt Brecht's *Galileo* and Eric Bogosian's *Talk Radio*. Tickets can be reserved about two weeks before opening night. Call 651-2225 to get on their mailing list.

Georgia Tech Theatre for the Arts
- 349 Ferst Dr. N.W., Atlanta; 894-2787

Ticket prices here are higher than those of other area colleges; but then, the caliber of performances is also higher. Paying $15-$18 may seem extravagant for a campus dance concert, but to see the internationally-acclaimed dance troupe Pilobolus Dance Theatre it is quite reasonable—tix cost a lot more when these dancers perform in New York, for instance. Discounted tickets, of course, are available for Georgia Tech students, faculty, and staff. Other events with similarly priced tickets have included theAmerican Indian Dance Theatre; comedienne Brett Butler; Chanticleer, one of America's premier vocal ensembles; and the hot South African rock band Mahlathini and the Mahotella Queens.

GT's Theatre for the Arts also sponsors a children's theater program. They present about three plays a year, geared to various age groups from kindergarten to eighth grade. Tickets to these shows are just $5 each. Call the above number for more info.

Kennesaw State College
- 3455 Frey Lake Rd. N.W., Kennesaw; 423-6151

There's more culture going on here than you can shake a stick at! Kennesaw State College offers events in music and theater, but that's not all. They also have lectures by poets, authors, and leaders in the business world; they even have two art galleries. The best part is that most of the events here are free!

KSC's "Musical Arts Series" offers free concerts and recitals on an almost weekly basis throughout the school year. Features in this series include the KSC Jazz Ensemble, the KSC Chorale, and the KSC Brass Ensemble. Information on this series is available by calling 423-6650.

Another series which isn't free, but still quite reasonable, is the "Cobb Symphony Concerts." Tickets to these concerts are in the $13-$15 range; the series presents about ten per year. Call 424-5541 for info. Then there are the "Premiere Series Concerts," which bring in musicians from the national circuit. There are only a few of these each year, and tickets can be as high as $20; but even great orchestras like the Atlanta Brassworks can be seen for just $10. Call 423-6650 for info.

Theater events are not as abundant as music events, but they certainly are cheap. Tickets to performances in the "Classic Theaterworks" series are just $10, and recent productions have included *The Mikado* and *Romeo and Juliet*. Other recent theatrical presentations include *Stories for a Winter Night,* and the Ninth Georgia Performance Festival, both of which were free.

Kennesaw State has two regular lecture series. "The Chautauqua Lectures" bring distinguished guests to speak on diverse topics. This series has featured poet Maya Angelou and Native American author Scott Momaday. For more information on this series, call 423-6235. "The Tetley Distinguished Leaders Lectures" feature notable business people from a variety of industries. Recent guests in this series included Dennis Berry, publisher of the *Altanta Journal-Constitution,* and Bernard Marcus, chairman and CEO of Home Depot. For more information about this series, call 423-6425.

For general information about music and performing arts at Kennesaw State College, call 423-6151. If you ask, they'll be happy to send you a calendar of events listing all of the above info, and more.

Morehouse College
- 830 Westview Dr. S.W., Atlanta; 215-2601

Morehouse College doesn't have as much going on as some of the other schools around, but the offerings they do have are free and open to the public. They present about three or four music events each semester, most of which are recitals and classical music concerts. They also have an annual Christmas Carol Concert, performed by the Glee Clubs of Morehouse and Spelman College. Call the number above for more info about music at Morehouse.

Oglethorpe University
• 4484 Peachtree Rd. N. E., Atlanta; 364-8555 or 364-8329

Oglethorpe University presents dozens of music concerts and lectures, plus an ambitious lineup of theater performances, for admission prices that'll make you want to do a little singing and dancing of your own.

Mad about music? Oglethorpe presents a number of concerts, featuring university music students, which are free and open to the public. In addition, they sponsor the "Skylight Gallery Concert Series," which presents beautiful music in a beautiful setting—the elegant, acoustically designed Skylight Gallery. These concerts are just $5 and have included performances by James Zellers, the Quintetto Barocco, and the Brookhaven Trio.

If you're more interested in lectures, they have plenty to choose from. The Rikard Lectures are free and open to the public, offering you the chance to hear ideas from the best and brightest in the field of business. Other lectures take place throughout the year on the subjects of science, art, and literature, again, free.

While there aren't quite as many theater offerings here, they are certainly worth checking out, especially

with tickets priced at $5 to $6 (and only $2 to $3 for children's theatre shows, and matinees of regular productions). Recent presentations have included Shakespeare's *Love's Labours Lost*; and, speaking of the Bard, a pair of original one-act comedies, *When Shakespeare's Ladies Meet* and *The Show Must Go On*. For more information about theater events call 364-8343.

And if all that isn't enough for you, there's more. Check out the Oglethorpe University Museum, housed in the school's Philip Weltner Library. Along with art exhibits, this museum presents its own slate of lectures and concerts at reasonable prices, usually around $5. For more information call 364-8555.

Spelman College
• 350 Spelman Lane S.W., Atlanta; 681-3643

The music department at Spelman College presents about a half-dozen concerts per semester, and they're all free of charge. Pianists Althea Waites and Richard Fields have given recitals here, along with such annual events as the Spelman College Faculty Chamber Music Concert.

Spelman's performance departments produce about six shows each year; these include a mix of theater and dance events. Tickets for these shows are $5, and $2.50 for students with ID. Recent productions include *Before It Hits Home*, a play about the homecoming of a son living with AIDS; and *Dancefest*, featuring choreography by the Spelman College dance faculty.

COMEDY

For standup comedy, the best cost-cutter in the biz remains the "Open Mike" night, when you can get in for a very low cover charge and see up-and-coming "stars of tomorrow." Guaranteed, there'll be plenty of klunkers (does the name Rupert Pupkin ring a bell, De Niro fans?); but the shows are hosted by headliners, so you're sure to get plenty of good laughs no matter what. Many clubs, some of which are listed here, have open mike shows; they tend to be early in the week. Call your favorite venue to see what they offer.

The Comedy Act Theatre
- 917 Peachtree St. N.E., Atlanta; 875-3550

Tickets to comedy shows can get pretty expensive, especially on weekends; but here at the Comedy Act Theatre, Friday and Saturday night shows are just $10. Better yet, on Tuesday through Thursday evenings, tickets are just $6. And Wednesday is "Ladies Night," when the first 100 women through the door get in free!

This venue bills itself as "the country's first major black stand-up and improv comedy theatre," with regional and national acts like Paul Mooney and D.L. Hughley. Enjoy the laughs Tuesdays, Wednesdays, and Thursdays at 8:30 p.m. and on Fridays and Saturdays at 8:30 p.m. and 11:30 p.m.

The Improv
- 247 Buckhead Ave. N.E., Atlanta; 364-9800

The Improv is in fashionable Buckhead and it is owned by the same people that own *the* Improv in Los Angeles, so it can't possibly by cheap, right? Wrong. On Tuesday, Wednesday, Thursday, and Sunday, tickets to the 8:30 p.m. show are just $6, and only a dollar more for reserved seats. On Fridays and Saturdays, meanwhile, tickets to either the 8:30 p.m. show or the 10:45 p.m. show go up to $10, and $11 for reserved seats.

Each show features not one, not two, but three, count 'em three, stand-up comics. There's an M.C. to keep things rolling, a feature act, and a headliner. And who will you see? Top-line national stars like Bobcat Goldthwait, or David Alan Grier from *In Living Color*. Call to find out what big names are coming up.

Laughing Matters
- Manuel's Tavern, 602 North Highland Ave. N.E., Atlanta; 525-3447

Here at this popular restaurant and watering hole, you can enjoy Laughing Matters, Atlanta's first improvisational comedy troupe. Improv is a concept that has become *really* big in cities like Chicago—in fact, some members from Laughing Matters have gone on to play one of Chi-town's most renowned improv comedy clubs, Second City. This kind of performance, sort of a cross between theater and standup, hasn't really caught on in Atlanta. But that hasn't stopped Laughing Matters from thriving; quite the opposite, and their run at Manuel's Tavern sure proves it.

For readers who are still unsure about just what improv is, allow Mr. C to explain. The comedians ask the audience to give them ideas for characters and situations, which the players then turn into (almost always) hilarious skits. The format employed at Manuel's is known as "Comedy Sports," which pits two teams of four comedians each against each other. They compete, with jokes, for the audience's favor. And all this fun can be had for a mere $5 per person, every Thursday and Saturday at 8 p.m.

For information, reservations, or to find out were else around town you can see Laughing Matters (comedians often feel the need to be moving targets), call their own telephone line, 717-4714.

Punchline Comedy Club
- The Balconies Shopping Center, 280 Hilderbrand Dr., Sandy Springs; 252-LAFF (5233)

This comedy venue is well-established—they've been around for twelve years—and they've presented national superstars like Jay Leno and Jerry Seinfeld, on their way up the ladder of stardom. Yet, the club's ticket prices are very down-to-earth.

On Tuesday, Wednesday, Thursday, and Sunday evenings at 8:30 p.m. you can get into the Punchline for just $7. On Fridays you have a choice of two shows, one at 8 p.m. and one at 10 p.m., for $10. The two Saturday shows, same times, are just $12.

Uptown Comedy Corner
- 2140 Peachtree Rd. N.W., Atlanta; 350-6990

Seven is definitely your lucky number here at the Uptown Comedy Corner. On most weeknights, tickets are just $7. And there's an even better deal to be had on Wednesdays, when the first 100 people in the door get in free (the 101st person pays $7). Once inside, *everyone* gets to partake of the free appetizer buffet. Thursday is "Ladies Night"; women get in for just $4 each, and men pay $7 (told you it was a lucky number!).

As you'd expect, tickets are more expensive on the weekends. Fridays and Saturdays, admission is $11; this

---

MR. CHEAP'S PICKS
Comedy

✔ **The Improv**—Three comics, six bucks. Good deal.

✔ **Laughing Matters**—Manuel's Tavern hosts this improv comedy troupe, and the cover charge will keep you giddy. Talk about cheap gags!

---

is, after all, when you'll see major national acts like Steve Harvey, host of television's "Showtime at the Apollo."

DANCE

Atlanta Ballet
- Atlanta Civic Center, 395 Piedmont Ave.N.E., Atlanta; 249-6400

If you think that you'll never be able to afford tickets to the Atlanta Ballet, being the premier ballet company in the area, think again. The AB presents five concerts per season, of classics such as "Giselle," along with its annual Christmas production of "The Nutcracker." Now, while it is true that the best seats in the house for an evening performance currently cost upwards of $36 apiece, Mr. C is here to point out that there *are* seats you can get for just $5 at all times, for all performances. What a bargain!

If you'd like to get a little closer, there are also discounts for students and senior citizens, though these are small savings, usually just a few dollars off the regular prices. (Nothing is cheaper than those $5 tix, which are available to all.) But, unlike other venues, the discounts are available at

any time, even weeks before the show opens, as long as you have the appropriate identification. And as Mr. C says, any savings is worth taking!

For a third option, the Atlanta Ballet also has rush tickets, which again are available to all. These are priced at $5 for all seats, when available. They're generally sold about one hour before curtain time, for that show only. If you have a chance to go directly to the box office around that time, and are willing to take that fifty-fifty chance on getting in, this can be your shot at the best seats for the lowest price.

Chappstick and the Cars Performance Duo
- Various locations; Information, 874-8710

No, it's not a rock band. Chappstick and the Cars actually consists of dancers Jim *Chapp*eleaux and Sherie *Car*son (get it?), who perform frequently at the 7 Stages Theatre in Little Five Points. They also turn up all around

MR. CHEAP'S PICKS
Dance

✔ **Atlanta Ballet**—You'll jump for joy (maybe even *pirouette*) over $5 tix for the high-class ensemble in town. Discounts for students and senior citizens, too.

✔ **Dancer's Collective**—This organization brings world-renowned modern dance troupes to Atlanta, at bargain rates.

✔ **Irish Arts of Atlanta**—Don't just watch dance, participate! This group will teach you *ceili* dancing, the roots of square dancing.

town, in an ongoing series of site-specific works. Their performances combine contemporary dance with monologues, theater, song, and more. They create about five productions a year, for which tickets are generally $7 to $10.

Recent site-specific works included a performance called "Equinox," held in a planetarium; here, they used stars to create "dancing" constellations. Many of their performances also tackle social issues, as in their recent "Paint a Rumor," about a painter who becomes obsessed with his models. This was presented at the Atlanta Arts Festival. Since these guys can be hard to catch up with, call them for information about upcoming shows.

Dance Force
• Various locations; Information, 892-8232

Dance Force is a modern troupe that likes to mix things up by performing in what can be best described as "non-traditional" performance spaces. One recent piece was performed in the swimming pool of the Buckhead

YWCA. Another piece has been presented annually in the Oakland Cemetery. This site-specific piece blends the music of Handl and Beethoven with the poetry of James Russell Lowell and Victorian-style dress.

Not everything Dance Force does is seen in such out-of-the-way places. When they're not dancing in cemeteries and swimming pools, the troupe can often be found at halls such as 7 Stages. They present about four major performances a year, with tickets generally in the $8 to $12 range.

Irish Arts of Atlanta
• Various locations; Information, 873-5621

Irish Arts of Atlanta sponsors participatory dances, where they'll teach you the fine art of *ceili* dancing. If this form of social group dancing seems very similar to square dancing, you're right—guess where the squares have their roots? Admission to these festive events is usually $4 or $5 per person. There is no set schedule for the dances, and the organization doesn't do a whole lot of advertising; call them to get on their mailing list for notices of upcoming dances and other events.

Dancer's Collective
• Various locations; Information, 233-7600

Dancer's Collective is a presenting organization, not an actual troupe; they bring national and international modern dance companies to Atlanta for performances and educational outreach. The dancers they bring in will not only give public performances, but they also teach master classes at local colleges and universities, along with conducting outreach classes with Atlanta's underprivileged youth. Each troupe generally gives two major performances during their stay, for which tickets range from $10 to $18. Subscriptions are also available.

Among the performers DC has brought to Atlanta are such internationally acclaimed ensembles as Pilobolus, David Dorfman Dance, and the BeBe Miller Company. In all, five or six companies take part in this program each year. Venues in which performances are held include the Georgia Tech Theatre for the Arts, the 14th Street Playhouse, and 7 Stages. Watch *Creative Loafing* for upcoming concerts, or give them a call for their schedule.

Ruth Mitchell Dance Theatre
* Various locations; Information, 237-8829

Many people love ballet but fear they would have to mortgage their home to afford tickets to a dance concert. Well, tickets to performances by the Ruth Mitchell Dance Theatre are a reasonable $15 for adults, and $10 for children and senior citizens, at all performances. Ruth Mitchell Dance Theatre includes professional dancers and dance students; their work incor-porates a number of ballet styles, from classical to modern. Recent concerts have included "An Evening with Sal Aiello" at the 14th St. Playhouse, and *The Nutcracker* at the Cobb Civic Center.

The troupe only presents four concerts per season, each with a run of only three or four nights. The advantage of a short season, though, is that season tickets are relatively inexpensive. For a little more than the cost of a single orchestra seat to see ballet at the Atlanta Civic Center, you can get the best seat in the house for all four Ruth Mitchell concerts. The price of $45 actually gets you four tickets for the price of three. For more info on individual or season tickets, call them at the number above.

Atlanta has several other small but dedicated local dance companies, each of which produce a handful of concerts per year. These performances are held at theaters throughout Atlanta, including 7 Stages, the 14th Street Playhouse, and 800 East Arts Center. Ticket prices depend on the venue, but most range from $6 to $12. Many of these companies also do "site-specific" works in public parks and other community settings; these may have cheaper tickets or may even be free. Watch the newspaper listings, and keep your eyes open for the following: **and Company** (yes, that's their name), **GardenHouse Dance Company, Moving in the Spirit Dance Company, Red Clay Performing Arts Group,** and **Several Dancers Core.**

MOVIES

Alas, there's not much to be done about the ever-rising prices of first-run Hollywood movies. Some theaters do cut the price a bit on their first shows of the day (see "Bargain Matinees" below). But don't despair! There are lots of alternative options for the budget moviegoer.

Cinéfest Film Theater
* 66 Courtland St. S.E., Atlanta; 651-2463

Cinéfest is a movie theater on the Georgia State University campus, with ticket prices that almost make you want to go back to school. The movies shown here include artsy-type films such as *Like Water For Chocolate* and *Orlando,* recent mainstream flicks like *The Firm* and *Rookie of the Year,* and documentaries such as *Manufacturing Consent: Noam Chomsky and the Media.* Of course, classic campus favorites also show up on the bill, from *Snow White and the Seven Dwarves* to *Monty Python's Life of Brian* ("classics," clearly, are in the eye of the beholder).

Everyone can agree on one thing: The ticket prices here are the main attraction. Admission is just $2 before 6 p.m., and $4 after 6 p.m. Such a deal! Of course, if you *are* a GSU student, show your ID and you get in free. Call them and they'll send you a copy of their calendar which includes showtimes and summaries of upcoming films. Cinéfest is open seven days a week.

Cinema Grill
- 7270 Roswell Rd., Sandy Springs; 395-0724

Here's a nifty concept: A movie theater with tables and chairs, where you can eat dinner while watching the picture. It's sort of like taking all the comfy aspects of renting a video and eating in front of the tube, and then taking a step *back* in the direction of spending an evening out. Better yet, make the movies as cheap as renting; add the option of beer and wine with your meal....and you have the Cinema Grill.

Located in the North Springs Center shopping plaza, CG has two different theaters showing second-run films—the hits you missed a couple of months ago—for just $2.50 per film. Each is shown twice a night; on weekends, they add a midnight movie, usually a horror flick.

The menu consists mainly of appetizers, burgers and sandwiches, salads, and individual pizzas. Nothing is terribly pricey, with most salads and sandwiches in the $4-$6 range; a hefty plate of chicken wings is $5.25, and a 12-inch pizza is $6.25. You can also get a basket of popcorn, which at $2.25 is no better or worse than "regular" movie prices. Of course, you are equally welcome to watch the film and order nothing at all.

There is a limited but decent selection of beers, most $2.25, also available in pitchers (many of the tables are group-sized); several wines are $2.95 a glass. An ID is required to order booze, though kids are welcome in the theater.

It's wise to show up a bit early, especially if you're going to the first showing, so that you can get your food before the movie starts. Otherwise, you'll run into the only downside of this fun concept; the waitstaff does continue to come around during the show. This is most annoying toward the end when, just as the story is building to a climax, someone taps you on the shoulder and says, "Your check will be $17.50...." Guess they're worried about being stiffed—too bad, because apart from this one glitch in the system, it's a great idea. After all, how often can you go out to dinner and a movie for around ten bucks a person?

Goethe-Institut Atlanta
- Colony Square, Plaza Level, 1197 Peachtree St. N.E., Atlanta; 892-2388

The Goethe-Institut is part of a program funded by the German government which brings the culture and language of Germany to other countries. Offerings include cultural events, German language courses and a library with books in German and English.

They have an extensive film schedule, and most screenings are free. Screenings include German films, such as *Kleine Haie* (*Acting it Out*), *Langer Samstag* (*Shop 'til You Drop*, a Mr. C fave), and *Yasemin*, as well as some American films, like *The Shining* and *Do the Right Thing,* shown with German subtitles.

They also present occasional music and dance concerts. While a few of these are free, the admission price depends on the venue with which Goethe is co-sponsoring the event. Past locations have included Briarcliff Baptist Church, Stone Mountain Park, and Emory University.

The Goethe-Institut also has an art gallery, bringing German art exhibits and related lectures to the city. Call them for more information and a calendar of events.

High Museum of Art
- 1280 Peachtree St. N.E., Atlanta; 892-3600

Museums, particularly art museums, afford you a wonderful opportunity to see movies that don't get distributed to commercial theatres—classic films, documentaries, and foreign films. The High Museum of Art has regular offerings for which admission is just $4 per ticket. A recent festival, "Les Films du Losange," was entirely dedicated to independent French cinema.

Occasionally, the High will show films in conjunction with one of its current exhibits; admission in these cases is free with your entry to the museum. For instance, the documentary *Sol LeWitt* was shown as part of a recent installation of that artist's wall drawings. Call the High Museum to get a calendar of upcoming events.

MR. CHEAP'S PICKS
Movies

✔ **Cinéfest Film Theater**—A movie theater on a college campus is not only convenient, it's cheap, too.

✔ **Cinema Grill**—Gives the phrase "dinner and a movie" a whole new meaning.

✔ **Goethe-Institut Atlanta, High Museum of Art**—If funky foreign films and avant-garde flicks are your thing, check the schedules at these museums. Not only will it be fun, it may well be free.

"SECOND-RUN" MOVIES

Many theaters exclusively show second-run features at bargain prices. These are movies which have already been at regular-price cinemas for a while, but hey—how many pictures can you see the night they open? If the picture was a flop, it will probably turn up in some of these places just weeks after its debut. Sometimes, a movie you'd *never* pay $7 to see is worth a try at $1.50. Second-run houses can come and go, or their prices may change; but here is a good sampling, at Mr. C's press time, of theaters to check out in the Greater Atlanta area.

Capital Cinemas Franklin Plaza
- 1033 Franklin Rd., Marietta; 916-0135

All shows 50¢.

Capital Cinemas Cobb Centre Six
- 2120 South Cobb Dr., Smyrna; 436-6352

All shows 99¢.

Capital Cinemas Fayette Place
- 383 Fayette Place, Fayetteville; 460-5413

All shows 99¢.

CineStar Theatres
- 1387 Roswell Rd., Marietta; 977-6887

All shows $1.

Greenbriar Cinema
- Greenbriar Mall, 2841 Greenbriar Pkwy., Atlanta; 629-9999

All shows $1.50.

Memorial Drive Cinema Four
- 6202 Memorial Dr., Stone Mountain; 469-4845

All shows $1.75.

Memorial Five Theatre
- 5610 Memorial Dr., Stone Mountain; 294-9096

All shows $1.75.

Northeast Plaza Cinema Twelve
- 3365 Buford Hwy. N.E., Atlanta; 248-0624

All shows $1.50.

Plaza Theatre
- 1049 Ponce de Leon Ave. N.E.,
  Atlanta; 873-1939

All shows $1.50.

Southlake Plaza Theatres
- 1053 Morrow Industrial Blvd.,
  Morrow; 968-1121

All shows $1.75.

Toco Hills Theatre
- 2983 North Druid Hills Rd. N.E.,
  Atlanta; 636-1858

All shows $1.50.

Tower Place Six Theatres
- 3340 Peachtree Rd. N.E., Atlanta;
  233-2151

All shows $1.

Town Center Theatres
- 400 Barrett Pkwy. N.W.,
  Kennesaw; 986-5050

All shows $1.25.

BARGAIN MATINEES

There are also ways to save money on first-run movies, if you can go during the daytime. These deals can change periodically, especially as the price of prime-time admission goes up. Call your local cinema to see if they're currently offering any bargain matinees. The following theaters are among the many which have recently advertised earlybird deals:

Friday's Plaza Theatres
- 6285 Peachtree Industrial Blvd.,
  Doraville; 458-5613

$3.75 before 6 p.m.

Market Square Four Theatres
- 2050 Lawrenceville Hwy.,
  Decatur; 636-0360

$3.75 before 6 p.m.

Memorial Square Theatres
- 5479 Memorial Dr., Stone
  Mountain; 292-2132

$3.75 before 6 p.m.

Merchants Exchange
- 4400 Roswell Rd., Marietta;
  986-5050

$3.75 before 6 p.m.

Southlake Festival Cinema Six
- 1564 Southlake Pkwy., Morrow;
  961-6840

$3.75 before 6 p.m.

Stonemont Theatres
- 5241 Memorial Dr., Stone
  Mountain; 292-2243

$3.75 before 6 p.m.

Twelve Oaks Quad
- 4162 Buford Hwy. N.E., Atlanta;
  321-3601

$2.75 before 6 p.m.

DRIVE-IN THEATERS

Finally, for something both cheap and romantic, there is the good ol' drive-in. Not much of this dying breed remains from its heyday of decades ago; the south, though, is one of the better parts of the country to find them. When you do come across one, it's often another place to films at bargain rates. Here are a couple of Mr. Cheap's finds:

Starlight Drive-In Theatre
- 2000 Moreland Ave. S.E., Atlanta;
  627-5786
  Tickets, for second-run movies,

are just $4.50 for adults; children under age ten are admitted free.

Storey North 85 Twin Drive-In Theatre
• 3265 Northeast Expressway Access Rd., Chamblee; 451-4570

North 85 has two separate screens, both showing the latest hot releases— not second-run films. Yet, the admis- sion price is only $4 for adults; and it's free for children under age 12. This also happens to be the site of a massive outdoor flea market on week- ends (see listing under "Flea Mar- kets").

MUSEUMS

Mr. C firmly believes that *all* museums are bargains. Consider how many treasures you can see, for less than the price of a movie! If you really enjoy a particular museum, by the way, consider becoming a member. This usually gets you free admission anytime, including per- haps your family, for the price of a couple of visits. It's a money-saver, and it helps out your beloved institution as well.

African-American Panoramic Experience
• 135 Auburn Ave. N.E., Atlanta; 521-APEX (2739)

Better known as APEX, the African- American Panoramic Experience pre- sents exhibits on local and national black history, famous black Atlan- tans, and prominent black artists. The aim of this museum is to better ac- quaint people of all races with the his- tory of African-Americans in the United States. APEX also houses the Paul Jones Collection of African Art, frequently displaying works from that continent as well.

Admission to APEX is just $2. Stu- dents pay just $1, while senior citi- zens and children under five are admitted free. It's open Tuesdays through Saturdays from 10 a.m. to 5 p.m., staying open an hour later on Wednesdays. In summer months, as well as February (Black History Month), it's also open on Sundays from 1 p.m. to 5 p.m.

Atlanta College of Art Gallery
• Robert W. Woodruff Arts Center, 1280 Peachtree St., N.W., Atlanta; 898-1157

You never know what you'll find here, since exhibits change fre- quently—about once a month. The Faculty Exhibition, full of collages, photographs, sculpture, and paint- ings, is worth checking out when it's running.

There's a wealth of talent in the student exhibits, too, so don't knock this place even though it's not a "pro- fessional" gallery—Mr. C thinks you'll be amazed at the quality of the work here.

Admission is free, although dona- tions are gladly accepted at the door. The gallery is supported in part by the Georgia Council for the Arts and by the the City of Atlanta Bureau of Cultural Affairs, but it also relies heavily on support from people like *you.*

Call the gallery or check the pa- pers for current information. The pub- lic is often invited to receptions, where you can often meet artists and designers.

The gallery is open from Monday through Saturday from 10 a.m. until 5 p.m., and Sunday from 2 p.m. to 6 p.m.

Atlanta Heritage Row
• Underground Atlanta, 55 Upper Alabama St. S.W., Atlanta; 584-7879

History buffs should certainly plan a visit to Heritage Row in the "Above Ground" section of Underground At- lanta. Six interactive exhibits take you directly through Atlanta's past, present, and future. From the wilderness of the late 1830s to a vision for the city's place in the year 2000, Heritage Row is a fascinating way to explore a city which continues to re-invent itself.

Tickets to Heritage Row are just $3 for adults, $2.50 for senior citizens and students, and $2 for children under age thirteen. Hours are Tuesday through Saturday from 10 a.m. to 5 p.m., and Sunday from 1 p.m. to 5 p.m. (closed on Mondays).

The Atlanta History Center
- 130 West Paces Ferry Rd. N.W., Atlanta; 814-4000

With the fall '93 opening of this vast new museum near central Buckhead, the Atlanta History Center has grown from a small, private group of historians into *the* premier authority on the history of the Piedmont Valley area, as well as the Civil War. The handsome, state-of-the-art facility now displays special and permanent exhibits in some 20,000 square feet of galleries—which is only a fraction of the available space still being developed.

In its "Metropolitan Frontiers" exhibit, you can trace the expansion of Atlanta from the 1830s through the present, and even into the future. Other exhibits currently focus on historical figures like Alonzo Herndon, the African-American who became one of Atlanta's first millionaire businessmen; on the immigration of Hispanics, Asians, and other ethnic groups into modern Atlanta; on local crafts and cultural activities; and much more.

And that's only the new building. The History Center is in fact a complex of several facilities, including period homes which you can tour. **The Swan House** is a stunning 1928 mansion, part of the original property here. **The Tullie Smith Farm** is a group of buildings from an 1840s plantation, which were moved here to join this 30,000-acre estate. The homes can be toured separately; each is surrounded by woods and gardens appropriate to its historical period.

There is also a library and archives building, open free to the public, for any kind of research uses; the Center's collection of Civil War archives is the most extensive one in the country.

With so much to see and do, you can easily spend an entire day wandering around here (they do have a restaurant, as well as a more informal cafe). Of course, because of all this new expansion, the Center is one of the pricier museums in town—though you certainly get more than your money's worth. Admission is $6.50 for adults; $5 for college students and seniors over 65; $4 for children ages 6-17; and free to kids under six. There is a small additional charge for the house tours, which actually allows you to pay for only what you've got time to see (tours can sell out in advance, so you should make these arrangements early in the day). And there is no charge to visit the library archives, or to stroll through the gardens and the beautiful wooded grounds.

Remember, also, that a membership is a better value if you expect to come here more than once or twice in a year (which is not hard to imagine). Members are admitted for free at all times. The museum is open from 9 a.m. to 5:30 p.m., Mondays through Saturdays, and from 12 noon to 5:30 on Sundays.

Atlanta History Center Downtown
- 140 Peachtree St. N.W., Atlanta; 814-4150

A former branch of the old C & S Bank in the heart of the city now houses the downtown branch of Buckhead's Atlanta History Center, offering free exhibits of photographs, artifacts, and video programs on a wide range of subjects. It's all packed into this elegant little building, with its interior of white marble, including the spiral staircase up to the second floor. Exhibits may cover any aspect of Atlanta's past and present—the campaign to make it the state capital the development of Hartsfield Airport, or even the beloved Braves. At the central desk, a trained volunteer is delighted to chat about the city and answer any questions; he or she can also set you up with one of several short videos, on subjects ranging from the Auburn Avenue historical district to *Gone With the Wind* author Margaret Mitchell. These are mostly five to twenty minutes in length.

Right outside the Peachtree Center MARTA station in Margaret Mitchell Square, the Atlanta History Center Downtown is open from 10 a.m. to 6 p.m., Mondays through Saturdays. It is also an official Atlanta Welcome Center, a good place for tourists to stop in for brochures on area attractions.

The Big Shanty Museum

- 2829 Cherokee St., Kennesaw; 427-2117

History buffs will love the Big Shanty Museum, home to the train involved in the Civil War incident known as "The Great Locomotive Chase of 1862." In a nutshell, the *General* was stolen by Union soldiers who were planning to destroy Confederate supply lines. Confederate soldiers gave chase in another steam locomotive, the *Texas* (which can be seen at the Cyclorama; see listing below), and eventually captured their foes. The *General* was used throughout the remainder of the war, and can now be seen in Kennesaw (which was called Big Shanty at that time), not far from where it was stolen.

Years later, in our own century, Buster Keaton created one of the greatest film comedies of all time, *The General*, based upon the same story.

The museum itself is a renovated cotton mill, and the tour of this facility includes exhibits and a slide show about that bygone era. Admission is just $2.50 for adults, $1 for children, and $2 for senior citizens (as well as for AAA members. Hmm...do they sell train insurance?). Big Shanty is open Mondays through Saturdays from 9:30 a.m. to 5:30 p.m., and Sundays from noon to 5:30 p.m. During

---

MR. CHEAP'S PICKS
Museums

✔ **African-American Panoramic Experience**—Aiming to bring this culture to people of all colors.

✔ **Michael C. Carlos Museum**—At Emory, 9,000 years of history come to life for $3.

✔ **The High Museum of Art**—The main branch is free on Thursday afternoons; their newly renovated downtown photo galleries are free all the time.

✔ **The Monetary Museum**—It doesn't cost a penny to discover this fascinating little center, hidden inside the Federal Reserve Building.

---

winter months, weekday hours are from 10 a.m. to 4 p.m.

Michael C. Carlos Museum

- 571 South Kilgo St. N.E., Atlanta; 727-4282

With over 12,000 objects from around the world, spanning 9,000 years of history, the Michael C. Carlos Museum at Emory University has an impressive collection indeed. You can explore the many fascinating exhibits the Carlos has to offer for a $3 donation.

Far from dry displays of bits of broken pottery, the museum takes a very modern approach to history. One recent exhibit was all about ancient perfumes, prepared with help from Emory's chemistry department. Similar cooperative exhibits have been undertaken with the departments of classics, philosophy, history, and theater studies.

At the Carlos, you'll see illuminated manuscript pages, drawings, and prints from the Middle Ages, 19th and 20th century works on paper, ancient Greek art including sculpture in marble, bronze, and terracotta and Corinthian and Attic vase painting, Pre-Colombian ceramics and metalwork, and more.

The museum is open seven days a week. Hours are from 10 a.m. to 5 p.m., Mondays through Thursdays, and also Saturdays; Fridays from 10 a.m. to 9 p.m.; and Sundays from 12-5. Call the number above for a 24-hour recorded message with more info on hours, exhibits, educational programs, and special events.

Cyclorama
- Grant Park, 800 Cherokee Ave. S.E., Atlanta; 658-7625

The Cyclorama offers visitors a chance to experience part of Atlanta's history in a unique way. You won't even have to spend a lot of greenbacks to do it; admission is only $3.50 for adults, $3 for seniors, and $2 for kids under twelve.

The name is slightly off; the Cyclorama is actually a huge diorama, done in the round. Okay, then what is a "diorama"? Mr. C wondered too, so he looked it up. A diorama is a three-dimensional scene with a realistically painted background. The scene depicted in this case is the Civil War siege of Atlanta. As you sit on a revolving viewing platform, you'll feel as if you're really a part of the conflict, thanks to music, narration, and those lifelike visuals.

This building also features a museum. Here you can see the *Texas*, one of the steam locomotives involved in the Great Locomotive Chase of 1862. There are many other artifacts from the Civil War, including weapons, maps and photographs, uniforms, and more.

The Cyclorama is open every day from 9:30 a.m. to 5:30 p.m., June through September; and from 9:30 a.m. to 4:30 p.m., October through May.

Fernbank Museum of Natural History
- 767 Clifton Rd. N.E., Atlanta; 378-0127

Fernbank makes it fun for people of all ages to explore the natural world around them. Exhibits include "A Walk Through Time in Georgia," which illustrates the development of the earth using various regions of Georgia as a model. A similar exhibit, geared specifically to children aged six to ten, is "The Georgia Adventure" which includes colorful recreations of five of the state's geographic regions.

Admission to Fernbank Museum of Natural History is just $5.50 for adults and $4.50 for children, students, and senior citizens. Children under two are admitted free.

This is a separate museum, by the way, from the Fernbank Science Center (see listing below). It's also the home of Atlanta's "IMAX" theatre, the five-story-high, seventy-foot-wide movie screen that surrounds you with sight and sound. Unfortunately, it requires an extra admission fee of $5.50 for adults and $4.50 for children, students, and senior citizens; this can add up to make your day here a costly one, especially for large families. You may come here for either the museum or the movie alone.

Fernbank Science Center
- 156 Heaton Park Dr. N.E., Atlanta; 378-4311

Owned and operated by the DeKalb County School System, the Fernbank Science Center dedicates itself to entertaining its visitors while educating them about science, technology, and the natural world. The best part about it is that it's almost completely free.

The only cost is for admission to the Planetarium, just $2 for adults and $1 for students. For this very reasonable price, you can enjoy a star show in one of the world's largest planetaria; it has a 70-foot projection dome over a 500-seat theater. Planetarium shows are held at 3 p.m. on Wednesday, Friday, Saturday, and

Sunday; and at 8 p.m. on Tuesday, Wednesday, Thursday, and Friday.

There is plenty more to see and do here. The Exhibition Hall features a wide range of permanent and changing exhibits: Study the natural environment and vanishing habitats of Georgia, an Apollo spacecraft, and the ever-popular dinosaur exhibit. "Treasures of the Earth" tours the geological history of Georgia, featuring a full-size model of a saber-toothed tiger. The Fernbank Forest gives you a chance to commune with nature more directly through self-guided tours of the two-mile trail.

And don't miss the Observatory. The Fernbank Observatory houses a 36-inch reflecting telescope, one of the largest in the world, which you can use to view all types of celestial beings. This observatory has a national reputation for research and science education. It's only open to the public on Thursday and Friday evenings, and only on clear nights, from about 8 p.m. to 10:30 p.m. When the skies are cloudy, they still give tours and explain the workings of this massive instrument. During inclement weather, the place closes up shop entirely.

Fernbank Science Center is open seven days a week. Hours vary for each exhibit; call for more info.

Georgia State Museum of Science and Industry
• Georgia State Capitol Building, Capitol Square S.W., Atlanta; 656-2844

This museum is definitely an unexpected treasure, and a free one at that. Tucked away on the fourth floor of the State Capitol building, it's a natural history museum combined with aviation and war displays, as well as tributes to past city and state leaders.

The nature side shows you preserved animals, fish and birds from all around the country—white-tailed deer, American buffalo, a 64-pound striped bass, and American bald eagles. The life-size snake, shark, alligator, and right whale models may be a bit *too* lifelike for very small children to enjoy; but there's always the mineral and seashell collections, and the Indian heritage exhibit featuring 2,500 year-old prehistoric relics.

Georgia industry is also highlighted, with interactive exhibits on kaolin mining and such; also on display is the world's oldest bale of cotton—from 1870.

Down on the first floor of the State Capitol building, the museum also features a chronological array of Georgia's flags, some of which were actually used in the Civil War, the Spanish-American War and World War I. Guns and other weapons used by Georgian soldiers are also shown.

Most of the exhibits in the museum are included as part of the free guided tours of the state house provided by the Capitol Guide Service. Tours are scheduled weekdays *and* weekends at 10 and 11 a.m. and 1 and 2 p.m.

High Museum of Art
• 1280 Peachtree St. N.W., Atlanta; 892-3600

Recent shows at the main branch of the High Museum have included "Annie Leibovitz Photographs, 1970-1990," displaying the Rolling Stone photographer's portraits of big-time celebrities; and "Crosscurrents: 20th-Century Art," a multi-themed display of self-portraits, dreamscapes, and abstract art. The museum's strikingly modern building is, in itself, worth checking out—and, with free hours on Thursday afternoons, you have no excuse but to go make yourself a little bit more cultured.

Every day the museum is open, tours are offered for free with the price of admission. These last about 45 minutes. They start at 11 a.m. and 1:30 p.m. Tuesdays through Fridays; on Fridays, when the museum is open later, there is an extra tour at 6 p.m. On weekends, the tours start at 1 and 3 p.m. Groups of six or more can call ahead and arrange tours at other times.

In addition to the museum's permanent displays and traveling exhibits, the High offers many lectures, workshops, and programs on the exhibits and artists themselves, and other topics of interest; some of these are free, while others get a bit pricey. Courses on art history, photography lectures and workshops, and family programs (including studio art workshops for $10 a person) are also scheduled regularly. Movies are also a mainstay of the High Museum's eclectic offerings (see listing under "Movies").

The museum is open Tuesdays through Thursdays from 10 a.m. until 5 p.m.; Fridays, from 10-9; Saturdays from 10-5, and Sundays from noon until 5. It's closed on Mondays. HMA members are always admitted free; if you visit often, membership is a good bargain! Regular admission is $5 for adults, $3 for students with IDs and senior citizens over 65, $1 for children ages 6-17, and free for those under 6.

And don't forget: The museum is free to all, every Thursday from 1 to 5 p.m. Why not make a day of it in Midtown and also visit the Botanical Gardens, which are also open to the public for free on Thursday afternoons (see listing under "Outdoors").

The Monetary Museum
- 104 Marietta St. N.W., Atlanta; 521-8020

This may be the only museum you'll ever go to which requires you to show identification just to go in. That's because the Monetary Museum is located inside the Federal Reserve Bank of Atlanta, a U.S. government building, just a block away from the CNN Center. The museum is on the third floor, and you must not only be signed in, but you'll have to wear a visitor's badge while you're inside. Just go to the security desk at the left side of the lobby, and ask to see the museum.

Upstairs, the museum itself is all of one large room, filled with fascinating displays about the history of money, the production of our currency, and the paths it follows whenever we spend it. See a gold ingot, whose daily value is written on a

chalkboard (on Mr. C's visit, it was worth a cool $43,619); see uncut sheets of dollar bills, and how a half-dollar goes from a sheet of metal to a round blank to the finished coin; test your ability to pick out counterfeit money.

You can also find out what really happens behind the scenes every time you write a check, or use a credit card. And, speaking of behind the scenes, a half-hour video gives you a tour of the whole building and all that goes on inside. One of the bank's functions is to take tired old paper bills out of circulation and shred them; would you believe five tons worth are destroyed every week? Yep. Some of these shreddings are packed into plastic baggies, and you're welcome to take some home with you.

So, not only does the Monetary Museum cost no money to visit, you can actually come away with some cash. It's open weekdays only, from 9:00 a.m. to 4:00 p.m.; closed on weekends and, of course, bank holidays.

Museum of the Jimmy Carter Library
- One Copenhill Ave. N.E., Atlanta; 331-3942

Just on the other side of Ponce de Leon Avenue from Virginia-Highland, the Carter Presidential Center has carved out a quiet, pastoral home for itself. Along with the official library archives and the Carter Center's offices and meeting halls—continuously humming with Mr. Carter's ongoing world peace activities—is this fine museum dedicated to his brief but busy term in office.

You begin with a half-hour film, in one of those super-comfy modern screening rooms, on the Carter presidency. This sets you up perfectly for the museum itself, with separate areas dedicated to the various issues in which he was involved: Camp David, the hostages in Iran, the Panama Canal treaty, strategic arms negotiations and more. Makes you realize, for someone whose presidency is often considered a "failure," just how many important events Carter dealt with. There are also videos of the many concerts held at the White House, from Horowitz to hoedowns; and a full-size replica of the Oval Office itself, complete with a recording of Carter giving you a personal guided tour.

Speaking of which, you are also free to tour the grounds of the Carter Center, beautifully landscaped with a Japanese garden, reflecting pools, and the like; the museum has a comfortable cafeteria as well. Neither of these require any admission fee. Admission to the museum is $2.50 for adults, $1.50 for senior citizens, and free to all under the age of sixteen. Open from 9 a.m. to 4:45 p.m., Monday through Saturday and from noon to 4:45 p.m. on Sunday.

Rhodes Hall
Georgia Trust for Historic Preservation

- 1516 Peachtree St. N.W., Atlanta; 881-9980

Rhodes Hall is an anachronistic figure in this Midtown stretch of Peachtree Street. Built over 90 years ago, this castle-like museum with its giant magnolia tree out front is listed in the National Register of Historic Places. It was once owned by Amos G. Rhodes, who became a successful "New South" businessman after coming to Atlanta with only $75 to his name.

The castle is modeled in Romanesque style; it was designed by archetect Willis Denny to remind Rhodes of the Rhineland castles he admired while visiting Europe. Gorgeous stained glass windows and a carved mahogany staircase adorn the inside. Most of this Victorian-era building's original features are intact, making for a lesson in art history as well.

Admission to Rhodes Hall is free, but donations are gladly accepted in the reception hall. The building is open for public tours on weekdays from 11 a.m. until 4 p.m.; group tours can be arranged by calling the mu-

seum ahead of time. You can also call the Trust for Historic Preservation's tour hotline at 876-2040 for information about other guided tours in the area.

Road to Tara Museum

- The Georgian Terrace, 659 Peachtree St. N.E., Atlanta; 897-1939

This museum is named for the original title that Atlanta's favorite daughter, Margaret Mitchell, gave to her book *Gone With The Wind*. Its home, the Georgian Terrace, served as accomodations for the cast of *Gone With The Wind* during the movie's 1939 premiere (note the museum phone number); it's also where Mitchell first gave her manuscript to Harold Latham, a representative of the MacMillan Publishing Company.

All that history before you even step inside! But that's only the tip of the iceberg—this place is full of such memorabilia as autographed first editions of the book, foreign editions, Mitchell's personal letters and papers, reproductions of the original movie costumes, GWTW dolls, and more. For anyone who ever fell in love with the story of Scarlett O'Hara and Rhett Butler, whether in the book or movie version, this museum is a must-see.

Admission is $5 for adults, $4.25 for seniors, and $3.50 for students; it's free for children under twelve. A special rate of $3.50 per person is available for groups of fifteen or more. Hours are Monday through Saturday, 10 a.m. to 6 p.m. and Sunday from 1 p.m. to 6 p.m.

SciTrek, The Science and Technology Museum of Atlanta

- 395 Piedmont Ave. N.E., Atlanta; 522-5500

Geared toward younger children, SciTrek emphasizes interactive exhibits and aims to help kids have fun while learning scientific principles (even if subconsciously). There are over 100 hands-on exhibits here, including the ever-popular "room-on-an-angle" and other optical illusions. Static machines, light bulbs, color displays, and mechanical contraptions are all part of the fun.

Also featured is a 40-foot tall Erector-set replica of the Eiffel Tower, and "Impact!," the museum's video-game-like exhibit that teaches children about skills required for driving.

Past traveling exhibits have included "Black Achievers in Science," "The Golden Age of Disney," "Sharks!," and "Light Dreams: The Art and Science of Holography."

SciTrek is open from 10 a.m. until 5 p.m., Tuesdays through Sundays, and from 12 to 5 on Sundays. Hours are generally extended in the summer; the museum suggests calling ahead to check.

General admission is $6.50 for adults; $4.25 for children, college students with ID, and senior citizens; and free for SciTrek members and children under age three. Weekdays during the school year, the museum offers a special reduced afternoon rate of $3.75 for admission from 1 to 5 p.m. Parking is available for $4 in lots behind the museum.

The Telephone Museum
- Southern Bell Center, 675 West Peachtree St. N.E., Atlanta; 529-7334

Oh, the treasures that lie hidden in the most unexpected places! Inside the BellSouth building, you'll find this interesting little museum which traces the development of that gizmo which we take so much for granted. You can hear an actual recording of Mr. Watson himself, describing the historic moment when Alexander Graham Bell spilled that jar of acid; watch a short film on the growth of the telecommunications system; and have a look at where it's all headed in the near future.

Admission to the museum is free to all. It's entered from the West Peachtree Street side of the building, at the corner of 3rd Street; or from the retail mall in the center of the building. One major drawback: The museum is only open on weekday lunch hours, Mondays through Fridays from 11:00 a.m. to 1:00 p.m. Hmmm....With all the money we send them every month, you'd think they could manage to keep the place open more than ten hours a week!

MUSIC

CLASSICAL

Atlanta Symphony Orchestra
- Symphony Hall, Woodruff Arts Center, 1280 Peachtree St. N.W., Atlanta; 892-2414

If you fear you'll need to refinance your house in order to enjoy a night of classical music with the internationally-acclaimed Atlanta Symphony Orchestra, Mr. C has come to the rescue. First of all, please note that reasonably priced seats are available for every concert: rear balcony seats average $17 or $18 apiece. But, if that's still too pricey for you, read on.

Rush Tickets: Students and senior citizens may purchase unsold tickets to some concerts for $13 on the day of the performance (rush tickets for matinees are available one day ahead of time). Tickets must be purchased at the Woodruff Arts Center; there is a limit of one ticket per person, and don't forget appropriate identification!

Sneak Preview Rehearsals: About half a dozen times per season, you can sit in as the ASO rehearses for particular concerts. You'd hardly think that musicians at the top of their game would *need* to practice, but they do; often, these are rehearsals with a guest artist or conductor, who needs a runthrough under full concert conditions. In any case, you always get the whole program. Most open rehearsals are scheduled on weekday mornings, and all take place in Symphony Hall. Tix are just $8 each, and may be purchased in advance.

Atlanta Symphony Youth Orchestra: The ASYO presents three concerts each year, in fall, winter, and spring. Hear the classical stars of tomorrow today—these teenagers are serious musicians, already considerably polished. Many will doubtless move up to the professional orchestra, or to others around the country. Tickets to these performances are just $5 for all seats; it's a great way to enjoy classical music inexpensively, and to support and encourage young artists.

Family Concerts: Subscribe to this special series, and tix are just $12 each. These concerts are designed to introduce children to the joys of classical music. There are about five concerts in the annual series, and some are designed around holidays such as Halloween and Christmas.

The Cathedral of St. Philip
- 2744 Peachtree Rd. N.W., Atlanta; 365-1050

The Cathedral of St. Philip presents weekly classical music concerts, all of which are free and open to the public. Most feature music played on the church's magnificent pipe organ. Other concerts present different instruments, such as the harpsichord, flute, or piano. Occasionally, larger groups perform here too, including Atlanta's International Youth Chorus and the Capitol City Opera Company. Concerts are held on Sunday afternoons at 3:30 p.m., from September through May; call for a schedule of upcoming events.

First Presbyterian Church
- 1328 Peachtree St. N.E., Atlanta; 892-8461

The First Presbyterian Church offers you an oppurtunity to enjoy classical music for free, though they do graciously accept donations. Concerts are held monthly during the school year, on Sundays at 2:15 p.m.

Recent concerts have included the Peachtree Brass, and violinist Timothy Schwartz with pianist Nancy Elton. One recent performance even included a performance by dancer Wendy Dixon. Give them a call to get a schedule of upcoming concerts.

Peachtree Christian Church
- 1580 Peachtree St. N.E., Atlanta; 876-5535

The Concert Series at the Peachtree Christian Church is chock full of fun and exciting performances. The concerts, which feature musicians from across the nation and around the world, are either free or very cheap.

One recent performance which required tickets for an advance cost of $8 ($10 at the door) featured the choir of the Coventry Cathedral in England. Recent freebie concerts included organist Nicholas Bowden; and a performance of Handel's *Messiah*, featuring the Peachtree Christian Church Sanctuary Choir, Soloists, and Orchestra.

Some events require only a "suggested donation," like the recent "Fine Arts of the Soviet Empire: A Concert and Arts Festival." For a suggested donation of $5, this event not only presented piano and operatic recitals, but also a display of visual arts, ethnic foods, and folk dancing from this now-defunct "empire."

MR. CHEAP'S PICKS
Music—Classical

✔ **Atlanta Symphony Orchestra**—The ASO offers a number of ways to enjoy classical music affordably, including rush tickets, sneak preview rehearsals, and family concerts.

199

Some events are benefits, so your donation goes toward helping a good cause. Call the church for a calendar of upcoming concerts and festivals.

COFFEEHOUSES

Oxford Espresso Cafe
• 360 Pharr Rd. N.E., 266-8350
The Oxford Espresso Cafe, at the Pharr Road branch of the Oxford Bookstore, hosts a singer-songwriter's showcase. "The Oxford Acoustic Cafe" happens every Sunday, Monday, and Tuesday at 8:30 p.m.; artists featured here recently include Kodac Harrison, Janet McLaughlin, and the Carvers. There's no cover charge, so the only money you'll spend is the price of cup of coffee and some pastry, if you're so inclined. If you really like what you hear, the music department downstairs may even have it on cassette or compact disc.

Cafe Diem
• 642 North Highland Ave. N.E., Atlanta; 607-7008
Sieze the day at Cafe Diem with poetry, classical guitar, hot coffee, and more. Cafe Diem hosts Amnesty International meetings, so they must be cool. Regular features include monthly poetry readings (the first Tuesday of the month) and classical guitar outside on the patio every Sunday. There is never a cover charge for

MR. CHEAP'S PICKS
Music—Coffeehouses

✔ **Homage Coffeehouse**—If Elvis really did come back, he'd stop in here.
✔ **Red Light Cafe**—Great local folk-rock and jazz, even better food.

any of these arts events.

A great hangout all around, Cafe Diem is open seven days a week, Monday through Thursday from 4 p.m. to 12:30 a.m., Friday and Saturday from 11 a.m. to 2:30 a.m., and Sunday from 11:30 a.m. to 12:30 a.m.

Homage Coffeehouse
• 255 Trinity Ave. S.W., Atlanta; 681-2662
Every Tuesday and Wednesday night, from about 9 p.m. into the wee small hours, this downtown club presents live jazz music with a cover charge of just $3. Located in a block of old industrial buildings, the Homage is sort of a cross between the gritty hipness of New York's art club scene with the potted plants/books and board games/wacky posters coffeehouses of the West Coast. If that sounds like a mouthful, or an eyeful, well, this place is a bit hard to describe; but it's fun. In addition to various coffees, beers and wines, there is a limited but equally eclectic food menu: Chips and guacamole, pita bread and hummus, brie and fruit—all between $3-$5. The Homage attracts a multi-ethnic and multi-generational crowd of friendly folks, who generally hang out until about 3:00 in the morning. The coffeehouse is open Tuesdays through Saturdays.

Liquid Bean
• 436 Ponce de Leon Ave. N.E., Atlanta; 874-0153
Liquid Bean is a grungy (as in grunge-scene) little hole-in-the-wall that features various forms of live entertainment on its small stage. Might be some jazz, some poetry, some performance art, some music, or whatever else folks are in the mood for. To say that these dudes are laid-back

is, like, a definite understatement. They open at 8 a.m. on Tuesdays, and then stay open 24 hours a day for the rest of the week. They are closed on Mondays, presumably to recuperate.

The cover charges here are equally laid-back. They generally charge only on Thurdays, Fridays, and Saturdays, and then it's usually about $3 to $5, depending on what's scheduled. Thursday features jazz; Friday and Saturday they present local bands,

the occasional national act, and maybe some performance art, for good measure.

Of course, since they're open 'round the clock, Mr. C just has to ask: couldn't you go in on a Wednesday, when there's no cover charge, and just *stay*, thus avoiding the Thursday, Friday, and Saturday charges? However you decide to divide up your time at the Bean, the entertainment starts around 10 p.m.

FOLK

County Cork Pub
• 56 East Andrews Dr. N.W., Atlanta; 303-1976
This Buckhead bar presents live Irish-American bands, playing music which varies from traditional Irish folk to more contemporary rock sounds (but often with a Celtic influence). Music generally takes place Tuesday through Saturday nights, but there is only a cover charge on Fridays and Saturdays.

Dante's Down the Hatch
• Underground Atlanta, 60 Upper Alabama St. S.W., Atlanta; 577-1800
• 3380 Peachtree Rd. N.E., Atlanta; 266-1600
See listing under "Jazz and Blues" below.

Eddie's Attic
• 515-B North McDonough St., Decatur; 377-4976
Eddie's Attic belongs to Eddie Owen and both have become quite legendary in these parts. This is where the Indigo Girls got their start, way back when they were just Emory University students eager to play gigs *anywhere*.

There is something going on at Eddie's every night of the week, usually two to three bands per evening, all for a cover charge of $3 to $7. In addition to the music, the club has a

game room for playing pool and further socializing.

Of particular interest is the "Writer's Format" on Sunday nights. A bunch of singers and songwriters are invited to come in and sit in a circle and do their thing. They describe it as "sort of like a living room jam." And you never know who you'll see here. Emily Saliers and Amy Ray, of the aforementioned Indigo Girls, must feel they owe the place because they stop in and jam fairly often.

In addition, Eddie's has an open-mike night every six weeks or so. Admission is free, and these give you a sneak peek at artists who may be up-and-coming in the acoustic music scene.

The Freight Room
• 301 E. Howard Ave., Decatur, 378-5365
For a kickin' time on the cheap, the Freight Room is a great place to check out. *Atlanta* magazine voted it 1992's best Bluegrass Club, and for good reason. Cover charges rarely exceed $10, and if they do, it's for Nashville acts like John Hartford, the Stockwell Brothers or Curtis Jones. Up-and-coming artists like Bill Sheffield and Ralph Luttrell played one Saturday for a cover of merely $3; so did Cedar Hill and Jan Smith.

Thursday is the night that draws the most well-known acts, but live

MR. CHEAP'S PICKS
Music—Folk

✔ **Eddie's Attic**—A veritable institution on the folk music scene. Come by and you may hear the next Indigo Girls.

✔ **Rainy Day Records**—Not only a great place to buy cheap CDs, Rainy Day is a great place to hear live music, free!

music plays here from Wednesdays through Saturdays, with an occasional Tuesday night gig—call ahead to check their schedule or pick up one of their postcard-size event listings the next time you visit. And you should expect almost anything during Open Mike night, held every Sunday. Admission to this bash is free—can't beat that!

The Freight Room was actually a train station in a former life, and you'd think that the old, exposed wooden rafters would snap from the beat of this music; but if anyone here is worried, they sure don't look it.

You can rustle up some good food while you're listening, too. The Freight Room serves up basics like burgers and wings, along with good beers. And, when the show starts its own cooking, popcorn seems to start flying all over the place. If you're in a rowdy mood, pull into the Freight Room.

Irish Arts of Atlanta
● 1288 North Morningside Dr. N.E., Atlanta; 873-5621
Irish Arts of Atlanta presents a monthly Irish music session at **Manuel's Tavern**, 602 North Highland Avenue, Atlanta (telephone 525-3447). This takes place on the second Sunday of each month from 3:30 p.m. to 6:30 p.m.; there is no cover charge, but donations are gratefully accepted. Manuel's, of course, has

plenty of the appropriate beers from the Emerald Isle on tap. It's a splendid way to pass a few merry hours. And, if you play Irish music yourself, give them a call to find out how you can get involved.

Limerick Junction Irish Pub
● 822 North Highland Ave. N.E., Atlanta; 874-7147
This bar bills itself as "a little bit of Ireland in the heart of Virginia-Highland." Having never been to Ireland himself, Mr. C can't say for sure if this is true, but it must come very close. The pub offers live music every night, mostly of the traditional Irish variety, though not exclusively.

What's more, there is never a cover charge during the week; and, on Fridays and Saturdays, it costs only $1 to get in. On Tuesday nights, Limerick Junction features an open-mike night with cash prizes for the best newcomers.

Rainy Day Records
● Toco Hills Promenade, 3005 North Druid Hills N.E., Atlanta; 636-6166
Along with being a great place to pick up some music on the cheap (see listing under "CDs, Records, and Tapes"), Rainy Day Records features live, in-house performances every Saturday at 3 p.m. and there is no cover charge. Artists featured here are generally locally-based folk and acoustic musicians. Many of the players who appear here also turn up at cafes and clubs like Eddie's Attic; so this is a good chance to get a free sneak preview. Stop in to get a list of the month's upcoming performances.

Red Light Cafe
● 553-I Amsterdam Ave. N.E., Atlanta; 874-7828
Part of the Midtown Outlets, and a fine place for a bite after a day of shopping, this place is also a worthy hangout on its own. The Red Light is a marvelous recent addition to the Atlanta cafe scene. Yes, it's next to the shops; yes, with such cavernous high ceilings, it might have been a warehouse too. But its owners have managed to turn the space into an artfully cozy room, with mission-style

wooden tables and chairs, a counter offering today's newspapers, and darkly atmospheric lighting.

Claiming to present "righteous California cooking," this is indeed a very West Coast mix of coffeehouse, restaurant, and music club, all at the same time. Sip a cup of strong Sumatra roast or espresso; have a sandwich, a full meal, or some homemade pastry; and peruse the artworks by local artists on the walls. Pick up a book or a board game from one of the side tables. Whatever, it's, you know, cool.

Folk and (mostly) acoustic rock groups play on Friday and Saturday nights from about 9 p.m., with a cover charge of $2-$3; the place usually jumps until 3:00 or 4:00 in the morning (and the kitchen stays open!). It's also the occasional setting for record release parties. Wednesday nights present a free showcase of singer/songwriters, while Sundays feature "Jazz at Sundown," live music to accompany dinner from 6-9 p.m., again with a small cover charge. The food itself is phenomenal. If you haven't heard about this cafe yet, or have been meaning to check it out, Mr. C urges you to do so.

JAZZ AND BLUES

Blues Harbor
* 2293-B Peachtree Rd. N.E., Atlanta; 605-0661

Blues Harbor is open Tuesday through Saturday, cranking out plenty of blues, zydeco, and even a little Louisiana swamp boogie. Cover charges average about $5 to $7. Seen here recently was Grammy Award-winner Luther "Guitar Jr." Johnson, a veteran of the Muddy Waters band. Music usually starts at 9:30 p.m., and rocks until around 1:30 to 2:00 in the morning.

Cafe 290
* The Balconies Shopping Cloister, 290 Hilderbrand Dr., Sandy Springs; 256-3942

Hot jazz in the suburbs? In a shopping plaza? Yes to both! Cafe 290 is located just off of Roswell Road, in something called the Balconies Shopping Cloister (shopping center, okay, shopping plaza, sure, but *cloister*? Well, for many, shopping *is* a religious experience). Anyway, this casual restaurant and bar presents jazz seven nights a week—usually blowing well into the night—and there's never a cover charge.

The menu, primarily steaks and seafood, zips out of Mr. C's price range (even at $15 for the average entree, the place is packed on weekends). But you're welcome to sit at the bar, with a good view of the musicians, and just have a drink or two. During the week, when it's less crowded, you can probably get a table, and have drinks or perhaps coffee and dessert. With its warm and cozy interior of dark wood decor and low lighting, plus that great music, this can be a romantic and inexpensive evening.

Dailey's
* 17 International Blvd. N.E., Atlanta; 681-3303

In the front bar room at this popular downtown restaurant, pianist/vocalist Jeni Michelson has a regular early evening gig at the keyboard, from 6-9 p.m. Mondays through Fridays. She plays a mix of her favorites and your requests, from jazz to pop to oldies; each table, in fact, has a booklet listing about 800 titles (!) in her repertoire.

The attractive bar has the feel of an outdoor courtyard, with its red brick and wrought-iron walls, and potted plants along the windows. It's a popular after-work gathering place for the suit-and-tie crowd (that includes women too, right?), many of whom will be going on into the dining room for dinner. Chances are, if you're reading this book, you will not be joining them. Even the drinks in the piano bar are overpriced; but the peanuts are free, and there are usually enough free tables so that you

can nurse your cocktail along without
feeling pressured.

Dante's Down the Hatch
- Underground Atlanta, 60 Upper
  Alabama St. S.W., Atlanta;
  577-1800
- 3380 Peachtree Rd. N.E., Atlanta;
  266-1600

When "Underground Atlanta" closed
for renovations, Dante's—a popular
restaurant—opened a Buckhead
branch. Now that "Underground Atlanta" is alive and thriving once
more, there are two Dante's from
which to choose. Both Dante's offer
live music seven nights a week, with
an interesting menu of fondues,
breads, and cheeses—though Mr. C
can't really say that these are cheap.

More reasonably priced, though,
are the cover charges to enjoy the entertainment. At the Buckhead location, admission to "the Wharf,"
where you can enjoy classical guitar,
is absolutely free. Admission to "the
Ship," which features a jazz trio, is
$4.

The touristy Underground location
is a bit more expensive but still quite
reasonable. Here, the Wharf features
acoustical guitar and other folk music, with admission just $1. Permis-
sion to board the Ship will cost you
$5, and you'll enjoy a jazz trio Mon-
day through Saturday and big band
jazz on Sundays.

Both locations are open until 11
p.m. on Sundays, 'til midnight Monday through Thursday, and 'til 1 a.m.
on Friday and Saturday nights.

Just Jazz
- 2101 Tula St. N.W., Atlanta;
  355-5423

In a building directly behind the
Buckhead branch of the ubiquitous
Mick's, Just Jazz is many things a
jazz club should be. You have to go
not only around the back, but up
some stairs and down the hall—
where the place suddenly opens up
into a funky, spacious and comfortable room. It's done completely in
black and white, mostly black, with
lots of tables covered with white
linen cloths. There's a nice, long bar

running down one side of the room.
And the stage is raised, so everyone
has a good view of the band.

Another part of the decor is a collection of saxes, trumpets and other
horns mounted on the walls as you
enter; but these are the only instruments that sit still in this club, known
for hard-hitting, traditional jazz.
Wednesdays through Saturdays feature a resident group, often joined by
guest musicians; while on Sundays
it's a jazz jam. Cover charge is usually $5 every night but Saturday,
when it goes up to $7 (a bit out of
Mr. C's range, though well worth it).
Occasional special bookings will go
even higher; Ramsey Lewis has
played here, as has Frank Foster's
version of the Count Basie Orchestra.

Sliding back down an octave or
two, Just Jazz does offer a happy
hour buffet, from 6:00 to 8:30 p.m.,
every Friday. Admission to the buffet, with entertainment by the house
band, is free.

Meno's New Orleans Cafe
- 113 E. Court Square, Decatur;
  377-4405

Just off of Ponce in the very center of
town, is this little parking lot lined
with shops and restaurants. Down at
the end, you'll find Meno's—a terrific little restaurant serving up authentic N'awlins food. On Fridays and
Saturdays, from 9:00 to about midnight or so, they also dish out generous portions of laid-back, traditional
jazz. It ain't Dixieland, just nice,
easygoing renditions of all the standards. There's no cover charge; you
can have a beer or some wine, or dig
into a plate of wonderful jambalaya
with andouille sausage, gumbo, or
shrimp etoufee. The dinners are reasonably priced, with truly large portions. The owner's wife personally
bakes their desserts, such as bourbon-
rum cake; or, for just a few bucks,
you can also get what may be the
best beignets and coffee this side of
the Mississippi.

Springy's Jazz Jam
- 710 Peachtree St. N.E., Atlanta;
  607-0021

Tuesdays from 9 p.m. til 1 a.m., Springy's Restaurant and Lounge plays relaxing jazz music in a classy yet casual atmosphere. You may think you're on the shores of Montego Bay, but you're actually smack dab in the Fox Theatre district of Midtown.

Their "Jazz Jam" series was once defunct, but was brought back last year by popular demand. There's no charge for the tunes on Tuesdays, and the authentic Jamaican food in the restaurant won't put you back much, either. The menu includes lots of moderately priced seafood entrees; desserts are a specialty at Springy's, too. If you're in the neighborhood for a show, this makes a great place to stop in afterwards for coffee and a creme caramel, a nightcap, and some tunes.

MR. CHEAP'S PICKS
Music—Jazz

✔ **Cafe 290**—Straight-ahead jazz seven nights a week, in a comfortable, suburban restaurant—with no cover charge.

✔ **Springy's**—Another restaurant, this one a Caribbean in Midtown, offers simple, elegant jazz on Tuesday nights—no cover.

ROCK/POP

American Pie
- 5840 Roswell Rd., Sandy Springs; 255-7571

Rock 'n roll and Top-40 hits are the favorite fillings at this Pie. Friday and Saturday nights, a mere $2 gets you in to dance your cares away with a DJ spinning your favorite tunes. On Sunday nights American Pie really cooks (or is that bakes?) with a live band. The cover on Sundays is still low, just $4. Music starts at about 10 p.m. and rocks until 3 a.m. on Saturdays, and 'til 4 a.m. Fridays and Sundays.

Botany's
- 898 Virginia Ave., Hapeville; 766-2545

No, this is not a place to buy azaleas. This is actually a bar, where live music can be heard Thursdays through Sundays. And there's never a cover charge. You could say Mr. C has a green thumb for finding free live music venues.

Anyway, Botany's presents a variety of musical styles, usually in the form of solo performers. Music starts around 9 p.m., and jams until 1 a.m. or so. Botany's also has a full-size

volleyball court and two dart boards. Hang around and get involved in the occasional dart league or volleyball tournament.

Buster's BBQ
- 4988 Memorial Dr., Stone Mountain; 297-9993

Buster's BBQ features live music on Friday and Saturday nights, without any cover charge. Mostly what you'll see (and hear) here is R & B, with some rock and country bands thrown in for good measure, and most of the performers are local artists. Music starts at 8 p.m. and the last set ends about 2 a.m.

CJ's Landing
- 270 Buckhead Ave., Atlanta; 237-7657

CJ's is a big hit among the trendy Buckhead crowd. It's more casual than many of the clubs in the Entertainment District—jeans are fine here. That's appropriate, since the place actually looks more like a treehouse than a bar, with a gigantic oak tree emerging from the center of the open deck area.

Expect a crowd from Thursday

through Saturday, when live reggae bands start to play at 10 p.m. The cover is usually no more than $3 or so, and if you get there early enough, there may be some room left on the teensy dance floor. If it's too noisy for you on the deck (conversation is nearly impossible so close to the loud bands), you can always retreat to the enclosed bar.

You can avoid the crowds altogether by coming in earlier; dance to recorded music (not all of it reggae, though) starting at 7 p.m., Wednesdays through Saturdays. If you get there before the band starts playing, there's no cover charge.

Dark Horse Tavern
• 816 North Highland Ave. N.E., Atlanta; 873-3607

Mr. C loves clubs that say their cover charge is "never more than" some nice, low dollar figure. Mr. C loves it even more when the cover charge usually stays even lower. The Dark Horse promises never to charge more than $5, but in fact, the cover charge is almost always just $2 or $3. The lineup ranges from rhythm and blues and rock to folk and acoustic music, playing seven nights a week in their large downstairs space.

Even on weekends, there are deals to be found here. Every Friday and Saturday from 8-10 p.m., before the main act, there is a separate "Acoustic Set" with an admission price of $1 per person. And, on Sunday evenings, the Dark Horse has an open-mike night with free admission.

Dave & Buster's
• 2215 D & B Dr., Smyrna; 951-5554

Every Wednesday through Saturday evening, this popular new restaurant features live dance bands. The only time there is ever a cover charge is on Fridays and Saturdays after 10 p.m., and even then it's only $1.

During the breaks, a DJ spins Top-40 hits so that you can keep right on dancing. However, should you need a little break yourself, there are plenty of other ways to stay amused here. D & B's has billiards, video games, virtual reality games, shuffle board, and more.

Dave & Buster's is open Monday through Thursday from 11 a.m. until 1 a.m., Friday from 11 a.m. until 2 a.m., Saturday from 11:30 a.m. 'til 2 a.m. and Sunday from 11:30 a.m. until 1 a.m. It's located near Delk Road, off of I-75.

Dr. Rib
• 1174 Euclid Ave. N.E., Atlanta; 525-5555

This restaurant and bar in Little Five Points has a side room in which blues musicians raise the roof every night of the week. Meanwhile, you can chow down on—what else?—ribs, chicken, beer by the pint or pitcher, and more. Prices are reasonable, and there is no cover charge for the music.

Fatt Matt's Rib Shack
• 1811 Piedmont Ave. N.E., Atlanta; 607-1622

Fatt Matt's also presents live blues every night with no cover charge. Mr. C does feel it important to note, though, that the musicians are paid through tips. If you've hung out for a little while and you've enjoyed the tunes, do toss a couple bucks into the hat. The musicians deserve it and it's still a great deal for you. Blues bands crank it up here from around 8:30 p.m., and they howl 'til 11 p.m. or so.

Frijoleros
• 1031 Peachtree St. N.E., Atlanta; 892-TACO (8226)

Along with its great (and cheap!) Mexican food, Frijoleros offers live music on Tuesday through Saturday nights. It's a loud, young scene, with the appropriate grunge decor. The bills feature rock 'n roll mostly, with some acoustic, country, and rockabilly mixed in, all from local bands. The cover charge is just $2 to $3.

The food is quite good, by the way (see listing under "Restaurants: Midtown"), and they've recently expanded into the storefront next door to add a narrow room with a bar at one end, and a small stage at the other. It gets pretty full. Music starts about 10-ish, and rocks until 1 or 2 a.m.

Groove Yard

- 691 Peachtree St. N.E., Atlanta; 873-0691

Most of the events here at the Groove Yard are album release parties. This is when record companies, like Sony, host a party to showcase a band that has just released an album on their label. Wouldn't these be more appropriately called CD release parties? The featured band, of course, plays some of the new tunes. Since these are mostly done for promotional purposes, admission is often free; when there is a charge, it is usually a minimal $2 to $5.

The Groove Yard hosts these groovy events as regularly as once or twice a week. Music starts about 9 p.m., and folks party well into the night, until two, three or even four in the morning. The club is located atop the Midtown branch of the Bridgetown Grill, a cool scene in itself (see listing under "Restaurants: Midtown") so you can combine great, cheap food and great, cheap entertainment with very little effort.

Jellyrolls

- 295 East Paces Ferry Rd. N.E., Atlanta; 261-6866

Jellyrolls ads tell you "this ain't no bake shop." Got *that* right. This is a good, cheap place to hang out and enjoy the rollicking sound of dueling pianos. Dueling pianos, for the uninitiated, are two pianos playing your requests, back and forth (like that banjo scene in *Deliverance*). People's requests range from Jerry Lee Lewis to the Spin Doctors to old television sitcom themes (Brady Bunch, anyone?) to Stone Temple Pilots. Whatever you crave, these quick-witted ivory-ticklers seem to know it. They'll even play the jingles from your favorite commercials.

The keys fly every Tuesday through Saturday night. Fridays and Saturdays are the only nights with a cover; just $2 before 9 p.m. and $3 after 9 p.m. The music goes until about 2 a.m. during the week, and 'til 3 a.m. on the weekends.

MR. CHEAP'S PICKS
Music—Rock/Pop

✔ **The Groove Yard**—Free or inexpensive rock, over the also-funky Bridgetown Grill in Midtown.

✔ **Midtown Music Hall**—Live rock and alternative music for just a few dollars.

✔ **Velvet**—Betcha didn't think you could afford such hipness. Don't forget your attitude, baby.

Johnny's Hideaway

- 3771 Roswell Rd. N.E., Atlanta; 233-8026

Johnny's Hideaway, in trendy Buckhead, can get crowded, but Mr. C usually considers that the sign of a pretty good hangout. And if Johnny's isn't a great place to hideaway, it is a great place to hangout, with dance music seven nights a week and never a cover charge. There is a two-drink minimum. The club opens every day at 11 a.m., and stays open all the way through to 4:00 in the morning.

The Masquerade

- 695 North Ave. N.E., Atlanta; 577-8178

The Masquerade is one of the big, showy places in town to hear cutting-edge alternative music by local and national bands. Depending on the act, tickets range from $5 up to $10 or so, with most groups checking in around $8.

During warmer months, check out the Masquerade Music Park. This is where you can see really big acts like Belly, Radiohead, the Cranberries, and House of Pain. Tickets to these concerts can be as much as $13.50 or more, but many fall into the $10 range.

Speaking of the fall, Masquerade itself is divided into three sections: Heaven, Purgatory, and Hell. Wednesdays through Sundays, you can go "Dancing in Hell," where cover charges are $2 to $3 during the week and $5 to $8 on the weekends.

Midtown Music Hall

• The Highlander, 931 Monroe Dr.N.E., Atlanta; 872-0060

Midtown Music Hall features live rock and alternative music Wednesdays through Saturdays. Weekday cover charges are just $1 to $2, and weekends aren't much more expensive at $3 to $5.

What could be better than live music for just a few dollars? Well, not much, but don't forget about the Highlander's free open-mike night on Sundays. There is also no cover charge on Mondays and Tuesdays, when DJs spin CDs all night.

The Point

• 420 Moreland Ave. N.E., Atlanta; 659-3522

The Point features live music Tuesday through Saturday, with ticket prices around $3 during the week and $5 on weekends. Exceptions are made, of course, for the occasional national act, like Smashing Pumpkins, when tickets can range from $12 to $14. But most of the time, the club hosts local alternative rock bands.

One night of the week is absolutely free: Sunday. Every week the Point invites you to "Psychodisco Sunday," with no cover charge. Definitely a reason to be late for work on Monday.

Velvet

• 89 Park Place N.E., Atlanta; 681-9936

Velvet was named one of the top nightclubs in America by *Newsweek* and was also mentioned in an article in *Details* about hot clubs around the country. How can Mr. C afford such hipness? Well, with cover charges of just $3 to $7, he *can* afford it, with attitude to spare.

The best deals are obviously early in the week, such as Mondays when cover charges are just $3. But even Fridays, when the DJs spin dance mu sic from the early 80s, aren't bad with a cover charge of $5.

Saturdays get pricey: $5 before midnight and $7 after (and we all know *no one* goes to the clubs before midnight). Also expensive, for reasons Mr. C may never comprehend, are Sundays—when the club hosts "70s Disco Hell." This music is worth good money to get *rid* of. Oh well, probably shouldn't argue with a hot trend.

Warehouse One

• 2115 Faulkner Rd. N.E., Atlanta; 636-8413

Warehouse One is a concert club featuring rock, blues, and alternative music. The really great news is that most shows are just $6. The occasional national act is going to cost anywhere from $8 to $15, but the majority of the bands seen here are strictly local. Concerts take place regularly Tuesdays through Saturdays; tickets are available at many Atlanta-area record stores.

OUTDOORS AND SPORTS ACTIVITIES

Atlanta Botanical Garden

• 1345 Piedmont Ave. N.E., Atlanta; 876-5858

The Atlanta Botanical Garden offers you the chance to explore the world of flora in settings that range from a tropical paradise to the surprisingly colorful desert. Admission is $4.50

for adults, $2.25 for seniors, students and children under 12. It's free for children under 6. Better yet, stroll in on Thursdays from 1 to 6 p.m., when admission is free to all.

At the Garden, you can see one of the world's few remaining urban hardwood forests, known as Storza

Woods. The Dorothy Chapman Fuqua Conservatory houses the aforementioned tropical paradise, which includes orchids, rare and endangered plants, as well as freely flying birds, and a waterfall. The Garden also sponsors educational programs, lectures, demonstrations, and plant shows. And if you need information on the care and feeding of your own plants, just call 888-GROW (4769).

The Atlanta Botanical Garden is open Tuesdays through Sundays from 9 a.m. until 6 p.m. (they stay open until 7 p.m. from April through September). It's closed on Mondays. Call the number above 24 hours a day for information about upcoming exhibits.

Chattahoochee Nature Center
* 9135 Willeo Rd., Roswell; 992-2055

The Chattahoochee Nature Center is a beautiful wooded preserve which you can enjoy for an admission price of just $2; kids get in for just a buck. Small price to pay for the pleasures to be found in this paradise of trees, fresh water ponds, and marshes, all so close to the city.

The Center itself houses activity rooms, live animal displays, and the Nature Store. Along with its merchandise, the store features a display of paintings by a different guest artist each month, for a true blend of life and art.

The CNC also offers classes in botany, river ecology, endangered species, and more. These classes are often conducted outside and include field trips; most require small additional fees. Call for more info and schedules.

Mr. C also wants to mention, for ardent nature lovers, that a CNC membership can provide you with significant savings and support a worthy cause at the same time. Individual memberships are just $20 a year; for this price, you get permanent free admission, a discount at the store, and many other benefits. If you want to make this place a regular hangout, it's definitely a worthwhile option.

MR. CHEAP'S PICKS
Outdoors and Sports Activities

✔ **Atlanta Botanical Gardens**—These blooms from all over the world are even lovelier on Thursdays, when admission is free.

✔ **Fernbank Greenhouses**—Commune with nature for free; you can even take a plant home to start your own greenhouse.

✔ **College Sports**—Exciting action, just like the pros, but for a fraction of the cost.

Fernbank Greenhouses
* 1256 Briarcliff Rd. N.E., Atlanta; 876-5947

The Fernbank Greenhouses are only open to the public on Sunday afternoons, but they're well worth setting aside the time for a trip. First of all, admission is free. But more importantly, this is a greenhouse in which you don't have to just look at the plants—you are actually encouraged to touch them! It's a rare opportunity for some real hands-on learning. And, as if all that weren't enough, you'll even get a small plant to take home as a souvenir. Then, you can start your own greenhouse.

To make more of a day of this outing, check out the nearby **Fernbank Rose Test Garden** at the corner of Ponce de Leon and Clifton Road. The Rose Test Garden is affiliated with the Fernbank Science Center, and admission again is free. The test garden displays different roses from around the world, as well as a "Garden of Excellence" for miniature roses, sponsored by the American Rose Society. They're open every day from daylight to dusk.

Atlanta Braves

- Atlanta-Fulton County Stadium,
521 Capitol Ave. S.W., Atlanta;
249-6400

"Take me out to the ball game. . . ."
You know how the song goes. But
did you know that, even though the
Braves have just raised their prices,
tickets to the upper pavilion can still
be had for a mere $5? This leaves
plenty of change for the requisite peanuts and Cracker Jacks.

If you're feeling lucky, and can
take a chance on getting in (or not) at
the last minute, there are extra savings for children. Day-of-game tickets in the upper pavillion, for kids
under the age of twelve, are just $1
apiece! At these prices, you can even
afford to bring the neighbors' kids as
well.

All of this may change, alas, when
the Braves move into their brand-
new stadium across the street, expected for the 1995 season. In the
meantime, the ticket window at Fulton County Stadium is open from
8:30 a.m. to 5 p.m. Monday through
Saturday and from 1 p.m. to 5 p.m.
on Sunday. Group discounts are also
available for parties of 30 or more.
Call 577-9100 for more info.

Atlanta Hawks

- The Omni, 100 Techwood Dr.
N.W., Atlanta; 827-DUNK (3865)

Basketball has become this country's
glamor sport. While tickets to Atlanta
Hawks games can be very expensive
(the top seats are a whopping $50),
you do still have some cheaper op-
tions.There are tickets available for
every game at just $10 each. Sure,
these are in nosebleed territory, but
you still get all the thrills of being at
the game. And high seats are better
than high prices any day.

Atlanta Knights Ice Hockey

- The Omni, 100 Techwood Dr.
N.W., Atlanta; 525-8900

Just because Atlanta is just a little bit
south of Canada doesn't mean you
can't enjoy the speed-skating action
of professional hockey. The Atlanta
Knights, members of the International Hockey League, play 41 regu-
lar-season home games in the Omni
Coliseum. They play every bit as
hard as their more celebrated counterparts in the National Hockey League.
And best of all, the most expensive
tickets in the house are just $16, and
some seats sell for as little as $8. Call
the number above for tix and schedule information.

College Sports

Just as local colleges and universities can offer performing arts at
a fraction of professional ticket prices, college sports can provide some
of the same high-flying action as professional sports for far less money.
You can enjoy college teams in just about any sport, all over Atlanta, and
in fact, all over Georgia. Mr. C has provided a sampling:

Georgia State University—If it's
NCAA Division I action you're looking for, head over to GSU. Tickets to
men's basketball games are just $4
for general seating and $5 for re-
served seats. Women's basketball tix
are a flat $3. Baseball and softball
games cost just $2. Call 651-2772 for
more info.

Georgia Institute of Technology—
Mr. C should point out that not *all*
college sports events are cheaper than
pro sports. Football tickets to see

"The Ramblin' Wreck from Georgia
Tech" are $21 apiece! Tickets to bas-
ketball games are a bit high, too,
about $14. But, women's basketball
is just $5 and men's baseball is just
$3. They even have some free events.
Call the ticket office at 894-5447 for
more info.

Kennesaw State College—At this
NCAA Division II school, you can
see basketball for $4 (tickets for chil-
dren are just $2). Baseball and soft-
ball tickets are $2 each, $1 for

children; and sports like cross-country, golf, and tennis are free. Call 423-6284 for more info.

Clayton State College—The big sports at this NAIA Division I school are men's and women's basketball and men's soccer. Tickets to any of these games are $3, and children under twelve are admitted free. Call the athletic department at 961-3450 for details.

Emory University—Emory is an NCAA Division III school with seventeen varsity sports, most of which can be seen for free. The main exceptions are men's and women's basketball; tix are $3 for adults, and $1 for children under twelve. Tickets must be purchased at the door; there are no advance sales. Call 727-6547 for ticket and schedule information.

READINGS AND LITERARY EVENTS

Barnes and Noble Booksellers
- 2900 Peachtree Rd. N.E., Atlanta; 261-7747
- 7660 North Point Pkwy., Alpharetta; 993-8340
- 4776 Ashford-Dunwoody Rd., Dunwoody; 393-9277

With three locations in greater Atlanta, some of which are sparkling and new, Barnes and Noble has a calendar that is full of ongoing and special events. All of them are free and open to the public.

Each store has regular story hours for children on Tuesday mornings and Thursday evenings. For grownups, B & N offers monthly "Booklover's Nights" and book discussion groups for singles. What better way to meet someone with a common interest? In addition, the Buckhead branch is planning monthly open mike poetry nights; these may already be up and running by the time you read this. Better brush up your Shakespeare.

But wait, that's not all! The Dunwoody branch recently presented the Handbell Choir from the Dunwoody United Methodist Church performing holiday carols. Holly Stevenson of the Theatre Gael performed scenes form her show, *Over the Garden Wall: Beatrix Potter and Her Friend.* A computer training specialist and an accountant joined forces to host a discussion on computer software for small businesses. Add to this traditional storytelling, acoustic music,

and the usual parade of authors-on-book-tours, and you have the makings of a great cultural center. All three stores are open seven days, 9 a.m. to 11 p.m.

Borders Bookshop
- 3655 Roswell Rd. N.E., Atlanta; 237-0707

Along with discounts and bargain books, Borders Bookshop is also a popular place to hear readings from well-known authors. Their newsletter/calendar of events, appropriately titled "FootNote," lists upcoming readings and special events, including many for kids. Authors who have visited here recently include Regina Barreca discussing her new book *Perfect Husbands and Other Fairy Tales*, Christina Baker Kline with her novel, *Sweetwater*, and Patricia Sprinkle signing her book *Death of a Dunwoody Matron*. Recent children's events included Dougal Dixon reading from *Dougal Dixon's Dinosaurs* and a Halloween storytelling night. Borders Bookshop is open 9 a.m. to 9 p.m. Monday through Saturday and from 11 a.m. to 6 p.m. on Sunday.

Charis Books
- 1189 Euclid Ave. N.E., Atlanta; 524-0304

Charis Books has a calendar that is chock full of author appearances and readings, which are geared to a feminist audience. There is something going on at Charis just about every week; most of these take place on

Thursday evenings at 7:30 p.m. The authors and discussions may deal with issues from lesbian politics to growing up male to dreadlock culture.

Notable authors such as Alice Walker, Kay Hagan, and poet Marjorie Agosin have all appeared here. Call or stop in to get a calendar of upcoming events.

Outwrite Books
- 931 Monroe Dr. N.E., Atlanta; 607-0082

Outwrite Books was just a wee three weeks old when Mr. C did his investigating, so it's difficult to say where this new shop will go. But the place has promise. It's a gay and lesbian bookstore, with an eye toward becoming a community center. Outwrite has a coffeehouse that is very much a part of, rather than separate from, the main store. At the time of this writing, their only regular program offers poetry readings on Monday nights at 7 p.m. These readings are free and open to the public; call to find out how you can get involved. They also bring in authors to do readings and book signings. So far, they've only presented local authors, but they have plans to bring in writers from the national scene as well. Keep your eyes on this place.

Oxford Book Stores
- 360 Pharr Rd. N.E., Atlanta; 262-3333
- 2345 Peachtree Rd. N.E., Atlanta; 364-2700
- 2395 Peachtree Rd. N.E., Atlanta; 262-3411
- 1200 West Paces Ferry Rd. N.W., Atlanta; 364-2488

With four locations, Oxford Books offers plenty of opportunities to rub elbows with the literati. Some of the authors who have been here to read and sign their work include President Jimmy Carter, with his book *Talking Peace*; James Earl Jones, reading from his autobiography *Voices & Silences*; and Bobbie Ann Mason, with

MR. CHEAP'S PICKS
Readings and Literary Events

✔ **Barnes and Noble Booksellers**—B&N has three locations in metro Atlanta, and all three have event calendars packed with readings, signings, book clubs, singles nights, and more.

✔ **Outwrite Books**—This gay and lesbian bookstore has an eye toward becoming a community center with lots of cool events. Definitely a place to watch.

✔ **Oxford Books at Pharr**—Atlanta's busiest stop on the author-appearance circuit, by Pharr.

her novel *Feather Crowns*. Most events are held at the main branch on Pharr Road, and there can be as many as two or three events per week.

Oxford also has some storytelling hours for children, and occasional special events. Recently they hosted a "Poetry Slam" workshop, at Oxford Too, co-sponsored with the Arts Festival of Atlanta.

And don't forget that the Pharr Road branch is also home to the **Oxford Acoustic Cafe,** featuring singers and songwriters every Sunday, Monday, and Tuesday at 8:30 p.m. Also at Pharr Road is the **Arts Connection,** an art gallery which features regular exhibits as well as workshops for photography, getting published, and more

And if you're visiting Oxford at Peachtree Battle, stop in for an espresso at their coffee shop, **Cup & Chaucer**.

THEATER

To save money on professional theater in town, consider a little-known option: **Volunteer ushering**. Many theaters use regular folks to help rip tickets, hand out programs, or guide people to their seats. In exchange for your services, you can watch the show for free. Responsibilities are light; you'll have to dress nicely, arrive a bit early to learn the layout of seats, and then go to it. As soon as the show begins, find a seat for yourself and enjoy the show—you're all done. Ushering can even make a fun cheap date—it's a guaranteed conversation starter afterwards! Best of all, you'll save yourself some cash *and* help that theater out at the same time. Call ahead to find out if that show you've been eyeing uses volunteers, and when they have slots available.

Meanwhile, here are some of the good, inexpensive theater companies around the Atlanta area:

A.R.T. Station
- 5384 Manor Dr., Stone Mountain; 469-1105

A.R.T. Station presents an eclectic mix of plays and concerts at very affordable ticket prices. Friday and Saturday performances are generally $14 for adults, and $10 for children. Thursday and Sunday performances are $12/$8 for kids.

While some of the plays produced here are family-oriented, A.R.T. Station also presents exciting and challenging pieces intended strictly for adult audiences—such as their recent *Lady Day at Emerson's Bar and Grill*, which portrayed the life of singer Billie Holiday.

Other shows have included concerts of contemporary folk music, gospel music, and storytelling. Give them a call to find out what they have coming up.

DeKalb Center for the Performing Arts
- Avondale High School, 1192 Clarendon Ave., Avondale Estates; 289-ARTS

The DeKalb Center for the Performing Arts consists of about 250 high school students studying dance, drama, and music. What does this have to do with you? Well, a couple of times a year they show off what they've learned in public performances which are open to the public at very low prices. Now, lest you think that means some two-bit recital which only a parent could love, Mr. C would like to point out that DCPA's choir was recently invited to sing at Carnegie Hall in New York City (How do you get to Carnegie Hall? Practice!).

Dramas and musicals, like *Godspell* and *Anything Goes*, are regularly presented here with ticket prices of about $6. Tickets to dance concerts and comedy nights are just $5 and $6, respectively. Student prices for all these events are $2 or $3. Check it out.

Down Right Theatre
- 3087 North Peachtree Rd., Duluth; 476-7926

For an actor, "down right" refers to the part of the stage that is closest to the audience and furthest to the actor's right side. For you, it refers to shows at this suburban theater, where prices are downright cheap. Admission for adults is just $11, while senior citizens and students get in for a nice, low $7. Recent productions have included *The Passion of Dracula* and Alan Acykbourn's oh-so-

British comedy, *Table Manners*. Certain special events have special (even lower!) ticket prices, such as storytelling shows for families at which admission is just $7 for all ages.

"Lunchtime With Kenny"
- Alliance Theatre, 1280 Peachtree St. N.E., Atlanta; 892-2414

Though shows at highly acclaimed Alliance Theatre are not as astronomically expensive as Broadway, they didn't exactly make Mr. Cheap's list. However, the Alliance does have an interesting free program Mr. C wants to share with you: It's called "Lunchtime with Kenny." Held on Tuesdays from noon to 1 p.m. in the Alliance Studio, the program is hosted by Artistic Director Kenny Leon. Bring a brown-bag lunch and join in.

There is one lunchtime seminar given for each new Alliance show, offering a behind-the-scenes look at how a script goes "from the page to the stage," as they say in show biz. It's a great chance for you to ask questions of the directors, actors, and designers, and to look at the set and costume designs. You'll even get to see a "sneak peek" of a scene from the show. Call them for a schedule of upcoming lunches.

Neighborhood Playhouse
- 430 West Trinity Place, Decatur; 373-5311

For something which sounds like community theater, the Neighborhood Playhouse is a professional troupe presenting high-quality dramas which are always very well-received. Recently seen on the boards here have been contemporary comedies and dramas such as *Steel Magnolias* and *A Few Good Men*, both of which were the basis for successful movies; classics, such as Noel Coward's *Present Laughter*; and many other hits.

Performances take place on Thursdays, Fridays, and Saturdays at 8 p.m. and on Sundays at 2 p.m. Tickets are just $12. On Thursdays and Sundays, discounted tickets are made available to students ($10) and sen-

iors ($7). Subscriptions are also available, which can bring the price down to about $10 for anyone.

Onstage Atlanta
- 420 Courtland St. N.E., Atlanta; 897-1802

Conveniently located in the Downtown area, Onstage Atlanta offers comedies, dramas, and musicals at prices that will allow you to see plenty of each genre. This ambitious troupe brings works by established playwrights to the city, while also acting as a showcase for unknown, original works.

Among the big hits they've presented have been such classics as *The Importance of Being Earnest*, as well as *Nunsense*, *Little Shop of Horrors*, and *Evita*. They also have a summer repertory of original shows, including local hits like *E.R. Emergency Room* and *E.R. II: Peachtree Memorial*.

Shows run Thursdays, Fridays, and Saturdays at 8 p.m., and Sundays at 5 p.m. Ticket prices range from $12 to $17; the summer rep shows have a top price of $14.

Roswell Village Theater
- Village Center Playhouse, 6117 Holcomb Bridge Rd., Roswell; 998-3526

At these two theaters, you can see any number of fun and lively performances without spending wads of cash to do so. General admission tickets to either venue are reasonably priced at $10 on the weekends, and only $6 on weeknights. And admission for seniors, students, and children is just $8 on weekends.

Recent shows at the Roswell Village Theater have included *Simply Broadway!*, *Man of La Mancha*, and *The Forgotten Carols*. At the Village Center Playhouse, a theater-in-the-round, playgoers have seen such ever-popular chestnuts as *Arsenic and Old Lace*, *Harvey*, and *A Christmas Carol*.

Shakespeare Tavern
- 499 Peachtree St. N.E., Atlanta; 874-5299

Home of the Atlanta Shakespeare Company, this is dinner theater such as you may never have seen before.

The ASC presents faithful renditions of plays by Shakespeare and his contemporaries, such as Christopher Marlowe, whose *Doctor Faustus* was recently produced. The atmosphere is indeed that of an old-fashioned tavern, not Elizabethan, but perhaps more Dickensian—a hollowed-out warehouse of exposed brick walls and wooden beams. At one end is a bar, serving up pints of Bass ale and Guinness stout; and all the seating is at tables, where you can eat dinner or just snack your way through the show.

After all, Shakespeare was never supposed to be stuffy and highbrow. It was written as pop entertainment for the gentry and common folk alike, and audiences brought food to the original Globe Theater—where the groundlings, as those in the cheap seats were called, had no hesitation in tossing orange rinds and other items onto the stage as they saw fit. Now, Mr. C is not suggesting that we bring back *all* historic customs, but it sure is nice to be able to sit back, relax, and eat during the show.

The food consists of some British pub offerings, like Cornish meat pies, along with a few not-so-Anglo items, like black bean chili. Many of these are in the $5 range, though you can have a full dinner at varying, slightly higher prices. Or, you can just have a beverage, or perhaps desserts, and watch the show. Ticket prices range up to $15, not the cheapest in town; but tix for the first few performances of any new show (each production usually runs a month or so) are generally half-price. On these nights especially, the Shakespeare Tavern is a true dinner theater bargain. Performances take place Thursday through Sunday evenings; food service begins an hour before showtime.

Southern Fried Productions
• Mercer University Fine Arts Auditorium, 3001 Mercer University Dr. N.E., Atlanta; 378-8646

Southern Fried Productions (great name, isn't it?) presents professional theater on the campus of Mercer Uni-

---

MR. CHEAP'S PICKS
Theater

✔ **"Lunchtime with Kenny"**—Preview new shows at the Alliance at these free brown-bag presentations.

✔ **Neighborhood Playhouse**—Top-quality recent hits, professionally done in Decatur.

✔ **Shakespeare Tavern**—The Bard comes vividly to life, while you down a pint of ale or sup royally at moderate prices.

✔ **Theatre in the Square**—Worth a drive to Marietta, especially if you can get weeknight rush tix.

---

versity—at college-level prices. Tickets for shows on Friday and Saturday evenings at 8 are just $10 for general admission, $7 for students and seniors. Better yet, Sunday matinees at 2 p.m. are always $5! Seen here recently have been dramas and comedies like *Talley's Folly*, *T-Bone and Weasel*, and *Master of Himself.*

Stage Door Players
• North DeKalb Cultural Center, 5339 Chamblee-Dunwoody Rd., Dunwoody; 396-1726

The Stage Door Players present professional productions at very reasonable ticket prices. Shows on Friday and Saturday evenings are $13, on Thursday evenings and Sunday afternoons they're just $10. Musicals are a bit more expensive, usually by a dollar per ticket.

And what might you see for so few dollars? Very ambitious shows indeed. Recent productions have included the British drama *Shadowlands*, Tim Rice and Andrew Lloyd Webber's musical *Joseph and the Amazing Technicolor Dreamcoat*, and Moliere's classic comedy *The Miser*.

Also interesting, and cheap, are special events like the New Play Series, with tickets just $5, as well as free staged readings of scripts still in development. You never know which of these may turn out to be a hit in the making!

Theater in the Square
- 11 Whitlock Ave., Marietta; 422-8369

Less than half an hour from downtown Atlanta, this fully-professional Equity company has a modern, comfortable theater that has recently been renovated (including wheelchair accessibility). It has a lobby as handsome as any Southern mansion's foyer, in keeping with the historic nature of Marietta's town square; the theater itself is intimate, only twelve rows deep, so that every plush seat has a perfect view.

The company presents five main productions annually, plus summer and Christmas shows. The plays range from such classics as *Death of a Salesman* to fresh-from-New York hits like *M. Butterfly* and *Lips Together, Teeth Apart*. It has even commissioned original works by emerging American playwrights, and offered many Atlanta-area premieres. Tickets are generally priced from $13-$20 or so, depending on the night, but there are several money-saving options.

For starters, you can subscribe to the entire season, and see the five main shows for as little as $57, less than $12 per show. Can't plan that far in advance? Then rush tickets are for you—at many weeknight performances, if tickets are still available an hour before showtime, you can walk up to the box office and get two for the price of one. It is a good idea to call earlier in the day to find out if rush tix are likely to be available.

Finally, there is Theatre in the Square's **Alley Stage**, presenting smaller-scale productions of experimental new works in a sixty-seat "black box" theater. These plays are a less-proven commodity, but then, many of the most successful new

scripts come from this kind of workshop. Ticket prices are also less expensive than the mainstage, ranging from $10 to $12. The schedule for these shows is not as regular; again, call the box office for info on upcoming Alley productions.

Theatrical Outfit
- 1012 Peachtree St. N.E., Atlanta; 872-0665

Always working along the fringes of mainstream theater, this Midtown company is dedicated to incorporating elements of music, visuals, performance art, dance, and literature into its dramatic offerings. The results are strikingly original works and new interpretations of classic pieces, such as their recent production of *Beowulf*. Heaven knows, anyone who remembers this thickly written medieval story from college days would hardly expect it to be the basis for a sold-out hit; such is the imaginative power of the Theatrical Outfit. Another example: During the holiday season, when it seems that everybody trots out their version of a certain Dickens warhorse, this group instead offers a home-grown musical entertainment called *An Appalachian Christmas*. It's an annual success.

And they do this all so affordably, with weekday ticket prices averaging $15 for adults, $10 for senior citizens, and $5 for students. Subscriptions are available, too; since many shows do become hot tickets, this is a good idea for theater fans *and* bargain fans.

Tri Cities Community Theatre
- 2750 East Point St., East Point; 681-6091

Mr. C believes that community theaters are a great way to enjoy live performance without paying exorbitant prices. This venue in East Point is a great example of that premise: All tickets at Tri Cities cost $10 for adults and $7 for children.

And for so little you get so much. Tri Cities performs such classics as *To Kill a Mockingbird* and *One Flew Over the Cuckoo's Nest*. They also present original works that give a lo cal flavor, like the recent hit, *Eula Mae's Beauty, Bait, and Tackle*.Tri Cities has also presented other special events, like a recent festival of one-act plays. Give them a call to find out about upcoming shows.

WALKS AND TOURS

Atlanta Institute of Architects
• 1197 Peachtree St. N.E., Atlanta; 873-3207

The Atlanta Institute of Architects sponsors free walking tours of interesting structures in and around the city. On the second Sunday of every month from February through November, a different building is chosen for exploration; selections are based upon up-and-coming trends in design, topical issues, or just whatever is new and hot. These may include city hall complexes, professional or medical facilities, high-rises, and arts centers. Each tour runs from 2 p.m. to 5 p.m.; call the AIA for their upcoming schedule.

The Atlanta Preservation Center
• The DeSoto, Suite 3, 156 7th St. N.E., Atlanta; 876-2040

The Atlanta Preservation Center offers tours of many of the city's historic districts, including the Fox Theatre district, Sweet Auburn, Inman Park, Ansley Park, Underground Atlanta, and historic Downtown. The cost for any one of these is never more expensive than $5 per person.

Tours are offered at various times, several days out of the week; most of these take place on Saturdays and Sundays. Each tour begins at a different location. Call the APC for a schedule of upcoming tours and locations. Admission is $5 for adults, $4 for senior citizens, and $3 for students. Groups of twenty or more can get a discounted rate of $4.50 per person.

Bulloch Hall
• 180 Bulloch Ave., Roswell; 992-1731

This impressive Greek Revival structure was the home of the Martha Bulloch, mother of President Theodore Roosevelt. Bulloch Hall survived the "War Between the States" by flying the French flag and confusing the Union Army; today, you can tour this antebellum house and its beautiful gardens for just $3.

But there are many other things to see and do here. Bulloch Hall also serves as a cultural center, gallery space, and reference library. Annual events include a March quilt show, a spring "Magnolia Ball," and special Christmas programs. Call for an upcoming schedule of art shows, musical and literary events, and exhibitions. Bulloch Hall also sponsors classes in various arts and crafts, including quilting, basketry, gardening, and folk art.

Tours are given Monday through Friday from 10 a.m. until 3 p.m.; appointments must be made for groups of ten or more. The cost for senior citizens is just $2, students $1, and under 6 are admitted free.

CNN Studio Tour
• CNN Center, Techwood Drive and Marietta St. N.W., Atlanta; 827-2300

So you want to find out just how the world's largest cable network really works, and maybe sneak a peek at Ted and Jane? For just $6 you can do all this by taking the CNN Studio tour. You'll get to see CNN's two live newsroom/TV studios, and learn about the rest of Ted Turner's empire—his library of MGM film classics, The Cartoon Network, and the Atlanta Braves and the Atlanta Hawks, and more.

Tours are given daily, every hour between 9 a.m. and 5 p.m.; they sell out quickly, and you'll probably have to buy tickets for tours an hour or two away unless you plan ahead give

24 hours notice for reservations. It's worth the wait, though, if you're starstruck. From a viewing deck above the newsroom, you can watch reporters scrambling for stories, and see a live broadcast in progress. Plus a few other surprises. Tour guides are well-informed of the company's workings and should be able to answer almost any questions you may have about the network.

Tours last nearly an hour, and CNN makes a point of informing people that the tour involves walking down several flights of stairs (handicapped-accesible tours can be arranged if you call ahead). The cost of the tour is $6 for adults, $4 for senior citizens, $3.50 for children age 12 and under, and free for kids under age 5. Groups of 30 people or more are asked to call in advance for arrangements.

The tour's well worth the price, though. Not only do you get an insider's view of the network, but you may just get to meet some of the stars, too. As Mr. C was leaving the tour area into the main area of the CNN Building, he almost walked smack into Bonnie Anderson, a CNN news anchor, as she came back from lunch.

DeKalb Historical Society Tours
• Old Courthouse on the Square, Decatur; 373-1088

Take a free walking tour of historic downtown Decatur. All you have to do is pick up a brochure—complete with a detailed map, historical facts, and trivia—and start walking. The brochure is available at touristy locations like Underground Atlanta, as well as vistor centers in Atlanta and Decatur.

The tour makes a total of 23 interesting stops, many of which are open to the public, so that you can also step inside and snoop around. Included on the tour are the Old Courthouse, Agnes Scott College, the Decatur Railroad Depot, and the Decatur Fire Station. The Old Courthouse even includes a free museum with more of this picturesque town's history.

It is estimated that the tour can be done in about two hours; obviously, you can do as much or as little as you wish. Mr. C recommends taking your time and exploring the various sites, both historical and commercial. The best part of this tour is that you can take it anytime you want to; but do bear in mind the hours of some of the attractions themselves.

The Georgia Governor's Mansion
• 391 West Paces Ferry Rd. N.E., Atlanta; 261-1776

The Georgia Governor's Mansion tour offers you a chance to peek into a home that not only holds social and historic value, but also serves as the home of the current governor; who can say, in the zany world of politics, who'll be living there by time you go.

On your tour you'll see the cherry-paneled library, the official state dining room and drawing room, the family living room, the guest bedroom, and more. The home features a collection of priceless Georgiana, such as manuscripts by Joel Chandler Harris, Flannery O'Connor, Erskine Caldwell, and Carson McCullers. The rarest piece in the house, though, is a 19th century French porcelain vase with a portrait medallion of Benjamin Franklin. Best of all the tour is completely free!

Since real people do live here, hours are limited: Tours are only offered between 10 a.m. and 11:30 a.m. on Tuesdays, Wednesdays, and Thursdays. Large groups are required to make reservations.

Georgia State Capitol Tours
• Georgia State Capitol Building, Capitol Square S.W., Atlanta; 656-2844

The Capitol Guide Service provides free tours of this historic building, where the state legislature works (occasionally) to this day. You may get a glimpse of Zell Miller dashing by. You can also sit in the Senate and House of Representatives galleries, and if they're in session, watch them wrestle bills to the ground. The first floor of the building also features a chronological display of Georgia's state flags, some of which were actually used in the Civil War, the Spanish-American War, and World War I. Guns and other weapons used by Georgian soldiers are also shown. See how a state project—the building of the Capitol itself—was actually completed within budget!

Also on the first floor are busts of prominent figures in Georgian history, including founding father James Edward Oglethorpe, Margaret Mitchell, and Juliette Gordon Low (founder of the Girl Scouts). Portraits of Martin Luther King, Jr., Jimmy Carter, and all former state governors also line the wall.

The tour winds up in the Georgia State Museum of Science and Industry, located on the fourth floor of the Capitol (see listing under "Museums"), which is also free. Tours are scheduled weekdays *and* weekends at 10 and 11 a.m. and 1 and 2 p.m.

The Herndon Home
- 587 University Place N.W., Atlanta; 581-9813

This magnificent Beaux Arts classical mansion was built in the early 1900s by Alonzo Herndon. Born as a slave, Herndon founded the Atlanta Life Insurance Company and went on to become Atlanta's wealthiest African-American man around the turn of the century. Yet, tours of his home are free!

Quite apart from its own social significance, this mansion boasts fine collections of antique furniture, Roman and Venetian glass pieces (some of which date back as far as 200 B.C.E.), silver, and other precious art. Tours are available Tuesdays through Saturdays from 10 a.m. to 4 p.m. Reservations are required for groups.

Oakland Cemetery
- 248 Oakland Ave. S.E., Atlanta; 577-8163

A short walk from the King Memorial MARTA station, the eighty-eight acre Oakland Cemetery is one of the finest examples of Victorian cemeteries in the country. This is where people still lay flowers at the grave of

---

MR. CHEAP'S PICKS
Walks and Tours

✔ **Atlanta Institute of Architects**—Free explorations of notable buildings all over town.

✔ **Georgia State Capitol Tour**—History, art, and politics come together in this free tour. Added bonus: The State Museum of Science and Industry, a hidden jewel upstairs.

✔ **Martin Luther King, Jr. Center/Sweet Auburn District**—Find out how truly current history can be.

Gone With the Wind author Margaret Mitchell Marsh, and golf balls at the stone of duffer Bobby Jones. Also laid to rest here are twenty-four past Atlanta mayors; Alexander Hamilton Stevens, who was vice president of the Confederacy during the Civil War; and nearly 3,000 Confederate soldiers.

The cemetery is a lesson in architecture, with its Gothic Revival and Neo-Classical mausoleums, Victorian carved tombstones, and fountain sculptures. Some of the oldest magnolia trees in the city loom over you as you walk around.

There is no admission fee. Guided tours can be arranged for a small charge of $1 for students, $2 for senior citizens, and $3 for adults. For groups of 25 or more, the charge is $2.50 per person. But it costs nothing to wander the grounds on your own; stop in at the visitor's center, a white two-story building with a small bell tower, in the middle of the cemetery. Here, you can get a free map and a few directions. The gates are open daily from 8:00 a.m. to 7:00 p.m. in spring and summer, closing up an hour earlier in fall and winter.

Kennesaw Mountain National Battlefield Park

- Old 41 Highway, Marietta; 427-4686

At Kennesaw Mountain, you can explore history and enjoy the great outdoors at the same time. The park preserves and commemorates the Battle of Kennesaw Mountain, a Civil War campaign which delayed the fall of Atlanta by two weeks. Listed on the National Register of Historic Places, the park has historical markers, cannon emplacements, monuments, and troop movement charts. Maps for self-guided tours are available, and special weekend programs are presented during the peak season. Stop in the Visitor Center for info.

What's that? Civil War history isn't your bag? No problem—there is still plenty to see and do here. Climb to the top of Kennesaw Mountain and enjoy a breathtaking view of northern Georgia. Activity areas are available for kite flying, sports, picnics, and just plain chilling out. Or, hit the trails; paths are designated for both hiking and horseback riding. Kennesaw Mountain is open daily from 8 a.m. to 5:30 p.m.; the Visitor Center opens at 8:30 a.m.

Martin Luther King, Jr. National Historic Site

- 449 Auburn Ave. N.E., Atlanta; 524-1956

Martin Luther King, Jr.'s passion for the civil rights movement lives on at this National Historic Site, with points of interest stretched along several blocks of Auburn Avenue.

King's tomb and eternal flame can be seen outside the Center for Nonviolent Social Change. Inside, the building features an audio-visual history of King's life and the development of his theory of non-violence.

The Center is also where tours meet to visit his birth home at 501 Auburn Avenue, and where you can pick up guides to the other sites in the Sweet Auburn area. You can also see the Ebenezer Baptist Church, where both King and his father preached, just down the street at 407-413 Auburn.

Admission to the Center is free, as are the tours of MLK's birth home, though donations are accepted.

The King Center is open daily during the fall and winter from 9 a.m. until 5:30 p.m., and in the spring and summer from 9 a.m. until 8 p.m. Guided tours are available; they must be arranged at least one month in advance, and the staff requests donations of $2 for persons 13 years old and up, and $1 for children and senior citizens.

Sweet Auburn District

- Auburn Ave. N.E., Atlanta; 524-1956

The entire Sweet Auburn area is rich in history, and the map obtained at the MLK Center (see listing above) can show you how to get to the houses and buildings in the area of particular interest. The **Herndon Building** at 231-245 Auburn Ave. was named for its builder, Alonzo F. Herndon, a former slave who eventually founded the Atlanta Life Insurance Company. The **Alexander Hamilton, Jr., Home** at 102 Howell St. (northwest of the MLK Center), with its Corinthian columns, was the home of Atlanta's leading black building contractor in the early part of this century. The "shotgun" row houses from 472 to 488 Auburn were built at that time, and are arranged in such perfect alignment that a gunshot could theoretically enter and leave the house through the doorways.

The World of Coca-Cola Pavilion

- 55 Martin Luther King, Jr. Dr. S.W., Atlanta; 676-5151

Museum or marketing juggernaut? Whichever way you see it, you can't fail to notice the World of Coca-Cola, located on the street level above Underground Atlanta; if you're in this vicinity, just look up. That famous, friendly logo, magnified about a thousand times, greets you in lights.

With its many audio-visual exhibits, including a model bottling line, a 90-seat theater and a wacky fountain that seems to shoot soda several feet before dispensing it, this shrine to soft drinks is sure to thrill the kids and impress young and older folks alike. Galleries show vintage magazine ads and commercials, and interactive television sets will give you a taste of how Coke's jingles sounded decades ago. The history of the soda is told from its earliest days as a headache cure to its development into the world's most recognized trademark.

Every fifteen minutes, a film takes you through some of the 200 countries in which Coke is sold, from Thailand to the Philippines to Africa. At the end of your visit, free samples of Coke, Diet Coke, and Fanta are proffered, along with some unusual sodas only sold in those other countries.

The Pavilion hours are 10 a.m. to 9:30 p.m. Monday through Saturday, and noon to 6 p.m. on Sunday. It's closed on major holidays. Admission is $2.50 for adults, $2 for senior citizens over 55, $1.50 for children aged 6-12 and free for children under 6 with an adult.

Tickets may be purchased in advance by calling weekdays from 9-5; and call 676-6074 to arrange for group tours. The Pavilion has elevators and special assistance is available for the hearing impaired.

RESTAURANTS

For the dining chapters of the book (which many folks consider to be its main course), Mr. C decided not to dig in alphabetically—but rather by geographical area. After all, when you're hungry, you want to eat *now*—no matter how appetizing some place halfway across town may sound. The city has been divided into six very broad sections, so that you can just pick up the book and find the cheap choices in your area. Or, the area where you're going to be...use this section with the "Entertainment" chapters to plan out a whole day or night on the town!

All of the restaurants in this book are places where you can eat dinner for under $10 per person (or, in many cases, far less), not including tax and tip. Lunch prices, of course, can be even lower. Even so, all of these eateries serve filling meals of "real" food, not phony fast food junk.

That $10 limit also does not include alcohol, which is going to be expensive just about anywhere. In fact, many of these places can afford to serve good, cheap food *because* they make their money on the drinks. If you're really tight on cash, you can always nurse one beer or an over-priced soda, eat well, and still come out ahead on the deal. And check out Mr. Cheap's special "Tip-Free" list for establishments where you can safely save an extra buck or two in that department. Enjoy!

MR. CHEAP'S PICKS
TIP-FREE RESTAURANTS

Atlanta Northeast/Decatur
(including Emory Village, North
Druid Hills, Toco Hills)
    Cedar Tree, 226
    Gold Burgers, 229
    Happy Herman's, 229
    Indian Delights, 230
    Lettuce Souprise You, 232
    Market Cafe at Your DeKalb
      Farmer's Market, 233
    Our Way Cafe, 237
    Touch of India, 241
    Varsity Jr., 241

Buckhead
    The Bread Market, 244
    Fellini's Pizza, 247
    Lettuce Souprise You, 249

**Downtown/Atlanta Southeast &
Southwest**
    The Beautiful Restaurant, 258
    Chanterelles, 258
    Delectables, 260
    South Fork Restaurant, 264
    Timberlake Sandwich Shop, 265

Little Five Points
(including Ponce area, Virginia-
Highland)
    Deacon Burton's Soul Food
      Restaurant, 269
    Eats, 270
    Fellini's Pizza, 271
    Tortillas, 277

Midtown
    C. W. Long Cafeteria at
      Crawford Long Hospital, 281
    Frijoleros, 283
    Lettuce Souprise You, 284
    Picnic Basket Deli, 287
    Touch of India, 290
    The Varsity, 290

Perimeter Suburbs
    Fellini's Pizza, 295
    Happy Herman's, 296
    Indian Delights, 296
    Lettuce Souprise You, 298

ATLANTA NORTHEAST/DECATUR
(including Emory Village, North Druid Hills, Toco Hills)

Athens Pizza House
- 1959 Lakewood Ave. S.E., Atlanta; 622-7911
- 246 Bobby Jones Expwy., Augusta; (706) 868-1508
- 5550 Peachtree Industrial Blvd., Chamblee; 452-8282
- 1565 Highway 138, Conyers; 483-6228
- 1341 Clairmont Rd., Decatur; 636-1100
- 1255 Johnson Ferry Rd., Marietta; 509-0099
- 6075 Roswell Rd. N.E., Sandy Springs; 257-0252

The Papadopoulos family has been making popular pizza in the Atlanta area since 1966. The prices are right, too; not only on the pizzas, but also on such appetizers as spinach pie ($1.50), Athens patatoes ($1.50), and fried kalamari ($4.40). Those last two *must* be good—they're spelled old-country style.

The pies themselves start at just $4.90 for an individual size. But why stop there? Go all out with a medium all-meat special (salami, sausage, pepperoni, ham, hamburger, and Canadian bacon) for $9.25. You won't have to eat again for a week.

Entrees like moussaka served with spinach pie, chicken parmesan, and spinach manicotti are each served with a Greek salad and garlic bread for $6.95. There's a children's section on the menu, too; the kids' spaghetti dinner is just $3.15, while you can join them with the gigantic regular spaghetti plate for $5.20.

Don't pass up the baklava for dessert, either. At $1.50 a slice, these nut-filled flaky pastries covered with honey are just the thing to end your meal on a sweet note.

Athens Pizza also offers many beers and wines (including Greek varieties like Kokino and Aspro), starting at $1.95 a glass.

If the crowds here get to be too much, though, consider visiting one of the Athens Pizza Express take-out locations, at 4060 Peachtree Road N.E., Atlanta (phone 365-8646) or at 1788 Clairmont Road, Decatur (634-8646).

Cafe 308
- 308-H West Ponce de Leon Ave., Decatur; 370-0308

Okay, so, the name isn't that original, but what this cafe in West Ponce Place lacks in verbal imagination, it makes up for with its creative sandwiches and laid-back, homey atmosphere.

Special sauces and fresh bread make memorable what could be an ordinary lunch. Try the grilled eggplant, piled on aromatic rosemary focaccia bread with bell pepper, smoked provolone cheese, honey mustard and crispy lettuce ($5.25). Their "P.L.T." is anything but everyday, made with fried provolone, arugula, and tomato with pesto mayo, also $5.25. Capered tuna salad sandwiches go for $4.75; or, how about a salad sampler of cilantro black beans and corn, roasted red potatoes, and tomato-dill pasta salads, all together for just $4.25.

Many local workers stop in for grub to go; but if you stay in, you'll enjoy the warm atmosphere from the cafe's real wicker chairs, mismatched tables and placemats, and gorgeous color photographs of nature scenes from the Okeefenokee to the western coastline.

Cafe 308 is open Mondays through Fridays from 9 a.m. into the early evening; they close at 4:00 on Saturdays, and all day Sundays.

Cedar Tree
- Emory Village Shopping Center, 1565 North Decatur Rd., Atlanta; 373-2118

Middle Eastern dishes are available at really cheap prices here. The breakfast selections are limited to bagels (50¢), croissants ($1.50), and omelettes ($1.99), but Emory students and professors alike come here at lunch for super vegetarian plates, shish kebabs, and sky-high club sandwiches.

Mr. C liked the baba ghanoush sandwich—baked eggplant with tahini (sesame seed) paste, just $2.75. Grape leaves and hummus wrapped in a pita is just $3.75, and the slightly spicy falafel sandwich is also $3.75.

Lamb or chicken kebab sandwiches are priced under $4.50. The kebab sampler platter tops the menu at $6.50, and comes with hummus, a salad, and pita for dipping. Student types seem to really go for the grilled pastrami, salami, and corned beef with mustard potato salad ($3.99) and the Meza Tray, a vegetarian plate with six different side orders from the menu. Enough to stuff three people, it sells for $14.99. Desserts include nine varieties of baklava (99¢ each), brownies, brioche, and flan.

Cedar Tree is open weekdays from 8 a.m. until 9 p.m., and Saturdays from 10 a.m. to 7 p.m. It's closed Sundays.

Chris's Pizza House
- Toco Hills Shopping Center, 2911 North Druid Hills Rd., Atlanta; 636-7544

Yeah, sure, you may think that pizza houses are a dime a dozen, but Mr. C thinks that Chris's is something special. Prices are super-cheap, and the food's quite good. This restaurant isn't what you'd call fancy, though ficus trees and skylights attempt to add a touch of class.

This is Greek pizza, by the way, not Italian (there is a difference, you know). Chris's pies come in four sizes, with prices starting at an incredibly low $2.85 for a plain individual size; a large plain 16" goes up to just

$8.90. Toppings include all the basics from anchovies to sausage, plus more unusual toppings like calamata olives, salami, and pepperoncini peppers. Calzones are $4.25, and can be made with the same extra ingredients as the pizzas.

The menu continues past pizza, though, to more traditional ethnic foods. Paynrl, a Greek dish made of dough, egg, and cheese, is $4.25. Or, go for souvlaki beef sandwiches for $3.85, and good ol' gyros for $3.60. Lasagna dinners, complete with Greek salad and garlic or pita bread, are only $6.25.

Spaghetti can be prepared several different ways—with butter, it's just $2.65, or $3.60 if you try it with one of several toppings like meatballs, peppers, mushrooms, eggplant parmesan, or sausage.

Chris's is open Mondays through Thursdays from 11 a.m. to 10 p.m., Friday and Saturdays from 11 a.m. to 11 p.m., and Sundays from 5 p.m. to 10 p.m.

Coco Loco Cuban & Caribbean Cafe
- 303 Peachtree Center Ave. N.E., Atlanta; 653-0070
- 2625 Piedmont Rd. N.E., Atlanta; 364-0212 and 261-0198
- 6301 Roswell Rd., Sandy Springs; 255-5434

Sure, Coco Loco may have a reputation as a yuppie hangout, but its prices are surprisingly *un*-yuppie. The Cuban sandwich, for instance, is just $3.75 for the regular size, and $4.50 for the super. Jamaican jerk chicken sandwiches go for $3.95, as does the *pan con lechon* (roast pork and grilled onions). For lighter appetites, or those who can't bear the hot spices, try grilled cheese with potato sticks for $2.25, or hot dogs and quarter-pound hamburgers, each just $2.50. The spicier Cuban hamburger, with onions, paprika, and Worcestershire sauce, is also just $2.50.

On the sweet side, tropical milkshakes, in flavors like papaya or mango ($1.95), and nectars (try the tamarind, just $1.50), will douse the flames of the Cuban spices.

Even entrees are reasonably priced, served with two side dishes like yucas, rice, or a salad. Cuban-style roast chicken with garlic and onions, fried sirloin steak, and pork chops are all just $5.95 each. Side dishes like black beans and rice ($1.75), sweet fried plantains or plantain chips (also $1.75) and home-made potato chips (95¢) won't break the bank, either, so you may just have enough money left for some (not so cheap) dessert, like key lime pie ($2.50), rice pudding ($1.95), or *pastelito de guayaba* (guava pastry), just 75¢ an order.

Domestic and imported beers, plus a limited wine selection, are also available.

Dooley's
• 1545 North Decatur Rd., Emory Village; 377-6598

Dooley is the ghoulish, yet legendary figure who "appears" on the Emory University campus half a dozen times or so a year. Students in any class he enters are free to leave, according to tradition, even if a test is taking place. Ah, those wacky college kids.

Actually, anyone who eats at Dooley's will be a happy camper, since you get lots of grub for your buck. This is another one of those bars that make a killing on booze, and can afford to sell food at super-cheap prices.

Don't miss the lunch specials, like the "Perfect 10", a list of ten items including a pita cheese grill, black beans and rice, a half-strip sandwich, and soup of the day. Pick any three for just $3.50; and the plate will be served in ten minutes or less. Mr. C got stuffed on spaghetti and marinara sauce, a giant baked potato, and vegetable soup. Definitely a deal.

All other entrees are served from 11:30 a.m. to 11:30 p.m. There's kind of a world-beat approach to the menu. French onion soup is $2.25 a cup, chili is $2.95, and char-grilled beefburgers or vegetarian burgers are $5.25. Falafel pita wraps and jerk chicken sandwiches are $5.95 each,

and served with fries, pasta salad, potato salad, nacho chips, or potato chips.

Dusty's Barbecue
• 1815 Briarcliff Rd. N.E., Atlanta; 320-6264

Suuuuuuueeeeet! Near Emory Village, Dusty's has won awards from *Creative Loafing* and other publications for its pork and beef barbecue. Some locals feel that the fare has fallen a notch or two in recent years, but the place still fills almost every wicker chair in the house during peak times.

If not for the sign out front, you'd think this was just a tiny little log cabin. Pictures of pigs and cows cover the walls, while gingham tablecloths and curtains add a homey touch.

Dusty's refers to itself as "Hog Heaven", but it's the customers who think they're dreaming once they see the low prices on the lunch and dinner items here. A regular size chopped pork barbecue dinner costs only $5.60 (the larger size is $6.80). All barbecue meals come with hush puppies and two vegetables on the side. Pork tenderloins are $6.75 an order. And, speaking of veggies, non-meat eaters can come here with their carnivorous friends and dine sumptuously on the four veggie plate. It's just $4.15, with choices like green beans, corn on the cob, baked beans, fried okra, and home-cooked potato chips.

Lunch items are actually served at any time of day, like the barbecued half-chicken or roast beef au jus (both $5.80). Dinner entrees include Dusty's baby back ribs, which are $8.50 for the regular (read: Paul Bunyan) size. Combination meals run about $7.95; this gives you the chance to try pork or beef barbecue, chicken and Brunswick stew, all in the same meal.

Dusty's is also known for its desserts, like peach, apple, or blackberry cobblers ($1.15), chocolate silk pie ($2.25), and carrot cake ($1.95).

Lunch and dinner are served seven

days a week. There is an odd-looking but serviceable drive-through area for those of you in a hurry.

Eddie's Attic
- 515-B North McDonough St., Decatur; 377-4976

If you can find Eddie's Attic (near East Trinity Place, below the courthouse), and make it up the staircase, you'll be in for a very pleasant surprise. Not only do they play super acoustic music at this tavern (the Indigo Girls got their start here), but the food is terrific, too.

Monterey Chicken quesadillas are just $4.50, and a hefty basket of nachos with plenty of sour cream is $4.95. The Attic Dog, grilled up and served with lots o' fries and slaw, is $3.95, and tostada salads are $5.95. Mr. C liked his huge bowl of Attic black bean soup, garnished with green onions and sour cream, for just $2.75; while red beans and rice, served with smoked sausage, is a big seller at just $4.95.

Eddie's opens at 4 p.m. daily. Even if you're not there to hear the bands and poets who troop through here each week, you can have fun hanging out and playing pool on the deck.

Evans Fine Foods
- 2125 North Decatur Rd., Emory Village; 634-6294

Evans is one of those friendly Ma n' Pa-owned places, making their customers feel right at home from the moment they walk in the door. They've been here since 1946; and while some of the waitresses seem to have been working here since around that time, the food makes up in taste what the service lacks in speed.

For breakfast, try a stack of hot cakes for $2.40, or a cheese omelette for $2.65. Add a side of hash browns (95¢), whole smoked sausage ($2.40), or corned beef hash ($1.50). Toast and jelly is just 85¢, while a bowl of cereal goes for $1.45.

At lunch or dinner, there's the egg sandwich for $1.35, grilled cheese for $1.35, and a quarter-pound hamburger for $2.30. A bowl of home-made soup (like green pea, or the yummy chicken gumbo) is $1.60. An open-faced roast beef or turkey sandwich with mashed potatoes is $3.95, while their famous (and tasty) chicken filet is yours for a mere $2.10. Evans also offers filet mignon ($5.95) and ribeye steak ($7.15), breaded veal ($4.35) and fried flounder ($4.45), all served with two kinds of freshly prepared vegetables.

Don't pass up Evans's homemade desserts, especially their pies: Chocolate or coconut cream, apple, or peach ($1.35-$1.45). You can also take a whole pie home for a cheap $6.75. Evans is open from 6 a.m. to 9 p.m., Mondays through Saturdays.

Everybody's Pizza
- 1040 North Highland Ave. N.E., Atlanta; 873-4545
- 1593 North Decatur Rd., Emory Village; 377-7766

Everybody loves Everybody's, not just for their great pizza, but for their starving-student prices, too.

One bonus right off the bat here is that you can choose from thirty amazing toppings—including basil, shrimp, sesame seeds, rosemary potatoes, feta cheese, and sun-dried tomatoes. Put 'em all on thick or thin crusts, too. A plain individual-size pie is just $3.25, going up to $5.85 for one with any four toppings. To be totally trendy, pesto sauce is 65 cents extra on the small, and $1.95 more on a large pizza.

You can also order one of Everybody's own combinations, which have been getting rave reviews for quite some time. How about one with shrimp and artichoke ($10.25), Florentine (with four kinds of cheese, spinach, and tomato slices for $8.25), or spicy-sweet jerk chicken for $9.75?

Or, try their lasagna ($6.25), fettucine carbonara ($6.75) or penne primavera ($6.50). Garlic-parmesan breadsticks are $1.25 for a small and $2.35 for a large order. And, just as with the pies, you can concoct your own salad, starting at $1.75.

Everybody's also serves beer and wine. They're open seven days a

RESTAURANTS ATLANTA NORTHEAST/DECATUR

week, closing at 1 a.m. Fridays and
Saturdays. Everybody got that?

Freight Room
- 301 East Howard Ave., Decatur;
  378-5365

The Freight Room is an aptly-named
train depot-turned country and blues
club and restaurant, located near the
entrance to Agnes Scott College near
East College Avenue. From the outside, the roof looks a bit unsturdy
(they do rock here, but thankfully
have yet to take the roof down), but
have no fear. The woodsy decor (lots
of wall-mounted fish and deer here)
and honest-to-goodness good food
and friendly service will take your
mind off its impending collapse.

Start your meal with some vegetarian refried beans for $2.25, or some
pub chips for $2.50. A big cobb salad
is $5.75, while the tuna and pasta
salad (try it with their poppyseed
dressing) is only $4.65.

California Sunshine sandwiches,
chock-full of sliced avocado, lettuce,
alfalfa sprouts, sliced black olives,
and Dijon mustard on sourdough
bread, are just $4.75, and the Freight-
Room stlye reuben, is $5.25. Bacon
and cheddar burgers are $5.25,
served with pub chips, lettuce and tomato, potato or fruit salad and a
pickle.

The sandwiches are so big, you'll
be tempted to split them, but be
aware that the Freight Room charges
$1 for each split entre.

Deep-dish, fresh-baked apple pie
slices are $2.50, and sour cream
brownies are $2.50. Carrot cake,
cheesecake, and sundaes are also
available for under $4.

Gold Burgers
- 3011 North Druid Hills Rd. N.E.,
  Atlanta; 325-9944

Atlanta's burgeoning food scene
seems to have at least one of every
kind of restaurant imaginable—including, yes folks, kosher fast food,
and this is it. Part of the Toco Hills
Promenade shopping center, Gold
Burgers is like a cross between a Middle Eastern deli and a certain
McChain. Meanwhile, everything

they serve is glatt kosher, the highest
of the high, all the way down to the
non-dairy "tofutti" ice cream for dessert.

The burgers themselves may be kosher, but they taste no better or worse
than any fast food burger, depending
on your view of such places. Personally, Mr. C cares little for the flat, frozen patty approach to burgerdom, but
it's good to know there is a kosher alternative for those who want it. The
basic quarter-pounders start at $3.45,
and $4.75 for a combo, which adds
fries and a drink. They also have turkey burgers for about the same price,
an option you won't find at most
chains.

You'll do far better, though, with
some of the other kinds of food
served here. Try their Mediterranean
specialties, like shawarma—a large
roll of ground lamb and spices,
slowly cooked on a rotisserie, from
which slices are shaved off and
stuffed into a pita bread sandwich
($3.99), or onto a bed of salad with
rice on the side ($5.89). Same
choices for grilled chicken ($4.39
sandwich, $6.29 platter), falafel
($2.99/$4.89), and others. Mr. C's dining companion was particularly
happy with a platter of grilled, marinated vegetables, which were moist
and tasty.

Add to all this a variety of
"Philly" steak sandwiches, hot dogs,
and salads; plus side orders ranging
from onion rings to hummus and pita
bread. There's also a kids' menu.
Gold Burgers may not be golden, but
it's quick, cheap, and can even be
fairly healthy. Though it's open every
day from 11 a.m. to 10 p.m., and 'til
1 a.m. on Saturday nights, do note
that, for religious reasons, it's closed
from two hours before sundown on
Friday until an hour after sunset on
Saturday.

Happy Herman's
- 2299 Cheshire Bridge Rd. N.E.,
  Atlanta; 321-3012
- 204 Johnson Ferry Rd., Sandy
  Springs; 256-3354

Best-known as a store for imported

gourmet treats and prepared foods for take-out, Happy Herman's is happy to have you sit at one of their few plastic tables near the entrance and nosh away. You can watch the traffic outside, or—much more interesting—inside the popular little shop.

Sip a tasty bowl of cream of mushroom soup ($1.89), or have them heat up a plate of cheese tortellini in tomato sauce ($5.99 per pound). Add a warm sourdough baguette or an individual-sized loaf of romano-parmesan bread, each 99 cents. Herman's also makes an exotic array of fresh sandwiches like "The Smokey," smoked turkey and smoked Gouda cheese on fresh-baked bread, with roasted peppers and grilled eggplant, all for $3.95. Or a New Orleans "Po' Boy" ($2.95), with layers of roast beef, turkey, ham, Swiss cheese, and thinly sliced pickles on a French roll.

And they have similarly wonderful salads, including the "Southwestern Grill" of grilled chicken breast, black beans, green peppers, cheddar cheese and pimientos—all on Romaine lettuce, all for $3.95. There are at least a dozen different salads to choose from, and almost as many dressings to put on top; the house flavor is a ranch dressing with feta cheese mixed in.

Finish off with some very elegant cakes and pastries, baked in the store, or perhaps something from the incredible-looking chocolate confectionery counter. Such great food, in such *hamish* surroundings, for a few bucks; you won't even have to leave a tip. After all this, you'll be happy too.

Indian Delights

- Scott Village Shopping Center, 1707 Church Street, Decatur; 296-2965
- Gwinnett Market Fair Shopping Center, 3675 Satellite Blvd., Duluth; 813-8212

How delightful—a non-smoking, tip-optional kind of restaurant with authentic Indian fare. Indian Delights has received kudos from *Creative Loafing*, the *Journal-Constitution*,

and *Atlanta* magazine, and all for good reason.

There are only eight tables here, so lots of local business people get their grub to go. Masala dhosa is a wonderful grilled combination of rice, white lentils, potatoes, and onions; it's served with a lentil-vegetable soup (Sambhar) and coconut chutney, all of which cost a mere $3.60. Vegetable biryani, a rice pilaf with spicy veggies, served with yogurt on the side, is also only $3.60. The most expensive item on the menu, in fact, is the $4.50 masala dhosa with rice cake (ioli) platter, which again is served with coconut chutney and Sambhar soup.

Appetizers will jazz up your meal for just a few bucks more. Bhel puri, which is fried whole wheat bread topped with potato, onions, and homemade noodles, is just $2.50. There's always the samosa, a northern Indian favorite, consisting of fried dough filled with potatoes and peas. It's served with sweet and spicy sauce, and you can get two for $1.80. Taro root leaves and chickpea pasta, topped with sesame seeds and cilantro, is $2.50. There's also the classic Mulligatwany soup ($1.50), and ganthia ($2.50), a spicy chickpea snack.

To cool off your taste buds after lunch or dinner, try the $1.25 dani vada, a white lentil ball covered in mild yogurt sauce; Mr. C prefers a sweet lassi (not the dog, but a sugar-yogurt shake), which sells for $2.25. Nut rolls with layers of phyllo leaves are two for $1.50, and cheese balls (ras malai) with syrup-flavored heavy cream is also two for $1.50.

Jagger's

- Emory Village Shopping Center, 1577 North Decatur Rd. N.E., Atlanta; 377-8888

You can't always get what you want in many restaurants, but Jagger's comes close—offering homemade soups, salads, roast turkey, pizza, fish, you name it—there's something for everyone in the family here, and at prices that make it possible to take the whole family out more often.

This is a self-described "neighbor-hood place", open since '72; they must be doing something right.

Jagger's can get crowded on the weekends with Emory students imbibing the hours away, but if you come at an off time or on a weekday, things are pretty quiet. Some professors even hold informal class discussions here.

Start off your meal with ten of Jagger's Buffalo wings ($4.25), a half-pound basket of raw vegetables ($2.50), or a cup of shrimp and crabmeat bisque ($2.95). Same price for a crock of their "Very Chunky Chili".

Dinners include such entrees as rainbow trout and roast turkey, each for $6.95. All dinners come with two choices of side dishes; choose from things like a dinner salad or cup of soup, vegetables, noodles, French fries, or mashed potatoes.

The Jagger Burger is served in a wine and mushroom sauce for $4.95; grilled chicken sandwiches, available plain, barbecued, or teriyaki style, are just $5.95 with fries. Individual-sized pizzas start at just $3.95. Desserts like French silk pie ($3.25) and amaretto cheesecake ($2.95) are big enough to share.

The children's menu features grilled cheese sandwiches and chips ($2.50), linguini ($2.25), turkey and mashed potatoes ($3.95), and Jagger's "award-winning" hot dog and fries ($1.95).

The Juice Factory
- 3092 Briarcliff Rd. N.E., Atlanta; 321-7775

Mr. C gives the Juice Factory thumbs up for its creative and super-healthy juice bar offerings, along with its light vegetarian menu. The atmosphere is nothing to jump up and down about (five booths and some posters on artificial food additives—oh joy), but there are copies of Vegetarian Times magazine to browse through. The noise from the juice maker leads many people to opt for take-out, but if you hit the Factory at an off-peak time of day, things do quiet down.

Plain juices cost $2.00 for eight ounces, and $4 for sixteen ounces. The usual apple and orange juices are here, plus oddities like watermelon, pineapple, cucumber, and even green pepper(!). The Factory also offers combinations ($2.75/$4.25) like the "Energizer II," with banana, papaya, coconut milk, almonds, and protein powder; or the "Ocean Cocktail," made with lemonade and honey. You can also make your own concoction with any of the ingredients, including lettuce, apple, beets, carrots, dates, wheat germ, kiwis, pears, and bananas. Other drinks include soy milk for $1.50.

Well, what to eat with these delectable drinks? Mr. C tried the falafel with tahini in a pita pocket, stuffed to overflowing with shredded carrot, lettuce, sprouts, and chunks of fresh tomato, all for $3.75. The avocado and tofu sandwich with tomatoes, scallions, and cheese is $5.95; and curried veggie soup, brown rice, and toast is a scrumptious $4.95.

Not to mention tabouli or tofu salads, vegetarian pizzas, and other healthy snacks. The Juice Factory is right near the corner of Clairmont, quietly hidden in a brick building next to a party supplies store.

Le Peep
- 2484 Briarcliff Rd. N.E., Atlanta; 325-7069
- 233 Peachtree St. N.E., Atlanta; 688-3782
- 3000 Windy Hill Rd., Marietta; 980-0898

And other suburban locations

Mr. Cheap loves Le Peep. The plates are piled so high with wonderful food that you'll find it *magnifique*, whether you come for breakfast, brunch, lunch, or dinner.

In spite of the French name, Le Peep actually serves food with a western flair. Why don't you come to your senses and try the "Desperado," Le Peep's skillet dish with eggs, cheese, chorizo sausage, green chilies and onions, mixed with salsa, for $6; or the Fiesta Skillet, full of "Peasant Potatoes," chunks of chicken, and diced onions covered with chili verde and cheddar. It's served up with two eggs for $5.75.

The aptly-named "Lumberjack Breakfast" lets you chop down eggs, two bacon strips, two sausage links, Peasant Potatoes, and a short stack of pancakes, for $5.85. For healthy palates, a huge fresh fruit plate is $4.20, and granola-dipped French toast is $4.95.

At lunch or dinnertime, LP's smoked turkey and bacon sandwich, with bacon, Muenster, lettuce, tomato and mayo, served with a garden salad or cup of soup or criss cross cut fries, is a winner for $5.35. A Philly cheese steak sandwich, with soup, salad, or fries, is just $6, and a jumbo 1/3-pound burger, also with choice of side dishes, is $4.75. And don't forget dessert: a sweet crepe, filled with blueberries, bananas, strawberries, or spiced apples, covered with whipped topping and cinnamon, is $1.95.

Le Peep has some of the best coffee and hot chocolate this side of the Divide (or should that be the Seine?), and serves breakfast any time of day. They also have a "Golden Years Club," which entitles anyone over 55 to a ten percent discount off any meal, seven days a week. Le *wow*!

Lettuce Souprise You
- 595 Piedmont Ave., N.E., Atlanta; 874-4998
- 2470 Briarcliff Rd. N.E., Atlanta; 636-8549
- 245 Pharr Rd. N.E., Atlanta; 841-9583
- 3525 Mall Blvd., Duluth; 418-9969
- 1475 Holcomb Bridge Rd., Roswell; 642-1601
- 5975 Roswell Rd., Sandy Springs; 250-0304
- 1109 Cumberland Mall, Smyrna; 438-2288

Here's a place after your humble author's own heart. At Lettuce Souprise You, one price gets you unlimited trips to their extensive salad bar, as well as the all-you-can-eat baked potato bar and pasta bar, plus homemade muffins, cornbread, and soups, and fresh fruit. Whew! Lettuce be thankful for places like this!

The salad bar is super-fresh and preservative-free; it features spinach, broccoli, tarragon tuna, spicy crab and pasta salad, and pineapple, along with dozens of other choices. Soups change daily, but always include at least one vegetarian recipe, such as potato-leek or lentil. Egg drop, chili, and vegetable soups are featured often, too.

How can they afford to offer such a bargain, you ask? Well, they do work on keeping costs down. For one thing, Lettuce Souprise You requests that you eat only in the restaurant—they don't allow anyone to leave with more than a muffin. If you'd like something to go, they will charge you for it. Well hey, that's only fair!

Meanwhile,the price for this entire sumptuous buffet is just $5.50 at lunchtime; $6.50 for brunch and dinner. Another cheap deal: Their "frequent buyer" club entitles you to a free meal when you've had twelve lunches, six dinners, or four brunches. Can it be any surprise that Lettuce Souprise You rates so highly with Mr. C?

Lucky China
- 2179 Lawrenceville Hwy., Decatur; 248-1288

Lucky for you, Lucky China serves up award-winning Chinese cuisine on the cheap. The atmosphere may not be spectacular (they're in the Cub Foods shopping center), but you can't beat their food. The lunch specials are especially bargain-priced, and take-outs are prepared lightning-fast.

An order of pot stickers is $3.65, and their super egg drop soup is $1.50. Neptune soup for two, made with scallops, shrimp, and vegetables, is $5.50. Combinations like chicken lo mein, moo goo gai pan, mandarin ribs, shrimp with Chinese vegetables, pork chow mein, and Szechuan dishes—each served with fried rice, chicken wing, and egg roll—are priced from $4.25 to $5.75.

A puu puu tray for two (isn't that just fun to say?) gives you and your date plenty to nibble on for just $10.

Broccoli with oyster sauce is $6.25, and curry shrimp is $8.50. Fried chicken with Cantonese vegetables is $8.75, and ma po bean curd with ground pork and Szechuan sauce is just $6.95. These dishes are all so big that you'll need to share, or bring a doggie bag home with you.

And, in the unlikely event that you have room for dessert, try Lucky China's jumbo orders of glazed bananas or glazed apples (a nice change from just fortune cookies), each $3.50.

Lucky China offers free delivery within the Decatur area on orders of $10.00 or more, from 4:30 to 9:30 p.m. only. They're open seven days a week, including a super Sunday lunch buffet from noon until 3 p.m.

Madras Cafe
- 3086 Briarcliff Rd. N.E., Atlanta; 320-7120

Near the intersection of Briarcliff and Clairmont Roads, the tiny Madras Cafe is a surefire bet for those of you who like Indian food. For those who've never cared for it, this may be the place to give it a try. If you're not into hot spices, just let the waiter know—the kitchen can adjust its recipes to fit your taste. Not only is the Indian cuisine healthy, but most dishes run in the $3 range.

Appetizers include the $1.50 "Mixture," a combination of chick pea noodles, peanuts, and cashews; or the Pakoda, a spicy, crispy Indian snack made from chick pea and rice flours and chilies. Steam-cooked rice cakes (*idli*) are $1.70, and masala dhosai (crepes filled with onions and potatoes) are $3.50.

Curried vegetable *kuruma*, a north Indian specialty, is $2, and fried masala vadai, a spicy, fried dish with chick pea flour, is served with sambar (lentil soup) and mint chutney for only $1.70.

Daily lunch or dinner specials start as low as $3.50; a variety of dishes are served with Basmati rice, vegetable curry sauce, yogurt salad, soft bread, and soda.

Traditional desserts include carrot

MR. CHEAP'S PICKS
Decatur

✔ **Our Way Cafe**—If Mr. C had *his* way, this homey place near Avondale Estates would be open seven days a week, and for dinner, too. Well worth going out of your way for.

✔ **Rainbow Restaurant**—You won't spend much green at this hangout, tucked in the back of Rainbow Natural Foods. A favorite of vegetarians and non-vegetarians alike.

✔ **Thumbs Up**—Two big ones for the quick service and tasty dishes at this neighborhood diner.

halwa (made with milk, butter, and sugar, spiced with cardamom) for $1, cheese balls for $1, and sweet buttery badhushas for $1.50.

To wash it all down, try a mango lassi or sweet lassi (sweetened yogurt shakes), each $2, or spicy masala tea. Mango juice is just 80¢, too.

The Madras Cafe is open seven days a week, until 8:00 p.m. only.

Market Cafe at Your DeKalb Farmer's Market
- 3000 East Ponce de Leon Ave., Decatur; 377-6400

For a salad bar beyond compare, freshly-prepared stir-frys and steamed veggies, fish-n-chips, and other meals under $5, you'll find it right here in the supermarket.

Huh? That's right. Not only is this one of the best supermarkets around, for both price and selection (see listing under "Shopping: General Markets"), but over to one side of the vast interior is a sit-down cafeteria which reflects the international mix of the staff and the surrounding Decatur community.

233

This is a good place for meat eaters and vegetarians alike. Entrees like chicken ($3.50 fried, $4.95 baked or grilled) are served with three side dishes, as are lamb stew ($4.95) and other daily specials. A hamburger and fries is $3.50, an eight-ounce New York strip steak is $6.99, and cold deli sandwiches are just $3.

Indian samosas, filled with beef or vegetables, are just $1.25. They're a hot, delicious, and rather greasy snack. Other items for vegetarians include a wonderful salad bar—a bargain at just 21 an ounce—and plain baked potatoes topped with broccoli and cheese for $1.50. The five veggie plate is a remarkable $3.

It's all served by a helpful, smiling staff. There is a separate bakery counter, selling delicious desserts, and that great coffee which Your DeKalb sells so inexpensively by the pound. While the food is hard to beat, there's not much atmosphere other than people watching; and the chairs are those plastic bucket-shaped types you may recall from grade school. Even so, the cafe fills up at lunchtime, and you may have to share your big, round table with fellow diners. Mr. C recommends that you bring a sweater, by the way, since the cafe is right across from the rather chilly dairy and fresh pasta departments of the supermarket.

The Market Cafe is open daily from 11:00 a.m. to 8:00 p.m.

Mary Mac's Tea Room and Restaurant
- 224 Ponce de Leon Ave. N.E., Atlanta; 876-6604
- 2205 Cheshire Bridge Rd. N.E., Atlanta; 325-7777
- 4431 Hugh Howell Rd., Tucker; 621-9935

And other suburban locations
Zell Miller and Jimmy Carter have eaten at Mary Mac's, considered to be Atlanta's oldest home cooking restaurant. Nothing's fancy here, really—you actually fill out the food slips yourself, since the waitresses are too busy helping the scores of folks who flock here at lunchtime.

Choose from a choice of entrees (baked chicken, country fried steak, baked fish almondine, beef tips on creole rice, sauteed chicken livers, etc.) with two side dishes for $6.50. Sweet potato cobbler is a popular choice, but Mr. C is partial to the cheese-whipped potatoes. Included in the price are tea, coffee, or punch, Mary Mac's cornbread, and ice cream in your choice of five flavors.

Meals are served in a flash; also, half portions can be ordered for those customers "under 12 or over 90." The Ponce location is currently open only for lunch, but may be reopening for dinner by the time you read this.

Mellow Mushroom
- 30 Pharr Rd. N.W., Atlanta; 233-3443
- 1679 Lavista Road N.E., Atlanta; 325-0330
- 931 Monroe Dr. N.E., Atlanta; 874-2291
- 6218 Roswell Rd. N.E., Sandy Springs; 252-5560

Hey, dudes, chill out at the Mellow Mushroom if you're looking for good pizza and calzones at better-than-good prices.

Small pizzas are just $4.95, and large ones are $9.75. Toppings include the basics (including mushrooms, of course) as well as some far-out stuff, like sun-dried tomatoes, pineapple, feta cheese, tofu, and artichoke hearts. Cool.

MM's "House Special" pizza is topped with pepperoni, mushrooms, ground beef, onions, sausage, green peppers, ham, tomatoes, bacon, extra cheese, and black olives—phew! You get them all for $14.95 (medium size) and $16.95 (large). Good luck finishing one. Meanwhile, white pizza—made without tomato sauce, and not often found in Atlanta—is just $7.95 for the small, $13.50 for the medium, and $15.50 for the large.

If pizza's not your passion, the Mushroom has other interesting and vaguely health-conscious items, such as teriyaki tofu sandwiches for $3.25, ham and cheese with sprouts for $3.95, and BLTs for $3.50.

234

Other goodies include orders of soft pretzels for $2.35, garlic bread for $1.50, and chef salads for $3.50.

Mick's

- 557 Peachtree Rd. N.E., Atlanta; 875-6425
- 2110 Peachtree Rd. N.W., Atlanta; 351-6425
- Peachtree Center, 229 Peachtree St. N.E., Atlanta; 688-6425
- Lenox Square Shopping Center, 3393 Peachtree Rd. N.E., Atlanta; 262-6425
- Underground Atlanta, 75 Upper Alabama St. S.W., Atlanta; 525-2825
- 116 East Ponce de Leon Ave., Decatur; 373-7797

And other suburban locations

Get to Mick's for one of the best milkshakes in town, great burgers, super desserts, and creative drinks. Stretching from Underground Atlanta to Buckhead and beyond, this yuppie haven seems determined to make the next siege of Atlanta a culinary one.

Prices here are not the absolute cheapest around, but you do get a lot of delicious food for the money. Start off with real fried green tomatoes ($5.75), chili-smothered French fries ($3.95), grilled carrots and broccoli ($2.50), or a cup of soup in flavors like tomato or "baked potato" ($1.95).

A half-pound hamburger, hickory grilled, with a generous side of fries or pasta salad, is $5.95. You can top it with cheddar or mozzarella cheese, guacamole, chili, barbecue sauce, or cracked pepper and mustard for 80¢ extra. Cheese-topped grilled boneless chicken is $7.50, and corn and tomato linguine with garlic bread is $6.95. Mick's chicken Reuben will completely stuff you for $7.95.

Do try to leave room for dessert, though. You'll probably want to share one of these monstrosities with a friend. Try the Oreo cheesecake ($3.95), the Giant Banana Split ($4.75), or Mr. C's favorite, the chocolate cream pie ($3.75). Yummy! Strawberry shortcake, homemade chocolate layer cake, and Heath Bar ice cream pie will all make delightful

MR. CHEAP'S PICKS
Druid Hills/Emory Village

✔ **Cedar Tree**—It's well worth a trip to Emory Village, just for this hangout's falafel sandwich alone.

✔ **Havana Sandwich Shop**—Filling platters of hot food, for around five bucks.

✔ **Papa Nick's**—Papa Nick knows Greek cuisine. A great place to bring the kids for pizza, while you feast on spanikopita and baklava.

ends to your meal, and all are under $4 apiece.

Besides the desserts, Mick's is known for its unusual mixed drinks—like "Frozen Pink Lemonade," "Frozen German Chocolate Cake," and "Peasant Coffee" (spiked with brandy, Grand Marnier, Kahlua, amaretto, and dark creme de cacao, and topped with whipped cream). These will doubtless not be cheap, but they are good. Most branches of Mick's have a separate bar area.

Nuts 'N Berries

- 4274 Peachtree Rd. N.E., Atlanta; 237-6829

You need not be a vegetarian to love the food at this cafe; but no matter what you like, you'll love their prices.

Attached to the Nuts 'N Berries health foods and vitamins store, this little hangout serves up classic American and Mexican dishes for a pittance. Try the chicken burrito for $3.65 (50¢ more with rice on the side), or a bean burrito for $3.05. Middle Eastern specialties include falafel burgers with tahini sauce, served with corn chips and dill pickle ($3.35), and hummus and pita bread for $3.35. If you're extra hungry, add a side of tabouli salad ($1.25), tofu salad ($1.50), or a garden salad with miso tahini or tofu dill dressing ($1.85).

Not to leave out the all-American tuna melt for $3.95, and a plain (but tasty, mind you) cheese sandwich piled with sprouts, tomato, and lettuce for $3.35.

The cafe serves lunch every weekday from 11 a.m. to 3:30 p.m., and brunch on Saturdays from 10 a.m. to 3 p.m.

Oasis Cafe

- 752 Ponce de Leon Ave. N.E., Atlanta; 881-0815
- Sage Hill Shopping Center, 1799 Briarcliff Rd. N.E., Atlanta; 876-0003

Get swept away to the Mediterranean with the good and cheap (not to mention good for you!) food at the Oasis. Start your day off right with an egg-pita "pizza" for $2.25—sort of a Middle Eastern answer to the Egg McMuffin. Or, perhaps a spinach onion omelette, served with toast, English muffin, and hash browns or fresh fruit, for $2.95.

Prices for lunch and dinner fare are worth relaxing over, too. Lamb or beef shish kabobs with rice and vegetables, served with barbecue or tahini sauce, are each $5.95; and the vegetarian combo consists of falafel, tabouli, hummus and baba ghannoush (a spiced eggplant puree), served with pita bread, all for just $5.25. If you're eating with a group of friends, try the mazza platter—a tray of dishes including those from the veggie combo, along with grape leaves, tahini, and tzatziki (yogurt salad)—for $12.95. It serves two or three people easily.

Of course, it wouldn't be a Mediterranean restaurant without gyros; the tasty gyro platter here is $4.95. The mjadra casserole (lentils, rice, and sauted onions) delicious and tummy-warming at $4.25.

For lighter appetites, Oasis also serves rotisserie chicken (a half-chicken plate is just $4.75). Also, lots of salad choices—fattoush with cucumbers, mint, and green peppers is

$3.50; a side of tabouli is $3.15. Sandwiches filled with things like hummus, baba ghannoush and tahini are all priced at $3.50 and under. Hitch up your camel and stay awhile.

Original Pancake House

- 1937 Peachtree Rd. N.E., Atlanta; 351-3533
- 4330 Peachtree Rd. N.E., Atlanta; 237-4116
- 2321 Cheshire Bridge Rd. N.E., Atlanta; 633-5712
- 501 Johnson Ferry Rd. N.E., Marietta; 977-5013
- 5099 Memorial Dr., Stone Mountain; 292-6914

The Original Pancake Houses sure won't leave you in the poor house. James Beard did name this one of the top ten restaurants in America, but you'd never know this from the prices. Quality runs high here—they use fresh juices, extra large Grade AA eggs, and pure whipping cream, plus all the cooking is done in pure butter.

The pancake recipe is a carefully-guarded secret, with good reason. They're light and fluffy, and just $3.55 an order. Georgia Pecan Waffles ($4.80) are delicious. If you're truly starving, Mr. C suggests the omelettes, served with three buttermilk pancakes, plus grits or toast, all for $6.95; or a four-ounce beef tenderloin steak for $4.50. Other good bets include French crepes with strawberry topping ($5.25). Side dishes include sweets like cinnamon applesauce ($1) and imported lingonberries in butter ($1.75).

Junior plates are available for children under ten. Two slices of French toast ($2.60), and three pancakes ($2.50) are served with milk, chocolate milk, or hot chocolate.

Meanwhile, to paraphrase the old orange juice commercials, "it's not just for breakfast anymore." OPH also serves a lunch menu of hamburgers ($4.25), soups (plus soup and half-sandwich specials for $4.95), and hot dogs (two for $2.95), along with salads and chili.

Senior citizens always get a 15%

discount here, and police and firemen also receive a discount off their meals. The Original Pancake Houses are open from 6:30 a.m. to 2:30 p.m. weekdays, and from 7 a.m. to 3 p.m. on weekends.

Our Way Cafe
- 303 East College Ave., Decatur; 373-6665

For home cooking away from home, make your way to Our Way. In the words of one server, "There's always meatloaf, some kinda chicken, and somethin' else" for main dishes, plus more veggies than you can shake a stalk at.

The scene is, as you'd imagine, pretty casual. Service is cafeteria style; patrons include lots of students from nearby Agnes Scott College, though you'll spot a few suits now and then. Our Way is decorated with pretty watercolor paintings, and there's a fireplace in the middle of the dining area.

For side dishes, try collard greens, pole beans, steamed cabbage, lima beans, sweet potato casserole, carrots, or macaroni and cheese. You'll get two or three sides with a main dish for under five bucks, like that meatloaf with two vegetables and bread, which is just $4.73. Same price for the four-veggie plate, served with fresh bread. Some of the similarly low-priced daily specials may include pork chops, stuffed cabbage, salmon croquettes, and chicken enchiladas.

Try to save room for the yummy homemade desserts, like banana pudding or fresh strawberry pie, each only $1.58 a slice. At these prices, "Our Way" is cheaper than staying home!

Strictly a lunchtime establishment, Our Way is open from 11:30 a.m. to 2:30 p.m., Monday through Friday only.

Papa Nick's Greek Pizza and Restaurant
- Sage Hill Shopping Center, 1799 Briarcliff Road N.E., Atlanta; 875-9677

Not your average pizza joint by far,

Papa Nick's adds a touch of class to a classic Greek menu—with its airy, chandeliered dining room and super service. Plates are piled high with food (even on the children's menu), and prices are pleasantly surprising.

Mr. C especially liked Papa's Greek herbed potatoes, which come with many of the entrees. Lunch specials (served weekdays from 11-3) include lasagna or a half-portion of one of their casseroles, such as fried eggplant or meatballs and cheese; these are served with garlic bread and a garden salad for $3.75. Gyros with French fries are $3.95, and super-big subs are just $3.50. Fried fish sandwiches are just $3.

If you're in the mood to stuff yourself silly, go for the grilled marinated chicken—served with potatoes, Greek salad and pita bread for $7.50. Moussaka (eggplant and beef) with spanikopita (feta and spinach) is $6.50, same sides; and Papa's Classico salad with gyro meat is $5.50 for the medium size. Nick's also sells wine and domestic and imported beer, including Aegean Beer, from (where else) Greece.

What about the pizzas? They get pretty fancy. Papa's Hawaiian pizza, topped with pineapple, is $12.50 for a medium-size, big enough to serve two or three people. If you'd rather make up your own pie, other unusual toppings include shrimp, pastrami, feta cheese and Greek peppers.

For the kids, Nick's has spaghetti plates ($2), a pita pizza ($2.25), chicken strips and fries ($3.50), plus hamburgers and lasagna. Again, these will keep the little ones occupied for quite a while.

PoFolks
- 2094 North Druid Hills Rd. N.E., Atlanta; 321-0300
- Market Square at North DeKalb, 2179 Lawrenceville Hwy., Decatur; 321-3948
- 825 Sandy Plains Rd., Marietta; 425-2322
- 4286 Lavista Rd., Tucker; 493-6925

- 5549 Old National Hwy., College Park; 761-3114
- 4909 Memorial Drive, Stone Mountain; 294-6444

And other suburban locations
Don't be fooled by the sky-high billboard signs—PoFolks may seem to be your typical family fast-food joint, but in fact it's a relaxing, friendly sort of place with an incredible selection of food.

If you like veggies (or even if you don't), try their Po' Plate, with any four side orders, plus cornbread or a biscuit for just $4.29. You have a choice from over two dozen sides, like sweet potato souffle, fried green tomatoes, cornbread, Brunswick stew, hobo beans, red beans and rice, or corn on the cob. You can also substitute a "garden patch" salad or vegetable soup for 69 cents extra.

Even po' folks can afford seafood here, like a plate of thirty fried Gulf shrimp for $6.69, southern-style catfish for $6.99, rainbow trout for $5.99, or the clam dinner for $5.49.

Other specialties, such as barbecued pork chops, hamburger steak, chicken n' dumplin's and chicken livers are all priced under $6 a plate, served with vegetables and a choice of breads.

PoFolks also makes a point of catering to the senior crowd, who can get some great bargains. Diners age 55 and over can choose from the Po Plate, fish dinners, fried chicken, and other platters, all served with vegetables and bread; most of these are specially priced at only $3.99 to $4.99.

This is a good place for them to bring the grandchildren, too. The children's menu includes things like the "Minner Dinner" with fish patty, hush puppies, and fries; plus country-fried steak, meatloaf, or chicken tenders, all under $3 each. And for everyone, all drinks except moo juice (guess what that is) are refilled for free. Not that you'll always need it; iced tea and lemonade are served in Mason jars.

Rainbow Natural Foods Restaurant
- 2118 North Decatur Rd., Decatur; 633-3538

See the light and try Rainbow for their super healthy breakfasts, lunches and dinners, and especially their incredible Sunday brunch. The teeny restaurant is way in the back of the Rainbow grocery (which has prices that aren't half-bad, either—see listing under "Food Stores").

There's usually a line for Sunday brunch—be sure to get there early if you want a seat. A bowl of yogurt and granola is $1.95; so is a whole wheat biscuit with scrambled egg and home fries. Egg dishes can be prepared with tofu instead for 50¢ extra. Banana nut smoothies, made with almonds, yogurt, nutmeg, and honey, are $1.95 each—protein powder and wheat germ is 75¢ extra. Mr. C tried the seven-grain French toast, topped with cinnamon, nutmeg, and honey, for $2.50 a half order (the whole order is gigantic). Huevos rancheros—made with poached eggs, beans, Monterey jack cheese, salsa, black olives, green olives, and sour cream, served with home fries—are just $4.25. Sides of tempeh bacon ($1.50) and yellow grits (60¢) will help you fill up without flattening your wallet.

For lunch and dinner, Rainbow has "Sunburgers" (made with vegetables, sunflower seeds, and potatoes), served with carrot sticks for $3.75, and a plate of steamed vegetables and brown rice plate for $2.95. Huge guacamole sandwiches are $4.95; peanut butter, apple, banana, and honey sandwiches are $2.75; and tuna hoagies are $6.50.

Don't pass up Rainbow's super desserts, either. Eggless cheesecake is $2.75, and slices of pecan or pumpkin pie are $1.50. Rainbow is open Monday through Saturday from 10 a.m. to 8 p.m., and Sundays for brunch from 11 a.m. to 3 p.m.

Robert's Place
- Piedmont Center, 3535 Piedmont Rd. N.E., Atlanta; 237-4839

Roberts is only open for breakfast

and lunch, but it's well worth waking up early for, with their famous cheese grits recipe and back-breakingly big sandwiches.

You can get a single order of those cheese grits for 90¢, or go for a grits, toast, and eggs platter for $2. The "Rob O'Muffin" sandwich, which Robert's claims as the original prototype of the Egg McMuffin, is $1.50. French toast is a mere $1.75, and a stack of pancakes with a side order of eggs is just $2.40.

For lunch, how about a baked potato with sour cream and butter for $1.40, chili & cheese for $2.10, or a turkey dog for $1.70? The salad bar's just 25¢ an ounce, too. Pimento cheese sandwiches are a favorite here, selling for just $2.80, kosher liverwurst sandwiches are just $3.30, and a half-pound burger is only $3.10. Finish off with a slice of carrot cake for 95¢.

And remember Robert's if you need party platters—for just $4.75 a person, you get enough roast beef, turkey, ham, pastrami, corned beef, Swiss and American cheese, cole slaw, potato salad, and pickles and condiments to feed the whole crew. Robert's is open from 7 a.m. to 3 p.m. only, Mondays through Fridays. In Piedmont Center, head for Building 14, Suite C-10.

Romeo and Juliet (R&J) Village Cafe

- 1569 North Decatur Rd. N.E., Atlanta; 378-4974

Okay, it sounds odd; but this is a coffeehouse-Chinese-Mexican restaurant all rolled into one. Talk about star-crossed! A favorite among Emory students, R&J keeps its food prices nice and low (keep in mind that the beer is a big profit maker, so the food's cheaper).

Mr. C liked the chicken stir-fry, which comes with miso soup and a side salad for $5.50. Veggie lo mein is $4.95. On the other side of the border, you'll find chicken, beef, or shrimp fajitas all priced under $6.25, with a salad included. Chicken quesadillas are just $4.95. And don't for-

get old standbys like teriyaki chicken sandwiches ($4.75), bacon cheeseburgers ($3.75), and good ol' grilled cheese sandwiches ($3).

Espresso ($1.35) and hot chocolate ($1.25) are especially good here, too. R&J has over twenty varieties of coffee at 95¢ a cup, but dessert is a little pricey ($1.95 for ice cream, and even more for slices of cake—but they "are" from some of the best bakeries in town).

St. Charles Deli

- 752 North Highland Ave. N.E., Atlanta; 876-3354
- Loehmann's Plaza, 2470 Briarcliff Rd. N.E., Atlanta; 636-5201

No need to pass "Go" and collect $200 before landing on *this* St. Charles. Brunch, lunch, and dinner are all good deals—if you can find a seat, that is, in this restaurant which takes New Orleans streetcars for its inspiration. Things sure get crowded, especially on weekends, so you may be wise not to "board" during rush hours.

Breakfast is served from 8-11 a.m., and includes treats like fluffy Belgian waffles for $4.25, make-your-own-omelettes starting at $5.25, and eggs with corned beef hash for $4.50. Mr. C enjoyed two eggs, with bagel, home fries, and juice (a mere $2.95); even with the busy crowd, everything was quickly delivered piping hot by one of the most unflappable waiters that Mr. C has ever seen in these parts.

Lunch features good ol' N'Awlins choices like the huge Muffaletta sandwich—cappicola ham, Genoa salami, mortadella and provolone cheese, topped with an antipasto salad, all on an Italian roll for $6.25. Try a soft-shell crab sandwich on an onion roll ($6.25), or the filling Philly cheese steak ($5.95). And there's always egg salad ($3.75), not to mention potato or macaroni salad, liverwurst, corned beef, and tuna salad sandwiches on pumpernickel, challah, whole wheat, Italian, or onion breads. Stanley and Stella never had it so good!

Get the office together and have a meal delivered—it's free on orders of $30 or more.

The Southern Star
- 231 West Ponce de Leon Ave., Decatur; 377-0799

This is a star in Mr. C's book, for sure. The lunch menu changes daily here, with great specials like pepper steak over rice ($4.35), baked pork ($4.35), and barbecued chicken ($4.20). All are served with your choice of vegetables on the side, including turnip greens, northern beans, or English peas. If you prefer, you can just have those; the three-vegetable plate is just $2.59.

Menu mainstays for breakfast include 99¢ egg sandwiches, three hotcakes for $3.10, and grilled smoked sausage for $1.50. Two eggs and a large pork chop make a hearty start to the day for $2.50, and country-style steak with two eggs, gravy, grits, and choice of bread is only $3.45. Or, have three eggs any style, with home fries, grits, and orange juice—plus your pick of bacon or sausage—all for an amazing $3.49.

The Southern Star is set up picnic-table style, and can accommodate very large parties. It does tend to fill up quickly during rush times. But, even amidst this old-style cooking, you can fax your order for take out by calling 377-2258.

Taco Mac
- 375 Pharr Rd. N.E., Atlanta; 239-0650
- 1006 North Highland Ave. N.E., Atlanta; 873-6529
- 771 Cherokee Ave. S.E., Atlanta; 624-4641
- 2120 Johnson Ferry Rd., Chamblee; 454-7676
- 1444 Oxford Rd., Emory Village; 377-2323
- 1570 Holcomb Bridge Rd., Roswell; 640-9598
- 5830 Roswell Rd. N.W., Sandy Springs; 257-0735
- 2845 Mountain Industrial Blvd., Stone Mountain; 621-3601

And other suburban locations

These guys claim that Buffalo wings were invented right here. Gee, wait'll the folks in Buffalo hear that. No matter—Taco Mac's spicy wings are for real, and they've also got the biggest beer selection this side of the Mississippi to wash them down. While the service can be slow as a sloth, Mr. C still thinks that the food and the prices make Mac a hit.

Appetizers include fried zucchini, cauliflower, or mushrooms for just $4 a plate; a jumbo basket of nachos with frijoles and cheese goes for $4.75. TM's guacamole salad is a mere $2.85. Basics include soft tacos for $1.55, super burritos for $3.25, quesadillas for $5.50, and chili for just $2.50; to go with these, beers from 28 different countries are reasonably priced, even though they come from as far away as New Zealand and the Ivory Coast.

Those Buffalo chicken wings come in sizes of ten for $4.75 or twenty for $7.05. Rustle them up in mild, medium, hot—or, for 50¢ extra, "Three Mile Island"-style. If you're having a party, here's an extra tip from Mr. C: You can get a 10% discount for platter orders of 250 wings or more.

Taco Mac has a kiddie menu too, with things like a burger and fries for $2.50, or a mini-fish and chips plate for the same price.

Thumbs Up Eatery
- 254 West Ponce de Leon Ave., Decatur; 377-5623

An aptly named neighborhood favorite, Thumbs Up features an extensive breakfast menu and delectable lunch entrees that won't break the bank. Their jams and preserves are homemade; so are the biscuits and buckwheat pancakes, and the syrup is pure maple. All *right*!

Early risers will like the smoked chicken omelette with onions, herbs, and mozzarella ($4.50), the Italian frittata with zucchini, onions, and marinara sauce ($4.25), or the combo breakfasts, like the "Country Lane Morning" (two eggs, O'Brien spuds or stone-ground grits, toast or biscuit for $3.50. Weekend brunch adds specials like "Eggs in Paradise"—tomatoes, basil, garlic, smoked sausage, and parmesan cheese, with choice of

Irish or Cajun potatoes, for $5.50.

For lunch, half-pound hamburgers are $4.50, blackened chicken is $5.25, and a big plate of super-spicy black beans and rice with sour cream is just $3.95. Tortellini salad will fill you up for $5.25, while a pair of cheese quesadillas with homemade salsa are $3.95.

Thumbs Up sells wine and beer, along with water-filtered coffees. Breakfast is served from 7:30 a.m. to 10:45 a.m., Monday through Friday, with weekend brunch from 8 a.m. to 2 p.m.; lunch is weekdays from 11 a.m. to 3 p.m., and dinner is served from 6-10 p.m.

Touch of India

- 962 Peachtree St. N.E., Atlanta; 876-7777
- 2065 Piedmont Rd. N.E., Atlanta; 876-7775

You'll wind up with a touch more money in your pocket if you eat at this restaurant, with locations in and just north of Midtown. The prices are right up Mr. C's alley; yet, the super samosas and tandoori dishes have attracted such celebrities as Mick Jagger, Sade, and Emilio Estevez.

Indian-style chicken fritters are $2.95, and prove Mr. C's theory that all ethnic groups really work from the same ideas. Mild lentil soup, or spicier Mulligatawny soup, is $1.95 a bowl. Chicken curry, $6.50, is available in three spice levels; and beef sheek kabab is $6.95. Sag aloo (spinach with potatoes) is $4.95; add some chapati bread for just $1.

Weekdays from 11:30-2:30, you can take advantage of the $4.25 lunch special ($3.95 for vegetarian dishes). The choices change from day to day, but usually include samosas (turnovers) or pakuras (fritters), a curry dish or other main entree with rice, and the sweet of the day to quell the spices (like homemade ice cream or rice pudding).

Touch of India also sells beer and wine. They're open for lunch Monday through Saturday from 11:30 a.m. to 2:30 p.m., and for dinner daily from 5:30 p.m. to 10:30 p.m.

Varsity Jr.

- 1085 Lindbergh Dr. N.E., Atlanta; 261-8843

"What'll ya have?" they'll ask you at The Varsity. Most likely, you'll have heartburn after a meal here; this is not a safe place for cholesterol counters. But then again, you'll also have change left in your pocket when you're done.

The Varsity's an oddball—an actual drive-in restaurant, a throwback to the 1950s. You can order from the car, or choose to eat inside, where you'll get to watch your burgers and fries travel along conveyor belts to your plastic orange tray. Then pick from several different dining areas, each with its own TV set showing news from CNN, sports on ESPN, or local Channel 11. Instead of tables, you sit at one of those attached desk-chair combinations we all remember so fondly from fifth grade.

Forget about your diet and get The Varsity's plain burgers for 75¢ (no extra charge for the grease) or double chili-cheese burgers ($1.60 each). Add some French fries for 85¢. Ten hot chicken wings are priced right at $3.10, while deviled egg sandwiches—just like the ones Mom used to put in your lunchbox—are $1.05. Extra toppings, like lettuce and tomato or cole slaw, are 25¢ each.

You get one hour of free parking at the North Avenue location, and the Varsity Jr. on Lindbergh (near the Cheshire Bridge Road intersection) has a good-sized lot, too. Gosh, Buffy, this'll be *perfect* for after the sock hop!

Yen Ching Restaurant

- Scott Village Shopping Center, 1707 Church St., Decatur; 296-0101

You may not expect much from Yen Ching, given its unimpressive strip-mall facade; but once you go inside, Mr. C thinks you'll be pleasantly surprised by its Mandarin, Szechuan, and Cantonese cuisine, good prices, and attentive service.

See for yourself and try their spring rolls ($1.95 for two), sizzling rice soup ($2.99), or "shrimp toast" ($3.95). Complete meals run under $8, like duck with plum sauce ($7.95), General Tso's chicken ($6.95), or pepper steak ($6.65). Sweet and sour shrimp is $7.50, while the vegetarian spicy bean curd with garlic sauce and celery, carrots, bean sprouts, bell pepper, and black mushrooms is merely $5.75. Egg foo young dishes start at $5.75.

The all-you-can-eat Sunday brunch buffet, running from 11:30 a.m. to 3 p.m., is $3.25 for children under 12 (free for those under 3), and $5.95 for adults. It's a dim-sum delight.

Calm down the fire in your mouth with a cooling dessert, such as fried carmelized apples or bananas; this unusual offering is just $1.95 for a generous half order, or $3.25 for a full.

Yen Ching is open seven days a week. Delivery is free to a limited area on orders of $10 or more at lunch, or $12.50 or more for dinner. MSG-free meals can be prepared upon request, too.

BUCKHEAD

Annie's Thai Castle
- 3195 Roswell Rd. N.E., Atlanta; 264-9546

They've really gone all out to make this a castle, with its fancy entranceway, lined with sunflower plants, and the super-polite staff. But believe Mr. C, you can have the budget of a serf and still dine like a king or queen here. Granted, some of the seafood dishes are priced over $10, but all other entrees will stuff you for $7 or so.

If you really feel like filling up, start off with appetizers like satay, the Thai chicken or beef kabobs, marinated in coconut milk. They come with peanut dipping sauce and a cucumber salad for $4.95. Or try the hot chicken wings, marinated and then deep fried, for $3.95.

Dinner entrees are so big, they should just come with doggie bags in advance. Broccoli chicken ($6.95), curried pork ($6.95), and rama beef (with curry paste, coconut milk, and ground spinach, served on a bed of steamed spinach for $7.95) are popular choices. Spicy Thai noodles or spaghetti are $7.95 each, and the mixed vegetable stir fry ($6.95) will fill you up without emptying your wallet.

Lunch specials are especially cheap, all served with rice, soup, or an eggroll. Pad Thai, $6.25, is a fine rendition of the popular rice noodle dish fried with bits of egg, shrimp, pork, bean sprouts, green onion, and peanuts. "Wings of the Angels," boneless chicken wings stuffed with pork, noodles, and onions, topped with sweet and sour sauce, is unique—and only $5.45. Curry-fried tofu and green beans, also with a choice of side dishes, is $4.95, and chili-flavored beef with basil leaves is only $5.45.

Annie's is open seven days a week, and is easily found in Buckhead, across the street from Rocky's Pizza.

Athens Pizza House
- 1959 Lakewood Ave. S.E., Atlanta; 622-7911
- 246 Bobby Jones Expwy., Augusta; (706) 868-1508
- 5550 Peachtree Industrial Blvd., Chamblee; 452-8282
- 1565 Highway 138, Conyers; 483-6228
- 1341 Clairmont Rd., Decatur; 636-1100
- 1255 Johnson Ferry Rd., Marietta; 509-0099
- 6075 Roswell Rd. N.E., Sandy Springs; 257-0252

The Papadopoulos family has been making popular pizza in the Atlanta area since 1966. The prices are right, too; not only on the pizzas, but also on such appetizers as spinach pie ($1.50), Athens patatoes ($1.50), and fried kalamari ($4.40). Those last two *must* be good—they're spelled old-country style.

The pies themselves start at just $4.90 for an individual size. But why stop there? Go all out with a medium all-meat special (salami, sausage, pepperoni, ham, hamburger, and Canadian bacon) for $9.25. You won't have to eat again for a week.

Entrees like moussaka served with spinach pie, chicken parmesan, and spinach manicotti are each served with a Greek salad and garlic bread for $6.95. There's a children's section on the menu, too; the kids' spaghetti dinner is just $3.15, while you can join them with the gigantic regular spaghetti plate for $5.20.

Don't pass up the baklava for dessert, either. At $1.50 a slice, these nut-filled flaky pastries covered with honey are just the thing to end your meal on a sweet note.

Athens Pizza also offers many beers and wines (including Greek varieties like Kokino and Aspro), starting at $1.95 a glass.

If the crowds here get to be too much, though, consider visiting one of the Athens Pizza Express take-out locations, at 4060 Peachtree Road N.E., Atlanta (phone 365-8646) and at 1788 Clairmont Road, Decatur (634-8646).

Baker's Cafe By Brownstone
• 1937 Peachtree Rd. N.E., Atlanta; 352-0202

For a great espresso or salad and sandwich on the run, zip on over to this Baker's Cafe—not to be confused with the Cajun-cookin' Baker's Cafe in Little Five Points.

BCBB, across the street from Piedmont Hospital, is a clear-your-own-table kinda place, which means you can save a bit by not having to leave a tip. But you may want to leave something for the counter help, since they work fast as lightning for you.

Saturdays and Sundays, folks warm in for the $5.99 all-you-can-eat breakfast bar, with omelettes,

eggs and hot fixings, a fruit and bagel bar, muffins, croissants, and other goodies. This deal runs from 9 a.m. to 1 p.m. only.

Try one of their hulking hoagies to get you going. Turkey po' boys, stuffed also with ham, salami, and pickle mustard on French bread, are $3.65; corned beef sandwiches are $3.85, and hummus, shrimp, or chicken salad sandwiches sell for $2.95 each. More out-of-the-ordinary choices here include the crab cake sandwich ($5.50) and knockwurst sandwich ($4.95).

Or, try one of their scores of salads, like tuna tarragon, chicken, grapes, and almonds, taboule or shrimp pasta ($5.99 to $8.99 a pound). Spinach and broccoli quiche or quiche Lorraine are just $1.95 a slice.

Desserts are a real attraction here, though, like the butter pecan cookies, fruit tarts (each $2), muffins (65¢), caramel brownies, petits-fours, and nutbreads. The cheesecake tastes as good as New York's, and is well worth it even at $2.50 a slice.

Now, here's something you never see in a restaurant: A money-back guarantee. If you're not satisfied with your order, for whatever reason, you'll get your cash back. Wow!

Baker's Cafe by Brownstone is open seven days a week—Mondays through Saturdays from 7 a.m. to 8 p.m., and Sundays from 8 a.m. to 4 p.m.

Bradshaw's Restaurant
• 35A West Paces Ferry Rd. N.W., Atlanta; 233-0134

Don't be turned off by the strip-mall location—Bradshaw's means good southern home cookin'. Located in the Buckhead Marketplace shopping center, the business crowd piles in for veggies and fried chicken that taste just like Mom used to make. If the line's out the door, you can get meals to go, but then you'd miss the sweet as pie waiters and waitresses who treat you like a long-lost relative.

Bradshaw's is also known as the Feedmill, but they're interested in try-

ing to get away from that name. As
one waitress said, "Every once in a
while, we get people callin' up trying
to sell us hay." No wonder they'd
like to change.

The old name is still fitting, in a
sense, since you're given enough
food on your plate to feed a horse.
Most entrees are priced at $4.95, and
you sure get your money's worth—
from choices like roast beef with
oven-browned potatoes, fried catfish,
stuffed bell peppers, and chuck
wagon steak with tomato sauce. All
of these are served with two generous
portions of veggies, like true southern-style homegrown sliced tomatoes, turnip greens, steamed cabbage,
black-eyed peas, incredible mashed
potatoes, and pickled beets.

For lighter appetites, try the grilled
ham and cheese sandwich with potato salad ($3.25), the tuna salad with
saltines ($4.25), or the homemade
chili ($1.25).

The Bread Market
- 3167 Peachtree Rd. N.E., Atlanta;
  816-8600

Don't let the name fool you—this is
a Buckhead sandwich shop and more.
Most business is take-out, but there's
a tiny eat-in area for you to enjoy the
Market's specialty items like tandoori
chicken ($4.75), grilled eggplant with
basil and mozzarella ($4.75), and
bleu cheese salad ($4.50).

Keep in mind that specials change
weekly, and the Market's homemade
soups sometimes sell out during the
course of the afternoon (gazpacho, vi-
chyssoise, turkey noodle, and mushroom are among the offerings, all at
only $2.25 a bowl). Pesto pasta salad,
sesame noodle salad, and focaccia
rounds are always available. And
their fresh chicken salad with grapes
and nuts mixed in ($4.75 a pound) is
hard to beat.

The Bread Market is also known
for its killer cookies and brownies,
but at $1.50 a pop, Mr. C found them
to be a little out of his price range.
Still, with the inexpensive prices on
the lunches, what the heck?

Cafe Gamay
- Swissotel Atlanta, 3391 Peachtree
  Rd. N.E., Atlanta; 365-0065

Want to impress a date or business
client without breaking your budget?
Try Cafe Gamay, which is cheaper by
far than its Swissotel neighbor, Opus,
but still quite dazzling. The post-mod-
ern art collection may be a little far
out for some tastes; but the food
prices, for this kind of quality, are far
from out-of-this-world.

You can dine inside, or on the
cafe's outdoor terrace overlooking
Peachtree Road.

Lunches and dinners start with appetizer choices like butternut squash
soup with smoked bacon and chives
($3.50), crispy calamari with spicy
marinara sauce ($4.75), and vegeta-
ble spring rolls with plum sauce
($3.50). Tuna salad nioise is $7.75,
oriental chicken salad with soba noodles and roasted cashews is $8, and a
chicken quesadilla with pico de gallo
is $7.50.

Light menu choices include the
swordfish steak with grilled vegetables ($10.75), chicken breast braised
in white wine, with cous cous
($10.75), and grilled salmon with yel-
low and green bean salad ($12).
Other specialties include fettuccine
pasta with shrimp and asparagus
($12.50), lump crab cake in a potato
crust with papaya mustard ($10.50),
and blackened mahi mahi with a cit-
rus relish ($11).

The cafe has a select wine list,
available by the glass. White wines
are priced from $3 a glass, for a Mon-
terey Vineyard chardonnay, reds start
at $4 for a Napa Ridge Pinot Noir,
and champagne choices include Piper
Sonoma Brut 1988 for $6.

No, it ain't cheap, but Mr. C had
to mention at least one place where
you can afford to splurge when you
have to. The Cafe is open from 6:30
a.m. to 11 p.m., seven days a week.

Cafe at Pharr
- Pharr Road Shopping Center, 316
  Pharr Rd. N.E., Atlanta; 238-9288

Within walking distance of Oxford
Books, the Cafe at Pharr is a no-non-

sense bakery which compensates for its plain decor with incredibly fresh homemade sandwiches and desserts.

Bakery selections vary slightly from day to day, but often include croissants for just 50¢, bleu cheese tartlettes for a mere 45¢, and fougasse for $1.25. Cheddar and tomato crostini at 45¢ each are also priced well in Mr. C's budget.

Lunch items include French bread pizza slices for $1.25, egg-potato salad for $4.25, and walnut chicken sandwiches for $4.75. Sandwiches can be made on fresh-baked white, French, or wheat bread or croissants. Whole wheat rolls, baguettes, brioche, and potato dill bread are great as lunch additions or as snacks on the go.

The cafe is open from 10 a.m. to 5 p.m., Mondays through Saturdays. It's closed Sundays.

Cafe Tu Tu Tango
- 220 Pharr Rd. N.E., Atlanta; 841-6222

It may take two to tango, but it doesn't take too much money to enjoy a superb *tapas* meal at this beatnik Buckhead eatery. They offer "food for the starving artist", which is always music to Mr. C's ears. If Andy Warhol were still around, this would his type of artsy scene. Wild jazz music blares all around, and you may even catch the sight of an artist or two at work—be sure to check the studio area upstairs.

Many of the paintings, tables, lamps, and sculptures decorating the room were created by local artists, and are for sale. But, to paraphrase the art world saying: If you have to ask how much, maybe you'd be better off sticking with the food.

It's all served in Spanish tapas style, so you start off with a pile of appetizer-sized plates at your table, and a paintbrush holder filled with utensils. Order a variety of small dishes to pass around. Each one only takes three to eight minutes to cook, and the sharp waitstaff checks back frequently to see if you've got room to order more. Naturally, this is a good place to bring friends.

Mr. C liked the hummus (this kind was made with black beans), served with rosemary flat bread, for just $3.75. Chili is $4.25, and shrimp ceviche is $6.95. Grilled chicken kebabs, served with a Thai peanut sauce, are only $5.25.

All gone? Time for another round. Mr. C tried the light and flaky brick-oven baked grilled chicken pizza, with cheddar cheese and poblano peppers, priced at just $5.95. Mmmm. Other good picks include alligator bites with chutney are $5.75, and calamari is just $3.95.

The fresh-baked rolls served with herbed butter with every order are worth a trip in themselves. Daily specials during Mr. C's visit included lobster and crayfish in phyllo dough, with champagne sauce ($6.50), and grilled lamb spareribs with mint barbecue sauce ($6.25), plus grilled grouper and pasta salad ($5.50).

Tu Tu Tango's sangria is $3.75 a glass, and a full liquor selection is also available. This is a fun scene for a night out in Buckhead, yet still moderately priced; watch out though, because all those little dishes can add up.

California Pizza Kitchen
- 181 14th St. N.E., Atlanta; 892-4220
- Lenox Square Shopping Center, 3393 Peachtree Rd. N.E., Atlanta; 262-9221

And other suburban locations
There's more than just pizza to be found at this growing national chain—things like potato leek soup, fresh pastas, lasagna, and Thai chicken. Don't get Mr. C wrong—the pizza's okay, too, especially the rosemary-chicken-potato pie with white wine and lemon for $8.95 (plenty here for two to share), and the southwestern burrito, made with lime, black beans, mild chilies, cheddar cheese, tomatillo salsa, sour cream, and white sweet onions (also $8.95). All pies are available without cheese, baked on either traditional or honey-wheat doughs. And unlike lots of other pizza houses in town, CPK uses no MSG.

Other entrees include angel hair, penne, or spaghetti, topped with tomato-herb sauce for $5.95, and spinach fettuccine with chicken, tri-color peppers, red onion, and cilantro in a tequila-lime sauce for $8.95. It's a large platter. Desserts are a bit pricey, in the unlikely event that you have room; try sharing a tiramisu ($4.50), Myers' Rum chocolate pecan pie ($3.95), apple crisp ($3.95), or tartufo—gelato balls rolled in chocolate chips, and served with vanilla bean sauce or berry puree ($3.50).

Coco Loco Cuban & Caribbean Cafe

* 303 Peachtree Center Ave. N.E., Atlanta; 653-0070
* 2625 Piedmont Rd. N.E., Atlanta; 364-0212 and 261-0198
* 6301 Roswell Rd., Sandy Springs; 255-5434

Sure, Coco Loco may have a reputation as a yuppie hangout, but its prices are surprisingly *un*-yuppie. The Cuban sandwich, for instance, is just $3.75 for the regular size, and $4.50 for the super. Jamaican jerk chicken sandwiches go for $3.95, as does the *pan con lechon* (roast pork and grilled onions). For lighter appetites, or those who can't bear the hot spices, try grilled cheese with potato sticks for $2.25, or hot dogs and quarter-pound hamburgers, each just $2.50. The spicier Cuban hamburger, with onions, paprika, and Worcestershire sauce, is also just $2.50.

On the sweet side, tropical milkshakes, in flavors like papaya or mango ($1.95), and nectars (try the tamarind, just $1.50), will douse the flames of the Cuban spices.

Even entrees are reasonably priced, served with two side dishes like yucas, rice, or a salad. Cuban-style roast chicken with garlic and onions, fried sirloin steak, and pork chops are all just $5.95 each. Side dishes like black beans and rice ($1.75), sweet fried plantains or plantain chips (also $1.75) and homemade potato chips (95¢) won't break the bank, either, so you may just have enough money left for some (not so

cheap) dessert, like key lime pie ($2.50), rice pudding ($1.95), or *pastelito de guayaba* (guava pastry), just 75¢ an order.

Domestic and imported beers, plus a limited wine selection, are also available.

East Village Grille

* 248 Buckhead Ave. N.E., Atlanta; 233-3345

The City of Atlanta, realizing just how fast Buckhead is growing, plans to split the area into East and West Villages by the turn of the century. So the East Village Grille is a bit ahead of its time, but that's okay. Folks come here (from wherever) for its super-friendly service, laid-back, neighborhood meeting place atmosphere, and reasonable prices. You'll find it next to the Raccoon Lodge, another popular Buckhead hangout.

Night owls (like your humble scribe) have gotta love the Grille's late-night breakfast specials. A plate of eggs, hash browns, toast, butter, and jelly is just $1.99. Cheese omelettes are $4.50, and sausage and eggs goes for just $4.75.

The regular dinner menu, for you non-vampires, offers a dozen hot chicken wings for $4.95, Caesar shrimp salad ($6.95), or turkey Rachel (with cole slaw, thousand island dressing and Swiss cheese on rye bread) for $5.95. All sandwiches come with a choice of side vegetables—the Grille's mashed potatoes are terrific. The bleu cheese burger is also popular (just $5.25, served with French fries, onion rings, or potato salad). And who could pass up the blue plate specials, all served with two veggie choices? Meat loaf, pork tenderloin, grilled fish, and rotisserie chicken are priced under $8, while the four-veggie plate with fresh-baked bread's just $5.25.

The EVG menu includes almost a dozen "Heart Smart" choices, low in fat and cholesterol. But for those of you who don't care about these things, don't miss their desserts. Hot apple pie and Stone Mountain pecan pies are $2.95 a slice.

EVG opens at 11 a.m. daily, and stays open until midnight Sunday through Wednesday (until 1 a.m. if it's really busy), until 2 a.m. Thursday, 'til 4 a.m. Friday, and until 3 a.m. Saturday. There's also a full liquor license.

Fellini's Pizza

- 2813 Peachtree Rd. N.E., Atlanta; 266-0082
- 923 Ponce de Leon Ave. N.E., Atlanta; 873-3088
- 422 Seminole Ave. N.E., Atlanta; 525-2530
- 4429 Roswell Rd. N.E., Atlanta; 303-8248
- 1991 Howell Mill Rd. N.W., Atlanta; 352-0799

And other suburban locations

While the scene at this pizza place would make for a great movie location, this is not a recommended place to take grandma or little tykes—it's loud, crowded, and the staff tends toward the slightly surly, under-employed-college-grad variety. The decor of brightly painted cinder-blocks and oddball celebrity portraits (Elvis lives!) helps the wild, Fellini-esque atmosphere along. The pizza's great, though, and two generously-large slices can fill you up for under three bucks.

Plain slices are just $1.10, believe it or not. Medium-sized cheese pies go for $7.50, and medium "white pizzas"—no tomato sauce, and plenty of garlic—are $11. Extra toppings (just the basics are offered here) are $1 each. Cheese calzones are $4.50. Wash it all down with 16-ounce domestic draft beers, which will put you back just $2.

While Fellini's is a take-a-number-and-we'll-bring-your-order-to-your-table joint, they do keep tip jars at the counters emblazoned with the label *In lieu of decent wages.* While it's optional, most customers do tip here, either at the counter or at their tables after they've eaten.

Good Ol' Days Cafe

- 3013 Peachtree Rd. N.E., Atlanta; 266-2597

MR. CHEAP'S PICKS
Buckhead

✔ **Bradshaw's**—Fill yourself up on fantastic southern cooking without emptying your wallet. Don't let the line out the door scare you away—it's well worth the wait.

✔ **Three Dollar Cafe**—That price is too good to be true, but Mr. C still loves this casual spot as an antidote to this neighborhood's prices.

✔ **Veggieland**—A Buckhead secret that should be kept no longer! Incredible miso soup and stir-fry—so good, you won't even realize you're eating vegetarian.

✔ **White House Restaurant**—This diner's *not* in a house, but they do make a point of making you feel at home, and you won't have to worry about a deficit.

- 401 Moreland Ave. N.E., Atlanta; 688-1006
- 5841 Roswell Rd. N.E., Sandy Springs; 257-9183

Good Ol' Days is a combination pool hall, sports bar, and caf, with wildly painted wall murals, pink and green vinyl tablecloths, and colored ceilings. With loud pop music pouring out of oversized speakers, it's a popular hangout with the twenty-some-things—casual, fun, and fit for limited budgets.

Appetizers tend toward the unusual, like fried whipped potatoes for $2.50, and sticky pots—cinnamon, brown sugar, and butter baked into flowerpot-shaped bread, topped with granola, cream cheese, and honey—for $1.95. During Mr. C's visit, apps were all half-price during happy hour.

If you've got more than the munchies, try their chicken quesadillas ($3.99) or New Orleans chicken ($5.49). The six-ounce "Uncomplicated" burger is a lean $3.49. Many of these have the signature flowerpot worked into their presentation. Is the name of this restaurant a thinly veiled reference to the 1960s "flower power" era? Are any of its patrons old enough to figure this out? Ah, nevermind.

Good Ol' Days also makes cheap breakfasts like no one else. Eggs, any style, are 60¢ each (80¢ for Eggbeaters); a bagel and cream cheese is $1.25; and the McFlowerpot sandwich (egg, cheese, and bacon on that specially shaped bread) will brighten your day for only $2.50. There are also classics like Belgian waffles ($3.15) and three-cheese omelettes, served with parmesan-topped sauteed red potatoes and toast, for $3.85. Good Ol' Days stays open well into the night, too, often with free live music from local rock bands.

Johnny Rockets

- 5 West Paces Ferry Rd., N.W., Atlanta; 955-6068
- Phipps Plaza, 3500 Peachtree Rd., Atlanta; 233-9867
- 6510 Roswell Rd., Sandy Springs; 257-0677
- 2970 Cobb Pkwy., N.W., Marietta; 955-6068

Go, go, go to Johnny's for huge portions of good ole American burgers and sandwiches at super value prices. The menu is limited, but you'll feel like you've been transported back in time to the 1950's.

Hamburger is the basic language spoken here. The "Original Burger," starting at $3.35, is topped with all the necessities: Lettuce, tomato, mustard, pickle, mayo, relish, and chopped onion. For a quarter more, you can add Johnny's cheddar cheese and "red, red sauce." Chili and bacon will add still more to the ticket, yet keep the burger under $6.

Hamburger haters can also find something for themselves here, like an egg salad sandwich ($2.45), the ever-popular BLT ($3.55), and a grilled cheese sandwich ($2.65). Throw some fries on the side for $1.45; better yet, try their chili fries for $2.75.

Johnny Rockets' "famous" malts and shakes are $2.95. For dessert, apple pie is $1.65; served a la mode, it's $2.40. It ain't like Mom's, but it's not bad. Basically, this is fast food with a bit more character than all your McChains, with its counter and stools, and sparkling white tile motif—an idealized "Happy Days" kinds joint.

Validated parking is available at the Buckhead location for just 50¢. JR is open Mondays through Thursdays from 11 a.m. to 10:30 p.m., and from 11 a.m. to 2 a.m. Fridays and Saturdays.

La Fonda Latina

- 2813 Peachtree Rd. N.E., Atlanta; 816-8311
- 1150-B Euclid Ave. N.E., Atlanta; 577-8317

Mr. C is fond of La Fonda for its incredible Mexican dishes and fun atmosphere. You can get stuffed (with food, that is) for under $6 or so, since this restaurant/bar makes big bucks off of its liquor sales.

An individual paella, the traditional Spanish casserole, is $5.95; it comes chock-full of calamari, chicken, shrimp, sausage, and peppers, served over rice. Gazpacho goes for $2.75, and big cheese quesadillas with a snappy salsa on top are $3.50. La Fonda's Cuban sandwich is just $4.25. Add a side of frijoles or extra tortillas for $1, and finish your meal with chocolate or vanilla flan ($2.25) or sweet guava cheesecake ($2.50).

La Fonda Latina is a noisy, people watching kind of restaurant. Don't even think about bringing a reading book with you. One recent Friday, in fact, Mr. C spotted a semi-famous band eating at the L5P branch before their late show at the Point; so, keep your eyes open when you eat here. Even if there aren't celebrities to check out, there are plenty of people trying to look just as interesting. No to mention the decor of fountains, hanging beads, and statues.

La Fonda Latina is open seven days a week, serving daily until 11 p.m. The L5P branch has some much-appreciated free parking in the back, too.

Lettuce Souprise You

- 595 Piedmont Ave., N.E., Atlanta; 874-4998
- 2470 Briarcliff Rd. N.E., Atlanta; 636-8549
- 245 Pharr Rd. N.E., Atlanta; 841-9583
- 3525 Mall Blvd., Duluth; 418-9969
- 1475 Holcomb Bridge Rd., Roswell; 642-1601
- 5975 Roswell Rd., Sandy Springs; 250-0304
- 1109 Cumberland Mall, Smyrna; 438-2288

Here's a place after your humble author's own heart. At Lettuce Souprise You, one price gets you unlimited trips to their extensive salad bar, as well as the all-you-can-eat baked potato bar and pasta bar, plus homemade muffins, cornbread, and soups, and fresh fruit. Whew! Lettuce be thankful for places like this!

The salad bar is super-fresh and preservative-free; it features spinach, broccoli, tarragon tuna, spicy crab and pasta salad, and pineapple, along with dozens of other choices. Soups change daily, but always include at least one vegetarian recipe, such as potato-leek or lentil. Egg drop, chili, and vegetable soups are featured often, too.

How can they afford to offer such a bargain, you ask? Well, they do work on keeping costs down. For one thing, Lettuce Souprise You requests that you eat only in the restaurant—they don't allow anyone to leave with more than a muffin. If you'd like something to go, they will charge you for it. Well hey, that's only fair!

Meanwhile, the price for this entire sumptuous buffet is just $5.50 at lunchtime; $6.50 for brunch and dinner. Another cheap deal: Their "frequent buyer" club entitles you to a free meal when you've had twelve

lunches, six dinners, or four brunches. Can it be any surprise that Lettuce Souprise You rates so highly with Mr. C?

The Mad Italian

- 2245 Peachtree Rd. N.E., Atlanta; 352-1368
- 2197 Savoy Dr., Chamblee; 451-8048
- East Lake Center, Marietta; 977-5209
- Windy Hill Plaza, Marietta; 952-1806

They're crazy about high quality at this South Buckhead and suburban eatery. The prices on Italian sandwiches, pasta, and calzones, in fact, are downright foolish. The Mad Italian is so nuts about fresh ingredients that his bread is flash frozen and trucked in all the way from New York; the folks here say that the Atlanta humidity and altitude are "improper" for good bread baking.

Anything you say, guys—the effort certainly pays off. Sandwiches, available in three sizes priced from $3.85 to just $5.50, include tuna hoagies, Italian sausage, meatball and cheese, cheese steak, and chicken salad varieties, along with the vegetable sautee with cheese. Pickles and potato chips come with sit-down orders (too bad for you take-out lovers). Whether you eat in or out, for just $1 more, you can enjoy the Mad Italian's house salad or spaghetti, or a cup of his soup of the day (Mr. C recommends the minestrone, but the *pasta e fagiole* is also highly touted by those in the know).

Cheese or meat calzones go for just $4.95; if you really feel like stuffing yourself, go for the baked cheese ravioli ($6.50), served with fresh bread and butter and house salad; or the pasta trio (cannelloni Florentine, spinach and cheese shells, and ricotta cheese shells) for $6.95, or fettucine Alfredo for $5.95.

Keep the kids happy with items like the kids' spaghetti plate (just $2.50). The Mad Italian is perfect for family dining, with a casual, wood-paneling, wicker-chair, gum-at-the-cash register kind of atmosphere. It's open seven days a week, including Fridays and Saturdays until midnight.

Metropolitan Pizza Bar
- 3055 Bolling Way N.E., Atlanta; 264-0135

Sure it's an upscale watering hole smack dab in the center of Buckhead, but since they make such a profit on the booze (imported beers start at $3.50 a bottle), the food is relatively cheap. You can actually get a super filling meal here for under $10.

Pizzas start at $5.95, and can be topped with everything from shiitake mushrooms and white clams to broccoli, pesto, roasted garlic, mixed peppers, and artichoke hearts. The "Neptune", made with gulf shrimp and pesto, is $7.95 for the 12" size.

"Metro Lasagna," stuffed with zucchini, mushrooms, and eggplant, is $6.50. So are the calzones, packed with proscuitto, ricotta, mozzarella, and mushrooms. Finish your meal the traditional Italian way with biscotti, available in honey, hazelnut, and chocolate flavors. Cappuccino and espresso are $2.50 and $1.75, respectively.

The Metropolitan Pizza Bar opens at 6 p.m. daily, and stays open until 1:30 a.m. Sundays through Thursdays; and until 2:30 a.m. on Fridays and Saturdays.

Mick's
- 557 Peachtree Rd. N.E., Atlanta; 875-6425
- 2110 Peachtree Rd. N.W., Atlanta; 351-6425
- Peachtree Center, 229 Peachtree St. N.E., Atlanta; 688-6425
- Lenox Square Shopping Center, 3393 Peachtree Rd. N.E., Atlanta; 262-6425
- Underground Atlanta, 75 Upper Alabama St. S.W., Atlanta; 525-2825
- 116 East Ponce de Leon Ave., Decatur; 373-7797

And other suburban locations
Get to Mick's for one of the best milkshakes in town, great burgers, super desserts, and creative drinks. Stretching from Underground Atlanta

to Buckhead and beyond, this yuppie haven seems determined to make the next siege of Atlanta a culinary one.

Prices here are not the absolute cheapest around, but you do get a lot of delicious food for the money. Start off with real fried green tomatoes ($5.75), chili-smothered French fries ($3.95), grilled carrots and broccoli ($2.50), or a cup of soup in flavors like tomato or "baked potato" ($1.95).

A half-pound hamburger, hickory grilled, with a generous side of fries or pasta salad, is $5.95. You can top it with cheddar or mozzarella cheese, guacamole, chili, barbecue sauce, or cracked pepper and mustard for 80¢ extra. Cheese-topped grilled boneless chicken is $7.50, and corn and tomato linguine with garlic bread is $6.95. Mick's chicken Reuben will completely stuff you for $7.95.

Do try to leave room for dessert, though. You'll probably want to share one of these monstrosities with a friend. Try the Oreo cheesecake ($3.95), the Giant Banana Split ($4.75), or Mr. C's favorite, the chocolate cream pie ($3.75). Yummy! Strawberry shortcake, homemade chocolate layer cake, and Heath Bar ice cream pie will all make delightful ends to your meal, and all are under $4 apiece.

Besides the desserts, Mick's is known for its unusual mixed drinks—like "Frozen Pink Lemonade," "Frozen German Chocolate Cake," and "Peasant Coffee" (spiked with brandy, Grand Marnier, Kahlua, amaretto, and dark creme de cacao, and topped with whipped cream). These will doubtless not be cheap, but they are good. Most branches of Mick's have a separate bar area.

MJ Pippin Chicago Style Pizza
- 3279 Roswell Rd. N.E., Atlanta; 231-9585

Lunch for $3.95 in Buckhead? You betcha. That's the price of the lunch specials offered every day here. They may include lasagna, pizza (of course), or pastas, served with a side salad and bread. What a deal!

Other house specialties include

spaghetti and meat sauce, with salad and garlic bread, for $5.95; also, manicotti for $7.50, fettucine Alfredo for $6.95, and chicken cacciatore with spaghetti for $8.95. Plus vegetable soup for just $1.95, and a variety of calzones.

Thick pan pizzas start at $7.95, but, as the restaurant's name implies, are done Chicago style. This means they're filling as heck—and that the small size is plenty for two people to share. Thin crust pies are also available for those of you with lighter appetites.

Additional toppings are 50¢ for vegetables and $1 for meat on small pies. The Veggie Pizza, covered with mushrooms, black olives, onions, sweet red peppers, green peppers, and sliced tomatoes, is just $11.95 for a small thick pan, and $16.95 for the large—which could feed an army.

MJ Pippin is definitely casual, with old Tiffany-style stained-glass lamps and well-worn wooden tables. Plus a pool table, as well. Kick back here Sundays through Thursdays from 11 a.m. to 1 a.m., and Fridays and Saturdays from 11 a.m. to 2 a.m.

OK Cafe
- 1284 West Paces Ferry Rd. N.W., Atlanta; 233-2888

Open twenty-four hours a day, the OK Cafe is popular with students and businesspeople during the daytime; by night, it's a haven for insomniacs and folks working the graveyard shift. You'll find it all the way over at the intersection of West Paces and the Northside Parkway.

Tropical forest print drapes, hand-painted glazed plates and wooden cut-out partitions between booths make for a cozy, albeit noisy, atmosphere. Breakfast items are served any time of day—a true sign of a great all-night diner. Be sure to try the buttermilk biscuits (95¢), blueberry-smothered multigrain griddle cakes ($4.95), or baked ham and eggs served with a biscuit or toast, and hash browns or grits, for $6.50). For a change of pace, sourdough French toast ($4.95) is a treat; and health

food fans will love the all eggwhite vegetable omelettes ($5.95).

In fact, the whole menu is a fun mix of traditional diner fare and trendy nouvelle. Start off your lunch with shaved fried onions ($1.95), sweet potato chips ($3.25), and a glass of the OK's incredible lemonade ($1.50). Tofu burgers, $5.25, joust with hefty (real) hamburgers for $4.75.

Country fried steak is served with two incredibly fresh vegetable sides and whole-kernel peppered corn muffins, all for $8.50. Mr. C got stuffed on the four-veggie platter, which consisted of right-off-the-cob corn, six-cheese macaroni, broccoli, and a whole baked sweet potato ($7). And the OK proves that the fifties are alive and well, with their big-selling real cherry cokes and black cows.

Desserts are too big to eat alone, so bring a friend and don't be put off by the prices: Hot apple strudel goes for $3.50, and hot fudge sundaes are $2.95. Race you to the bottom!

Original Pancake House
- 1937 Peachtree Rd. N.E., Atlanta; 351-3533
- 4330 Peachtree Rd. N.E., Atlanta; 237-4116
- 2321 Cheshire Bridge Rd. N.E. Atlanta; 633-5712
- 501 Johnson Ferry Rd. N.E., Marietta; 977-5013
- 5099 Memorial Dr., Stone Mountain; 292-6914

The Original Pancake Houses sure won't leave you in the poor house. James Beard did name this one of the top ten restaurants in America, but you'd never know this from the prices. Quality runs high here—they use fresh juices, extra large Grade AA eggs, and pure whipping cream, plus all the cooking is done in pure butter.

The pancake recipe is a carefully-guarded secret, with good reason. They're light and fluffy, and just $3.55 an order. Georgia Pecan Waffles ($4.80) are delicious. If you're truly starving, Mr. C suggests the omelettes, served with three buttermilk

pancakes, plus grits or toast, all for
$6.95; or a four-ounce beef tender-
loin steak for $4.50. Other good bets
include French crepes with strawberry topping ($5.25). Side dishes in-
clude sweets like cinnamon
applesauce ($1) and imported lingon-
berries in butter ($1.75).

Junior plates are available for children under ten. Two slices of French
toast ($2.60), and three pancakes
($2.50) are served with milk, choco-
late milk, or hot chocolate.

Meanwhile, to paraphrase the old
orange juice commercials, "it's not
just for breakfast anymore." OPH
also serves a lunch menu of hamburgers ($4.25), soups (plus soup and half-
sandwich specials for $4.95), and hot
dogs (two for $2.95), along with sal-
ads and chili.

Senior citizens always get a 15%
discount here, and police and firemen
also receive a discount off their
meals. The Original Pancake Houses
are open from 6:30 a.m. to 2:30 p.m.
weekdays, and from 7 a.m. to 3 p.m.
on weekends.

Oxford Books Espresso Cafe
• 360 Pharr Rd. N.E., Atlanta;
  266-8350
Tired of the Peachtree Road
lunchtime hustle and bustle? Chill
out upstairs at Oxford Books, in their
quiet little cafe. You can relax and
leaf through your latest purchase, or
eavesdrop on a book club meeting,
while you nosh on creative sandwich
combinations. Fresh flowers at each
table add a nice touch.

The breakfast menu is limited to
scones ($2.25), jumbo-sized muffins
($1.95) and bagels (85¢), but lunch is
something else again, with a creative
touch. Mr. C enjoyed the "Tale of
Tuna City" sandwich ($4.50), and
"The Breast Years of Our Lives"
(with avocado, sprouts, cheddar, and
garlic mayonnaise on whole wheat,
$4.75). Or how about the "Hot Ham-
let" ($4.25) with ham, Swiss cheese
and tomato grilled on egg bread with
honey mustard dressing. 'Course, it
should really be some cheese from
Denmark....

As the cafe's name implies, there
are all kinds of coffee drinks to go
with the food. Not only hot beverages, either: The cappuccino shake
($3.50) is super, even by itself. The
cafe also has a children's menu, with
things like peanut butter and jelly and
grilled cheese sandwiches.

It's almost like a throwback to the
days of beatnik coffeehouses. The
cafe is open Sundays through Thursdays from 9 a.m. until 11 p.m., and
Fridays and Saturdays from 9 a.m.
until midnight. The sandwich bar
closes at one hour before the cafe
does.

Ray's New York Pizza
• 3021 Peachtree Rd. N.E., Atlanta;
  364-0960
Greenwich Village has this little piz-
zeria, called Ray's, which is legendary for classic New York-style
pizza. So much so, that several
chains have arrived recently, trading
on very similar names. None can beat
the original, but actually, they all
come pretty close.

Now, this one sure looks like a
typical teenager pizza-joint hangout.
But Ray's makes great thin-crust
pizza and sells it at very un-Buckhead prices.

Weekdays from noon to 2:30,
Ray's offers an all-you-can-eat salad
and pasta bar with the purchase of
any entree (like pizza, calzones or lasagna) for just $4.99. Pizza slices sell
for just $1.15, and small pies start at
only $7.95. The ingredients get quite
fancy, like artichoke pesto pizzas,
which start at $13.95. Other popular
dishes include sandwiches like the
Hawaiian chicken ($5.25), turkey bur-
ger ($4.95), and eggplant hero
($4.50); sun-dried tomato and broc-
coli calzones sell for just $4.95, and
can be stuffed with any of the pizza
toppings for 35¢ an item.

Ray's also offers an amazing selection of domestic and imported beers,
from Pete's Wicked Ale, Red Stripe
and Whitbread to Guinness, Kronen-
berg, Peroni and Tecate.

Rio Grande Cantina
- 2257 Peachtree Rd. N.E., Atlanta; 352-8993

Not to be confused with the similarly low-priced (and ubiquitous) Rio Bravo Cantina, Rio Grande goes beyond the standard Mexican dishes and jazzes up its food with incredibly fresh ingredients and unusual combinations. The decor here does leave a bit to be desired (garish green-painted booths and suspiciously dim lighting). But there's a hopping weekend scene at this South Buckhead spot, thanks to the good grub—and popular musicians booked for no- or low-cover shows.

Start off your meal with sopa de pollo, a tomato-based chicken soup with rice, for $2.50 a bowl. *A la carte* orders like beef tostadas ($3.50), large bean burritos ($3.50), and hot tamales (yep, tamales—for $2) will get you going. Frijoles refritos (that's refried beans to us) are just $2 an order; and sides of salsa verde, pico de gallo, and jalapenos are just 95¢ each for generous sized bowls.

Lunch specials are served weekdays from 11 a.m. all the way to 5 p.m. Huevos rancheros (Mexican eggs, served with rice) are just $4.50; same price for a bean burrito and cheese enchilada plate with rice. *Arriba!*, the "Speedy Gonzalez" lunch, consists of a taco, an enchilada, and rice or frijoles, for a mere $3.50.

House specialties include chimichangas for $7.75 (enough for two to share), enchiladas (beef, cheese, bean, or chicken) starting at $4.25, and a half-order of chicken or beef burritos—with beans and jalapeno cheese sauce—for $4.50. Fajitas with rice go up to $8.75 (with shrimp for $9.50), while tostadas deluxe, filled with refried beans, chicken breast, sour cream and Rio Grande's special sauce, is $6.95.

Rio Grande also serves children's meals for those under 12, like the taco, rice, and refried bean plate, beef burrito and rice, or Mexican hamburger, each $2.95.

To end your spicy meal on a sweet note, try RGC's flan ($2.50), or the sopapilla, a fried tortilla with honey, priced right at just $1.25 ($2.25 a la mode). RGC's fresh fruit margaritas, available in lime, strawberry, raspberry, banana, and peach, start at $3.75.

Rio Grande Cantina is open from 11 a.m. to 11 p.m. weekdays, and Saturdays and Sundays from noon to 11 p.m.

Rocky's Brick Oven Pizza
- 1770 Peachtree St. N.E., Atlanta; 876-1111
- 3210-A Roswell Rd. N.E., Atlanta; 262-ROCK (7625)

And other suburban locations
Yo. Rocky's has fought the good fight to gain a share of Atlanta's burgeoning pizza market, and the result is lower prices for you. Brick-fired ovens produce a slightly smoky-flavored, crunchy European pizza, and there are lots of fresh, unusual toppings to jazz these up. Homemade mozzarella and impeccably fresh ingredients have helped Rocky's win international awards for their food; and it's been voted the best inexpensive restaurant in town by Fodor's Guides.

Make up your own individual pizza (prices start at $4.95), by topping it with fried breaded eggplant, Italian sausage, sauteed chicken, or other goodies, for $1 each. Rocky's big Neapolitan (thin-crust) pie, enough for three people to share, starts at $14.95; Sicilian-styles, enough for four people, are $17.95. These gargantuan pies make this a good place to come with the gang.

Some of Rocky's more creative combinations include "The Gardenia"—broccoli and artichoke hearts, white glazed garlic sauce, mozzarella, gorgonzola, tomatoes and pesto. "Chicken Bianca Oreganato," with fresh garlic, white wine, red onions, and lemon, and "Eggplant Florentine" pizzas are also good choices.

They have great calzones here, too. All are priced at $8.50 each, such as the "Beau Bock," stuffed to overflowing with salami, prosciutto ham, pepperoni, provolone, and cappicola. Rocky's offers delivery on orders over $10.

Silver Spoon Cafe
- 2040 Peachtree Rd. N.W., Atlanta; 351-8433
- Phipps Plaza, 3500 Peachtree Rd. N.E., Atlanta; 237-8335
- 1 Galleria Pkwy. N.W., Smyrna; 916-1976

And other suburban locations

So, you weren't born with one of these in your mouth; you can still get a great meal at the Silver Spoon. Some entrees get a bit pricey, but the cafe does have items like fresh quiche for $4.99, Cajun chicken sandwiches for $6.49, big Caesar salads for $4.99, and fettuccine Alfredo for $7.99. Not to mention delicious five cheese pizzas for $5.99.

The children's menu, served to those ten years old and younger, features proven kid-pleasers like grilled cheese sandwiches ($1.99), pepperoni pizza ($2.99), chicken fingers ($2.99), and corn dogs ($1.99). The little ones are also given a game-covered menu to keep them busy.

Desserts include mocha or cappuccino freezes for $2.99, and apple walnut crisps for $3.29. This popular place gets pretty busy, especially around lunchtime; to avoid the rushes, you can actually call ahead to the Silver Spoon for preferred seating.

Steamhouse Lounge Seafood Bar
- 3041 Bolling Way N.E., Atlanta; 233-7980

You'll be happy as a clam with this dining choice. It's a watering hole in every sense of the word (and self-appointed as "The best little dump in Buckhead"), with bar regulars' names engraved on tiny plates and affixed to "their" seats at the bar.

To start off, try "Uncle Sherman's famous" crab dip, served with warm pita bread ($2.95), or the seafood nachos, laced with baby shrimp, crabmeat, bay scallops, jalapeños, and tomato ($6.25). Their super chili's a deal at $2.95 a bowl, as is lobster bisque is $3.25 a bowl. Fresh corn on the cob, in season, and the terrific potato salad are just 75¢ a side.

A dozen raw oysters can be shucked to order for $5.95; the "U-Shuck-'Em" bucket of two dozen oysters is $9.95; and the famous Frogmore Skillet, heaped high with steamed oysters, shrimp, Polish sausage, potatoes, and corn on the cob, all in butter sauce, is a huge bargain at $8.95. The "Steam Pot" is a popular item with groups, filled as it is with every varieties of shellfish that the Lounge sells. (Steamhouse sells shellfish by the seashore...) It serves up to four people and is reasonably priced at $24.95.

Less daring souls (like your children, perhaps?) tend to stick to the basics like the deli salad ($5.25), turkey-bacon sandwiches ($4.95), and chili dogs ($3.25).

Reel something in for yourself, Mondays through Saturdays from 11:30 a.m. to 2 a.m., and Sundays from 12:30 p.m. to midnight. The bar stays open until 4 a.m. weekdays, til 3 a.m. Saturday, and til 2 a.m. Sunday.

Sunny Garden
- Around Lenox Shopping Center, 340 Wooddale Dr. N.E., Atlanta; 262-1191

If you're looking for some cheap eats as an antidote for a day of shopping at Lenox Square shopping center, Sunny Garden may just do the trick. Lunch specials, offered daily from 11 a.m. to 4 p.m., include over two dozen combination plates: Everything from moo goo gai pan to sauteed baby shrimp with chicken to Mandarin pork. Nearly all are served with white or brown rice and eggroll, for just $4.65.

Other classic dishes like egg drop soup ($1.25), chop suey ($5.75), and egg foo young ($6.50) are priced right. Full dinners like shrimp with garlic sauce ($7.95), Hunan beef ($6.95), and orange chicken ($8.50) are prepared quickly and served by a super-polite waitstaff.

The restaurant also has a "diet" menu of specialties made without oil, salt, or cornstarch. Steamed bean curds and broccoli, steamed mixed vegetables and the like are just $5.95

each—or $1 more with chicken.

Sunny Garden, open seven days a week, also offers free delivery on orders of $12 or more.

Sweet Stuff Dessert Cafe
• 3102 Roswell Rd. N.E., Atlanta; 841-6612

Stuff yourself at Sweet Stuff. Considering the gargantuan size of the goods here, you had better arrive starving—or bring along a friend or two to help you tackle the towering treats. By sharing, you really won't end up spending that much in this Buckhead bakery.

That is, if you can make up your mind from the dazzling array of cakes and pies spinning in the glass display cases. Sacher torte, marble cheesecake, black forest cake, chocolate mousse, coconut lemon pie, and the ultimate "Death By Chocolate" cake will all tempt you, and each goes for $3.95 a slice. Selection varies from day to day, but you're always sure to find something to try.

Ice cream desserts are, for lack of a better word, huge. The "Chocoholic" (a chocolate candy shell with chocolate ice cream, hot fudge and whipped cream) and the "V.I.P. Chocolate Chip" (a jumbo sized cookie topped with the same) are $6.95 each. On the lighter side (who are we kidding, really), you can try the raspberry peach melba or a strawberry sundae for $4.95 each.

Sweet Stuff also has cappuccino, espresso, herbal teas, milk shakes, and fruit juices.

Taco Mac
• 375 Pharr Rd. N.E., Atlanta; 239-0650
• 1006 North Highland Ave. N.E., Atlanta; 873-6529
• 771 Cherokee Ave. S.E., Atlanta; 624-4641
• 2120 Johnson Ferry Rd., Chamblee; 454-7676
• 1444 Oxford Rd., Emory Village; 377-2323
• 1570 Holcomb Bridge Rd., Roswell; 640-9598
• 5830 Roswell Rd. N.W., Sandy Springs; 257-0735

• 2845 Mountain Industrial Blvd., Stone Mountain; 621-3601
And other suburban locations
These guys claim that Buffalo wings were invented right here. Gee, wait'll the folks in Buffalo hear that. No matter—Taco Mac's spicy wings are for real, and they've also got the biggest beer selection this side of the Mississippi to wash them down. While the service can be slow as a sloth, Mr. C still thinks that the food and the prices make Mac a hit.

Appetizers include fried zucchini, cauliflower, or mushrooms for just $4 a plate; a jumbo basket of nachos with frijoles and cheese goes for $4.75. TM's guacamole salad is a mere $2.85. Basics include soft tacos for $1.55, super burritos for $3.25, quesadillas for $5.50, and chili for just $2.50; to go with these, beers from 28 different countries are reasonably priced, even though they come from as far away as New Zealand and the Ivory Coast.

Those Buffalo chicken wings come in sizes of ten for $4.75 or twenty for $7.05. Rustle them up in mild, medium, hot—or, for 50 extra, "Three Mile Island"-style. If you're having a party, here's an extra tip from Mr. C: You can get a 10% discount for platter orders of 250 wings or more.

Taco Mac has a kiddie menu too, with things like a burger and fries for $2.50, or a mini-fish and chips plate for the same price.

Three Dollar Cafe
• 3002 Peachtree Rd. N.E., Atlanta; 266-8667
• 8595 Roswell Rd., Dunwoody; 992-5011
• 2580 Windy Hill Rd., Marietta; 850-0868
The Three Dollar Cafe is not your average Buckhead watering hole. That's because it's much more like anywhere else's watering hole. Mr. C likes the very casual, un-Buckhead atmosphere (feel free to wear your oldest T-shirt). And while you *will* have to spend a little over three bucks on dinner here, alas, the name isn't all

that far off. Portions are so huge, in fact, that you'll most likely get two meals out of whatever you order.

Three Dollar Cafe's chicken wings are real crowd pleasers at just $3.78 an order—feel free to get messy, too, since each table is thoughtfully provided with rolls of paper towels for post-pigout cleanups. Or, try an order of sauted mushrooms for $3.86.

Mr. C got quite stuffed on the salad and steamed veggie platter, which comes with new potatoes, lots of carrots, and darn near a whole head each of broccoli and cauliflower—all for just $4.98.

Steak and cheese sandwiches are only $4.25, reubens are $4.78, and beef kabobs are $6.86. Chicken Oscar, made with crabmeat topping, white asparagus and Hollandaise sauce, is served with squash casserole *and* rice and gravy, complete for $6.95.

Don't forget dessert, either, with treats like key lime pie, cheesecake, and ice cream-topped brownies, each under $2.50.

Three Dollar has a children's menu, too, with spaghetti, burgers and fries, chicken wing and fries, or a grilled cheese sandwich, for just $1.95 each. Kids three and under get a free peanut butter and jelly sandwich. Now, *there's* a deal!

Uncle Tai's

- 3500 Peachtree Rd. N.E., Atlanta; 816-8888

Yep, okay, this *is* the Uncle Tai's you may have seen advertised in Atlanta magazine, the one that gives those fancy cooking classes and all, right in the middle of Phipps. Granted, dinner here doesn't exactly fit into the Mr. C scheme of things, but lunch here is a relative bargain.

From 11 a.m. to 2:30 p.m. each weekday, Uncle Tai's offers a super deal: A "Cafe Platter" of shrimp with zucchini, beef with green peppers, or curried chicken. Whichever you choose, it comes with the soup of the day, a vegetable spring roll, and fried rice, all for $6.50. Not bad!

Other lunch entrees, served from 11 a.m. to 4:30 p.m. daily, include

moo shu pork with bamboo shoots and tree-ear mushrooms ($6.75), sweet and sour shrimp ($7.25), fish with black bean sauce (also $7.25), and lamb with scallions ($7.25). Hunan-style noodles with shrimp and chicken are $6.25, as is eggplant in garlic sauce. Hot tea, steamed rice, and soup (hot and sour or corn) are served with all of these.

Traditionally hot and spicy dishes are clearly marked; the chef can alter the spices if requested. Uncle Tai's is open from 11 a.m. to 10 p.m., Mondays through Thursdays, and from 11 a.m. to 11 p.m. Fridays and Saturdays. That lunch deal may make it easier for you to impress a date, or your boss, with good food in elegant surroundings.

Veggieland

- 211 Pharr Rd. N.E., Atlanta; 231-3111
- 209 Sandy Springs Circle, Sandy Springs; 252-1165

You don't have to be a vegetarian to like the food here—you'll never notice that there's no refined sugar or dairy products used in any of the menu items. Veggieland is a place for real purists—jars of no-salt spice mixtures and non-irradiated cayenne pepper flakes sit at each table, and even the ice cubes are made with filtered water. It's a well-kept Buckhead secret, undeservingly overshadowed by a certain (more expensive) leafy chain located right down the street.

Mr. C liked the cashew and soy strip veggie stir-fry, its perfectly steamed snow peas, broccoli, carrots, red and green peppers, and bean sprouts sitting atop a mound of basmati rice. This was enough for two meals, really, priced at a healthy $4.75. It's also available with baked tofu and almonds, instead of the cashews and soy strips, for the same price. Whole-grain pasta primavera with pesto is another hearty entree, perfect for vegetarians and non-vegetarians alike, is just $5.95.

The "Veggie Burger" is made from nuts, beans, and spices, topped with tomato, lettuce, sprouts and onion on a whole wheat bun, for $3.40; top it with soy cheese for 35¢ extra. The tofu-chicken sandwich, served with fried sweet potatoes, is just $3.95. Soup selections change daily; the potato leek soup is super, and just $1.25 for a good-sized cup.

The restaurant itself is tiny, with a small patio, and a laid-back, take-your-time atmosphere. Colorful Caribbean-scene paintings and classical music make for peaceful surroundings, while the attentive service makes you feel right at home.

Veggieland is open weekdays from 11:30 a.m. to 3 p.m., and again from 5 p.m. to 9 p.m.; Saturdays from 11:30 a.m. to 9 p.m., and Sundays (in the Buckhead location only) from noon to 8 p.m.

White House Restaurant
- 3172 Peachtree Rd. N.E., Atlanta; 237-7601

Mr. C will bet that you've driven by this treasure a hundred times without noticing, since it's wedged into a strip mall with a furniture and shoe stores, near the Buckhead IHOP. White House is the kind of diner where you get treated like a head of state, even though the food prices are more appropriate for the guy who cleans the windows.

Breakfast is served any time of day—gotta love it. And you'll love the prices, too—two eggs any style, grits, biscuits or toast, and butter and jelly are just $2.90. Hotcakes with syrup are $2.20, oatmeal is $1.90, and the "Working Man's Breakfast" (tsk tsk, we're supposed to say working *person* now), consists of a hefty-sized pork chop, with two eggs, grits, and biscuit, for $5.30.

For lunch, Mr. C tried the three-vegetable platter, with whole okra, potato salad, and steamed spinach for $3.60, while a friend enjoyed an open-faced hot turkey sandwich with mashed spuds for $4.85. Specials change daily, but include some Greek mainstays (like pastitsio or moussaka, each $5.90), as well as Irish beef stew, filet mignon, and barbecued pork (all under $7, including veggies and fixin's). Even seafood is inexpensive here, like fried flounder, perch, or trout dinners, all under $6.

And, if you've got room left over for dessert, don't miss the cheesecake ($1.30) or homemade peach cobbler ($1.20).

The White House (the one in Buckhead, that is) is open from 6 a.m. to 3 p.m., Monday through Saturday. Perhaps President Bill—no stranger to cobbler himself—could somehow use this to help close the national deficit?

DOWNTOWN/ATLANTA SOUTHEAST & SOUTHWEST

Athens Pizza House
- 1959 Lakewood Ave. S.E., Atlanta; 622-7911
- 246 Bobby Jones Expwy., Augusta; (706) 868-1508
- 5550 Peachtree Industrial Blvd., Chamblee; 452-8282
- 1565 Highway 138, Conyers; 483-6228
- 1341 Clairmont Rd., Decatur; 636-1100
- 1255 Johnson Ferry Rd., Marietta; 509-0099
- 6075 Roswell Rd. N.E., Sandy Springs; 257-0252

The Papadopoulos family has been making popular pizza in the Atlanta area since 1966. The prices are right, too; not only on the pizzas, but also on such appetizers as spinach pie ($1.50), Athens patatoes ($1.50), and fried kalamari ($4.40). Those last two *must* be good—they're spelled old-country style.

The pies themselves start at just $4.90 for an individual size. But why stop there? Go all out with a medium all-meat special (salami, sausage, pepperoni, ham, hamburger, and Canadian bacon) for $9.25. You won't have to eat again for a week.

Entrees like moussaka served with spinach pie, chicken parmesan, and spinach manicotti are each served with a Greek salad and garlic bread for $6.95. There's a children's section on the menu, too; the kids' spaghetti dinner is just $3.15, while you can join them with the gigantic regular spaghetti plate for $5.20.

Don't pass up the baklava for dessert, either. At $1.50 a slice, these nut-filled flaky pastries covered with honey are just the thing to end your meal on a sweet note.

Athens Pizza also offers many beers and wines (including Greek varieties like Kokino and Aspro), starting at $1.95 a glass.

If the crowds here get to be too much, though, consider visiting one of the Athens Pizza Express take-out locations, at 4060 Peachtree Road N.E., Atlanta (phone 365-8646) and 1788 Clairmont Road, Decatur (634-8646).

The Beautiful Restaurant
- Wheat Street Plaza South, 397 Auburn Ave. N.E., Atlanta; 223-0080
- 2260 Cascade Rd. S.W., Atlanta; 752-5931

The decor may not be beautiful here (unless you like fake wood paneling, orange vinyl booths and second-grade classroom style tables), but the bargain-priced food sure is a gorgeous deal. Servings are generously sized, and you can get a full meal for under $5—a great place to eat in after visiting the MLK Center down the street.

Starting with breakfast, a stack of pancakes is just $1.35 (whole wheat version, $1.50), and bacon omelettes are $2.95. Grilled cheese sandwiches go for just 90¢, while the rib-eye steak breakfast tops out the menu at $7.05.

For lunch, police sergeants and other regulars file in to fill up on the house special—any three vegetables, plus fresh bread and soda or tea, for just $2.99. Choose from Brussels sprouts, squash, rutabagas, turnips, okra, corn on the cob, rice, creamed potatoes, collard greens, broccoli casserole, yams, and more.

They charge you for little extras (like lemon or butter will cost you 5¢), but that helps the place keep prices down on main dishes—thus, you can get spaghetti and meat sauce for a mere $2.97, Brunswick stew for $1.89, grilled liver for $2.77, oxtails for $3.77, and the homemade soup of the day for $1.50. Bigger appctites will like the filet of sole ($4.27), chipped barbecue beef ($2.97), baked or fried chicken ($2.52), and pepper steak ($4.27). Desserts include fresh carrot cake for a mere 90¢ a slice.

Service is cafeteria style. The Beautiful Restaurant is open from 7 a.m. to 8:30 p.m. daily.

Chanterelles
- 646 Evans St. S.W., Atlanta; 758-0909

Just around the corner from the West End MARTA station, Chanterelles is a cozy, humble, neighborhood spot where local folks relax over home-cooked meals assembled in cafeteria style. The pricing is simple: Most entrees are $4. Add one vegetable on the side, and it's $5.35. Two veggies are $6.25. Or, you can have a platter of just vegetables, four of your choice, for $5.25. Just point to what you want!

Entrees change daily, but you'll always find about a half-dozen to choose from. Surprisingly, these are not always "down home" dinners, but rather things like baked fish Florentine (with cheese and spinach over the top), chicken teriyaki, rosemary chicken, and others. There are also a couple of dinners which are a tad more expensive, such as shrimp and rice ($5.65) or broiled lamb and two vegetables ($6.45). And there at least ten different vegetables available.

It's all hot and delicious; but beyond this easygoing menu, there are few other amenities. There are no hot beverages served, and no alcohol—but the cold drinks do include ginger beer, IBC root beer, lemonade, and sodas. The dining room consists of ordered rows of small, plastic-topped tables, with cushioned easy chairs on wheels. Kinda different, and certainly comfortable. And, while there is no waiter service, someone does come around to help set you up, remove your tray, and get you any little missing extras.

Being in a neighborhood that is still in the process of gentrification, the restaurant closes up around 8:00 p.m.

Coco Loco Cuban & Caribbean Cafe

- 303 Peachtree Center Ave. N.E., Atlanta; 653-0070
- 2625 Piedmont Rd. N.E., Atlanta; 364-0212 and 261-0198
- 6301 Roswell Rd., Sandy Springs; 255-5434

Sure, Coco Loco may have a reputation as a yuppie hangout, but its prices are surprisingly *un*-yuppie. The Cuban sandwich, for instance, is just $3.75 for the regular size, and $4.50 for the super. Jamaican jerk chicken sandwiches go for $3.95, as does the *pan con lechon* (roast pork and grilled onions). For lighter appetites, or those who can't bear the hot spices, try grilled cheese with potato sticks for $2.25, or hot dogs and quarter-pound hamburgers, each just $2.50. The spicier Cuban hamburger, with onions, paprika, and Worcestershire sauce, is also just $2.50.

On the sweet side, tropical milk-shakes, in flavors like papaya or mango ($1.95), and nectars (try the tamarind, just $1.50), will douse the flames of the Cuban spices.

Even entrees are reasonably priced, served with two side dishes like yucas, rice, or a salad. Cuban-style roast chicken with garlic and onions, fried sirloin steak, and pork chops are all just $5.95 each. Side dishes like black beans and rice ($1.75), sweet fried plantains or plan-

tain chips (also $1.75) and home-made potato chips (95) won't break the bank, either, so you may just have enough money left for some (not so cheap) dessert, like key lime pie ($2.50), rice pudding ($1.95), or *pastelito de guayaba* (guava pastry), just 75 an order.

Domestic and imported beers, plus a limited wine selection, are also available.

Cowan's Sandwich Shoppe

- 124 Spring St. S.W., Atlanta; 521-2190

Let's face it, folks—just about *any* sandwich shop is going to have low prices. But Mr. Cheap felt he had to include this tiny diner, "sandwiched" among hulking federal buildings, because the joint is near-legendary among downtown office workers and blue-collar types.

Little more than an snack stand with just a narrow counter and a few tables inside, Cowan's has been here for over forty years. When the weather is good, picnic tables spilling into the parking lot add a few more seats (there are plans to enclose this area, someday).

The menu is limited, but the fare is warm and filling. Mr. C's fave is the barbeque sandwich, with a stew of pork and beans slathered onto a fresh roll for only $2.65. The "Golden Nugget," a few cents more, offers

---

MR. CHEAP'S PICKS
Downtown

✔ **Delectables**—The name says it all, doesn't it? This is a bright spot in the often dull downtown lunch scene—in the library, of all places.

✔ **Delights of the Garden**—Ultra-vegetarian heaven. This food is delicious; and it's so healthy, it's not even *cooked*!

fried chicken pieces instead. Ham and cheese biscuits are another hearty homemade winner, just 90 cents for a single order, $1.80 for a double. And pimento cheese sandwiches ($2) are popular, with a pile of them pre-wrapped and waiting for hurried regulars.

The atmosphere, as far as it can possibly go, is boisterous and friendly—a good place for small talk with the owner, or conversation with your co-workers (if you can get in). Cowan's is open weekdays only, naturally, from 6:00 a.m. until about 2:00 in the afternoon.

Delectables
- One Margaret Mitchell Square N.W., Atlanta; 681-2909

Who would expect a great restaurant on the lower floor of the Atlanta-Fulton County Library? Super eateries like this may be a fading breed, but certainly aren't entirely gone with the wind yet.

Come on in when you've got the lunch-hour blahs. Sure, the food is served cafeteria-style, but the chef livens up the menu with special sauces, homemade soups, and fresh bread, all prepared perfectly. Flowers decorate each table; pretty pastel tablecloths, classical music, and ficus trees perk up the place, too.

Choices here change weekly. Recent specials included vegetarian lasagna, Crab Louis pasta, and an asparagus, goat cheese, and prosciutto strudel. Mr. C liked one of the menu mainstays: Smoked turkey on an onion roll, served with potato bread, and an organic vegetable salad topped with vinaigrette, with a total price under $7. Shrimp and scallop pesto pasta will fill you up for $7.50. Those with lighter appetites will like the small plates, like a $2.50 Waldorf salad, Delectables' gazpacho ($3.25) or its much talked-about chili.

If you have room left for dessert, Mr. C suggests the white chocolate brownie ($1.75), or their incredibly fresh chunky chocolate chip cookies ($1.25 each). Delectables also brews cappuccino, espresso, and several varities of tea, such as jasmine and Ceylon.

Delectables is open weekdays only, from 11 a.m. to 2:30 p.m. To hear their list of specials, call 421-8353. A delightful surprise!

Delights of the Garden
- 136 Marietta St. N.W., Atlanta; 524-5744
- 1081 Juniper St. N.E., Atlanta; 876-4307

For a change, a restaurant claiming to offer "a new concept in eating" is probably correct. Delights of the Garden does standard vegetarian cooking one better; this food is not even cooked. Fruits, vegetables, and grains "cooked only by the sun" are the staple ingredients here, and they're turned into a surprising array of truly creative dishes.

For instance, the kitchen turns out an item called "Veggie Tuna." There is, of course, no fish involved; it's made from carrots, food-processor-shredded to within a millimeter of their lives. These are then mixed with a touch of mayonnaise and seasonings just as tuna would be, and the result has exactly the same moist texture—and even, to some degree, the taste—of tuna salad. And there's certainly no need to worry about it being dolphin-safe!

You can have this as an appetizer, on a bed of *very* fresh lettuce, for $2.50; or, as part of several combination platters. Another unusual appetizer is "Sprout Spaghetti" (also $2.50), in which raw bean sprouts stand in for cooked pasta; y'know, from a slight distance, they even look the same. A good-sized bed of sprouts is topped with a sauce of ground tomato and spices, plus a couple of grain "meatballs"—and again, it all works.

The trick here, it seems, is one of helping the veggies go down by preparing them in sauces and spices which give them a lot of taste. The most frequently-used staple is kush, a nutty grain derived from bulgur wheat. On its own, kush is rather dry and, well, grainy; but when the chef

spikes it with a various flavors, it becomes a succession of delicious, and
certainly healthy, entrees. You can
have "Spicy Kush," which has a
tangy bite to it; "Nori Rolls," kush
wrapped in seaweed sheets just like
sushi; or a mild kush which you can
flavor up with their delicious house
dressing, a smoothly blended spinach
tahini sweetened with chopped raisins. (Mr. C doesn't even *like* raisins,
but he sure loved this sauce.)

Not everything is unfamiliar.
You'll find marinated vegetables, garden salads, chips and salsa, guacamole, and other yummy foods. Wash
them down with fresh juices or
herbal teas; perhaps they'll have
whipped up a batch of their special almond cocoa, too.

The pricing is very simple, as
these and other creations are combined into several different platters
("Garden Sampler," "Nubian Delight"), which are all available in
small ($4.95) or large ($6.95) sizes.
Each plate has three to six items; you
can even create your own sampler.
Believe it or not, this stuff is really
filling. And, not only is it all good for
you, but the fully explanatory menu
even notes which vitamins and minerals you get from each food. The
friendly staff, all dedicated to this
kind of food, will patiently answer
any questions you may have.

In his many travels, Mr. C had
never before seen many of these
dishes; if you're into healthy eating
(heck, even if you aren't), he suggests that you give this place a try.

Fat Tuesday
• Underground Atlanta, 50 Upper
  Alabama St., S.W.; 523-7404
• 3167 Peachtree Rd. N.E., Atlanta;
  233-9584
• 2321 Windy Hill Rd. S.E.,
  Marietta; 952-2070
Cheap food in Underground Atlanta?
Believe it. A popular after-work hangout, Fat Tuesday will help you keep
you *and* your wallet fat. Their Cajun
sandwiches and soups fill you up
nicely for under $5.

Mr. C liked the big plate of just-

right spiced black beans & rice
($4.95). Ham-cooked red beans and
rice, served with house salad, bread
and butter, are only $5.50. And the
tasty seafood gumbo is a big seller at
$5.25.

Pretend that it's Mardi Gras time
and try a ham po'boy, piled high with
toppings on a French roll and served
with fries ($4.95), or the fried bayou
chicken sandwich ($5.95). If you just
want to nibble on appetizers, the veggie platter is good at $2.95, as are
spicy-hot chicken wings at $3.95.
And here's an extra tip from Mr. C:
Mondays through Fridays from 5 to 7
p.m., FT offers its appetizers at two
for the price of one!

Of course, all these spices are going to get you thirsty, and nobody
mixes a drink like Fat Tuesday. Their
daiquiri mixing machines look like
something out of a laundromat, but
make for great coladas and other
punchy mixed drinks with names like
"Swampwater." These can be a bit on
the pricey side, but then, this is how
they can keep the food cheap.

Le Peep
• 233 Peachtree St. N.E., Atlanta;
  688-3782
• 2484 Briarcliff Rd. N.E., Atlanta;
  325-7069
• 3000 Windy Hill Rd., Marietta;
  980-0898
And other suburban locations
Mr. Cheap loves Le Peep. The plates
are piled so high with wonderful food
that you'll find it *magnifique*,
whether you come for breakfast,
brunch, lunch, or dinner.

In spite of the French name, Le
Peep actually serves food with a western flair. Why don't you come to
your senses and try the "Desperado,"
Le Peep's skillet dish with eggs,
cheese, chorizo sausage, green chilies
and onions, mixed with salsa, for $6;
or the Fiesta Skillet, full of "Peasant
Potatoes," chunks of chicken, and
diced onions covered with chili verde
and cheddar. It's served up with two
eggs for $5.75.

The aptly-named "Lumberjack
Breakfast," lets you chop down eggs,

two bacon strips, two sausage links, Peasant Potatoes, and a short stack of pancakes, for $5.85. For healthy palates, a huge fresh fruit plate is $4.20, and granola-dipped French toast is $4.95.

At lunch or dinnertime, LP's smoked turkey and bacon sandwich, with bacon, Muenster, lettuce, tomato and mayo, served with a garden salad or cup of soup or criss cross cut fries, is a winner for $5.35. A Philly cheese steak sandwich, with soup, salad, or fries, is just $6, and a jumbo $\frac{1}{3}$-pound burger, also with choice of side dishes, is $4.75. And don't forget dessert: a sweet crepe, filled with blueberries, bananas, strawberries, or spiced apples, covered with whipped topping and cinnamon, is $1.95.

Le Peep has some of the best coffee and hot chocolate this side of the Divide (or should that be the Seine?), and serves breakfast any time of day. They also have a "Golden Years Club," which entitles anyone over 55 to a ten percent discount off any meal, seven days a week. Le *wow*!

Mick's
- 557 Peachtree Rd. N.E., Atlanta; 875-6425
- 2110 Peachtree Rd. N.W., Atlanta; 351-6425
- Peachtree Center, 229 Peachtree St. N.E., Atlanta; 688-6425
- Lenox Square Shopping Center, 3393 Peachtree Rd. N.E., Atlanta; 262-6425
- Underground Atlanta, 75 Upper Alabama St. S.W., Atlanta; 525-2825
- 116 East Ponce de Leon Ave., Decatur; 373-7797

And other suburban locations
Get to Mick's for one of the best milkshakes in town, great burgers, super desserts, and creative drinks. Stretching from Underground Atlanta to Buckhead and beyond, this yuppie haven seems determined to make the next siege of Atlanta a culinary one.

Prices here are not the absolute cheapest around, but you do get a lot of delicious food for the money. Start off with real fried green tomatoes

($5.75), chili-smothered French fries ($3.95), grilled carrots and broccoli ($2.50), or a cup of soup in flavors like tomato or "baked potato" ($1.95).

A half-pound hamburger, hickory grilled, with a generous side of fries or pasta salad, is $5.95. You can top it with cheddar or mozzarella cheese, guacamole, chili, barbecue sauce, or cracked pepper and mustard for 80¢ extra. Cheese-topped grilled boneless chicken is $7.50, and corn and tomato linguine with garlic bread is $6.95. Mick's chicken Reuben will completely stuff you for $7.95.

Do try to leave room for dessert, though. You'll probably want to share one of these monstrosities with a friend. Try the Oreo cheesecake ($3.95), the Giant Banana Split ($4.75), or Mr. C's favorite, the chocolate cream pie ($3.75). Yummy! Strawberry shortcake, homemade chocolate layer cake, and Heath Bar ice cream pie will all make delightful ends to your meal, and all are under $4 apiece.

Besides the desserts, Mick's is known for its unusual mixed drinks— like "Frozen Pink Lemonade," "Frozen German Chocolate Cake," and "Peasant Coffee" (spiked with brandy, Grand Marnier, Kahlua, amaretto, and dark creme de cacao, and topped with whipped cream). These will doubtless not be cheap, but they are good. Most branches of Mick's have a separate bar area.

Our Daily Bread and Cobbler Shop
- 879B Ralph D. Abernathy Blvd. S.W., Atlanta; 753-2777

This bright, cozy cafe in the West End is kind of a cross between a bakery and a luncheonette. Stop in for a quick muffin or a just-baked meat pie, or order up a full hot lunch and find a table by the big glass window. The food is wonderful, the service comes with a smile and it's all done fast and cheap.

For the fastest deal in the West (End), try the "Sandwich Bar Express." This goes salad bars one better by offering a selection of fresh, well-stuffed, ready-made sandwiches such as ham, cheese, turkey, and salami on a roll, veggies in pita bread, and turkey on whole wheat—plus chips, a pickle, and a drink—all for $3.99. Or, go for the daily special, a variety of hot entrees served up as a complete meal for $4.99. These can range from something found in our own backyard, like Brunswick stew, to something from far away lands, such as chicken curry.

Soups and salads include a bowl of chili for just $1.85, Caesar salad topped with chicken for $3.99, and minestrone for 95 cents a cup. And there are lots of smaller hot items, available either as side dishes (marinated vegetables, 85¢, corn soufflé, 95¢) or as individual snacks (a spicy West Indian meat patty, $1).

And we haven't even gotten to the second half of the store's name yet! There's something here for every kind of sweet tooth, from walnut-oatmeal-raisin cookies (50 cents each) to German chocolate cake ($1.55 a slice) to—of course—cobblers, cobblers, cobblers. Oh sure, they've got your basic apple, cherry, and so forth. But how about pear almond? Or plum custard, banana rum, or even mango? They're all about $1.50 per slice, and all yummy.

ODB opens up at 11:30 in the morning (presumably, they're baking like mad until then); they only serve until 5:00 in the afternoon. However, being near the West End MARTA station, they do sell food to take out until 7:30 on weeknights. Closed all day Sunday.

Paschal's Restaurant
- 830 Martin Luther King, Jr. Drive S.W., Atlanta; 577-3150

Located in front of a motor hotel of the same name (see listing under "Hotels and Lodging"), Paschal's is a longtime landmark for down home eating for businessmen and an older local crowd. Most of the patrons seem to be regulars from this non-gentrified neighborhood west of the Omni; the city's rampant development hasn't reached this far yet, and

the streets around here can get pretty tough at night. Inside this restaurant, though, the folks who work and eat here go out of their way to be friendly.

The front room is your traditional luncheonette, with a counter and comfortably padded booths. To the rear, leading into the hotel, you come into a vastly different environment: A pair of darkly elegant, formal dining rooms. Whichever setting you choose, you'll find the same great soul food menu.

That food, meanwhile, is wonderful and cheap. Southern fried chicken is perhaps the house specialty; at $5.50 (25 cents more for white meat), it's fantastic; and it comes with your choice of two vegetables—things like candied yams, June peas, collard greens, or rice and gravy. The crust is crunchy and tasty all by itself—the true test—with grains of black pepper mixed into the batter.

Most other lunch/dinner entrees are priced between $6-$9, including such choices as broiled chopped sirloin, pork chops, country fried steak, broiled catfish, flounder stuffed with crabmeat, and many others. All of these come with two vegetables, as well as little bread and cornbread rolls. There is a more formal listing of steaks and chops, but these prices do rise out of Mr. C's range.

For smaller appetites, try a plate of "Paschal Style" chicken hash, served with creamed potatoes and one egg any style for $5.50; or a fried chicken sandwich, just $3.75. There are muffins and homemade soups, and salads too. One thing is certain: They won't let you leave hungry.

Reggie's
- CNN Center, 100 Techwood Dr., Atlanta; 525-1437

Reggie Mitchell is something of a living legend, having traveled through Thailand, Burma, and India with the Royal Marines and the Indian army. His restaurant is covered with memorabilia from these exploits, as well as related English lithographs. The menu is pretty interesting, too, a mix of traditional pub specialties and American foods.

Appetizers like fried peppered cheese balls or seafood chowder ($4.25 each) won't break the bank. Have a plate of "bangers and mash," the traditional English pork sausage and potatoes, for $6.95. Vegetarian lasagna is $6.50, and curried chicken is $6.95. Reggie's hefty sandwiches, like the grilled marinated chicken with Swiss cheese ($6.45), will keep you fortified for any long march.

If you're lucky, Reggie just may greet you at the door; he'll be happy to show you his original watercolor of Winston Churchill or family pictures of his ancestor, Lord Cornwallis, and perhaps regale you with stories of faraway lands.

Reggie's is open Monday through Saturday from 11:30 a.m. to 11 p.m., and Sundays from noon to 11 p.m. These hours are usually extended following games at the nearby Omni.

Soul Vegetarian
- 879-A Ralph D. Abernathy Blvd. S.W., Atlanta; 752-5194
- 652 North Highland Ave. N.E., Atlanta; 875-0145

The very name of these restaurants sounds like a contradiction in terms. Soul food is not generally thought of as being light and healthy. One imagines some kind of tofu ribs or such. In fact, the menu does not differ much from that of any vegetarian restaurant; it's the atmosphere, complete with jazz music, a very homey welcome, and a bit of scripture on the walls which sets the place apart from the city's other sprout palaces.

Everything here is all-natural and cholesterol-free, right on down to the soy ice cream that's always offered as your meal is cleared. The entrees themselves, in an unliklely turn, tend toward Middle Eastern delicacies. "Soups from Jerusalem" feature marak alfunah, a garlicky split-pea; it's only $1 a cup, or $1.90 a bowl. Add some cornbread—yes, this works— for another buck.

Most of the entrees are salads and sandwiches, with one daily lunch or

---

MR. CHEAP'S PICKS
West End

✔ **Our Daily Bread**—Cheap lunch specials, plus wonderful breads and pastries.

✔ **Paschal's Restaurant**— There's no question, this soul food is as authentic as it gets.

---

dinner special added, like spaghetti with a tomato-vegetable sauce. At $7.95, the dinners include salad and cornbread. Otherwise, sandwiches are all $3.70; make any one into a platter for $5, adding a side salad and hand-cut French fries or onion rings—however healthy *those* can be. The unique specialty of the house is something called kalebone, made from wheat grain (plenty of protein) into a tasty concoction which can be made into burger patties or sliced into a gyro-like pita sandwich. Flavored with a few different sauces, it's moist and filling.

Salads range from $2.75 to $5.75, in small and large sizes; these are based around carrots or tofu, along with your basic garden salad. A platter of steamed vegetables with a salad is $5.50. Finish off with the above-mentioned "ice cream"; a baked cobbler of some variety is also usually on the menu. Everything's very simple here, but done quite well

South Fork Restaurant
- Martin Luther King Center, 449 Auburn Ave. N.E., Atlanta; 526-8920
- 737 Ralph McGill Blvd. N.E., Atlanta; 522-4809

Fans of the TV show "Dallas" will b in for a big surprise if they come to these cheap eats havens—which hap pen to share the name of J.R. Ewing's ranch. These are *slightly* small

Why go to a McChain when you can get a full meal here for under $

This is honest-to-goodness home cooking, whether it's a $1.79 fish fillet or a $2.50 fried chicken dinner. Choose from the many freshly made side dishes set up at the steam table—the real mashed potatoes and fried okra are especially good.

South Fork will please the kids (and whoever's paying for them) too, with grilled cheese sandwiches ($2.29), hamburgers ($1.79), and tuna salad sandwiches ($2.85).

The South Forks open up bright and early for breakfast, even offering specials for early risers. You can get two eggs, grits, bacon or sausage, a biscuit and toast, all for a tiny $2.49.

South Fork offers an additional bonus: If you buy any four meals in one week, they'll give you a fifth meal for free.

The South Fork on McGill is open weekdays from 6:30 a.m. to 4 p.m. only, while the MLK Center location is open seven days a week from 8 a.m. to 7 p.m.

Taco Mac
- 375 Pharr Rd. N.E., Atlanta; 239-0650
- 1006 North Highland Ave. N.E., Atlanta; 873-6529
- 771 Cherokee Ave. S.E., Atlanta; 624-4641
- 2120 Johnson Ferry Rd., Chamblee; 454-7676
- 1444 Oxford Rd., Emory Village; 377-2323
- 1570 Holcomb Bridge Rd., Roswell; 640-9598
- 5830 Roswell Rd. N.W., Sandy Springs; 257-0735
- 2845 Mountain Industrial Blvd., Stone Mountain; 621-3601

And other suburban locations
These guys claim that Buffalo wings were invented right here. Gee, wait'll the folks in Buffalo hear that. No matter—Taco Mac's spicy wings are for real, and they've also got the biggest beer selection this side of the Mississippi to wash them down. While the service can be slow as a sloth, Mr. C still thinks that the food and the prices make Mac a hit.

Appetizers include fried zucchini, cauliflower, or mushrooms for just $4 a plate; a jumbo basket of nachos with frijoles and cheese goes for $4.75. TM's guacamole salad is a mere $2.85. Basics include soft tacos for $1.55, super burritos for $3.25, quesadillas for $5.50, and chili for just $2.50; to go with these, beers from 28 different countries are reasonably priced, even though they come from as far away as New Zealand and the Ivory Coast.

Those Buffalo chicken wings come in sizes of ten for $4.75 or twenty for $7.05. Rustle them up in mild, medium, hot—or, for 50¢ extra, "Three Mile Island"-style. If you're having a party, here's an extra tip from Mr. C: You can get a 10% discount for platter orders of 250 wings or more.

Taco Mac has a kiddie menu too, with things like a burger and fries for $2.50, or a mini-fish and chips plate for the same price.

Timberlake Sandwich Shop
- 60 Luckie St. N.W., Atlanta; 525-5265

It'll be your lucky day when you eat at the 25-year-old Timberlake Sandwich Shop, located just a couple of blocks from the Peachtree Center MARTA stop. They call themselves "A New York style deli with southern hospitality", a description Mr. C found to be right on the mark.

Daily specials are super-cheap, like the the turkey breast sandwich ($2.50), egg salad sandwich ($1.75), and hot pastrami ($2.50). Cuban sandwiches sell big here, and come with a cup of black bean soup for $3.95. Any day, you can get a "soup and half-sandwich" deal for $2.95. And all sandwiches come with cole slaw and pickles.

Po'boys ($2.95), turkey ham ($2.50), mile-high Reubens ($3.95), kosher salami sandwiches ($2.95), and shrimp salad ($3.70) are also popular picks. Soup choices may include clam chowder, vegetable beef, chili, chicken noodle, and black bean, with some starting as low as just 90 for a cup.

Desserts, like New York style cheesecake ($1.50), carrot cake ($1.45), and devil's food cake ($1.45) won't set you back much, either. The shop's open weekdays only, until 4 p.m.

Wall St. Deli
- Peachtree Center Building, 303 Peachtree Center Ave. N.E., Atlanta; 223-6885 (fax 223-3354)
- Equitable Building, 100 Peachtree St. N.W. (Mezzanine floor), Atlanta; 681-5542 (fax 681-4652)

It's almost as busy in here as the floor of the stock exchange, but the food they sell is not a blue-chip commodity at all. Their super-fresh, salad bar has over seventy different items, rivaling even those of Lettuce Souprise You; it won't cost you an arm and a leg either. Each container costs up to $4.29 at the most—no matter how high you pile it with Wall St.'s regular salad bar items, or even the pastas and sauces, fruits, garlic bread, veggies, and delicious mini chocolate muffins covered with confectioner's sugar. Wow!

Other popular lunch choices include the "make your own" one-pound baked potato ($3.49), which you can stuff with various ingredients like cheese and broccoli; and the fresh sandwiches, like the "Bronx" (hot corned beef and pastrami with melted Swiss on rye) and the "Brooklyn" (hot roast beef, smoked cheddar, mild peppers with Russian dressing), each just $4.39. The "Vegetarian" (of no particular borough, apparently) is piled high with avocado, American and Swiss cheeses, sprouts, lettuce, tomato, peppers, onions, and mayo, all for just $4.09.

Soup choices include split pea, pinto bean, chicken noodle, black-eyed pea, and cream of spinach, plus chili, all starting at just $1.59 for the small size. Wall St. also offers "soup and half sandwich of the day" deals, starting at $3.99. For dessert, along with the above-mentioned muffins, Mr. C liked the peanut butter cookies (49¢ each); while cinnamon rolls, at $1.29 each, are also popular.

Many busy corporate types fax ahead their orders to save time. Mr. C has generously provided you with this insider trading info, above.

LITTLE FIVE POINTS
(including Ponce area, Virginia-Highland)

Addis Ethiopian Restaurant
- 453 Moreland Ave. N.E., Atlanta; 523-4748

Addis, in Little Five Points, is a most unusual and interesting—as well as inexpensive—way to dine. The heart of most any Ethiopian meal is not so much the cooked food itself, but the *injera* bread you use to eat it. This is a flat, crepe-like pancake; tear a piece off, and use it to pick up a portion of the various stews like lemon-marinated chicken and ginger root ($7.50), or beef in berbere (red pepper) sauce ($7).

Some of the other platters you can get with the bread include herbed lentils in berbere sauce ($5.50), yellow split peas with curry, green peppers, and herbs ($5), and vegetable stew with cabbage, carrots, and potatoes ($5.50). They're all yummy, and many are not too spicy-hot. Order a single entree per person at your table and share as you would in a Chinese restaurant.

Appetizers are also reasonably priced. Mr. C loved the pastry shells filled with cumin-spiced beef and green onions ($2.00 each). And all entrees are served with two vegetable side dishes, like gomen (spiced collard greens), bulgur (cracked wheat), or seneg karya (hot green peppers).

Here's where North Africa meets the American South—you wouldn't find collard greens in an Ethiopian restaurant in, say, New York City.

Addis's desserts include lemon sherbet and baklava ($1.95 each); sweet and simple. Addis is open from 4 p.m. to 10 p.m. Monday through Thursday, Friday 4 p.m. to 11 p.m., Saturday noon to 11 p.m., and Sunday 1 p.m. to 10 p.m.

American Roadhouse

- 842 North Highland Ave. N.E., Atlanta; 872-2822
- 1317 Dunwoody Village Pkwy., Dunwoody; 512-8114

Kitsch is king of the road at American Roadhouse. Heavily decorated with traffic signs, license plates, and even full-size, old-fashioned gasoline pumps, these folks work hard to imbue the restaurant with a sense of nostalgic fun. Mr. C found this style a bit forced, but all this memorabilia is certainly interesting to check out.

Of course, you may simply want to ignore it all and look at the vast menu instead, which is loaded with food that's as all-American as apple pie and Chevrolet. Breakfast is served from 7:00 a.m. throughout the day and evening; pull up to a plate of pecan waffles for $3.95, or a sausage and cheese omelette with home fries and a bagel for $4.25. They even have "Egg Beater" breakfasts with fresh fruit and a bran muffin ($3.95), as well as banana shakes and Slim-Fast shakes (now, *that's* American).

Lunch and dinner choices seem as endless as a Nebraska highway. A variety of burgers start at $4.50 and up, whether made from beef, turkey, or tofu; or, try the grilled chicken, bacon, and cheddar sandwich ($5.95), the pulled pork sandwich ($5.25), or—wouldja believe—a po'boy made with deep-fried oysters ($6.25).

There are also plenty of appetizers, soups, and salads. Three-cheese quesadillas are $2.95; blackened salmon pasta salad is $6.25; Roadhouse chili is $1.75 a cup, $2.75 a bowl.

Then, there are the "Blue Plate

Specials"—a dozen of 'em, priced about $2 lower at lunchtime than at dinner, but all quite reasonable. Chicken pot pie, one of Mr. C's favorites, is $5.50 at lunch, $7.50 at dinner; other meals include country-fried steak ($4.95/$6.95), homemade meatloaf ($5.25/$7.25), and trout almondine ($5.50/$7.50). These can get a bit pricey, but all plates do come with two side dishes, in over fifteen choices from Granny Smith applesauce to sesame carrots to Waldorf salad.

Big desserts range from apple pie (of course) to chocolate mousse pie, each priced at $2.75. Basically, ARH tries to cover all the bases, doing a decent job of having something for everyone. It's open seven days a week until 11 p.m., and an hour later on weekends.

Baker's Cafe

- 1134 Euclid Ave. N.E., Atlanta; 223-5039

Good gumbo! The Baker's Cafe is the place For creative Cajun favorites at fantastic prices. Breakfast, served from 7:30 a.m. to 11 a.m. weekdays, includes a Mr. C favorite: "Budget Helpers"! One includes two eggs and two bacon strips, with homefries or grits, toast, and coffee, all for just $2.95. Or two pancakes and coffee for $2.50 (blueberries and whipped cream are $1 extra).

Homemade buttermilk biscuits are just 50¢ a pop, and omelettes start at $2.95, again served with grits or homefries, and toast or a biscuit. Corned beef hash with eggs and toast is a steal at just $3.25, while a side of honey-cured ham is a sweet deal indeed at $1.50. Or take yourself to the bayou country with a Creole-sauce covered frittata with peppers and onions, served with French bread and homefries, all for $4.95.

Brunch, served on weekends from 9 a.m. to 2:30 p.m., features a (truly) jumbo fresh fruit bowl, topped with yogurt and granola, for $3.95; and eggs Sardu, a novel twist on ol' Benedict—with artichoke hearts, spinach, and Hollandaise sauce on an

English muffin, for $5.95.

Lunch and dinner specials include many unique creations. Start with a "mug 'a beans & rice" for $1.95; then move on to boneless horseradish-grilled chicken with homefries for $6.25, Creole eggplant lasagne for $5.95, Cajun catfish for $6.95, or jambalaya (chicken, ham, and Creole sausage with vegetables and rice) at $6.95. The Muffaletta sandwich (with ham, salami, cheese and olive salad) is a popular N'Awlins specialty at just $5.50. Vegetarians, meanwhile, will like the marinated tofu with homefries ($4.95).

Get the idea, y'all? It's good stuff. The Baker's Cafe is open weekdays from 7:30 a.m. to 11 a.m. for breakfast, 11:30-2:30 for lunch, and from 5-9 p.m. for dinner. It's open until 10 p.m. on Fridays and Saturdays, and closed on Sundays after brunch.

Bridgetown Grill
- 1156 Euclid Ave. N.E., Atlanta; 653-0110
- 689 Peachtree St. N.E., Atlanta; 873-5361

Hey now, this is where Ziggy Marley would eat if he visited Atlanta. The reggae's loud, the Caribbean dishes hearty and healthy. The Little Five Points location is pretty tiny inside, with lots of two-seater booths, but in good weather you can try to get a seat on the patio. The Midtown branch is roomier—with a dance club, the Groove Yard, up on the second floor.

Granted, Bridgetown's menu selection isn't exactly vast; but everything is prepared just right. At lunch, you can get a meal for under $5, like the $4.95 jerk chicken with tangy raspberry sauce (Mr. C's favorite), the vegetarian "garden burger" plate ($4.50), or apricot honey-glazed pork chops ($4.95). Seafood lovers should check out the grilled salmon salad ($7.50), piled high with pineapple, oranges, red onions, tomatoes, and jack cheese.

Prices on many of the same items go up slightly on the dinner menu. If you're just looking for appetizers, try the scrumptious pineapple egg brioche bread with guava butter ($1.25); or an order of *ceviche* ($4.50)—scallops marinated in lime juice with sweet peppers. All entrees are served with a side of black beans and rice plus an Island salad.

Cafe Diem
- 640 North Highland Ave. N.E., Atlanta; 607-7008

In what seems like no time at all, Cafe Diem has pretty much become the city's focal point for the trendy, artsy coffeehouse scene. The food is wonderful, and the coffee and desserts are intense; come to think of it, so are the waiters and waitresses. Don't come here if you're in a hurry. Come here to see and be seen—by everyone but the staff.

The reasonably priced menu runs to sandwiches, salads, and pastas, augmented by two or three daily specials. Start with a bowl of homemade vegetable soup for $2.50, or soup and a salad for $4.25; a fresh Caesar salad is $4.50, and you can top it with grilled chicken for another $1.25.

Sandwiches are served on large, crusty baguettes, with potato salad and fruit garnish; conveniently for this review, all are priced at $4.95. Turkey muenster seems a popular favorite, with lean, thin-sliced meat, melted cheese, alfalfa sprouts, tomato slices and honey-mustard dressing. The veggie melt, of course, also ranks highly with the black-clothing-and-patchouli-oil crowd.

Pastas start at the same price, for a platter of cheese tortellini in tomato sauce, served with garlic bread; special entrees check in a bit higher, but very much worth it—you may find dishes like chicken jambalaya ($5.45) or the frequent fave, chicken in red wine sauce ($7.95).

Do try to save room for the incredible desserts and coffees, or make a separate trip for these alone; raspberry linzertorte, mocha cappuccino cake, chocolate mousse cake...these vary from day to day, but as you can see, the choices sway heavily (very heavily) toward chocolate. Prices range from $2.50 to $3.50 for a good-sized wedge. Espressos come in single, double, latte (with milk added), mocha—about a dozen varieties in all, and available in decaffeinated form as well. Lots of herbal teas, too, for you non-caffaholics.

When weather permits, you have your choice of sitting inside, amongst the local artworks on the walls, or on the patio, amongst local scenery. The cafe is open every day, until midnight; and until 2:00 a.m. on weekends.

Calcutta Tandoori & Curry Restaurant
• 1138 Euclid Ave. N.E., Atlanta; 681-1838

Mr. C was asked to not print Calcutta's prices, but suffice it to say that you won't break your budget here, by a long shot.

Appetizers include goodies like Mulligatawny soup (lentils and spices), papadum bread, and tandoori chicken. Main courses include traditional shrimp, lamb, and chicken, in sauces made with tomato and pepper, coconut, or curry; these can be adjusted to your personal taste in the fiery spices department. Okra, mixed vegetables, spinach, mango chutney, and basmati rice are among the favorite side dishes.

Calcutta is open for lunch Mondays through Saturdays, and dinner every night of the week. Free parking is available at the Sevananda lot down Euclid Avenue.

Curry House
• 451 Moreland Ave. N.E., Atlanta; 688-0005

A popular Little Five Points hangout for adults (and not the skateboard crowd hanging out near the Point), Curry House will spice up your life without burning a hole in your back pocket.

Start off by trying their onion bhaji (fritters) or chana bhaji (spiced chickpeas) for $2 each. Mulligatawny soup (made with lentils) is also just $2.

Among the main dishes Mr. C liked were chicken and lentils for $6, tandoori chicken for $6.50, beef

curry for $6.50, and coconut shrimp for $7.50. There's also a variety of lamb dishes, spicy sauted vegetables, and different varieties of basmati rice, priced from $2-$6.50.

Desserts include traditional kulfi (light pistachio ice cream), and gulab jamun (syrup and cheese), for $2 a pop. Lassi yogurt drinks are $1.50, and mango lassi is just $1.75.

Curry House is open for lunch on weekdays only, and for dinner seven nights a week.

Deacon Burton's Soul Food Restaurant
• 1029 Edgewood Ave., N.E., Atlanta; 658-9452

You won't feel guilty after eating with Atlanta's deacon of soul food. The original Deacon Burton has left us, but this award-winning restaurant carries on just as it always has. Nobody should visit town without trying their incredible fried chicken. It's easily found across the street from the Reynoldstown MARTA stop, so you have no excuses!

Burton's is a simple, unpretentious family restaurant with old plastic tablecloths and mismatched chairs, and cafeteria-style steam tray service (tips are optional, but appreciated, at the register). There's no loud music, either, only the sizzling sound of frying chicken. Ambiance is not the priority here. The food is.

They don't even use any menus; trust Mr. C when he says that you can get a full meal here for under $4. A lunch of chicken, corn bread, okra, and iced tea is just $3.18. Fritters, baked beans, and pork chops are among the many other good bets. At breakfast time, long lines form for the grits, biscuits, and sausage.

Keep in mind that "waste not, want not" is the golden rule here; you'll be charged for any extra condiments like lemon slices or butter. But then, if you don't use these, it's a few more nickels in your own pocket!

Deacon Burton's Grill is open from 7 a.m. to 5 p.m. weekdays only.

Eat Your Vegetables
- 438 Moreland Ave. N.E., Atlanta; 523-2671

Attention veggie haters: You'll like EYV, really. They've been open since 1979 and definitely know what they're doing, offering vegetarian and non-vegetarian entrees that even a seven-year-old could like.

Yes, they have tofu sandwiches; but barbecued tofu on whole wheat ($3.75) is not your average dry deal! Focaccia pizza pie ($4.25), veggie burgers ($3.75) and miso soup ($1.75) are other tasty non-meat choices. Meanwhile, this is not strictly a vegetarian restaurant. Grilled chicken ($4.50) and turkey burritos ($4.95) come highly recommended, too. Lunch is the true bargain here; dinners get a bit more pricey, though the carefully prepared food and hearty portions still make this a good value.

As if the food isn't impressive enough, popular local acoustic musicians like Rusty Johnson, Cass Kennedy, and Caroline Aiken play Thursday through Sunday nights, and a deck overlooking L5P adds to the fun. EYV is a smoke-free establishment; it's open for lunch Monday through Friday, for dinner Monday through Saturday, and for Sunday brunch from 11 a.m. to 3 p.m. In between lunch and dinner, a limited menu is offered with dishes like hummus and fresh vegetable plates.

Eats
- 600 Ponce de Leon Ave. N.E., Atlanta; 888-9149

New in '93, this fun joint on Ponce—across from City Hall East—is something like a world-beat cafeteria, or perhaps a funky soup kitchen. The atmosphere is comfortably downscale, enough to attract a mixed crowd of yuppies and hippies alike. Antique photos and paintings by local artists hang on the walls. There is an old, upright piano, which may or may not work. It matters little, as the sound system plays an eclectic mix ranging from Billie Holiday to Bob Marley to zydeco.

Walk up to one of several stations along the side of the restaurant, and grab a tray; one area serves up pastas, another meats and veggies, another is a bar where you can get a bottle of Samuel Adams or New Amsterdam beer for just $2.15 (domestics are $1.65; pitchers are available too) or a bottle of "Cheep Chianti" for a dollar.

The pastas begin with your choice of spaghetti, ziti, linguine, or fettucine; top this with basic marinara for a mere $2.30, pesto for $2.75, alfredo for $3.35, or marinara and sausage for $3.50. All come with garlic bread. Hey kids, it's chow time.

At the meat counter, the choice is even simpler: Jamaican-style jerk chicken. It's delicious, marinated with that tantalizing blend of mild spices and sweet cinnamon. Have it all by its lonesome—an entire half-bird—for $3.75; or as a platter with white rice, black beans, and real cornbread (as denoted by the kernels of real corn), all for $4.50. This may be the largest plate of home-cooked food you'll ever get for a price like that.

There are a few other offerings, including a vegetarian plate (natch), but you have the basic scenario. For dessert, have a slice of applebread for 80 cents (who else gives you dessert for less than a dollar?) with an espresso for 90 cents. Cappuccinos are $1.30. All this makes for a cool hangout, but alas, the food lines shut down at 10:00 p.m.

Euclid Avenue Yacht Club
- 1136 Euclid Ave. N.E., Atlanta; 688-2582

This couldn't be further from the typical haughty yacht-club atmosphere. It's more of a yacht *pub*, really meant for you darts lovers and Harley owners.

Preserved swordfish hang from the ceiling, and paper money from all over the world decorates the wall behind the bar. There's a noisy, chaotic crowd that hangs out here, for both the fun and the food.

Menu favorites include the $3.50 chef salad, their award-winning Brunswick stew ($2.50 a cup), Philly cheese steak sandwiches for $4.25, and the "Land Shark" sandwich (for fans of that classic "Saturday Night Live" skit) stuffed with ham, roast beef, turkey, and cheese for $5. Appetizers, like the tasty quesadillas ($3.25), are good catches, too.

Lunch and dinner specials change weekly, but these may include delicious blue-plates like the Club's grilled pork chops, served with squash, onions, and bread, for $4.95; also, smaller deals such as burritos for $3.25, or a bowl of black beans and rice for just $2.75.

The Club opens at 11 a.m. daily (noon on weekends) and has a license to stay open until 4 a.m. every night (3 a.m. on Saturdays). If things are slow, though, they'll put 'er in to port a little earlier than that. Can you blame them?

Everybody's Pizza
1040 North Highland Ave. N.E., Atlanta; 873-4545
1593 North Decatur Rd., Emory Village; 377-7766

Everybody loves Everybody's, not

MR. CHEAP'S PICKS
Virginia-Highland

✔ **Everybody's Pizza**—If everybody tried Everybody's Pizza, the world would be a much happier place. Their pizza crisps are *amazing*.

---

just for their great pizza, but for their starving-student prices, too.

One bonus right off the bat here is that you can choose from thirty amazing toppings—including basil, shrimp, sesame seeds, rosemary potatoes, feta cheese, and sun-dried tomatoes. Put 'em all on thick or thin crusts, too. A plain individual-size pie is just $3.25, going up to $5.85 for one with any four toppings. To be totally trendy, pesto sauce is 65 cents extra on the small, and $1.95 more on a large pizza.

You can also order one of Everybody's own combinations, which have been getting rave reviews for quite some time. How about one with shrimp and artichoke ($10.25), Florentine (with four kinds of cheese, spinach, and tomato slices for $8.25), or spicy-sweet jerk chicken for $9.75.

Or, try their lasagna ($6.25), fettucine carbonara ($6.75) or penne primavera ($6.50). Garlic-parmesan breadsticks are $1.25 for a small and $2.35 for a large order. And, just as with the pies, you can concoct your own salad, starting at $1.75.

Everybody's also serves beer and wine. They're open seven days a week, closing at 1 a.m. Fridays and Saturdays. Everybody got that?

Fellini's Pizza
- 2813 Peachtree Rd. N.E., Atlanta; 266-0082
- 923 Ponce de Leon Ave. N.E., Atlanta; 873-3088
- 422 Seminole Ave. N.E., Atlanta; 525-2530

- 4429 Roswell Rd. N.E., Atlanta;
  303-8248
- 1991 Howell Mill Rd. N.W.,
  Atlanta; 352-0799

And other suburban locations
While the scene at this pizza place
would make for a great movie location, this is not a recommended place
to take grandma or little tykes—it's
loud, crowded, and the staff tends toward the slightly surly, under-employed-college-grad variety. The
decor of brightly painted cinder-
blocks and oddball celebrity portraits
(Elvis lives!) helps the wild, Fellini-
esque atmosphere along. The pizza's
great, though, and two generously-
large slices can fill you up for under
three bucks.

Plain slices are just $1.10, believe
it or not. Medium-sized cheese pies
go for $7.50, and medium "white piz-
zas"—no tomato sauce, and plenty of
garlic—are $11. Extra toppings (just
the basics are offered here) are $1
each. Cheese calzones are $4.50.
Wash it all down with 16-ounce domestic draft beers, which will put
you back just $2.

While Fellini's is a take-a-number-
and-we'll-bring-your-order-to-your-table joint, they do keep tip jars at the
counters emblazoned with the label
In lieu of decent wages. While it's optional, most customers do tip here,
either at the counter or at their tables
after they've eaten.

George's
- 1041 North Highland Ave. N.E.,
  Atlanta; 892-3648

As Mr. C always says, bars make the
money on the booze, so they can afford to serve food cheap. It certainly
pays to try places like George's for
lunch and dinner. It has been a Vi-Hi
fixture since 1961, and no wonder.
They've got nearly three dozen beers
to pick from, plus good food to boot.

George's is a popular watering
hole for the Emory crowd (and Mr. C
does mean *crowd*), so you may be
hard-pressed to get a good seat on
weekends. It's worth a venture,
though, for thick sandwiches like
French-dip roast beef ($4.95), the

reuben ($4.75), and chicken filet
sandwiches ($3.95). Basics like
grilled cheese ($2.25), or ham, tur-
key, corned beef, or roast beef sandwiches ($3.25 each), can be served
up with French fries for just $1 extra.

Quarter-pound hot dogs sell for
$2.25, pasta salad is $3.95, and a big
bowl of cheese-topped chili is $2.95.
Giant half-pound hamburgers
($5.75), come with fries, cole slaw,
potato salad, or onion rings. Popcorn
shrimp, served with the same choice
of sides, is $5.50. Good food, good
hangout.

Good Ol' Days Cafe
- 3013 Peachtree Rd. N.E., Atlanta;
  266-2597
- 401 Moreland Ave. N.E., Atlanta;
  688-1006
- 5841 Roswell Rd. N.E., Sandy
  Springs; 257-9183

Good Ol' Days is a combination pool
hall, sports bar, and cafe, with wildly
painted wall murals, pink and green
vinyl tablecloths, and colored ceilings. With loud pop music pouring
out of oversized speakers, it's a popular hangout with the twenty-some-
things; casual, fun, and fit for limited
budgets.

Appetizers tend toward the unusual, like fried whipped potatoes for
$2.50, and sticky pots—cinnamon,
brown sugar, and butter baked into
flowerpot-shaped bread, topped with
granola, cream cheese, and honey—
for $1.95. During Mr. C's visit, apps
were all half-price during happy hour

If you've got more than the
munchies, try their chicken quesadillas ($3.99) or New Orleans chicken
($5.49). The six-ounce "Uncompli-
cated" burger is a lean $3.49. Many
of these have the signature flowerpot
worked into their presentation. Is the
name of this restaurant a thinly veiled
reference to the 1960s "flower
power" era? Are any of its patrons
old enough to figure this out? Ah,
nevermind.

Good Ol' Days also makes cheap
breakfasts like no one else. Eggs, any
style, are 60¢ each (80¢ for Eggbeaters); a bagel and cream cheese is

$1.25; and the McFlowerpot sandwich (egg, cheese, and bacon on that specially shaped bread) will brighten your day for only $2.50. There are also classics like Belgian waffles ($3.15) and three-cheese omelettes, served with parmesan-topped sauteed red potatoes and toast, for $3.85. Good Ol' Days stays open well into the night, too, often with free live music from local rock bands.

La Fonda Latina

- 2813 Peachtree Rd. N.E., Atlanta; 816-8311
- 1150-B Euclid Ave. N.E., Atlanta; 577-8317

Mr. C is fond of La Fonda for its incredible Mexican dishes and fun atmosphere. You can get stuffed (with food, that is) for under $6 or so, since this restaurant/bar makes big bucks off of its liquor sales.

An individual paella, the traditional Spanish casserole, is $5.95; it comes chock-full of calamari, chicken, shrimp, sausage, and peppers, served over rice. Gazpacho goes for $2.75, and big cheese quesadillas with a snappy salsa on top are $3.50. La Fonda's Cuban sandwich is just $4.25. Add a side of frijoles or extra tortillas for $1, and finish your meal with chocolate or vanilla flan ($2.25) or sweet guava cheesecake ($2.50).

La Fonda Latina is a noisy, people-watching kind of restaurant. Don't even think about bringing a reading book with you. One recent Friday, in fact, Mr. C spotted a semi-famous band eating at the L5P branch before their late show at the Point; so, keep your eyes open when you eat here. Even if there aren't celebrities to check out, there are plenty of people trying to look just as interesting. Not to mention the decor of fountains, hanging beads, and statues.

La Fonda Latina is open seven days a week, serving daily until 11 p.m. The L5P branch has some much-appreciated free parking in the back, too.

Majestic

- 1031 Ponce de Leon Ave., Atlanta; 875-0276

MR. CHEAP'S PICKS
Ponce Area

✔ **Eats**—Downscale becomes trendy at this cool cafeteria, from the folks who brought you Tortillas.

✔ **Manuel's Tavern**—This sprawling, watering-hole hangout serves up good beer, good company, and good food cheap.

"Food That Pleases" are the words emblazoned in neon along the curving facade of the Majestic. It's a good thing that this is true, since the surroundings here will hardly make you feel like royalty. Little seems to have changed at this luncheonette since its opening in 1929, including quite possibly some of the staff; but, before you conclude that this is going to be an unfavorable writeup, read on.

Y'see, Mr. Cheap happens to love a good dive. And this *is* a good one. If you feel the same way about fading, homey, come-as-you-are, leave-a-bit-heavier places, then Majestic is one for the books. Certainly this book, anyway.

For starters, the joint is open 24 hours a day. That's great already. Another plus is that you can get breakfast at any time of day or night, like freshly browned pecan waffles for $3.50; add ham, bacon, or sausage for another dollar. Omelettes, eggs, pancakes, you know the territory.

Lunch and dinner entrees are served from 10:30 in the morning until 9:00 at night, and these are the true bargains. Most are in the $4-$5 price range, including your choice of two vegetables on the side. Chicken breast filet with gravy, and London broil in mushroom sauce, are both $4.40; Southern fried chicken is $4.50, while a grilled ham steak in red-eye gravy jumps up to $5.25. Choose a pair from candied yams, fried zucchini squash, pickled beets, creamed potatoes, or even macaroni and cheese, among others, to go along with your meal.

Of course, you can always get sandwiches (hot open-face roast beef, $3.95), burgers, salads, and a variety of other entrees at all hours. Homemade vegetable soup is a winner at $1.50 a bowl. And try to save room for fresh-baked apple pie, a mere $1.45 a slice, or $2 with ice cream; you can even take home a whole pie for just $5.50. Ah, but then, you'd miss that Majestic ambiance.

Manuel's Tavern
● 602 North Highland Ave. N.E., Atlanta; 296-6919

For almost forty years, this restaurant and bar has been a popular hangout—and something of an antidote to the trendy neighborhood in which it somehow co-exists with chi-chi cafes and boutiques. Perhaps the yuppies who frequent Manuel's are the sort who find "downscale" to be trendy, too. For that matter, this *was* one of the places in which Steve Martin was spotted during some filming he recently did in town. Oh, it's so hard to know where anything stands these days.

Anyway, it's no hardship to get a good meal cheap here, that's for sure. Like so many pubs, Manuel's can afford to give the food away, thanks to its busy bar scene. There's a large menu of casual eats, from such appetizers as chili and cheese nachos ($4.75), Buffalo wings ($3.95 for a plate of ten), and deep-fried mushrooms with horseradish ($3.75), to bowls of potato-leek soup or chili for $2.25 each.

There are lots of sandwiches, both hot and cold. Have a chicken salad melt for $4.25, a nice, big Reuben for $4.75, or a fresh, six-ounce burger with chips for just $2.95. Can't beat that!

Bigger dinners include Manuel's smoked honey chicken, a tasty half-bird for $5.95; a half-rack of ribs for $6.25; and, on Friday nights only, an eight-ounce prime rib roast for $7.25. Dinners all come with "Texas Toast" and your choice of potatoes, vegetables, or black beans and rice.

Needless to say, there are lots of great beers on tap, along with a full bar. The restaurant itself has a bar room, with several other dining rooms which sprawl in all directions from this first (most important?) room. The atmosphere is always lively, bustling with folks who are clearly enjoying themselves.

Murphy's Round the Corner
● 997 Virginia Ave. N.E., Atlanta; 872-0904

This Virginia-Highland landmark is open for breakfast, lunch, and dinner, and offers traditional Irish fare, vegetarian items, and unique entree combinations at super prices. You'll doubtless leave here stuffed, especially if you try one of their many decadent desserts.

For breakfast, pecan waffles are $3.25, and two eggs any style—with Irish potatoes and a biscuit or muffin—are just $2.95. A New Mexico breakfast tortilla (this *is* an Irish restaurant, don't forget), is served with spuds or grits for $4.75, and it can be made with tofu instead of eggs if you prefer. Fresh-baked honey wheat doughnuts, 55 cents each, make at least an attempt to "healthen up" the South's favorite food.

Lunch specials, served weekdays from 11:30 a.m. to 4 p.m., offer red beans and rice for $5.25, boneless grilled rainbow trout for $4.95, and chicken quesadillas for only $5.95. The quiche of the day is $5.95, and Mr. C liked the three-salad sampler, a unique deal, also $5.95.

Dinner choices include more traditional Irish specialties. Almond raspberry chicken, served with rice and veggies, is $8.95, a gingered roast beef sandwich is $5.25, and Murphy's pesto hoagie sandwich is $5.

Dieters beware: Murphy's has some of the best-looking cakes, pies, and dessert treats in the city. Triple layer carrot cake is $3.25 a slice; as are "trio chocolate torte," raspberry white chocolate cheesecake, and sour cream apple pie.

If you get a Murphy's card, and get it stamped every time you spend $3 or more, you'll get a coupon for a $5 discount off your next meal when the card is fully stamped ($54 worth).

Murphy's is open Mondays through Thursdays from 7 a.m. to 10 p.m., Fridays 7 a.m. to 12:30 a.m., Saturdays from 8 a.m. to 12:30 a.m., and Sundays from 8 a.m. to 10 p.m. There's free designated parking in areas around the restaurant, and additional free parking evenings after 6 p.m. in the Highland Hardware parking lot at the corner of Los Angeles and North Highland Avenues.

St. Charles Deli
- 752 North Highland Ave. N.E., Atlanta; 876-3354
- Loehmann's Plaza, 2470 Briarcliff Rd. N.E., Atlanta; 636-5201

No need to pass "Go" and collect $200 before landing on *this* St. Charles. Brunch, lunch, and dinner are all good deals—if you can find a seat, that is, in this restaurant which takes New Orleans streetcars for its inspiration. Things sure get crowded, especially on weekends, so you may be wise not to "board" during rush hours.

Breakfast is served from 8-11 a.m., and includes treats like fluffy Belgian waffles for $4.25, make-your-own-omelettes starting at $5.25, and eggs with corned beef hash for $4.50. Mr. C enjoyed two eggs, with bagel, home fries, and juice (a mere $2.95); even with the busy crowd, everything was quickly delivered piping hot by one of the most unflappable waiters that Mr. C has ever seen in these parts.

Lunch features good ol' N'Awlins choices like the huge Muffaletta sandwich—cappicola ham, Genoa salami, mortadella and provolone cheese, topped with an antipasto salad, all on an Italian roll for $6.25. Try a softshell crab sandwich on an onion roll ($6.25), or the filling Philly cheese steak ($5.95). And there's always egg salad ($3.75), not to mention potato or macaroni salad, liverwurst, corned

beef, and tuna salad sandwiches on pumpernickel, challah, whole wheat, Italian, or onion breads. Stanley and Stella never had it so good!

Get the office together and have a meal delivered—it's free on orders of $30 or more.

Soul Vegetarian
- 879-A Ralph D. Abernathy Blvd. S.W., Atlanta; 752-5194
- 652 North Highland Ave. N.E., Atlanta; 875-0145

The very name of these restaurants sounds like a contradiction in terms. Soul food is not generally thought of as being light and healthy. One imagines some kind of tofu ribs or such. In fact, the menu does not differ much from that of any vegetarian restaurant; it's the atmosphere, complete with jazz music, a very homey welcome, and a bit of scripture on the walls which sets the place apart from the city's other sprout palaces.

Everything here is all-natural and cholesterol-free, right on down to the soy ice cream that's always offered as your meal is cleared. The entrees themselves, in an unlikely turn, tend toward Middle Eastern delicacies. "Soups from Jerusalem" feature marak alfunah, a garlicky split-pea; it's only $1 a cup, or $1.90 a bowl. Add some cornbread—yes, this works— for another buck.

Most of the entrees are salads and sandwiches, with one daily lunch or dinner special added, like spaghetti with a tomato-vegetable sauce. At $7.95, the dinners include salad and cornbread. Otherwise, sandwiches are all $3.70; make any one into a platter for $5, adding a side salad and hand-cut French fries or onion rings—however healthy *those* can be. The unique specialty of the house is something called kalebone, made from wheat grain (plenty of protein) into a tasty concoction which can be made into burger patties or sliced into a gyro-like pita sandwich. Flavored with a few different sauces, it's moist and filling.

Salads range from $2.75 to $5.75, in small and large sizes; these are based around carrots or tofu, along with your basic garden salad. A platter of steamed vegetables with a salad is $5.50. Finish off with the above-mentioned "ice cream"; a baked cobbler of some variety is also usually on the menu. Everything's very simple here, but done quite well.

Taco Mac

- 375 Pharr Rd. N.E., Atlanta; 239-0650
- 1006 North Highland Ave. N.E., Atlanta; 873-6529
- 771 Cherokee Ave. S.E., Atlanta; 624-4641
- 2120 Johnson Ferry Rd., Chamblee; 454-7676
- 1444 Oxford Rd., Emory Village; 377-2323
- 1570 Holcomb Bridge Rd., Roswell; 640-9598
- 5830 Roswell Rd. N.W., Sandy Springs; 257-0735
- 2845 Mountain Industrial Blvd., Stone Mountain; 621-3601

And other suburban locations
These guys claim that Buffalo wings were invented right here. Gee, wait'll the folks in Buffalo hear that. No matter—Taco Mac's spicy wings are for real, and they've also got the biggest beer selection this side of the Mississippi to wash them down. While the service can be slow as a sloth, Mr. C still thinks that the food and the prices make Mac a hit.

Appetizers include fried zucchini, cauliflower, or mushrooms for just $4 a plate; a jumbo basket of nachos with frijoles and cheese goes for $4.75. TM's guacamole salad is a mere $2.85. Basics include soft tacos for $1.55, super burritos for $3.25, quesadillas for $5.50, and chili for just $2.50; to go with these, beers from 28 different countries are reasonably priced, even though they come from as far away as New Zealand and the Ivory Coast.

Those Buffalo chicken wings come in sizes of ten for $4.75 or twenty for $7.05. Rustle them up in mild, medium, hot—or, for 50¢ extra, "Three Mile Island"-style. If you're having a party, here's an extra tip

from Mr. C: You can get a 10% discount for platter orders of 250 wings or more.

Taco Mac has a kiddie menu too, with things like a burger and fries for $2.50, or a mini-fish and chips plate for the same price.

Tapatio Restaurante Mexicano

- 1091 Euclid Ave. N.E., Atlanta; 688-8903

You've heard of the "Treasure of the Sierra Madre"? Here it is. This cozy, colorful restaurant near the Variety Playhouse is a bit of buried Mexican treasure right in Little Five Points.

You have a good choice of entrees; or, you can create your own combination from over twenty side orders. Cheese quesadillas ($4.50), or guacamole and chips ($2.95) make good starters.

Dinner entrees may not be named too originally (Numero Uno, Numero Dos, etc.), but are definitely good values. Number Five combines a chicken and cheese enchilada and a beef burrito with chili relleno, rice, and beans, all for $6.95; while Number Fifteen offers a big taco and burrito platter with rice and beans for $6.75. Or, dine *a la carte* with tacos ($1.50 each), tostados ($3.25), seafood enchiladas ($3.50), beef or bean burritos ($3.25), or tamales ($2.50). An oversized seafood salad, laced with crabmeat and shrimp, is $7.50.

For every two people dining at your table, you'll get a complimentary basket of nacho chips. Tapatio also sells domestic and imported beers, wine, sangria, and margaritas. Desserts are also good deals, like Mexican fried ice cream ($2.75), and fried dough ($1.75).

Lunch specials, served weekdays from 11:30 a.m. to 3 p.m., are worth a trip in themselves. A taco with rice and frijoles is $3.25, a taco with a chicken enchilada, rice, and beans is $3.95, and a vegetarian enchilada, chalupa, and a taco is $4.50.

They're open Monday through Thursday from 11:30 a.m. to 10 p.m. Friday and Saturday until midnight, and Sunday from 4-10 p.m.

Tortillas
- 774 Ponce de Leon Ave. N.E., Atlanta; 892-3493

This place takes low-maintenance dining to the max—or rather, to the Mex—and really has some fun with it. The food here is super-cheap, but also super-fresh; and, best of all, they have A Gimmick. When you order your food at the counter up front, they'll give you your drinks and appetizers, which you bring to your table. They also give you a toy; a large, plastic iguana, perhaps, or a racing car. When your hot food is ready, they'll bring it to you by finding the right toy. Cute, huh? It adds an extra element of fun to this raucous, no frills restaurant.

The menu, geared toward fast and easy prep, could hardly be simpler. Choose a soft taco, burrito, or "super burrito" (which adds rice on the inside). Choose the filling—chicken, pork, beef, or vegetarian beans and cheese. If you wish, choose some extras, like guacamole or hot sauce. The whole entree can cost you as little as $1.85, for a bean and cheese taco; and no more than $5 or so for

the works. In fact, there is even a cheese and tomato quesadilla for just $1.55, grilled up nice and crunchy, and folded over into something like a big, Mexican slice of pizza.

All of the food sampled by Mr. C and his dining companion was very fresh, especially the guacamole, made with chunks of avocado and topped with diced tomato. Get an order with lots of salty chips for $2.85, or a fresh greens salad for $1.40; add any of these to a taco or burrito, and you've got a full meal. There's also a decent selection of not-overpriced beers on hand.

Unlike some of the other funky industrial-approach burrito joints around, Tortillas attracts a mixed young crowd of students and locals. The place was packed on a recent weeknight, and everybody was definitely having a good time. Check out the upstairs deck too, especially during good weather when they roll up the plastic screens for a lovely view of scenic Ponce. As Mr. C's friend pointed out, a cold beer and a taco up here on a warm evening can be a fine state of affairs.

MIDTOWN

Bangkok Restaurant
- 1492-A Piedmont Rd., N.E., Atlanta; 874-2514

Hidden (to the uninitiated) within the rather ordinary shopping center of Ansley Square, Bangkok lays claim to being the very first Thai restaurant in the entire state of Georgia. Having opened in 1977, this may well be true. Back then, Bangkok was a brand-new president—doesn't *that* feel like a long time ago! Did any of us know, back then, of the Thai food revolution that was to come?

Anyway, Bangkok is a small restaurant with a surprisingly large menu, and these folks certainly know what they're doing. With its natural wood decor and comfortable high-backed chairs, the place has a kind of

humble elegance—proving, as some places do, that "less is more." And their service, from the moment they greet you at the door, is extra-friendly (even if you are just ordering take-out) and quick.

Most entrees are in the $6-$8 range. These include, naturally, several different varieties of curry dishes, from "Ruby curry" ($6.75), made with beef or chicken, to "Jade shrimp curry" ($7.95). Spice is considered nice all over the menu; other piquant dishes include "Spicy catfish" ($7.50), and "Sorcerer's Apprentice" ($6.75), a frighteningly hot stir-fry of chicken and veggies in chili sauce. For less spicy tastes, "Gingerine" ($6.25) is a zingy but not tongue-lashingly hot ginger chicken dish; and "Octet" ($6.95) mixes chicken, shrimp, and vegetables.

Vegetarian, rice, and noodle dishes, by the way, are even cheaper and every bit as good. Traditional pad Thai ($5.95), curry fried rice with beef or chicken ($5.25), and "Market Place Noodles" ($5.95), also with beef or chicken, are heaping platters indeed. Even the "Mee-Krob" appetizer, crispy fried noodles with pork, shrimp, and bean sprouts with an orange-tamarind sauce, is huge and only $5.50. Plenty of other good appetizers and soups, by the way, as well as two dozen lunch combination specials all under $5.00.

Also in the Ansley Square shopping center, across from Bangkok, is another longtime Asian favorite, **The King and I** (1510-F Piedmont Rd. N.E., Atlanta; 892-7743). The surroundings here are even less to sing about, but "getting to know you" in this case means getting to know good, filling food that's super-cheap and served up super-quick. The menu is a mixture of Chinese and Thai specialties. They also have a second, newer location in the Buckhead area, at 4058-C Peachtree Rd., N.E.; telephone 262-7985.

The Black-eyed Pea
- 1901 Peachtree Rd. N.E., Atlanta; 351-5580
- 4370 Roswell Rd. N.E., Marietta; 971-7708
- 925 Holcomb Bridge Rd., Roswell; 640-1877
- 2590 Spring Rd. S.E., Smyrna; 319-7166
- 1905 Rockbridge Rd., Stone Mountain; 413-6042

And other suburban locations
The Black-eyed Pea is a classic family restaurant, the sort where the waiters and waitresses are accustomed to handling parties of oh, say, twelve people at a time. Seniors and short-on-cash college students also swear by this chain, with its generously-sized servings of food at low prices.

Fill up on red beans and rice, brought to you with fresh cornbread for just $2.39, or BEP's cheese-broccoli soup ($1.85). Massive $\frac{1}{3}$-pound hamburgers on whole wheat buns are $3.99, as are their popular chicken fried "steakwiches." Mr. C liked the veggie platter, giving you five (yep, *five*) dishes with rolls and cornbread for $4.99. Skin-on mashed spuds, fried corn, turnip greens, and the broccoli casserole are among Mr. C's faves. Wash it all down with a quart of Lipton iced tea for 99¢, plus free refills to boot; they have a full liquor license, too.

Most daily specials, like liver and onions, chicken and dumplings, and beef tips, are priced $6 or lower, served with two veggies and cornbread. And (as if you'll have room), the homemade apple pie ($2.25) and banana pudding ($1.65) are both good bets.

The good ol' days are very much alive here, with old-fashioned quilts, antique washboards, and black-and-white photographs covering the walls. And don't worry about finding a parking spot in busy Buckhead—this location offers plenty of free parking in the back. Black-eyed Peas are open Sundays through Thursdays from 11 a.m. to 10 p.m., and Fridays and Saturdays from 11 a.m. to 11 p.m.

Bobby and June's Kountry Kitchen
- 375 14th St. N.W., Atlanta; 876-3872

Bobby and June's is a true, family-run roadside diner. It's a working-class version of the Silver Skillet just a few blocks down the street, which is so downscale as to be considered trendy. There's no kitsch at the Kountry Kitchen, where lifelong waitresses in beehive hairdos make sure you are well taken care of. The building itself is a wooden cabin whose interior is divided into a small counter and a couple of rooms filled with booths. Several of Bobby's prize fishing catches are stuffed and mounted on the walls, along with steer horns (which, presumably, he did not catch himself), old gee-tars, and vintage soda bottles.

The Kitchen starts up early—6:00 a.m., six days a week. Have a couple of eggs—"Any way you want 'em, honey"—with several strips of bacon, two biscuits, and grits, for $3.45. Lots of folks also stop in for a variety of "breakfast sandwiches" to go; everything here is made up right quick.

For lunch and dinner (the place closes up at 8:00 p.m.), the specialty is barbecued ribs. Have a rack with one vegetable for $4.75, with two for $5.25, three for $6.10, are all by their lonesome for a paltry $3.25. The veggies change daily, but may include rice and gravy, turnip greens, fried okra, pinto beans, stewed squash, corn on the cob, and so on. Other meat platters also vary as daily specials, like steak and gravy, beef tips and rice, fried chicken...you know, the basics. These tend to be a bit less than the ribs, starting at $4 for a plate with one veg.

Homemade soups are a heartwarmingly cheap $1.85 per bowl, and of course there are sandwiches and burgers as well. And don't forget a slice of pecan pie afterwards, just $1.25, or apple cobbler for a mere 80 cents. Can you beat that for homemade desserts? Mr. C doubts it.

The restaurant closes after lunch on Saturdays, and all day Sundays.

Bridgetown Grill

- 1156 Euclid Ave. N.E., Atlanta; 653-0110
- 689 Peachtree St. N.E., Atlanta; 873-5361

Hey mon, this is where Ziggy Marley would eat if he visited Atlanta. The reggae's loud, the Caribbean dishes hearty and healthy. The Little Five Points location is pretty tiny inside, with lots of two-seater booths, but in good weather you can try to get a seat on the patio. The Midtown branch is roomier—with a dance club, the Groove Yard, up on the second floor.

Granted, Bridgetown's menu selection isn't exactly vast; but everything is prepared just right. At lunch, you can get a meal for under $5, like the

---

MR. CHEAP'S PICKS
Midtown

✔ **Brother Juniper's**—Gigantic breakfasts and lunches, laid-back atmosphere.

✔ **Red Light Cafe**—In the Midtown Outlets, unlikely though it is, you'll find one of Atlanta's best coffeehouses—serving incredibly fresh, creative food.

✔ **Silver Grill**—Huge "meat and three" platters in a comfy diner.

✔ **Touch of India**—Add a touch of spice to your life without burning a hole in your wallet. In Buckhead, too.

$4.95 jerk chicken with tangy raspberry sauce (Mr. C's favorite), the vegetarian "garden burger" plate ($4.50), or apricot honey-glazed pork chops ($4.95). Seafood lovers should check out the grilled salmon salad ($7.50), piled high with pineapple, oranges, red onions, tomatoes, and jack cheese.

Prices on many of the same items go up slightly on the dinner menu. If you're just looking for appetizers, try the scrumptious pineapple egg brioche bread with guava butter ($1.25); or an order of *ceviche* ($4.50)—scallops marinated in lime juice with sweet peppers. All entrees are served with a side of black beans and rice plus an Island salad.

Brother Juniper's

- 1037 Peachtree St. N.E., Atlanta; 881-6225

A Midtown fixture since 1978, Brother Juniper's is a breakfast and lunch haven for vegetarians and other laid-back folks. They come here for the relaxing, airy atmosphere as much as for the healthy food.

The place is not strictly vegetarian, by any stretch. Juniper's offers a "Decent Breakfast" which consists of far more than its name implies—two eggs, plus choices of bacon or sausage, toast or biscuits, grits or home fries with cheese, all for just $4.25. They make a scrambled egg biscuit for the commuter crowd; it's just $1, and a lot less greasy than the ones at McDonald's.

Or, sit and have "Le Popular Low Cal Breakfast," with a dry-scrambled or poached egg, toast, cantaloupe or orange juice and cup of yogurt and blueberries, all for $2.95. For the same price, you can try the "Bishop's Platter" of two pancakes and two eggs—add bacon or sausage for a dollar extra.

The lunch hours fill up early for deals like the "Friar Tuck Sandwich," made with avocado, Swiss cheese, bacon, tuna, and sprouts. Just one half of this creation, for $2.95, may be enough for some appetites, though of course you're welcome to get the whole thing for $5.50. A huge chef salad is $4.75; top it with shrimp for $2 extra. Homemade chili is just $1.45 a cup, and delicious vegetarian soups are $1.50 a bowl. You certainly won't feel sinful if you finish up with Brother J's homemade frozen yogurt, which is just $1.25.

Breakfast is served from 7 a.m. to 11 a.m., and lunch from 11 a.m. to 2:30 p.m., Mondays through Fridays only.

California Pizza Kitchen

- 181 14th St. N.E., Atlanta; 892-4220
- Lenox Square Shopping Center, 3393 Peachtree Rd. N.E., Atlanta; 262-9211

And other suburban locations
There's more than just pizza to be found at this growing national chain—things like potato leek soup, fresh pastas, lasagna, and Thai chicken. Don't get Mr. C wrong—the pizza's okay, too, especially the rosemary-chicken-potato pie with white wine and lemon for $8.95 (plenty here for two to share), and the southwestern burrito, made with lime,

black beans, mild chilies, cheddar cheese, tomatillo salsa, sour cream, and white sweet onions (also $8.95). All pies are available without cheese, baked on either traditional or honey-wheat doughs. And unlike lots of other pizza houses in town, CPK uses no MSG. And that's A-OK with Mr. C.

Other entrees include angel hair, penne, or spaghetti, topped with tomato-herb sauce for $5.95, and spinach fettuccine with chicken, tri-color peppers, red onion, and cilantro in a tequila-lime sauce for $8.95. It's a large platter. Desserts are a bit pricey, in the unlikely event that you have room; try sharing a tiramisu ($4.50), Myers' Rum chocolate pecan pie ($3.95), apple crisp ($3.95), or tartufo—gelato balls rolled in chocolate chips, and served with vanilla bean sauce or berry puree ($3.50).

Cha Gio

- 966 Peachtree St. N.E., Atlanta; 885-9387

This Vietnamese restaurant in the midst of Midtown is a hit for its fantastic spring rolls. Come here for Cha Gio's lunch and dinner specials, which make it easy to sample several dishes without spending your life savings.

Start off with a pair of those spring rolls for just $1.25, available in meat or vegetarian varieties; and six fried chicken wings are just $1.95, and Vietnamese-style wonton soup is only $1.50.

You won't break the bank with main dishes like sliced beef with ginger root and snow peas ($5.95), sweet and sour chicken ($5.75), or lemon grass pork chops ($6.50). Marinated red snapper, served with vegetables and rice, is only $6.50, and five spicy shrimp dishes sell for under $7.

Daily lunch specials include a $4.50 buffet, with fried rice and a choice of two meat dishes, or noodle dishes and crepes. And the restaurant's special dinners—for two, three, four or five people—are a great pick if you're out with friends. For well under $10 a person, you're served wonton soup, spring rolls, sliced beef with broccoli, sweet and sour shrimp, and fried rice, with a dessert of Vietnamese egg custard (*Banh flant*) or lychee fruit, and tea.

Cha Gio's chef will be happy to prepare any special dish request, or to tone down the spices in the hotter menu items. Cha Gio is open from 11 a.m. to 10 p.m., Mondays through Saturdays, and from noon to 9 p.m. Sundays.

C. W. Long Cafeteria at Crawford Long Hospital
• 449 Peachtree Rd. N.E., Atlanta; 686-4411

Who says you have to work there to eat there? As far as hospital food goes, this stuff is actually good, and the staff sees to it that there are actually some healthy menu items. The clear-your-own-table cafeteria setting also means there's no tipping necessary, saving another buck or two.

Breakfast, served until 10 a.m., features items like salmon croquettes for $1.79, biscuits for just 35¢ (take *that*, McDonald's!), and pancakes for a mere 70¢ a plate. Make your own breakfast combo with plain grits (45¢ an order), turkey patties (49¢ apiece), hash browns (55¢) and sausage links (39¢).

For lunch, help yourself to the salad bar and pay just 19¢ an ounce. Chicken salad sandwiches are $1.70, pimento cheese sandwiches go for $1.39, and honey ham sandwiches are $1.99. Vegetarian burgers are also just $1.99, and grilled cheeses are a whopping (hardly!) $1.09. Frozen yogurt, available in six flavors, is just $1 for a big bowlful.

The cafeteria is open from 7:30 a.m. to 4 p.m. Monday through Friday.

Delights of the Garden
• 136 Marietta St. N.W., Atlanta; 524-5744
• 1081 Juniper St. N.E., Atlanta; 876-4307

For a change, a restaurant claiming to offer "a new concept in eating" is probably correct. Delights of the Garden does standard vegetarian cooking

one better; this food is not even cooked. Fruits, vegetables, and grains "cooked only by the sun" are the staple ingredients here, and they're turned into a surprising array of truly creative dishes.

For instance, the kitchen turns out an item called "Veggie Tuna." There is, of course, no fish involved; it's made from carrots, food-processor-shredded to within a millimeter of their lives. These are then mixed with a touch of mayonnaise and seasonings just as tuna would be, and the result has exactly the same moist texture—and even, to some degree, the taste—of tuna salad. And there's certainly no need to worry about it being dolphin-safe!

You can have this as an appetizer, on a bed of *very* fresh lettuce, for $2.50; or, as part of several combination platters. Another unusual appetizer is "Sprout Spaghetti" (also $2.50), in which raw bean sprouts stand in for cooked pasta; y'know, from a slight distance, they even look the same. A good-sized bed of sprouts is topped with a sauce of ground tomato and spices, plus a couple of grain "meatballs"—and again, it all works.

The trick here, it seems, is one of helping the veggies go down by preparing them in sauces and spices which give them a lot of taste. The most frequently-used staple is kush, a nutty grain derived from bulgur wheat. On its own, kush is rather dry and, well, grainy; but when the chef spikes it with a various flavors, it becomes a succession of delicious, and certainly healthy, entrees. You can have "Spicy Kush," which has a tangy bite to it; "Nori Rolls," kush wrapped in seaweed sheets just like sushi; or a mild kush which you can flavor up with their delicious house dressing, a smoothly blended spinach tahini sweetened with chopped raisins. (Mr. C doesn't even *like* raisins, but he sure loved this sauce.)

Not everything is unfamiliar. You'll find marinated vegetables, garden salads, chips and salsa, guacamole, and other yummy foods. Wash them down with fresh juices or herbal teas; perhaps they'll have whipped up a batch of their special almond cocoa, too.

The pricing is very simple, as these and other creations are combined into several different platters ("Garden Sampler," "Nubian Delight"), which are all available in small ($4.95) or large ($6.95) sizes. Each plate has three to six items; you can even create your own sampler. Believe it or not, this stuff is really filling. And, not only is it all good for you, but the fully explanatory menu even notes which vitamins and minerals you get from each food. The friendly staff, all dedicated to this kind of food, will patiently answer any questions you may have.

In his many travels, Mr. C had never before seen many of these dishes; if you're into healthy eating (heck, even if you aren't), he suggests that you give this place a try.

Erica's Cafe
- 1027 Peachtree St. N.E., Atlanta; 885-9011

For Caribbean cuisine on the cheap, venture no further than Midtown, because Erica's is where it's at. Owner Erica Nyong, a native of Nigeria, adds an African accent to the dishes; her fruit salsas, made from mango, papaya, and oranges, are worth the trip all by themselves. But do try them on the food.

Appetizers include fried escargot for $4.99, fish cakes for $2.99, and yellow or green plantain slices for just $1.99. Grilled shrimp in a pita pocket is also $4.99, and the "Herbed Island Salad," with shrimp, chicken, or tuna, mixed with seasoned broccoli and carrots and served in a pineapple boat, is a fun treat at $6.25. Who says salads have to be boring?

Entrees include Jamaican jerk chicken for only $5.25, and chicken covered in peanut sauce is just $1 more. Spicy deep-fried conch seasoned with cayenne, cilantro, and curry is only $7.99, and sauted shrimp, scallops, and fish in a ginger sauce is $8.99. Caribbean marinated

beef is $6.99, and "Island Omelettes" filled with chicken, beef or seafood—with a spicy tomato sauce—go for $6.25.

All entrees are served with two side dishes, like African-style spinach, cous cous, rainbow pasta, or red rice; plus a roll or peppery cornbread muffin. Children's portions are also available.From the purple ceiling to pink-painted fans to the odd artwork like one entitled, "My Darling Metropolis", there's no shortage of atmosphere, which is matched by the far-out food. Erica's Cafe is open from 11 a.m. to 11 p.m. Mondays through Thursdays, 11 a.m. until "whenever" on Fridays, 4 p.m. 'til whenever on Saturdays, and 4 p.m. until 11 p.m. on Sundays.

Fox's Stage Door Deli & Saloon
- 654 Peachtree St. N.E., Atlanta; 881-0223

With a name like this, where else could it be but next to the Fox Theatre? Fox's Stage Door makes a great place to have dinner before the show, dessert after the show, or lunch anytime. In fact, the restaurant only opens for dinner on evenings when there is an event next door (about 200 nights out of the year), but it serves lunch every weekday, regardless.

The atmosphere is half the story. Located in this ornate, nostalgic old building, FSD has the artsy, sophisticated mood you might easily expect from a cafe near Carnegie Hall or the theatres of Broadway. A small grand piano is tucked into a corner by the front door, and popular melodies unobtrusively waft into the air. Tables are small and intimate, lending themselves to good conversation or a touch of romance. Lighting is mellow and warm, coming from small lamps spread around the room. At the center, there is a small, handsome bar.

What's missing is the New York prices. At lunch, there is an array of sandwiches from $3.95 to $5.95, all stuffed with Boar's Head meats (a well-known butcher in New York): Black Forest ham, honey glazed turkey, lean corned beef, and pastrami. On the hot side, you've got your Reubens, your open-faced roast beef, tuna melts served on sliced bagels, and more. All come with sides of cole slaw, potato salad, macaroni, or French fries.

There are always several hot pasta dishes, priced at $4.95, like fettucine Alfredo, or such daily specials as eggplant Parmigiana, served with soup or salad. Speaking of which, there are plenty of these as well: Chef's, Caesar's, a tomato stuffed with chicken salad, and so on.

Dinners get a bit more expensive, though for much the same menu. Open-faced roast beef and turkey sandwiches are $7.95, served with French fries; daily pasta and chicken dinner specials are $8.95 and $9.95, respectively.

After your meal—or perhaps instead—have a slice of New York cheesecake ($2.75) and a caffe latte ($2). If you are planning to dine before the show, be sure to arrive early enough to allow for the crowds of people who are doing the same thing. There are plenty of tables; but, as large as the place is, the Fox itself is so much larger.

French Quarter Food Shop
• 923 Peachtree St. N.E., Atlanta; 875-2489

This place is almost as noisy as its namesake section of New Orleans, and the food's just as good, too.

Start your meal with etouffee, a dish of seasonal seafood and vegetables served with Louisiana white rice ($4.95), or perhaps an order of red beans in sausage stock ($1.95), or kettle-cooked potato chips (75¢). The "Garden District" salad, with Mandarin oranges, roasted pecans, and poppy seed dressing, is yummy for $2.95, while the chef's gumbo of the day (chicken, seafood, etc.) is also $2.95.

Among the main courses, fried oysters are a good bet ($6.25), as is the muffaletta sandwich (salami, baked ham, provolone and Swiss cheeses, with antipasto, on French

bread), at $5.95. Beers and wines are reasonably priced, too.

The above-mentioned red beans and rice, with andouille sausage or blackened chicken tenderloins, is $6.95, while other traditional N'awlins dishes include shrimp creole and classic jambalaya. Either one will fill you up for $7.95.

Kids under age six can try the kiddie plate, with fried chicken fingers or shrimp, plus Cajun fries and mandarin oranges, for $2.95. As if you'll have room for dessert, allow Mr. C to suggest the pecan praline cheesecake ($3.25) or creme caramel ($2.25).

Lunch and dinner are served six days a week. The French Quarter is closed on Sundays.

Frijoleros
• 1031 Peachtree St. N.E., Atlanta; 892-TACO (8226)

You'd have to say that "low" is the operative word here. Low, as in prices; also selection, decor, hospitality....but hey, you wanna be coddled? Go eat at the Ritz! This is *cheap* dining, remember. The tip alone at such a high-falutin' establishment could buy you an entire meal here. And you don't even *have* to leave a tip at this place, though you're welcome to do so.

And besides, not everything is low here. The volume of the heavy rock music, for instance—that's way up there, whether it's on the sound system by day or from one of the local bands which play in the newly expanded bar area by night. The quality of the food is right up there, too. Tacos and burritos are the staples of the limited menu; they are hearty, stuffed with beans, cheese, salsa, and your choice of additional fillings. The basic bean and cheese, in either taco or burrito form, is $2.45 for the small size, $3.45 for the large; add green chili ($2.95/$3.95), barbecued beef or chicken ($3.25/$4.25); and so on. Mr. C found the small size to be nearly a meal in itself, but you can always add a salad ($1.75), black beans and rice ($1.95) or other appetizers on the side.

Draft beers are just $1.75, with pitchers available; there are some good imports here, including Tecate and Foster's Lager. And yes, there are a *few* other entrees, such as fajitas with beef or chicken ($3.25 small, $4.25 large), and a "loaded" quesadilla ($3.25) with the same basic choices. But, as you can see, everything's simple here. It's a great place for speedy take-out service, which may also be a good idea if the acid-inspired decor isn't your cup of salsa.

Gorin's Diner
- 1170 Peachtree St. N.E., Atlanta; 892-2500

This is the site of the original Gorin's, and with its shiny stainless steel exterior, the diner may make you think you've just stepped back into the 1950s.

The prices on the classic menu items will take you back in time, too. At breakfast, the "Midtowner" gives you two eggs any style, plus your choice of bacon, ham or sausage; grits or potatoes; and toast or a bagel, all for an incredible $2.65. That's cheaper than staying home!

For lunch or dinner, beer-battered onion rings in a basket big enough for two or three people to share are $2.95. Gargantuan deli sandwiches, made with sliced turkey, chicken salad or tuna salad on an egg roll, served with a choice of side dishes like wild rice or cole slaw, are $5.25. A grilled cheese sandwich with tomatoes, cucumbers, mushrooms, and sprouts is $4.95, including French fries; same with the California burger, topped with guacamole and Monterey jack cheese, for $6.25.

Gorin's, meanwhile, has built its reputation just as much from ice cream and soda fountain treats. Vanilla syrup- flavored Cokes, root beer floats ($2.25), apple pie, mud pie, and numerous other classic homemade desserts are mostly priced under $3. These have also become the focus of Gorin's franchise chain, turning up all over the city; but this location is the one with the full menu and full charm.

Gorin's Diner doesn't allow smoking of any sort, so you can breathe easy here. It's open at 7:00 a.m. daily, serving until midnight Sundays through Thursdays and until 2:00 a.m. Fridays and Saturdays. Hallelujah late-nighters!

Lettuce Souprise You
- 595 Piedmont Ave., N.E., Atlanta; 874-4998
- 2470 Briarcliff Rd. N.E., Atlanta; 636-8549
- 245 Pharr Rd. N.E., Atlanta; 841-9583
- 3525 Mall Blvd., Duluth; 418-9969
- 1475 Holcomb Bridge Rd., Roswell; 642-1601
- 5975 Roswell Rd., Sandy Springs; 250-0304
- 1109 Cumberland Mall, Smyrna; 438-2288

Here's a place after your humble author's own heart. At Lettuce Souprise You, one price gets you unlimited trips to their extensive salad bar, as well as the all-you-can-eat baked potato bar and pasta bar, plus homemade muffins, cornbread, and soups, and fresh fruit. Whew! Lettuce be thankful for places like this!

The salad bar is super-fresh and preservative-free; it features spinach, broccoli, tarragon tuna, spicy crab and pasta salad, and pineapple, along with dozens of other choices. Soups change daily, but always include at least one vegetarian recipe, such as potato-leek or lentil. Egg drop, chili, and vegetable soups are featured often, too.

How can they afford to offer such a bargain, you ask? Well, they do work on keeping costs down. For one thing, Lettuce Souprise You requests that you eat only in the restaurant— they don't allow anyone to leave with more than a muffin. If you'd like something to go, they will charge you for it. Well hey, that's only fair!

Meanwhile, the price for this entire sumptuous buffet is just $5.50 at lunchtime; $6.50 for brunch and dinner. Another cheap deal: Their "frequent buyer" club entitles you to a free meal when you've had twelve lunches, six dinners, or four brunches. Can it be any surprise that Lettuce Souprise You rates so highly with Mr. C?

Mary Mac's Tea Room and Restaurant

- 224 Ponce de Leon Ave. N.E., Atlanta; 876-6604
- 2205 Cheshire Bridge Rd. N.E., Atlanta; 325-7777
- 4431 Hugh Howell Rd., Tucker; 621-9935

And other suburban locations
Zell Miller and Jimmy Carter have eaten at Mary Mac's, considered to be Atlanta's oldest home cooking restaurant. Nothing's fancy here, really—you actually fill out the food slips yourself, since the waitresses are too busy helping the scores of folks who flock here at lunchtime.

Choose from a choice of entrees (baked chicken, country fried steak, baked fish almondine, beef tips on creole rice, sauteed chicken livers, etc.) with two side dishes for $6.50. Sweet potato cobbler is a popular choice, but Mr. C is partial to the cheese-whipped potatoes. Included in the price are tea, coffee, or punch, Mary Mac's cornbread, and ice cream in your choice of five flavors.

Meals are served in a flash; also, half portions can be ordered for those customers "under 12 or over 90." The Ponce location is currently open only for lunch, but may be reopening for dinner by the time you read this.

Meatballs

- 1365 Peachtree St. N.E., Atlanta; 874-2691

Meatballs is a tiny, eight-table place near the Arts Center MARTA stop. You'll really be lucky to get a seat during the lunch rush when workers from Midtown Plaza create a line that spills right out the front door. You can wait and watch the cooks toss their pizza pies into the air, or order ahead for take-out.

The breakfast menu isn't expansive, but it isn't expensive, either. The prices, for this stretch of Midtown, are simply super. Bagels are just 75 cents, croissants are just 70

cents, and a cuppa joe is only 60 cents.

You'll love the lunch prices, too. The house specialty—a meatball super sub—will more than fill you up for just $3.50. Calzones or lasagna are $4.50 each, and pasta salad for only $3.95. Spaghetti with marinara sauce is just $3.95 ($4.25 with meatballs), and that includes a side of garlic bread. Large-size pizzas start at $9.50, and can be topped with spinach, pepperoni, peppers, and, of course, meatballs; or, grab a slice for $1.25.

Don't miss dessert, either—big, yummy cream cheese brownies ($1.50) and chocolate chip cookies (90 cents) are, as they say, "to die for." Meatballs is open Mondays through Fridays from 7:30 a.m. to 4 p.m. only. They also offer catering.

Mick's

- 557 Peachtree Rd. N.E., Atlanta; 875-6425
- 2110 Peachtree Rd. N.W., Atlanta; 351-6425
- Peachtree Center, 229 Peachtree St. N.E., Atlanta; 688-6425
- Lenox Square Shopping Center, 3393 Peachtree Rd. N.E., Atlanta; 262-6425
- Underground Atlanta, 75 Upper Alabama St. S.W., Atlanta; 525-2825
- 116 East Ponce de Leon Ave., Decatur; 373-7797

And other suburban locations
Get to Mick's for one of the best milkshakes in town, great burgers, super desserts, and creative drinks. Stretching from Underground Atlanta to Buckhead and beyond, this yuppie haven seems determined to make the next siege of Atlanta a culinary one.

Prices here are not the absolute cheapest around, but you do get a lot of delicious food for the money. Start off with real fried green tomatoes ($5.75), chili-smothered French fries ($3.95), grilled carrots and broccoli ($2.50), or a cup of soup in flavors like tomato or "baked potato" ($1.95).

A half-pound hamburger, hickory grilled, with a generous side of fries or pasta salad, is $5.95. You can top it with cheddar or mozzarella cheese, guacamole, chili, barbecue sauce, or cracked pepper and mustard for 80¢ extra. Cheese-topped grilled boneless chicken is $7.50, and corn and to-mato linguine with garlic bread is $6.95. Mick's chicken Reuben will completely stuff you for $7.95.

Do try to leave room for dessert, though. You'll probably want to share one of these monstrosities with a friend. Try the Oreo cheesecake ($3.95), the Giant Banana Split ($4.75), or Mr. C's favorite, the chocolate cream pie ($3.75). Yummy! Strawberry shortcake, homemade chocolate layer cake, and Heath Bar ice cream pie will all make delightful ends to your meal, and all are under $4 apiece.

Besides the desserts, Mick's is known for its unusual mixed drinks—like "Frozen Pink Lemonade," "Frozen German Chocolate Cake," and "Peasant Coffee" (spiked with brandy, Grand Marnier, Kahlua, amaretto, and dark creme de cacao, and topped with whipped cream). These will doubtless not be cheap, but they are good. Most branches of Mick's have a separate bar area.

Ming Wah Chinese Restaurant
- 1371 Peachtree St. N.E., Suite 103, Atlanta; 875-6585

While many restaurants have come and gone on this stretch of Peachtree near Midtown Plaza, Ming Wah has been around since '72. And no won-der, with super deals like their week-day lunch buffet: For $3.95, you get plenty of rice, an eggroll, and a choice of dishes such as chicken chow mein, almond chicken, chicken wings, moo goo gai pan, or moo shi pork. For just a dollar more, you can visit the all-you-can-eat buffet, which includes a salad bar and your choice of traditional classic Chinese dishes.

Among the menu entrees: Egg foo young, served with white rice, ranges from $5.25 (for plain vegetable) up to $6.25 (with shrimp). Vegetable lo mein is $4.95, and the Ming Wah spe-cial Cantonese chow mein—with

chicken, shrimp, pork, and pan-fried noodles—is $7.95. Tasty almond chicken is $6.25, and spare ribs with black bean sauce are $6.75.

One frown from Mr. C: Extra for-tune cookies are 15¢ each. Come on, we all know this is the most impor-tant part of any Chinese restaurant meal! But then, they do have some-thing unusual for dessert—eggroll fried ice cream ($1.55), kind of a var iation on the dessert often found in Mexican restaurants. Open seven days a week.

Original Pancake House
- 1937 Peachtree Rd. N.E., Atlanta; 351-3533
- 4330 Peachtree Rd. N.E., Atlanta; 237-4116
- 2321 Cheshire Bridge Rd. N.E., Atlanta; 633-5712
- 501 Johnson Ferry Rd. N.E., Marietta; 977-5013
- 5099 Memorial Dr., Stone Mountain; 292-6914

The Original Pancake Houses sure won't leave you in the poor house. James Beard did name this one of the top ten restaurants in America, but you'd never know this from the prices. Quality runs high here—they use fresh juices, extra large Grade AA eggs, and pure whipping cream, plus all the cooking is done in pure butter.

The pancake recipe is a carefully-guarded secret, with good reason. They're light and fluffy, and just $3.55 an order. Georgia Pecan Waf-fles ($4.80) are delicious. If you're truly starving, Mr. C suggests the om elettes, served with three buttermilk pancakes, plus grits or toast, all for $6.95; or a four-ounce beef tender-loin steak for $4.50. Other good bets include French crepes with straw-berry topping ($5.25). Side dishes in clude sweets like cinnamon applesauce ($1) and imported lingon berries in butter ($1.75).

Junior plates are available for chil dren under ten. Two slices of French toast ($2.60), and three pancakes ($2.50) are served with milk, choco-late milk, or hot chocolate.

Meanwhile, to paraphrase the old orange juice commercials, "it's not just for breakfast anymore." OPH also serves a lunch menu of hamburgers ($4.25), soups (plus soup and half-sandwich specials for $4.95), and hot dogs (two for $2.95), along with salads and chili.

Senior citizens always get a 15% discount here, and police and firemen also receive a discount off their meals. The Original Pancake Houses are open from 6:30 a.m. to 2:30 p.m. weekdays, and from 7 a.m. to 3 p.m. on weekends.

Picnic Basket Deli

- Georgia Federal Bank Building, 1447 Peachtree St. N.E., Atlanta; 876-4213

Ok, this Midtown deli doesn't have baskets and blankets (there's a TV playing soap operas instead), but the hearty sandwiches are as good as if you'd made them at home. They also serve super breakfasts for you "gotta run" types. Egg biscuits are under a buck—so are the blueberry, banana nut, raisin bran and chocolate chip muffins. Super-fresh bagels are just 85¢. And a stack of three pancakes costs—get this—$1.25. Add some hash browns for just 50¢ more.

For lunch, the Basket's sandwiches are available hot or cold, on ten different types of bread. Ham and cheese ($2.80), liverwurst ($2.50), pimento cheese ($1.85), pastrami ($2.95), and chicken filet ($2.75) sandwiches are definitely priced right. Gyros, souvlaki, falafel and other Greek favorites are all available for under $3. Mr. C liked their Philly cheese steak sandwich ($2.75), which actually comes Atlanta-style on a hoagie roll.

For extra-large appetites, try the gourmet specials, all priced under $4. "The Dome" is piled high with turkey, cheese, ham, lettuce, and tomato on an onion roll; and the "Olympic Turkey" on rye with lettuce, tomato, and Thousand Island dressing, is just 3.50. All of these are served with potato chips or a salad.

At these prices, you can afford to stick around for dessert, too. New York or Black Forest cheesecakes are just $1.25 a slice, and the fresh fudge brownies are a treat at 99¢ each. Hot coffee's just 50¢ too. The Deli is open from 7:30 a.m. to 6:30 p.m., Mondays through Fridays only.

Red Light Cafe

- 553-I Amsterdam Ave. N.E., Atlanta; 874-7828

Whether you need to fortify yourself after a day of shopping at the Midtown Outlets, or you've discovered this place as a worthy hangout on its own, the Red Light is a marvelous recent addition to the Atlanta cafe scene. Yes, it's next to the shops; yes, with such cavernous high ceilings, it might have been a warehouse too. But its owners have managed to turn the space into an artfully cozy room, with mission-style wooden tables and chairs, a counter offering today's newspapers, and darkly atmospheric lighting.

Claiming to present "righteous California cooking," this is indeed a very West Coast mix of coffeehouse, restaurant, and music club, all at the same time. Sip a cup of strong Sumatra roast or espresso; have a sandwich, a full meal, or some homemade pastry; and peruse the artworks by local artists on the walls. Pick up a book or a board game from one of the side tables. Whatever, it's, you know, cool.

The food itself is phenomenal. Every ingredient is fresh, from the crisp and colorful garden salad to delightfully creative and delicious entrees. Mr. C was ecstatic over "Angel Hair alla Checca," thin spaghetti tossed with wedges of tomato, basil, and fresh garlic; it's topped with mozzarella and romano cheeses, all of which make a wonderfully tasty combination. Pastas are the only real entrees; otherwise, the menu consists of interesting nouvelle sandwiches and salads, like "corn-fed ham" with pesto, on wheat or sourdough bread, served with a garnish of fresh fruit for $5.25; the Garden sandwich, like, totally California, a mix of fresh vegetables in a parmesan vinaigrette; not to mention pesto boboli pizza ($4.25) and turkey black bean chili ($4.50). Oh, and peanut butter and jam sandwiches with apple or banana for $2.25.

Food is served from 5 p.m. on Tuesday, Wednesday, and Thursday; from noon on Friday, Saturday, and Sunday. No closing times are posted, but the cafe is usually open until 3:00 or 4:00 in the morning—and that includes the kitchen! If you haven't heard about this cafe yet, or have been meaning to check it out, Mr. C urges you to do so.

Rocky's Brick Oven Pizza
- 1770 Peachtree St. N.E., Atlanta; 876-1111
- 3210-A Roswell Rd. N.E., Atlanta; 262-ROCK (7625)

And other suburban locations
Yo. Rocky's has fought the good fight to gain a share of Atlanta's burgeoning pizza market, and the result is lower prices for you. Brick-fired ovens produce a slightly smoky-flavored, crunchy European pizza, and there are lots of fresh, unusual toppings to jazz these up. Homemade mozzarella and impeccably fresh ingredients have helped Rocky's win international awards for their food; and it's been voted the best inexpensive restaurant in town by Fodor's Guides.

Make up your own individual pizza (prices start at $4.95), by topping it with fried breaded eggplant, Italian sausage, sauteed chicken, or other goodies, for $1 each. Rocky's big Neapolitan (thin-crust) pie, enough for three people to share, starts at $14.95; Sicilian-styles, enough for four people, are $17.95. These gargantuan pies make this a good place to come with the gang.

Some of Rocky's more creative combinations include "The Gardenia"—broccoli and artichoke hearts, white glazed garlic sauce, mozzarella, gorgonzola, tomatoes and pesto. "Chicken Bianca Oreganato," with fresh garlic, white wine, red onions, and lemon, and "Eggplant Florentine" pizzas are also good choices.

They have great calzones here, too. All are priced at $8.50 each, such as the "Beau Bock," stuffed to overflowing with salami, prosciutto ham, pepperoni, provolone, and cappicola. Rocky's offers delivery on orders over $10.

Silver Grill Restaurant
- 900 Monroe Dr., Atlanta; 876-8145

The Silver Grill may be the quintessential Southern roadside diner. It's been around for forty years or more; it's simply staggering to think of how much hash has been slung by this meal-a-minute joint in that time. Actually, what gets served up here the most seems to be good ol' southern fried chicken—plump, meaty breasts of it, deep-fried to a crackly crunch. For $6.25, one of these will be the centerpiece to a platter, along with your choice of three cooked vegetables. Plus a basket of fresh baked rolls and cornbread. Plus coffee. Full yet?

The veggies change daily, but you'll usually see things like real mashed potatoes and gravy, lima beans, cole slaw, creamed white corn, mustard greens, and perhaps their "Pear and Cheese Salad"—you can even get a platter of just sides, your choice of four, for $5. Mainly, though, people go for the basic "meat and three." In addition to the chicken, that may include country fried steak, veal cutlets, or pork chops, all for the same $6.25. Or, shoot the works with filet mignon for $7.

If you have a smaller appetite than these hearty and heavy meals would suggest, perhaps you should look elsewhere. Well, that's not entirely true; there are sandwich versions of the fried chicken or steak, each $2.75; as well as hamburgers for $2.50, and grilled cheese sandwiche for $1.75. These may possibly help you save room for dessert. Peach cobbler is the specialty of the house (did you guess?), topped with your choic of one other fruit, such as apple or cherry, for $1.25. Throw a scoop of ice cream on it for $2.75. Hey, you may bust a gut here, but you sure won't bust a wallet.

Sit at the old-style counter, and you can watch what appears to be a culinary circus moving in fast-forward mode. Service can be brusque at times, like the lunch rush, but it never fails to be brisk as well. When they can catch their breath, the staff can be quite friendly. The place may not win any prizes for decor, but it's clean, bright, and definitely funky. Open for weekday lunch and dinner only; Mondays through Fridays from 10:30 a.m. to 9:00 p.m.

The Silver Skillet
- 200 14th St. N.W., Atlanta; 874-1388

Here's another of Atlanta's great greasy spoons, serving up hot breakfasts and meat-and-veg lunches in a delightful setting of yellow and olive green. It's a particularly hot spot on weekends, for a mixed crowd of dressed-down yuppies, students from nearby Georgia Tech, and older folks who've been finding the Skillet a comfortable and dependable place for over thirty years.

The place opens at 6:00 a.m. on weekdays, an hour later on weekends. You can belly up to the counter, or sidle into a booth, and begin your day with a couple of biscuits and gravy ($2.50; add a scrambled egg for an extra fifty cents). The gravy is thick and creamy, with just a dash of black pepper. Two eggs and bacon, any way you like 'em, are $3.85; and just about all breakfast dishes include your choice of grits, toast, and gravy, or a biscuit on the side. For brunch, if you're supremely hungry, try the weekend special of two pork chops, two eggs, grits, and biscuits—all for $5.95. Better be prepared to lay low somewhere for a while, though.

Which brings us to lunch. All the classics are here—country fried steak, baked or fried chicken, chicken and dumplings, each of which are $4.75 with two vegetables. Broiled Cajun catfish, same price, seems to be the only concession to the yupsters. The vegetables offer many choices, from potatoes baked, creamed, or au gratin, to broccoli cas-serole or macaroni and cheese. And if you're just looking for a quick (but equally heavy) bite, Skillet burgers are $2 (cheeseburgers $2.50), and the Skillet country ham sandwich is $3.95. Add a cup or bowl of home-made vegetable soup, or finish off with a slice of ice box pie, and you shouldn't have to eat again for a week.

The Silver Skillet only serves until 3:00 p.m. on weekdays, 'til 1:00 on Saturdays and 2:00 on Sundays. During the week, you can also eat in "The Little Skillet," which is part of the same building; it too has a counter and tables, not to mention some actual silver in its decor.

Sitar
- 884 Peachtree St. N.E., Atlanta; 885-9949

Alas, there are no sitar players to serenade you here, at least there weren't any when Mr. C dropped in; but there sure is plenty of good, cheap Indian food in this eatery, lo-cated in a rather desolate stretch of Midtown.

Sitar is a popular place (despite its lack of air conditioning). The restau-rant's name was actually inspired by the soothing music of the sitar, and the wait staff does see to it that each customer is treated to a special, relax-ing meal.

Lunch specials, served with rice and dessert of the day, are priced no higher than $3.75. These may include dishes like tarka-dal (mixed vegeta-bles and lentils) for $3.25, or chicken curry and vegetables for just $3.75. Both are served with samosas (vege-table-stuffed crispy pastries). Other cheap (but good!) choices include the "Light Lunch" special, with chapati bread with spiced mixed veggies ($3.25), or the regular menu's al-mond lamb ($4.95) and spiced shrimp ($5.25).

Side dish choices feature creamy smooth spinach and cheese ($3.75), Bombay aloo (spicy potatoes) for $3.50, or stuffed paratha bread filled with potatoes and peas ($1.50).

Desserts include homemade

mango sherbet ($2) and mango lassi ($1.50). Gulab jamun, Indian deep-fried cheese balls in syrup, are also a good finish to a meal at $1.50 each. Some of these are included in the lunchtime specials.

Sitar is open for lunch every day but Sunday (with specials on week-days only), and for dinner seven nights a week.

Springy's
• 710 Peachtree St. N.E., Atlanta; 607-0021

Hey mon, if you want real (but cheap!) Jamaican food, get yourself to Springy's for lunch. Dinnertime gets a bit pricier, though the values are good; but the lunch hour is where the real deals are.

Jerk chicken tenders will start your meal off right for $3.95; jerk pork is $4.50. (Jerk's a tasty, sweet blend of grilled spices—not your boss!). Homemade soups, like beef or red kidney bean, are just 95¢ a cup, $1.95 a bowl. Salads are jumbo-sized, like the "Caribbean," with jerk chicken or pork, cheese, and pineapple ($6.50), the shrimp and spinach ($6.50), or the "Chef's Special" (smoked turkey, ham, cheeses, and pineapple, $6.95). Grilled fish sand-wiches are $6.50, fried fish filets (of telapia fish) are $6.95. Oxtail, as tra-ditional a Jamaican delicacy as it is southern, is served with red beans and rice for $6.95. During Mr. C's visit, the special of the day was enough to feed an army—cod fish and callaloo, jerk chicken, "journey cakes," fried plantain, vegetable salad, and rolls, all for $8.95.

Desserts feature goodies like creme caramel or Jamaican bread pudding, flavored with rum, each $2.95. Springy's also features Ameri-can and Jamaican jazz music on cer-tain nights of the week (see listing under "Music"). Call ahead for up-coming shows. They're located right in the Fox Theatre district of Mid-town.

Touch of India
• 962 Peachtree St. N.E., Atlanta; 876-7777

• 2065 Piedmont Rd. N.E., Atlanta; 876-7775

You'll wind up with a touch more money in your pocket if you eat at this restaurant with locations in and just north of Midtown. The prices are right up Mr. C's alley; yet, the super samosas and tandoori dishes have at-tracted such celebrities as Mick Jag-ger, Sade, and Emilio Estevez.

Indian-style chicken fritters are $2.95, and prove Mr. C's theory that all ethnic groups really work from the same ideas. Mild lentil soup, or spicier Mulligatawny soup, is $1.95 a bowl. Chicken curry, $6.50, is avail-able in three spice levels; and beef sheek kabab is $6.95. Sag aloo (spin-ach with potatoes) is $4.95; add some chapati bread for just $1.

Weekdays from 11:30-2:30, you can take advantage of the $4.25 lunch special ($3.95 for vegetarian dishes). The choices change from day to day, but usually include samosas (turnovers) or pakuras (fritters), a curry dish or other main entree with rice, and the sweet of the day to quell the spices (like homemade ice cream or rice pudding).

Touch of India also sells beer and wine. They're open for lunch Mon-day through Saturday from 11:30 a.m. to 2:30 p.m., and for dinner daily from 5:30 p.m. to 10:30 p.m.

The Varsity
• 61 North Ave. N.W., Atlanta; 881-1706

"What'll ya have?" they'll ask you at The Varsity. Most likely, you'll have heartburn after a meal here; this is not a safe place for cholesterol count-ers. But then again, you'll also have change left in your pocket when you're done.

The Varsity's an oddball—an ac-tual drive-in restaurant, a throwback to the 1950s. You can order from the car, or choose to eat inside, where you'll get to watch your burgers and fries travel along conveyor belts to your plastic orange tray. Then pick from several different dining areas, each with its own TV set showing news from CNN, sports on ESPN, or local Channel 11. Instead of tables, you sit at one of those attached desk-chair combinations we all remember so fondly from fifth grade.

Forget about your diet and get The Varsity's plain burgers for 75¢ (no extra charge for the grease) or double chili-cheese burgers ($1.60 each). Add some French fries for 85¢. Ten hot chicken wings are priced right at $3.10, while deviled egg sand-wiches—just like the ones Mom used to put in your lunchbox—are $1.05. Extra toppings, like lettuce and to-mato or cole slaw, are 25¢ each.

You get one hour of free parking at the North Avenue location, and the Varsity Jr. on Lindbergh (near the Cheshire Bridge Road intersection) has a good-sized lot, too. Gosh, Buffy, this'll be *perfect* for after the sock hop!

PERIMETER SUBURBS

American Roadhouse
- 842 North Highland Ave. N.E., Atlanta; 872-2822
- 1317 Dunwoody Village Pkwy., Dunwoody; 512-8114

Kitsch is king of the road at Ameri-can Roadhouse. Heavily decorated with traffic signs, license plates, and even full-size, old-fashioned gasoline pumps, these folks work hard to im-bue the restaurant with a sense of nos-talgic fun. Mr. C found this style a bit forced, but all this memorabilia is cer-tainly interesting to check out.

Of course, you may simply want to ignore it all and look at the vast menu instead, which is loaded with food that's as all-American as apple pie and Chevrolet. Breakfast is served from 7:00 a.m. throughout the day and evening; pull up to a plate of pecan waffles for $3.95, or a sausage and cheese omelette with home fries and a bagel for $4.25. They even have "Egg Beater" breakfasts with fresh fruit and a bran muffin ($3.95), as well as banana shakes and Slim-Fast shakes (now, *that's* American).

Lunch and dinner choices seem as endless as a Nebraska highway. A va-riety of burgers start at $4.50 and up, whether made from beef, turkey, or tofu; or, try the grilled chicken, ba-con, and cheddar sandwich ($5.95), the pulled pork sandwich ($5.25), or—wouldja believe—a po'boy made with deep-fried oysters ($6.25).

There are also plenty of appetiz-ers, soups, and salads. Three-cheese quesadillas are $2.95; blackened salmon pasta salad is $6.25; Road-house chili is $1.75 a cup, $2.75 a bowl.

Then, there are the "Blue Plate Specials"—a dozen of 'em, priced about $2 lower at lunchtime than at dinner, but all quite reasonable. Chicken pot pie, one of Mr. C's favor-ites, is $5.50 at lunch, $7.50 at din-ner; other meals include country-fried steak ($4.95/$6.95), homemade meat-loaf ($5.25/$7.25), and trout al-mondine ($5.50/$7.50). These can get a bit pricey, but all plates do come with two side dishes, in over fifteen choices from Granny Smith applesauce to sesame carrots to Wal-dorf salad.

Big desserts range from apple pie (of course) to chocolate mousse pie, each priced at $2.75. Basically, ARH tries to cover all the bases, doing a de-cent job of having something for eve-ryone. It's open seven days a week until 11 p.m., and an hour later on weekends.

Anne & Bill's Restaurant
- 424 Forest Pkwy., Forest Park; 366-4477

Yum. Anne & Bill's is one of Mr. C's favorites. You'd be foolish to miss this gem on the way to or from the airport. All types—produce growers from the nearby Farmer's Market, businesspeople, and locals—crowd into the lobby to wait for a table. But service is swift, even during rush times, and once you taste Anne & Bill's apple betty, homemade cornbread, super fresh veggies or "broasted" chicken, you'll be glad you stayed.

For you jumbo-sized appetite types, try the Texas breakfast: An eight-ounce steak, two eggs any style, and grits, toast or biscuits, all for $5.95. Scrambled eggs and salmon, with grits or bread, is $4.05; and a stack of three frisbee-sized hot cakes is just $2.15. Three-egg omelettes served with grits start at just $3.25. And you've got to love their coffee, just 55¢ a cup with a free refill.

Show up early to beat the lunch crowd, and try the veggie plate for just $2.95, which comes with as many of Anne & Bill's cornbread mini muffins and yeast rolls as you can eat. Choose from such sides as incredible mashed potatoes, rutabagas, spinach, macaroni salad, carrot salad, and fried squash.

Hot roast beef with mashed potatoes, gravy, and sliced tomato, served on light bread, is $4.25. Quarter-pound burgers are only $1.60, hash browns, homefries or French fries are 95¢, and turkey sandwiches go for only $2.75. And the half-bird broasted chicken with salad, fries and rolls is a bargain at $5.50.

The most expensive item on the menu is the T-bone steak, priced at $7.50; with it, you also get French fries or two vegetables, tossed salad, and homemade rolls.

If you don't have room for dessert (and believe Mr. C—you probably won't!), you should definitely get something for later. Homemade pound cake is $1.15 a slice, peach cobbler is just 95¢, and pies are only $1.35 a slice, including sweet potato, lemon meringue, banana, coconut and chocolate cream pies, key lime, or pecan pies.

Anne & Bill's opens bright and early at 5:30 a.m weekdays, and closes up around 3:00 in the afternoon. On Saturdays, they're open 7 a.m. to 2 p.m. It's closed Sundays.

Athens Pizza House

- 1959 Lakewood Ave. S.E., Atlanta; 622-7911
- 246 Bobby Jones Expwy., Augusta; (706) 868-1508
- 5550 Peachtree Industrial Blvd., Chamblee; 452-8282
- 1565 Highway 138, Conyers; 483-6228
- 1341 Clairmont Rd., Decatur; 636-1100
- 1255 Johnson Ferry Rd., Marietta; 509-0099
- 6075 Roswell Rd. N.E., Sandy Springs; 257-0252

The Papadopoulos family has been making popular pizza in the Atlanta area since 1966. The prices are right, too; not only on the pizzas, but also on such appetizers as spinach pie ($1.50), Athens patatoes ($1.50), and fried kalamari ($4.40). Those last two *must* be good—they're spelled old-country style.

The pies themselves start at just $4.90 for an individual size. But why stop there? Go all out with a medium all-meat special (salami, sausage, pepperoni, ham, hamburger, and Canadian bacon) for $9.25. You won't have to eat again for a week.

Entrees like moussaka served with spinach pie, chicken parmesan, and spinach manicotti are each served with a Greek salad and garlic bread for $6.95. There's a children's section on the menu, too; the kids' spaghetti dinner is just $3.15, while you can join them with the gigantic regular spaghetti plate for $5.20.

Don't pass up the baklava for dessert, either. At $1.50 a slice, these nut-filled flaky pastries covered with honey are just the thing to end your meal on a sweet note.

Athens Pizza also offers many beers and wines (including Greek varieties like Kokino and Aspro), starting at $1.95 a glass.

If the crowds here get to be too much, though, consider visiting one of the Athens Pizza Express take-out locations at 4060 Peachtree Road N.E., Atlanta (phone 365-8646) or at 1788 Clairmont Road, Decatur (634-8646).

Bien Thuy
- 5095-F Buford Hwy., Doraville;
  454-9046

Like so many highway shopping centers in and around Atlanta, North-
woods Plaza hides a very popular
ethnic restaurant among its storefronts. Bien Thuy serves up Vietnamese food, so creatively that the cafe
has frequently been cited as one of
the city's best. It certainly makes for
an unusual meal, even if you're a veteran of other Asian cuisines; it's also
very filling and quite inexpensive.

The setting attempts to be a bit
more than your average hole-in-the-
wall, with potted palms and a couple
of secluded booths. The sound system may treat you to Viet versions of
American pop tunes. Ignore these,
and proceed directly to the spring roll
appetizers—large, tightly rolled hand-
fuls of vermicelli noodles, various
greens, sliced pork, and whole
shrimps—served fresh and cold with
a tangy peanut sauce for dipping. You
get a pair of these for $2.50.

To be honest, if you're not *au fait*
with Viet restaurants, the menu here
can be daunting. There seem to be
endless selections of what look like
the same things over and over, thanks
partly to poor translation. Not to
worry. Unlike the menu, the waitresses tend to speak fluent English,
and what's more, they are happy to
explain what various items consist of.
They'll even make suggestions for
you, if you wish.

What you should know is that the
bulk of Vietnamese entrees are
soups—but these are definitely *not*
appetizers. They are vast bowls
packed with various meats, vegetables and noodles, all in a tasty, somewhat salty broth. They are meals in
themselves, and with most priced
around $4.50, darned cheap ones. Mr.
C enjoyed "Beef balls and rice noodles," filled with meatballs of such
finely ground beef that they have the
texture of paté; there were tons of
'em swimming around in this bowl,
along with scallions, bok choy, and a
mass of rice noodles at the bottom.
You also get a plate of fresh, crisp

MR. CHEAP'S PICKS
Suburbs

✔ **Anne & Bill's**—Down home
  cookin' doesn't get much better
  than this Forest Park eatery,
  y'all.

✔ **Bien Thuy**—Incredibly
  creative Vietnamese food in a
  Doraville strip mall.

✔ **Lettuce Souprise You**—Let us
  say you'll be surprised by their
  all-you-can eat smorgasbord of
  fresh, healthy soups and salads,
  plus pasta, the baked potato bar,
  and the best chocolate chip
  muffins this side of heaven.
  Located all over the place.

bean sprouts to toss in.

Other combinations include thinly
sliced steak, shrimp, tripe, barbecued
pork, egg noodles instead of rice noodles, and so on—over two dozen
choices, all under $5. You'd never ex-
pect to have trouble finishing off a
bowl of soup, but it could happen
with any one of these.

Of course, there are other kinds of
entrees, like chicken chow mein
($7.50 for a big platter), several tofu
dishes (all $6.75), and quite a variety
of seafood. We're not just talking
shrimp here. We're talking clams,
eel, octopus, and—yes—jellyfish.
Mr. C has spent too many childhood
summers at the beach to even contem-
plate "jellyfish with mixed vegetables," but the way these folks can
cook, it's probably wonderful.

The Black-eyed Pea
- 1901 Peachtree Rd. N.E., Atlanta;
  351-5580
- 4370 Roswell Rd. N.E., Marietta;
  971-7708
- 925 Holcomb Bridge Rd., Roswell;
  640-1877

- 2590 Spring Rd. S.E., Smyrna; 319-7166
- 1905 Rockbridge Rd., Stone Mountain; 413-6042

And other suburban locations
The Black-eyed Pea is a classic family restaurant, the sort where the waiters and waitresses are accustomed to handling parties of oh, say, twelve people at a time. Seniors and short-on-cash college students also swear by this chain, with its generously-sized servings of food at low prices.

Fill up on red beans and rice, brought to you with fresh cornbread for just $2.39, or BEP's cheese-broccoli soup ($1.85). Massive ⅓-pound hamburgers on whole wheat buns are $3.99, as are their popular chicken fried "steakwiches." Mr. C liked the veggie platter, giving you five (yep, *five*) dishes with rolls and cornbread for $4.99. Skin-on mashed spuds, fried corn, turnip greens, and the broccoli casserole are among Mr. C's faves. Wash it all down with a quart of Lipton iced tea for 99¢, plus free refills to boot; they have a full liquor license, too.

Most daily specials, like liver and onions, chicken and dumplings, and beef tips, are priced $6 or lower, served with two veggies and cornbread. And (as if you'll have room), the homemade apple pie ($2.25) and banana pudding ($1.65) are both good bets.

The good ol' days are very much alive here, with old-fashioned quilts, antique washboards, and black-and-white photographs covering the walls. Black-eyed Peas are open Sundays through Thursdays from 11 a.m. to 10 p.m., and Fridays and Saturdays from 11 a.m. to 11 p.m.

Coco Loco Cuban & Caribbean Cafe

- 303 Peachtree Center Ave. N.E., Atlanta; 653-0070
- 2625 Piedmont Rd. N.E., Atlanta; 364-0212 and 261-0198
- 6301 Roswell Rd., Sandy Springs; 255-5434

Sure, Coco Loco may have a reputation as a yuppie hangout, but its

prices are surprisingly *un*-yuppie. The Cuban sandwich, for instance, is just $3.75 for the regular size, and $4.50 for the super. Jamaican jerk chicken sandwiches go for $3.95, as does the *pan con lechon* (roast pork and grilled onions). For lighter appetites, or those who can't bear the hot spices, try grilled cheese with potato sticks for $2.25, or hot dogs and quarter-pound hamburgers, each just $2.50. The spicier Cuban hamburger, with onions, paprika, and Worcestershire sauce, is also just $2.50.

On the sweet side, tropical milkshakes, in flavors like papaya or mango ($1.95), and nectars (try the tamarind, just $1.50), will douse the flames of the Cuban spices.

Even entrees are reasonably priced, served with two side dishes like yucas, rice, or a salad. Cuban-style roast chicken with garlic and onions, fried sirloin steak, and pork chops are all just $5.95 each. Side dishes like black beans and rice ($1.75), sweet fried plantains or plantain chips (also $1.75) and homemade potato chips (95¢) won't break the bank, either, so you may just have enough money left for some (not so cheap) dessert, like key lime pie ($2.50), rice pudding ($1.95), or *pastelito de guayaba* (guava pastry), just 75¢ an order.

Domestic and imported beers, plus a limited wine selection, are also available.

Dawat Indian Cafe

- 4025 Satellite Blvd., Duluth; 623-6133

Here's Mr. C's choice if you're up in this neck of the suburban woods. Dawat is a popular vegetarian cafe located across the street from Harry's Farmers Market. They serve a dynamite all-you-can-eat weekday lunch buffet for just $4.99 ($6.49 on weekends). Vegetables, rice, raita (spiced yogurt), salads, parathas (vegetable-stuffed breads), and masalas (potato patties with lentils) are among the offerings.

Even if you're not taking advantage of their bargain buffet, the other menu offerings won't break the bank, either. Try the vegetable biryani (rice with spicy vegetables, topped with tomatoes and cilantro, served with mint yogurt), for $3.25; or an order of dosas—golden crepes with coconut chutney, served with lentil soup, just $2.99. Combo platters are priced at $5.25, like the dosa and idli (rice and lentil cake) platter, served with coconut chutney, or the chickpea-dahi bade plate (deep fried lentils with cashews and raisins), same price.

Bhel puri is a popular side dish both in Bombay and here at the Dawat Cafe. It's made from deep fried puffed rice tortillas, thin noodles, and bits of potato, topped with onions and cilantro and chutneys. Add an order for just $2.50.

Dawat is open Sunday through Thursday from 11:30 a.m. to 8:30 p.m. (Mondays until 2:30 p.m. only), and Friday and Saturday from 11:30 a.m. to 9:30 p.m.

Fat Tuesday

- 3167 Peachtree Rd. N.E., Atlanta; 233-9584
- Underground Atlanta, 50 Upper Alabama St., S.W.; 523-7404
- 2321 Windy Hill Rd. S.E., Marietta; 952-2070

Fat Tuesday will help you keep you *and* your wallet fat. Their Cajun sandwiches and soups fill you up nicely for under $5.

Mr. C liked the big plate of just-right spiced black beans & rice ($4.95). Ham-cooked red beans and rice, served with house salad, bread and butter, are only $5.50. And the tasty seafood gumbo is a big seller at $5.25.

Pretend that it's Mardi Gras time and try a ham po'boy, piled high with toppings on a French roll and served with fries ($4.95), or the fried bayou chicken sandwich ($5.95). If you just want to nibble on appetizers, the veggie platter is good at $2.95, as are spicy-hot chicken wings at $3.95. And here's an extra tip from Mr. C: Mondays through Fridays from 5 to 7 p.m., FT offers its appetizers at two for the price of one!

Of course, all these spices are going to get you thirsty, and nobody mixes a drink like Fat Tuesday. Their daiquiri mixing machines look like something out of a laundromat, but make for great coladas and other punchy mixed drinks with names like "Swampwater." These can be a bit on the pricey side, but then, this is how they can keep the food cheap.

Fellini's Pizza

- 2813 Peachtree Rd. N.E., Atlanta; 266-0082
- 923 Ponce de Leon Ave. N.E., Atlanta; 873-3088
- 422 Seminole Ave. N.E., Atlanta; 525-2530
- 4429 Roswell Rd. N.E., Atlanta; 303-8248
- 1991 Howell Mill Rd. N.W., Atlanta; 352-0799

And other suburban locations
While the scene at this pizza place would make for a great movie location, this is not a recommended place to take grandma or little tykes—it's loud, crowded, and the staff tends toward the slightly surly, under-employed-college-grad variety. The decor of brightly painted cinderblocks and oddball celebrity portraits (Elvis lives!) helps the wild, Fellini-esque atmosphere along. The pizza's great, though, and two generously-large slices can fill you up for under three bucks.

Plain slices are just $1.10, believe it or not. Medium-sized cheese pies go for $7.50, and medium "white pizzas"—no tomato sauce, and plenty of garlic—are $11. Extra toppings (just the basics are offered here) are $1 each. Cheese calzones are $4.50. Wash it all down with 16-ounce domestic draft beers, which will put you back just $2.

While Fellini's is a take-a-number-and-we'll-bring-your-order-to-your-table joint, they do keep tip jars at the counters emblazoned with the label *In lieu of decent wages.* While it's optional, most customers do tip here, either at the counter or at their tables after they've eaten.

Good Ol' Days Cafe
- 3013 Peachtree Rd. N.E., Atlanta; 266-2597
- 401 Moreland Ave. N.E., Atlanta; 688-1006
- 5841 Roswell Rd., Sandy Springs; 257-9183

Good Ol' Days is a combination pool hall, sports bar, and cafe, with wildly painted wall murals, pink and green vinyl tablecloths, and colored ceilings. With loud pop music pouring out of oversized speakers, it's a popular hangout with the twenty-somethings; casual, fun, and fit for limited budgets.

Appetizers tend toward the unusual, like fried whipped potatoes for $2.50, and sticky pots—cinnamon, brown sugar, and butter baked into flowerpot-shaped bread, topped with granola, cream cheese, and honey—for $1.95. During Mr. C's visit, apps were all half-price during happy hour.

If you've got more than the munchies, try their chicken quesadillas ($3.99) or New Orleans chicken ($5.49). The six-ounce "Uncomplicated" burger is a lean $3.49. Many of these have the signature flowerpot worked into their presentation. Is the name of this restaurant a thinly veiled reference to the 1960s "flower power" era? Are any of its patrons old enough to figure this out? Ah, nevermind.

Good Ol' Days also makes cheap breakfasts like no one else. Eggs, any style, are 60¢ each (80¢ for Eggbeaters); a bagel and cream cheese is $1.25; and the McFlowerpot sandwich (egg, cheese, and bacon on that specially shaped bread) will brighten your day for only $2.50. There are also classics like Belgian waffles ($3.15) and three-cheese omelettes, served with parmesan-topped sauteed red potatoes and toast, for $3.85. Good Ol' Days stays open well into the night, too, often with free live music from local rock bands.

Happy Herman's
- 2299 Cheshire Bridge Rd. N.E., Atlanta; 321-3012

- 204 Johnson Ferry Rd., Sandy Springs; 256-3354

Best-known as a store for imported gourmet treats and prepared foods for take-out, Happy Herman's is happy to have you sit at one of their few plastic tables near the entrance and nosh away. You can watch the traffic outside, or—much more interesting—inside the popular little shop.

Sip a tasty bowl of cream of mushroom soup ($1.89), or have them heat up a plate of cheese tortellini in tomato sauce ($5.99 per pound). Add a warm sourdough baguette or an individual-sized loaf of romano-parmesan bread, each 99 cents. Herman's also makes an exotic array of fresh sandwiches like "The Smokey," smoked turkey and smoked Gouda cheese on fresh-baked bread, with roasted peppers and grilled eggplant, all for $3.95. Or a New Orleans "Po' Boy" ($2.95), with layers of roast beef, turkey, ham, Swiss cheese, and thinly sliced pickles on a French roll.

And they have similarly wonderful salads, including the "Southwestern Grill" of grilled chicken breast, black beans, green peppers, cheddar cheese and pimientos—all on Romaine lettuce, all for $3.95. There are at least a dozen different salads to choose from, and almost as many dressings to put on top; the house flavor is a ranch dressing with feta cheese mixed in.

Finish off with some very elegant cakes and pastries, baked in the store, or perhaps something from the incredible-looking chocolate confectionery counter. Such great food, in such *hamish* surroundings, for a few bucks; you won't even have to leave a tip. After all this, you'll be happy too.

Indian Delights
- Scott Village Shopping Center, 1707 Church Street, Decatur; 296-2965
- Gwinnett Market Fair Shopping Center, 3675 Satellite Blvd., Duluth; 813-8212

How delightful—a non-smoking, tip-optional kind of restaurant with authentic Indian fare. Indian Delights has received kudos from *Creative Loafing*, the *Journal-Constitution*, and *Atlanta* magazine, and all for good reason.

There are only eight tables here, so lots of local business people get their grub to go. Masala dhosa is a wonderful grilled combination of rice, white lentils, potatoes, and onions; it's served with a lentil-vegetable soup (Sambhar) and coconut chutney, all of which cost a mere $3.60. Vegetable biryani, a rice pilaf with spicy veggies, served with yogurt on the side, is also only $3.60. The most expensive item on the menu, in fact, is the $4.50 masala dhosa with rice cake (ioli) platter, which again is served with coconut chutney and Sambhar soup.

Appetizers will jazz up your meal for just a few bucks more. Bhel puri, which is fried whole wheat bread topped with potato, onions, and homemade noodles, is just $2.50. There's always the samosa, a northern Indian favorite, consisting of fried dough filled with potatoes and peas. It's served with sweet and spicy sauce, and you can get two for $1.80. Taro root leaves and chickpea pasta, topped with sesame seeds and cilantro, is $2.50. There's also the classic Mulligatwany soup ($1.50), and ganthia ($2.50), a spicy chickpea snack.

To cool off your taste buds after lunch or dinner, try the $1.25 dani vada, a white lentil ball covered in mild yogurt sauce; Mr. C prefers a sweet lassi (not the dog, but a sugar-yogurt shake), which sells for $2.25. Nut rolls with layers of phyllo leaves are two for $1.50, and cheese balls (ras malai) with syrup-flavored heavy cream is also two for $1.50.

Johnny Rockets
- 5 West Paces Ferry Rd., N.W., Atlanta; 955-6068
- Phipps Plaza, 3500 Peachtree Rd., Atlanta; 233-9867
- 6510 Roswell Rd. N.W., Sandy Springs; 257-0677
- 2970 Cobb Pkwy., N.W., Marietta; 955-6068

Go, go, go to Johnny's for huge portions of good ole American burgers and sandwiches at super value prices. The menu is limited, but you'll feel like you've been transported back in time to the 1950s.

Hamburger is the basic language spoken here. The "Original Burger," starting at $3.35, is topped with all the necessities: Lettuce, tomato, mustard, pickle, mayo, relish, and chopped onion. For a quarter more, you can add Johnny's cheddar cheese and "red, red sauce." Chili and bacon will add still more to the ticket, yet keep the burger under $6.

Hamburger haters can also find something for themselves here, like an egg salad sandwich ($2.45), the ever-popular BLT ($3.55), and a grilled cheese sandwich ($2.65). Throw some fries on the side for $1.45; better yet, try their chili fries for $2.75.

Johnny Rockets' "famous" malts and shakes are $2.95. For dessert, apple pie is $1.65; served a la mode, it's $2.40. It ain't like Mom's, but it's not bad. Basically, this is fast food with a bit more character than all your McChains, with its counter and stools, and sparkling white tile motif—an idealized "Happy Days" kinds joint.

Validated parking is available at the Buckhead location for just 50¢. JR is open Mondays through Thursdays from 11 a.m. to 10:30 p.m., and from 11 a.m. to 2 a.m. Fridays and Saturdays.

Joli-Kobe Bakery & Cafe
- The Prado, 5600 Roswell Rd., Sandy Springs; 843-3257

If you can find a parking spot in the super-busy Prado complex, be sure to try the super-big deli sandwiches and homemade soups at Joli-Kobe. The place itself is nothing fancy, with a casual, local hangout feel; but the fare is healthier than you'll find at most typical delis. All sandwiches are piled high with fresh lettuce, tomato, and sprouts, plus fresh fruit and a pickle on the side.

Joli-Kobe's shrimp sandwich is a

_ᴖain at $5.50, served on your choice of croissant, baguette, or whole wheat bread. The almond curry chicken and sauteed chicken are also $5.50 each; egg salad sandwiches are $3.95; and you can also get any of these choices on a child-size croissant for $2.95.

Joli is becoming well-known for its creative and value-sized salads, like pasta ham, teriyaki chicken and turkey salads, served with vinaigrette or ginger dressing. Needless to say, the cafe is good to know about for quality take-out food; you can even bring an eight-ounce bottle of those delicious dressings home for $1.50.

Le Peep

- 2484 Briarcliff Rd. N.E., Atlanta; 325-7069
- 233 Peachtree St. N.E., Atlanta; 688-3782
- 3000 Windy Hill Rd., Marietta; 980-0898

And other suburban locations
Mr. Cheap loves Le Peep. The plates are piled so high with wonderful food that you'll find it *magnifique*, whether you come for breakfast, brunch, lunch, or dinner.

In spite of the French name, Le Peep actually serves food with a western flair. Why don't you come to your senses and try the "Desperado," Le Peep's skillet dish with eggs, cheese, chorizo sausage, green chilies and onions, mixed with salsa, for $6; or the Fiesta Skillet, full of "Peasant Potatoes," chunks of chicken, and diced onions covered with chili verde and cheddar. It's served up with two eggs for $5.75.

The aptly-named "Lumberjack Breakfast," lets you chop down eggs, two bacon strips, two sausage links, Peasant Potatoes, and a short stack of pancakes, for $5.85. For healthy palates, a huge fresh fruit plate is $4.20, and granola-dipped French toast is $4.95.

At lunch or dinnertime, LP's smoked turkey and bacon sandwich, with bacon, Muenster, lettuce, tomato and mayo, served with a garden salad or cup of soup or criss cross cut fries,

is a winner for $5.35. A Philly cheese steak sandwich, with soup, salad, or fries, is just $6, and a jumbo $1/3$-pound burger, also with choice of side dishes, is $4.75. And don't forget dessert: a sweet crepe, filled with blueberries, bananas, strawberries, or spiced apples, covered with whipped topping and cinnamon, is $1.95.

Le Peep has some of the best coffee and hot chocolate this side of the Divide (or should that be the Seine?), and serves breakfast any time of day. They also have a "Golden Years Club," which entitles anyone over 55 to a ten percent discount off any meal, seven days a week. Le *wow*!

Lettuce Souprise You

- 595 Piedmont Ave., N.E., Atlanta; 874-4998
- 2470 Briarcliff Rd. N.E., Atlanta; 636-8549
- 245 Pharr Rd. N.E., Atlanta; 841-9583
- 3525 Mall Blvd., Duluth; 418-9969
- 1475 Holcomb Bridge Rd., Roswell; 642-1601
- 5975 Roswell Rd., Sandy Springs; 250-0304
- 1109 Cumberland Mall, Smyrna; 438-2288

Here's a place after your humble author's own heart. At Lettuce Souprise You, one price gets you unlimited trips to their extensive salad bar, as well as the all-you-can-eat baked potato bar and pasta bar, plus homemade muffins, cornbread, and soups, and fresh fruit. Whew! Lettuce be thankful for places like this!

The salad bar is super-fresh and preservative-free; it features spinach, broccoli, tarragon tuna, spicy crab and pasta salad, and pineapple, along with dozens of other choices. Soups change daily, but always include at least one vegetarian recipe, such as potato-leek or lentil. Egg drop, chili, and vegetable soups are featured often, too.

How can they afford to offer such a bargain, you ask? Well, they do work on keeping costs down. For one thing, Lettuce Souprise You requests that you eat only in the restaurant—

they don't allow anyone to leave with more than a muffin. If you'd like something to go, they will charge you for it. Well hey, that's only fair!

Meanwhile, the price for this entire sumptuous buffet is just $5.50 at lunchtime; $6.50 for brunch and dinner. Another cheap deal: Their "frequent buyer" club entitles you to a free meal when you've had twelve lunches, six dinners, or four brunches. Can it be any surprise that Lettuce Souprise You rates so highly with Mr. C?

The Mad Italian
- 2245 Peachtree Rd. N.E., Atlanta; 352-1368
- 2197 Savoy Dr., Chamblee; 451-8048
- East Lake Center, Marietta; 977-5209
- Windy Hill Plaza, Marietta; 952-1806

They're crazy about high quality at this South Buckhead and suburban eatery. The prices on Italian sandwiches, pasta, and calzones, in fact, are downright foolish. The Mad Italian is so nuts about fresh ingredients that his bread is flash frozen and trucked in all the way from New York; the folks here say that the Atlanta humidity and altitude are "improper" for good bread baking.

Anything you say, guys—the effort certainly pays off. Sandwiches, available in three sizes priced from $3.85 to just $5.50, include tuna hoagies, Italian sausage, meatball and cheese, cheese steak, and chicken salad varieties, along with the vegetable sautee with cheese. Pickles and potato chips come with sit-down orders (too bad for you take-out lovers). Whether you eat in or out, for just $1 more, you can enjoy the Mad Italian's house salad or spaghetti, or a cup of his soup of the day (Mr. C recommends the minestrone, but the pasta e fagiole is also highly touted by those in the know).

Cheese or meat calzones go for just $4.95; if you really feel like stuffing yourself, go for the baked cheese ravioli ($6.50), served with fresh

bread and butter and house salad; or the pasta trio (cannelloni Florentine, spinach and cheese shells, and ricotta cheese shells) for $6.95, or fettucine Alfredo for $5.95.

Keep the kids happy with items like the kids' spaghetti plate (just $2.50). The Mad Italian is perfect for family dining, with a casual, wood-paneling, wicker-chair, gum-at-the-cash register kind of atmosphere. It's open seven days a week, including Fridays and Saturdays until midnight.

Mary Mac's Tea Room and Restaurant
- 224 Ponce de Leon Ave. N.E., Atlanta; 876-6604
- 2205 Cheshire Bridge Rd. N.E., Atlanta; 325-7777
- 4431 Hugh Howell Rd., Tucker; 621-9935

And other suburban locations

Zell Miller and Jimmy Carter have eaten at Mary Mac's, considered to be Atlanta's oldest home cooking restaurant. Nothing's fancy here, really—you actually fill out the food slips yourself, since the waitresses are too busy helping the scores of folks who flock here at lunchtime.

Choose from a choice of entrees (baked chicken, country fried steak, baked fish almondine, beef tips on creole rice, sauteed chicken livers, etc.) with two side dishes for $6.50. Sweet potato cobbler is a popular choice, but Mr. C is partial to the cheese-whipped potatoes. Included in the price are tea, coffee, or punch, Mary Mac's cornbread, and ice cream in your choice of five flavors.

Meals are served in a flash; also, half portions can be ordered for those customers "under 12 or over 90." The Ponce location is currently open only for lunch, but may be reopening for dinner by the time you read this.

Mick's
- 557 Peachtree Rd. N.E., Atlanta; 875-6425
- 2110 Peachtree Rd. N.W., Atlanta; 351-6425
- Peachtree Center, 229 Peachtree St. N.E., Atlanta; 688-6425

- Lenox Square Shopping Center, 3393 Peachtree Rd. N.E., Atlanta; 262-6425
- Underground Atlanta, 75 Upper Alabama St. S.W., Atlanta; 525-2825
- 116 East Ponce de Leon Ave., Decatur; 373-7797

And other suburban locations
Get to Mick's for one of the best milkshakes in town, great burgers, super desserts, and creative drinks. Stretching from Underground Atlanta to Buckhead and beyond, this yuppie haven seems determined to make the next siege of Atlanta a culinary one.

Prices here are not the absolute cheapest around, but you do get a lot of delicious food for the money. Start off with real fried green tomatoes ($5.75), chili-smothered French fries ($3.95), grilled carrots and broccoli ($2.50), or a cup of soup in flavors like tomato or "baked potato" ($1.95).

A half-pound hamburger, hickory grilled, with a generous side of fries or pasta salad, is $5.95. You can top it with cheddar or mozzarella cheese, guacamole, chili, barbecue sauce, or cracked pepper and mustard for 80¢ extra. Cheese-topped grilled boneless chicken is $7.50, and corn and tomato linguine with garlic bread is $6.95. Mick's chicken Reuben will completely stuff you for $7.95.

Do try to leave room for dessert, though. You'll probably want to share one of these monstrosities with a friend. Try the Oreo cheesecake ($3.95), the Giant Banana Split ($4.75), or Mr. C's favorite, the chocolate cream pie ($3.75). Yummy! Strawberry shortcake, homemade chocolate layer cake, and Heath Bar ice cream pie will all make delightful ends to your meal, and all are under $4 apiece.

Besides the desserts, Mick's is known for its unusual mixed drinks—like "Frozen Pink Lemonade," "Frozen German Chocolate Cake," and "Peasant Coffee" (spiked with brandy, Grand Marnier, Kahlua, amaretto, and dark creme de cacao, and topped with whipped cream). These will doubtless not be cheap,

but they are good. Most branches of Mick's have a separate bar area.

Original Pancake House
- 1937 Peachtree Rd. N.E., Atlanta; 351-3533
- 4330 Peachtree Rd. N.E., Atlanta; 237-4116
- 2321 Cheshire Bridge Rd. N.E., Atlanta; 633-5712
- 501 Johnson Ferry Rd. N.E., Marietta; 977-5013
- 5099 Memorial Dr., Stone Mountain; 292-6914

The Original Pancake Houses sure won't leave you in the poor house. James Beard did name this one of the top ten restaurants in America, but you'd never know this from the prices. Quality runs high here—they use fresh juices, extra large Grade AA eggs, and pure whipping cream, plus all the cooking is done in pure butter.

The pancake recipe is a carefully-guarded secret, with good reason. They're light and fluffy, and just $3.55 an order. Georgia Pecan Waffles ($4.80) are delicious. If you're truly starving, Mr. C suggests the omelettes, served with three buttermilk pancakes, plus grits or toast, all for $6.95; or a four-ounce beef tenderloin steak for $4.50. Other good bets include French crepes with strawberry topping ($5.25). Side dishes include sweets like cinnamon applesauce ($1) and imported lingonberries in butter ($1.75).

Junior plates are available for children under ten. Two slices of French toast ($2.60), and three pancakes ($2.50) are served with milk, chocolate milk, or hot chocolate.

Meanwhile, to paraphrase the old orange juice commercials, "it's not just for breakfast anymore." OPH also serves a lunch menu of hamburgers ($4.25), soups (plus soup and half-sandwich specials for $4.95), and hot dogs (two for $2.95), along with salads and chili.

Senior citizens always get a 15% discount here, and police and firemen also receive a discount off their meals. The Original Pancake Houses are open from 6:30 a.m. to 2:30 p.m. weekdays, and from 7 a.m. to 3 p.m. on weekends.

PoFolks
- 2094 North Druid Hills Rd., Atlanta; 321-0300
- Market Square at North DeKalb, 2179 Lawrenceville Hwy., Decatur; 321-3948
- 825 Sandy Plains Rd., Marietta; 425-2322
- 4286 Lavista Rd., Tucker; 493-6925
- 5549 Old National Hwy., College Park; 761-3114
- 4909 Memorial Drive, Stone Mountain; 294-6444

And other suburban locations
Don't be fooled by the sky-high billboard signs—PoFolks may seem to be your typical family fast-food joint, but in fact it's a relaxing, friendly sort of place with an incredible selection of food.

If you like veggies (or even if you don't), try their Po' Plate, with any four side orders, plus cornbread or a biscuit for just $4.29. You have a choice from over two dozen sides, like sweet potato souffle, fried green tomatoes, cornbread, Brunswick stew, hobo beans, red beans and rice, or corn on the cob. You can also substitute a "garden patch" salad or vegetable soup for 69 cents extra.

Even po' folks can afford seafood here, like a plate of thirty fried Gulf shrimp for $6.69, southern-style catfish for $6.99, rainbow trout for $5.99, or the clam dinner for $5.49.

Other specialties, such as barbecued pork chops, hamburger steak, chicken n' dumplin's and chicken livers are all priced under $6 a plate, served with vegetables and a choice of breads.

PoFolks also makes a point of catering to the senior crowd, who can get some great bargains. Diners age 55 and over can choose from the Po Plate, fish dinners, fried chicken, and other platters, all served with vegetables and bread; most of these are specially priced at only $3.99 to $4.99.

This is a good place for them to bring the grandchildren, too. The children's menu includes things like the "Minner Dinner" with fish patty, hush puppies, and fries; plus country-fried steak, meatloaf, or chicken tenders, all under $3 each. And for everyone, all drinks except moo juice (guess what that is) are refilled for free. Not that you'll always need it; iced tea and lemonade are served in Mason jars.

Silver Spoon Cafe
- 2040 Peachtree Rd. N.W., Atlanta; 351-8433
- Phipps Plaza, 3500 Peachtree Rd. N.E., Atlanta; 237-8335
- 1 Galleria Pkwy. N.W., Smyrna; 916-1976

And other suburban locations
So, you weren't born with one of these in your mouth; you can still get a great meal at the Silver Spoon. Some entrees get a bit pricey, but the cafe does have items like fresh quiche for $4.99, Cajun chicken sandwiches for $6.49, big Caesar salads for $4.99, and fettuccine Alfredo for $7.99. Not to mention delicious five cheese pizzas for $5.99.

The children's menu, served to those ten years old and younger, features proven kid-pleasers like grilled cheese sandwiches ($1.99), pepperoni pizza ($2.99), chicken fingers ($2.99), and corn dogs ($1.99). The little ones are also given a game-covered menu to keep them busy.

Desserts include mocha or cappuccino freezes for $2.99, and apple walnut crisps for $3.29. This popular place gets pretty busy, especially around lunchtime; to avoid the rushes, you can actually call ahead to the Silver Spoon for preferred seating.

Spaghetti Warehouse
- 2475 Delk Rd., Marietta; 953-1175
Having heard the name, Mr. C was expecting to check out some shop offering deals on dried pastas. Instead, he was equally delighted to find a rather lavish restaurant, fun and glitzy, yet not at all expensive.

In front of, but not connected to a Marriott hotel just east of I-75, this place is suitable for a mixed crowd—

funky enough for a date, but not too boisterous for the older folks. It's also a haven for business people, promising lunches in ten minutes—or they're on the house. Service is indeed prompt and friendly.

There are several large, high-ceilinged rooms, done in an inviting wood-and-brass tavern style. But the decor only gets crazier from there. Every square inch of the walls is lined with signs, turn-of-the-century advertisements and other bits of Americana. One room is dominated by a full-size San Francisco trolley car, with tables inside; or, you may find yourself in a "booth" fashioned from brass bed headboards and red velvet upholstery. And you thought you had to stay home to eat in bed.

The food, meanwhile, is plentiful and, yes, cheap! A small loaf of warm sourdough bread is served as soon as you sit, and another is brought as soon as it's finished. You can start with an antipasto, minestrone, or just a cup of sauteed mushrooms. The entrees themselves consist of basic spaghetti with your choice of over a dozen sauces and toppings. Among these are a basic meatless marinara ($5.45); white wine clam sauce ($5.95); seafood marinara (also $5.95), laced with shrimp and crabmeat; even chili ($5.65), made with beer as an ingredient—don't worry, there's not enough to impair your driving. Whichever you choose, you'll get a heaping mound that's hard to finish.

There are other pasta dishes, including a tasty, homemade 15-layer lasagna ($7.95), meat or cheese ravioli ($6.25), and fettucine alfredo ($5.95). And the place wouldn't be Italian without a few veal and chicken dishes; one of Mr. C's dining companions was quite happy with the evening's special of chicken piccata, which was served with spaghetti for $8.95. All entrees, by the way, include your choice of minestrone or a large, crisp garden salad.

A good selection of American and imported beers is on hand, as well as several basic varieties of wines by

the glass or bottle, or pitchers of sangria.

It all makes for a fun and splashy kind of meal, an outing which looks like it should cost a lot more than it does. For Mr. C's readers in town, this is a fine way to start or finish a day of bargain hunting in the northern suburbs.

Taco Mac

- 375 Pharr Rd. N.E., Atlanta; 239-0650
- 1006 North Highland Ave. N.E., Atlanta; 873-6529
- 771 Cherokee Ave. S.E., Atlanta; 624-4641
- 2120 Johnson Ferry Rd., Chamblee; 454-7676
- 1444 Oxford Rd., Emory Village; 377-2323
- 1570 Holcomb Bridge Rd., Roswell; 640-9598
- 5830 Roswell Rd. N.W., Sandy Springs; 257-0735
- 2845 Mountain Industrial Blvd., Stone Mountain; 621-3601

And other suburban locations

These guys claim that Buffalo wings were invented right here. Gee, wait'll the folks in Buffalo hear that. No matter—Taco Mac's spicy wings are for real, and they've also got the biggest beer selection this side of the Mississippi to wash them down. While the service can be slow as a sloth, Mr. C still thinks that the food and the prices make Mac a hit.

Appetizers include fried zucchini, cauliflower, or mushrooms for just $4 a plate; a jumbo basket of nachos with frijoles and cheese goes for $4.75. TM's guacamole salad is a mere $2.85. Basics include soft tacos for $1.55, super burritos for $3.25, quesadillas for $5.50, and chili for just $2.50; to go with these, beers from 28 different countries are reasonably priced, even though they come from as far away as New Zealand and the Ivory Coast.

Those Buffalo chicken wings come in sizes of ten for $4.75 or twenty for $7.05. Rustle them up in mild, medium, hot—or, for 50¢ extra, "Three Mile Island"-style. If you're having a party, here's an extra tip from Mr. C: You can get a 10% discount for platter orders of 250 wings or more.

Taco Mac has a kiddie menu too, with things like a burger and fries for $2.50, or a mini-fish and chips plate for the same price.

Three Dollar Cafe
- 3002 Peachtree Rd. N.E., Atlanta; 266-8667
- 8595 Roswell Rd., Dunwoody; 992-5011
- 2580 Windy Hill Rd., Marietta; 850-0868

Though it got its start in Buckhead, the Three Dollar Cafe is not your average Buckhead watering hole. That's because it's much more like anywhere else's watering hole. Mr. C likes the very casual atmosphere (feel free to wear your oldest T-shirt). And while you *will* have to spend a little over three bucks on dinner here, alas, the name isn't all that far off. Portions are so huge, in fact, that you'll most likely get two meals out of whatever you order.

Three Dollar Cafe's chicken wings are a real crowd pleaser at just $3.78 an order—feel free to get messy, too, since each table is thoughtfully provided with rolls of paper towels for post-pigout cleanups. Or, try an order of sauted mushrooms for $3.86.

Mr. C got quite stuffed on the salad and steamed veggie platter, which comes with new potatoes, lots of carrots, and darn near a whole head each of broccoli and cauliflower—all for just $4.98.

Steak and cheese sandwiches are only $4.25, reubens are $4.78, and beef kabobs are $6.86. Chicken Oscar, made with crabmeat topping, white asparagus and Hollandaise sauce, is served with squash casserole *and* rice and gravy, complete for 6.95.

Don't forget dessert, either, with treats like key lime pie, cheesecake, and ice cream-topped brownies, each under $2.50.

Three Dollar has a children's menu, too, with spaghetti, burger and

fries, chicken wing and fries, or a grilled cheese sandwich, for just $1.95 each. Kids three and under get a free peanut butter and jelly sandwich. Now, *there's* a deal!

Veggieland
- 211 Pharr Rd. N.E., Atlanta; 231-3111
- 209 Sandy Springs Circle, Sandy Springs; 252-1165

You don't have to be a vegetarian to like the food here—you'll never notice that there's no refined sugar or dairy products used in any of the menu items. Veggieland is a place for real purists—jars of no-salt spice mixtures and non-irradiated cayenne pepper flakes sit at each table, and even the ice cubes are made with filtered water. It's a well-kept Buckhead secret undeservingly overshadowed by a certain (more expensive) leafy chain located right down the street.

Mr. C liked the cashew and soy strip veggie stir-fry, its perfectly steamed snow peas, broccoli, carrots, red and green peppers, and bean sprouts sitting atop a mound of basmati rice. This was enough for two meals, really, priced at a healthy $4.75. It's also available with baked tofu and almonds, instead of the cashews and soy strips, for the same price. Whole-grain pasta primavera with pesto is another hearty entree, perfect for vegetarians and non-vegetarians alike, at just $5.95.

The "Veggie Burger" is made from nuts, beans, and spices, topped with tomato, lettuce, sprouts and onion on a whole wheat bun, for $3.40; top it with soy cheese for 35¢ extra. The tofu-chicken sandwich, served with fried sweet potatoes, is just $3.95. Soup selections change daily; the potato leek soup is super, and just $1.25 for a good-sized cup.

The restaurant itself is tiny, with a small patio, and a laid-back, take-your-time atmosphere. Colorful Caribbean-scene paintings and classical music make for peaceful surroundings, while the attentive service makes you feel right at home.

Veggieland is open weekdays from

11:30 a.m. to 3 p.m., and again from 5 p.m. to 9 p.m.; Saturdays from 11:30 a.m. to 9 p.m., and Sundays (in the Buckhead location only) from noon to 8 p.m.

HOTELS AND LODGING

Always on the lookout for a bargain, Mr. C has tried to wade through the tricky waters of the hotel biz to find rooms where you can stay for well under $100 a night. These waters are tricky because hotel rates ebb and flow. And don't forget that taxes are always going to be added on top of any quoted price. Below, then, are the results of his not-necessarily scientific survey.

Two important tips: First of all, you should always, *always* ask about discounts. Remember: No hotel room ever has only one price. Take advantage of any discounts you can—including corporate, AAA, military, American Association of Retired Persons, and others. Furthermore, if you're going to be in town long enough, ask about weekly rates.

Finally, Atlanta is convention central. If you're planning to stay in a hotel, motel, or bed and breakfast, be sure to make reservations—and make them *early*. Convention business also means that many rooms are empty come Friday, so you can get a great weekend package deal at almost any hotel in the city. Even ritzier places like the Westin may run under $100 a night with one of these deals.

HOTELS

Best Western American Hotel
- 160 Spring St. N.W., Atlanta;
  688-8600 or 1-800-621-7885

This hotel is across the street from the Westin Peachtree Plaza, but it sure doesn't have Westin-style prices, by far. Call it "Best Westin."

The American has been around since 1962, and though this is a funny thing to mention, the mortgage is actually paid off (imagine!), allowing them to charge attractive discount rates. It became affiliated with Best Western only four years ago, joining a national reservation system.

Some of the original employees are still working here; owner Dr. Marvin Goldstein estimates that more than twenty percent of the employees have been with the hotel over fifteen years. His concierge staff is particularly knowledgeable about Atlanta and tending to your business or travel needs.

The American was one of the first integrated hotels in the city, long before civil rights laws ordered all Atlanta hotels to do so. Some well-known guests have stayed here over the years, including Martin Luther King, Jr., Elvis Presley, Pearl Bailey, Richard Nixon, and even Zorba the Greek (but not Anthony Quinn).

The American features a pool, cable television, and a small exercise room. Rooms run about $70 for a single and $80 for a double. There are over 300 rooms in the hotel, but it often fills up, especially during popular tourist times, so call early for reservations. There is a fee for parking; however, if you're car-free, the Peachtree Center MARTA station is just a short walk up the hill.

Cheshire Motor Inn
- 1865 Cheshire Bridge Rd. N.E.,
  Atlanta; 872-9628; or
  1-800-827-9628

A bit cozier than your typical motor lodge, the Cheshire Motor Inn has modern rooms which start as low as $30 a night. Even at such low prices, these rooms have a double bed, and color TV with cable. They are clean, comfortable, and well-kept. There are two rows of these cottage-style rooms; across the parking lot, CMI has larger, more typical motel rooms at higher rates.

It's conveniently located just north of Piedmont Park, quite central to the northern half of the city; though there is bus service, it's better to have a car here. You can be downtown, or out to the northern suburbs, in twenty minutes or so. Also, located on the same premises, is the Colonnade Restaurant—a popular and moderately priced dining spot that is as well known for its traditional Southern cuisine as for the crowds that make it hard to get a table. Many other good restaurants, stores, and a movie theater can also be found up and down Cheshire Bridge Road.

Comfort Inn Buckhead
- 2115 Piedmont Rd. N.E., Atlanta;
  876-4365; or 1-800-221-2222

Singles are just $49, and doubles just $55, at this Spanish villa-style motel. There's not much doing on this stretch of Piedmont, unless you count the Denny's down the street; but business travelers like the easy access to I-75/85, and the late (12 noon) checkout time. Lenox Square is just a short drive away, too, as is the Buckhead Diner and the hopping Buckhead Avenue/Bolling Way area of town.

Days Inn Peachtree
- 683 Peachtree St. N.E., Atlanta;
  874-9200; or 1-800-325-3535

Days Inn is a name folks trust; and this one, located almost directly across the street from the Fox Theatre, is quite a bargain for a hotel in town. Single rooms start around $60, and doubles around $70, with even better corporate rate deals for business travelers. Oh, and you also get complimentary coffee with that, too.

This is a distinctive, classic southern-style brownstone building, with an ornate exterior, and Oriental carpets and fancy chandeliers in the lobby. Such graceful elements are holdovers from its pre-Days days. Don't let this overwhelm you, though; rooms are decorated simply and tastefully. An added bonus is the security system at the front door—this is Atlanta's entertainment district, after all, and you should be aware that there are a few unsavory characters wandering around at night. Things tend to stay pretty quiet, for the most part.

In addition to being centrally located to both the business district and the fun of Midtown clubs, this Days Inn is within walking distance of the North Avenue MARTA station. For drivers, there is a parking garage in the rear. And don't worry about keeping the kids happy and fed; a Wendy's Restaurant sits right off the hotel lobby.

Another good Days Inn location in the Atlanta area is their Downtown hotel, located at 300 Spring Street (telephone 523-1144).

Emory Inn
- 1641 Clifton Rd. N.E., Atlanta; 712-6700 or 1-800-933-6679

Affiliated with world-renowned Emory University, the Emory Inn is far from the bustle of downtown, yet still within easy access of Interstates 85 and 20. Ponce de Leon Avenue is just a few blocks away, which can take you either straight into Midtown, or out to Stone Mountain. The Lenox Square Shopping Center, Phipps Plaza and central Buckhead are short drives away.

Of course, you can stay right where you are and explore the Emory

MR. CHEAP'S PICKS
Hotels/Motels

✔ **Cheshire Motor Inn**— Super-cheap, yet comfy and modern.
✔ **Comfort Inn Buckhead**—Well, it's *near* Buckhead, but not even close to Buckhead prices.
✔ **Emory Inn**—Luxury surroundings at very moderate rates.
✔ **Travelodge Hotel Atlanta**— Not a motel, but a full-service hotel at comparable rates.

campus itself, including the Michael C. Carlos Museum, Theatre Emory (see listings in the "Entertainment" section of this book), and the Glenn Memorial Auditorium.

The Inn is where many dignitaries stay when visiting the university, and it's also preferred by researchers working with the nearby Centers for Disease Control and the national headquarters for the American Cancer Society.

Rooms in the three-floor inn run about $85, which includes use of the pool, whirlpool, and exercise room. (A note to handicapped individuals: there are no elevators at the Inn.)

Hampton Inns
- General information and reservations: 1-800-HAMPTON
- Hampton Inn Buckhead: 3398 Piedmont Rd. N.E., Atlanta; 233-5656
- Hampton Inn Hotel, 3400 Northlake Pkwy., Northlake; 493-1966
- Hampton Inn-Druid Hills Road, 1975 North Druid Hills Rd. N.E., Atlanta; 320-6600
- Hampton Inn Marietta, 455 Franklin Rd., Marietta; 425-9977

- Hampton Inn Southlake, 1533 Southlake Pkwy., Morrow; 968-8990
- Hampton Inn-Atlanta Airport, 1888 Sullivan Rd., College Park; 996-2220

At $55-$62 for a single, and $67 for a double, this national chain is a definite bargain. Mr. C especially likes that at Hampton Inn, the "continental breakfast"—which usually consists of just coffee and danish—also offers cereals, bagels, toast, and juice.

Mr. C also likes the fact that all Hampton Inns provide free parking, free local phone calls, and free cable television. Business travelers also appreciate that rooms are equipped with data jacks to attach to personal computers.

Most Hamptons have outdoor swimming pools open in season. Plenty of non-smoking rooms are also offered, and kids and the third and fourth adult in each room stay for free. What a deal! Hampton Inns are all well-located, whether you want to stay near the airport, enjoy the trendy Buckhead shopping at Phipps Plaza and Lenox Square, or take in a Braves game. Note: The Washington Street branch, which faces Fulton County Stadium, also puts it next to the major construction site which will become the Braves' new stadium in 1995. Daytimes are a bit noisy and dusty at the moment.

But then, don't forget that Hampton Inns offer a 100% satisfaction guarantee: If you're not happy with your stay for any reason, you don't have to pay. But since Hampton Inns tend to be immaculately clean and comfortable, with staffs to accommodate your every need, it's an unlikely scenario.

Holiday Inn Atlanta-Decatur Conference Plaza
- 130 Clairmont Ave., Decatur; 371-0204 or 1-800-225-6079

This is a great place for the whole family to stay, since it's well removed from the noise and crowds of Downtown and Midtown, and away from Buckhead's traffic, yet still

close to lots of fun spots. It's handicapped-accessible, with two floors of non-smoking rooms available. There's an indoor swimming pool with whirlpool, and an exercise room, too. Of course, this place is a favorite of business travelers, thanks to the 25,000-square foot conference plaza adjoining the hotel.

Downtown is just five miles away, a short and easy drive; or, the Decatur MARTA station is an even shorter distance by foot. Two of Mr. C's favorite inexpensive restaurants, the Southern Star and Thumbs Up, are located just down Ponce de Leon Avenue (see listings under "Restaurants: Atlanta Northeast/Decatur"). There are lots of flea markets and salvage shops in the area for him, not to mention Your DeKalb Farmer's Market (see listing under "Shopping: Food Stores"), Emory University's cultural life and museums, plus the historic downtown Decatur area. The lively Little Five Points and Virginia-Highland neighborhoods are surprisingly close, too.

You may not even need a rental car, since MARTA's so close. The hotel provides complimentary van service to business destinations within a five mile radius; the hotel's also a designated stop for the Atlanta Airport Shuttle.

With all these amenities, not to mention the fancy marble decorations, you'd expect to pay a lot more than the going rates, which range from $69 for a room on weekends to $94 weekdays. Not cheap, but definitely reasonable.

The Inn at the Peachtrees
- 330 West Peachtree St., Atlanta; 577-6970 or 1-800-242-4642

Weekend rates run $70 for a single, and $80 for a double room at this cute little downtown motel (rates increase about $10 during the week). Corporate and government rates and AAA discounts are also available.

It's just a couple of blocks from the Civic Center and Peachtree MARTA stations, making it a favorite among school tours and business travlers alike (on-site parking is limited, so keep this in mind).

Underground Atlanta, Macy's, Peachtree Center, and the World Congress Center are also right nearby. There's no pool, but visitors do have visiting rights to a health club nearby.

The 100 rooms are far from huge but have recently been renovated, giving the hotel a warm, homey atmosphere. Cable TV is included in the room price, and pay-per-view movies are also available.

Paschal's Motor Hotel, Restaurant and Lounge

- 830 Martin Luther King, Jr. Drive, S.W., Atlanta; 577-3150

(See listing under "Restaurants: Downtown/Atlanta South" also)

Paschal's is a name long-famous not only for its soul food restaurant, but also for its great-rate hotel. Rooms are large and comfy, and just $45 a night (including tax) for a single, $50 for a double, or $56 for a triple occupancy room.

While the West End neighborhood may not be the safest—it's thought by many Atlantans to be on the rise again, actually—there is an extensive security system plus a security staff on duty. The hotel also houses Paschal's Coffee Shop and La Carousel Lounge (where Aretha Franklin and Lou Rawls have performed). Live jazz is heard in the lounge several nights a week.

Downtown is just a few minutes' drive from here, and the Ashby MARTA station is two blocks away. Clark-Atlanta University is right down the street.

Quality Inn Habersham/Downtown

- 330 Peachtree St. N.E., Atlanta; 577-1980 or 1-800-228-5151

Singles and doubles start as low as $59 at this prime-located, European-style hotel. The common parlor area, complete with large-screen TV, is so comfortable that Mr. C saw a tourist snoozing there, right in the middle of the afternoon.

The Habersham's rooms are comfortably sized, many with extra chairs and sofas, and handsome cherrywood-finish fixtures. Each room has a wet bar, coffee maker, huge walk-in closets, and a separate vanity area, making it easy for families to get ready in the morning without everyone having to fight for bathroom time. An added bonus is the complimentary continental breakfast, which includes fruit, muffins and other pastries, juices, coffee, and more.

The hotel also has a sauna and exercise room, and limited free parking. Within walking distance are the Hard Rock Cafe, the Georgia Dome, Civic Center, Omni, Underground Atlanta, and Peachtree Center.

Pets can stay here too, with a $100 deposit ($80 is refundable).

Travelodge Hotel Atlanta

- 2061 North Druid Hills Rd. N.E., Atlanta; 321-4174 or 1-800-255-3050

This hotel is conveniently located near the intersection of the Northeast Expressway (Interstate 85) and North Druid Hills Road. It's about a five minute drive to Buckhead, about ten minutes down the highway to downtown, and less than half an hour to Hartsfield Airport (unless it's rush-hour, in which case, you'll be lucky to get there at all). More importantly for Mr. Cheap's readers, it's very close to the Outlet Mall on Buford Highway!

While you may think of Travelodges as teeny tiny motels, this one is a real live nine-floor *hotel*, complete with an outdoor heated pool, a sauna, and a small universal gym. Cable TV with HBO is free, and they even have room service. There's plenty of free parking in the lot, too.

Nightly rates range from $49 for a single room with queen-size bed to $59 for a king or two queens. These should help you avoid financial checkmate, and leave you with some cash for Stone Mountain Park (just fifteen minutes west of the hotel) or, of course, bargain shopping.

For those who don't mind the noisy Downtown area, the **Atlanta Downtown Travelodge**, located at

311 Courtland St. N.E., (telephone 659-4545), also offers low rates—about $78 for a two-double bed room, with singles as low as $49. Plus free parking, many rooms which open up onto balconies, and free continental breakfast. It's just blocks away from the Civic Center, SciTrek, Underground Atlanta, and the CNN Center.

Villager Lodge
- 144 14th St. N.W., Atlanta; 873-4171

Villager Lodge is a chain of independently franchised motor hotels, of which there are a couple in the city. In both cases, these are establishments which have been taken over from previous operators, renovated, and run separately. Both are available for "extended stay lodging," meaning they offer weekly rates as well as daily, and many of the rooms include kitchenettes.

Beyond that, the two places are as different as night and day. The one at the above address is clean, neat, very newly renovated, and well run. There is another Villager Lodge on Peachtree Street in Midtown; but, un-

less you are particularly tough and resilient, you don't want to stay at that one. It's a run-down flop house in a run-down area. Mr. C hates to bad-mouth a business, but he feels it's important to draw the distinction, since anyone would assume that two motels with the same name will be run the same way. No way.

The 14th Street Villager, however, is much more worth looking into. Many rooms—especially those rented by the week—include microwave ovens and small refrigerators, so that you can save money on dining out. There is an outdoor swimming pool open during the warmer months, and cable television. The motel's location, at the nicer, northern end of Midtown, is convenient whether you have a car or not. It's right off of the I-75/85 highway; if you're traveling on foot, the Woodruff Arts Center—and the similarly named MARTA station—is right around the corner.

Rates for a double occupancy room, when Mr. C inquired, were about $40 per night, and $147 per week—about half the daily rate.

ALTERNATIVE LODGING

Atlanta Dream Hostel
- 222 East Howard Ave., Decatur; 370-0380

The sixties live on, man. Not affiliated with the International Youth Hostel circuit, this most unusual place is closer in style to a commune, making this a colorful place to stay for those who don't mind, um, a loose atmosphere. At just $10 per night, it's certainly cheap enough.

Formerly located in a rough part of downtown Atlanta, ADH recently moved out to this idyllic suburban spot, two blocks south of the Decatur MARTA station. The building was originally a livery stable, and still has a rustic look to it, with high, wooden-

beam ceilings and sliding barn doors on the side. It's divided into a large central room, which has some of the hostel's twenty beds, plus a lounge area with couches and a television, and several smaller rooms. A couple of cats roam freely. A covered side patio functions as a "biergarten"; nearby, there's a vegetable patch, complete with mulch pile.

Being a non-regulated hostel, the standard rules governing such places are more lax here. ADH is open 24 hours a day; there is no curfew, and no "closed" period during the day. Late-night entry is overseen by the manager, who lives on the premises (and sleeps near the door). Sleeping is dormitory style, like any hostel; men are separated from women, although there is a loft with a double bed for couples. There is a kitchen area with some well-worn apparatus; laundry facilities, and a few bikes for rent. A free limousine service is available for pickups from the airport, with advance notice.

The location, near the MARTA, makes zipping in and out of town very convenient—though, alas, with train tracks literally outside the front door, it can also be noisy on occasion. Well, whaddaya want for ten bucks a night? Remember, that price includes taxes, plus linens and blankets (they're uh, still working on insulating the building), free coffee, tea and local phone calling, and the chance to meet some very laid-back folks. The Atlanta Dream Hostel—the lodging which begs the question, "Whose dream is it, anyway?"—may just be the place for you.

Atlanta Youth Hostel
- 229 Ponce de Leon Ave., N.E. Atlanta; 875-2882

This is Atlanta's branch of the International Youth Hostel network, where travelers (mostly college-age or so) from as far away as Australia know they can stay for almost no money. You can do the same, whether you're visiting from Athens, Greece, or Athens, Georgia; even if you're not a member of the network. The cost for members is a microscopic $12.50 per night, plus tax; nonmembers will get a $3 extra charge added on. That, plus a one-time linen rental fee of $2 if you didn't bring your own (savvy hostelers do), is the entire cost. Can't beat it.

These, of course, are no-frills accommodations, dormitory-style; you'll be sharing your room with several other folks. Bathrooms are shared, as well. And one other factor to note is that you *can't* hang out in the hostel between the hours of 12 noon and 5:00 p.m. They kick you out so that they can clean house. There's also a midnight curfew, though you can arrange to get a key

---

MR. CHEAP'S PICKS
Alternative Lodging

✔ **Atlanta Youth Hostel**—$12.50 a night. Can't beat it.
✔ **Midtown Manor**—A nice alternative to motels, this Victorian-style rooming house offers great weekly rates.

---

to get in after hours.

The common areas aren't as no-frills. There's a TV lounge and kitchen facilities, so that you can save more money by doing your own cooking. It's all tastefully decorated, and quite lively. Part of the charm of a hostel, obviously, is meeting foreign travelers and exchanging stories about faraway places. The folks who work here are also ready to provide tons of information about local attractions and transportation.

The Atlanta Youth Hostel has fifty beds, which can easily fill up during peak times; it's always a good idea to call ahead and make reservations. You can even use a credit card. The North Avenue MARTA station is just a few blocks away.

Bed & Breakfast Atlanta
- 1801 Piedmont Ave. N.E., Suite 208, Atlanta; 875-0525

This isn't a bed and breakfast in itself, but rather a matchmaking service that can place you in any of the over eighty B&Bs in the Atlanta area. Bed & Breakfasts can sometimes be even cheaper than discount-rate hotels and motels (since they don't have to pay a staff to remain on duty 24-hours a day). Size, location, and amenities also lead to a wide variety in prices.

High quality is guaranteed by *Bed & Breakfast, The National Network*, and these folks are also members of the Georgia Hospitality & Travel Association and the Georgia Bed & Breakfast Council. Many of the participating inns are actually private homes, making you feel right at home by using the living room and other areas of the house. All are near public transportation, and offer private baths, air conditioning, and continental breakfasts. Because of B&B Atlanta's detailed information, accommodations for special needs—like for those with allergies to pets or foods—can be made especially for you.

Rates run anywhere from $40-$100 a night for single rooms and $48 to $140 for a double, with a $12 charge for the third person over the age of three in a room with parents. Weekly and monthly rates are also available; a small service fee is also worked into the cost.

You can even purchase gift certificates for the service; keep in mind that B&Bs usually cost $80-$120 for two people. B&B Atlanta's business hours are from 9 a.m. to noon and 2 p.m. to 5 p.m., weekdays. Messages can be left at other times, and will be promptly returned.

Midtown Manor
- 811 Piedmont Ave. N.E., Atlanta; 872-5846

This is a nice alternative to hotels and motels, especially if you're staying for a week or longer. Midtown Manor is, in fact, a group of individual Victorian-era houses on a tree-lined street just a couple of blocks from Peachtree Street. That short walk makes quite a difference; at once, a commercial (and somewhat rundown) area gives way to a pleasant, quieter residential neighborhood.

Rooms at the Manor are fully furnished in turn-of-the-century style. They are all carpeted, and include a color TV (no cable) and a refrigerator; laundry, and microwave ovens are also available in each building. Some quarters have their own bathrooms, but the more inexpensive rooms require you to share a hallway bathroom. You also get a private phone, one crucial difference from

the average hotel; if you are out when someone tries to call you, there is no switchboard operator to take a message.

Daily rates start at $35 a night, and range up to $85, depending on the size of the room; weekly rates begin at $125, though these tend to be occupied on very long-term schedules. The average room rents for $150 per week. Prices include a breakfast of coffee and doughnuts, available in the lobby each morning. When you register, you get a set of keys—one for your room, and one for the front door of the house. This gives you 24-hour access, as well as 24-hour security. A manager also resides in each building, and there is a front office open during business hours. The staff is very friendly, taking care of any little needs very promptly. Off-street parking is available, too.

Woodruff Bed & Breakfast Inn
- 223 Ponce de Leon Ave. N.E., Atlanta; 875-9449; or 1-800-473-9449

For just $65 for a single room or $75 for a double, you can get treated to some real southern hospitality at this inn which, by the way, happens to be a former brothel. No, Mr. C isn't joking—this handsomely restored, multi-level Midtown abode had a former life as a true blue, er, cathouse. But honestly, the only traces of the past you'll see are antique photos of the former lady of the house, Bessie Woodruff, along with her framed degree in "Physio- and Massage Therapy". Yeah, *right*, Bessie.

Within walking distance, you'll find Mary Mac's Tea Room, the Fox Theatre, the Varsity Restaurant, and Georgia Tech. The North Avenue MARTA station is also nearby. Since you'll be saving big bucks on lodging, you may even be able to afford dinner at one of the fancier establishments nearby, like the Abbey or the Crab House.

While this stretch of Ponce looks bit seedy, rest assured that the Woodruff is a safe and sound place to stay. The rooms are fully furnished, some with Oriental lace curtains, and many of them open up onto porches. This particular bed and breakfast is slightly European in style; most rooms have private baths. Some require that guests share bathrooms, but this is the exception, not the rule (and usually applies to the two double-bed rooms, which are a real deal at just $85 a night).

The Woodruff is a popular place for wedding parties to stay in, since there's plenty of common space in the foyer and living room for hanging out. Breakfasts can be served in the main dining area, or brought to your room. Who would've thought you could find such service at a place listed in this book?

ALPHABETICAL INDEX

315

SUBJECT INDEX

Amplifiers, See "Musical Instruments"
Appliances, major
  air conditioners, 12
  bathroom, 13
  dishwashers, 12, 13
  kitchen, 12, 13, 14
  lawnmowers and outdoor equipment, 14
  microwaves, 13, 14, 74
  refrigerators & freezers, 12, 13, 14
  sewing machines, 14
  small, used, 66, 79
  stoves and ranges, 12, 13
  washers and dryers, 12, 13, 14
  vacuum cleaners, 14, 74
Art gallery exhibits
  African-American artists, 172
  American artists, 170
  art centers, 168, 169, 169-170
  Asian, 176
  Atlanta area artists, 170, 173, 174, 176
  Central American, 176
  contemporary art, 170, 172, 176
  European artists, 171
  folk art,
  Haitian, 172
  international, 171, 176
  jewelry, 173
  Mexican, 174
  mixed media/experimental, 171
  festivals, 168
  folk art, 170, 173, 174, 176
  glass-176
  paintings, 171, 175, 176
  performance art, 175
  photography, 171, 172, 173-174, 175
  sculpture, 170, 175, 176
Art supplies, 155-158
Athletic shoes, See "Shoes and Sneakers"
Audio equipment, See "Electronics"
Baby clothes

New, 56, 57, 71
  Secondhand, 60, 61
Baby Equipment & furniture, 61, 63, 71-72
Bakeries, 89-93
  French, 91
  Greek, 91
  New York style, 93
  outlets, 89, 90, 92
  thrift, 89, 90, 92
Bedding
  adjustable beds, 17
  Bed frames, 15, 16
  daybeds, 18
  futons, 15 (Also see "Furniture")
  headboards, 16
  mattresses, 15-18
  waterbeds, 16
Beer, See "Liquor"
Books, 19-27
  art and photography, 20, 22, 23, 26
  automobile, 21
  bargain books & overstocks, 20, 21
  biography and autobiography, 19, 21, 23, 25, 26, 27
  children's, 21, 22, 23, 24-25, 25, 26, 27
  classics, 20
  comics, 21, 22
  computer, 21, 22
  cookbooks, 21, 22, 23, 24, 26, 27
  fitness, 21
  gardening, 21
  gay & lesbian, 19
  health and psychology, 21, 23, 24, 25, 26
  history & civil war, 19, 20, 21, 27
  horror, 19, 23, 25
  humor, 20, 23, 26
  local & southern authors, 19
  magazines (back issues), 19, 22, 16
  mysteries, 19, 23, 25
  out-of-print, 19

poetry, 26
  rare & unusual, 19
  romances, 19, 22
  science fiction, 19, 21, 26
  sports, 25
  textbooks, used, 20, 27
  travel, 20, 25, 27
Breads, thrift, 89, 90, 92 (Also see "Bakeries")
Cameras and photography
  supplies, 35-39
  cameras, new, 36, 37, 38
  cameras, used, 35-39
  equipment, used, 35, 36, 37, 38
  supplies, new, 38-39
  movie & camcorders, 36, 39
  panoramic, 36
  supplies, used, 37
Camping equipment, See "Sporting and Fitness Equipment"
Candy and nuts, 93-95
  bulk, 93
  candy-making supplies, 93
  chocolate, 93-95
  nuts, 94, 95
  outlets, 94
  sugarfree and diabetic, 93, 94
Carpeting and rugs, See "Rugs and carpeting"
Cassettes, See "Compact discs"
Cheese, 95
Children's activities
  arts & crafts, 178
  educational projects, 177, 178
  music, 178
  plays/theater, 177, 178, 179, 183
  puppet shows, 177
  storytelling, 177, 178
  tours, 179
  videos & cartoons, 179
  workshops, 178
Clothing, new, 42-59, 71-72
  athletic, 44, 51, 52, 59, 61, 65
  baby, 56-57, 61
  belts & suspenders, 43, 44, 46, 50, 58, 65

Other Titles of Interest from Bob Adams, Inc.

AVAILABLE AT YOUR LOCAL BOOKSTORE

Mr. Cheap's Boston

Mr. Cheap's Chicago

Mr. Cheap's New York

Mr. Cheap's San Francisco
(available May, 1994)

Mr. Cheap's Washington, DC
(available August, 1994)

If you cannot find these titles at your bookstore, you may order them directly from the publisher.

BY PHONE: Call 1-800-872-5627 (in Massachusetts 617-767-8100). We accept Visa, Mastercard, and American Express. $4.50 will be added to your total order for shipping and handling.

BY MAIL: Write out the full title of the books you'd like to order and send payment, including $4.50 for shipping and handling to: Bob Adams, Inc., 260 Center Street, Holbrook, MA 02343.

PLEASE CHECK AT YOUR LOCAL BOOKSTORE FIRST